KRESGE'S KATALOG

TRADE MARK

5¢ AND 10¢
MERCHANDISE

The Original Parcel Post
5 and 10 cent Store

S. S. KRESGE CO.
DETROIT, MICHIGAN, U.S.A.

COPYRIGHT 1913 S.S.KRESGE CO.

KRESGE'S
KATALOG
OF 5¢ & 10¢
MERCHANDISE

KRESGE'S KATALOG OF 5¢ & 10¢ MERCHANDISE

S.S. KRESGE COMPANY

DETROIT, MICHIGAN

1913

RANDOM HOUSE · NEW YORK · 1975

Manufactured in the United States of America
Facsimile Edition

Library of Congress Cataloging in Publication Data

Kresge (S. S.) Company.
Kresge's katalog of 5¢ and 10¢ merchandise.

Photoreprint of the 1913 ed.
1. Variety stores—United States—Catalogs.
2. Manufactures—Catalogs. 3. Kresge (S. S.) Company.
I. Title.
HF5465.U6K745 1975   381′.45′00029   75-20184
ISBN 0-394-73151-4 pbk.

INTRODUCTION

On October 8, 1957, Stanley S. Kresge, the son of the founder of the Kresge Company, addressed the Newcomen Society in Detroit, Michigan. His subject was "S. S. Kresge Company and Its Builder Sebastian S. Kresge." Stanley Kresge said:

"During the last half of the nineteenth century, the stage was set for the developments of our wonderful twentieth century.

"With imagination unfettered, slowly but surely, American ingenuity began to find ways for making new things and ways to distribute them, and, simultaneously, the American people acquired a desire to have these new things, which were, despite their frequent crudeness, an improvement over the things which people had used in the pioneer days when the first necessity was to tame the wilderness.

"It is well to remember that this was the period in which . . . customers were intrigued by what a nickel or a dime could buy."

And you will be, too, as you browse through the pages of this "Katalog" issued by the Kresge Company in 1913 when the firm briefly entered the mail-order business, and also had over a hundred five-and-ten stores in the eastern and midwestern sections of the United States.

Everything in the "Katalog" sold for a nickel or a dime and you could buy human hair switches for only 10¢; Rosewood pipes—10¢; "extra good quality" bleached huck towels—5¢; "linen finish ink" tablets with 55 leaves—5¢; printed muslin U.S. flags, 11x17 inches—5¢.

But this little "Katalog" is also an absorbing chronicle of the needs and desires of the people of the early twentieth century. For sale were watch fobs, smelling salts "invaluable for ladies traveling," gauze stockings, breakfast caps, satin palm fans, wool powder puffs, "books for red-blooded boys by Horatio Alger, Jr.," nickeloid flutes, salt safes, gas globes, lamp wicks and tiddlywinks.

The latest popular sheet music included "Always Take a Girl Named Daisy," "He Wants Someone to Call Him Papa" and "In the Harbor of Home Sweet Home."

Today the Kresge Company is a multi-billion-dollar mass merchandiser. The firm's K marts are the most successful discount department stores in the world. But the strength of the company today is rooted in this nostalgia of the early 1900's. Kresge's "Katalog" promised "every article is useful and of a dependable quality." Over sixty years have passed since the "Katalog" was issued, and the Kresge Company still promises this today.

Robert E. Dewar

Robert E. Dewar
Chairman of the Board
S. S. Kresge Company

KRESGE'S
KATALOG
OF 5¢ & 10¢
MERCHANDISE

The Connecting Link
between YOU and ECONOMY

KRESGE'S
PARCEL POST
FIVE AND TEN CENT STORE
DOUBLES THE BUYING POWER OF YOUR NICKELS AND DIMES

COPYRIGHT 1913 S.S. KRESGE CO.

Announcement

Our new Parcel Post 5c and 10c Store is now ready to serve you—ready to fill all orders you send us for merchandise illustrated in this Katalog, representing as it does *the world's best 5c and 10c Bargains.*

Our object in publishing this Katalog is to make it possible for *you to have a modern 5c and 10c store in your home;* to enable you to order by mail the very things you need for yourself, family and home at 5c and 10c.

Just think! You hold in your hands a Katalog that is filled from cover to cover with *useful and practical merchandise—the very things you would readily buy in your home town if it were possible for you to do so.*

Every line of merchandise shown in this Katalog is produced with the utmost care, *and fully guaranteed to be as represented.*

Millions of people in almost every walk of life are buying Kresge 5c and 10c merchandise from our chain of more than 100 retail stores, because it is what they need, *for every article is useful, and of a dependable quality.*

You, too, will be a Kresge customer after you look through this Katalog and see the *wonderful bargains you can get from us at 5c and 10c.* And remember, *we guarantee to please you or return your money promptly.*

Look through the Katalog now—before you lay it down—make out and send us a trial order. *Let us prove to you that the Kresge Parcel Post 5c and 10c Store doubles the buying power of your nickels and dimes; that it really is the connecting link between you and economy.*

All orders you send us will be filled carefully and shipped promptly.

S. S. KRESGE COMPANY
*The Original Parcel Post 5c and 10c
Store With Over 100 Branch Stores*

You will save money every time you order from this Katalog

SEND US A TRIAL ORDER

Every order you send us is accepted with the understanding and agreement that if you do not find the merchandise just as represented and described in this Katalog, you may return it to us and we will promptly return your money and pay transportation charges both ways. Send us a trial order and be convinced that you can double the buying power of your nickels and dimes by ordering from this Katalog. We will give you prompt service and the best values at 5 and 10 cents that you have ever seen. This Katalog is a modern 5 and 10 cent store in your home. Keep it where you can refer to it at any time, for it means a saving of many dollars each year on dependable merchandise for yourself, family and home.

Our great chain of over 100 retail stores gives us an enormous buying power, enables us to buy direct from manufacturers, very often contracting for their entire output, thereby eliminating the commissions of the jobber and wholesaler which saves us from 25 to 50 per cent.

We in turn share this saving with you. That is why you can get such good 5 and 10 cent bargains from us. We really make it possible for you to buy for 5 and 10 cents useful and practical merchandise that is often sold as high as 15 and 25 cents.

QUALITY OF KRESGE MERCHANDISE IS FULLY GUARANTEED

The quality of Kresge 5 and 10 cent merchandise is worthy of your most careful consideration. We could not afford to guarantee satisfaction or to promptly return money on all orders if we were not sure our merchandise was of a dependable quality, and just as represented in every way. We handle only dependable merchandise, and every article we sell is fully guaranteed, even though our prices are limited to 5 and 10 cents.

All merchandise is carefully inspected by expert inspectors and checkers before being shipped, thus eliminating mistakes in filling your orders. Of course, now and then an error will creep in, no matter how careful we may be, and should you receive any merchandise from us that proves unsatisfactory to you, just send it right back and we will promptly exchange it for other merchandise or return your money.

Remember, when ordering from us, you take no chance whatever as we guarantee to please you or promptly refund your money. Our guarantee on the inside page of Katalog cover fully protects you against an unsatisfactory purchase.

You will find it a wonderful lot of satisfaction to deal with us for you will get just what you order, and every item will prove to be a bargain.

S. S. KRESGE CO. ARE RELIABLE

We are reliable—ask your banker or any express or mercantile agency about us. We have been established for more than sixteen years and are today one of the largest as well as one of the most successful business enterprises in the world. Not only are we well rated commercially speaking, but have over 100 retail stores in the principal cities of the United States, through which we serve millions of customers.

You take no risk whatever when ordering from us. We will promptly return money sent us for merchandise and all transportation charges, if any, should you be displeased with your order for any reason whatever. Read our "Money Back Guarantee" on the inside second cover page. It is the fairest and broadest guarantee ever written, fully protecting you against loss.

KRESGE'S LIBERAL POLICY

No matter how large or small your order may be, we want you to be so well pleased with our merchandise and service, that you will tell your friends and neighbors about the wonderful bargains they can buy from us. It is our aim to render such efficient nd intelligent service that you will order from us year after year; to please you so well that you will tell your friends about the wonderful bargains you got from Kresge's new Parcel Post 5 and 10 cent store.

In no instance shall your wishes be overlooked. We want you to feel that each order you send us will be looked after as carefully as if you were to make a personal selection from one of our many stores.

All that is necessary on your part to enjoy our liberal policy to the fullest extent, is to state your wants plainly when ordering.

KRESGE SERVICE IS PROMPT

Every order you send us will be filled and shipped promptly. Every letter you write us regarding your order or about merchandise will be answered courteously and without delay. We know that prompt service is one of our greatest assets; that it will win the confidence of those who order from us to the same extent that sending them good merchandise will; therefore we have established the most up-to-date methods in our mail order store so that we can ship all orders just as quickly as possible. We want you to feel that you can send to us, for merchandise by mail, in the confidence that you know you will receive your order promptly.

Kresge service will make it a pleasure for you to order merchandise by mail from our new Parcel Post 5 and 10 cent store, and we are certain that you will be delighted with every article you receive.

Extra Special Free Delivery Offer On Orders Amounting to $10.00 or More—

IF YOU LIVE IN ONE OF THE STATES MENTIONED BELOW

Read This Offer. You Can Get Your Order Delivered Free

We will pay the freight to all points in the states mentioned in the list below, *on all orders amounting to Ten Dollars ($10.00) or more*, provided at least one-third of the order consists of dry goods, notions, etc., and the balance of hardware, tinware, woodenware, glassware, etc. We will not prepay the freight if the order consists only of hardware, woodenware, tinware, enamelware or glassware.

It will be no trouble at all to get your friends and neighbors to club with you and make up a $10.00 order. *This wonderful prepay offer on shipments amounting to $10.00 or more will save you and your friends all the cost of transportation charges.* By clubbing together in this way you can make up an order for the necessary amount without any trouble.

This is indeed a liberal offer and should appeal to everyone desiring to *reduce the high cost of living.* Any order you send us amounting to $10.00 or more, and consisting of the merchandise named above, will be shipped to you, all charges paid, if you live in one of the following states:

Connecticut	Maine	New Hampshire	Ohio	Vermont
Delaware	Maryland	New Jersey	Pennsylvania	West Virginia
Illinois	Massachusetts	New York	Rhode Island	Wisconsin
Indiana	Michigan			

Kresge Helps You Pay the Freight—

IF YOU DO NOT LIVE IN ONE OF THE STATES MENTIONED ABOVE

This is a Special Offer—One That Will Save You Money

To all customers living in the states not mentioned in the above list, *we make the following liberal allowance to help pay the freight charges:* On all orders you send us, *amounting to $10.00 or more,* and at least one-third of the order consists of dry goods and notions, and the balance of hardware, glassware, dinnerware, woodenware, etc., as you may desire, *we will allow you 50c per 100 lbs.* This amount may be deducted from the amount of the transportation charges you send us with the order. You make an additional saving in either case. If you live in one of the states mentioned above, you save the entire cost of transportation on orders amounting to $10.00 or more, or if you live in one of the states not mentioned in the above list *you save 50c per 100 lbs.* on all orders amounting to $10.00 or more.

Get your friends and neighbors to order with you. You can save money for them and yourself, and in addition you can earn one of the beautiful premiums offered on the back cover of this Katalog.

It is Easy to Order 5 and 10 Cent Merchandise from this Katalog

Buying 5 and 10 cent merchandise by mail is indeed very simple and easy—so easy that any-one who can read and write can do it. The following simplified instructions will make everything so perfectly clear to you that you can order from this Katalog with as much satisfaction as if you were to go to one of our many stores and personally select the merchandise.

It's easy to order from Kresge's New Parcel Post 5 & 10c Store.

We have prepared a special order blank for you to use when ordering, one of which is enclosed with this Katalog. Should you not have one of our order blanks, use a piece of plain paper, writing only on one side of the paper. We will cheerfully send a supply of order blanks upon request.

In writing your order, use every precaution to make your wants plain and there will be no danger of our misunderstanding you. It is important that you write your order according to the following instructions.

OUR TERMS

Our terms are cash with the order. This method enables us to conduct our business with the least expense, therefore making it possible for us to give you better values for your money than we could, were our systems not based on the most economical methods of conducting each department. It is much better for you to send the full remittance with your order because you have no extra expense to pay the express company for returning the money to us. There is no advantage in having your merchandise sent C. O. D. as in many instances the express agent will not permit examination of merchandise until the full amount has been paid, including all charges. You positively take no risk in sending full payment with your order, because we absolutely guarantee to please you or refund your money. Make all money orders and checks payable to S. S. Kresge Company.

HOW TO SEND MONEY

There are several safe methods by which you can send money. We advise you to remit by post office money order, express money order, New York bank draft, or by registered mail. The safest and one of the most convenient ways is by post office money order. We do not advise the sending of cash by letter, but if it is inconvenient for you to remit in any other way, be sure to use a strong envelope, seal it securely, and have it registered. DO NOT SEND POSTAGE STAMPS in payment of your order as we cannot dispose of them except at a loss, and handling stamps is a great inconvenience.

WRITE YOUR NAME AND ADDRESS PLAINLY

The first thing to do when making out your order is to write your name, town, county, state, R. F. D.

or post office box as plainly as you possibly can, as it is of very great importance to have your name and address correct and plainly written.

If you are married, always sign your husband's initials. Should you change your address, please advise us, stating your old as well as new address.

ACKNOWLEDGMENT OF ORDERS

As we endeavor to ship all orders within from 6 to 12 hours after same have been received, we will not send acknowledgments of orders except in instances where a slight delay is occasioned by either lack of information, or where the order will be temporarily delayed for a few days waiting for a new supply of merchandise. In this case we will always advise you just when your order will be shipped. Should it happen that you do not receive your order within a reasonable time, please write us promptly, stating the exact date you sent the order and the amount enclosed, and how you sent the money, whether by post office or express money order, bank draft or registered letter.

SHIPPING POINT

If your shipping point is different from your post office, be sure to advise us to what point you desire shipment made, as well as giving us your post office address. Always give full Katalog number of article or articles you are ordering, sizes and colors, and any other information that will enable us to handle your order promptly.

Be sure to advise us just how and to what point you desire to have your order shipped. That is, state by what railroad or nearest express office. If you want your order shipped by freight be sure to tell us whether or not there is a freight agent at your shipping point. If there is no agent at your station and you desire charges prepaid, it will be necessary for you to send us a sufficient amount of money to prepay freight charges. Should you send us more than enough to cover charges, we will promptly refund you the difference. It is always advisable to send us a little more money than will be needed rather than not to send enough, as in that case your order would be delayed until we could write you for the additional amount needed to prepay freight charges.

PROTECTION FROM LOSS OF MERCHANDISE IN SHIPMENT

We absolutely guarantee safe delivery of all merchandise you order from us without any extra cost to you whatever, no matter whether same was shipped by parcel post, express or freight. We will refill all orders that fail to reach you, just as quickly as we can secure the proper information from the post office department, express company, or railroad company, regarding the non-delivery of said merchandise. Please bear in mind that you pay nothing extra for this protection as we feel that it is our duty to see that all merchandise ordered from us reaches you safely regardless of where you live or how you ordered it shipped.

Please read these instructions before writing out your order

CLUB ORDERS SAVE YOU MONEY

In order to help you share to the fullest extent the benefits of the low prices quoted in this Katalog, we suggest the use of the club order plan—that is, allowing your friends and neighbors to order merchandise with you, thus making the greatest possible saving in transportation charges. Club orders can either be shipped by parcel post, express or freight, the latter method offering the greatest saving. The freight charges on a 20-pound order often amount to as much as a 100-pound order, so you see that by having your friends order with you, you reduce your part of the freight charges to a very small amount. Remember that we prepay freight charges on all orders, amounting to $10 or more to the states mentioned in the prepay list on page 3. Also remember that we help you pay freight charges to any state in the U. S. not mentioned in the prepay list, the average allowance being 50c on every 100 pounds on orders amounting to $10 or more, consisting of dry goods, hardware, crockery, etc. By getting your friends and neighbors to club with you, you can have a large order come by freight at about the usual cost of a 20 or 25-pound package. You, in turn, giving each one ordering with you, their part of the merchandise and sharing the expense of freight charges according to their part of the order, which would be a fair and very economical way to order your merchandise and a method assuring all the greatest economy in every instance.

HOW TO RETURN MERCHANDISE

It is our aim to fill each and every order so carefully, and to give such good values and dependable merchandise, that you will not have to return any part of your order. But in transacting a large business it is almost impossible to keep mistakes from creeping in now and then, and should you find it necessary to return merchandise to us for exchange or refund, do not, under any circumstances, put any money in the package, whether you send it by parcel post, freight or express. If it is necessary to write a letter regarding the merchandise you are returning, send same in a separate letter by mail, making sure to enclose with it a memorandum of the merchandise you are returning, and any other particulars pertaining to the order. When returning the merchandise to us, be sure to address package plainly, writing your name and address on the outside of the package in the upper left hand corner, or use an express tag, tying same to the package.

Before returning goods please notify us that it is necessary for you to return same and we will advise you just how we desire to have you return the package. We cannot adjust complaints promptly, or refill orders, unless you notify us so we can give you the proper instructions regarding the merchandise to be returned. We cannot be responsible for the delay of merchandise being returned, unless you have first communicated with us, and we have informed you how we want same returned.

REGARDING THE RETURNING OF MERCHANDISE TO US

Do not return goods by parcel post if the package weighs more than 5 pounds, and do not return merchandise by express should the package weigh more than 20 pounds, unless we advise you to the contrary. Should you send returned goods to us by express, we pay the charges when the merchandise is received. Should you return merchandise by parcel post, you pay the postage and as soon as we receive the goods you have returned, we will forward you the amount of postage you have paid.

OMISSION OF MERCHANDISE ORDERED

We carry enormous stocks of the merchandise shown in this Katalog and expect to fill 99 out of every 100 orders promptly—that is, from within 6 to 12 hours after we receive them. We shall endeavor to fill all orders from first choice selection. However it may occasionally occur that we are temporarily sold out of some particular item, in which case, rather than delay your order for any length of time, we will ship all merchandise you have ordered except the item or items which we might be sold out of, unless you give second choice selections.

SMALL ORDERS MAKE VERY UNPROFITABLE SHIPMENTS

We will promptly fill any order sent us, regardless of how small it is, but ask you to please make your orders amount to a dollar or more, as smaller orders are very unprofitable both to you and ourselves, as the transportation charges and packing expense on orders for less than a dollar are often as great as on those amounting to from $3 to $5. It is to your advantage to make your order as large as possible, thereby reducing the transportation charges to the lowest amount. Transportation charges can be greatly reduced by ordering a quantity of merchandise at one time. For instance, the freight charges on a package weighing 25 or 50 pounds will be as much as on a package weighing 100 pounds.

WRITE US FOR INFORMATION

Write us as often as necessary for any information you may want about our merchandise, transportation charges, etc. We will promptly answer all correspondence.

HOW TO FIGURE WEIGHT OF MERCHANDISE

Throughout the Katalog we mention the weight of each article listed, except where average weights are quoted for a certain line of merchandise, or the average weight of merchandise on the page. It is an easy matter for you to figure up the total weight of merchandise you desire to order. Simply add together the weights of the numbers you are ordering, and you will have the total net weight of the merchandise. The weight quoted under each item is for merchandise only, as we have not added the necessary weight to cover packing boxes, etc. If your order is to be shipped by parcel post, be sure to allow an extra amount for postage charges. Should there be an amount left after paying postage we will promptly return same to you.

How to have your order shipped

We recommend that you have your order shipped by parcel post or freight; however, we will ship orders by express if you desire to have us do so. We give parcel post and freight rate tables on opposite page. These tables show the approximate charges. When ordering shipment sent by parcel post, be sure to include an extra amount of money to pay postage. Shipments by freight may be sent prepaid or collect. If prepaid, be sure to send an extra amount of money to cover same. When goods are shipped by freight the rate is the same, no matter what road the shipment is sent over. Our Traffic Department routes all freight shipments so that they will reach our customers with the least delay. We pack all goods carefully so that they will reach you in good condition.

WHEN TO HAVE YOUR ORDER SHIPPED BY PARCEL POST

All shipments weighing twenty pounds or less, when the entire outside measurements are not more than 72 inches in circumference, may be sent by parcel post at the zone rate in which you live. For instance, if you live in zone 5 and your order weighs 10 pounds, the transportation charges would be 62 cents. Or if you live in zone 2 and your package weighs 3 pounds, the cost would be 7 cents. The rate for all merchandise weighing 4 ounces or less, is 1 cent per ounce regardless of distance. Packages weighing more than 4 ounces up to and including 20 pounds, take the rate of the zone in which you live. No matter what zone you live in, if you desire to have your order shipped by parcel post, you can tell just what it will cost you, by figuring up the total weight of all the merchandise you have selected. In order that you may clearly understand how to use the parcel post to the best advantage when ordering merchandise, we give on the opposite page a rate table for parcel post packages. This table shows the cost of packages weighing over 4 ounces to 20 pounds in all the different zones. Parcel post rates apply only to merchandise such as dry goods, household utensils, hardware, glassware and crockery, etc. Books, etc., are carried as third class matter regardless of distance. The rate is 3 ounces for 1 cent. When ordering merchandise shipped by parcel post, be sure to include the necessary postage to cover same. It is better for you to send too much postage than not enough, as if you should not send a sufficient amount we would hold your order until we wrote for the additional amount.

WHEN TO HAVE YOUR ORDER SHIPPED BY FREIGHT

This is the most economical method of shipping merchandise but a little slower than parcel post—therefore the great difference between parcel post and freight charges. Small orders should not be sent by freight as an order weighing 10 to 20 pounds can be shipped by parcel post as cheaply as by freight. Should your order consist of dry goods, tinware, hardware, crockery, etc., and weigh from 25 to 100 pounds or more it should be shipped by freight. Always remember that the freight charges on orders weighing 25 pounds will cost as much as one weighing 100 pounds. If you desire to take advantage of the saving offered by having your order shipped by freight, you should make it as large as possible. Freight charges are based on the 100-pound rate.

HOW TO FIGURE FREIGHT CHARGES

It will be very easy for you to figure freight charges if you consult the freight rate table given on opposite page. In this table we have given the names of the principal cities in various states. Freight rates are figured with the larger cities in each state as a basis. All other towns located in the same section of the state near one of the cities mentioned take practically the same rate, or perhaps a few cents more or less per 100 pounds than the rate given to the large city mentioned. If your town is not in the list, the rate will be about the same as the rate to the nearest city mentioned. By consulting your nearest freight agent you can find out just what the rate to your town is per 100 pounds.

Transportation charges do not amount to very much

Parcel post, express or freight charges do not amount to very much when you consider the great saving you make by ordering your merchandise from us. There would be no object in our issuing this Katalog if we could not save you money on all the merchandise you bought of us, regardless of where you live, providing the order amounted to enough to make a profitable shipment. For instance, orders amounting to less than one dollar make very unprofitable shipments if the customer lives beyond the third zone. We guarantee to save you from 25 to 50 per cent on all the merchandise you order from this Katalog. You can see from these figures that you do not have to order many dollars' worth of goods to more than make up express or freight charges. Read our special prepay offer on orders amounting to $10 or more on page 3. If you wish to make the greatest saving in transportation charges, order merchandise for the entire family at one time and have it all shipped together. Do not fail to show this Katalog to your friends as they will, no doubt, want to order merchandise with you, which will help you make a still greater saving in transportation charges.

Things to remember when ordering

All orders weighing from 4 ounces to 20 lbs. can be shipped by parcel post to any point in the U. S.

Packages weighing 4 ounces or less can be shipped by parcel post at the rate of 1c per ounce to any zone.

Packages weighing over 20 lbs., and not more than 50 lbs., can be shipped by parcel post to points within zones 1 and 2.

All printed books, such as fiction, toy books, etc., can be shipped by mail at the rate of 3 ounces for 1c, to any point in the U. S.

When ordering, be sure to state Katalog numbers of the articles you desire, as well as sizes and colors, if this information is required.

Be sure to enclose an extra amount of money to pay transportation charges if you want your order shipped by parcel post, freight or express, when it is necessary to prepay charges

POSTAGE RATE TABLE FOR PARCEL POST PACKAGES

This table shows the amount of postage by parcel post, according to the weight of the package and according to the zone.	ZONE 1 Not over 50 Miles From DETROIT	ZONE 2 51 to 150 Miles From DETROIT	ZONE 3 151 to 300 Miles From DETROIT	ZONE 4 301 to 600 Miles From DETROIT	ZONE 5 601 to 1,000 Miles From DETROIT	ZONE 6 1,001 to 1,400 Miles From DETROIT	ZONE 7 1,400 to 1,800 Miles From DETROIT	ZONE 8 Over 1,800 Miles From DETROIT
Weight of Package	Amount of Postage Required	Amount of Postage Required	Amount of Postage Required	Amount of Postage Required	Amount of Postage Required	Amount of Postage Required	Amount of Postage Required	Amount of Postage Required
Over 4 oz. up to 1 lb	$0.05	$0.05	$0.06	$0.07	$0.08	$0.09	$0.11	$0.12
Over 1 lb. up to 2 lbs	.06	.06	.08	.11	.14	.17	.21	.24
Over 2 lbs. up to 3 lbs	.07	.07	.10	.15	.20	.25	.31	.36
Over 3 lbs. up to 4 lbs	.08	.08	.12	.19	.26	.33	.41	.48
Over 4 lbs. up to 5 lbs	.09	.09	.14	.23	.32	.41	.51	.60
Over 5 lbs. up to 6 lbs	.10	.10	.16	.27	.38	.49	.61	.72
Over 6 lbs. up to 7 lbs	.11	.11	.18	.31	.44	.57	.71	.84
Over 7 lbs. up to 8 lbs	.12	.12	.20	.35	.50	.65	.81	.96
Over 8 lbs. up to 9 lbs	.13	.13	.22	.39	.56	.73	.91	1.08
Over 9 lbs. up to 10 lbs	.14	.14	.24	.43	.62	.81	1.01	1.20
Over 10 lbs. up to 11 lbs	.15	.15	.26	.47	.68	.89	1.11	1.32
Over 11 lbs. up to 12 lbs	.16	.16	.28	.51	.74	.97	1.21	1.44
Over 12 lbs. up to 13 lbs	.17	.17	.30	.55	.80	1.05	1.31	1.56
Over 13 lbs. up to 14 lbs	.18	.18	.32	.59	.86	1.13	1.41	1.68
Over 14 lbs. up to 15 lbs	.19	.19	.34	.63	.92	1.21	1.51	1.80
Over 15 lbs. up to 16 lbs	.20	.20	.36	.67	.98	1.29	1.61	1.92
Over 16 lbs. up to 17 lbs	.21	.21	.38	.71	1.04	1.37	1.71	2.04
Over 17 lbs. up to 18 lbs	.22	.22	.40	.75	1.10	1.45	1.81	2.16
Over 18 lbs. up to 19 lbs	.23	.23	.42	.79	1.16	1.53	1.91	2.28
Over 19 lbs. up to 20 lbs	.24	.24	.44	.83	1.22	1.61	2.01	2.40

NOTE: If you live in the first or second zone, or within 150 miles of Detroit, we can ship orders, weighing from 21 to 50 pounds, by parcel post at the following rates:

21 pounds	$0.25	29 pounds	$0.33	37 pounds	$0.41	44 pounds	$0.48
22 pounds	.26	30 pounds	.34	38 pounds	.42	45 pounds	.49
23 pounds	.27	31 pounds	.35	39 pounds	.43	46 pounds	.50
24 pounds	.28	32 pounds	.36	40 pounds	.44	47 pounds	.51
25 pounds	.29	33 pounds	.37	41 pounds	.45	48 pounds	.52
26 pounds	.30	34 pounds	.38	42 pounds	.46	49 pounds	.53
27 pounds	.31	35 pounds	.39	43 pounds	.47	50 pounds	.54
28 pounds	.32	36 pounds	.40				

TABLE OF FREIGHT RATES

Showing freight rates per 100 pounds on goods shipped from Detroit to a number of cities in each state, these cities being used by the railroads as a basis for figuring rates for all towns in the immediate vicinity.

City and State	First Class Freight Per 100 Lbs.	City and State	First Class Freight Per 100 Lbs.	City and State	First Class Freight Per 100 Lbs.	City and State	First Class Freight Per 100 Lbs.
ALABAMA		**INDIANA**		**MONTANA**		**RHODE ISLAND**	
Birmingham	$1.27½	Evansville	$0.45	Helena	$3.05	Providence	$0.65½
Mobile	1.16	Indianapolis	.38½	Missoula	3.05	**SOUTH CAROLINA**	
Selma	1.46½	South Bend	.30	**NEBRASKA**		Charleston	1.20
ARIZONA		**IOWA**		Chadron	2.09	Greenville	1.16
Prescott	3.05	Des Moines	.83	Lincoln	1.06	Sumter	1.37
Yuma	3.48	Dubuque	.55	North Platte	1.79	**SOUTH DAKOTA**	
ARKANSAS		Sioux City	1.01	**NEVADA**		Aberdeen	1.50
Fort Smith	1.50	**KANSAS**		Austin	3.80	Bellefourche	2.30
Little Rock	1.40	Abilene	1.57	**NEW HAMPSHIRE**		Sioux Falls	1.04
Texarkana	1.67	Dodge City	1.93	Concord	.65½	Watertown	1.20
CALIFORNIA		Emporia	1.50	**NEW JERSEY**		**TENNESSEE**	
Los Angeles	3.50	Fort Scott	1.20	Belvidere	.58½	Chattanooga	1.14½
San Francisco	3.50	Winfield	1.71	Toms River	.58½	Jackson	1.08½
COLORADO		**KENTUCKY**		**NEW MEXICO**		Memphis	.91
Colorado Springs	2.08	Frankfort	.63	Gallup	3.05	**TEXAS**	
Denver	2.08	Jackson	1.12½	Santa Fe	2.58	Dallas	1.87
Durango	3.63	Louisville	.43	Silver City	2.66	El Paso	1.99
CONNECTICUT		**LOUISIANA**		**NEW YORK**		Houston	1.87
To all points	.65½	Lake Charles	1.80	Albany	.56	**UTAH**	
DELAWARE		New Orleans	1.16	Buffalo	.36	Marysvale	3.23
Dover	.55½	Shreveport	1.65	New York	.55½	Salt Lake City	2.73
Georgetown	.55½	**MAINE**		Rochester	.41½	**VERMONT**	
D. C.		Bangor	.65½	**NORTH CAROLINA**		Bennington	.65½
Washington	.55½	**MARYLAND**		Albemarle	1.23	**VIRGINIA**	
FLORIDA		Baltimore	.55½	Raleigh	1.16½	Marion	.54
Jacksonville	1.33½	**MASSACHUSETTS**		**NORTH DAKOTA**		Richmond	.54
Miami	2.30½	Boston	.65½	Bismarck	1.83	**WASHINGTON**	
Pensacola	1.33	**MINNESOTA**		Fargo	1.38	Seattle	3.50
GEORGIA		Albert Lea	.83	Grand Forks	1.47	Spokane	3.05
Atlanta	1.36½	Duluth	.83	Williston	2.22	**WEST VIRGINIA**	
Macon	1.41½	Minneapolis	.83	**OHIO**		Charleston	.41
Nashville	.81	Rochester	.83	Bellefontaine	.31½	Wheeling	.41
Waycross	1.53½	**MISSISSIPPI**		Cleveland	.30	**WISCONSIN**	
IDAHO		Jackson	1.33	Columbus	.31½	Ashland	.83
Boise	3.05	Vicksburg	1.16	**OKLAHOMA**		Green Bay	1.43
Twin Falls	3.05	**MISSOURI**		Tulsa	1.60	Milwaukee	.43
ILLINOIS		Springfield	1.08	**OREGON**		**WYOMING**	
Cairo	.50½	St. Louis	.46	Portland	3.50	Cheyenne	2.08
Danville	.37	Sedalia	.99	**PENNSYLVANIA**		Green River	2.73
Galesburg	.50			Harrisburg	.55½	Sheridan	2.78
Peoria	.43			Philadelphia	.56½		
				Pittsburgh	.41		

MICHIGAN RATES: First-class freight rates, per 100 lbs. from Detroit to Grand Rapids, 30c per 100 lbs.; Mackinaw City, 49c per 100 lbs.; Hancock, 76c per 100 lbs. Freight charges to other points in proportion.

Index to the World's Best 5 and 10 cent Bargains

NOTE: Owing to lack of space it is impossible for us to index all the merchandise illustrated in this Katalog.

Extra Special Bargains—Nothing Over Ten cents

Ladies' Fine Ribbed Cotton Vests 10c
AX126—Ladies' Fine Ribbed Cotton Vests. Low neck, sleeveless. Mercerized insertion trimmed front and back. Sizes to fit bust measurements from 32 to 40 inches. State size wanted. Weight 3 ounces.
Price.....................10c

Ladies' Good Quality Gauze Stockings, per pr. 10c

AX103—Ladies' Gauze Stockings. Made of good quality light weight cotton yarn, 4 inch garter top. Colors: black, tan or white. Well shaped ankle and seamless heel and toe. Will not shrink. Sizes 8½, 9, 9½ and 10. State size and color wanted. Weight per pair, 2 ounces. Price per pair....10c

For other bargains in hosiery see pages 47, 48, 49. Nothing over 10c

OUR GUARANTEE
Every order you send us is accepted with the understanding and agreement that if you do not find the merchandise just as represented and described in this Katalog, you may return it to us and we will exchange it for other goods, or promptly return your money and pay transportation charges both ways.

Splendid Quality Percale Apron 10c
AX50—Splendid Quality Percale Apron. Bib style, neatly bound all round with white tape. Comes in choice patterns, popular checks, neat figures or stripes, in the most durable colors. Weight 3 ounces.
Price.....................10c

Every Article Illustrated in this Katalog is a Special Bargain—Nothing Over Ten Cents

CHAMPION FLY SWATTER, 10c

HX1409—Champion Fly Swatter. Made of good screen, bound with heavy felt. Twisted wire and varnished wood handle. About 17 inches long over all. Weight 2 ounces. Price....10c

LONG NURSING BOTTLES, 2 for 5c

EE151 — Long Nursing Bottles. Made of best quality plain, clear glass. Graduated scale on side from 1 to 8 ounces. Weight, each, 7 ounces. Price, 2 for.........5c

SQUAT NURSING BOTTLES, 2 for 5c

EE152 — Squat Nursing Bottles. Made of best quality plain, clear glass. Graduated scale on side from 1 to 8 ounces. Weight, each, 7 ounces. Price, 2 for...........5c

BRIGHT TIN FUNNELS, 2 for 5c

HH640—Bright Tin Funnels. Rounded edge. Used for filling nursing bottles, 3½ inches over all. Weight, each, 1 ounce. Two for...............5c

NICKEL PLATED CORKSCREW, 10c

HX1410—Nickel Plated Cork Screw. Self puller, with strong spring and enameled wood handle. About 6½ inches over all. Weight 4 ounces. Price.......................10c

BLUE SEAL WHITE VASELINE, 10c

BX332 — Blue Seal White Vaseline. An excellent remedy for burns, scalds, sunburn, colds, etc. Guaranteed under the Pure Food and Drugs Act. Medium size glass jar with metal top. Weight 5 ounces. Price.....10c

SPRING BOTTOM INSECT GUN, 10c

HX1224—Spring Bottom Insect Gun Stamped from sheet brass and enameled tin. Leather bellows top. For the destruction of insects in the house and garden. Weight 3 ounces. Price....10c

SPRING STEEL CARLISLE HOOKS, BOX, 10c

HX1450—Spring Steel Carlisle Hooks. Sizes: Nos. 1, 3, 5 and 7. Illustration shows two actual sizes. Packed 100 in a box. State size wanted. Weight, per box, 4 ounces. Price, per box 10c

SINGLE GUT FISH HOOKS, PACKAGE, 5c

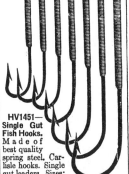

HV1451—Single Gut Fish Hooks. Made of best quality spring steel. Carlisle hooks. Single gut leaders. Sizes: 1, 3 and 5. Six in package. State size wanted. Weight, 1 ounce. Package.....5c

HX1451—Same as above, but double gut leader. Sizes: 1, 2, 3 and 5. Six in package. State size wanted. Weight, 1 ounce. Package.......................10c

EMPIRE CITY TROLLING SPOON, 10c

HX1452—Empire City Trolling Spoon. Fluted spoon, heavily nickel plated. Treble hook attached. Swivel end. A very effective spoon. Sizes: 4, 4½ and 5. State size wanted. Weight, each, 1 ounce. Price. 10c

RING LEAD SINKERS, 6 for 5c

H1453—Ring Lead Sinkers. Have brass wire loops in end. 2 inches over all. Weight, six, 3 ounces. 6 for. 5c

H14533—Same as above, but smaller. Weight, 12, 5 ounces. 12 for.....................5c

PAINTED EGG SHAPE FLOATS, 2 for 5c

HH1455—Painted Egg Shape Floats. 2 inches long. White top, green bottom. Solid wood center. Weight, each, ½ ounce. 2 for....5c

DOUBLE GUT LEADERS, EACH 10c

HX1454—Double Gut Leaders. Each leader 3 feet long. Made of extra heavy double gut. Weight, two, 1 ounce. 2 for.........5c

BRAIDED HANK LINES, 2 for 5c

HH1456—Braided Hank Lines. Made of good quality Egyptian cotton. Green color. 25 feet in a hank. Weight, two, 1 ounce. Price, 2 for...........5c

AMATEUR CASTING LINE, 10c

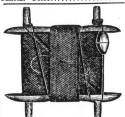

HX1459—Amateur Casting Line. A good quality line, hard braided. No. 6. 75 feet on a spool. Colors: mixed green and white. Unusual strength. Weight per spool, 2 ounces. Price..............10c

FURNISHED FISHING LINE, 5c

HV1458—Furnished Fishing Line. Complete with 50 feet sea green line, heavy sinker and gut hook. All wound on 4½x5 inch wood winder. Weight, 3 ounces. Price.......5c

FURNISHED FISHING LINE, 5c

HV1457—Furnished Fishing Line. Complete with 15 feet good white line. Good hook, sinker and colored float. All wrapped on black enameled wood winder. Weight, 2 ounces. Price.................5c

WOOD CHOKER MOUSE TRAP, 5c

HV1637—Wood Choker Mouse Trap. Made from solid block of wood with coppered wire spring chokers. Catches four mice at one time. Weight, 5 ounces. Price 5c

LEATHER DOG COLLARS, 10c

HX1400—Leather Dog Collars. Tanned leather, felt lined, metal bell and name plate. ⅜ inch wide, 10 to 12 inches long. Weight, 1 ounce. Price.....................10c

HX1401—Same as above, but no bell. ⅝ inch wide, 12 to 14 inches long. Nickeled ring for chain. Weight, 1 ounce. Price.......10c

HX1402—Same as above, but 1 inch wide, 17 to 19 inches long. Nickeled chain ring. Weight 3 ounces. Price.............10c

LEATHER DOG HARNESS, 10c

HX1403—Leather Dog Harness. Good quality leather, felt lined. 3½ inch neck. 4½ inch shoulder. Nickeled buckle. 12 spots and 2 brass bells. A very attractive and well-made harness. Weight, 2 ounces. Price..............10c

LEATHER DOG LEAD, 10c

HX1404—Leather Dog Lead. Good quality tanned leather with nickel plated swivel snap. ⅜ inch wide, 48 inches long, with hand loop. Weight, 2 ounces. Price.....10c

HARDWOOD NAIL BRUSH, 5c

HV1529—Hardwood Nail Brush. Made of best white tampico. Solid hardwood block with raised and grooved hand hold. Weight, 4 ounces. Price, each.............5c

TAMPICO NAIL BRUSH, 5c

HV1528—Tampico Nail Brush. Made of best quality white tampico. 3½ x 4½ inches. Polished block, rounded corners, oblong shape. Weight, 4 ounces. Price.......5c

NAIL BRUSHES, 2 for 5c

HH1526—Nail Brushes. 4 x 15 row white tampico. Sanded hardwood block. A strong, well-made and dependable brush. Weight, each, 4 ounces. Two for......5c

EXTRA SPECIAL BARGAINS—nothing over 10c

NAINSOOK EDGE, YARD 5c.
AV300—Fine Quality Nainsook Edge. About 1½ inches wide. This edge makes a splendid trimming. Pattern as illustrated. Weight yard, ⅔ ounce. Price yard......5c

SWISS VEINING, YARD 5c.
AV310—Fine Quality Swiss Veining. About 1 inch wide. Pattern as illustrated, and very showy. This is an exceptional value for the money. Weight yard, ½ ounce. Price yard......5c

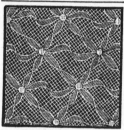

ALLOVER NET, ½ YARD 10c.
AZ530—Fancy Allover Net. About 18 inches wide. Heavy floral design as illustrated. Comes in white or ecru. State color wanted. Weight ½ yard, 1 ounce. Price ½ yard......10c

For other bargains in laces and embroideries, see pages 17 to 24. We import our laces and embroideries direct and save you the middlemen's profits. Nothing over 10c.

RENAISSANCE DOILIES, EACH 10c.

AX601—Renaissance Doilies. Made of good Battenburg braid with pure white muslin center. These doilies are about 12 inches square. Weight 1 ounce. Price......10c

LADIES' WASH BELT, 10c.
AX248—Ladies' Wash Belt. Made of good quality white lawn, heavily embroidered. 2½ inches wide. Fitted with pearl buckle. Sizes 24 to 36. State size wanted when ordering. Weight 2 ounces. Price 10c

We pay the freight on all orders amounting to $10 or more if ordered as indicated on page 3. You save money by buying your merchandise from us and also on transportation charges. Read our offer on page 3.

BEST QUALITY SILK HAIR NET Superior Finish 2 FOR 5¢

SILK HAIR NETS 2 FOR 5c.
BB112—Extra Large Imported Silk Hair Nets. Each net equipped with elastic band, and guaranteed perfect in every respect. Each net in separate envelope. State shade wanted. Weight two nets, 1 ounce. Price 2 for......5c
See page 71 for special bargains in Hair Goods.

EMBROIDERED DOILY, 10c.
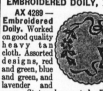
AX4289—Embroidered Doily. Worked on good quality heavy tan cloth. Assorted designs, red and green, blue and green, and lavender and green. State color wanted. Weight, each 1 ounce. Price......10c

LADIES' FANCY RING, 10c.

DX4544—Ladies' Fancy Ring. Split shank, set with three first quality white brilliants. See directions for ordering on page 55. Weight 1 ounce. Price......10c

BEAUTY PINS, CARD 10c.

DX374—Beauty Pins. Half of pin fancy chased design, half plain. Round or square ends. Nicely finished. Come 6 on a card. Illustration shows actual size. Weight per card, 2 ounces. Price, card......10c

BEAUTY PINS, 12 FOR 5c.

DX376—Beauty Pins. Chased finish. One piece. A well made and durable pin. Exceptional value for the price. Above illustration shows actual size. Weight 12, 2 ounces. Price 12......5c

BEAUTY PINS, CARD 10c.

DX373—Beauty Pins. Flat shape with fancy design in center. Well made with rich finish. 6 pins on a card. Above illustration full size. Weight card, 2 ounces. Price......10c

VEIL OR BAR PIN, 10c.

DX327—Veil or Bar Pin. Made of best quality imitation Persian ivory, set with six first quality white brilliants. Illustration shows ⅞ actual size. Weight 1 ounce. Price......10c
A complete line of bar pins, beauty pins, jewelry, etc., for men, women and children will be found on pages 50 to 58. Many retail jewelers charge as high as 25c for the same items. Our price, nothing over 10c.

MEN'S CUFF LINKS, 10c.
DX502—Men's Cuff Links. Finished in Roman or silver color. Large lover's knot design. Strong lever ends. Specify color wanted when ordering. Weight pair, 1 ounce. Price......10c

MEXICAN OUTING HATS, 10c.
DX998—Mexican Outing Hats. Made from good quality straw. Medium wide rolling brim. Very light and serviceable. Suitable for outings, fishing trips, picnics etc. Can be worn by men, women or children. Weight, packed, 7 ounces. Price......10c

BOYS' INDIAN OUTFIT.

EX639—Indian Suit. Blouse only. Trimmed Indian fashion and comes in sizes 2 to 8. State size wanted. Weight 2 ounces. Price.10c
EX640—Indian Suit. Trousers only. Trimmed Indian fashion and matches EX639. Weight 2 ounces. Price.10c
EX641—Indian Suit. Headdress only. Made of assorted colored feathers and matches above. Weight 1 ounce. Price..10c
Order suit complete. Not sold separately. Complete......30c

FANCY VASES, EACH 10c.
EX157—Fancy Vases. Made of good quality opal glass, and stand about 8½ inches high. Can be had in green tint with rose design; brown tint with elk design; or blue tint with violet decoration. State design wanted when ordering. These vases are nicely made and well finished. Weight each 16 ounces. Price each..10c

EX162
EX162 — Heart-shape bon-bon dish. 6 inches long. Very attractive. Beautiful Nu-cut glass pattern. Weight, 18 ounces. Price, each......10c

HEAVY CUT CREAMER 10c
EX131 — Heavy Cut Creamer. Good quality heavy glass. Cut wreath design. Good heavy handle, and neatly turned lip. Matches EX-130. Weight, 9 ounces. Price.....10c

HEAVY CUT SUGAR, 10c.
EX130 — Heavy Cut Sugar. Good quality heavy glass. Cut wreath design. Neat attractive pattern. Matches EX131. Weight, 10 ounces. Price......10c

CUP AND SAUCER, 5c.
EV-183—Holland Tea-Cup and Saucer. Best white crockery. High-grade finish. Cup has round smooth handle. Weight, complete, 12 ounces. Cup and saucer.....5c

ENAMEL PRESERVING KETTLE, 10c.

HX812—Preserve Kettle. Of heavy gray enamel, rolled edge, tipping handle and lip. Strong wire bail securely attached. Four sizes, 2 quart, 2½ quart, 3½ quart, and 4 quart. Always mention size wanted. Average weight, 14 ounces. Price, each......10c

CHECKER BOARDS, EACH, 10c.
EX613—Checker Boards. Folding wood frame with strong board top, covered with bright colored heavy paper. Size when open, 14x14 inches. Complete with checkers and dice box for playing parchesi. A strong, durable board. Weight complete 12 ounces. Price complete......10c

5 and 10 Cent Bargains in Towels

FRINGED TURKISH WASH CLOTHS, 2 FOR 5c.
AA250—Fringed Turkish Wash Cloths. These cloths are 11 inches square and have a fine Terry center. Nicely fringed on edges. Weight 2 cloths 2 ounces. Price 2 for..**5C**

TURKISH WASH CLOTHS, 2 FOR 5c.

AA251—Turkish Wash Cloths. Good quality cloths, double Terry, crocheted edge. Very soft and absorbent. Cloth loop for hanging up. The cloths are 9½ inches square. Weight two cloths 3 ounces. 2 for....**5C**

TURKISH WASH CLOTH, 5c.

AV252—Turkish Wash Cloth. Good quality wash cloth, heavy Terry. Has fancy border and overlocked edges. Size of cloth 11 inches square. Very soft and will not irritate the skin. Weight 2 ounces. Price............**5C**

TURKISH WASH CLOTHS, 5c.

AV253—Turkish Wash Cloths. These cloths are made of heavy Terry and nicely hemmed. Have fancy interwoven border of pink or blue. Size of cloth is 12x13 inches. State color of border wanted when ordering. Weight 3 ounces. Price, each.......**5C**

LARGE SIZE GOOD QUALITY TURKNIT SPECIAL WASH CLOTHS, 5c.

AV254—Turknit Wash Cloth. A very popular brand. Cloth is made of Terry on one side, the other side plain. Has fancy overlocked edges and cloth loop for hanging up. Size is 12x13 inches. Weight 3 ounces. Price, each......**5C**

BLEACHED CRASH TOWELING, PER YARD 5c.

CRASH TOWELING

AV255—Bleached Crash Toweling. Best quality bleached crash toweling about 16 inches wide. Has woven red border on both sides. This is an extra quality toweling at a special price. Weight per yard. 3 ounces. Per yard......................**5C**

GOOD QUALITY TOWELS, EACH 5c.

AV256—Good Quality Towels. Made of best quality absorbent cloth. Suitable for hotel, barber, kitchen, and other uses. Edges are nicely hemmed and towels have woven red border. Size 14x24 inches. Weight 3 ounces. Price, each..........**5C**

GOOD QUALITY HUCK TOWELS, 5c.

AV257—Good Quality Huck Towels. Towels have fine woven red border on both sides and edges are very neatly hemmed. Size of towel is 14x24 inches. These towels are suitable for the bathroom, barbers, hotels, and others who require a good wearing, serviceable towel. For these purposes they will give entire satisfaction. Weight 3 ounces. Price...........**5C**

EXTRA GOOD QUALITY BLEACHED HUCK TOWELS, EACH 5c.

AV258—Good Quality Bleached Huck Towels. Size of towel is 14x28 inches, and has a fine woven red border. The ends are neatly hemmed. This is a strong, durable towel for every day use and is an exceptional value at the price. Weight per towel 4 ounces. Special price, each.....................**5C**

LARGE SIZE HUCK TOWELS, 10c.

AX259—Large Size Huck Towels. These towels are made of very good quality bleached huck and have fancy woven red border on both sides. The ends are neatly and strongly hemmed. The size of towel is 17½x36 inches. This is a soft absorbent towel of extra size. Weight each 4 ounces. Price, each......................**10C**

EXTRA QUALITY PURE WHITE FANCY HUCK TOWELS, 10c.

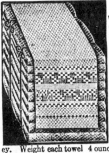

AX260—Extra Quality Pure White Huck Towels. Have neatly woven border on both sides with nice, strong hemstitched ends. These towels are pure white throughout and of the best quality. Each towel is 17½x36 inches in size. They are an exceptional value at the price. Weight 4 ounces. Price, each......................**10C**

FANCY HEM-STITCHED WOVEN BORDER GOOD QUALITY HUCK TOWELS, 10c.

AX261—Good Quality Huck Towels. The size of towel is 18x34 inches. Have fancy hemstitched ends and artistic woven red border. Made of good quality bleached huck. This is a very fine towel for the money. Weight each towel 4 ounces. Price..**10C**

LARGE SIZE FANCY HEM-STITCHED GOOD QUALITY HUCK TOWELS, 10c.

AX262—Large size Huck Towels. These towels have fancy hemstitched ends with a pure white woven border throughout the entire towel. The size of this towel is 18x34 inches. An exceptional value for the price. Cannot be duplicated at the price. Weight each 6 ounces. Price.....................**10C**

EXTRA QUALITY LARGE SIZE HEAVY WEIGHT HUCK TOWELS, 10c.

AX263—Heavy Weight Huck Towels. The size of these towels is 17½x38 inches. Made of extra quality heavy weight huck. Have fancy woven red border, and strong neatly hemmed ends. This is an extra large size towel. Weight 5 ounces. Price...........**10C**

EXTRA QUALITY BLEACHED TURKISH BATH TOWELS, 5c.

AV264—Turkish Bath Towels. Made of fine quality Terry cloth. Size of towel 14x28 inches. Pure white throughout. Has long fringed ends. A very special value at the price. Weight each towel 2 ounces. Price............**5C**

HEAVY TERRY BATH TOWELS, LONG FRINGED ENDS, EACH 10c

AX265—Heavy Terry Bath Towels. Size of towel 17½x38 inches. Has fancy woven white border with long fringed ends. Made of heavy Terry, perfectly bleached. An exceptionally fine towel for the bathroom. Extra length. Weight each towel 5 ounces. Price..**10C**

PURE WHITE HEAVY TERRY HEMMED BATH TOWELS, EACH 10c.

AX266—Heavy Terry Bath Towels. Size of towel 17½x34 inches Made of best quality heavy Terry, pure white throughout. Has strong neatly hemmed ends and fancy woven border. This is a very soft and absorbent towel. A remarkable value. Weight each 5 ounces. Price............**10C**

5 and 10 Cent Bargains in Handkerchiefs

LADIES' FINE INITIAL HANDKERCHIEFS, EACH 10c.

AX155—Ladies' Fine Initial Handkerchiefs. Made of fine quality sheer cloth. ¼-inch edge neatly hemstitched. Nicely embroidered Old English initials in fancy wreath design. Choice of any initial. An exceptional value for the money. State initial wanted. Weight, 1 ounce. Each.. **10C**

LADIES' SWISS EMBROIDERED HANDKERCHIEFS, 10c.

AX158—Ladies' Swiss Embroidered Handkerchiefs. A good quality imported handkerchief. Can be supplied in a great variety of beautiful patterns. Finest quality cloth, and very neat embroidering. May be had in scalloped or hemmed edges. Hemmed edge ¼-inch wide and neatly hemstitched. You will find this handkerchief to be a special value for the money. State whether you prefer hemstitched or scalloped edge. Weight, 1 ounce. Price, each...... **10C**

LADIES' EMBROIDERED HANDKERCHIEFS, EACH, 10c.

AX157—Ladies' Embroidered Handkerchiefs. Made of excellent quality sheer cloth. Beautiful embroidered design of full blown rose and other flowers in corner. ¼-inch edge neatly hemstitched. A very dainty handkerchief at the price. Weight, 1 ounce. Each..................... **10C**

LADIES' CROSSBAR HANDKERCHIEFS, 2 FOR 5c.

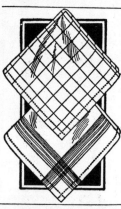

AA145—Ladies' Crossbar Handkerchiefs. Made of good quality white lawn. Measure full 12 inches square. Assorted crossbar designs woven in white throughout handkerchief. ¼-inch edge neatly hemstitched. A dainty handkerchief for ladies. Weight, 1 ounce. 2 for........ ....**5C**

CORDED BORDER HANDKERCHIEFS, 2 FOR 5c

AA147—Corded Border Handkerchiefs. Full size. Made of good quality white lawn. Have double corded border woven through handkerchief in white. ¼-inch edge neatly hemstitched. A very good value for the money. Weight, two 1 ounce. Price, 2 for.....................**5C**

LADIES' PLAIN WHITE HANDKERCHIEFS, EACH, 5c.

AV149—Ladies' Plain White Handkerchiefs. Made of best quality sheer mercerized cloth. ¼-inch edge, neatly hemstitched. This is a pure white handkerchief and a good value. A dainty handkerchief for ladies and misses. Weight, 1 ounce. Price, each.....................**5C**

FANCY WOVEN BORDER HANDKERCHIEFS, EACH, 10c.

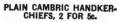

AX156—Fancy Woven Border Handkerchiefs. Made of best quality sheer Shamrock cloth. ¼-inch woven colored edge, neatly hemstitched. Double woven border, one white and the other colored. Pink, blue or lavender borders. State color wanted. Weight, 1 ounce. Price, each............**10C**

LADIES' PURE LINEN HANDKERCHIEFS, EACH, 10c.

AX154—Ladies' Pure Linen Handkerchiefs. These handkerchiefs are warranted all pure linen and of the very best quality. Have ¼-inch edge very neatly hemstitched. One of the very best values offered in this style. Weight 1 ounce. Price, each........**10C**

CHILDREN'S PRINTED BORDER HANDKERCHIEFS, 2 FOR 5c.

AA146—Children's Printed Border Handkerchiefs. Made of good quality white lawn with ¼-inch edge very neatly hemstitched. The border is printed in an assortment of very neat designs and in various colors. Weight, two, 1 ounce. Price, 2 for..............**5C**

LADIES' FINE EMBROIDERED HANDKERCHIEFS, 5c.

AV152—Ladies' Fine Embroidered Handkerchiefs. These handkerchiefs are made of very fine quality lawn. Edge is ¼-inch wide, neatly hemstitched. Heavily embroidered design of grape and other patterns in one corner. Unusual value. Weight, 1 ounce. Each...................**5C**

PLAIN CAMBRIC HANDKERCHIEFS, 2 FOR 5c.

AA144—Plain Cambric Handkerchiefs. Full size, made of good quality cambric. ¼-inch edge, neatly hemstitched. This is a very exceptional value for the price. These handkerchiefs are suitable for either ladies or children. Weight, two, 1 ounce. Price, 2 for..................**5C**

LADIES' INITIAL HANDKERCHIEFS, EACH, 5c.

AV151—Ladies' Initial Handkerchiefs. These handkerchiefs are full size and made of good quality white lawn. Have neatly embroidered Roman initial in one corner. ¼-inch edge neatly hemstitched. State initial wanted when ordering. Weight, 1 ounce. Each.................**5C**

LADIES' MOURNING HANDKERCHIEFS, EACH, 5c.

AV153—Ladies' Mourning Handkerchiefs. Made of good quality white lawn. These handkerchiefs have ¼-inch border neatly hemstitched. Good, fast color. This is a good quality mourning handkerchief for ladies and misses. Weight, 1 ounce. Special price, each..................**5C**

LADIES' FINE CAMBRIC HANDKERCHIEFS, EACH, 5c.

AV148—Ladies' Fine Cambric Handkerchiefs. These handkerchiefs are made of a fine quality soft finish cloth. Have ¼-inch edge very neatly hemstitched. Just the right size for ladies. Very attractive value. Weight each, 1 ounce. Price..................**5C**

FANCY BORDER HANDKERCHIEFS, EACH, 5c.

AV150—Fancy Border Handkerchiefs. Ladies' handkerchiefs with fancy border in a variety of very neat printed patterns. White lawn center with faint corded effect throughout. ¼-inch edge very neatly hemstitched. A very good quality handkerchief. Weight, 1 ounce. Price.....................**5C**

Special Bargains at 5c and 10c Each

GOLD LOOP PATTERN

FLOW BLUE PATTERN   **MORNING GLORY PATTERN**

The above illustrations are actual reproductions of the three patterns of beautiful crockery fully described on pages 108, 109.   These numbers come in all the most useful pieces at 10c each.

JAPANESE HAND DECORATED SALT AND PEPPER SHAKERS

FX150—Creamer
Each 10c.

FX149—Sugar
Each 10c.

DX162
10c.

DV164
5c.

DX163
10c.

FX147—Sugar
Each 10c.

FX148—Creamer
Each 10c.

See page 28 for descriptions, sizes and weights of all the above articles

SPECIAL VALUE IN SHAVING CUPS, EACH 10c.

FX138
Novelty vase, each 10c.

FX152
Each 10c.

FX153
Each 10c.

FX151
Each 10c

FX139
Fancy vase, each 10c.

Complete descriptions giving sizes and weights of above numbers on page 28.

FANCY
SHELF
VASE

FANCY
SHELF
VASE

FX156
Fancy plate, each 10c.

FX146
10c.

FX140
10c.

FX145
10c.

FX141
10c

FX144
10c

FX157
Fancy plate 10c.

For descriptions, sizes and weights of above articles, see page 28.

FX143
Ash tray, 10c.

FX154
Bon Bon dish, 10c.

FX170
Fancy vase, 10c.

FX155
Bon Bon dish, 10c.

FX142
Basket, 10c.

For descriptions, sizes and weights of the above articles, see page 28.

Stamped Pillow Tops, Centerpieces, etc., 10c

AX400—Pillow Top stamped American Beauty Rose and motto design. Each 10c.

AX401—Pillow Top stamped white daisy design. Works up beautifully. 10c.

AX402—Pillow Top stamped forget-me-not and motto design. Very attractive. 10c.

AX403—Pillow Top stamped flag design. Words, OLD GLORY in large letters. 10c.

Complete descriptions, sizes and weights of the above pillow tops are given on page 27.

AX404—Pillow Top stamped Poppy design. Cross stitch work in corners. 10c.

AX405—Pillow Top stamped violet in conventional design. Very easy to work. 10c.

AX406—Pillow Top stamped American Beauty Rose design in fancy effect. 10c.

AX407—Pillow Top stamped Water Lily design. Very effective when worked. 10c.

Complete descriptions, sizes and weights of the above pillow tops are given on page 27.

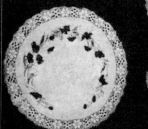

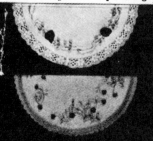

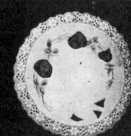

AX417—Centerpiece stamped daisy design. Each 10c.

AX418—Stamped strawberry design. Each 10c.
AX419—Stamped Rose design. Each 10c.

AX420—Stamped Rose design. Each 10c.
AX421—Stamped strawberry design. Each 10c.

AX422—Centerpiece stamped rose design. Each 10c.

Complete descriptions, sizes and weights of the above centerpieces are given on page 27.

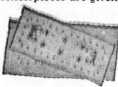

AX423—Stamped handkerchief case. Each 10c.

AX424—Stamped pin cushion cover. Each 10c.

AX425—Stamped pin cushion cover. Each 10c.

AX426—Stamped pin cushion cover. Each 10c.

AX427—Stamped work bag. Each 10c.

Complete descriptions of AX423-424-425-426-427 on page 27.

Embroidery silks of equal quality usually retail at 4c and 5c per skein.

IMPERIAL EMBROIDERY SILKS, 2 skeins for 5c.
See page 26 for complete list of colors, etc.

We can furnish Imperial Embroidery silks in floss or rope sizes.

Stamped Pillow Tops, Pennants, etc., at 10c

AX408—Pillow top stamped Elks Lodge Emblem. Elks head and B. P. O. E. Each 10c.

AX409—Pillow top stamped Odd Fellows Emblem. Eye and I. O. O. F. plainly outlined. Each 10c.

AX410—Pillow top stamped Loyal Order of Moose Emblem. Head of Moose with lettering. Each 10c.

AX411—Pillow top stamped **Masonic Emblem.** Makes a very effective pillow when worked. Each 10c.

Complete descriptions, sizes and weights of the above pillow tops on page 27.

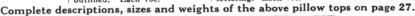

AX412—Pillow top stamped Modern Woodmen of America Emblem. Very attractive. Each 10c.

AX413—Pillow top stamped Knights of Columbus Lodge Emblem. Easily worked. Each 10c.

AX414—Pillow top stamped American Beauty Rose and cross stitch design. Very attractive. Each 10c.

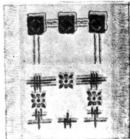

Oblong pillow tops, 10c.
AX415—Pretty Rose design.

AX416—Arts and Crafts design.

Complete descriptions, sizes and weights of the above pillow tops on page 27.

AX430—Table Scarf stamped conventional design on each end. For description, size and weight, see page 28.

AX4288—Embroidered doily. 12 in. in diameter. Worked on good quality heavy tan cloth. Assorted designs. Colors, red and green, blue and green, lavender and green. State color. Weight 1 oz. Each 10c.

AX429—Centerpiece stamped forget-me-not design. Makes a very beautiful centerpiece when worked. Each 10c. For description, size, weight, etc., see page 28.

AX4299—Embroidered doily. 10 in. in diameter. Worked on good quality linen crash. Trimmed with ecru torchon lace. Comes in design illustrated above. Weight, 1 oz. Price, each 10c.

AX428—Table Scarf stamped Arts and Crafts design. Each 10c. For description, size and weight, see page 28.

FRATERNAL PILLOW TOPS IN COLORS, EACH 10c
EX569—We can furnish pillow tops for all leading fraternal societies at 10c each. See page 28 for descriptions and list of societies we can furnish.

COLLEGE PILLOW TOPS IN COLORS, EACH 10c
EX570—We can furnish pillow tops of all the leading colleges with the college seal in rich colors for 10c each. For list of colleges we can furnish, see page 28.

STATE SEAL PILLOW TOPS IN COLORS, EACH 10c
EX571—We can furnish pillow tops for all the States. State seals printed in rich colors. 10c each. See page 28, for description and how to order.

Fraternal Pennants, 10c.
EX574—We can furnish this pennant with emblems of all leading fraternal societies printed in rich colors at 10c each. See page 28 for list of societies we can furnish.

College Pennants, 10c.
EX572—We can furnish this pennant for all leading colleges in rich colors for 10c each. For description and list of colleges we can furnish, see page 28.

Patriotic Pennants, 10c.
EX573—We can furnish this pennant for all the States (army, navy, etc.), printed in rich colors, at 10c each. See page 28 for description and how to order.

Special Bargains in Ribbons, Flowers, 10c.

DX220, 10c	DX209, 10c	DX214, 10c	DX212, 10c	DX216, 10c
Beautiful cotton and silk rose.	Cluster of full blown roses.	Bunch of silk and cotton violets.	Large cherry cluster and foliage.	Bunch of beautiful geraniums.

Descriptions, giving colors, etc., of the flowers illustrated above will be found on pages 31 and 32.

DX221, 10c	DX228, 10c	DX224, 10c	DX238, 10c	DX234, 10c
Large extra quality cotton and silk rose.	Cluster of four large poppy blossoms.	Cluster of six pretty open roses.	Two beautiful full blown roses.	Cluster of six beautiful poppies.

Descriptions, giving colors, etc., of the flowers illustrated above will be found on pages 32 and 33.

AX725, per yd., 10c	AX726, per yd., 10c	AX728, per yd., 10c	AX727, per yd., 10c	AX721, per yd., 10c
Extra good quality moire ribbon.	Extra quality fancy silk ribbon.	Extra quality fancy floral ribbon.	Fine quality fancy floral ribbon.	Fine quality satin dot ribbon.

For complete descriptions, giving colors, widths, etc., of above ribbons, see pages 34 and 35.

DX116, 10c	DX106, 10c	DX110, 10c	DX100, 10c	DX115, 10c
Men's knitted four-in-hand tie. 45 in. long.	Men's silk poplin club tie. All popular colors.	Men's fancy four-in-hand tie. A special value.	Men's four-in-hand tie in solid colors.	Men's knitted four-in-hand tie. 45 in. long.

Descriptions of the above neckwear will be found on page 44. We offer many special bargains in men's neckwear.

DX337 Beauty pins. 10c.	DX308 Hand painted bar pin, fancy setting. Each 10c.	DX338 Beauty pins. 10c.
DX362 Beauty pins. 10c.	DX407 Fancy bar pin, enameled in beautiful colors, 10c.	DX364 Beauty pins. 10c.
	DX303 Bar pin in rich colors hand painted. Each 10c.	

For complete descriptions of above numbers see pages 50, 52 and 53. The illustrations above show goods actual size.

EMBROIDERIES AT 5¢ & 10¢

All of our Embroideries are imported direct from Europe, saving you the usual middlemen's profits. This is the reason we can offer such remarkable values. The patterns are carefully selected and the designs worked in a skilful manner on the best quality cloth. Special attention is called to the patterns selling at 10c per half yard. These same grades are sold by other dealers at prices ranging from 25c to 39c per yard. Our prices—nothing over 10c.

AV301—PER YARD, 5c.
A fine quality medium cambric edge. Width, 2½ inches. Heavily embroidered edge with eyelet and artistic leaf design. Makes a pretty trimming. Weight, ½ ounce. Per yard.....**5¢**

AV302—PER YARD, 5c.
Fine quality cambric embroidery edge, 2⅜ inches wide. Neatly scalloped edge with raised leaf pattern and eyelet design as illustrated. Weight, ½ ounce. Per yard.............**5¢**

AV303—PER YARD, 5c.
A good quality cambric edge, full 3 inches wide. Has heavy scalloped edge, open work pattern and raised leaf design. A very neat pattern. Weight, ½ ounce. Per yard............**5¢**

AV304—PER YARD, 5c.
Fine Cambric embroidery edge, 3½ inches wide. Has fancy scalloped edge and beautiful raised design as illustrated. A very high quality embroidery. Weight, ½ ounce. Per yard.....................**5¢**

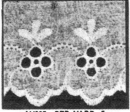

AV305—PER YARD, 5c.
Fine cambric embroidery edge of best quality, full 4 inches wide. Has fancy scalloped edge and design is 1½ inches deep. A very neat pattern. Weight, ½ ounce. Per yard.............**5¢**

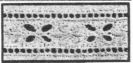

AV306—PER YARD, 5c.
Medium cambric insertion, 4½ inches wide. Beautiful pattern of open work and raised design full ¾ inches wide. A very neat design. Weight, ½ ounce. Per yard.....................**5¢**

AV307—PER YARD, 5c.
Good quality fine cambric insertion, 2½ inches wide. Very neat open work and raised design, full 1½ inches wide. A very showy pattern. Weight, ½ ounce. Per yard.............**5¢**

AV308—PER YARD, 5c.
Ribbon beading insertion, 1¼ inches wide. Pattern of neat open work design with opening for ½-inch ribbon. Design embroidered on best quality cambric. Weight, ½ ounce. Per yard.....................**5¢**

AV309—PER YARD, 5c.
Fine Swiss veining, full 1-inch wide. Made of best quality Swiss with neatly embroidered pattern running through center. A very special value. Weight, ½ ounce. Per yard.............**5¢**

AX320—PER YARD, 10c.
A very fine quality Swiss edge, 2¾ inches wide. The pattern is an eyelet and raised flower design with neatly scalloped edge. Weight, ½ ounce. Price, per yard ....**10¢**

AX321—PER YARD, 10c.
This is a fine quality nainsook edge, full 2¾ inches wide. Has neatly embroidered scalloped edge and raised floral design as illustrated. Weight, ½ ounce. Price, per yard.. ....**10¢**

AX322—PER YARD, 10c.
Fine quality Swiss embroidery edge, 3½ inches wide. Has neatly embroidered scalloped edge with eyelet and raised floral design, as illustrated. Weight, ½ ounce. Price, per yd.**10¢**

AX323—PER YARD, 10c.
A fine quality medium cambric edge, full 3¾ inches wide. Has heavily embroidered scalloped edge and open work pattern with raised fleur-de-lis design. A very beautiful pattern. Weight, ½ ounce. Per yard ....**10¢**

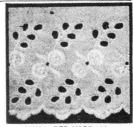

AX324—PER YARD, 10c.
Fine quality cambric embroidery edge, full 6 inches wide. Heavily embroidered scalloped edge with open work and raised pattern design, as illustrated. Weight, ½ ounce. Per yard....................**10¢**

AX325—PER YARD, 10c.
Fine cambric embroidery edge, 6½ inches wide Has neatly scalloped edge and open work pattern, as illustrated. Pattern is full 3 inches deep. A very showy piece. Weight, ½ oz. Per yard ....**10¢**

AX326—PER YARD, 10c.
Fine quality cambric embroidery skirting, 9½ inches wide. Has neatly embroidered scalloped edge with eyelet and raised pattern design. Pattern 4½ inches deep. Weight, ½ ounce. Per yard.......................**10¢**

Be sure to state Katalog Number of embroideries desired when ordering.

Embroideries, Galloons, Edgings, Etc., Yd. 10c

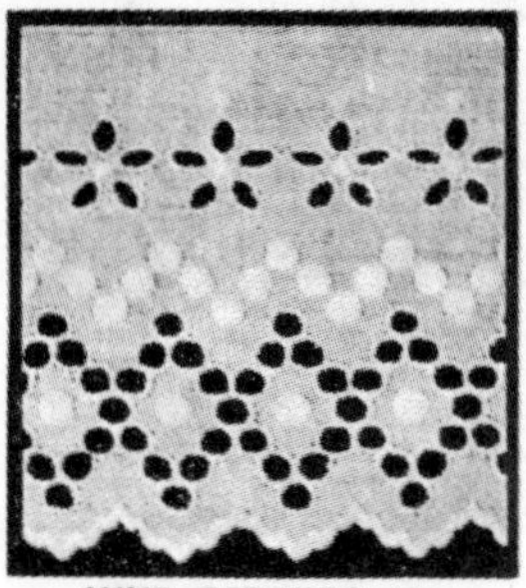

AX327—PER YARD, 10c.
Fine quality cambric skirting, 8½ inches wide. Has large eyelet and raised work design, 4 inches deep. All on best quality cambric. A very showy pattern. Weight, ½ ounce. Per yard........................**10c**

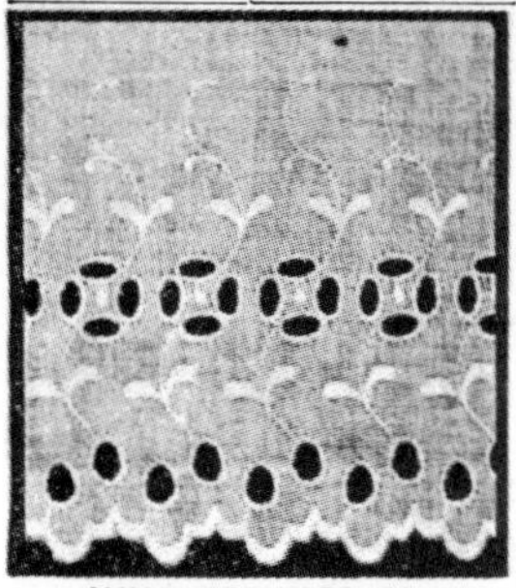

AX328—PER YARD, 10c.
Flouncing made of best quality cambric and measures full 16 inches. Heavily embroidered edge, eyelet and raised floral design. A very special value. Weight, 1 ounce. Per yard........................**10c**

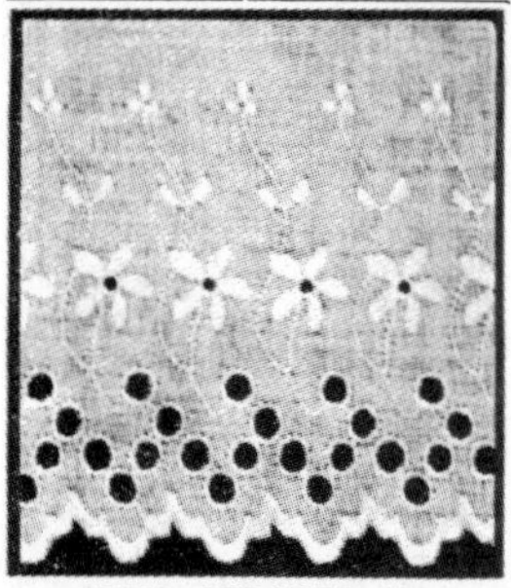

AX329—PER YARD, 10c.
Fine quality cambric embroidery flouncing, full 16 inches wide. Neatly embroidered scalloped edge. Large eyelet and raised floral design as illustrated. Weight, 1 ounce. Per yard........................**10c**

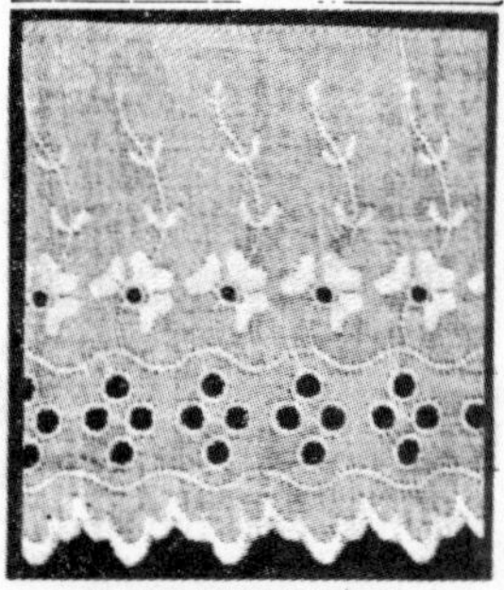

AX330—PER YARD, 10c.
Embroidery flouncing of best quality fine cambric, full 16 inches wide. Has neat eyelet and raised floral pattern with neatly embroidered edge. Weight 1 ounce. Price, per yard......**10c**

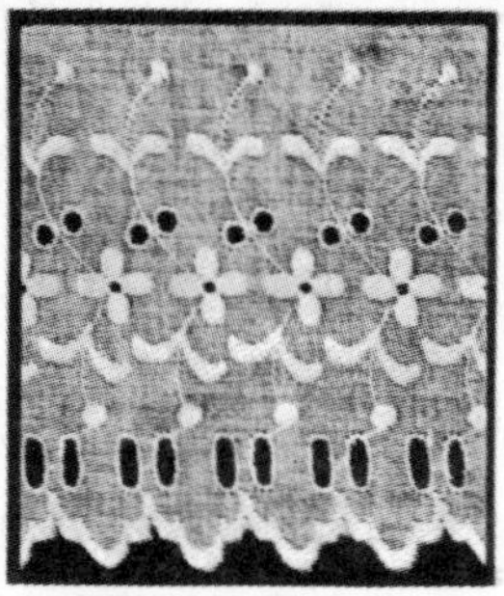

AX331—PER YARD, 10c.
Corset cover embroidery of fine quality cambric. Has eyelet and raised floral design with ½-inch ribbon beading. A very unusual value. Wt., 1 ounce. Price, per yard......**10c**

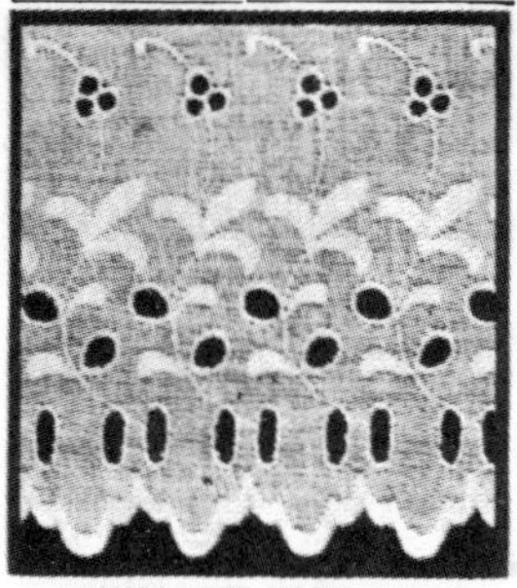

AX332—PER YARD, 10c.
Showy cambric corset cover embroidery, full 16 inches wide. Has raised floral and large eyelet design with neatly scalloped edge. ½-inch ribbon beading. Weight, 1 ounce. Per yard........................**10c**

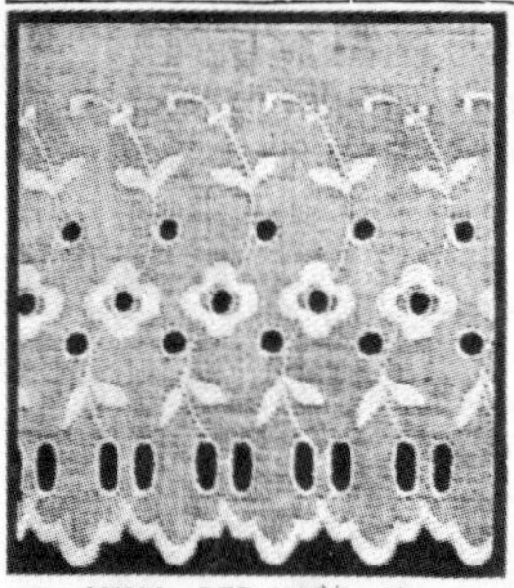

AX333—PER YARD, 10c.
Fine quality cambric corset cover embroidery. 15 inches in width. Scalloped embroidered edge with raised floral and eyelet design, 5 inches deep. Weight, 1 ounce. Per yard....**10c**

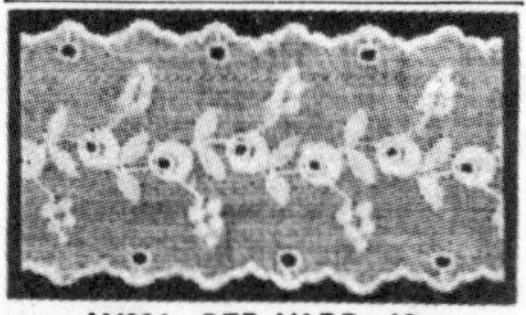

AX334—PER YARD, 10c.
Fine Swiss dress galloon, 1½ inches wide. Neatly embroidered edge with raised floral design through center. A very neat pattern. Special value. Weight, ½ ounce. Per yard.....**10c**

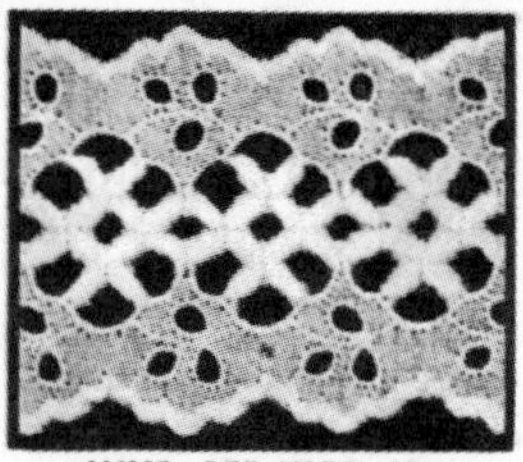

AX335—PER YARD, 10c.
Good quality Swiss dress galloon, 3¾ inches wide. Has neatly embroidered edge with open work and raised figure design throughout. Very showy pattern. Weight, ½ ounce. Per yard........................**10c**

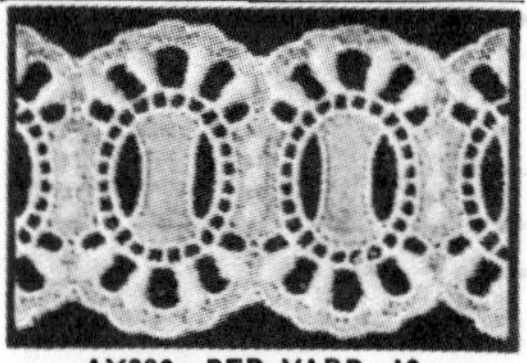

AX336—PER YARD, 10c.
Beautiful ribbon galloon, 1¾ inches wide. This is a very artistic pattern and represents a succession of oval designs. ½-inch ribbon beading. Wt., ½ ounce. Per yard..........**10c**

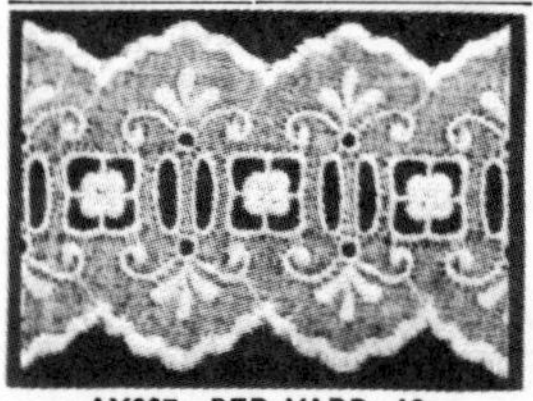

AX337—PER YARD, 10c.
Extra quality cambric ribbon galloon, 2 inches wide. Neatly embroidered scalloped edge with beautiful raised design through center. Ribbon beading, ½-inch wide. Weight, ½ ounce. Per yard............**10c**

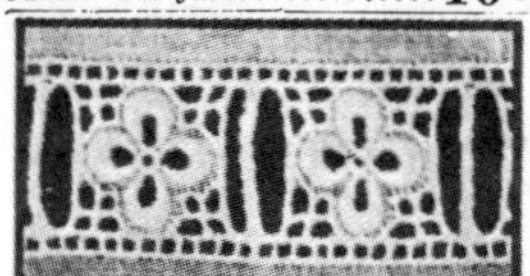

AX338—PER YARD, 10c.
Fine quality Swiss ribbon beading, 1¾ inches wide. Very beautiful open work and raised design as illustrated. Ribbon beading, 1¾ inches wide. Wt., ½ ounce. Per yard..........**10c**

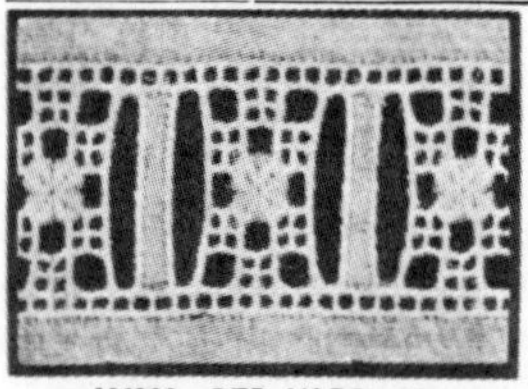

AX339—PER YARD, 10c.
Fine quality cambric ribbon beading, 2½ inches wide. A neat open work pattern with raised figures. Ribbon beading is 1-inch wide. Weight, ½ ounce. Per yard............**10c**

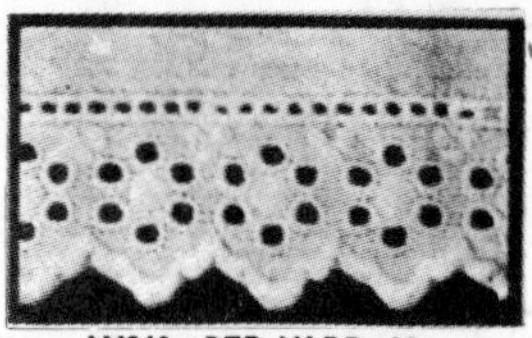

AX340—PER YARD, 10c.
Fine nainsook baby edge, 1¾ inches wide. Has neatly embroidered scalloped edge with eyelet and raised figure design. A very dainty pattern. Weight, ½ ounce. Per yard....**10c**

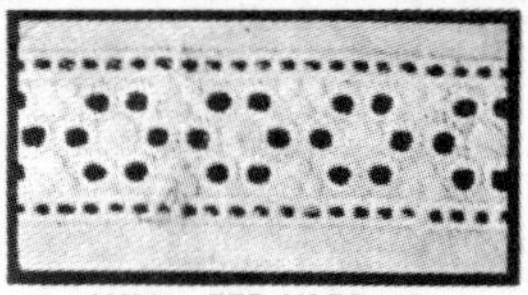

AX341—PER YARD, 10c.
Fine quality nainsook insertion, 1½ inches wide. Has eyelet and raised figure design and matches pattern No. AX340. A special value. Weight, ½ ounce. Per yard **10c**

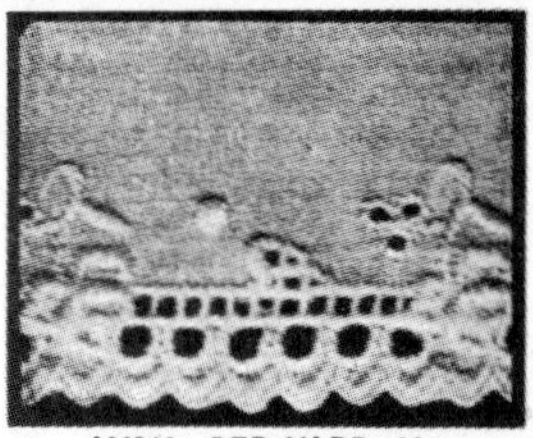

AX342—PER YARD, 10c.
Fine quality nainsook embroidery edge, 1¾ inches wide. Has neatly embroidered scalloped edge with eyelet and raised floral design pattern. Adapted for use on infants' wear. The illustration gives a slight idea of this number. Weight, ½ ounce. Per yard........................**10c**

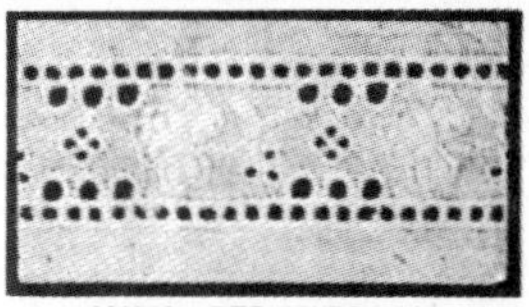

AX343—PER YARD, 10c.
Fine quality nainsook insertion, 1½ inches wide. Has very neat open work and raised floral pattern and matches pattern No. AX342 perfectly. Weight ½ ounce. Per yard............**10c**

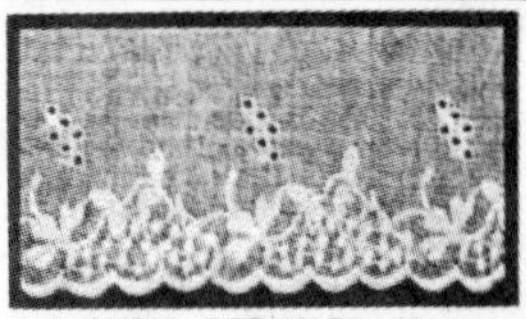

AX344—PER YARD, 10c.
Fine Swiss Baby Edge, 2¼ inches wide. Neatly embroidered scalloped edge with small eyelet and raised floral design, as illustrated. Weight, ½ ounce. Per yard............**10c**

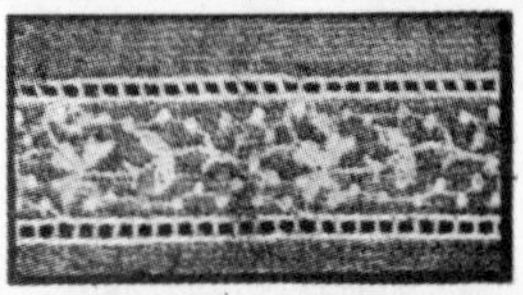

AX345—PER YARD, 10c.
Best quality Swiss insertion, 1½ inches wide. Has small eyelet and raised floral design and matches No. AX344 perfectly. Weight, ½ ounce. Price, per yard........................**10c**

NOTE—We do not send samples of embroideries or laces. The illustrations shown are actual pictures of the goods and show the patterns as they appear in the merchandise. We guarantee everything to be just as represented or will return your money.

Fine Quality Embroideries, per ½ Yard 10c

AZ363—PER ½ YARD, 10c.
Fine Swiss embroidery insertion or band, 6 inches wide. Pattern is in eyelet and heavy raised figure effect, as illustrated. Very showy. Weight, ½ ounce. Per ½ yard **10C**

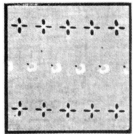

AZ364—PER ½ YARD, 10c.
Fine quality cambric all-over embroidery, about 16 inches wide. Pattern in embroidered eyelet and raised figure effect, as illustrated. Special value. Weight, 1 ounce. Per ½ yard **10C**

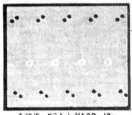

AZ365—PER ½ YARD, 10c.
All-over embroidery of fine quality cambric full 16 inches wide. Has neat pattern of eyelet and raised figure design throughout. See illustration. Weight, 1 ounce. ½ yard **10C**

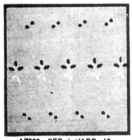

AZ366—PER ½ YARD, 10c.
Fine cambric all-over embroidery, full 16 inches wide. Best quality cambric. Eyelet and neat raised figure pattern throughout, as illustrated. Weight, 1 ounce. Per ½ yard . . **10C**

AZ361—PER ½ YARD, 10c.
Showy Swiss dress galloon, 3½ inches wide. Neatly embroidered edges with open work and raised figure pattern. Baby Irish effect. Very showy. Wt., ½ ounce. ½ yard **10C**

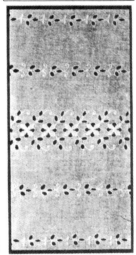

AZ368—PER ½ YARD, 10c.
Swiss embroidery waist fronts, about 17 inches wide. Neat pattern in eyelet and raised figure design. Pattern is about 11 inches deep. Weight, 1 ounce. Per ½ yard **10C**

AZ370—PER ½ YARD, 10c.
Fine quality cambric corset cover embroidery, 16 inches wide. Neatly scalloped edge, open work and raised figure pattern. ½-inch ribbon beading. Weight, 1 ounce. ½ yard **10C**

AZ362—PER ½ YARD, 10c.
Fine quality Swiss band, full 4 inches wide. Beautiful open work and raised figure design throughout, 2½ inches wide. See illustration. Weight, ½ ounce. Price, per ½ yard **10C**

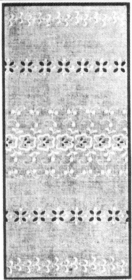

AZ369—PER ½ YARD, 10c.
Best quality Swiss all-over embroidery waisting. 17 inches wide. Beautiful design in open work and heavy raised figures. A very showy and effective pattern. Weight, 1 ounce. ½ yard **10C**

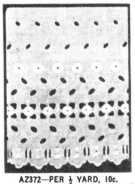

AZ372—PER ½ YARD, 10c.
Cambric corset cover embroidery, full 16 inches wide. Design as illustrated, 8 inches deep. Weight, 1 ounce. Per ½ yard **10C**

NOTE—We do not send samples of laces or embroideries. We guarantee satisfaction or will return your money.

AZ360—PER ½ YARD, 10c.
Fine Swiss galloon, full 3¾ inches wide. Heavily embroidered edges with open work and raised floral design throughout, as illustrated. Very showy. Weight, ½ ounce. ½ yard **10C**

AZ367—PER ½ YARD, 10c.
Swiss all-over embroidery waisting, about 17 inches wide. Heavy showy pattern as illustrated. Weight, 1 ounce. Per ½ yard **10C**

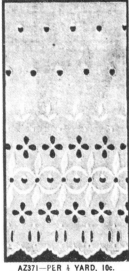

AZ371—PER ½ YARD, 10c.
Cambric corset cover embroidery, 15 inches wide. Neatly embroidered scalloped edge, open work and heavy raised pattern. ½-inch ribbon beading. Wt., 1 ounce. ½ yard **10C**

Fine Quality Flouncings, per ½ Yard 10c

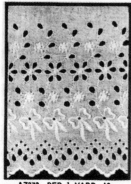

AZ373—PER ½ YARD, 10c.
Cambric embroidery flouncing of fine quality, full 16 inches wide. Made of best quality cambric with neat open work design and beautiful raised figure pattern. Has nicely embroidered scalloped edge. Pattern is about 6½ inches deep. Weight, 1 ounce. ½ yd. **10C**

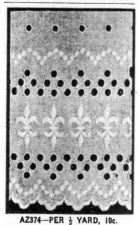

AZ374—PER ½ YARD, 10c.
Fine quality cambric embroidery flouncing. 16 inches wide. Made of best quality cambric with nicely embroidered scalloped edge, eyelet design with raised fleur-de-lis figures. Pattern is 9½ inches deep. Weight, 1 ounce. Price, per ½ yard............**10C**

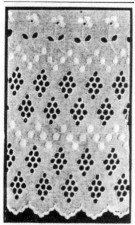

AZ375—PER ½ YARD, 10c.
Fine cambric embroidery flouncing, 16 inches wide over all. Has showy eyelet and raised figure design with neatly embroidered scalloped edge, as illustrated. Pattern is full 8 inches deep. Weight, 1 ounce. Per ½ yard......................**10C**

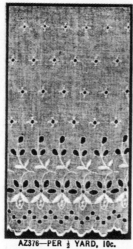

AZ376—PER ½ YARD, 10c.
Fine quality Swiss embroidery flouncing, 26 inches wide. Has heavily embroidered scalloped edge with neat open work and raised figure design throughout. Weight, 1 ounce. ½ yard........................**10C**

AZ377—PER ½ YARD, 10c.
Showy Swiss embroidery flouncing, full 26 inches wide. Heavy embroidered scalloped edge with eyelet and raised figure design throughout. Weight, 1 ounce. Per ½ yard..**10C**

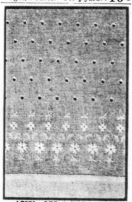

AZ379—PER ½ YARD, 10c.
27-inch Swiss embroidery flouncing. Very dainty pattern, as illustrated. Suitable for infants' apparel, etc. Body of best quality Swiss. Weight, 1 ounce. ½ yard..............**10C**

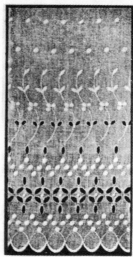

AZ378—PER ½ YARD, 10c.
Fine Swiss embroidery flouncing, full 26 inches wide. Very showy pattern of open work and raised figure design as illustrated. Neatly embroidered scalloped edge. Weight, 1 ounce. ½ yard......................**10C**

AZ380—PER ½ YARD, 10c.
Hemstitched Swiss embroidery flouncing, 27 inches wide. Very dainty pattern, 10½ inches deep, with 2½-inch hemstitching. A special value. Wt., 1 ounce. ½ yard..............**10C**

AZ381—PER ½ YARD, 10c.
Japanese flouncing of best quality sheer mercerized cloth. Beautiful heavy pattern with nicely embroidered scalloped edge. Full 18 inches wide. Weight, 1 ounce. ½ yard......**10C**

AZ382—PER ½ YARD, 10c.
Japanese flouncing, full 18 inches wide. Heavy embroidered design with neat scalloped edge. Mercerized cloth. Popular for summer clothes. Preferred to voile. An attractive pattern at a special value. Weight, 1 ounce. ½ yard.....................**10C**

AZ383—PER ½ YARD, 10c.
Best quality Japanese flouncing. Full 17 inches wide. Embroidered on sheer mercerized cloth. Beautiful raised floral design and embroidered scalloped edges, as illustrated. This is certainly an unusual value at the price. Weight, 1 ounce. ½ yard **10C**

AX739—PER YARD 10c.
Best Quality Muslin Flouncing. 17 inches wide. Made with two rows of five pin tucks each, row of lace insertion, and heavy torchon lace edge. Weight, 1 ounce. Per yard..**10C**
AX740—Same quality as above, except ruffle containing three rows of hemstitching. 19 inches wide. Weight yard 1 ounce. Per yard..**10C**

LACES AT 5 & 10¢

THE laces shown on this and the following pages represent the cream of the stock of the English, German and French lace makers. The new tariff schedule makes it possible for us to offer you almost unheard of values. The patterns represented on these pages are the best selections of the 1914 offerings. The lace Department of the Kresge Stores is one of our most talked of features owing to the exceptional values and wide range of beautiful patterns. Nothing over 10c.

Round mesh Val lace. Good quality. Edge and insertion to match. 1 inch wide.
A400—Edge. 3 yards for .....**5 C**
A401—Insertion. 3 yards for...**5 C**

Val. lace. Round mesh. Fine quality. Edge and insertion to match. 1 inch wide.
A402—Edge. 3 yards for.....**5 C**
A403—Insertion. 3 yards for...**5 C**

Square mesh Val. lace. High quality. Edge and insertion to match. Width ⅞ inches.
A404—Edge. 3 yards for .....**5 C**
A405—Insertion. 3 yards for...**5 C**

Round mesh Val. lace. Edge and insertion to match. Extra value. 1 inch wide.
A406—Edge. 3 yards for......**5 C**
A407—Insertion. 3 yards for....**5 C**

A408—Fine quality beading. ⅜ inches wide.
Splendid value. 3 yards for......**5 C**

A409—Round mesh Val. beading. ¾ inches wide. As illustrated. 3 yards for..........................**5 C**

A410—Fancy Val. beading. Extra value. ⅜ inches wide. 3 yards for.**5 C**

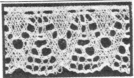

A411—Fast edge German torchon lace. 1¼ inches wide. Good quality. 3 yards for ....**5 C**

A412—Linen finish torchon lace. 1 inch wide. Extra value. 3 yards for..........................**5 C**

A413—All linen torchon lace. ¾ inches wide. Fine quality. 3 yards for..........................**5 C**

A414—German cotton torchon lace. Fine quality. 1 inch wide. 3 yards for..........................**5 C**

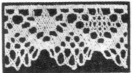

A415—Good quality German torchon lace. 1½ inches wide. 3 yards for.**5 C**

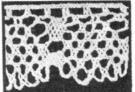

A416—Heavy cotton torchon lace. Special value. 1½ inches wide. 3 yards for..........................**5 C**

Showy Val. lace. Good quality. Edge and insertion to match. ⅝ inches wide.
AA417—Edge. 2 yards for .....**5 C**
AA418—Insertion. 2 yards for.**5 C**

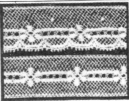

Neat Val. lace. Special value. Edge and insertion to match. ¾ inches wide.
AA419—Edge. 2 yards for.....**5 C**
AA420—Insertion. 2 yards for.**5 C**

Fine quality Val. lace. Neat design. Edge and insertion to match. ⅝ in. wide.
AA421—Edge. 2 yards for.....**5 C**
AA422—Insertion. 2 yards for.**5 C**

Showy Val. lace. Good quality. Edge and insertion to match.
AA423—Edge. 2 yards for.....**5 C**
AA424—Insertion. 2 yards for.**5 C**

Fine quality Val. lace. 1½ inches wide. Edge and insertion to match.
AA425—Edge. 2 yards for....**5 C**
AA426—Insertion. 2 yards for.**5 C**

Fine round mesh Val. lace. Rosebud pattern. Edge and insertion to match. 1 inch wide.
AA427—Edge. 2 yards for.....**5 C**
AA428—Insertion. 2 yards for.**5 C**

Showy round mesh Val. lace. 1½ inches wide. Edge and insertion to match.
AA429—Edge. 2 yards for....**5 C**
AA430—Insertion. 2 yards for.**5 C**

When ordering laces we recommend that you include embroideries, embroidering cotton, stamped pillow tops, centerpieces, dry goods, etc., as a large order of these goods can be sent at a very small cost for transportation. The average weight of above laces is 1 ounce per yard.

Extra Quality Laces at 2 yds. 5c and per yd. 5c

Neat Cluny Pattern lace. Edge and insertion to match. ¾ inches wide. Good quality.
AA431—Edge. 2 yards for.... 5c
AA432—Insertion. 2 yards for 5c

Baby Irish design lace. Width ¾ inches. Edge and insertion Special value.
AA433—Edge. 2 yards for.... 5c
AA434—Insertion. 2 yards for 5c

AA435—Plain Val. beading. ⅝ inches wide. Good value. 2 yards for..... 5c

AA436—Round mesh Val. beading. ¾ inches wide. As illustrated. 2 yards for........ 5c

AA437—Good quality Val. edge, beading top. ¾ inches wide. 2 yards for............ 5c

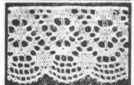

AA438—Heavy German torchon lace. Fast edge. 1⅞ inches wide. 2 yards for....... .... 5c

AA439—Finest quality linen torchon lace. ¾ inches wide. 2 yards for . 5c

AA440—Fine German linen torchon lace. 1½ inches wide. 2 yards for. 5c

AA441—Heavy German cotton torchon lace. 2 inches wide. 2 yards for........................5c

AA442—Best quality mercerized torchon lace. 1½ inches wide. 2 yards for 5c

AV499.—Heavy cotton torchon lace. Extra good quality. 4½ inches wide, Wt. per yard, 2 oz. Per yard.. 5c

AA443—Extra fine quality linen beading. ⅝ inches wide. 2 yards for..................... 5c

Cotton torchon lace. Filet style. Edge and insertion to match. ¾ inches wide.
AA444—Edge 2 yards for..... 5c
AA445—Insertion. 2 yards for. 5c

Fine quality cotton torchon lace. Edge and insertion to match. 1 inch wide.
AA446—Edge, 2 yards for.....5c
AA447—Insertion. 2 yards for. 5c

Showy cotton torchon lace. Edge and insertion to match. Width 2 inches. Weight per yard, 1 oz.
AA448—Edge. 2 yards for.... 5c
AA449—Insertion. 2 yards for. 5c

Fine quality cotton torchon lace. Edge and insertion to match. 2 inches wide. Weight per yard, 1 oz.
AA450—Edge. 2 yards for..... 5c
AA451—Insertion. 2 yards for. 5c

Extra good quality Val. lace. Edge and insertion to match. ⅝ inches wide.
AV452—Edge. Per yard...... 5c
AV453—Insertion. Per yard . 5c

Extra quality Val. lace. Edge and insertion to match. ⅞ inches wide
AV454—Edge. Per yard......5c
AV455—Insertion. Per yard. 5c

NOTE—We do not send samples of laces or embroideries.

Be sure to send an extra amount of money for Postage Charges. Average weight of laces on this page, per yard, ½ ounce; except where otherwise stated.

Fine quality Val. lace. Edge and insertion to match. 1½ inches wide. ⅞ inch insertion.
AV456—Edge. Per yard....... 5c
AV457—Insertion. Per yard.... 5c

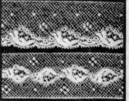

Val. lace, extra fine quality. About ⅞ inches wide. Edge and insertion to match.
AV458—Edge. Per yard....... 5c
AV459—Insertion. Per yard.... 5c

Good quality Val. lace. About 1½ in. wide. Edge and insertion to match.
AV460—Edge. Per yard....... 5c
AV461—Insertion. Per yard... 5c

Round hole Val. lace. Edge and insertion to match. Fine quality. 1½ inches wide.
AV462—Edge. Per yard...... 5c
AV463 Insertion. Per yard... 5c

Ivory color Mechlin lace. Good quality. Edge and insertion to match. About ⅞ inches wide.
AV469—Edge. Per yard 5c
AV470—Insertion. Per yard.... 5c

These Laces are Wonderful Bargains

Extra quality round mesh Val. lace. Edge and insertion to match. 2⅜ inches wide.
AV464—Edge. Per yard......5 C
AV465—Insertion. Per yard...5 C

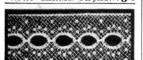

AV466—**Fine quality Val.** beading. ⅞ inches wide. Per yard.........5 C

AV467—**Val. beading.** Special value. ¾ inches wide. Per yard.........5 C

AV468—**Fine quality Val.** lace, with beading top. 1⅜ inches wide. Per yard.........5 C

Fine quality lace, Baby Irish design. 1 inch wide. Edge and insertion to match.
AV471—Edge. Per yard......5 C
AV472—Insertion. Per yard...5 C

Cluny pattern extra quality lace. 1⅜ inches wide. Edge and insertion to match.
AV473—Edge. Per yard......5 C
AV474—Insertion. Per yard..5 C

Mercerized cluny lace. Fine quality. 1 inch wide. Edge and insertion to match.
AV475—Edge. Per yard......5 C
AV476—Insertion. Per yard...5 C

Fine quality cotton cluny lace. 1⅞ inches wide. Edge and insertion to match.
AV477—Edge. Per yard......5 C
AV478—Insertion. Per yard...5 C

Heavy cotton cluny lace. Extra quality. 2¼ inches wide. Edge and insertion to match. White or ecru. State which.
AV479—Edge. Per yard.....5 C
AV480—Insertion. Per yard...5 C

Heavy cotton cluny lace. Good quality. 2⅜ inches wide. Edge and insertion to match. White or ecru. State which.
AV483—Edge. Per yard......5 C
AV484—Insertion. Per yard...5 C

Good quality English cotton torchon lace. 2 inches wide. Edge and insertion to match.
AV487—Edge. Per yard......5 C
AV488—Insertion. Per yard...5 C

Good quality cotton torchon lace, with small cluny design. Edge 2½ inches wide. Insertion 1⅞ inches wide
AV489—Edge. Per yard......5 C
AV490—Insertion Per yard...5 C

Fine cotton torchon lace. Neat design. Good quality. About 2 inches wide. Edge and insertion to match.
AV491—Edge. Per yard......5 C
AV492—Insertion. Per yard...5 C

AV495—**Fine quality** German torchon lace. 1⅞ inches wide. Per yard.........5 C

AV496—**Mercerized torchon** lace. Fine quality. 2¾ inches wide. Per yard.........5 C

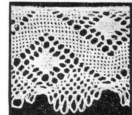

AV497—**Heavy cotton** torchon lace. Special value. 3 inches wide. Per yard.........5 C

AV498—**Good quality** heavy cotton torchon lace. 3½ inches wide. Per yard.........5 C

Cotton torchon lace. Very showy pattern. About 4 inches wide. Edge and insertion to match.
AV493—Edge. Per yard......5 C
AV494—Insertion. Per yard...5 C
Weight, per yard, 2 ozs.

Be sure to send an extra amount of money for postage charges when ordering. Average weight of above laces per yard, 1 oz., except where otherwise stated.

We do not send samples of laces or embroideries. The illustrations shown are actual pictures of the laces. We guarantee to please you or return your money.

Unequaled Bargains in Laces, Etc. at 10c

Fine quality Cluny, real lace shade. 3 inches wide. Edge and insertion to match. AX504—Edge. Per yard **10c**
AX505—Insertion. Per yard.. **10c**

Heavy cotton cluny lace. Good quality. 5¼ inches wide. Edge and insertion to match. White or ecru.
AX514—Edge. Per yard...... **10c**
AX515—Insertion. Per yard... **10c**

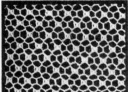

AZ527—Good quality all-over net. 18 inches wide. White only. Per ½ yard........................ **10c**

AZ528—All-over net, tucked pattern. White or ecru. 18 inches wide. Per ½ yard..................... **10c**

Be sure to inclose an extra amount of money to pay postage charges. Average weight of laces on this page per yard, 2 ounces; nets, per ½ yard, 1 ounce.

AX524—White Oriental edge. Neat pattern on fine quality net. About 6 inches wide. Per yard........ **10c**

Heavy cotton Cluny lace. Special value. Edge and insertion to match. Edge, 5 inches wide. Insertion, 4 inches wide. White or ecru.
AX506—Edge. Per yard...... **10c**
AX507—Insertion. Per yard.. **10c**

Showy fancy cotton lace. Very good quality. Edge and insertion to match.
AX420—4¾-inch edge. Per yard **10c**
AX421—4-inch insertion. Yard. **10c**

All pure linen Cluny lace. 2½ inches wide. Edge and insertion to match.
AX500—Edge. Per yard.... **10c**
AX501—Insertion. Yard ... **10c**

Heavy Cotton Cluny lace. Good quality. Edge and insertion to match. White or ecru. Edge 4½ inches wide. Insertion, 5 inches wide.
AX510—Edge. Per yard...... **10c**
AX511—Insertion. Per yard... **10c**

Neat shadow lace. Good quality. Design as illustrated. Edge and insertion to match.
AX522—4½-inch edge. Per yard. **10c**
AX523—3½-inch insertion. Yard **10c**

Medium cotton Cluny Lace. Good quality. 2⅛ inches wide. Edge and insertion to match.
AX502—Edge Per yard...... **10c**
AX503—Insertion. Per yard... **10c**

Extra fine quality shadow lace. 5 inches wide. Edge and insertion to match. AX518—Edge. Per yard **10c**
AX519—Insertion. Per yard.. **10c**

AZ525—Extra quality plain all-over net. Fine mesh. 36 inches wide. White or ecru. Per ½ yard.... **10c**

AZ532—All over net. Cluny design. 18 inches wide. White or ecru. Per ½ yard...................... **10c**

Special Bargains in Art Goods at 10c Each

CROCHETED DOILIES, EACH, 10c.

AX600—Crocheted Doilies. These doilies are hand made of pure white mercerized cotton. Very neat star design border with large design in middle. Special value. Weight, 1 ounce. Each................10C

RENAISSANCE DOILIES, EACH, 10c.

AX601—Renaissance Doilies. Made of good Battenberg braid with pure white muslin center. These doilies are about 12 inches square. Weight, 1 ounce. Price.....................10C

SQUARE RENAISSANCE DOILIES, EACH, 10c.

AX602—Square Renaissance Doilies. All-over design, made from good quality Battenberg braid. Can be washed. About 12 inches square. Weight, 1 ounce. Price. 10C

EMBROIDERED CENTERPIECES, EACH, 10c.

AX603—Embroidered Centerpieces. Good quality art cambric. Pure white embroidery work with neatly embroidered scalloped edge. Diameter, 15 inches. Weight, 1 ounce. Price.......10C

STAMPED CENTERPIECES, EACH, 10c.

AX604—Stamped Centerpieces. Neat eyelet design and scalloped edge stamped on good quality cambric. Will measure about 20 inches when completed. Weight, 2 ounces. Price...................10C

CENTERPIECE OUTFIT COMPLETE, 10c.

AX609—Centerpiece Outfit. Contains one stamped white cambric 18-inch centerpiece with diagram lesson sheet, and enough mercerized cotton to complete. Wt., 2 ounces. Price..............10C

CENTERPIECE AND DOILIE OUTFIT, 10c.

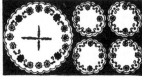

AX610—Centerpiece and Doilie Outfit. One 12-inch centerpiece, four 6-inch doilies, stamped on white cambric. Lesson sheet and mercerized white cotton to complete. Weight, 2 ounces. Price..............10C

SHOPPING BAG OUTFIT, 10c.

AX611—Shopping Bag outfit. Contains one stamped shopping bag pattern on heavy white cloth, lesson sheet, and white mercerized cotton to complete. Price...............10C

WHISK BROOM HOLDER OUTFIT, EACH, 10c.

AX612—Whisk Broom Holder Outfit. Contains one stamped design on heavy art duck, lesson sheet, and sufficient white mercerized cotton to complete. Weight, 2 ounces. Price......10C

LACE TRIMMED APRON, 10c.

AX621—Lace Trimmed Apron. Artistic design stamped on good quality lawn, trimmed with lace, long tie strings. Requires only embroidering to complete. Weight, 1 ounce. Price....................10C

FANCY APRON OUTFIT, 10c.

AX619—Fancy Apron Outfit. Stamped on good quality white lawn. Contains lesson sheet and white mercerized floss to complete the embroidery. Weight, 2 ounces. Price. 10C

STAMPED CORSET COVERS, EACH, 10c.

AX620—Stamped Corset Covers. Neat eyelet design, stamped on good quality white lawn. Needs only embroidering to complete. Weight, 2 ounces. Price...10C

BREAKFAST CAP OUTFIT, 10c.

AX616—Breakfast Cap Outfit. Neat design stamped on good quality white lawn, lesson sheet, and white mercerized cotton to complete. Weight, 2 ounces. Price............10C

BABY BIB OUTFIT, 10c.

AX618—Baby Bib Outfit. Contains neat eyelet design stamped on white mercerized suiting, lesson sheet and white mercerized floss to complete. Weight, 2 ounces. Price....10C

BABY CAP OUTFIT, 10c.

AX617—Baby Cap Outfit. Contains one cap, stamped on fine quality white cambric, lesson sheet and enough white mercerized cotton to complete. Weight, 2 ounces. Price..............10C

HANDKERCHIEF CASE OUTFIT EACH, 10c.

AX614—Handkerchief Case Outfit. Neat eyelet pattern, stamped on heavy white cloth, lesson sheet and enough white mercerized cotton to complete. Weight, 2 ounces. Price............10C

PIN CUSHION COVER OUTFIT, 10c.

AX615—Pin Cushion Cover Outfit. Neat design stamped on heavy art duck, full instructions, and enough white mercerized floss to complete design. Weight, 2 ounces. Price.......10C

GLOVE CASE OUTFIT, 10c.

AX613—Glove Case Outfit. Stamped pattern on heavy white art duck, lesson sheet, and white mercerized cotton to complete. Weight, 2 ounces. Price.....................10C

STAMPED SHOE BAG, 10c.

AX623—Stamped Shoe Bag. Stamped on good quality tan drill, tape bound, with hangers. Holds 2 pair of shoes. Weight, 2 ounces. Price........10C

STAMPED LAUNDRY BAG, 10c.

AX624—Stamped Laundry Bag. Design stamped on white cambric center. Tan sides with drawstring at top. Size, 19x27 inches. Wt. 4 ounces. Price......10C

WHITE FLANNEL BABY SHAWLS, EACH, 10c.

AX622—White Flannel Baby Shawl. Made of good quality flannel with word "Baby" stamped in one corner. Overlocked edges. 25 inches square. Weight, 2 ounces. Price......10C

STAMPED HUCK TOWELS, EACH, 10c.

AX606—Stamped Huck Towels. Eyelet floral pattern one end, stamped for scalloping. Size, 18x36 inches. Weight, 3 ounces. Price..............10C

State Katalog number and inclose an extra amount of money to pay postage charges when ordering. We will promptly return your money if we fail to please you.

We illustrate above many useful pieces of art goods and each number is a wonderful bargain. Be sure to include some of the above items in your order.

THE ORIGINAL PARCEL POST **KRESGE'S KATALOG** FIVE AND TEN CENT STORE

Art Goods, Etc. Nothing Over 10c

PILLOW FRINGE, PER YARD, 10c.

AX633— Pillow Fringe. Heavy quality cotton fringe, 4 inches wide. Ecru color only. For trimming oblong pillow tops. Weight, yard, 1 ounce. Price, yard.... **10C**

NOTTINGHAM LACE PILLOW SHAMS, EACH, 10c.

AX608—Nottingham Lace Pillow Shams. Very showy floral design with overlocked edges. Comes in white only. These shams are full 30 inches square. These pillow shams will wash well and give very good satisfaction. Weight, each, 3 ounces. Price........ **10C**

DRESSER SCARFS, 10c.

AX605 — Dresser Scarfs. Made of extra quality lawn, hemstitched ends with stamped floral design. Size, 18x40 inches. Weight, each, 3 ounces. Price **10C**

PILLOW BACKS, 10c.

A X 6300 — Pillow Backs. Made of plain heavy art cloth. Colors, tan or green. 21 inches square. State color wanted. Weight, 2 ozs. Price... **10C**

CORONATION BRAID, PER BUNCH, 10c.

A X 6 2 5 — Coronation Braid. Best quality mercerized braid, large size, white only, six yards in a bunch. Weight, 1 ounce. Per bunch...... **10C**

SPOOL SILK, 100 YARDS, 5c.

AV637—Spool Silk. Our special brand sewing silk, guaranteed best quality and full length. All staple colors. State color wanted when ordering. Weight, per spool, 1 ounce. Price.. **5C**

NOTTINGHAM LACE DRESSER SCARF, 10c.

AX607—Dresser Scarf. Neat floral pattern, pure white. Size, 17x50 inches. Good wearing quality. Weight, each, 3 ounces. Price............. **10C**

SILK DRAPERY LOOPS, EACH, 5c.

AV627 — Silk Drapery Loops. Medium cord, 3 inch silk bound tassel. Colors, white, ecru, red, or green. State color wanted when ordering. Weight, 1 ounce. Price........ **5C**
AX628 — Same as above, except heavier. Has mercerized ruff. Weight, each, 2 ounces. Price. **10C**

WHITE COTTON CURTAIN LOOPS, 5c.

AV629 — White Cotton Curtain Loops. Made of best quality plain white cotton, heavy cord, 4 inch tassels. Weight, 2 ounces. Price........ **5C**
AA626 — Same as above, except medium size. Plain white cotton cord with 3 inch tassel. Weight, 1 ounce each. Price, 2 for.. **5C**

MERCERIZED CROCHET COTTON, PER BALL, 10c.

AX636 — Mercerized Crochet Cotton. 6-ply, hard twisted yarn. Very brilliant lustre. For all kinds of crochet work. Size, 3-75 yds. Size, 5-120 yds. Size, 10-130 yds. Size, 20-170 yds. Size, 30-220 yds. Size, 40-250 yds. State size wanted. White only. Weight, ball 2 ounces. Price............ **10C**

SCRIM PILLOW RUFFLING, PER YARD, 5c.

AV634 — Scrim Pillow Ruffling. Conventional edge worked with mercerized yarn. Draw-string at top to produce ruffle effect. Colors, cream body with green, red, green and red, yellow and blue edges, or black body with yellow or red edges. This is the ruffling shown on pillow tops, pages 14 and 15. State combination desired. Weight, per yard, 1 ounce. Price, per yard.................. **5C**

EXTRA QUALITY PILLOW GIRDLES, EACH, 10c.

AX630 — Extra Quality Pillow Girdles. Heavy 3-ply cotton cord with tassels to match. Length, 3 yards. Colors, red, green, yellow, red and green, yellow and white, black and yellow or red, white and blue. State color wanted. Weight, each, 3 ounces. Price.................... **10C**

MERCERIZED PILLOW EDGE, PER YARD, 5c.

AV632 — Mercerized Pillow Edge. Made of good quality yarn, 1¼ inches wide. Comes in ecru color only. Weight, yard, 1 ounce. Per yard................. **5C**

FELT LINED EMBROIDERY HOOPS, PAIR, 10c.

AX635 — Felt Lined Embroidery Hoops. Smooth finished wood, close fitting. Inside hoop felt covered to prevent slipping. Oval shape, 4½x9 inches, and 6x12 inches. Round shape, 5, 6, 7 and 8 inches. State shape and size wanted. Weight, pair, 2 ounces. Price.................... **10C**

BALL CURTAIN FRINGE, PER YARD, 5c.

AV631 — Ball Curtain Fringe. Suitable for curtains, upholstering, etc. Medium chenille balls on good quality tape. Colors, white, ecru, green, or red. State color wanted. Weight, per yard, 1 ounce. Price...... **5C**

"Imperial Brand" Embroidery Silks—2 Skeins 5c

We heartily recommend the use of our special "Imperial Brand" Embroidery Silks. The low price at which we offer our "Imperial Brand" Embroidery Silks is not to be construed in any way as a lack of merit. A careful comparison of our silks with other brands which ordinarily retail at 4c and 5c per skein will convince you of the superiority of our "Imperial Brand" Embroidery Silks.

We can furnish "Imperial Brand" Embroidery Silks in floss or rope size. When ordering be sure to state whether floss or rope is desired. We furnish "Imperial Brand" Embroidery Silks in complete assortments as listed below to work the Pillow Tops, Centerpieces, etc., illustrated on pages 14 and 15. The assortments listed below contain all necessary silks in the proper colors to work designs on Pillow Tops and Centerpieces in beautiful natural looking colors. When ordering be sure to state the Number of assortment you desire, also Katalog Number of Pillow Top or Centerpiece.

ASSORTMENT 1.—For working Pillow Top AX400. Consists of 18 skeins, complete assortment.....**45C**	**ASSORTMENT 11**—For working Pillow Top AX410 Consists of 14 skeins, complete assortment.....**35C**	**ASSORTMENT 21**—For working Centerpiece AX420. Consists of 14 skeins, complete assortment.....**35C**
ASSORTMENT 2.—For working Pillow Top AX401. Consists of 12 skeins, complete assortment.....**30C**	**ASSORTMENT 12**—For working Pillow Top AX411. Consists of 12 skeins, complete assortment.....**30C**	**ASSORTMENT 22**—For working Centerpiece AX421. Consists of 14 skeins, complete assortment.....**35C**
ASSORTMENT 3—For working Pillow Top AX402. Consists of 14 skeins, complete assortment.....**35C**	**ASSORTMENT 13**—For working Pillow Top AX412. Consists of 12 skeins, complete assortment.....**30C**	**ASSORTMENT 23**—For working Centerpiece AX422. Consists of 12 skeins, complete assortment.....**30C**
ASSORTMENT 4—For working Pillow Top AX403. Consists of 16 skeins, complete assortment.....**40C**	**ASSORTMENT 14**—For working Pillow Top AX413. Consists of 14 skeins, complete assortment.....**35C**	**ASSORTMENT 24**—For working Case AX423. Consists of 6 skeins, complete assortment.....**15C**
ASSORTMENT 5—For working Pillow Top AX404. Consists of 16 skeins, complete assortment.....**40C**	**ASSORTMENT 15**—For working Pillow Top AX414. Consists of 16 skeins, complete assortment.....**40C**	**ASSORTMENT 25**—For working Cover AX424. Consists of 6 skeins, complete assortment.....**15C**
ASSORTMENT 6—For working Pillow Top AX405. Consists of 12 skeins, complete assortment.....**30C**	**ASSORTMENT 16**—For working Pillow Top AX415. Consists of 10 skeins, complete assortment.....**25C**	**ASSORTMENT 26**—For working Cover AX425. Consists of 6 skeins, complete assortment.....**15C**
ASSORTMENT 7—For working Pillow Top AX406. Consists of 14 skeins, complete assortment.....**35C**	**ASSORTMENT 17**—For working Pillow Top AX416. Consists of 12 skeins, complete assortment.....**30C**	**ASSORTMENT 27**—For working Cover AX426. Consists of 8 skeins, complete assortment.....**20C**
ASSORTMENT 8—For working Pillow Top AX407. Consists of 16 skeins, complete assortment.....**40C**	**ASSORTMENT 18**—For working Centerpiece AX417. Consists of 8 skeins, complete assortment.....**20C**	**ASSORTMENT 28**—For working Bag AX427. Consists of 4 skeins, complete assortment.........**10C**
ASSORTMENT 9—For working Pillow Top AX408. Consists of 8 skeins, complete assortment.....**20C**	**ASSORTMENT 19**—For working Centerpiece AX418. Consists of 14 skeins, complete assortment.....**35C**	**ASSORTMENT 29**—For working Scarf AX428. Consists of 10 skeins, complete assortment.....**25C**
ASSORTMENT 10—For working Pillow Top AX409. Consists of 10 skeins, complete assortment.....**25C**	**ASSORTMENT 20**—For working Centerpiece AX419. Consists of 16 skeins, complete assortment.....**40C**	**ASSORTMENT 30**—For working Centerpiece AX429. Consists of 18 skeins, complete assortment.....**45C**
		ASSORTMENT 31—For working Scarf AX430. Consists of 16 skeins, complete assortment.....**40C**

Descriptions of Pillow Top Outfits, Etc.

We describe on this page the beautiful Pillow Tops, Centerpieces, etc. illustrated on pages 14 and 15

DESCRIPTION OF AX400.

American Beauty Rose and Motto Design, stamped on best quality tan art ticking. 21 inches square 10c
One drill back 10c
4 yards No. AV634 ruffling, on page 26, yd., 5c 20c
To completely work above design order assortment No. 1 of Imperial Embroidery Floss, consisting of 18 skeins, 2 skeins, 5c 45c
Weight of above outfit complete, 5 ounces.

DESCRIPTION OF AX401.

White Daisy design, stamped on tan ticking. 21 inches square 10c
One drill back 10c
4 yards No. AV634 ruffling on page 26, yd., 5c 20c
To completely work above design order assortment No. 2 of Imperial Embroidery Floss, consisting of 12 skeins, 2 skeins, 5c 30c
Weight of above outfit complete, 5 ounces.

DESCRIPTION OF AX402.

Forget-me-not Design, stamped on tan art ticking. 21 inches square 10c
One tan drill back 10c
4 yards No. AV634 ruffling on page 26, yd., 5c 20c
To completely work above design order assortment No. 3 of Imperial Embroidery Floss, consisting of 14 skeins, 2 skeins, 5c 35c
Weight of above outfit complete, 5 ounces.

DESCRIPTION OF AX403.

Popular "Flag" Design, stamped on best quality tan art ticking. 21 inches square 10c
One drill back 10c
4 yards No. AV634 ruffling on page 26, yd., 5c 20c
To completely work above design order assortment No. 4 of Imperial Embroidery Floss, consisting of 16 skeins, 2 skeins, 5c 40c
Weight of above outfit complete, 5 ounces.

DESCRIPTION OF AX404.

Poppy Pattern stamped on best quality tan ticking. 21 inches square 10c
One drill back 10c
4 yards No. AV634 ruffling on page 26, yd., 5c 20c
To completely work above design order assortment No. 5 of Imperial Embroidery Floss, consisting of 16 skeins, 2 skeins, 5c 40c
Weight of above outfit complete, 5 ounces.

DESCRIPTION OF AX405.

Violet Design stamped on tan ticking. 21 inches square 10c
One drill back 10c
4 yards No. AV634 ruffling, on page 26, yd., 5c 20c
To completely work above design order assortment No. 6 of Imperial Embroidery Floss, consisting of 12 skeins, 2 skeins, 5c 30c
Weight of above outfit complete, 5 ozs.

DESCRIPTION OF AX406.

American Beauty Pattern stamped on best quality tan ticking. 21 inches square. 10c
One drill back 10c
4 yards No. AV634 ruffling on page 26, yd., 5c 20c
To completely work above design order assortment No. 7 of Imperial Embroidery Floss, consisting of 14 skeins, 2 skeins 5c 35c
Weight of above outfit complete, 5 ounces.

DESCRIPTION OF AX407.

Water Lily Design on tan ticking. 21 inches square 10c
One drill back 10c
4 yards No. AV634 ruffling on page 26, yd., 5c 20c
To completely work above design order assortment No. 8 of Imperial Embroidery Floss, consisting of 16 skeins, 2 skeins, 5c 40c
Weight of above outfit complete, 5 ounces.

DESCRIPTION OF AX408.

Elk's Lodge Pillow Top, stamped with B. P. O. E. and Elk head design on best quality tan ticking. 21 inches square. 10c
One drill back 10c
4 yards No. AV634 ruffling on page 26, yd., 5c 20c
To completely work above design order assortment No. 9 of Imperial Embroidery Floss, consisting of 8 skeins, 2 skeins, 5c 20c
Weight of above outfit complete, 5 ounces.

In the description of each number we specify the various materials, and price of same, necessary to completely work and finish all numbers illustrated on pages 14 and 15. When ordering be sure to specify Katalog Number and enclose money enough to cover the price of the outfit desired.

DESCRIPTION OF AX409.

Odd Fellow's Pillow Top, stamped with I. O. O. F. and emblem on best quality tan art ticking. 21 inches square 10c
One drill back 10c
4 yards No. AV634 ruffling on page 26, yd., 5c 20c
To completely work above design order assortment No. 10 of Imperial Embroidery Floss, consisting of 10 skeins, 2 skeins, 5c 25c
Weight of above outfit complete, 5 ounces.

DESCRIPTION OF AX410.

Loyal Order of Moose Pillow Top, stamped with proper emblem on best quality tan art ticking. 21 inches square 10c
One drill back 10c
4 yards No. AV634 ruffling on page 26, yd., 5c 20c
To completely work above design order assortment No. 11 of Imperial Embroidery Floss, consisting of 14 skeins, 2 skeins, 5c 35c
Weight of above outfit complete, 5 ounces.

DESCRIPTION OF AX411.

Masonic Pillow Top with proper emblem stamped on best art ticking. 21 inches square 10c
One drill back 10c
4 yards No. AV634 ruffling on page 26, yd., 5c 20c
To completely work above design order assortment No. 12 of Imperial Embroidery Floss, consisting of 12 skeins, 2 skeins 5c 30c
Weight of above outfit complete, 5 ounces.

DESCRIPTION OF AX412.

Modern Woodmen of America emblem, stamped on best tan art ticking. 21 inches square 10c
One drill back 10c
4 yards No. AV634 ruffling on page 26, yd., 5c 20c
To completely work above design order assortment No. 13 of Imperial Embroidery Floss, consisting of 12 skeins, 2 skeins 5c 30c
Weight of above outfit complete, 5 ounces.

DESCRIPTION OF AX413.

Knights of Columbus emblem stamped on best quality tan art ticking. 21 inches square 10c
One drill back 10c
4 yards No. AV634 ruffling on page 26, yard, 5c 20c
To completely work above design order assortment No. 14 of Imperial Embroidery Floss, consisting of 14 skeins, 2 skeins, 5c 35c
Weight of above outfit complete, 5 ounces.

DESCRIPTION OF AX414.

American Beauty Rose, cross-stitch design, stamped on best quality basket weave cloth. 21 inches square 10c
One drill back 10c
4 yards No. AV634 ruffling on page 26, yd., 5c 20c
To completely work above design order assortment No. 15 of Imperial Embroidery Floss, consisting of 16 skeins, 2 skeins 5c 40c
Weight of above outfit complete, 5 ounces.

DESCRIPTION OF AX415.

Conventional Rose Design Pillow Top, stamped on best quality art crash. 17x22 inches 10c
One drill back 10c
One yard Ecru fringe No. AX633 on page 26 .... 10c
To completely work above design order assortment No. 16 of Imperial Embroidery Floss, consisting of 10 skeins, 2 skeins, 5c 25c
Weight of above outfit complete, 5 ounces.

DESCRIPTION OF AX416.

Arts and Crafts Pillow Top stamped on heavy tan art crash. 17x22 inches 10c
One drill back 10c
One yard Ecru fringe No. AX633 on page 26 .... 10c
To completely work above design order assortment No. 17 of Imperial Embroidery Floss, consisting of 12 skeins, 2 skeins 5c 30c
Weight of above outfit complete, 5 ounces.

DESCRIPTION OF AX417.

Centerpiece, Yellow Daisy Design, stamped on heavy white basket weave cloth. 22 inches in diameter 10c
2 yards white Cluny lace, yd., 5c 10c
To completely work above design order assortment No. 18 of Imperial Embroidery Floss, consisting of 8 skeins, 2 skeins 5c 20c
Weight, of above outfit complete, 3 ounces.

DESCRIPTION OF AX418.

Centerpiece, Strawberry Design, stamped on best quality heavy white drill. 27 inches in diameter 10c
3 yards white Cluny lace, yd., 5c 15c
To completely work above design order assortment No. 19 of Imperial Embroidery Floss, consisting of 14 skeins, 2 skeins 5c 35c
Weight of above outfit complete, 3 ounces.

DESCRIPTION OF AX419.

Centerpiece, American Beauty and Leaf Design, stamped on heavy tan drill. 27 inches in diameter 10c
3 yards Ecru Cluny lace, yd., 5c 15c
To completely work above design order assortment No. 20 of Imperial Embroidery Floss, consisting of 16 skeins, 2 skeins, 5c 40c
Weight of above outfit complete, 5 ounces.

DESCRIPTION OF AX420.

Centerpiece, Rose Design, stamped on heavy white drill. 27 inches in diameter 10c
3 yards white Cluny lace, yd., 5c 15c
To completely work above design order assortment No. 21 of Imperial Embroidery Floss, consisting of 14 skeins, 2 skeins 5c 35c
Weight of above outfit complete, 3 ounces.

DESCRIPTION OF AX421.

Centerpiece, Strawberry Design, stamped on heavy tan drill. 27 inches in diameter 10c
3 yards Ecru Cluny lace, yd., 5c 15c
To completely work above design order assortment No. 22 of Imperial Embroidery Floss, consisting of 14 skeins, 2 skeins 5c 35c
Weight of above outfit complete, 5 ounces.

DESCRIPTION OF AX422.

Centerpiece, American Beauty Rose Design, stamped on heavy white basket weave cloth. 22 inches in diameter 10c
2 yards white Cluny lace, yd., 5c 10c
To completely work above design order assortment No. 23 of Imperial Embroidery Floss, consisting of 12 skeins, 2 skeins, 5c 30c
Weight of above outfit complete, 3 ounces.

DESCRIPTION OF AX423.

Handkerchief Case, Butterfly Design, stamped on heavy ecru Paris cloth. Edges stamped for escalloping. 8x10 inches. 10c
To completely work above design order assortment No. 24 of Imperial Embroidery Floss, consisting of 6 skeins, 2 skeins 5c 15c
Weight of above outfit complete, 2 ounces.

DESCRIPTION OF AX424.

Pin Cushion Cover, Forget-me-not Design, stamped on heavy white art linen. Edges and eyelets stamped. Two 4x12-inch forms 10c
To completely work above design order assortment No. 25 of Imperial Embroidery Floss, consisting of 6 skeins, 2 skeins 5c 15c
Weight of above outfit complete, 2 ounces.

DESCRIPTION OF AX425.

Pin Cushion Cover, Wreath Design stamped on good quality brown linen. Stamped edges and eyelets. 4x10 inches 10c
To completely work above design order assortment No. 26 of Imperial Embroidery Floss, consisting of 6 skeins, 2 skeins 5c 15c
Weight of above outfit complete, 2 ounces.

DESCRIPTION OF AX426.

Pin Cushion Cover, Neat Floral Pattern, stamped on heavy Paris cloth, edges stamped for escalloping. 9x12 inches 10c
To completely work above design order assortment No. 27 of Imperial Embroidery Floss, consisting of 8 skeins, 2 skeins 5c. 20c
Weight of above outfit complete, 2 ounces.

DESCRIPTION OF AX427.

Shopping or Work Bag, Wreath Design, stamped on heavy tan Paris cloth. Bag equipped with metal eyelets and draw-string. 9x12 inches 10c
To completely work above design order assortment No. 28 of Imperial Embroidery Floss, consisting of 4 skeins, 2 skeins 5c 10c
Weight of above outfit complete, 2 ounces.

Descriptions of the Pillow Tops, Centerpieces and Pennants Shown on page 15

DESCRIPTION OF EX569.

Fraternal Pillow Tops. All appropriate color combinations with emblem of each fraternity reproduced in colors. Size, 18x18 inches. Extra good grade felt. List includes Royal Arcanum, F. O. E., A. O. H., A. F. & A. M., K. of Maccabees, Knights Templar, K. of C., K. of P., Moose, Woodmen of America, W. O. W., Shriners, B. P. O. E., G. A. R., I. O. O. F., and U. S. A. State kind wanted. Weight, each, 2 ounces. Price.............................. 10c

DESCRIPTION OF EX570.

College Pillow Tops. Made of good grade felt with college emblem in appropriate color combinations. Size, 18x18 inches. List includes Princeton, Pennsylvania, Yale, Columbia, Chicago, Army, Navy, Carlisle, Cornell, Harvard, Dartmouth, Brown, Vassar, Wisconsin, Nebraska and Bucknell. State college wanted. Weight, each, 2 ounces. Price.............................. 10c

DESCRIPTION OF EX571.

Pillow Tops. Seals and names of states in appropriate colors on good quality felt. List includes every state in the Union. Size of pillow top, 18x18 inches. Weight, each, 2 ounces. Price 10c

NOTE:—We furnish the above Pillow Tops as described only. Be sure to state the number and title of each Pillow Top you desire when ordering.

DESCRIPTION OF AX428.

Table Scarf, Arts and Crafts Design, both ends stamped. Heavy crash cloth. Material required to complete design as illustrated on page 15. One stamped scarf, 17x36 inches 10c

One yard fringe AX633, page 26.... 10c

To completely work above design order assortment No. 29 Imperial Embroidery Floss, consisting of 10 skeins, 2 skeins,5c 25c

Weight of above outfit complete, 4 ounces.

DESCRIPTION OF AX429.

White Centerpiece, Conventional Design, stamped on heavy white basket weave cloth. Edge stamped for escalloping. Material required to complete design as illustrated on page 15:

One stamped Centerpiece, 22 inches in diameter........................ 10c

Above design may be embroidered with white only, or in colors, using assortment No. 30, Imperial Embroidery Floss, consisting of 18 skeins, 2 skeins 5c.............. 45c

Weight of above outfit complete, 2 ounces.

DESCRIPTION OF AX430.

Table Scarf, Conventional Design, stamped on each end of heavy tan crash. Material required to complete design as illustrated on page 15:

One stamped scarf, 17x36 inches.... 10c

One yard ecru fringe AX633, page 26 10c

To completely work above design order assortment No. 31 of Imperial Embroidery Floss, consisting of 16 skeins,2 skeins 5c 40c

Weight of above outfit complete, 5 ounces.

DESCRIPTION OF EX572.

Felt College Pennants. College name and emblem in appropriate color combinations on good grade felt. Size of pennant, 13x34 inches. List includes Yale, Columbia, Chicago, Purdue, Illinois, Nebraska, North Dakota, Army,Dartmouth, Michigan, U. of P., Carlisle, Kansas, Colorado, Wyoming, Ohio, Princeton, Iowa, Harvard,Minnesota, Indiana, Pennsylvania, Notre Dame, West Point, Cornell, Virginia, Wisconsin, W. & J., Penna. State, New Mexico, Denver, Michigan (Mascot), Texas, Vermont, Maine, Boston, Brown University, G. A. R., Knights of Malta. State kind wanted. Weight, each, 2 ounces. Price.............................. 10c

DESCRIPTION OF EX573.

Patriotic Pennants. Appropriate color combinations on good grade felt. Size of pennant, 13x34 inches. List includes U. S. A., Army, Navy, Boy Scouts and state seals of every state in the Union. State kind wanted. Weight, 2 ounces. Price...... 10c

DESCRIPTION OF EX574.

Fraternal Pennants. Correct emblems and mottoes in rich color combinations on good grade felt. Size, 13x34 inches. List includes A. O. H., Moose, I. O. O. F., Shriners, B. P. O. E., A. F. & A. M., Knights Templar, Royal Arcanum and K. of C. State kind wanted. Weight, each, 2 ounces. Price.............................. 10c

NOTE:—We furnish the above Pennants as described only. State kind wanted when ordering.

Descriptions of the Fancy Vases, Plates, Creamers and Sugars Shown on Page 13

The illustrations of the articles described below are shown on page 13 in actual colors. They are indeed very special bargains—nothing over 10c.

FX138—Imported Colonial Bisque Figure. Girl with vase. 4x5 inches. Gold trimmed. Matches FX139. Weight, 5 ounces. Price.............................. 10c

FX139—Imported Colonial Bisque Figure. Boy with vase. 4x5 inches. Gold trimmed. Matches FX138. Weight, 5 ounces. Price.............................. 10c

FX140—Imported Colonial Bisque Figure. Girl with match holder. 4½ inches high. Matches FX141. Gold trimmed. Weight, 5 ounces. Price.................. 10c

FX141—Imported Colonial Bisque Figure. Boy with match holder. 4½ inches high. Gold trimmed. Matches FX140. Weight, 5 ounces. Price 10c

FX142—Imported Novelty Basket. Bunch of grapes in raised design on basket, finished in natural colors. Size, 3½x4 inches. Weight 5 ounces. Price 10c

FX143 — Imported Ash Tray. Small pig. Tray finished in rich colors, highly glazed. Size, 3x4 inches. Weight, 5 ounces. Price.............................. 10c

FX144—Imported China Vase. Brown shaded and highly glazed. Has picture of "Angelus" or "Reaper." 6 inches high. Weight, 8 ounces. Price........... 10c

FX145—Imported China Vase. Brown and green shaded, highly glazed. Has picture of "Shepherd" in rich colors. 6 inches high. Weight, 6 ounces. Price 10c

FX146—Imported China Vase. Brown shaded and glazed. Has picture of "Reaper" or "Angelus." Novel shape. 6 inches high. Weight, 6 ounces. Price 10c

FX147—Imported Sugar Bowl. Colored rose border, highly glazed. Artistic pattern. Matches FX148. 4 inches high. Weight, 9 ounces. Price.......................... 10c

FX148—Imported Creamer. Colored rose border, highly glazed. Very neat pattern. Matches FX147. 3 inches high. Weight, 6 ounces. Price 10c

FX149—Imported Sugar Bowl. Rich gold border on bowl and cover, highly glazed. 4 inches high. Matches FX150. Weight, 10 ounces. Price.......................... 10c

FX150 — Imported Creamer. Rich gold border and stripe decoration. 3 inches high. Matches FX149.Weight,6 ounces. Price 10c

FX151 — Imported Shaving Mug. China mug with fancy edge and head of horse in rich colors. Strong handle. 3½ inches high. Weight, 9 ounces. Price........... 10c

FX152 — Imported Shaving Mug. China mug with fancy edge and dog's head in rich colors. Highly glazed. 3½ inches high. Weight, 9 ounces. Price........... 10c

FX153—Imported Shaving Mug. China Mug with fancy edge and lady's head in rich colors. Large handle. 3½ inches high. Weight, 9 ounces. Price............ 10c

FX154 — Imported Bon Bon Dish. Perforated, heart shape with floral decorations and gold edge. Size, 2½x4½ inches. Weight, 5ounces. Matches FX155. Price... 10c

FX155 — Imported Bon Bon Dish. Perforated, oblong shape, floral decorations and gold edge. Size, 4x6 inches. Matches FX154. Weight, 4 ounces. Price........... 10c

FX156—Imported China Plate. Perforated edge with floral decoration and gold rim. Diameter, 7 inches. Weight, 6 ounces. Price.......................... 10c

FX157—Imported Fancy Plate. Floral decorations on black, brown or dark brown backgrounds. Hand painted effects. Diameter 6½ inches. State color background preferred. Weight, 7 ounces. Price........... 10c

DX162—Assorted Salts and Peppers. Plain shapes, hand decorated. Direct importation from Japan. Well perforated tops with cork stopper in bottom. Weight, each, 3 ounces. Price.............................. 10c

DX163—Assorted Salts and Peppers. Fancy shapes, hand decorated. Imported from Japan. Perforated top, cork stopper in bottom. Weight, each, 3 ounces. Price....... 10c

DV164 — Assorted Salts and Peppers. Plain and fancy shapes. Hand decorated. Imported from Japan. Perforated tops with cork stopper in bottom. Weight, each, 2 ounces. Price.............................. 5c

FX170—Imported Jardinieres or Vase. Rich Oriental design and pattern. Dark green and bronze colors. 3x5½ inches, oval shape. Weight, 9 ounces. Price........... 10c

When ordering Chinaware, etc., it is advisable to make your order large enough to have same shipped by freight, thereby reducing transportation charges

SHOW THIS KATALOG TO YOUR FRIENDS AND ASK THEM TO ORDER WITH YOU. SEE OUR SPECIAL CLUB OFFER ON THE BACK COVER PAGE OF THIS KATALOG.

DX913

DX900

DX908

DX906

DX909

DX911

DX912

DX910

DX907

DX905

Here are the latest Spring and Summer styles in women's hat frames at 10c each. All frames are made of good quality rice net, except Nos. DX912 and DX913, which are made of good quality crinoline.

You can save a lot of money by ordering your millinery goods from us. Hundreds of thousands of women who live within shopping distance of one of the many Kresge 5c and 10c Stores find it profitable and practical to buy their shapes and trimmings from us, because they save money—often as much as from $1.00 to $2.00 on a hat, by doing the trimming themselves.

HOW TO ORDER HAT FRAMES

We illustrate on this page ten of the latest styles for the coming season. Select the style you prefer and order by Katalog Number.   In order to make it a profitable shipment, we advise you to order, at least, one dollar's worth of dry goods with your millinery order, as the transportation charges will not amount to very much more, owing to the manner in which we have to pack the shapes in order to insure safe delivery of same.   For instance, the average weight of hat frames when boxed ready for shipment is about 2 pounds, and by ordering dry goods and millinery trimmings the weight will not be increased very much, thus assuring the greatest possible saving on transportation charges.

See our Special Bargains in Flowers and Ribbons on pages 31 to 35.

Be sure to order at least one dollar's worth of dry goods or millinery trimmings when ordering hat frames; as a single hat frame makes an unprofitable shipment.

We guarantee satisfaction or will return your money.

Weight of one Hat Frame boxed, ready to ship, 2 pounds.

Latest Style Rice Net Hat Frames, 10c Each

DX901—10c. DX902—10c. DX903—10c. DX904—10c.

The above hat frames are for children and girls. They are made of good quality rice net, in the season's latest styles. When ordering state Katalog Number desired.

Be sure to order at least one dollar's worth of dry goods or millinery trimmings when ordering hat frames as a single hat frame makes an unprofitable shipment.

Children's Latest Style Straw Hats, 10c Each

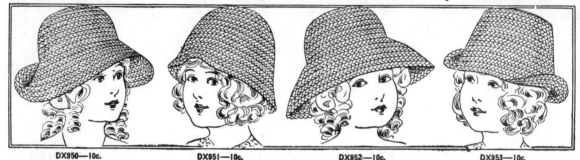

DX950—10c. DX951—10c. DX952—10c. DX953—10c.

The four styles illustrated above are for children and girls. They are made in the latest styles, of good quality straw. All are made of Cream Color Straw.

Be sure to order at least one dollar's worth of dry goods or millinery trimmings when ordering straw hats, as a single hat makes an unprofitable shipment.

Special Bargains in Hat Braids and Silk and Cotton Covered Brace Wire at 5c and 10c

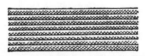

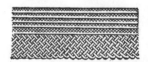

STRAW BRAID, 4½ YARDS TO BUNCH, 10c.

DX919—Good Quality Straw Braid. 1½ inches wide, coarse weave. Comes in white, black, navy, brown, red and natural color. 4½ yards to the bunch. Weight, 3 ounces. Price, per bunch 10C

STRAW BRAID, 5½ YARDS TO BUNCH, 10c.

DX918 — Good Quality Straw Braid. 1½ inches wide. Close weave. Can be had in the following colors: navy, brown, red and natural color; also black or white. State color desired. Weight, 3 ounces. Price, per bunch....................10C

GOOD QUALITY SILK HEMP BRAID, PER YARD, 5c.

DV921 — Good Quality Silk Hemp Braid. 1½ inches wide. Can be had in the following colors; navy, brown, red and natural color; also black or white. Weight, per yard, 1 ounce. Price, per yard..........................5C

FINE QUALITY SILK HEMP BRAID, PER YARD, 5c.

DV920 — Good Quality Silk Hemp Braid. Closely woven in style illustrated above. 1½ inches wide. Colors; navy, brown, red and natural color; also black or white. Weight, per yard, ½ ounce. Price, per yard......5C

SILK COVERED BRACE WIRE, 8 YARDS, 5c.

DV915—Good Quality Silk Covered Brace Wire. Medium size. We can furnish this number in black or white. Comes 8 yards to the piece. Weight, per piece, 2 ounces. Price, per piece of 8 yards...................5C

SILK COVERED BRACE WIRE, PER PIECE OF 8 YARDS, 5c.

DV914—Good Quality Silk Covered Brace Wire. Small size. We furnish this number in black or white. State which is desired. Comes 8 yards to the piece. Weight, 1 ounce. Price, per piece of 8 yards...........5C

COTTON COVERED BRACE WIRE, 14 YARDS FOR 5c.

DV916—Good Quality Medium Size, Cotton Covered Brace Wire. Comes 14 yards to the piece. Can be had in black or white. State which is desired. Weight, per piece, 3 ounces. Our special price, for 14 yard piece....5C

COTTON COVERED RIBBON WIRE, 12 YARDS FOR 10c.

DX917—Bolt of Cotton Covered Ribbon Wire. Comes put up in bolts of 12 yards to the piece. Black or white. State which is desired when ordering. Weight, per bolt, 2 ounces. Our special price for 12 yard bolt 10C

Wonderful Bargains in Flowers at 10c Each

DAISY WREATH, 10c.
DX200 — Beautiful Daisy Wreath. Contains 45 white blossoms with yellow centers. Green foliage. Length, 24 inches. Weight, 2 ounces. Price, each......**10C**

ROSE BUD WREATH, 10c.
DX201 — Rose Bud Wreath. Contains 35 small rose buds with green foliage. Length, about 24 inches. Comes in pink or red. Weight, 2 ounces. Price, each. **10C**

FORGET-ME-NOT WREATH, 10c.
DX202 — Forget-Me-Not Wreath. Contains 54 small blossoms with green foliage. Length, 24 inches. Comes in all blue or blue and pink combination. Weight, 2 ounces. Price, each......**10C**

DAISY WREATH, 10c.
DX203 — Wreath of Daisies. Contains five large yellow daisies with brown centers and five large green leaves. Length of wreath, about 20 inches. Weight, 2 ounces. Price, each...........**10C**

JUNE ROSE CLUSTER, 10c.
DX204 — Cluster of Roses. Contains eight buds and eight large leaves. Length, 6 inches. Comes in pink or red. Weight, 1 ounce. Price, per bunch, only...............**10C**

MOSS ROSE, 10c.
DX205 — Bunch of Moss Roses. Contains 15 buds with green foliage. To be had in either pink or red. State color. Extra value. Weight 1 ounce. Price......**10C**

FORGET-ME-NOT SPRAY, 10c.
DX206 — Forget-Me-Not Spray. Contains 44 bunches and 96 blossoms. Blue color only. Length, about 7 inches. Extra value. Weight, 1 ounce. Price, each...**10C**

BUNCH OF LILACS, 10c.
DX207 — Bunch of Imported Lilacs. Contains eight large sprays and green leaves. Comes in white and natural color. Length, about 8 inches. Weight, 1 ounce. Price, each. **10C**

LILIES OF THE VALLEY, 10c.
DX208 — Bunch of Lilies of the Valley. Contains 13 branches and 54 blossoms. White only, green foliage. Length, about 8 inches. Weight, 1 ounce. Each **10C**

HALF BLOWN ROSES, 10c.
DX209 — Cluster of Half Blown Roses. Contains nine buds and six leaves in variegated colors, in red or pink. Extra special value. Weight, 1 ounce. Price, each. **10C**

MOSS ROSES, 10c.
DX210 — Bunch of Moss Roses. Contains 12 buds and 4 large leaves. Comes in white and pink. State color. Special value. Weight, 1 ounce. Price, each . **10C**

JUNE ROSES, 10c.
DX211 — Bunch of June Roses. Contains nine buds and six leaves in black only. Favorite mourning flower. Extra value. Weight, 1 ounce. Price, each ..**10C**

CHERRY CLUSTER, 10c.
DX212 — Cherry Cluster. Contains nine cherries in natural shade and six large leaves. A very popular spring trimming. Weight, 1 ounce. Price, each **10C**

GRAPE CLUSTER, 10c.
DX213 — Grape Cluster. Contains 12 grapes and 5 leaves. Comes in natural grape colors of green and red. Length, about 8 inches. Weight, 1 ounce. Price **10C**

BUNCH OF VIOLETS, 10c.
DX214 — Bunch of Silk and Cotton Violets. Contains 11 large blossoms and 4 leaves. In beautiful natural violet colors. Weight, 2 ounces. Price............**10C**

BUNCH OF VIOLETS, 10c.
DX215 — Special value in large bunch of violets. Contains 24 double blossoms and 4 leaves. Comes in natural color only. Weight, 2 ounces. Price...........**10C**

BUNCH OF GERANIUMS, 10c.
DX216 — Bunch of Geraniums. Contains six large imitation plush blossoms with five natural colored leaves. Comes in variegated green colors. Weight, 2 ounces. Price.**10C**

LARGE ROSE, 10c.
DX217 — Large double Rose with two small buds and five large leaves. Length, about 8 inches. An extra value and very popular. Weight, 2 ounces. Price. **10C**

These Beautiful Flowers Are Only 10c Each

DOUBLE ROSE, 10c.
DX218 — Beautiful double cotton **rose** with one plush and two silk petals, three natural leaves. Comes in black only. Weight, 2 ounces. Price, each.....................**10¢**

BEAUTIFUL ROSE, 10c.
DX219 — Large Open Rose with nine leaves. Comes in red or pink. Imitation rubber stems. An excellent value. Weight, 2 ounces. Price, each.....................**10¢**

LARGE ROSE, 10c.
DX220 — Beautiful Cotton Rose with silk and plush petals, one bud and four leaves. Comes in variegated colors of red and pink. Weight, 2 ounces. Price, each..........**10¢**

LARGE ROSE, 10c.
DX221 — Large cotton Rose with two silk and one plush petal and nine leaves. Variegated colors of pink, red and wine. State color. Weight, 2 ounces. Price, each..........**10¢**

MOSS ROSE BUDS, 10c.
DX222 — Large Moss Rose Buds. Contains six half blown roses and nine leaves. A very popular number. Length, about 8 inches. Colors; pink or red. Weight, 2 ounces. Price, each. ....**10¢**

ROSE CLUSTER, 10c.
DX223 — Rose Cluster of three medium size roses, two buds and five leaves. Length, about 8 inches. Colors: pink, red or yellow. State color. Weight, 2 ounces. Price, each..................**10¢**

ROSE CLUSTER, 10c.
DX224 — Rose Cluster. Contains 6 open roses and 9 leaves. Length about 8 inches. Comes in red or pink. Dark centers. Special bargain. Weight, 2 ounces. Price, each...................**10¢**

ROSE BUD CLUSTER, 10c.
DX225 — Cluster of Roses. Contains five large half blown buds. Length about 7 inches. Can be had in red or pink. A special bargain. Weight, 2 ounces. Price, each.. **10¢**

ROSE CLUSTER, 10c.
DX226 — Beautiful Rose Cluster. Contains four nice natural looking leaves. Length about 8 inches. Comes in red or yellow. Weight, 2 ounces. Price, each. ....**10¢**

ROSE BUD SPRAY, 10c.
DX227 — Rose Bud Spray. Contains six half blown buds, six buds and six leaves. A handsome trimming. Length, 10 inches. Weight, 2 ounces. Price, each. ....**10¢**

POPPY SPRAY, 10c.
DX228 — Handsome Poppy Spray. Contains four large blossoms, silk petal and five leaves in natural poppy color. Length, about 12 inches. Weight, 2 ounces. Price, each. ....**10¢**

MOSS ROSE SPRAY, 10c.
DX229 — Moss Rose Spray. Contains nine moss buds and nine leaves. Pink or red with green foliage. Very pretty trimming. Weight, 2 ounces. Price, each. ....**10¢**

ROSE CLUSTER, 10c.
DX230—Moss Rose Cluster. Contains six large half blown buds and four large leaves. Length, about 8 inches. Comes in pink or red with green foliage. Weight, 2 ounces. Price, each.. **10¢**

ROSE BUD SPRAY, 10c.
DX231—Beautiful Rose Bud Spray. Contains three large half blown blossoms and four natural color leaves. Length, about 10 inches. Weight, 2 ounces. Price.......**10¢**

Extra Quality Flowers and Foliages at 10c

CORN FLOWERS, 10c.
DX232 — Cluster of Corn Flowers. Contains 7 large blossoms and natural color foliage. Length about 9 inches. Comes in natural blue only. An excellent value. Weight, 2 ounces. Price, each **10C**

CLUSTER OF DAISIES, 10c.
DX233 — Daisy Cluster. Contains 7 large blossoms. Comes in either white or yellow with brown centers. Length, about 9 inches. Very popular number. An excellent value. Weight, 2 ounces. Price **10C**

POPPY CLUSTER, 10c.
DX234 — Cluster of Poppies. Contains 6 large blossoms and full centers. Length about 8 inches. One of our best values. Comes in natural color only. Weight, 2 ounces. Price, each **10C**

CLUSTER OF GERANIUMS, 10c.
DX235—Bunch of Geraniums. Contains 9 natural looking blossoms with wood silk petals and 4 natural looking leaves. Length about 8 inches. Special bargain. Weight, 2 ounces. Price, each **10C**

BUNCH OF ROSES, 10c.
DX236 — Bunch of Roses. Contains two large double roses with one moss covered bud and one large natural looking leaf. Length about 8 inches. Comes in red or pink. A very attractive trimming. Weight, 2 ounces. Price, each **10C**

ROSE SPRAY, 10c.
DX238 — Very Attractive Rose Spray. Contains two large open roses and four natural looking leaves. Length about 8 inches. Colors, red or pink. Be sure to state color desired when ordering. Wt., 2 ounces. Price, each . **10C**

MOURNING ROSES, 10c.
DX237 — Mourning Roses. Two in a bunch. Large open flowers and three natural looking leaves. Come in black only. Very popular number for mourning trimming and a special bargain at the price. Weight, 2 ounces. Price, each **10C**

ROSE SPRAY, 10c.
DX239 — Pretty Rose Spray. Contains 4 medium size full blown roses and 6 natural looking leaves. Length about 12 inches. Can be had in red or pink. A very attractive trimming and an unusual value. Weight, 1 ounce. Price, each ... **10C**

ROSE SPRAY, 10c.
DX240 — Beautiful Rose Spray. Contains two nice full blown roses with one silk and one plush petal. Two small buds and three natural looking leaves. Comes in variegated shades of pink and red. Length, about 8 inches. Weight, 1 ounce. Price, each **10C**

ROSE FOLIAGE, 10c.
DX241 — Large Bunch of Rose Foliage. Contains 27 natural looking green leaves. Length, about 12 inches. Special bargain. Weight, 1 ounce. Price, each. **10C**

ROSE FOLIAGE, 10c.
DX242—Bunch of Rose Foliage. Contains 15 shaded leaves and 6 moss rose buds. Length, about 12 inches. An exceptional value. Weight, 1 ounce. Price, per bunch...... **10C**

BUNCH OF FOLIAGE, 10c.
DX243 — Large Natural Looking Spray. Contains 18 shaded leaves in natural color, 12 small pink buds. Length, about 8 inches. Weight, 1 ounce. Price, each **10C**

BLACK FOLIAGE, 10c.
DX244 — Bunch of Beautiful Mourning Foliage. Contains 27 natural looking leaves. Length, about 8 inches. Comes in black only. Weight, 1 ounce. Per bunch **10C**

Special Bargains in Ribbons at 5 and 10¢

SATIN BABY RIBBON, PER SPOOL, 10c.

AX700—Satin Baby Ribbon. No. 1 satin ribbon about ¼ inch wide. Comes in the following colors: white, pink, blue and cardinal. A very fine quality baby ribbon for all purposes. Each spool contains 10 yards. State color wanted. Per spool......**10¢**

BEST QUALITY BABY RIBBON SPOOL, 10c.

AX701—Best Quality Baby Ribbon. Fine quality satin ribbon in the following colors: white, pink, light blue, and cardinal. Width 5-16 inch. 5 yards to spool. Price................**10¢**
AX702—Same as above, but ⅜ inch wide. State color wanted. Per spool.......**10¢**

WASH RIBBON BLOCK DESIGN PER SPOOL, 10c.

AX703—Wash Ribbon. Block Design. This is an all silk quality ribbon and our most popular pattern. Colors come in white, pink, light blue and cardinal. Width ½ inch. 10 yard piece. State color desired. Per spool................**10¢**
AX704—Same as above, but 5-16 inch wide. 5 yard piece................**10¢**
AX705—Same as above, but ⅜ inch wide. 5 yard piece................**10¢**

SATIN DOT WASH RIBBON S POOL, 10c.

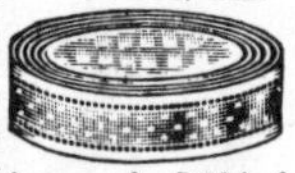

AX706—Satin Dot Wash Ribbon. This is an attractive all silk messaline ribbon. Has neat raised dot design. Comes in the following colors: white, pink, light blue and cardinal. 5 yards in a spool. 5-16 inch wide. State color wanted. Per spool.........**10¢**
AX707—Same as above, but ⅜ inch wide. Per spool................**10¢**

SATIN TAFFETA RIBBON PER YARD, 5c.

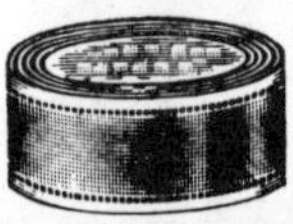

AV708—Satin Taffeta Ribbon. Best quality all silk satin taffeta. An exceptional value. Comes in one width only, about ⅞ inch. Colors: white, pink, light blue, and cardinal. State color wanted. Price per yard......**5¢**

SATIN TAFFETA RIBBON PER YARD, 5c.

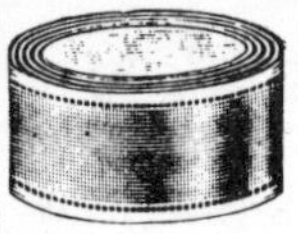

AV709—Satin Taffeta Ribbon. This is a good quality satin taffeta ribbon, but not as heavy as AV708. Comes in the following colors: white, pink, light blue, and cardinal. Width about 1⅛ inches. State color wanted. Per yard................**5¢**

2¼-INCH SATIN TAFFETA RIBBON YARD, 10c.

AX710—Satin Taffeta Ribbon. This is a heavy quality all silk satin taffeta ribbon. Comes in the following colors: white, blue, pink and red. Highly suitable for a large variety of uses. This ribbon is 2¼ inches wide. State color wanted when ordering.
Per yard................**10¢**

GOOD QUALITY SATIN TAFFETA RIBBON, YARD 10c.

AX711—Good Quality Satin Taffeta Ribbon. Fast edge. A very high quality ribbon. Comes in the following colors: white, pink, blue, violet, red, and black. 2¾ inches wide. State color wanted.
Per yard................**10¢**

We take pride in offering you this splendid line of ribbon values. Not only do we enable you to save from 25 to 50% by ordering your ribbons from this Katalog but we also offer you qualities that cannot be approached by ordinary dealers. By placing large contracts we secure the very lowest possible prices thereby enabling us to give you Special Bargains at 5 and 10c. We carry a large stock of these ribbons at all times.

SATIN TAFFETA RIBBON, PER YARD 10c.

AX712—Satin Taffeta Ribbon. This is one of the best values we offer. Comes in the following colors: white, pink, light blue, navy, red, violet, and black. Ribbon is about 3⅛ inches wide State color wanted when ordering.
Yard................**10¢**

GOOD QUALITY SATIN RIBBON, PER YARD 10c.

AX713—Good Quality Satin Ribbon. This is a medium quality satin faced ribbon. May be had in the following colors: white, pink, blue, red and black. Ribbon is 3¼ inches wide. State color wanted when ordering. Per yard......**10¢**

WIDE SATIN RIBBON PER YARD, 10c.

AX714—Wide Satin Ribbon. This is a medium quality satin ribbon, fast edge. Comes in the following colors: white, pink, light blue, red, and black. This ribbon is about 4 inches wide. State color wanted when ordering. Per yard................**10¢**

ALL SILK TAFFETA RIBBON YARD 5c.

AV715—All Silk Taffeta Ribbon. This is the best quality made in this width. All silk taffeta. Colors: white, pink, light blue and red. Ribbon is about ⅞ inch wide. State color wanted when ordering. Per yard................**5¢**

ALL SILK TAFFETA RIBBON PER YARD 5c.

AV716—All Silk Taffeta Ribbon. This is an exceptional quality. Colors: white, pink, light blue, red and black. Ribbon is about 1⅛ inches wide. A splendid value. State color wanted when ordering.
Price per yard................**5¢**

BEST QUALITY TAFFETA RIBBON PER YARD 10c

AX717—Best Quality Taffeta Ribbon. This is an all silk taffeta ribbon of unexcelled quality. Comes in the following colors: white, pink, blue, red and black. This ribbon is about 2¾ inches wide. State color wanted. Price, per yard...**10¢**

ALL SILK TAFFETA RIBBON PER YARD 10c.

AX718—All Silk Taffeta Ribbon. This is an exceptional quality all silk taffeta ribbon. Guaranteed to please. Can be furnished in the following colors: white, pink, blue, red, navy and black. 3¼ inches wide. State color wanted. Per yard................**10¢**

ALL SILK TAFFETA RIBBON PER YARD 10c.

AX719—All Silk Taffeta Ribbon. Fast edge. Good quality. Colors: white, pink, blue, red, navy and black. About 3⅝ inches wide. A very good value for the money. State color wanted. Per yard................**10¢**

PIN DOT SATIN TAFFETA RIBBON 5c.

AX720—Pin Dot Satin Taffeta Ribbon. This is an all silk ribbon in a very popular and attractive pattern. Colors: white, blue, pink, red, and lavender. About ⅞ inch wide. State color wanted. Per yard................**5¢**
AX721—Same as above, but medium quality. Colors: white, blue, pink and red. About 3⅛ inches wide. State color wanted. Per yard................**10¢**

ALL SILK MOIRE TAFFETA RIBBON 10c.

AX723—All Silk Moire Taffeta Ribbon. Finished with watered effect and is very popular for millinery purposes. Colors: white, blue, pink, Alice blue and black. About 3⅛ inches wide. State color wanted. Per yard........**10¢**

CORDED HAIR-BOW TAFFETA RIBBON PER YARD 10c.

AX724—Corded Hair-Bow Taffeta Ribbon. Specially made for hair-bow purposes. Colors: white, pink, red, blue and black. About 3⅛ inches wide. State color wanted when ordering. Price per yard................**10¢**

PLAIN MOIRE RIBBON PER YARD 10c.

AX725—Plain Moire Ribbon. Extra wide, medium quality, pressed edge. Colors: white, blue, pink, red and black. Ribbon is about 5 inches wide. State color wanted when ordering.
Price per yard................**10¢**

SHEPHERD CHECK RIBBON PER YARD 10c.

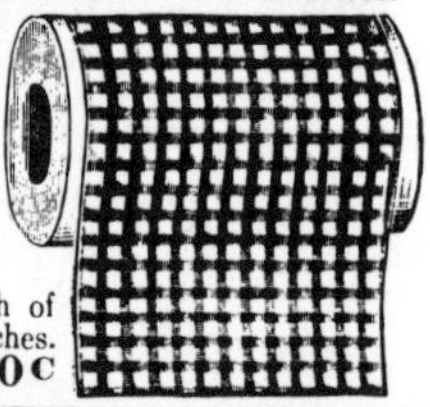

AX729 — Shepherd Check Ribbon. This is a very popular all silk black and white checked ribbon. Preferred by many as a pleasing change to solid colors. A very high quality ribbon. Width of ribbon about 3⅛ inches. Price, per yard.....**10¢**

SCOTCH PLAID RIBBON PER YARD 10c.

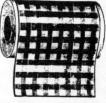

AX730—Scotch Plaid Ribbon. This is a high quality all silk ribbon. May be had in neat combinations in which the most prominent colors are red, green and blue. The ribbon is about 3⅛ inches wide. State color wanted. Per yard......**10¢**

FANCY EMBOSSED RIBBON PER YARD 10c.

AX726—Fancy Embossed Ribbon. Neat embossed pattern on medium quality ribbon. Comes in the following colors: white, blue, pink, cardinal and black. A good value. Ribbon is about 4 inches wide. State color wanted when ordering. Price per yard................**10¢**

Average weight of ribbons, per yard or spool, 1 oz. State color and number when ordering.

Don't Overlook These Bargains at 5 and 10c

FANCY WARP PRINT TAFFETA RIBBON, YARD, 10c.

AX727 — F a n c y Warp Print Taffeta Ribbon. This is an all silk ribbon printed with neat floral pattern. About 3¼ inches wide. Combinations white and light blue, white and yellow, white and pink, white and lavender. State which. Weight, per yard, 1 ounce. Price, per yard...................**10c**

MEDIUM QUALITY FLORAL PRINT RIBBON, PER YARD, 10c.

A X 7 2 8 — Medium g o o d Quality Floral Print Ribbon. About 5 inches wide. Can be had in white and red, or white and blue combinations. State which combination wanted. A very good value for the money. Weight, per yard, 1 ounce. Price, per yard **10c**

The two numbers of ribbons shown above are illustrated in actual colors on page 16.

ALL SILK BLACK VELVET RIBBON, PER YD, 10c.

AX731 — All Silk Black Velvet Ribbon. Heavy velvet face with all satin back. An exceptional quality. Black only. About 1 inch wide. Weight, yard, 1 ounce. Price, yard.....................**10c**
AX732 — Same as above, except about 1⅜ inches wide. Weight, yard, 1 ounce. Price, yard.........**10c**

EXTRA GOOD QUALITY BLACK VELVET RIBBON, PER YARD, 10c.

AX733 — Black Velvet Ribbon. Heavy velvet face with black satin finish back. This is a very good quality velvet ribbon and an exceptional value at the price. About 2 inches wide. Weight, per yard, 1 ounce. Price, per yard.....................**10c**

BLACK VELVETEEN RIBBON, 2½ INCHES WIDE, PER YARD, 10c.

AX734 — Black Velveteen Ribbon. Especially adapted for sashes, or millinery purposes. A very good quality. Has cotton back. Comes in black only. About 2½ inches wide. Weight, yard, 1 ounce. Price...**10c**
AX735 — Same as above, except about 3 inches wide. Weight, yard, 1 ounce. Price...............**10c**

MOIRE GROS-GRAIN BELTING, 27-INCH LENGTHS, 10c.

AX7366 — Moire Gros-Grain Belting. This is a heavy ribbed belting of good quality. Can be had in either black or white. State color wanted. This belting is about 1¾ inches wide. Weight for length of 27 inches, 2 ounces. Price, per length........**10c**

WATERPROOF SILK MALINE, IN FAST COLORS, PER YARD, 10c.

AX741 — Waterproof Silk Maline. Full 27 inches wide, and can be had in the following colors; black; white, pink, light blue, red, brown, green, or navy. This goods is imported direct from one of the best French manufacturers. Fast colors and fine mesh. State color wanted when ordering. Weight, per yard, 1 ounce. Price, per yard **10c**

PLAIN WHITE DOTTED SWISS, SPECIAL PRICE PER YARD, 10c.

AX737 — Plain White Dotted Swiss. This is a clean c l o s e l y woven fabric of good quality. Medium size dots. Full 27 inches wide. Suitable for window c u r t a i n s, etc. Comes in white only. Weight per yard, 2 ounces. Price, per yard **10c**

GOOD QUALITY SHEER INDIAN LINON, PER YARD, 10c.

AX738 — Sheer Indian Linon. This is a very fine quality cloth suitable for making children's dresses, aprons, caps, etc. Goods full 30 inches wide. Comes in pure white color only. This is an exceptional value for the money and you will have to pay much more at the regular stores. Weight, per yard, 2 ounces. Price per yard **10c**

SPECIAL BARGAINS IN HAT PINS, EACH, 10c.

DX575 — 9 inches l o n g. Head set with 19 first quality white brilliants. Good v a l u e. Each...**10c**

DX576 — 8 inches l o n g. Head set with large imitation pearl slug. For small hats. Price....**10c**

DX577 — 9½ inches l o n g. Head set with large, genuine gold-stone. Extra value. Price....**10c**

Average weight of the above pins, 1 ounce each.

DX578 — 7 inches l o n g. Head set with large imitation pearl and 15 white b r i l - liants. Price....**10c**

DX579 — 8 inches l o n g. Signet s t y l e, open w o r k head, finished in rich gilt color. Price....**10c**

DX580 — 9 inches l o n g. Head set with very large imitation pearl and 12 large brilliants. Price....**10c**

Average weight of the above pins, 1 ounce each.

FINE QUALITY JAPANESE FOLDING FANS, EACH, ONLY 10c.

BX702 — Fine quality Japanese Folding F a n s. These fans come in artistic designs a n d colorings, consisting of Japanese scenes and floral decorations. Some on parchment paper. About 9 inches long when folded. Values up to 25c. Weight, each, 1 ounce. Price.**10c**

JAPANESE FOLDING FANS, FANCY WOOD FRAMES, EACH, 5c.

BV701 — Japanese Folding Fans. Fancy wood frames. E x t r a f i n e quality. Assorted colors a n d designs of Japanese scenes and flowers. A strong, durable fan and an exceptional v a l u e for the price. Worth double the money. Weight, each, 1 ounce. Price, each. **5c**

JAPANESE FOLDING FANS, ASSORTED COLORS, 2 FOR 5c.

BB700 — Japanese F o l d i n g Fans. Come in assorted colors a n d designs. Frames of wood, covered with good strong p a p e r in a beautiful range of patterns and colors on one side. 8½ inches long when folded. Weight, each, 1 ounce. 2 for...................**5c**

PYRALIN IVORY FOLDING FAN, GOOD QUALITY EACH, 10c.

BX703 — Pyralin Ivory Folding Fan. Fancy cut out design. Made of good quality Pyralin ivory stock. Each fan has 13 leaves. Size, open, 5x9 inches. A very neat and attractive fan for ladies or children. Weight, each, 1 ounce. Price.....................**10c**

BEAUTIFUL JAPANESE GEISHA SILK FANS, EACH, 10c.

BX704 — Beautiful Japanese Geisha Silk Fans. Assorted shapes and designs. Fan is made of silk stretched on heavy metal frame. This silk covering is painted with beautiful Japanese scenes and flowers, in rich natural colors. Has black enameled handle. A good range of shapes and decorations. Weight, each 2 ounces. Price....................**10c**

GOOD QUALITY SATIN PALM FANS, 2 FOR 5c.

EE245 — Good Quality Satin Palm Fans. These fans are made of best quality palm leaves, round shape, about 12 inches in diameter. A good value. Wt., of 2, 2 ounces. Price, 2 for **5c**
EE246 — Same as above, except fancy shape. Made of best quality imported palm, with strongly sewed edges. Weight of 2, 2 ounces. Price, 2 for **5c**

Unusual Values —— Nothing Over 10c Each

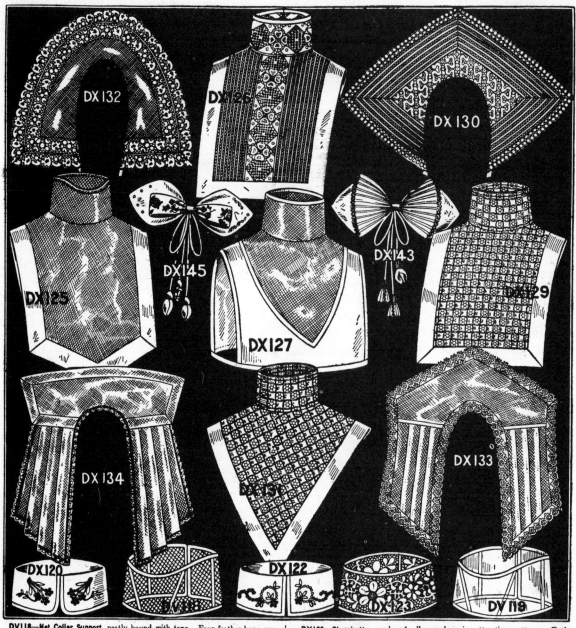

DV118—Net Collar Support, neatly bound with tape. Four feather-bone supports. 3 inches high. Sizes, 12 to 15 neck. State size desired. Weight, ½ ounce. Each **5c**

DV119—Chiffon Collar Foundation, neatly bound with tape. 2¾ inches high. Sizes, 12 to 15 neck. State size. Weight, ½ ounce. Each **5c**

DX120—Standing Collar, neatly embroidered corners and back. 2 inches high. Sizes, 12 to 15 neck. State size. Weight, 1 ounce. Each **10c**

DX122—Standing Embroidered Collar. 2 inches high. Comes in assorted patterns. An excellent value. Sizes, 12 to 15 neck. State size. Weight, 1 ounce. Each **10c**

DX123—Imported Lace Stock Collar, heavy pattern. Comes in 12 beautiful styles, similar to illustration. About 2½ inches high. Weight, 1 ounce. Special price, each **10c**

DX125—Chemisette, made of fine net with medium high collar. Two collar supports. Entire length, 16 inches by 10 inches wide across front. Well made. Weight, 1 ounce. Our special price, each **10c**

DX126—Chemisette, made of plain net with 18 rows of fine tucking. Lace insertion center. Collar to match. Entire length, 16 inches by 10 inches across front. Special value. Weight, 1 ounce. **10c**

DX127—Guimpe, made of net and lawn, finished with draw-string around waist. Tape bound, well made. Extraordinary value. Weight, 2 ounces. Price, **10c**

DX129—Chemisette, made of all-over lace in attractive patterns. Entire length, 15 inches by 9 inches across front. One of our most extraordinary values. Weight, 1 ounce. Price, each **10c**

DX130—Dutch Collar, made of all-over plaited net. Lace trimmed. Insert of fancy net in back of collar. White or ecru. Weight, 1 ounce. Price, each **10c**

DX131—Chemisette, all-over lace pattern. Length, 16 inches by 14 inches wide across shoulders. A special value. Weight, 1 ounce. Each **10c**

DX132—Dutch Collar, made of fine quality net. Trimmed with row of lace insertion and lace edge. Width, 5 inches. Weight, 1 ounce. Each **10c**

DX133—Fichu, made of fine quality net, lace trimmed. Plaited ends. Length, 18 inches from back to front. About 15 inches wide over shoulders. Weight, 1 ounce. Each **10c**

DX134—Fichu, made of good quality net, trimmed with narrow lace edge. Plaited ends. Measures about 17 inches from back to front. 12 inches wide over shoulders. Wonderful value. Weight, 1 ounce. Each **10c**

DX143—Novelty bow with pink satin ribbon background, plaited white chiffon front with scalloped silk edge. Three novelty pendants. Extraordinary value. Weight, 1 ounce. Each **10c**

DX145—Novelty Bow. Pink satin ribbon background, center of floral pink ribbon. Bow trimmed with three pendants. Safety fastener. Weight, ½ ounce. Price, each **10c**

THE ORIGINAL PARCEL POST **KRESGE'S KATALOG** FIVE AND TEN CENT STORE

Page 36

DX124—Mercerized Cord Ruching. White, blue, pink, lavender, 42 in. for **10C**

DX128—Jabot of fine quality lawn, trimmed with imitation hand-made lace. 10 inches long, 6 inches wide. Each............................**10C**

DX135—Dutch Collar of good quality lawn. Finished with pretty lace edge. 12 inches wide across shoulders. Width, 4 inches. Extra special value. Ea.**10C**

DX136—Attractive Jabot of fine net, trimmed with lace. About 10 inches long, 8 inches wide. Special value. Each........................**10C**

DX137—Medici Ruff of extra quality chiffon and all-over lace. 20 inches long, 2½ inches wide. Price.......................**10C**

DX138—Dutch Collar of imitation hand made lace and lawn. About 3½ inches wide. Exceptional value. Each.....................**10C**

DX139—Medici Ruff of plaited net, beautiful all-over lace top. Width, 1½ inches. Length, 20 inches. Each......................**10C**

DX140—Jabot of fine quality lawn, lace edge. 10 inches long by 6 inches wide. Extra special value. Each.......................**10C**

DX141—Medici Collar, one narrow and one wide row of extra quality plaited chiffon. 1½ inches wide. 20 inches long. Each................**10C**

DX142—Novelty Bow of pink satin with black velvet background. Three fancy pendants. Extra special value. Each................**10C**

DX144—Satin and Velvet Bow. 18 French knots. Safety fastener. Comes in assorted colors. Special at......................**10C**

DX146—Novelty Rose, pink silk flower, green silk leaves, trimmed with four pink satin pendants. Special value at.....................**10C**

DX148—Novelty Ribbon Rosette of extra quality narrow silk ribbon. Eight hand tied streamers. Each...........................**10C**

DX149—2½-inch Net Ruffling, lace edge. White, ecru or black. Yard....**10C**

DZ150—2½-inch Net Ruffling, dainty lace edge. White or ecru. ½ yard..**10C**

DX151—2-inch Net Ruffling, lace edge. White or ecru. Yard...........**10C**

DX152—2-inch Shadow Lace Ruffling, white or ecru. Yard..........**10C**

DX153—1¾-inch plaited Net Ruffling, white, ecru or black. Yard......**10C**

DX154—2½-inch Lace Trimmed Net Ruffling. White or ecru. Yard....**10C**

DX155—1¾-inch plaited Chiffon Ruffling. White only. Yard.........**10C**

DZ156—3-inch pointed Net Ruffling. White or ecru. ½ yard.........**10C**

DZ157—2½-inch scalloped Net Ruffling. White, ecru or black. ½ yard**10C**

DZ158—2-inch double Chiffon Ruff. White, black, navy or ecru. ½ yard**10C**

DZ160—2½-inch shadow Lace Ruffling. White, ecru or black. ½ yard..**10C**

DZ162—3-inch plaited Net Ruffling. White, ecru or black. ½ yard.....**10C**

DX163—Latest style Net Collar, trimmed with 3½-inch lace and plaited net. Each..........................**10C**

DX164—Jabot of fine quality net trimmed with insert of pretty lace. Length, 8 inches. Width, 6 inches. Price, each.......................**10C**

Average weight of Jabots, Collars, etc., 1 ounce; Ruching per ½ yard, ½ ounce. Be sure to send an extra amount of money to pay postage when ordering.

Remarkable Bargains in Beads at 10c Each

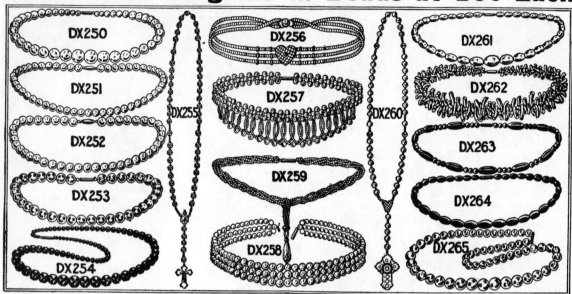

DX250—**Graduated bead necklace.** About 13 inches long. Imitation gold or pearl color. State color. Weight 1 ounce. Price, each................**10c**

DX251—**Bead necklace.** Uniform size beads. About 13 inches long. Strong fastener. Gold or pearl color. State color. Weight 1 ounce. Price, each.**10c**

DX252—**Bead necklace.** Uniform size beads. About 13 inches long. Strong fastener. Gold or pearl color. State color. Weight 1 ounce. Price, each..**10c**

DX253—**Necklace of heavy glass beads.** About 13 inches long. Strong fastener. Turquoise or amber color. State color. Weight 1 ounce. Price, each.......**10c**

DX254—**Necklace of English cut graduated beads.** About 18 inches long. Colors: Amber, ruby, or red. State color. Weight 1 ounce. Price, each.**10c**

DX255—**Rosary of glass beads** with silver color chain links, and silver finish metal cross pendant. 25 inches long. Comes in colors of blue, green, amethyst and white. State color. Weight 1 ounce. Price, each...........................**10c**

DX256—**Three-strand fancy necklace.** About 12 inches long. Strong fastener. Comes in white only, trimmed with silver and coral-color beads. Weight 1 ounce. Price, each..**10c**

DX257—**Novelty bead necklace** in fancy woven design as illustrated above. About 12 inches long. Strong fastener. Comes in assorted colors of amethyst, turquoise, etc. State color. Weight 1 ounce. Price, each............. **10c**

DX258—**Three-strand glass bead necklace.** Uniform size beads. About 12 inches long. Strong fastener. Comes in colors of dark blue, amber, turquoise and white. State color. Weight 2 ounces. Price, each......................**10c**

DX259—**Three-strand twisted bead necklace,** made of white seed beads, trimmed with pressed glass pendant. About 14 inches long. Strong fastener. Comes in silver-color only. Weight 1 ounce. Price, each..............................**10c**

DX260—**Rosary of ivory-finish bone beads.** Gilt color metal chain links with fancy carved pendant. About 25 inches long. Comes as described only. A special value. Weight 2 ounces. Price, each.......................................**10c**

DX261—**Necklace of oval-shaped imitation coral beads.** Highly finished. About 13 inches long. Strong fastener. Weight 1 ounce. Coral-color only.......**10c**

DX262—**Necklace of real rough coral.** Made in fancy design as illustrated above. 13 inches long. Strong fastener. Weight 2 ounces. Price, each.........**10c**

DX263—**Necklace of fancy black beads.** Dull finish. Very attractive necklace. About 13 inches long. Strong fastener. Weight 1 ounce. Price, each..........**10c**

DX264—**Necklace of black oval-shaped beads.** About 13 inches long. Strong fastener. Weight 1 ounce. Color black only. Price, each.................**10c**

DX265—**Opera bead necklace.** 18 inches long. Made of graduated beads. Comes colors of blue, coral and also white. State color. An excellent value. Weight 2 ounces. Price, each...**10c**

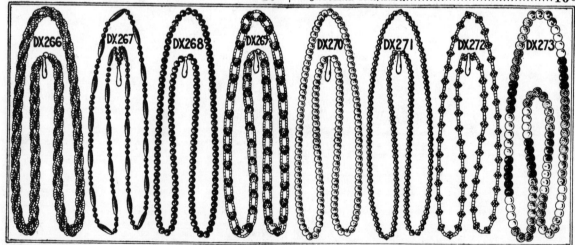

DX266—**Braided locket or fan chain** made of seed beads. 48 inches long. Comes in blue, white, or blue and white combination. State color. An excellent value. One of our best sellers. Weight 2 ounces. Price, each..................**10c**

DX267—**Fan or locket chain** made of fancy shaped black beads. Dull finish. About 48 inches long. An excellent chain at the price. Weight 2 ounces. Color black only. Price, each......................................**10c**

DX268—**Fan chain.** Uniform size beads. About 48 inches long. Dull black color only. A popular style chain. Weight 2 ounces. Price, each..........**10c**

DX269—**Fancy fan chain.** Double links of small silver-color beads, with pressed fancy-shaped ruby color beads between links. About 48 inches long. Comes as described only. Weight 2 ounces. Price, each...........................**10c**

DX270—**Fan or locket chain.** Uniform size beads. About 48 inches long. Colors: White, coral, golden or turquoise. State color. Weight 2 ounces. Price, each..**10c**

DX271—**Fan or locket chain,** made of fancy pressed glass beads. About 48 inches long. Comes in colors of amethyst, green, amber or ruby. State color. Weight 2 ounces. Price, each....................................**10c**

DX272—**Fancy fan or locket chain,** made of small and large beads. About 48 inches long. Comes in colors of amethyst, green, amber, or ruby. State color. A very attractive chain. An excellent value. Weight 2 ounces. Price......**10c**

DX273—**200 Kindergarten beads.** Strung on heavy cord. Size of beads about ⅜ inch in diameter. Just the thing for the children. Popular colors of green, blue, yellow and white. Weight 5 ounces. Price, each.........................**10c**

Extra Special Bargains—Nothing Over 10c

Good Quality Knit Vests, Etc., Nothing Over 10c

AX185

AX133

AX131

AX129

AX186

MUSLIN BRASSIERE

MUSLIN CORSET COVER

AX126

AX132

AX128

AX127

AX130

AX126 — Ladies' Fine Ribbed Cotton Vests. Low neck, sleeveless. Mercerized insertion trimmed front and back with mercerized tape. Made in sizes to fit bust measurements from 32 to 40 inches. State size wanted. Weight, 3 ounces. Each..10c

AX127 — Ladies' "Fitrite" Vests. Designed to prevent falling shoulder straps. Neat lace edge trimming. Mercerized wash braid. Sleeveless. Sizes, to fit bust measurements 32 to 40 inches. State size wanted. Weight, 3 ounces.10c

AX128 — Ladies' Straight Vests. Trimmed with silk tape, elastic ribbed. Low neck and sleeveless. Sizes to fit bust measurements from 32 to 40 inches. State size wanted. Weight, 3 ounces. Price, each........................10c

AX129 — Ladies' Extra Fine Ribbed Vests. 1x1 rib. V-neck, sleeveless. Lace trimmed. Mercerized wash braid. An exceptional quality for the price. Sizes to fit bust measurements from 32 to 40 inches. State size wanted. Weight, 3 ounces. Price, each. 10c

AX130 — Ladies' Extra Size Vests. Lace insertion trim front and back. Low neck, sleeveless. Good quality tape ribbon. One of the best values we offer. Sizes to fit bust measurements from 42 to 48 inches. State size wanted. Weight, 3 ounces. Price, each 10c

AX185—Ladies' Brassiere. Made of good quality Muslin trimmed with fancy embroidery and edged with good quality lace. A very exceptional value for the price. Sizes to fit bust measurements from 34 to 44 . State size wanted. Weight, 2 ounces. Price, each 10c

AX131—Ladies' Extra Size Vests. Fine ribbed. Neatly trimmed neck and armholes. Good quality tape ribbon. Elastic ribbed, sleeveless, low neck. A good value for the money. Made in sizes to fit bust measurements from 42 to 48 inches. State size wanted. Weight, 3 ounces. Price.........................10c

AX132—Ladies' Extra Size Vests. Elastic ribbed, low neck, sleeveless. Full mercerized trimmed and mercerized wash tape. Designed for stout women. This garment is in big demand. Sizes to fit bust measurements from 42 to 48 inches. State size wanted. Weight, 3 ounces. Price, each...........10c

AX133—Ladies' Extra Size Vests. Similar to AX132, but made with wing sleeves. Come in sizes to fit bust measurements from 42 to 48 inches. State size desired. Weight, 3 ounces. Price, each 10c

AX186—Ladies' Muslin Corset Cover. Made of good quality muslin, trimmed with lace. Has tape drawstring. Bust measurements 34 to 44 inches. State size wanted. Weight, 2 ounces. Price, each.........................10c

We offer Extra Special Bargains in Women's Knit Vests, Corset Covers and Brassieres at 10c each. When ordering be sure to state size desired; also Katalog Number.

Women's Good Quality Aprons, 10c Each

AX201 DUSTING CAP

AX193 GOOD QUALITY CHAMBRAY

AX187 LAWN TEA APRON

AX199 GOOD QUALITY CAMBRIC

AX195 GOOD QUALITY GINGHAM

AX189 LAWN TEA APRON

AX194 GOOD QUALITY PERCALE

AX188 LAWN TEA APRON

AX200 CHILD'S ALLOVER DRESS APRON

AX198 SATEEN

AX192 LAWN TEA APRON

AX190 CROSSBAR LAWN

AX196 GOOD QUALITY LAWN

AX202 DUSTING CAP

AX191 LAWN TEA APRON

AX197 SATEEN

AX187—Ladies' Tea Apron, made of good quality lawn. Scalloped edges. Neatly embroidered. Long tie streamers. Weight, 1 ounce. Each......**10¢**

AX188—Ladies' Tea Apron, made of good quality lawn. Neatly embroidered. Scalloped edges. Long tie streamers. Weight, 1 ounce. Price, each....**10¢**

AX189—Ladies' Tea Apron of white lawn. Neatly embroidered in colors of pink, blue or lavender. State color desired. Weight, 1 ounce. Price, each.**10¢**

AX190—Ladies' Tea Apron of cross-bar lawn, trimmed with 2½-inch ruffle. Full size. Long waist streamers. Weight, 1 ounce. Price, each...........**10¢**

AX191—Ladies' Tea Apron of good quality white lawn. Trimmed with lace. Pocket trimmed to conform. Waist tie streamers. Weight, 1 ounce. Price, each.......**10¢**

AX192—Ladies' Tea Apron, made of good quality white lawn. Trimmed with two rows of lace insertion. Edged with lace. Long waist tie streamers. Full size. Weight, 1 ounce. Price, each..................**10¢**

AX193—Ladies' Apron, made of good quality blue chambray with pocket. Tape bound all around. Large size. Tie streamers. Weight, 3 ounces. Ea.**10¢**

AX194—Ladies' Apron, made of good quality percale. Large bib. Entire apron tape-bound. Comes in assortment of neat dark checks and stripes. Exceptional value. Long waist tie streamers. Weight, 3 ounces. Price, each.**10¢**

AX195—Ladies' Apron of extra good quality gingham in popular size blue and white check. 30 inches long, 26 inches wide. Waist tie streamers. Weight, 3 ounces. Price, each..................**10¢**

AX196—Ladies' Apron of extra quality white lawn; 32 inches long, 27 inches wide. Hemstitched hem and five rows of pintucks at bottom of apron. Weight, 3 ounces. Price, each..................**10¢**

AX197—Ladies' Apron, made of good quality black sateen. 32 inches long, 27 inches wide. Hemstitched. Tie streamers. Weight, 3 ounces. Each....**10¢**

AX198—Ladies' Circular Apron of good quality black sateen. 3½ inch ruffle. Large size pocket. Tie streamers. Weight, 3 ounces. Price, each........**10¢**

AX199—Ladies' Round Apron. Large size. Made of good quality high lustre black cambric. Large pocket. Weight, 3 ounces. Price, each..........**10¢**

AX200—Children's All-Over Dress Apron of good quality percale. Tape bound. Pocket trimmed to conform. Very desirable garment for children from 3 to 6 years old. Comes in neat pin checks and figures in medium dark colors. Weight, 2 ounces. Price, each..................**10¢**

AX201—Ladies' Dusting Cap, made of good quality percale. Trimmed with embroidered washable insertion. Large size. Elastic at back. Neat patterns in light colors. Weight, 2 ounces. Price, each........................**10¢**

AX202—Ladies' Dusting Cap, made of good quality percale. Turn-back front. Scalloped edge. Well made throughout and full size. Elastic at back. Comes in neat patterns in light colors. Weight, 2 ounces. Price, each........**10¢**

Special Bargains in Children's Wear at 10c

AX140 AGES 2 TO 12

AX139 AGES 2 TO 12

AX136 AGES 2 TO 12

AX138 AGES 2 TO 12

AX133 DRAWERS ONLY AGES 6 TO 14

AX142 DRAWERS ONLY AGES 8 TO 18

AX143 AGES 2 TO 12

AX135 AGES 2 TO 12

AX137 DRAWERS ONLY AGES 2 TO 12

AX141 DRAWERS ONLY AGES 2 TO 12

AX134 AGES 2 TO 12

AX1333—Child's Ribbed Cotton Drawers. Strong muslin waistband. Lace trimmed. Made to fit ages 6 to 14. State size wanted. Weight, 3 ounces. Price, each...**10C**

AX134—Children's Low Neck Vests. Made with wing sleeves. Mercerized trim, with good quality mercerized wash tape. Fine ribbed. Made in sizes to fit ages 2 to 12. A very special value. State size wanted. Weight, 2 ounces. Price, each...**10C**

AX135—Children's High Neck Vests. Made of good quality yarn, fine ribbed. Good quality mercerized trim, mercerized wash tape. Short sleeves and high neck. A very good value at the price. Sizes to fit ages 2 to 12. State size wanted. Weight, 2 ounces. Price...........................**10C**

AX136—Children's High Neck Ribbed Vests. Long sleeves. Mercerized trim, with good mercerized wash tape. High neck. Buttons down front, five good quality pearl buttons. Made in sizes 2 to 12. State size wanted. Weight, 2 ounces. Price...........................**10C**

AX137—Children's Cotton Knee Pants. Strong muslin waistband. Buttons at side. Made to fit ages, 2 to 12. State size wanted. Weight, 2 ounces. Price...........................**10C**

WHEN ORDERING CHILDREN'S GARMENTS, BE SURE TO STATE AGE DESIRED; ALSO KATALOG NUMBER.

AX138—Children's Knit Waists. For boys or girls. Taped front and back, and over shoulders. Double row of buttons and pin-tubes for hose supporters. Sizes, to fit ages 2 to 12. State size wanted. Weight, 4 ounces. Price..**10C**

AX139—Children's Cambric Underwaists. Made of heavy material. Corded, tape bound, and hose supporter attachments. Made in sizes to fit ages 2 to 12. State size wanted. Weight, 3 ounces. Price.........................**10C**

AX140—Children's Underwaists. Made of heavy material, tape bound with hose supporter attachments. Good agate buttons attached with mercerized tape. Sizes, to fit ages 2 to 12. State size wanted. Weight, 3 ounces. Price, ea.**10C**

AX141—Children's Cambric Drawers. Hemstitched ruffle with five pin tucks. Buttons at side. Strong muslin waistband. Sizes to fit ages 2 to 12. A very good value at a low price. State size wanted. Weight, each, 3 ounces. Price..**10C**

AX142—Misses' Muslin Drawers. Made from good quality cloth, neatly hemstitched ruffle. Buttons at side. Strong muslin waistband. Full sizes to fit ages 8 to 18. A very good value. State size wanted when ordering. Weight, 3 ounces. Price..**10C**

AX143—Children's Cambric Underskirts. Made of good quality cambric. Long waisted. Neat hemstitched ruffle with three pin tucks. Tape bound edges. Agate buttons. Sizes, to fit ages 2 to 12. One of the best values in this line. State size wanted. Weight, 4 ounces. Price.........................**10C**

See our special bargains in children's hosiery on pages 48 and 49.

THE ORIGINAL PARCEL POST KRESGE'S KATALOG FIVE AND TEN CENT STORE

Page 42

Bargains for Infants—Nothing Over 10c

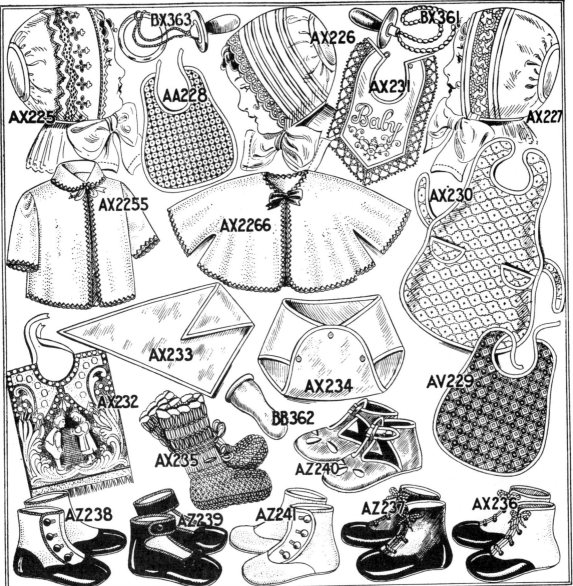

AX225 — **Infant's Lawn Cap.** Made from sheer quality lawn with embroidery revere and lace edge. Caps are full size, tie strings. Weight, 1 ounce. Each....**10C**

AX226 — **Infant's Lawn Cap.** Fine quality material with three narrow and four wide tucks. Lace edge. Long tie strings. Weight, 1 ounce. Each....**10C**

AX227 — **Infant's Lawn Bonnet.** Fine quality lawn with lace insertion trimming. Long tie strings. Weight, 1 ounce. Each....**10C**

AA228 — **Infant's Oil-cloth Bib.** Selected patterns, best quality oil-cloth. Bound edges. 7x10 inches. Weight, 1 ounce. 2 for....**5C**

AV229 — **Infant's Oilcloth Bib.** Same quality as AA228, but larger. 11x14 inches. Good assortment of patterns. Weight, 1 ounce. Price....**5C**

AX230 — **Child's Large Apron Bib.** Best quality oilcloth. Light patterns. Tape bound edges. Two pockets and waist strap. Weight, 3 ounces. Each....**10C**

AX231 — **Embroidered Bib.** The word "Baby" is embroidered on good quality lawn, duck lined. Lace trim. Weight, 1 ounce. Each....**10C**

AX232 — **Turkish Bib.** Imported Jacquard weave, neat design. 10½x14 inches. Colors, pink and blue. State color. Weight, 2 ounces. Each....**10C**

AX233 — **Triangular Diaper.** Made of best quality rubberized cloth, bound with tape. Weight, 2 ounces. Each....**10C**

AX234 — **Waterproof Diaper Cover.** Best quality rubberized cloth, bound with tape. Three agate buttons. Weight, 2 ounces. Each....**10C**

AX2255 — **Infant's Flannelette Sacque.** Embroidered front, sleeves and collar in pink or blue. Comes in cream or pure white. State combination wanted. Weight, 2 ounces. Each....**10C**

AX2266 — **Infant's Kimono.** Good quality flannelette, circular shape. Edges embroidered pink or blue. Colors, cream or pure white. State combination wanted. Weight, 2 ounces. Each....**10C**

AX235 — **Infants' Bootees.** Best quality wool yarn. Hand crocheted. Pink and white, or blue and white. State color. Weight per pair, 1 ounce. Per pair....**10C**

AX236 — **Infants' Soft Sole Shoes.** Patent leather toe. Upper in white, black, pink, blue, or red. Sizes, 1 to 4. State color and size wanted. Lace only. Weight, per pair, 2 ounces. Per pair....**10C**

AZ237 — **Infants' Lace Shoes.** Soft sole. Patent leather. Soft tops in black, white, pink or blue. Sizes, 1 to 4. State size and color. Weight, per pair, 2 ounces. Price per pair....**20C**

AZ238 — **Infants' Button Shoes.** Soft sole. Patent leather. Soft tops in black, white, pink, blue or red. Sizes, 1 to 4. State size and color. Weight, per pair, 2 ounces. Price per pair....**20C**

AZ239 — **Infants' Soft Sole Slippers.** Black patent leather, ankle straps. Sizes, 1 to 3. State size wanted. Weight, per pair, 2 ounces. Price per pair....**20C**

AZ240 — **Infants' Tan Barefoot Sandals.** Calfskin soft sole. Fine for outdoors. Sizes, 1 to 4. State size. Weight, per pair, 2 ounces. Price per pair....**20C**

AZ241 — **Infants' Button Shoes.** Soft sole. Solid colors, white, black, pink, blue or red. Sizes, 1 to 4. State color and size. Weight, per pair, 2 ounces. Price per pair....**20C**

BX361 — **Baby Pacifier.** Black rubber nipple, bone guard, 12-inch strand polished shell beads. Weight, 1 ounce. Each....**10C**

BB362 — **Rubber Nipple.** Extra heavy. 1½ inches long. Weight, 1 ounce. 2 for....**5C**

BX363 — **Transparent Rubber Pacifier** with Bone Shield, and 1½-inch bone ring attached to 7-inch double cord. Weight, 1 ounce. Each....**10C**

Latest Style Neckwear for Men and Boys, 10c

DX100—**All Silk Four-in-Hand Tie.** 42 inches long, 2 inches wide. French end. Colors, red, black, white, navy, green, light blue. Weight, 1 ounce. Each . . . . **10¢**

DX101—**Silk Four-in-Hand Tie.** 42 inches long, 2 inches wide. Fancy weaves. Comes in red, black, white, navy, green, light blue. Weight, 1 ounce. Each . . **10¢**

DX102—**Silk Poplin Four-in-Hand Tie.** 42 inches long, 1½ inches wide. Comes in red, black, white, navy, green, light blue and lavender. Worn on either side. Weight, 1 ounce. Price, each . . . . **10¢**

DX103—**Silk Shield Bow Tie,** 3¾ inches long. Comes in fancy colors and designs. State predominating color wanted when ordering. Weight, ½ ounce. Each. **10¢**

DX104—**Mercerized Poplin Bow-Tie.** 3¼ inches long with covered shield and covered back. Black only. Weight, ½ ounce. Price, each . . . . **10¢**

DX105—**Boys' Shield Bow-Tie.** Fancy colors and designs. 3¼ inches long. Covered shield, patent back. State predominating color wanted. Weight, ½ ounce. Each . . . . **10¢**

DX106—**Fancy Silk Poplin Club Ties.** 32 inches long, 1½ inches wide. Colors, red, black, white, navy, green, light blue and lavender. Weight, 1 ounce. Each. . . . . **10¢**

DX107—**Shield Teck Tie of Fine Quality Material.** Fancy patterns and stripes. 12 inches long. State predominating color when ordering. Weight, 1 ounce. Each . . . . **10¢**

DX108—**Silk Poplin Shield Teck tie.** 12 inches long. Colors, black, red, navy, green, light blue and brown. 25c value. Weight, 1 ounce. Each . . . . . . **10¢**

DX109—**Shield Teck Four-in-Hand Tie** of fine quality material. One of our best values. Black only. Weight, 1 ounce. Each . . . . **10¢**

DX110—**Washable Four-in-Hand Tie,** about 48 inches long, 2¼ inches wide. French open end. Double stitched back. Made of silk and linen, in light colors with dainty colored stripes. Wonderful value. Weight, 1 ounce. Each . . **10¢**

DX111—**Washable Four-in-Hand Tie,** about 48 inches long, 1½ inches wide. Worn on either side. Light, dainty colors with cross stripes and fancy figures. State color when ordering. Weight, 1 ounce. Each . . . . **10¢**

DX112—**Washable Four-in-Hand Tie.** 46 inches long, 2 inches wide. Light colors, fancy figures and stripes. Weight, 1 ounce. Each . . . . **10¢**

DX113—**Windsor Tie.** 37 inches long, 4 inches wide. Made of silk poplin, hemmed edges. Comes in white, black, light blue, pink, scarlet, cardinal, navy. Weight, 1 ounce. Price, each . . . . **10¢**

DX114—**Washable Four-in-Hand Tie.** Reversible. About 47 inches long, 1½ inches wide. Made of highly mercerized cotton in light colors with colored stripes. Weight, 1 ounce. Price, each . . . . **10¢**

DX115—**Knitted Four-in-Hand Tie.** 45 inches long, 1½ inches wide. Beautiful colors with cross stripes. Made of fibre silk and cotton. Gives excellent satisfaction. Special bargain. Weight, 1 ounce. Price, each . . . . **10¢**

DX116—**Knitted Four-in-Hand Tie.** 45 inches long, ½-inch wide. Fancy mixed colors. Made of fibre, silk and cotton. One of our best values. Weight, 1 ounce. Price, each . . . . **10¢**

DX117—**Men's and Boys' soft collars.** 2 inches high. Made of good quality washable material. Colors: white, cream or blue. Sizes, 12 to 16. ½ sizes included. State size. Weight, 1 ounce. Each . . . . **10¢**

Men's and Boys' Suspenders, 10c Per Pair

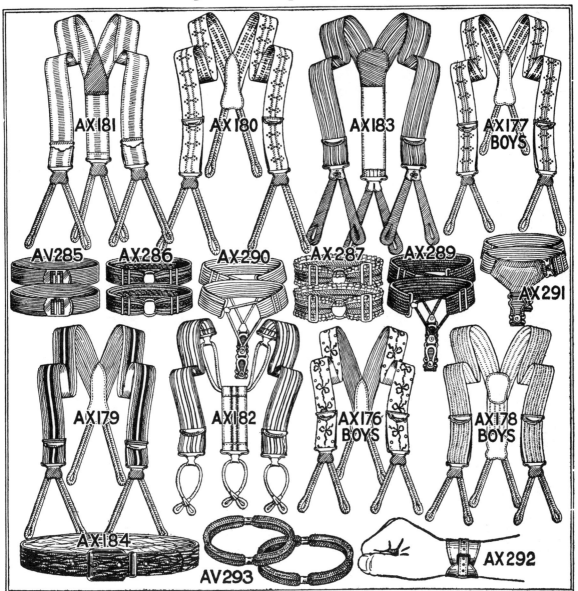

AX181 AX180 AX183 AX177 BOYS

AV285 AX286 AX290 AX287 AX289 AX291

AX179 AX182 AX176 BOYS AX178 BOYS

AX184 AV293 AX292

AX176—Boys' Suspenders. Made of good quality 1¼ inch lisle webbing. Reinforced leather back and front. Good sliding buckles. All metal parts heavily nickel plated and polished. Mohair ends. Weight, 2 ounces. Price........**10c**

AX177—Boys' Suspenders. Good quality lisle webbing 1¼ inches wide. Leather front and back, strongly sewn. Mohair ends. Strong sliding buckles. All metal parts heavily nickel plated and polished. Weight, 2 ounces. Price........**10c**

AX178—Boys' Police Style Suspenders. Made extra strong. Best quality lisle webbing. Heavy leather back and front. Mohair ends. Strong sliding buckles. All metal parts heavily nickel plated and polished. Weight, 2 ounces. Price **10c**

AX179—Men's Suspenders. Made of 1⅛ inch lisle webbing. Front and back of die cut tanned leather. Mohair ends. Strong sliding buckle. All metal parts highly polished and nickel plated. 36 inches long. Weight 3 ounces. Price..**10c**

AX180—Men's Light Weight Suspenders. Made of good quality 1¼ inch lisle webbing. Front and back of tanned leather. Sliding buckle. All metal parts heavily nickel plated and polished. Mohair ends. Full length size. Weight, 3 ounces. Price..**10c**

AX181—Men's Police Suspenders. Made of good quality lisle webbing 1⅛ inches wide. Front and back of die cut tanned leather. Mohair ends. Strong sliding buckle. All metal parts heavily nickel plated and highly polished. Weight, 3 ounces. Price..**10c**

AX182—Self Adjusting Suspenders. Made of good quality web elastic with strong cord attachment. Strong sliding buckles. All metal parts are highly polished and heavily nickel plated. Full length size. Weight, 2 ounces. Price........**10c**

AX183—Men's Heavy Police Suspenders. Made of good quality heavy web elastic with strong leather back and ends. Strong sliding buckle, heavily nickel plated. Especially made for policemen, firemen, and postmen. Weight, 3 ounces. Price..**10c**

AX184—Men's Leather Belts. 1 inch wide. Colors, black, with gunmetal buckle and loop, or brown with brass buckle and loop. Sizes to fit 30 to 46 inch waist measure. A regular 25c value. State size and color wanted. Weight, 3 ounces. Price..**10c**

AV285—Flat Elastic Arm Bands. Made of ¾ inch lisle webbing. Nickel trimmed. Colors, black, white, brown, pink, light blue. State color wanted. Weight, pair 2 ounces. Price..**5c**

AX286—Flat Elastic Arm Bands. Best quality ¾ inch fancy lisle webbing. Sliding buckles and ring strongly made and heavily nickel plated. Weight, pair 2 ounces. Price..**10c**

AX287—Fancy Arm Bands. 1 inch frilled mercerized elastic. Nickeled sliding buckles. Black, white, pink, and light blue. State color wanted. Weight, pair 2 ounces. Price..**10c**

AX289—Men's Garters. Made of ⅞ inch mercerized cable webbing, strong cord, flat loop. Full size. Colors, black, white, light blue, brown, or red. State color. Weight pair, 3 ounces. Price..**10c**

AX290—Men's Garters. Made of ⅞ inch plain lisle webbing. Strong cord, flat loop, rubber button. Black, white, light blue, brown or red. State color. Weight pair, 3 ounces. Price..**10c**

AX291—Men's Pad Garters. Full length. Double stitched. Good quality elastic. Strong button. Nickeled trimmings. Black, white, light blue, brown or lavender. Weight pair, 2 ounces. Price..**10c**

AV293—Round Arm Bands. Good quality round elastic. Come in the following colors: blue, white, brown, or black. State color wanted. Weight pair, 2 ounces. Price..**5c**

AX292—Leather Wrist Bands. Made of good quality tanned leather, lined, strongly sewn. Adjustable. Colors, black or tan. Weight, 1 ounce. Price..**10c**

Extra Special Bargains—Nothing Over 10c

MEN'S FANCY BORDER HANDKERCHIEFS, 10c.

AX164 — Men's Fancy Border Handkerchiefs. Made of extra quality soft finish cotton cloth. Woven borders of assorted colors in blue, pink and lavender. Ends neatly hemstitched. Full size. State color wanted. Weight, 1 ounce. Each....... **10C**

MEN'S PLAIN COTTON HANDKERCHIEFS, 5c.

AV159 — Men's Plain Cotton Handkerchiefs. Made of good quality plain white cotton cloth. Edges are ¼-inch wide and neatly hemstitched. Size of handkerchief, 17½ inches square. Color is pure white throughout, and come in plain white only. Weight, 1 ounce. Each................**5C**

COLORED BORDER HANDKERCHIEFS, 5c.

AV161 — Colored Border Handkerchiefs. Made of good quality white cotton cloth. Have neat colored border, 1-inch wide, nicely hemstitched. Handkerchiefs are full size. The borders are assorted and the illustration shows one of these styles. Can be placed in the outside coat pocket. Weight, each, 1 ounce. Price........**5C**

MEN'S NOVELTY WHITE HANDKERCHIEFS, 10c.

AX167 — Men's Novelty White Handkerchiefs. Made of extra quality corded cloth. Satin stripe design and border. The satin stripe design is woven all through the handkerchief. Edges are ½-inch wide, neatly hemstitched. A very popular style. Weight, 1 ounce. Price........**10C**

PLAIN WHITE LINEN HANDKERCHIEFS, 10c.

AX166 — Plain White Linen Handkerchiefs. Made of extra quality pure linen cloth, bleached to a pure white. Handkerchiefs are full size. Edges are ¼-inch wide and are neatly hemstitched. A special value. Weight, 1 ounce. Price, each................**10C**

MEN'S INITIAL HANDKERCHIEFS, 10c.

AX169 — Men's Initial Handkerchiefs. Made of fine quality white cotton cloth. Full size. ½-inch edge neatly hemstitched. Fancy embroidered initial in one corner. State initial wanted. Weight, 1 ounce. Price, each **10C**

MEN'S BLUE HANDKERCHIEFS, EACH, 5c.

AV162 — Men's Blue Handkerchiefs. Made of best quality, heavy cotton cloth with polka dot design throughout. Handkerchiefs are 21 inches square. Best quality indigo dye. Wt., each, 1 ounce. Price,..............**5C**

MEN'S JAPONETTE INITIAL HANDKERCHIEFS, 5c.

AV160 — Men's Japonette Initial Handkerchiefs. Made of soft finished cream-white color cloth. Has large silk embroidered initial in one end. ½-inch edges neatly hemstitched. State initial desired. Wt., 1 ounce. Price, each................**5C**

SILK EMBROIDERED INITIAL HANDKERCHIEFS, 10c.

AX168 — Silk Embroidered Initial Handkerchiefs. Made of best quality cream-white color mercerized cloth. Silk embroidered initial of latest design. ½-inch edges neatly hemstitched. State initial wanted. Wt. 1 ounce. Price, each...........**10C**

MEN'S TURKEY RED HANDKERCHIEFS, 5c.

AV163 — Men's Turkey Red Handkerchiefs. Made of best quality cotton cloth. Neat black and white figures on red center with fancy scroll border. Edges are neatly hemmed. Weight, each, 1 ounce. Price **5C**

MEN'S PLAIN WHITE HANDKERCHIEFS, 10c

AX165 — Men's Plain White Handkerchiefs. Made of best quality fine cotton cloth. Full 20 inches square. Pure white throughout. ¼-inch edges neatly hemstitched. A very special value. Weight, 1 ounce. Price, each...... **10C**

BOYS' OR LADIES' KNIT WRIST GLOVES, PAIR, 10c.

AX175 — Boys' or Ladies' Knit Wrist Gloves. Made of extra heavy quality canton flannel. Edges strongly sewed with good thread. Close fitting wrists knitted from good quality brown yarn. Weight, per pair, 3 ounces. Price.................**10C**

MEN'S WHITE CANTON FLANNEL GLOVES, PER PAIR, 10c.

AX170—Men's White Canton Flannel Gloves. Made of heavy quality 11-ounce cloth. Has cloth wrists with woven red border. Edges strongly sewed with good thread. Wide enough to permit the hand to move freely. Weight, per pair, 3 ounces. Price **10C**

MEN'S CANTON FLANNEL KNIT WRIST GLOVES, PER PAIR, 10c.

AX171—Men's Canton Flannel Knit Wrist Gloves. Made of 10-ounce bleached canton flannel. Edges strongly sewed with good thread. Perfect fitting. Close fitting wrist of woven brown yarn. A very good value. Weight, per pair, 3 ounces. Price......**10C**

MEN'S HEAVY CANTON FLANNEL GAUNTLET GLOVES, PAIR, 10c.

AX172—Men's Heavy Canton Flannel Gauntlet Gloves. Made of heavy canton flannel. Edges strongly sewed with good thread. Easy fitting. Gauntlet is of heavy stiffened duck with red all-over edge. Specially made to protect the hand and wrist. Weight, per pair, 3 ounces. Price.. **10C**

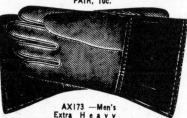

MEN'S EXTRA HEAVY BROWN GAUNTLET GLOVES, PAIR, 10c.

AX173 —Men's Extra Heavy Brown Gauntlet Gloves. Made of extra heavy quality brown canton flannel. Edges strongly sewed with good thread. Gauntlet is of heavy black oil cloth, lined with canvas. Reinforced edges. Special value. Wt., per pair, 4 ounces. Price **10C**

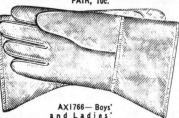

BOYS' AND LADIES' STRONG GAUNTLET GLOVES, PAIR, 10c.

AX1766— Boys' and Ladies' Strong Gauntlet Gloves. Made of heavy bleached canton flannel. Edges strongly sewed with good thread. Easy fitting. Gauntlet is made of stiff duck cloth, crocheted edge to prevent ravelling. Weight, per pair, 3 ounces. Price.................**10C**

HOSIERY for MEN, WOMEN & CHILDREN PER PAIR 10¢

GUARANTEED HOSIERY AT 10c

Numbers AX100, AX113 and AX114, on this and the following pages are Guaranteed Hose for Men, Women and Children. We absolutely guarantee these numbers to give satisfactory wear, or to replace them without extra cost. Our Guarantee Ticket is attached to every pair. Nothing over 10c.

On this and the following pages we show the same good qualities in hosiery that have contributed to the success of the Kresge Stores. The values are so great that many of our customers purchase hosiery in lots of a dozen or more pairs. We are sure that you will be so pleased with your first order that you will do likewise. The variety shown in these pages enable you to order for every member of the family. The wearing quality of our hosiery will surprise you.

We have made a specialty of strong school stockings for children. Boys and girls attending school need a good strong wearing stocking, and we have selected our lines with this in mind. In our ladies' hosiery we have a variety of weights from light gauze to the heaviest grades, and a variety of styles and weigths in men's hosiery to please everyone.

The numbers bearing our Guarantee ticket are positively guaranteed, and we will send you a new pair for any that give unsatisfactory wear. When returning our guaranteed hosiery for exchange it is necessary to return the guarantee ticket from the original pair with the stockings.

All of the numbrs shown on these pages are seamless, with two exceptions, and these are mentioned in the description. The patent toes are so well made that they can be worn with as much comfort as full seamless goods.

When ordering be sure to give correct style number, color and size. If in doubt about the size, tell us the size of the shoe you wear and we will fit you perfectly. Remember —Nothing over 10c.

Ladies' Plain Cotton Guaranteed Stockings, Special Per Pair 10c

AX100 — Ladies' Plain Cotton Stockings. Under this number we offer one of the best values in ladies' stockings. Each pair bears our guarantee as to quality. Fast colors: black or tan. Sizes, 8½, 9, 9½ and 10. Full seamless heel and toe with extra heavy top to prevent tearing. The stocking is strongly reinforced at the heel and toe. Very fine close ribbed and made from good quality soft cotton yarn. These stockings are so woven that they will stretch easily and not have that tight, cramped feeling. State size and color wanted. Weight, 3 ounces. Per pair..................**10C**

Ladies' Black Cotton Stockings With White Feet, Per Pair 10c

AX105 — Ladies' Black Cotton Stockings with white feet. Under this number we offer a very attractive value. The stockings have strongly hemmed top to prevent tearing with patent seamless heel and toe. Made of good quality soft cotton yarn. Will stretch easily and not bind the leg. Well shaped ankles. Foot is of pure white cotton yarn of extra good quality. Preferred by many to the solid color stocking. Will not shrink or lose color when washing. Sizes, 8½, 9, 9½ and 10. Come in black only. State size wanted when ordering. Weight, per pair, 3 ounces. Price, per pair......**10C**

Ladies' Extra Size Black Stockings, Per Pair 10c

AX102 — Ladies' Extra Size Black Stockings. This number comes in black only for extra large shaped leg. Full seamless stocking with spliced heel and toe. Have extra strong reinforced toe where stockings are usually weakest. Fine close weave and made of good quality soft cotton yarn in lisle finish. Good quality dye is used and color will not come out. Each pair bears our guarantee. Will not shrink with washing. No seams or knots to bother tender feet. Sizes, 8½, 9, 9½ and 10. Be sure to state size when ordering. Special value. Weight, 3 ounces. Price, per pair........**10C**

Ladies' Ribbed Top Cotton Stockings, Per Pair 10c

AX101 — Ladies' Ribbed Top Cotton Stockings. This is a very exceptional value and one we think cannot very well be duplicated at this price. Each pair is well made throughout. They come in fast colors, black or tan, with strong reinforced heel and toe, the places that are most liable to wear. Good, heavy ribbed top, about 5 inches deep. Woven from good quality soft cotton yarn. Will not cramp or feel tight on the feet. Guaranteed to hold their color and will not shrink. Sizes, 8½, 9, 9½ and 10. State size and color wanted. Weight, 3 ounces. Per pair.....................**10C**

Good Quality Hosiery for Women and Children at 10c Per Pair

Ladies' Plain Tan Cotton Stockings, Special Price Per Pair 10c

AX107—Ladies' Plain Tan Cotton Stockings. This is a very special value in a tan cotton stocking. Made from selected yarn of good quality, very soft and agreeable to the skin. Has well shaped ankles with double heel and toe of strong seamless construction. Good strong double tops to prevent tearing. Fine close weave with plenty of stretch. Will not cramp or bind the leg. Come in sizes, 8½, 9, 9½ and 10. Come in tan color only, just the proper shade. State size wanted when ordering. Weight per pair 3 ounces. Price........**10C**

Ladies' Selected Cotton Yarn Fancy Embroidered Hose, Per Pair 10c

AX104—Ladies' Selected Fancy Embroidered Hose. Made of best quality selected soft cotton yarn, full seamless hemmed top. Ankle and half of leg neatly embroidered in fancy design, colors white, blue or red on black ground. These designs are very neat and not too flashy. Have well shaped ankles and good seamless double heel and toe. This is one of our guaranteed stockings and a very special value for the money. Come in following sizes: 8½, 9, 9½, and 10. State size and color of embroidery desired. Weight per pair 3 ounces. Price.....................**10C**

Be sure to state Size and Katalog Number desired when ordering.

Ladies' Gray Mixed Stockings, Per Pair 10c

AX108—Ladies' Gray Mixed Stockings. Appeals especially to elderly women. Color is a neat gray mixed, made of best quality very soft cotton yarn with good hemmed top. Well shaped ankle and seamless double heel and toe. Sizes, 8½, 9, 9½ and 10. State size wanted. Weight 3 ounces. Per pair....**10C**

Ladies' Pure White Cotton Stockings, Per Pair 10c

AX106—Ladies' Pure White Cotton Stockings. Very fine quality, pure all white color. Seamless heel and toe. Well shaped ankle, strong hemmed top. Sizes, 8½, 9, 9½, and 10. A very special value in a pure white cotton stocking. State size wanted. Weight per pair 2 ounces. Price per pair. **10C**

Ladies' Fine Quality Gauze Stockings, Per Pair 10c

AX103—Ladies' Gauze Stockings. Made of fine quality cotton yarn, light weight. 4 inch garter top. Colors: black, tan or white. Well shaped ankle and seamless heel and toe. Will not shrink. Sizes, 8½, 9, 9½ and 10. State size and color wanted. Weight per pair 2 ounces. Price, per pair **10C**

Children's Guaranteed Ribbed Cotton Stockings, Per Pair 10c

AX114—Children's Guaranteed ribbed cotton Stockings. Suitable for either boys or girls. Full seamless, elastic leg, extra durable. Colors, black or tan. Sizes 5, 5½, 6, 6½, 7, 7½, 8, 8½, 9 and 9½. State size and color wanted. Weight per pair 4 ounces. Price......**10C**

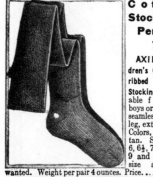

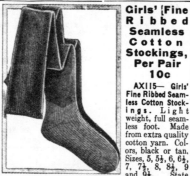

Girls' Fine Ribbed Seamless Cotton Stockings, Per Pair 10c

AX115—Girls' Fine Ribbed Seamless Cotton Stockings. Light weight, full seamless foot. Made from extra quality cotton yarn. Colors, black or tan. Sizes, 5, 5½, 6, 6½, 7, 7½, 8, 8½, 9 and 9½. State size and color wanted. Weight per pair 3 ounces. Price, per pair...................**10C**

Boys' Heavy Ribbed Black School Stockings, Per Pair 10c

AX116—Boys' Heavy Ribbed Black School Stockings. Double strength knee, full seamless. One of our best values. Comes in black only. Sizes, 5, 5½, 6, 6½, 7, 7½, 8, 8½, 9 and 9½. State size wanted. Weight per pair 4 ounces. Price per pair......**10C**

Children's Fine Ribbed Stockings, Per Pair 10c

AX117—Children's Fine Ribbed Stockings. Extra strong, full seamless, elastic ribbed leg. Colors, tan or white. Sizes, 5, 5½, 6, 6½, 7, 7½, 8, 8½, 9 and 9½. A special value in children's stockings. State size and color wanted. Weight per pair 2 ounces. Price.......**10C**

Boys' Extra Heavy School Hose, Per Pair 10c

AX118—Boy's Extra Heavy School Hose. Made of good quality cotton, triple strength knee, shaped ankle, full seamless. Double heel and toe. A special value. Sizes 5, 5½, 6, 6½, 7, 7½, 8, 8½, 9 and 9½. Black only. State size wanted. Per pair 2 ounces. Price, per pair.............**10C**

TRIPLE KNEE

Misses' Fine Ribbed Lisle Stockings, Per Pair 10c

AX119—Misses' Fine Ribbed Lisle Stockings. Full, seamless, light weight, shaped ankle and leg. Woven from good quality cotton yarn. Sizes 6, 6½, 7, 7½, 8 and 8½. Colors, black, tan or white. State color and size wanted. Weight pair 2 ounces. Price, per pair.......**10C**

MISSES SIZES

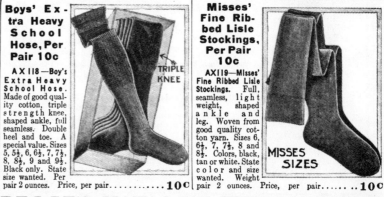

Men's Good Wearing Socks, Only 10c Per Pair

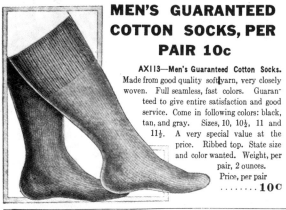

MEN'S GUARANTEED COTTON SOCKS, PER PAIR 10c

AX113—Men's Guaranteed Cotton Socks. Made from good quality soft yarn, very closely woven. Full seamless, fast colors. Guaranteed to give entire satisfaction and good service. Come in following colors: black, tan, and gray. Sizes, 10, 10½, 11 and 11½. A very special value at the price. Ribbed top. State size and color wanted. Weight, per pair, 2 ounces. Price, per pair 10C

Men's Embroidered Socks, Per Pair, 10c.

AX112—Men's Embroidered Socks. Neat embroidery on black or gray ground. Assorted stripe and other designs. Full seamless, double strength heel and toe. Sizes, 10, 10½, 11 and 11½. State size and color wanted. Weight, per pair, 2 ounces. Price, per pair....................................10C

Per Pair **10c**

Per Pair **10c**

Per Pair **10c**

Men's Medium Weight Cotton Socks, Per Pair, 10c.

AX109—Men's Medium Weight Cotton Socks. Knitted from good quality soft yarn with elastic top. Comes in black only with cream colored feet. Full seamless. Sizes, 10, 10½, 11 and 11½. State size wanted when ordering. Weight, per pair, 2 ounces. Price, per pair.................................10C

Men's Black Cotton Socks, Per Pair, 10c.

AX110—Men's Black Cotton Socks. A good heavy weight, well knitted sock with good elastic top. A fine sock for mechanics. Comes in black only. Sizes, 10, 10½, 11 and 11½. State size wanted when ordering. Weight, per pair, 3 ounces. Price, per pair....10C

Men's Light Weight Cotton Socks, Per Pair, 10c.

AX111—Men's Light Weight Cotton Socks. Made from extra quality yarn, full seamless. Guaranteed to give satisfaction. Colors: black, tan, gray, navy, and lavender. Sizes, 10, 10½, 11 and 11½. State size and color wanted. Weight, per pair, 2 ounces. Price, per pair..................................10C

Infants' and Children's Hosiery—Special at 10c Per Pair. State Size Desired

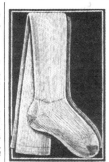

Infants' Fine Ribbed Stockings, Per Pair, 10c.

AX120 — Infants' Fine Ribbed Stockings. Medium weight, full seamless. Colors: black, tan, pink, light blue and white. Sizes, 4½, 5, 5½ and 6. State size and color wanted when ordering. Weight per pair, 2 ounces. Price, per pair..10C

Infants' Cashmerette Stockings, Per Pair, 10c.

AX121 — Infants' Cashmerette Stockings. Toes tipped with pink or blue mercerized yarn. Cream color only. Sizes, 4, 4½, 5, 5½ and 6. Special value. State size wanted. Weight, per pair, 2 ounces. Price, per pair.......10C

Infants' Silk Finish Stockings, Per Pair, 10c.

AX122 — Infants' Silk Finish Stockings. Good quality mercerized yarn. Full seamless. Colors: white, pink, light blue, tan or black. Sizes, 4, 4½, 5, 5½ and 6. State size and color wanted. Weight, per pair, 2 ounces. Price, per pair.......10C

Infants' Fancy Top Socks, Per Pair, 10c.

AX123 — Infants' Fancy Top Socks. Best quality soft white yarn. Seamless heels and toes. Woven ribbed top. Pure white body with dainty black stripes around top. The tip of toe and heel is woven in black. Sizes, 4½, 5, 5½, 6 and 6½. State size wanted. Weight, 1 ounce. Per pair.............10C

Infants' Fancy Top Socks, Per Pair, 10c.

AX124 — Infants' Fancy Top Socks. Best quality soft white cotton yarn. Pure white body with dainty pink or light blue stripes around top. Tips of toe and heel same color as stripes. Sizes, 4½, 5, 5½, 6 and 6½. State size and color wanted. Weight, 1 ounce. Per pair....10C

Infants' Fancy Socks, Per Pair, 10c.

AX125 — Infants' Fancy Socks. Best quality soft white yarn. White body with dainty stripe in pink or blue color throughout. Colored tops to match. Tips of heel and toe same color as stripe. Sizes, 4½, 5, 5½, 6 and 6½. State size and color wanted. Weight, per pair, 1 ounce. Price.............10C

See our special bargains for Infants on page 43—nothing over 10c

OUR GUARANTEE

We absolutely guarantee the jewelry shown on this and the following pages to be exactly as represented, and we will cheerfully refund your money if for any reason you are not satisfied with your purchase.

On this and the following pages we show exceptional bargains in jewelry for women and men. Our buyers regularly visit the country's largest jewelry markets for the latest novelties and designs, and our immense buying power enables us to sell these articles to you at about half of what retail jewelers charge. Everything shown in our Jewelry Department is dependable, and we guarantee that you will find everything to be as represented. When we state that we guarantee an article to wear one year we mean absolutely what we say—that we absolutely guarantee that article to wear to your satisfaction for one year. The engraving, hand painting and settings will give satisfactory wear. When purchasing bar pins or beauty pins, do not fail to include a few items for the gentlemen. On pages 56, 57 and 58 you will find exceptional bargains in cuff links, collar buttons, stick pins, scarf sets, coat and vest chains, watch fobs, etc., nothing over 10c. Bracelets, La Vallieres, rings, neck chains, etc., for women and children will be found on the following pages—exceptional values at 5c and 10c each. Read our guarantee above.

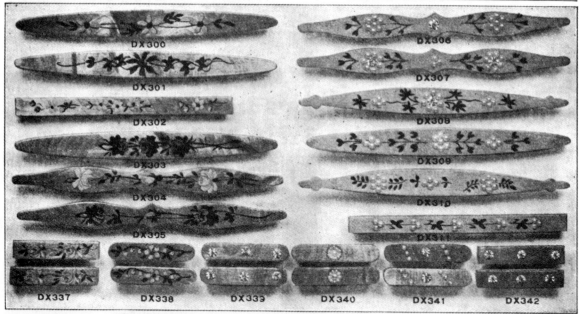

The illustrations above show goods about two-thirds actual size.

DX300—Veil or bar pin.......10c	DX303—Veil or bar pin.......10c
DX301—Veil or bar pin.......10c	DX304—Veil or bar pin.......10c
DX302—Veil or bar pin.......10c	DX305—Veil or bar pin.......10c

These veil or bar pins are made of the best quality Persian imitation ivory on good celluloid foundation. They are beautifully hand painted in floral designs such as Roses, Violets, Forget-me-nots, Poinsettas, and other flowers. They come in assorted shapes such as straight bar design, long oval design, fancy bar design, and others. Exceptional values, and easily worth 25c each.

DX306—Veil or bar pin.......10c	DX309—Veil or bar pin.......10c
DX307—Veil or bar pin.......10c	DX310—Veil or bar pin.......10c
DX308—Veil or bar pin.......10c	DX311—Veil or bar pin.......10c

These pins are made of good quality white celluloid, highly finished. Have hand painted sprays and leaves. They are set with imitation seed pearls and fine quality white brilliants. Come in assorted shapes, such as straight bar, oval, round ends, and others. These beautiful pins are unquestionably excellent values and are the most advanced styles for the coming spring season. Be sure to state number desired when ordering.

Hand Painted Beauty Pins Set With Imitation Pearls and Brilliants

DX337 — Celluloid beauty pins. Hand painted designs. Straight bar shape. Roses or other patterns. Come mounted two on a card. Price...........10c

DX338 — Celluloid beauty pins. Beautiful hand painted designs of floral sprays. Straight bar shape with round edges. 2 on card. Price...........10c

DX339 — Celluloid beauty pins. Persian imitation ivory finish, set with three large white brilliants. Come 2 on a card. Price....10c

DX340 — Celluloid beauty pins. Persian imitation ivory finish. Set with imitation seed pearls in clusters. 2 on a card. Price...10c

DX341 — Celluloid beauty pins. Persian imitation ivory finish. Set with six imitation seed pearls and one large white brilliant. 2 on card............10c

DX342 — Celluloid beauty pins. Imitation Persian ivory finish. Set with three first quality brilliants. Good value. 2 on a card. Price..10c

Beautiful Bar Pins and Tie Clasps, 10c

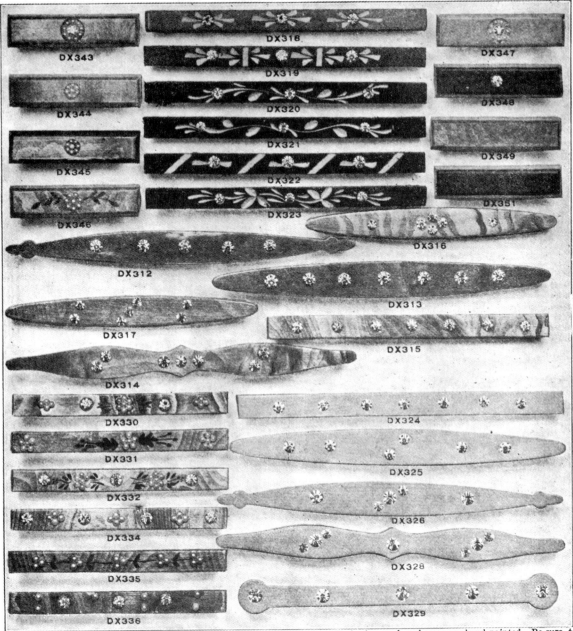

These popular bar pins and tie clasps are something entirely new. They are made of the best quality imitation Persian ivory, and are set with beautiful white brilliants or imitation seed pearls. Some have black backgrounds with white engraving, others a plain white background, and some are hand painted. Be sure to state number of style wanted when ordering. They are exceptional values and some jewelers retail them at 25c. Our prices—nothing over 10c.

DX312 to DX317. Veil or bar pins. Imitation Persian ivory finish, set with brilliants.

DX312—Veil or bar pin	10c
DX313—Veil or bar pin	10c
DX314—Veil or bar pin	10c
DX315—Veil or bar pin	10c
DX316—Veil or bar pin	10c
DX317—Veil or bar pin	10c

DX318 to DX323. Veil or bar pin, hand engraved, black backgrounds, set with brilliants.

DX318—Veil or bar pin	10c
DX319—Veil or bar pin	10c
DX320—Veil or bar pin	10c
DX321—Veil or bar pin	10c
DX322—Veil or bar pin	10c
DX323—Veil or bar pin	10c

DX343 to DX351. Tie clasps with plain white or hand painted backgrounds, set with brilliants or imitation seed pearls.

DX343—Tie Clasp	10c
DX344—Tie Clasp	10c
DX345—Tie Clasp	10c
DX346—Tie Clasp	10c
DX347—Tie Clasp	10c
DX348—Tie Clasp	10c
DX349—Tie Clasp	10c
DX351—Tie Clasp	10c

When ordering veil or bar pins do not fail to include rings, la vallieres, necklaces, etc., which will be found on the following pages. Cuts show goods about actual size. Weight ea. 1 oz.

DX324 to DX329. Veil or bar pins. Plain white imitation ivory finish, set with fine quality brilliants.

DX324—Veil or bar pin	10c
DX325—Veil or bar pin	10c
DX326—Veil or bar pin	10c
DX328—Veil or bar pin	10c
DX329—Veil or bar pin	10c

DX330 to DX336. Medium size veil or bar pins. Imitation Persian ivory finish, plain and hand painted backgrounds, set with brilliants or imitation seed pearls.

DX330—Veil or bar pin	10c
DX331—Veil or bar pin	10c
DX332—Veil or bar pin	10c
DX334—Veil or bar pin	10c
DX335—Veil or bar pin	10c
DX336—Veil or bar pin	10c

Beauty Pins, Pin Sets and Bar Pins, 10c

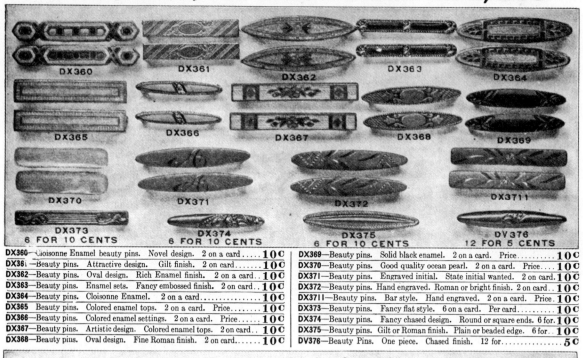

DX360
DX361
DX362
DX363
DX364
DX365
DX366
DX367
DX368
DX369
DX370
DX371
DX372
DX3711
DX373
6 FOR 10 CENTS
DX374
6 FOR 10 CENTS
DX375
6 FOR 10 CENTS
DV376
12 FOR 5 CENTS

DX360—Cloisonne Enamel beauty pins. Novel design. 2 on a card.....**10¢**
DX361—Beauty pins. Attractive design. Gilt finish. 2 on card......**10¢**
DX362—Beauty pins. Oval design. Rich Enamel finish. 2 on a card..**10¢**
DX363—Beauty pins. Enamel sets. Fancy embossed finish. 2 on card..**10¢**
DX364—Beauty pins. Cloisonne Enamel. 2 on a card...............**10¢**
DX365—Beauty pins. Colored enamel tops. 2 on a card. Price....**10¢**
DX366—Beauty pins. Colored enamel settings. 2 on a card. Price..**10¢**
DX367—Beauty pins. Artistic design. Colored enamel tops. 2 on card.**10¢**
DX368—Beauty pins. Oval design. Fine Roman finish. 2 on a card....**10¢**

DX369—Beauty pins. Solid black enamel. 2 on a card. Price.........**10¢**
DX370—Beauty pins. Good quality ocean pearl. 2 on a card. Price....**10¢**
DX371—Beauty pins. Engraved initial. State initial wanted. 2 on card..**10¢**
DX372—Beauty pins. Hand engraved. Roman or bright finish. 2 on a card..**10¢**
DX3711—Beauty pins. Bar style. Hand engraved. 2 on a card. Price.........**10¢**
DX373—Beauty pins. Fancy flat style. 6 on a card. Per card.........**10¢**
DX374—Beauty pins. Fancy chased design. Round or square ends. 6 for.**10¢**
DX375—Beauty pins. Gilt or Roman finish. Plain or beaded edge. 6 for..**10¢**
DV376—Beauty Pins. One piece. Chased finish. 12 for...............**5¢**

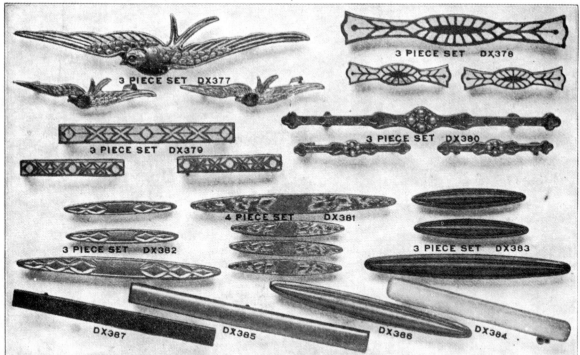

3 PIECE SET DX377
3 PIECE SET DX378
3 PIECE SET DX379
3 PIECE SET DX380
4 PIECE SET DX381
3 PIECE SET DX382
3 PIECE SET DX383
DX387
DX385
DX386
DX384

DX377—Three piece veil or waist set. Lucky Bluebird pattern. Set consists of one large and two small bluebirds. Good, quality baked enamel finish. Per set... **10¢**

DX378—Three piece enamel waist set. Has novel Egyptian pattern. Finished in assorted enameled colors. One large and two small pins in set. Per set.. **10¢**

DX379—Three piece waist or veil set. Has quaint Oriental pattern, finished in gilt and colored enamel. Set consists of one large and two small pins. Per set **10¢**

DX380 — Three piece veil or waist set. Novel bar design. Each pin set with four imitation seed pearls, or white stones. A very attractive set. Per set. **10¢**

DX381—Four piece veil or waist set. Consists of one large and three small pins. Chased design. Bright or Roman finish. Per set......................**10¢**
DX382—Three piece veil or waist set. One large and two small pins in rolled plate finish. Old English design. Bright color. Per set.................**10¢**
DX383—Three piece veil or waist set. Comes in black color only. Can be had in plain or beaded edge. One large and two small pins. Per set...........**10¢**
DX384 Pearl shell bar pin. 2 inches long. Clear bright finish. Each..**10¢**
DX385—Polished bar pin. Bright gold color. 12K finish. Price......**10¢**
DX386—Roman finish bar pin. Fancy raised design. Rolled plate finish.**10¢**
DX387—Real goldstone bar pin. 2¼ inches long. Very popular number.**10¢**

Note: The illustrations on this page show goods about actual size. Average weight 1 oz.

Stylish Brooches and Bar Pins, 10c Each

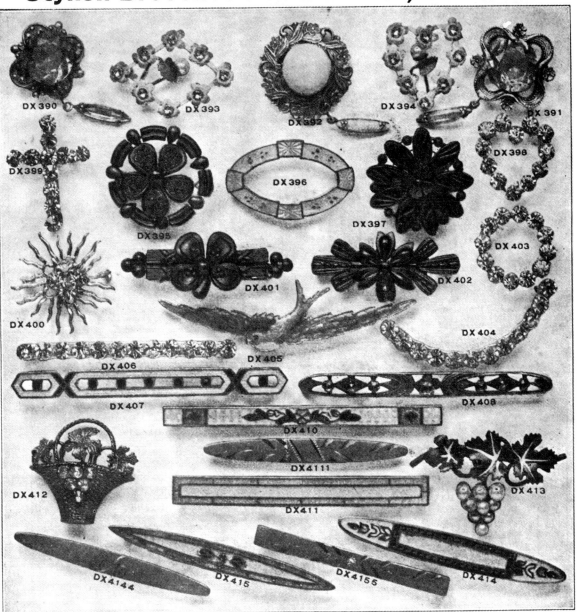

DX390—Brooch, set with fancy-shape sapphire and pendant. Price, each **10C**

DX393—Imported brooch pin, set with 8 brilliants and 1 imitation pearl. Fancy blue enamel finish. Price, each....................................**10C**

DX392—Novelty brooch pin, with turquoise setting and pendant. Special value. Each....................................**10C**

DX394—Heart-shape imported brooch, set with 8 brilliants and one imitation pearl. Fancy blue enamel finish. Each....................................**10C**

DX391—Fancy shape brooch. Amethyst setting and pendant. Each..**10C**

DX399—Brooch pin. Cross design, set with 11 first quality brilliants. Price, Each....................................**10C**

DX395—Fine quality black enamel brooch pin, as illustrated. Each....**10C**

DX396—Oval collar pin, enameled in dainty assorted colors and designs. Each....................................**10C**

DX397—Black enamel brooch pin. Style as illustrated. Each........**10C**

DX398—Heart-shape brooch pin set with 12 first quality brilliants. Excellent value. Each....................................**10C**

DX400—Sunburst set with 4 first quality brilliants. Bright silver finish metal mounting. Price, each....................................**10C**

DX401—Black enamel brooch pin. Design as illustrated. Special at, each **10C**

DX402—Black enamel brooch pin as illustrated. Each..............**10C**

DX403—Brooch pin set with 12 first quality brilliants. Silver finish mounting. Each....................................**10C**

DX406—Bar pin set with 12 brilliants with silver finish metal frame. Each **10C**

DX405—Blue bird collar pin trimmed with gilt. Each................**10C**

DX404—Crescent-shape brooch set with 12 first quality brilliants. Silver finish metal frame. Excellent value. Each....................................**10C**

DX407—Fancy shape enamel bar pin. Highly finished. Most popular color combinations. Price, each....................................**10C**

DX408—Novelty bar pin set with 7 fancy shape colored stones. Bronze finish metal frame. Each....................................**10C**

DX412—Imported basket-shape brooch. Assorted colors and designs. Ea.**10C**

DX410—Enamel Bar Pin. Fine quality enamel finish in beautiful designs and color. Special value at, each....................................**10C**

DX4111—Engraved bar pin comes in Roman or bright finish. Warranted to wear 5 years. Each....................................**10C**

DX411—Enamel bar pin in fancy design. Beautiful finish and color. Each **10C**

DX413—Collar Pin. Represents clusters of grapes. Each........**10C**

DX415—Fancy enamel bar pin. Fine finish. Beautiful colors. Each..**10C**

DX414—Fancy enamel bar pin. Exquisite coloring, and attractive design. Each....................................**10C**

DX4144—Initial bar pin. Roman or bright finish. Warranted to wear 5 years. Any initial. State initial when ordering. Each....................................**10C**

DX4155—Hand engraved bar pin. Comes in Roman or bright finish. Warranted to wear 5 years. Each....................................**10C**

Average weight of above articles, each 1 oz. Illustrations show goods about actual size.

Extraordinary Values in Jewelry at 10c

DX425
DX421   DX424   DX427   DX426   DX423   DX422   DX420

DX420—Neck Chain and Heart Shape Pendant. Gilt or silver color. Set with 12 rhinestones. Weight, 1 ounce. Price..........................**10C**

DX422—Neck Chain and Cross Pendant. Comes in gilt or silver color. 10 good quality rhinestones. Weight, 1 ounce. Price..........................**10C**

DX423—Neck Chain and Graduated Pendant. Gilt or silver color. 7 graduated rhinestones. Beautiful pattern. Weight, 1 ounce. Price............**10C**

DX427—Foxtail Fan Chain. Comes in silver, gunmetal, or gilt color. 48 inches long. Strong snap. Weight, 1 ounce. Price.........................**10C**

DX424—Neck Chain and Cluster Pendant. Gilt or silver color. 7 brilliant rhinestones. Strong clasp. Weight, 1 ounce. Price...................**10C**

DX425—Neck Chain and Drop Pendant. Gilt or silver color. Four rhinestones and imitation pearl drop. Weight, 1 ounce. Price....................**10C**

DX426—Gilt Shot Necklace. 14 inches long. Has strong fastener. Finished in a beautiful gilt color. Weight, 1 ounce. Price....................**10C**

DX421—Neck Chain and Spray Pendant. Gilt or silver color. 7 large rhinestones. Beautiful design. Weight, 1 ounce. Price....................**10C**

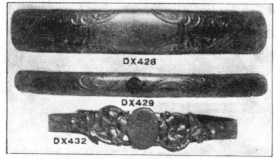

DX428
DX429
DX432

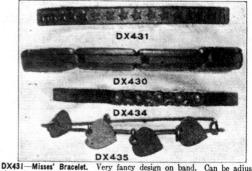

DX431
DX430
DX434
DX435

DX428—Ladies' Bracelet. Beautiful embossed design. Patent catch. Gilt color. A heavy bracelet in an attractive pattern. Weight, 1 ounce. Price. **10C**

DX429—Ladies' Bracelet. Beautiful embossed design, set with birthstone. Patent clasp. Gilt color. State color stone desired. Weight, 1 oz. Price.**10C**

DX432—Misses' Bracelet. Fancy raised design with signet top. Adjustable. Gilt color. Fancy design around band. Weight, 1 ounce. Price........**10C**

DX431—Misses' Bracelet. Very fancy design on band. Can be adjusted to various sizes. Comes in gilt color. Weight, 1 ounce. Price...........**10C**

DX430—Ladies' Bracelet. Patent spring links which can be adjusted to various sizes. Bright gilt finish. Weight, 1 ounce. Price....................**10C**

DX434—Misses' Bracelet. Adjustable. Fancy raised design, set with five imitation pearls. A very popular pattern. Weight, 1 ounce. Price....**10C**

DX435—Gilt Wire Bracelet. Adjustable pattern with four heart spangles attached. Suitable for children and misses. Weight, 1 ounce. Price......**10C**

DX437— Imitation Coral Snake Bracelet. Narrow pattern. Three coils. Eyes set with brilliant rhinestones. This is a very attractive pattern and closely resembles genuine coral. This is a very popular style and is suited for both misses and children. Weight, 1 ounce. Price.................**10C**

DX436 — Imitation Coral Bracelet. Double bands in round pattern with large fancy knot. This is a very attractive bracelet and can be adjusted as desired. Suitable for either children or misses. Has a genuine coral color. Weight, 1 ounce. Price.............................**10C**

DX438— Imitation Coral Snake Bracelet. This is a medium weight bracelet and made in three coils. Can be adjusted as desired. Suitable for ladies, misses or children. Weight, 1 ounce. Price..**10C**

DX441 — Screw Back Earrings. Finished in bright gilt color with well finished adjustable screws. Will not pierce or injure the ear. Settings may be had either in jet or turquoise. Weight, pair, 1 ounce. Price......**10C**

DX439 — Earrings. Finished in bright gilt with fine adjustable screw backs. Settings are large brilliant rhinestones securely mounted. These earrings usually sell in retail jewelry stores at from 25c to 50c. Weight, pair, 1 ounce. Price.............**10C**

DX440 — Ear Drops. Set with large imitation pearls in patent mounting. Adjustable screw back. Nicely finished in bright gilt color. A very attractive pattern and an exceptional value for the money. Weight, pair, 1 ounce. Price.**10C**

The above illustrations, except Coral Bracelets, show goods about actual size.

Extra Quality Rings, Special at 10c Each

All of our set rings are plated with 1-20th stock 10K gold, and we fully guarantee them to wear one year. Any ring purchased from us that does not wear for one year can be returned for a new one. Our trade mark is stamped on the inside of each one of our set rings

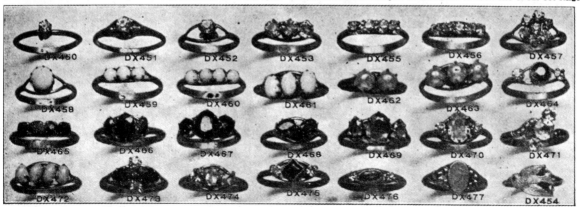

DX450—10c.
Ring. First quality white stone, mounted in high setting. Price **10C**

DX451—10c.
Ring. First quality white stone in Belcher setting. Price........**10C**

DX452—10c.
Ring. Split shank, with first quality white stone in high setting. Price **10C**

DX453—10c.
Ring. Split shank, Set with three brilliant rhinestones. Price........**10C**

DX455—10c.
Ring. Split shank. Mounted with four brilliant settings. Price........**10C**

DX456—10c.
Ring. Split shank, set with five first quality white stones. Price........**10C**

DX457—10c.
Ring. Split shank, seven white stones in cluster. Price........**10C**

DX458—10c.
Ring. Split shank set with one large imitation opal. Price........**10C**

DX459—10c.
Ring. Split shank, set with three small imitation opals. Price........**10C**

DX460—10c.
Ring. Split shank, set with four imitation opals. Price, each........**10C**

DX461—10c.
Ring. Split shank. High setting, three good size imitation opals........**10C**

DX462—10c.
Ring. Split shank. Set with two imitation pearls. Price, each........**10C**

DX463—10c.
Ring. Split shank, set with three large imitation pearls. Price........**10C**

DX464—10c.
Ring. Split shank imitation ruby, two first quality white stone brilliants. Price........**10C**

DX465—10c.
Ring. Split shank set with four imitation rubies. Price........**10C**

DX466—10c.
Ring. Split shank. Large and two small imitation ruby settings. Price..**10C**

DX467—10c.
Ring. Split shank. Large and two small imitation garnet settings **10C**

DX468—10c.
Ring. Split shank. Set with two imitation rubies. Price........**10C**

DX469—10c.
Ring. Split shank, one large, two small imitation amethysts. Price........**10C**

DX470—10c.
Ring. Split shank, large imitation sapphire. Two white brilliants **10C**

DX477—10c.
Ring. "Signet pattern. We guarantee this ring to wear one year and will stamp any one initial you desire on same free of charge. Price........**10C**

DX471—10c.
Ring. Serpentine shank, one large, two small imitation sapphires ...**10C**

DX472—10c.
Ring. Split shank, four imitation turquoise sets. Price........**10C**

DX473—10c.
Ring. Split shank, set with two imitation emeralds and two small white stones **10C**

DX474—10c.
Ring. Split shank. Set with three small imitation amethysts. Price.**10C**

DX475—10c.
Ring. Split shank. Set with one imitation emerald and two first quality brilliants ...**10C**

DX476—10c.
Ring. Split shank, one imitation amethyst, two fine brilliants **10C**

DX454—10c.
Fine enamel Blue Bird ring, with sterling shank. Price........**10C**

Average Weight of the above rings 1 ounce. Illustrations are about actual size.

How To Order Rings: Cut a narrow strip of thick paper long enough to go around second joint of finger on which you want to wear the ring. Place one end of the paper on top of the joint and draw the strip tightly around the finger. Make a pencil mark where the paper meets this end; then cut off at pencil mark and send us the part that was wrapped around finger.

Men's Link and Scarf Sets at 10c

MEN'S LINK AND SCARF SETS, 10c.
DX490 — Men's Link and Scarf Set. Beautiful sapphirine setting, consisting of two link buttons with beautiful scarf pin to match. A splendid combination. Weight, 2 ounces. Price....................**10C**

MEN'S SCARF SETS, 10c.
DX493—Men's Scarf Set. Elegant imitation blister pearl setting in plain mounting. Link buttons and scarf pin match perfectly. Splendid value. Weight, 2 ounces Price **10C**

MEN'S LINK AND SCARF SETS, 10c.
DX491—Men's Link and Scarf Set. Beautiful goldstone setting in plain mounting. Links and scarf pin match perfectly. Can be worn with almost any color scarf. Weight, 2 ounces. Price........**10C**

LINK AND SCARF SETS, EACH, 10c.
DX494 — Link and Scarf Set. Consists of link buttons and scarf pin in lover's knot design with white stone setting. A very popular number. Weight, 2 ounces. Price **10C**

MEN'S LINK AND SCARF SETS, 10c.
DX492—Men's Link and Scarf Set. Consists of link buttons and scarf pin to match, and set with colored cut stones, very fancy mounting. Weight, 2 ounces. Price....................**10C**

INITIAL LINK AND SCARF SETS, 10c.
DX495—Initial Link and Scarf Set. Consists of link buttons and scarf pin to match, Roman finish. Hand engraved initial. State initial wanted when ordering. Weight, 2 ounces Price........**10C**

Illustrations show sets about actual size. State number when ordering.

Bargains in Jewelry For Men at 5c and 10c

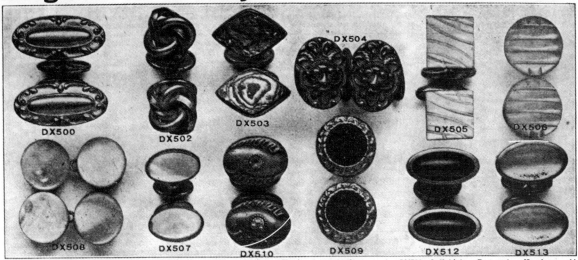

DX500—Cuff Links. Made in bright gilt finish. Have long oval top in fancy raised and embossed design. Have lever ends. Weight pair 1 ounce. **10C**

DX502—Cuff Links. Finished in Roman or silver color. Large lover's knot design. Strong lever ends. Specify color wanted. Weight 1 ounce. Price. **10C**

DX503—Cuff Links. Abalone shell sets securely mounted. Have strong lever ends. Comes in silver finish color. Price, pair 1 ounce. Price...... **10C**

DX504—Cuff Links. These links have embossed heads in assorted designs. Rose gold finish. Strong lever ends. Weight, pair 1 ounce. Price.... **10C**

DX505—Cuff Links. Heads of square shape, engraved pearl shell. Strong metal lever backs. Finished in gilt color. Weight, per pair 1 oz. Price.... **10C**

DX506—Cuff Links. Post-style buttons. Tops of round shape engraved shell pearl. Strong posts and lever backs. Weight, pair 1 ounce. Price...... **10C**

DX508—Cuff Links. Both ends of round shell pearl with chain link. For soft shirts and shirt waists. Very popular number. Weight, pair 1 ounce. **10C**

DX507—Cuff Links. Solid link with strong bar, gilt finish. Shell pearl sets in both ends. A very popular shirt waist number. Weight, 1 ounce. Price.... **10C**

DX509—Cuff Links. Post style. Has large goldstone, set in fancy embossed mounting. Lever ends. Weight pair, 1 ounce. Price.................. **10C**

DX510—Cuff Links. Embossed design, top set with first quality brilliants. Lever back. Gilt or green gold finish. Weight pair, 1 ounce. Price.......... **10C**

DX512—Cuff Links. Plain oval mounting with large red carbuncle setting. Strong lever back. Rich gilt finish. Weight, 1 ounce. Price................ **10C**

DX513—Cuff Links. Plain long oval mounting, set with imitation moonstones. Strong lever back, bright gilt finish. Weight, 1 ounce. Price............ **10C**

DX478—Stick Pin. Horsewhip style. Gold filled wire with brilliant rhinestone set. Weight ½ ounce. **10C**

DX479—Stick Pin. Made of gold filled wire. Question mark design, set with rhinestone. Weight ½ ounce. Price................................... **10C**

DX480—Stick Pin. Gold filled wire. Wishbone design. Set with rhinestone. Weight ½ ounce. **10C**

DX481—Stick Pin. Large rhinestone in Tiffany setting. A popular number. Weight ½ ounce. **10C**

DX482—Stick Pin. Large oval goldstone setting. Weight ½ ounce. Price.................. **10C**

DX483—Stick Pin. Colored stone set surrounded with ten brilliants. Rich design. Weight ½ ounce. Price................................... **10C**

DX484—Stick Pin. Horseshoe shape set with ten first quality brilliants. Weight ½ ounce. Price.. **10C**

DX485—Stick Pin. Real opal in Tiffany setting. Weight ½ ounce. Price.................. **10C**

DX486—Stick Pin. Oval shape, set with eight brilliants. Weight ½ ounce. Price.......... **10C**

DX487—Stick Pin. Double horsehead chased design in gilt color. Weight ½ ounce. Price.......... **10C**

DX488—Stick Pin. Large fresh water pearl with first quality brilliant. Weight ½ ounce. Price.... **10C**

DX489—Stick Pin. Crescent shape design of fine quality shell pearl. Weight ½ ounce. Price..... **10C**

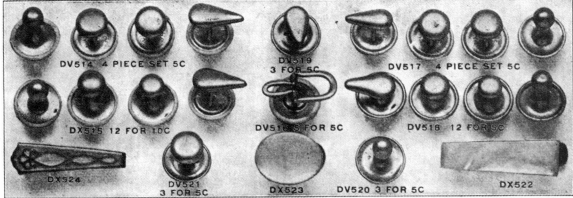

DV514—Collar Button Set. Celluloid backs. Four pieces on card. Weight, 1 ounce. Price.......... **5C**

DX515—Collar Buttons. Celluloid backs. 12 assorted styles on card. Weight, 1 ounce. Price.... **10C**

DV516—Patent Collar Buttons. Celluloid backs. Five buttons on card. Weight, 1 ounce. Price.... **5C**

DV517—Collar Button Set. Aluminum backs. Lever ends. Four on card. Weight, 1 ounce. Price.... **5C**

DV518—Collar Buttons. One piece, gilt color. 12 buttons on card. Weight, 1 ounce. Price........ **5C**

DV519—Collar Buttons. Gooseneck pattern, lever ends. Plated back. Three on card. Weight, 1 oz. **5C**

DV520—Collar Buttons. Post style, plated back. Three on a card. Weight, 1 ounce. Price........ **5C**

DV521—Collar Buttons. Flat head, lever ends, plated back. Three on card. Weight, 1 ounce. **5C**

DX522—Tie Clip. 1½ inches long. Shell pearl mounting. Bar shape. Weight, 1 ounce. Price. **10C**

DX523—Tie Clip. Small oval style with fine pearl shell mounting. Weight, 1 ounce. Price...... **10C**

DX524—Tie Clip. Cloisonne enamel, bar shape, 1½ inches long. Assorted designs and finishes. Weight, 1 ounce. Price............................ **10C**

The above illustrations show goods about actual size. State Katalog Number when ordering.

Latest Style Coat and Vest Chains, 10c Each

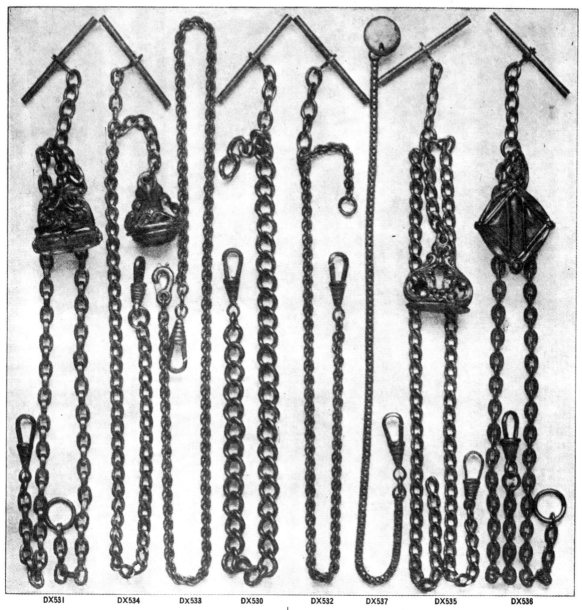

DX531   DX534   DX533   DX530   DX532   DX537   DX535   DX536

PLAIN LINK VEST CHAINS, 10c.

DX530—Plain Link Vest Chains. This chain is about 11 inches long and formed of large heavy links in a popular style. Finished in Roman color. Can be worn with any style of charm. One end is equipped with a strong snap for attaching to watch. A good value for the money. Weight 1 ounce. Price.....................**10C**

DOUBLE VEST CHAIN GILT FINISH, 10c.

DX531—Double Vest Chain. This chain is full 14 inches long and composed of good heavy links finished in a rich gilt color. One end is equipped with a strong snap and the other has a large round ring. Has a heavy charm attached set with a large colored stone. Weight 1 ounce. Price.....................**10C**

SINGLE VEST CHAINS, EACH 10c.

DX532—Single Vest Chains. This is one of the popular rope style chains, finished in Roman color. Chain is about 10½ inches long. Has good strong snap at one end for attaching to watch. Can be worn with any style of charm desired. This is one of the prettiest chains in our line. Weight 1 ounce. Price............**10C**

ROMAN FINISH WALDEMAR CHAIN, 10c.

DX533—Roman Finish Waldemar Chain. This chain comes in the popular Waldemar style and is full 15 inches long. Has a fine Roman color finish. One end has a good strong snap for attaching to watch and the other end is equipped with patent closing ring. Weight 1 ounce. Price.....................**10C**

SINGLE VEST CHAIN, STONE CHARM, 10c.

DX534—Single Vest Chain. This chain is about 11 inches long and made of flattened links with a rich gilt finish. One end is equipped with a strong snap for fastening to watch. This chain has a fancy stone set charm. Stones may be had in Turquoise, Sapphire, Ruby, Emerald, etc. Weight 1 ounce. Price.... ....**10C**

FANCY SIGNET VEST CHAIN, 10c.

DX535—Fancy Signet Vest Chain. This is a double vest chain of good quality flattened gilt links. Chain is 14 inches long over all. Charm is of a very fancy signet style, Roman color finish. One end is equipped with a good strong snap for attaching to watch. The other end is plain. Weight 1 ounce. Price.............**10C**

DOUBLE VEST CHAINS, EACH 10c.

DX536—Double Vest Chains. Good quality gilt chain with strong fancy links. Has a very fancy stone charm set in gilt metal. Length of chain is 14 inches over all. Has good snap on one end and heavy ring on the other. This is a very high grade chain and a popular number. Weight 1 ounce. Price..............**10C**

SHELL BUTTON COAT CHAIN, 10c.

DX537—Shell Button Coat Chain. This chain is about 9 inches long and comes in the popular snake link. Has a Roman color finish. One end is equipped with a dark shell button and the other end with a good strong snap for attaching to watch. Just the chain for dress wear when the watch is worn on the coat. Weight 1 ounce. Price.....................**10C**

NOTE—The illustrations on this page show goods about actual size.

Ribbon and Leather Fobs Special at 10c

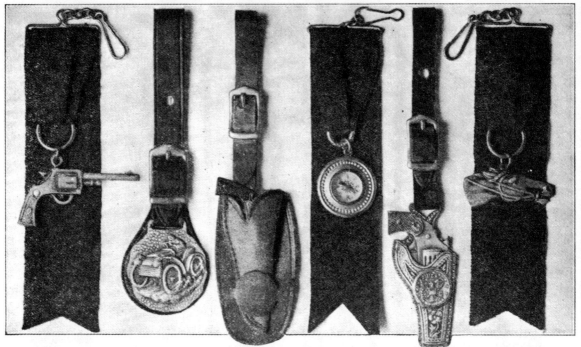

IVORY REVOLVER FOB, 10c.	AUTOMOBILE LEATHER FOB, 10c.	COWBOY FOB, 10c.	COMPASS CHARM FOB, 10c.	METAL REVOLVER FOB, 10c.	RIBBON WATCH FOB, 10c.
DX540—Ivory Revolver Fob. Mercerized ribbon fob with ivory colored revolver charm, set with white stone. Weight 1 ounce. Price........10C	DX541 — Automobile Leather Fob. Good quality black leather fob with nicely stamped metal automobile charm. Weight, 1 ounce. Price,..........10C	DX542—Cowboy Fob. Leather fob with small metal gun in leather holster. Good quality nickeled buckle. Weight 1 ounce. Price.........10C	DX543—Compass Charm Fob. Good mercerized ribbon. Compass charm nicely gilted. Gilt buckle and snap. Weight 1 ounce. Price...........10C	DX544—Metal Revolver Fob. Leather strap with revolver charm. Fine quality die work. Gun in holster. Weight 1 ounce. Price...........10C	DX545—RibbonWatch Fob. Black mercerized ribbon with light colored imitation ivory horsehead charm. Weight 1 ounce. Price...........10C

HORSESHOE FOB, 10c.	BOY SCOUT FOB, 10c.	LINCOLN PENNY FOB, 10c.	BASEBALL FOB, 10c.	INITIAL WATCH FOB, 10c.	AIRSHIP DESIGN FOB, 10c.
DX546—Horseshoe Fob. Good leather fob with horseshoe charm and horse's head stamped in metal. Very pretty. Weight 1 ounce. 10C	DX547—Boy Scout Fob. Leather fob with Boy Scout charm stamped in metal. Very popular with boys. Weight 1 ounce.........10C	DX548—Lincoln Penny Fob. A good leather fob, with American shield. Genuine Lincoln penny in each shield. Weight 1 ounce.........10C	DX549—Baseball Fob. Good leather fob with baseball player nicely stamped in metal. A very popular charm. Weight 1 ounce. 10C	DX550—Initial Watch Fob. Leather fob with solid stamped gilt initial. Specify initial wanted when ordering. Weight 1 ounce.........10C	DX551—Airship Design Fob. Fine leather fob with airship charm nicely stamped in metal. Good nickeled buckle. Weight 1 ounce. 10C

The above Illustrations of Fobs show goods about one-half actual size.

Special Bargains for Men—Nothing Over 10c

LEATHER TOBACCO POUCH,
10c.

BX524—Tobacco Pouch. Made of extra quality soft finish brown leather. Closes with draw string and snap fastener. Well made throughout. Size, 4½x5½ inches. Weight, 1 ounce. Price, each....**10C**

LEATHER TOBACCO POUCH,
10c.

BX525—Tobacco Pouch. Made of extra quality brown calf skin. Closes with draw string and snap fastener. Exceptional value. Size, 4½x5 inches. Weight, 1 ounce. Price, each............**10C**

LEATHER TOBACCO POUCH,
10c.

BX526—Tobacco Pouch. Made of imitation buckskin leather. Light weight in light tan color. Closes with draw string. Size, 5½x5½ inches. Weight, 1 ounce. Special price....**10C**

RUBBER TOBACCO POUCH,
10c.

BX527 — Tobacco Pouch. Made of fine quality red rubber with automatic closing top. See illustration above. An unusual value. 3½ inches in diameter. Weight, 1 ounce. Each.**10C**

ALUMINUM MATCH SAFE,
10c.

BX528—Aluminum Match Safe. Made of best quality white aluminum. Satin finish over all. Will not tarnish or corrode. Size, 1½x3 inches. Weight, 1 oz. Price, each........**10C**

COMBINATION PIPE CLEANERS, 5c.

BB646 — Combination Pipe Cleaners. 12 cotton covered wire stem cleaners and scraper for bowl. Stem cleaners are 7 inches long. Weight, 1 ounce. Price, 2 packages for.....**5C**

CALABASH PIPES, EACH, 10c.

BX529 — Calabash Pipe. Finished in rich brown color, hard rubber bent stem, nickel plated metal ferrule. Length over all, about 5 inches. Assorted shapes. State style wanted. Weight, 2 ounces. Price, each..**10C**

ROSEWOOD PIPES, EACH, 10c.

BX530—Rosewood Pipe. Assorted shapes; straight or bent, amber or black stems. Pipes are nicely finished and have full size bowl. Nickel plated metal ferrule. State style wanted. Weight, 1 ounce. Price......**10C**

FRENCH BRIAR PIPES, 10c.

BX531 — Briar Pipes. Assorted shapes. Straight or bent stems in amber or black. These pipes are nicely turned and insure a cool, sweet smoke. Extra special value. State style wanted. Weight, 1 ounce. Each**10C**

MEDIUM BRIAR PIPES, 10c.

BX532—Briar Pipes. Made in assorted shapes, medium small size, straight and bent with amber stem. A high grade pipe at a special price. State proper stem wanted. Weight, 1 ounce. Each...........**10C**

LARGE SIZE POCKET KNIFE, 10c.

HX410 — Pocket Knife. Large size, with stag handle. 3-inch blade of good quality steel, highly polished, sharp edge. A strong well made knife. Entire length opened, 6½ inches. Weight, 2 ounces. Price, each.**10C**

STAG HANDLE JACK KNIFE, 10c.

HX411—Jack Knife. Heavy stag handle with shield. 2½ inch blade. Thumb cutout on handle permitting blade to be easily opened. Made of best quality steel. Length opened, 6 inches. Weight, 2 ounces. Price......**10C**

BEST QUALITY POCKET KNIFE, 10c.

HX412 — Pocket Knife. Two blades, heavy stag handle, brass lined. Fancy shaped handle with shield. Blades are made of best quality steel, highly polished. High tempered, keen cutting edge. Weight, 1 ounce. Special value at..............**10C**

BLACK HANDLED PEN KNIFE, 10c.

HX413—Pen Knife. With two blades, hardwood black handle, finished with shield. Thumb cutout in handle, permitting blades to be easily opened. 2-inch blade. Length over all, 5 inches. Weight, 1 ounce. Price......**10C**

ALUMINUM PEN KNIFE, 10c.

HX414—Aluminum Pen Knife. With two blades, patriotic decorations on handle. Made of best quality steel, highly polished. Length both blades open, 6 inches. Weight, 1 ounce. Price, each. **10C**

PEN KNIFE, HARDWOOD HANDLE,
10c.

HX415—Pen Knife. Two blades. Black hardwood handle with brass shield, brass lined. Fancy shaped. Blades of fine quality steel. Length when opened, 6 inches. Weight, 1 ounce. Price...............**10C**

HIGH GRADE PEN KNIFE, 10c.

HX416 — High Grade Pen Knife. With two blades, imitation pearl handle, brass lined. Blades of fine quality steel, highly polished. Length when opened, 5½ inches. Weight, 1 ounce. Price.................**10C**

PEARL HANDLED PEN KNIFE, 10c.

HX417 — Pearl Handled Pen Knife. With two blades of fine quality, highly polished steel. Length over all when blades are opened, 5 inches. Weight, 1 ounce. Extra value at.......**10C**

EBONY HANDLE SHAVING BRUSH, 10c.

HX418—Shaving Brush. Filled with medium white bristles, securely set, will not fall out. Round ebony handle, highly nickel plated ferrule. Weight, 2 ounces. An extra special value at..**10C**

SQUARE HANDLE SHAVING BRUSH, 10c.

HX419 — Shaving Brush. Large size, filled with white bristles, firmly set. Square block shaped ebony handle. Well made and will give satisfaction. Weight, 2 ounces. Price.....**10C**

State Katalog number when ordering.

CHERRY HANDLE SHAVING BRUSH, 10c.

HX420 — Shaving Brush. Imitation badger bristles, firmly set. Cherry handle, nickel trimmed mounting, black wood ferrule. A brush that readily retails at 25 cents. Weight, 2 ozs. Special at.......**10C**

MEDIUM SIZE SHAVING BRUSH, 10c.

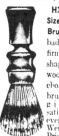

HX421—Medium Size Shaving Brush. Imitation badger bristles, firmly set. Fancy shaped, round wood handle, ebony finish. A brush that will give thorough satisfaction in every particular. Weight, 2 ounces. Price, each **10C**

BADGER HAIR SHAVING BRUSH, 10c.

HX422 — Shaving Brush. Medium size; imitation badger bristles, firmly set. Fancy hardwood handle, ebony finish; trimmed with highly nickel plated band. Weight, 2 ounces. An extra special value at ..**10C**

THE ORIGINAL PARCEL POST KRESGE'S KATALOG FIVE AND TEN CENT STORE

Good Quality Leather Purses, etc., 10c Each

MEN'S COIN PURSE, 10c.

BX500 — Men's Coin Purse. 3¾ inches wide by 3 inches deep. Best calf skin body. Highly polished nickel frame. Three compartments. Weight, 1½ ounces. Price, each....**10c**

EXTRA STRONG COIN PURSE, 10c.

BX501 — Extra Strong Coin Purse. Selected calf skin body. Stitched with welt seam. Fine nickel plated frame. Two compartments. Weight, 1½ ounces. Price, each...........**10c**

MEN'S CALF SKIN PURSE, 10c.

BX502. — Men's Calf Skin Purse. Extra strong, heavy and wide nickel plated frame. Durable catch. A serviceable purse. One compartment. Weight, 1¼ ounces. Price, each....**10c**

DOUBLE COIN PURSE, 10c.

BX503 — Double Coin Purse. Black calf skin body. Made with special heavy nickeled brass overlapping frame. Coins cannot possibly slip out. Weight 2 ounces. Price, each...**10c**

MEN'S SEAL GRAIN PURSE, 10c.

BX504 — Single Pocket Purse. Oval shape. Looks like genuine seal leather. Will give good service. Weight, 1½ ounces. Price, each............**10c**

SEAL GRAIN PURSE 10c.

BX504 — .....se. Double .....e. Welt stitche.....ion of genuine sea.. Weight, 1½ ounces. Price, each....**10c**

DOUBLE LEATHER PURSE, 5c.

BV506 — Double Purse. Strong, serviceable frame. Good quality leather throughout. Size, 2¾x3 inches. Weight, 1 ounce. Price, each....**5c**

OVAL COIN PURSE, 5c.

BV507 — Oval Coin Purse. Single pocket. Nickel plated overlapping frame. Size, 3x3½ inches. A strong light purse. Weight, 1 ounce. Price, each..................**5c**

LADY'S COIN PURSE, 10c.

BX508 — Lady's Coin Purse. Small size. Single pocket. Seal grain leather. Welt seam. Oblong shape. Strong nickel plated frame and catch. Size, 2½x3½ inches. Weight, 1 ounce. Price, each..................**10c**

MEN'S EXTRA LARGE COIN PURSE, 10c.

BX509 — Men's Extra Large Coin Purse. Single pocket. Selected calf skin body. Strong catch. Nickel plated overlapping frame. Size, 3½x4½ inches. Extra value. Weight, 1½ ounces. Price, each....**10c**

LADY'S LEATHER COIN PURSE, 10c.

BX510 — Lady's Leather Coin Purse. Imitation seal grain. Single pocket. Size, 4½x2½ inches. Just right for use in handbag. Weight, 1½ ounces. Price, each............**10c**

LADY'S LEATHER PURSE, 10c.

BX511 — Lady's Seal Grain Leather Coin Purse. Lacquered brass frame. Oblong shape. Leather lined. Size, 4½x2½ inches. Extra value. Weight, 1 ounce. Price, each **10c**

SMALL DOUBLE PURSE, 10c.

BX512 — Small Double Purse. Size, 3x2½ inches. Seal grain leather. Strong, double frame highly nickel plated. Weight, 1 ounce. Price, each....**10c**

CHILD'S COIN PURSE, 5c.

BV513 — Child's Coin Purse. Single pocket. Oval shape. Ornamental frame. Made in a wide assortment of leathers and desirable colors. Weight, ½ ounce. Price, each.......**5c**

LADY'S MEDIUM SIZE PURSE, 10c.

BX514 — Lady's Medium Size Leather Coin Purse. Single pocket. Oblong shape. Durable frame and catch. Size, 4x2½ inches. Extra value. Weight, 1½ ounces. Price, each.**10c**

CHILD'S OVAL SHAPE PURSE 10c.

BX515 — Child's Purse. Oval shape. Fancy embossed gilt frame. Has 15-inch double chain attached. Comes in green, brown, maroon, grey, etc. State color wanted. Wt. 1½ ounces. Price, each.**10c**

MEN'S EXTRA DEEP COIN PURSE, 10c.

BX516 — Men's Extra Deep Coin Purse. Size, 3¾x5½ inches. Double pocket. Made of selected leather. Extra strong frame. Weight, 1½ ounces. Price, each..................**10c**

LEATHER CARD CASE, 10c.

BX517 — Card Case. 3⅛x5 inches, folded. Has celluloid inside pocket for identification card, and compartment for cards or bills. Comes in black only. Weight, 1 ounce. Price, each..................**10c**

EXTRA DEEP COIN PURSE, 10c.

BX518 — Extra Deep Coin Purse. Made of suede leather. Single pocket. Heavily nickel plated overlapping frame. Size, 3½x4½ inches . Weight, 1 ounce. Price, each............**10c**

SILVER GILT PURSE WITH CHAIN 10c.

BX519 — Silver Gilt Purse with Chain. Imitation mesh. Looks like a mesh bag. Double inside pocket. Weight, 3 ounces. Price, each....**10c**

BILL-FOLD WITH COIN POCKET, 10c

BX522 — Bill-Fold with Coin Pocket attached. Made of extra selected soft black calf skin with double snap fastener. Weight, 1 ounce. Price, each...................**10c**

COMBINATION BILL-FOLD, 10c.

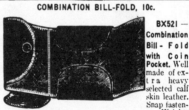

BX521 — Combination Bill-Fold with Coin Pocket. Well made of extra heavy selected calf skin leather. Snap fastener. Weight, 1 ounce. Price, each...................**10c**

BILL-FOLD AND CARD CASE, 10c.

BX523 — Combination Bill-Fold and Card Case. Has inside pocket for identification card, two card pockets and large pocket for bills. Size, folded, 2¾x4¾ inches Weight, 1 ounce. Price, each..............**10c**

COSMETICS & TOILET ARTICLES AT 5¢ & 10¢

GREASELESS PEROXIDE CREAM PER JAR, 10c.

BX250— Greaseless Peroxide Cream. A cream which is very popular at the present time. Snow white in color and has a very pleasant odor. Comes put up in 2 ounce opal glass jars with nickel plated top. Weight 10 ounces. Price. **10¢**

EXTRA QUALITY MASSAGE CREAM PER JAR, 10c.

BX253—Extra Quality Massage Cream. A perfect rolling massage cream of extra quality. Cream is delicately perfumed and sealed with parafine to retain its freshness. Directions for using on each jar. Put up in handsome glass jars with aluminum screw top. A generous supply in each jar. Weight 5 ounces. Price. **10¢**

WITCH HAZEL AND LEMON CREAM, 10c.

BX258—Witch Hazel and Lemon Cream. Made of best double distilled witch hazel and lemon cream. Its use insures a beautiful complexion. Full directions on each bottle. Excellent after shaving. Weight 11 ounces. Price. **10¢**

EXTRACT WITCH HAZEL PER BOTTLE, 10c.

BX259—Extract Witch Hazel. Made of best quality double distilled. Invaluable for sprains, bruises, bites of insects, swellings, and after shaving. Should be in every home. Weight 10 ounces. Price. **10¢**

Toilet articles are quite heavy and should be ordered with other merchandise in order to make a profitable shipment.

SUPERIOR QUALITY COLD CREAM PER JAR, 10c.

BX251—Superior Quality Cold Cream. A most delightful preparation, especially for dry, rough or chapped skin. Delicately perfumed. Put up in opal glass jars with nickel plated top. Its use opens the pores and makes the skin soft and healthy. Directions on each jar. Weight 7 ounces. Price. **10¢**

COLGATE'S COLD CREAM PER TUBE, 10c.

BX255—Colgate's Cold Cream. Put up in medium size tubes. A strictly high grade cold cream, delicately perfumed. Weight 1 ounce. Price. **10¢**

EYEBROW PENCILS, EACH, 10c.

BX257—Eyebrow Pencil. Put up in convenient aluminum case. Can be carried in purse or handbag. Colors black or brown. State color wanted. Weight 1 ounce. Each. **10¢**

PURE ROUGE STICK, 10c.

BX256—Pure Rouge Stick. Put up in convenient aluminum case. Can be carried in purse or handbag. Rich red color. Weight 1 ounce. Price. **10¢**

DELICATE LAVENDER ODOR SMELLING SALTS PER BOTTLE, 10c.

BX262—Smelling Salts. Has a very delicate lavender odor. Will last for a very long time without deteriorating. A convenient size to carry in the handbag. Invaluable for ladies traveling. Comes in a very attractive square bottle with large glass stopper. Best quality ingredients. Weight per bottle 5 ounces. Price per bottle. **10¢**

MOORAC ROUGE PASTE PER JAR, 10c.

BX254—Moorac Rouge Paste. This is a very superior quality rouge paste. It is of a rich red color which gives perfect results. Round opal glass jar with opal glass lid. A generous quantity in each jar. Weight 5 ounces. Price. **10¢**

MOORAC GREASELESS CREAM PER JAR, 10c.

BX252—Moorac Greaseless Cream. A high grade delicately scented cream which has all the advantages of the regular creams, but is not greasy. Its use is very beneficial to the skin. Put up in square opal jars with nickel plated tops. Directions on each jar. Weight 9 ounces. Price. **10¢**

CAMPHORATED CREAM PER JAR, 10c.

BX2522 — Camphorated Cream. A superior quality cold cream with the soothing and healing qualities of pure champor added. Full directions for using on each jar. Excellent for chapped hands, face, or lips, also for use after shaving. Put up in round opal glass jar with aluminum top. Weight 7 ounces. Price. **10¢**

MOORAC LIQUID SHAMPOO, 10c.

BX260—Moorac Liquid Shampoo. Made of highest quality ingredients. Keeps the scalp in a healthy condition. Full 8 ounce bottle. Weight 16 ounces. Price. **10¢**

FLORIDA WATER PER BOTTLE, 10c.

BX263—Florida Water. This well known toilet water has a very delicate odor. Comes in 3½ ounce tall bottle. Weight 10 ounces. Price. **10¢**

HAIR TONIC AND DANDRUFF REMEDY, 10c.

BX261—Hair Tonic and Dandruff Remedy. A superior quinine hair tonic or preparation. Destroys the dandruff germs. Weight 9 ounces. Price. **10¢**

We guarantee the toilet articles sold by us to conform to the Pure Food and Drugs Act.

Complexion Powders, Etc.—Nothing over 10c

VIOLET WITCH HAZEL, BOTTLE, 10c.

BX2622 — Violet Witch Hazel. Made of best quality distilled witch hazel with delicate violet fragrance. Highly suitable for use after shaving, bathing, etc. Also for general toilet use. Comes put up in neat shape bottle. Wt., 13 ounces. Price, per bottle **10C**

VIOLET AND LILAC TOILET WATER, 10c.

BX2633 — Violet and Lilac Toilet Water. A rare product for general toilet use. Your choice of two odors; violet and lilac. The fragrance is very delicate. Put up in a handsome bottle with artistic glass stopper. State odor wanted. Weight of bottle, 8 ounces. Price, each..........**10C**

MOORAC BAY RUM, PER BOTTLE, 10c.

BX264 — Moorac Bay Rum. Best quality bay rum. Invaluable for general toilet purposes, after shaving, bathing, etc. A generous quantity in each bottle. This bay rum is put up in an attractive glass bottle holding 4 ounces. Each bottle weighs 10 ozs. Price, per bot. .**10C**

HIGH GRADE PERFUME, PER BOTTLE, 10c.

BX265 — High grade Perfume. Choice of four permanent odors; rose, lilac, lily of the valley and violet. This high grade perfume is put up in 1 ounce fluted bottles. State odor wanted when ordering. Weight, per bottle, 5 ounces. Price..**10C**

SPECIAL QUALITY PERFUME BOTTLE, 10c.

BX266 — Special Quality Perfume. Choice of four delicate odors; rose, lilac, lily of the valley, violet. A special value. Perfume is put up in 1 ounce square bottles with fancy glass stopper. Weight, per bottle, 5 ounces. Price, per bottle **10C**

EXTRA QUALITY PERFUME BOTTLE 10c.

BX267 — Extra Quality Perfume. Odors equal to perfume sold at much higher prices. Comes in six odors; violet, white rose. China rose, lily of the valley, lilac, and Jockey Club. State odor wanted when ordering. Weight, per bottle, 3 ounces. Price, per bottle **10C**

LIQUID ROUGE, PER BOTTLE, 10c.

BX268 — Liquid Rouge. This rouge is the best quality. Perfect lasting color, and easily applied. Preferred by many to other forms of rouge. Put up in an attractive package. Weight, 3 ounces. Price..**10C**

PERSIAN NAIL BLEACH, PER BOTTLE, 10c.

BX269 — Persian Nail Bleach. A very high quality bleach for removing discolorations and stains of every description from the finger nails. Full directions for using on each bottle. Attractive package. Weight, 4 ounces. Price.**10C**

PERSIAN NAIL PASTE, 10c.

BX270 — Persian Nail Paste. A brilliant polishing paste for the finger nails, put up in opal glass jar. Full directions for using on each jar. Weight, 2 ounces. Price..................**10C**

PERSIAN NAIL STONE, 10c.

BX271 — Persian Nail Stone. A perfect preparation for polishing the finger nails. Contains no acid, pumice, or dust. Economical to use. Weight, per box, 1 ounce. Price..................**10C**

NAIL POLISH

HIGH GRADE NAIL POLISH, 10c
BX272 — High Grade Nail Polish. Best quality German nail polish put up in stick form in celluloid box. One of the highest grade polishers on the market. Weight, 1 ounce. Price **10C**

TETLOW'S COMPLEXION POWDER 5c.

BV280 — Tetlow's Perfect Complexion Powder. Comes in white and flesh tints. One of the best known complexion powders. State tint wanted. Weight, 1 ounce. Price........**5C**

VENESE ROSE COMPLEXION POWDER, 10c.

BX281 — Venese Rose Complexion Powder. One of the finest grade complexion powders on the market. Comes in white and flesh tints. State tint wanted when ordering. Weight, 4 ounces. Price.**10C**

AIR-FLOAT FACE POWDER, 10c.

BX282 — Air-Float Face Powder. A strictly high class face powder; rich delicate perfume. Comes in white or flesh tint. State tint wanted. Weight, 4 ounces. Price, per box **10C**

TOKETA FACE POWDER, 10c.

BX283 — Toketa Face Powder. Extra fine quality and has a very delicate odor. Comes in two tints; white or flesh. State tint wanted. Weight, per box, 4 ounces. Per box............**10C**

FINE RICE POWDER, 10c.

BX284 — Fine Rice Powder. Violette Poudre de Riz Complexion Powder. An extra fine rice powder, delicately perfumed. Comes in two tints; flesh or white. State tint wanted when ordering. Weight, per package, 2 ounces. Price...**10C**

CORYLOPSIS TALCUM POWDER BOX, 10c.

BX273 — Corylopsis Talcum Powder. Best quality talcum powder scented with a very delicate and lasting Japanese odor. Comes in 8 ounce can with patent sprinkler top, nickel plated. Each can weighs 10 ounces. Price, per can....**10C**

VIOLET TALCUM POWDER CAN, 5c.

BV274 — Violet Talcum Powder. This talcum powder is of a superior quality and has a very delicate violet perfume. Excellent for general toilet use. 8-ounce can with patent sprinkler top. Weight, per can, 10 ounces. Price, per can..............**5C**

WILDWOOD VIOLET TALCUM POWDER, 10c.

BX275 — Wildwood Violet Talcum Powder. This is a very high class talcum powder with a delicate wildwood violet perfume. This powder is put up in an attractive brass dome top can, containing 14 ounces of talcum. Weight, 16 ozs. Price...**10C**

TRAILING ARBUTUS TALCUM POWDER, 10c.

BX276 — Trailing Arbutus Talcum Powder. This is a special quality with the delicate Trailing Arbutus odor. Comes put up in a special lithographed pyramid can with sprinkler top. A very special value. Weight, 7 ounces. Price, per can.......**10C**

AIR-FLOAT TALCUM POWDER, 10c.

BX277 — Air-Float Talcum Powder. An extra fine quality talcum powder. Delicately perfumed. Oval shape can with brass sprinkler top. White or flesh tint. State tint wanted. Wt. per can, 5 ounces. Price......**10C**

FOREST FRINGE VIOLET TALCUM POWDER, 10c.

BX278 — Forest Fringe Violet Talcum Powder. A very good grade of talcum powder with a delicate violet perfume. Comes in attractive oval shape can with sprinkler top. Special value. Weight, 5 ounces. Price.....**10C**

ROYAL TALCUM POWDER, 10c.

BX279 — Royal Talcum Powder. One of the highest grade talcum powders on the market. Violet borated. Comes in attractive oval shape cans with nickeled sprinkler top. Weight, per can, 5 ounces. Price, per can.......**10C**

We guarantee all toilet preparations sold by us to be made in accordance with the Pure Food and Drugs Act. We guarantee each article to be as represented or will promptly refund your money.

High Grade Toilet Articles at 5c and 10c

IMPORTED DOWN POWDER PUFF, 10c.

BX285—Imported Down Powder Puff. Made of finest quality imported down with strong silk back and extra quality white bone handle. A very exceptional value. Puff is 3½ inches in diameter. Weighs 1 ounce. Price........10C

SMALL SIZE POWDER PUFF, 5c.

BV288 — Small Size Powder Puff. Made of best quality imported down with strong silk back and extra quality white bone handle. A very convenient small size puff. 2 inches in diameter. Weighs 1 ounce. Price, each. 5C

WOOL POWDER PUFF, 10c.

BX287 Wool Powder Puff. Made of best quality pure white wool. Extra large size. Has strong silk ribbon in back. Each puff is packed in a sanitary transparent envelope. Weight, 1 ounce. Price, each...................10C

SMALL WOOL POWDER PUFF, FINE QUALITY, 5c.

BV288 — Small Wool Powder Puff. Made of best quality white merino wool. 1½ inches in diameter. Has good silk ribbon sewn in back. Each puff is packed in a sanitary transparent envelope. Weight, 1 ounce. Price, each..........5C

LARGE SIZE TOILET CHAMOIS, 10c.

BX289 — Large size Toilet Chamois. Each chamois is of the finest texture and made only of the best selected skins. Size of chamois is 8x10 inches. Easily worth double the price. Weight, 1 ounce. Price, each......10C

MEDIUM SIZE TOILET CHAMOIS, 5c.

BV290 — Medium Size Toilet Chamois. Each chamois is of the finest texture and made only of the best selected skins. Size of chamois, is 6x8 inches. A very soft and flexible piece of goods. Weight, 1 ounce. Price, each..................5C

CELLULOID PUFF BOX, 10c.

BX291—Celluloid Puff Box. Made of best quality celluloid with fancy cover to match. Diameter, 2½ inches by 1¾ inches high. three colors; pink, blue, and white. State color wanted. Weight, 1 ounce. Price, each. 10C

CELLULOID SOAP BOX, 10c.

BX292—Celluloid Soap box. Made in two pieces of best quality celluloid. A very neatly designed box. Size, 2½x3½ inches. Come in three colors, pink, blue, and white. Give color wanted. Weight, 1 ounce. Price, each..................10C

Fine Quality Tooth Brushes Only 10c Each

BONE HANDLED TOOTH BRUSH, 10c.

BX293—Bone Handled Tooth Brush. Made in the prophylactic shape of the finest quality white bristles. Ventilated back. Best quality. Weight, 1 ounce. Price, each. 10C

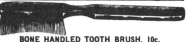

BONE HANDLED TOOTH BRUSH, 10c.

BX294—Bone Handled Tooth Brush. Made in assorted shaped handles. Hand drawn Japanese brush. Extra fine quality white bristles, securely fastened in black. Weight, 1 ounce. Price..............10C

CHILD'S TOOTH BRUSH, 10c.

BX295 — Child's Tooth Brush. Good quality bristles securely fastened in handle. Handle is made of best quality celluloid. 5 inches long. Weight, 1 ounce. Price.....................................10C

CELLULOID HANDLED TOOTH BRUSH, 10c.

BX296—Celluloid Handled Tooth Brush. Made in the prophylactic style of best quality white bristles, drawn by hand and securely fastened. Weight, 1 ounce. Price.....................................10C

LARGE SIZE TOOTH BRUSH, 10c.

BX297—Large Size Tooth Brush. German make. Best quality white bristles, best celluloid handle. Bristles are securely fastened. Weight, 1 ounce. Price, each. 10C

BEST QUALITY TOOTH BRUSH, 10c.

BX298—Best Quality Tooth Brush. Made of best grade bone handle and comes in assorted shapes. Bristles are fine quality and hand drawn. Weight, each, 1 ounce. Price, each.....................10C

A PERFECT PREPARATION FOR THE TEETH—MOORAC TOOTH WASH, 10c.

BX299 — Moorac Tooth Wash. A perfect preparation for cleansing the teeth, perfuming the breath, and preserving the gums. Its daily use is a necessity. Comes in convenient shaped bottle with metal screw top. One of the best grades of tooth wash on the market. Weight, per bottle, 6 ounces. Price, each. 10C

FOR BEAUTIFYING AND PRESERVING THE TEETH—ROYAL TOOTH POWDER, 10c.

BX300 — Royal Tooth Powder. A strictly pure tooth powder which contains no acid or grit. Has a delightful fragrance and its use keeps the teeth white, destroys tartar and preserves the gums. Packed in an attractive lithographed box with handsome nickeled top. Very economical to use. Weight, per box, 4 ounces. Price, per box....10C

A POWDER CONTAINING NEITHER ACID NOR GRIT—MOORAC TOOTH POWDER, 10c.

BX301—Moorac Tooth Powder. A strictly high grade tooth powder containing no acid or grit. Pleasant to use. Keeps the teeth white and sound, removes all tartar and destroys all harmful germs. Put up in convenient glass bottle with nickel plated top. Weight, 7 ounces. Price, per bot..10C

A HIGH QUALITY ECONOMICAL DENTAL CREAM — COLGATE'S RIBBON DENTAL CREAM, 10c.

BX302 — Colgate's Ribbon Dental Cream. A high quality of dental cream which is thoroughly antiseptic. The ribbon top makes it very economical to use. Perfumes the breath. Weight, 2 ounces. Price....10C

LARGE SIZE TUBE HIGH QUALITY ROYAL DENTAL CREAM, 10c.

BX303 — Royal Dental Cream. One of the best dental creams on the market. Comes in the new ribbon top tube which makes it very economical to use. Large size tube. Weight, 3 ounces. Price....10C

Big Bargains in Toilet Soaps at 5c

EGYPTOL TOILET SOAP, 2 BARS FOR 5c.

BB304. — Egyptol Toilet Soap. A strictly pure toilet soap. Oval shaped bars. Comes in two colors and odors; buttermilk, white, and carnation, pink. State kind wanted when ordering. Weight, 2 bars 7 ounces. Price, 2 for..................5C

GLYCERINE TOILET SOAP, 2 BARS FOR 5c.

BB305—Glycerine Toilet Soap. A high grade transparent glycerine soap, put up in oval shaped, 2½ ounce bars. Preferred by many who want a pure transparent glycerine soap. Weight, 2 bars 5 ounces. Price, 2 bars for..................5C

PINEY WOOD TAR HAND SOAP, 2 BARS, 5c.

BB306 — Piney Wood Tar Hand Soap. This soap is hard milled which prevents it from wasting away too rapidly. Comes in the convenient oval shaped 3 ounce bars. Weight, 2 bars 6 ozs. Price, 2 bars...................5C

SUPERFINE TOILET SOAP, 2 BARS FOR 5c.

BB307 — Superfine Toilet Soap. Comes in 3 ounce bars, convenient oval shape. Two odors; witch hazel and buttermilk. A very hard milled soap. Unexcelled for the bath. State odor wanted. Weight, 2 bars 6 ounces. Price 2 bars 5C

NOTE—It pays you to order other merchandise with soaps.

Fine Quality Toilet Soaps at 5c and 10c

WITCH HAZEL TOILET SOAP, 5c.

BV309 — Witch Hazel Toilet Soap. A pure witch hazel soap of extra quality. Comes in convenient oval shape for the toilet and bath. The soap is hard milled. Weight, 6 ounces. Price.........5C

FLOTILLA BATH SOAP, 5c.

BV312 — Flotilla Bath Soap. Especially prepared for the toilet and bath, and comes in convenient oval cake to fit the hand. Each cake is packed in a separate box. Weight, each, 6 ounces. Price, per cake.......5C

TOKETA BUTTERMILK SOAP, 5c.

BV315—Toketa Buttermilk Soap. Large cake of special good quality. Made in oval shape and convenient for the toilet and bath. Fits the hand. This soap is hard milled. Weight, per cake, 6 ounces. Price......5C

MECHANICS' PUMICE HAND SOAP, 5c.

BV318 — Mechanics' Pumice Hand Soap. This is a very desirable soap for mechanics, printers, machinists, etc., as it cuts grease and grime. Bar is hard milled. Convenient oval shape. Weight, 7 ounces. Price.............5C

TOILET SOAP, PER BOX, 10c.

BX321—Toilet Soap. An extra high quality toilet soap with a very delicate odor, lily of the valley. Three hard milled, oval shape cakes in each box. An exceptional value. Weight, per box, 10 ounces. Price....................................10C

WILLIAMS' SHAVING STICK, 10c.

BX327 — Williams' Shaving Stick. A very popular shaving soap. The stick is very economical to use and will last a long time. Put up in an attractive nickel plated box, paper lined. Delicately perfumed. Weight per box, 2 ounces Price.....10C

Do not forget to enclose postage when ordering.

HOFFMAN HOUSE TOILET SOAP, 5c.

BV310—Hoffman House Toilet Soap. An all pure white bath and toilet soap of extra quality. Comes in oblong shape, convenient for the bath. Soap is hard milled. Weight, 6 ounces. Per cake.5C

ALLPURE BUTTERMILK SOAP, 5c.

BV313 — Allpure Buttermilk Soap. This is a very high quality buttermilk soap especially prepared for the toilet and bath. Comes in convenient oval cake to fit the hand. Weight, per cake, 6 ounces. Price.....................5C

INDUSTRIAL TAR SOAP, 5c.

BV316 — Industrial Tar Soap. This is a very good quality tar soap. Made in convenient oblong shape cake. Just the thing for mechanics, and workmen. Each cake packed in separate box. Weight, 6 ounces. Price..5C

CASTILE TOILET SOAP, 5c.

BV319 — Castile Toilet Soap. An extra high quality pure castile toilet soap. Made of the very best ingredients. Unexcelled for the toilet and bath. This soap is cut in square cake. Weight, per cake, 7 ounces. Price.............5C

TOILET SOAP, PER BOX, 10c.

BX322 — Toilet Soap. Three oval shape bars of the very highest quality in each box. Soap has a very delicate lilac odor. Each bar is wrapped separately. Very convenient size. Weight, per box, 10 ounces. Price....................................10C

PURE TOILET SOAP, 10c.

BX324 — Pure Toilet Soap. Colgate's, in convenient guest room size, delicately perfumed with sandalwood or dactylis odor. State odor wanted. Weight, 2 ounces. Price.............10C

ALLPURE OATMEAL SOAP, 5c.

BV311—Allpure Oatmeal Soap. Best quality for the toilet and bath. Comes in oval shape and fits the hand. One of the best soaps of the kind on the market. Weight, 6 ounces. Price, per cake................5C

FAIRY FLOATING BATH SOAP, 5c.

BV314—Fairy Floating Bath Soap. One of the best quality floating soaps. Convenient oval size for the toilet and bath. Each cake is packed in an attractive paper box. Weight, per cake, 4 ounces. Price.................5C

SWEETHEART TOILET SOAP, 5c.

BV317 — Sweetheart Toilet Soap. This well-known soap is of a special high quality and comes in convenient oval shape bars. Each cake is hard milled. Packed in separate box. Weight, 3 ounces. Price........5C

TRANSPARENT GLYCERINE SOAP, 5c.

BV320 — Transparent Glycerine Soap. A very high grade pure glycerine toilet soap. Made in convenient oval shape. Fine for the toilet or bath. Cake fits the hand nicely and is hard milled. Weight, 6 ounces Price.............................5C

TOILET SOAP, PER BOX, 10c.

BX323—Toilet Soap. Three guest room size bars in each box. Soap is delicately perfumed with marsh violet odor. Each bar is wrapped separately. This is a hard milled soap. Weight, per box, 10 ounces. Price....................10C

ANTISEPTIC SHAVING CREAM, FINE QUALITY AT 10c. PER TUBE

BX328 —Antiseptic Shaving Cream. High quality shaving cream, put up in a convenient tube. No danger of dust, grit or other impurities getting into it. Economical to use. Wt., per tube, 2 ounces. Price......10C

PURE TOILET SOAP, 10c.

BX325 — Pure Toilet Soap. Colgate's Pure Toilet Soap in convenient guest room size, delicately perfumed with monad violet odor. Weight, per cake, 2 ounces. Price 10C

WILLIAMS' SHAVING SOAP, 5c.

BV326 — Williams' Shaving Soap. One of the best known shaving soaps on the market. Each cake contained in a separate paper box. Weight, 2 ounces. Price.......5C

It will pay you to order soaps with dry goods, etc. You run no risk whatever when ordering from us. We guarantee to please you or return your money including all transportation charges.

THE ORIGINAL PARCEL POST **KRESGE'S KATALOG** FIVE AND TEN CENT STORE

Dependable Toilet Articles, at 5 and 10c

MECHANICS' SOAP PASTE, 10c.

BX329—Mechanic's Soap Paste. Can be used in either warm or cold water. Removes grease and grime from the hands. Invaluable for mechanics, printers, and others. No injurious substances. Weight, 12 ounces. Price.... **10C**

REFINED PETROLEUM JELLY, 10c

BX330 — Refined Petroleum Jelly. A valuable remedy for wounds, burns, skin diseases, etc. Guaranteed under the Pure Food and Drugs Act. Put up in a large glass jar with a metal cover top. Weight of jar, 27 ounces. Price, per jar. **10C**

BLUE SEAL VASELINE, 10c.

BX331 — Blue Seal Vaseline. One of the best quality vaselines on the market. An excellent remedy for burns, scalds, sunburn, colds, sore throat, etc. Guaranteed under the Pure Food and Drugs Act. Packed in large glass jar. Weight, 9 ounces. Price **10C**

BLUE SEAL WHITE VASELINE, 10c.

BX332 — Blue Seal White Vaseline. Packed in a medium size glass jar with metal top. Weight, per jar, 5 ounces. Price...... **10C**

BV333 — Same as above, except yellow in color. Wt., 5 ounces. Price...... **5C**

PEROXIDE OF HYDROGEN, 10c.

BX334 — Peroxide of Hydrogen. The well-known antiseptic. Guaranteed full U. S. P. strength. 12-ounce capacity. Weight, 16 ounces. Price.... **10C**

BV334A— Same as above, except 6 ounce capacity. Weight, 9 ounces. Price... **5C**

STERILIZED ABSORBENT COTTON, 10c.

BX335 — Sterilized Absorbent Cotton. Just the thing to have around the house for emergency cases. Large box. An exceptional value. Weight, 5 ounces. Price **10C**

LARGE SIZE SPONGE, 10c.

BX336 — Large Size Sponge. Large No. 1 yellow sponge, suitable for bathroom and other purposes. Solid piece. Weight, each, 1 ounce. Price, each...................... **10C**

FLORIDA YELLOW SPONGES, 5c.

BV337 — Florida Yellow Sponges. All good quality No. 1 sponges. Suitable size for bathroom and other purposes. Solid round trimmed sponge. Fine texture. Weight, 1 ounce. Price.... **5C**

CUP SPONGES, EACH, 10c.

BX338 — Cup Sponges. First quality silk eye or cup sponges. Just the right size for sponge cup. Fine close texture. Weight, 1 ounce. Price, each....................... **10C**

RED RUBBER SPONGE, 10c.

BX339 — Red Rubber Sponge. The celebrated Wearever red rubber sponge. One of the best quality rubber sponges on the market. A very special value. Weight, each, 1 ounce. Price, each... **10C**

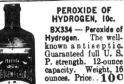

RUBBER COMPLEXION BRUSH, 10c.

BX340 — Rubber Complexion Brush. Made of first quality rubber. Has glove fastener snap on back. Fits the hand. Usual price, 25 cents. Weight, 2 ounces. Our price.......... **10C**

BENT POINT MANICURE SCISSORS, 10c.

BX347—Bent Point Manicure Scissors. Made of first quality steel, highly nickel plated. 4 inches long. Weight, 1 ounce. Price...................... **10C**

EXTRA HEAVY NAIL SCISSORS, 10c.

BX348—Extra Heavy Nail Scissors. Made of high grade steel, finely nickel plated. 3½ inches long. Weight, 1 ounce. Price....................... **10C**

TEMPERED STEEL NAIL FILE, 10c.

BX352 — Tempered Steel Nail File. Finest grade tempered steel double cut, 6, 7 and 8 inches. State size. Weight, 1 ounce. Price.......... **10C**

HIGH GRADE NAIL FILE, 10c.

BX353 — High Grade Nail File. Tempered steel, pointed end. High grade double cut. Good value. Wt., 1 ounce. Price..................... **10C**

PATENT NAIL CLIP, 10c.

BX354 — Patent Nail Clip. Made of high grade tempered steel, heavily nickel plated. Weight, 1 ounce. Price............................. **10C**

GOOD QUALITY TWEEZERS, 5c.

BV355 — Good Quality Tweezers. Made of good quality steel, pointed or blunt ends. State kind wanted. Wt., 1 ounce. Price.................. **5C**

EBONY HANDLE CORN KNIFE, 10c.

BX349 — Ebony Handle Corn Knife. Made of high grade steel tempered blade. 4 inches long. Weight, 1 ounce. Price.................... **10C**

EBONY HANDLE NAIL FILE, 10c.

BX350 — Ebony Handle Nail File. Good sharp cutting file, 2¼ inches long. Ebony handle. Weight, 1 ounce. Price............................. **10C**

BONE HANDLE NAIL FILE, 10c.

BX351 — Bone Handle Nail File. Handle made of best quality white bone. Sharp cutting edge. Weight, 1 ounce. Price.................. **10C**

DOUBLE CUT NAIL FILE, 10c.

BX351I—Double Cut Nail File. Good quality steel. Each file in leatherette case. Weight, 1 ounce. Price.. **10C**

SANITARY MANICURE OUTFIT, 10c.

BX356 — Sanitary Manicure Outfit. Five instruments mounted on card, as follows: one nail file, six emery boards, one orange stick, one pair of tweezers, one combination blackhead extractor and earspoon. Weight, 1 ounce. Price.................. **10C**

EMERY NAIL BOARDS, 5c.

BB357 — Emery Nail Boards. 12 to a package. Double faced; one side smooth, the other side coarse. Weight, 1 ounce. 2 packages............ **5C**

PEARL NAIL CLEANER, 10c

BX358 — Pearl Nail Cleaner. A useful article for the toilet table. Weight, 1 ounce. Price, each **10C**

ORANGE WOOD STICKS, 6 FOR 5c.

B359 — Orangewood Sticks. For care of the nails. Straight and hoof style. 5 inches long. Weight 1 ounce. 6 for **5C**

Every page of this Katalog is full of wonderful bargains. Nothing over 10c.

CHAMOIS NAIL BUFFER, 10c.

BX360 — Chamois Nail Buffer. Padded chamois with fine ebony finish handle, bound with silk braid. 4 inches long. Weight, 1 ounce. Price....................... **10C**

NAIL SCRUB BRUSHES, 10c.

BX341 — Nail Scrub Brushes. Japanese brushes made in various shapes and sizes, with solid and assorted color bristles. Finished hardwood handle. Weight, 2 ounces. Price........................ **10C**

VENTILATED NAIL BRUSH, 10c.

BX342 — Ventilated Nail Brush. Made of best quality all white bristles with open or ventilated back. Back made of best hardwood. Weight, 2 ounces. Price................ **10C**

BONE HANDLED NAIL BRUSH, 10c.

BX344 — Bone Handled Nail Brush. Made with five rows of best quality white bristles. Good white bone handle. Bristles set solidly. Weight, 1 ounce. Price........................ **10C**

BONE HANDLED NAIL BRUSH, 10c.

BX343 — Bone Handled Nail Brush. best quality white bristles, four rows in center, one row on each side. 5½ inches long. Weight, 1 ounce. Price........................ **10C**

WOOD HANDLED NAIL BRUSH, 10c.

BX346 — Wood Handled Nail Brush. Made of best quality black and white bristles. One row of bristles on each side. Varnished back. Weight, 1 ounce. Price................ **10C**

INFANTS' HAIR BRUSH, 10c.

BX345 — Infants' Hair Brush. Made with extra long real soft bristles. Handle extra quality white bone. Length 5 inches. Weight, 1 ounce. Price........................ **10C**

WIRE HAIR BRUSH, 10c.

HX1500 — Wire Hair Brush. Best quality wire securely set in rubber. Ebony finish back. Weight, 3 ounces. Price........................ **10C**

HX15001 — Same as above, but natural finish. Weight, 3 ounces. Price........................ **10C**

Extra Quality Brushes and Combs, 5 and 10c

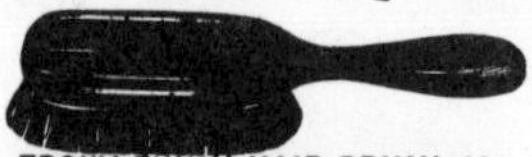

EBONY FINISH HAIR BRUSH, 10c.
HX1501 — Ebony Finish Hair Brush. Made of good quality black bristles, set in cement. Concave back, ebony finish. Medium size. Weight, 4 ounces. Price **10c**

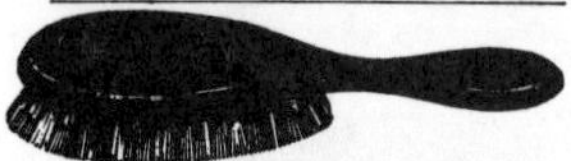

LARGE OVAL HAIR BRUSH, 10c.
HX1502 — Large Oval Hair Brush. Black fibre center, white bristle edge. Ebony finish back and handle. Oval shape. Large size. Weight, 4 ounces. Price........................ **10c**

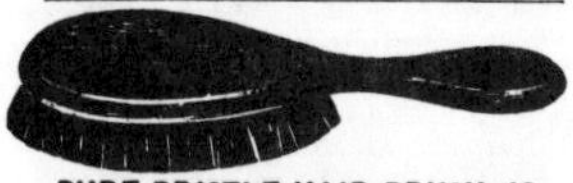

PURE BRISTLE HAIR BRUSH, 10c.
HX1503 — Pure Bristle Hair Brush. Large oval shape, best quality black bristles set in cement. Natural finish wood back. Weight, 5 ounces. Price........................ **10c**

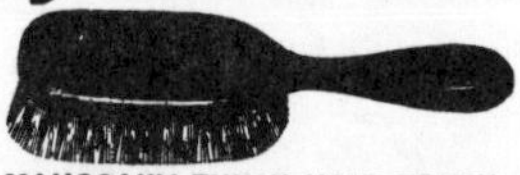

MAHOGANY FINISH HAIR BRUSH, 10c.
HX1504 — Mahogany Finish Hair Brush. Fox back. Pure white bristles set in cement. Medium size. Back highly finished in mahogany. Weight, 4 ounces. Price **10c**

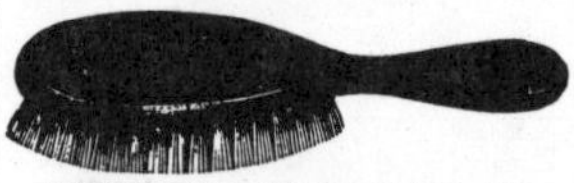

LARGE OVAL HAIR BRUSH, 10c.
HX1505 — Large Oval Hair Brush. Made with best quality all white bristles, set in cement. Large oval back, highly finished in mahogany. Weight, 4 ounces. Price **10c**

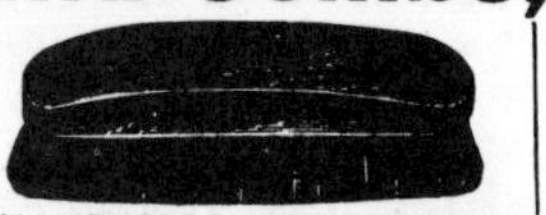

ALL BRISTLE CLOTH BRUSH, 10c.
HX1506 — All Bristle Cloth Brush. Made of good quality black bristles, set in cement. Extra heavy back finely finished in mahogany. Weight, 5 ounces. Price **10c**

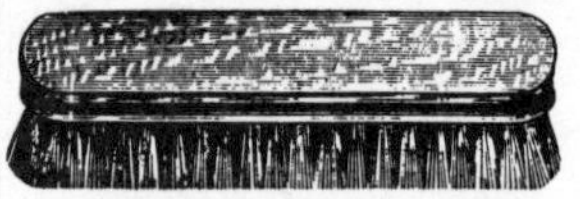

LARGE CLOTH BRUSH, 10c.
HX1507 — Large Cloth Brush. Made of good black fibre center, gray bristle edge. Back finished in yellow, highly polished. Grooved edges. Weight, 5 ounces. Price...... **10c**

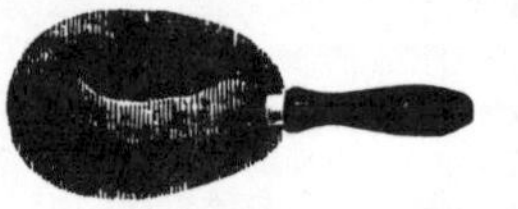

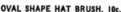

OVAL SHAPE HAT BRUSH, 10c.
HX1509 — Oval Shape Hat Brush. Made of best quality fibre, wire drawn. Cloth or hat brush. Mahogany finish handle. Weight, 3 ounces. Price **10c**

Special Bargains in Whisk Brooms at 10c Each.

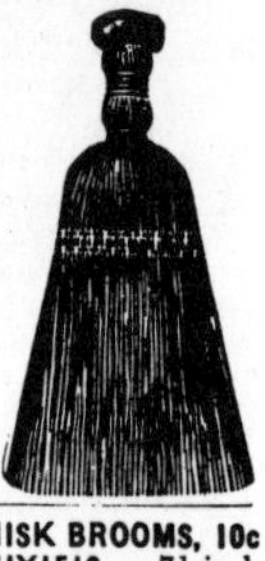

HX1511 — Extra stock Corn sewed. Wire bound handle. Weight, 3 ozs. Price.. **10c**
HX1511A — Same as above, 9 inches. Weight, 7 ounces. Price **10c**

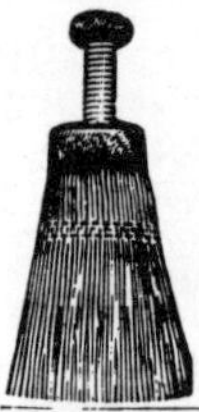

WHISK BROOMS, 10c
HX1510 — 7½-inch Whisk Broom. Best white Tampico, velvet top. Wire bound handle. Weight, 3 ounces. Price... **10c**

Remember, you can have your money back if you are not pleased with the merchandise you order from this Katalog.

Every Comb Guaranteed to be as Represented

HORN FINE COMBS, 10c.

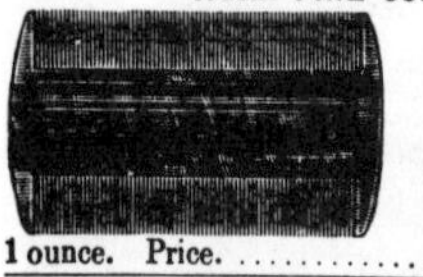

BX400 — Horn Fine Combs. Perfectly cut from best quality genuine horn. 3¼ inches long by 1⅞ inches wide. Needle teeth. An excellent comb. Weight, 1 ounce. Price.......................... **10c**

POCAHONTAS FINE COMB, 5c.
BV401 — Pocahontas Fine Comb. Double cut from high grade hard rubber. 3½ inches long and 1⅞ inches wide. Fine sharp teeth. Weight, 1 oz. Price........................ **5c**

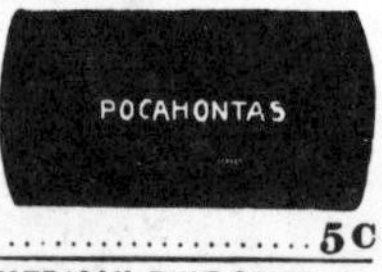

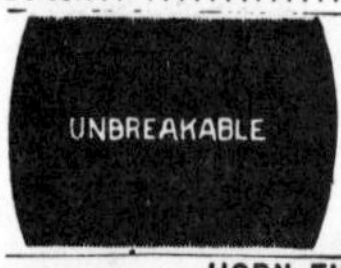

AMERICAN FINE COMB, 5c.
BV402 — American Fine Comb. Size, 2x3 inches. Double cut from extra quality hard rubber. Smooth sharp teeth. Weight, 1 ounce. Price, each... **5c**

HORN FINE COMB, 5c.
BV403 — Horn Fine Comb. 3½ inches long by 1⅞ inches wide. Double cut from fine selected horn. Fine smooth teeth. Weight, 1 ounce. Price.......................... **5c**

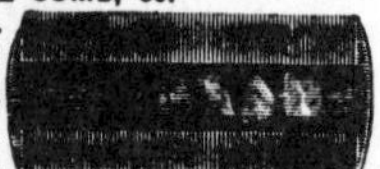

UNBREAKABLE FINE COMB, 10c.

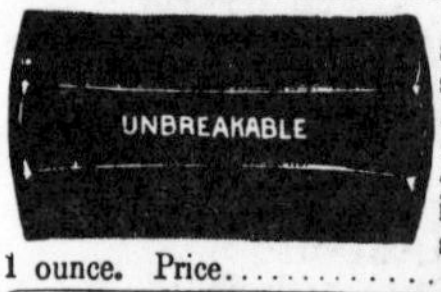

BX404 — Unbreakable Fine Comb. Large size. Concave center. Double cut from selected hard rubber. 4 inches long by 2¼ inches wide. Good sharp teeth. Weight, 1 ounce. Price.......................... **10c**

PERFECT FINE COMB, 10c.
BX405 — Perfect Fine Comb. Large size. Double cut of extra quality fine hard rubber. Unbreakable. Size, 3¾x2¼ inches. Smooth finish, perfect fine comb. Weight, 1 ounce. Price............ **10c**

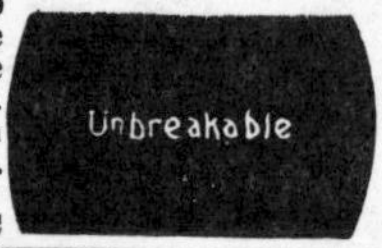

CONCAVE FINE COMB, 10c.

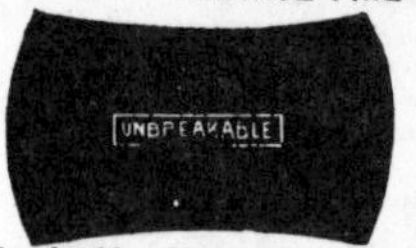

BX406 — Concave Fine Comb. Double cut from extra quality fine hard rubber. Has extra smooth concave edges. Size, 3½ x 2 inches. A perfect finish hard rubber fine comb. Weight, 1 ounce. Price. **10c**

All of the combs listed below are of fine selected stock and perfectly finished. We show wonderful bargains in horn, hard rubber and aluminum combs at 5 and 10c, on Page 67.

IMPORTED FINE COMB, 10c.

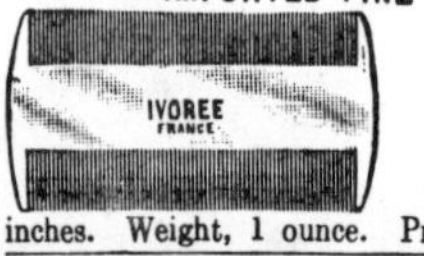

BX407 — Imported Fine Comb. Made of best French ivoree. Double cut with very fine teeth. Imitation ivory. Size, 3½x1¾ inches. Weight, 1 ounce. Price........... **10c**

ALUMINUM FINE COMB, 10c.
BX408 — Aluminum Fine Comb. Double cut from fine quality aluminum. Will last a life time. 3 inches long by 1¾ inches wide. Fine sharp teeth. Weight, 1 ounce. Price.......................... **10c**

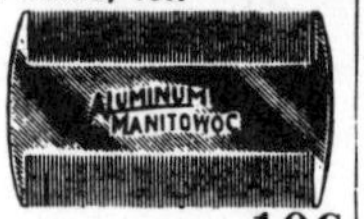

INFANTS' COMBS, EACH, 10c.

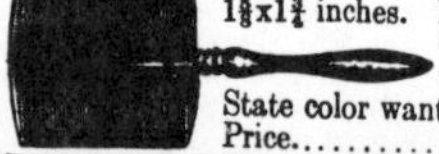

BX409 — Infants' Combs. Size, 1⅝x1¾ inches. Handle 2½ inches long. Come in three colors: white, blue or pink. State color wanted. Weight, 1 ounce. Price.......................... **10c**

FOLDING POCKET COMB, 10c.
BX410 — Folding Pocket Comb. Size, 1x3½ inches folded. 7 inches long when open. One end fine, the other end coarse. Made of best quality fine black rubber. Weight, 1 ounce. Price........... **10c**

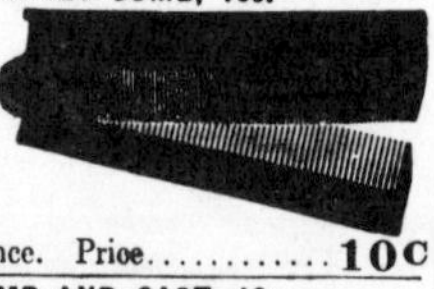

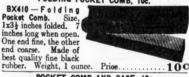

POCKET COMB AND CASE, 10c.

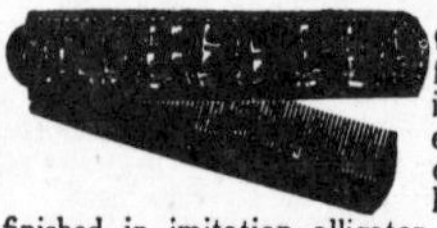

BX411 — Pocket Comb and Case. Comb folds in knife style. 3½ inches long when folded. Comb and case cut from best quality hard rubber. Case is finished in imitation alligator. Weight, 1 ounce. Price.......................... **10c**

ALUMINUM POCKET COMB, 5c.
BV412 — Aluminum Pocket Comb. Made of best quality aluminum. Has coarse and fine teeth. Length, 4¾ inches. Leatherette case. Weight, 1 ounce. Price, each... **5c**

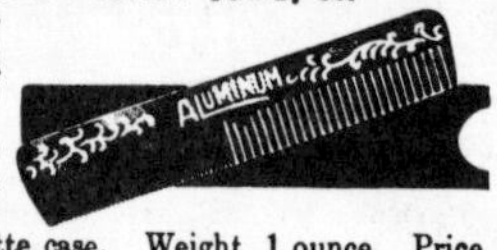

EXTRA QUALITY POCKET COMB, 5c.

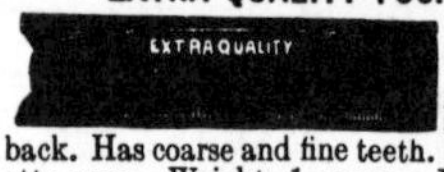

BV413 — Extra Quality Pocket Comb. Made from best quality hard rubber. Oval back. Has coarse and fine teeth. 4 inches long. Leatherette case. Weight, 1 ounce. Price........... **5c**

HORN POCKET COMB, 10c.
BX414 — Horn Pocket Comb. Has coarse and fine teeth. 5 inches long. Leatherette case, metal bound. Weight, 1 ounce. Price.......................... **10c**

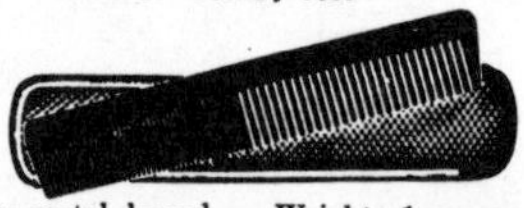

HORN POCKET COMB, 5c.

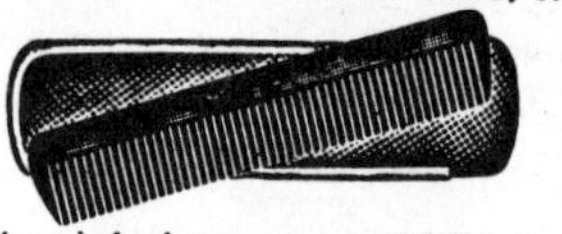

BV415 — Horn Pocket Comb. All coarse teeth. 4½ inches long. Has metal bound leatherette case. Weight, 1 ounce. Price each.......................... **5c**

UNBREAKABLE POCKET COMB, 10c.
BX416 — Unbreakable Pocket Comb. Best quality hard rubber, all coarse teeth. Heavy oval back. 5 inches long. Leatherette case. Weight, 1 ounce. Price.......................... **10c**

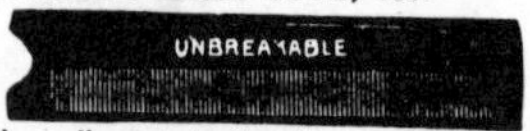

WIDE POCKET COMB, 10c.

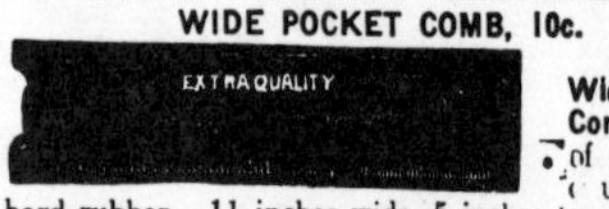

BX417 — Wide Pocket Comb. Made of extra quality hard rubber. 1¼ inches wide, 5 inches long. Coarse and fine teeth. Leatherette case. Weight, 1 ounce. Price.......................... **10c**

HORN DRESSING COMB, 5c.
BV418 — Horn Dressing Comb. Made of best quality select horn. 1¼ inches wide by 4½ inches long. All coarse teeth. Heavy straight back. Weight, 1 ounce. Price.......................... **5c**

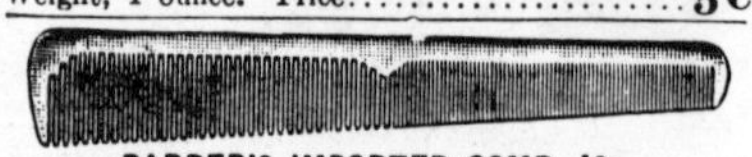

BARBER'S IMPORTED COMB, 10c.
BX419 — Barber's Imported Comb. 6¾ inches long, tapering shape. Has coarse and fine teeth. Cream colored stock. Weight, 1 ounce. Price, each.. **10c**

Exceptional Values in Combs, 5c and 10c

On this page we show a variety of combs so large that we can please every one. Wonderful values in horn, hard rubber or aluminum. The material is of the best, carefully selected, perfectly cut teeth and smoothly finished. Nothing over 10c.

HORN DRESSING COMB, 10c.

BX420—Horn Dressing Comb, Metal Back. Made of selected highly polished horn. Entire back and end teeth reinforced with nickel plated metal casing. 7½ inches long by 1½ inches wide. Has both fine and coarse teeth. Weight, 1 ounce. Price, each....**10C**

HARD RUBBER DRESSING COMB, 10c.

BX421—Hard Rubber Dressing Comb. Made of high grade selected Gutta Percha, highly polished. All coarse teeth, perfectly cut by special machinery. Back and ends reinforced with nickel plated metal casing. Weight, 1 ounce. About 7½ inches long, 1½ inches wide. Price, each....................**10C**

REINFORCED HARD RUBBER COMB, 10c.

BX422—Hard Rubber Dressing Comb. Made of high grade selected Gutta Percha, highly polished. Has both coarse and fine teeth, perfectly cut and shaped by special machinery. Back and ends reinforced with nickel plated casing. About 7½ inches long by 1½ inches wide. Weight, 1 ounce. Price, each....**10C**

ALUMINUM BARBER'S COMB, 10c.

BX423—Aluminum Barber's Comb. Bright finish. Has both coarse and fine teeth. Is tapered toward the fine tooth end, is 7 inches long. A light, durable, well balanced comb for barber's use. Weight, 1 ounce. Price, each. **10C**

ALUMINUM DRESSING COMB, 10c.

BX424—Aluminum Dressing Comb. A strong, highly polished pure aluminum comb. Perfectly cut and shaped teeth, both coarse and fine. Is made with extra heavy back with added metal in center to give strength. 7 inches long by 1½ inches wide. Weight, 1 ounce. Price, each....................**10C**

ALUMINUM DRESSING COMB, 10c.

BX425—Aluminum Dressing Comb. A strong, highly polished pure aluminum comb. Perfectly cut and shaped teeth, both coarse and fine. Is made with extra heavy back with added metal in center to give strength. 7½ inches long by 1½ inches wide. Weight, 1 ounce. Price, each........................**10C**

ALUMINUM DRESSING COMB, 10c.

BX426—Aluminum Dressing Comb. A very fine model, has extra heavy back with stiffening ridge. Perfectly cut and shaped coarse and fine teeth. Is made from highly polished selected aluminum. 7 inches long by 1½ inches wide. Weight, 1 ounce. Price, each...................................**10C**

BARBER'S HORN COMB, 10c.

BX427—Barber's Horn Comb. Carefully cut from hard selected horn. Extra sharp, coarse and fine specially grailed teeth. Tapered shape. Very highly polished. A comb that will give perfect satisfaction and will stand the hardest kind of usage. 7 inches long by 1 inch wide. Weight, 1 ounce. Price, each.......................................**10C**

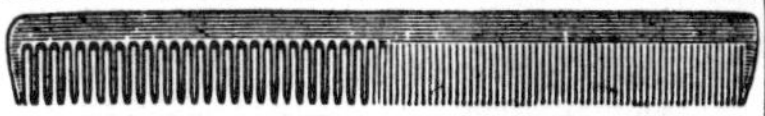

BARBER'S MOTTLED HORN COMB, 10c.

BX428—Barber's Comb. Made of finest selected mottled horn. Straight shape. Has both fine and coarse teeth. Carefully cut and finished. A light excellent comb at a very low price. 7½ inches long by ⅞ inches wide. Weight, 1 ounce. Price, each..**10C**

CELLULOID DRESSING COMB, 10c.

BX429—Celluloid Dressing Comb. This comb, made of the best grade of extra hard imitation ivory is 7¾ inches long by 1½ inches wide. The teeth have been carefully cut and grailed, and while light the comb is very stiff. A great favorite with hair dressers and others. Weight, 1 ounce. Price, each........**10C**

LADY'S HIGHLY FINISHED COMB, 10c.

BX430—Lady's Comb. A genuine selected horn comb, made with long coarse and fine teeth. This comb is very highly finished and will give lasting satisfaction to the purchaser. 7⅝ inches long by 1¾ inches wide. Weight, 1 ounce. Price, each.................**10C**

LADY'S SELECTED HORN COMB, 10c.

BX431—Lady's Comb. A genuine selected horn comb, made with long, coarse and fine teeth. This comb is very highly finished and will give lasting satisfaction to the purchaser. Length, about 8 inches by 1¾ inches wide. Weight, 1 ounce. Price, each.**10C**

HAND MADE DRESSING COMB, 10c.

BX432—Dressing Comb. Hand made. Particular care has been taken in selecting the horn from which these excellent combs have been cut by hand. They are very highly finished, come with very long all coarse teeth. Measure 7½ inches long by 1¾ inches wide. Weight, 1 ounce. Price, each........**10C**

HARD RUBBER DRESSING COMB, 5c.

BV433—Hard Rubber Dressing Comb. Made of very good quality hard rubber, has medium heavy oval back, medium fine and coarse teeth. 7 inches long by 1½ inches wide. Weight, 1 ounce. Price, each..**5C**

BARBER'S HARD RUBBER COMB, 10c.

BX434—Barber's Hard Rubber Comb. Made of the famous Goodyear Gutta Percha, with very strong back. Has both coarse and fine teeth, is practically unbreakable. 7 inches long by ⅞-inch wide. Weight, 1 ounce. Price, each.......................**10C**

EXTRA HEAVY DRESSING COMB, 10c.

BX435—Extra Heavy Dressing Comb. Our Dreadnought model. Made of fine quality hard rubber, very strong back, long, perfectly cut teeth, both coarse and fine, measures 8x1½ inches. Weight, 1 ounce. Price, each....................................**10C**

HARD RUBBER DRESSING COMB, 10c.

BX436—Extra Heavy Dressing Comb. Our Dreadnought model. Made of fine quality hard rubber, very strong back, long, perfectly cut teeth, all coarse, measures 8x1½ inches. Weight, 1 ounce. Price, each.....................................**10C**

UNBREAKABLE DRESSING COMB, 10c.

BX437—Unbreakable Dressing Comb. Made of extremely hard rubber, has extra heavy oval back, is very highly polished, has perfectly cut teeth. A most durable comb. 8 inches long by 1½ inches wide. Weight, 1 ounce. Price, each.................**10C**

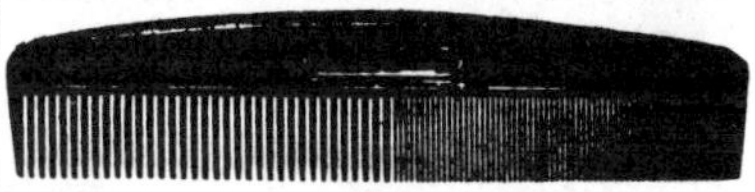

LARGE SIZE DRESSING COMB, 10c.

BX438—Large Size Dressing Comb. Unbreakable. Has heavy arch double concave back, carefully cut and shaped coarse and fine teeth, highly polished. A very popular model, 8 inches long by 1¾ inches wide. Weight 1 ounce. Price, each...................**10C**

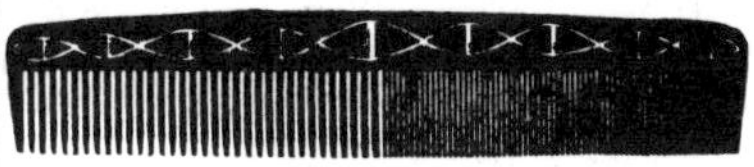

FANCY DRESSING COMB, 10c.

BX439—Fancy Dressing Comb. A very well made comb. Comes in hard black rubber only, is very highly polished, long, coarse and fine teeth. Fancy design, heavy oval back, as illustrated. 8 inches long by 1¾ inches wide. Weight, 1 ounce. Price, each....**10C**

LADY'S EXTRA LARGE COMB, 10c.

BX440—Lady's Extra Large Comb. Made from first quality hard rubber and entire comb is very highly polished. Extra high heavy oval back, finished in fancy design as illustrated. Made with coarse and fine teeth. 8 inches long by 1¾ inches wide. Weight, 1 ounce. Price, each **10C**

We guarantee to please you or return your money

We guarantee the merchandise illustrated and described in this Katalog to be as represented in every instance, and should you purchase anything from us that fails to please you we will exchange it for other goods or refund your money.

THE ORIGINAL PARCEL POST KRESGE'S KATALOG **FIVE AND TEN CENT STORE**

Extra Quality Stylish Back Combs, 10c

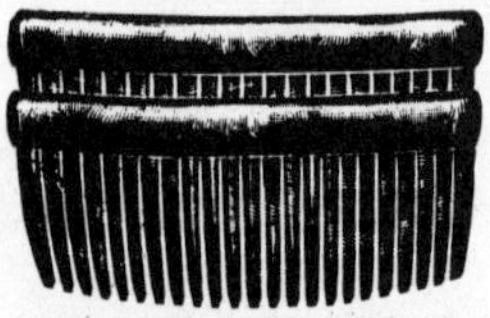

SIDE COMBS, PER PAIR, 10c
BX113—Side Combs. Size 2x4 inches. Highly polished. Heavy patch back. Oval top. Made from extra quality celluloid. Weight 1 ounce. Price per pair...... **10c**

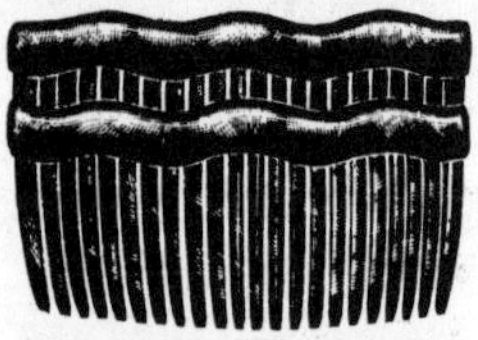

SIDE COMBS, PER PAIR, 10c.
BX114—Side Combs. Size, 2x4 inches. Brilliant polish. Heavy patch back. Waved top. Made from selected quality celluloid. Weight, ½ ounce. Price, per pair........ **10c**

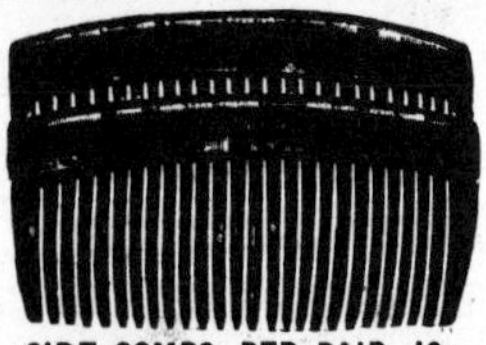

SIDE COMBS, PER PAIR, 10c.
BX115—Side Combs. Size, 2x4¾ inches. Finely polished. Heavy oval top. Made from finest celluloid. Weight, 1 ounce. Price, per pair **10c**

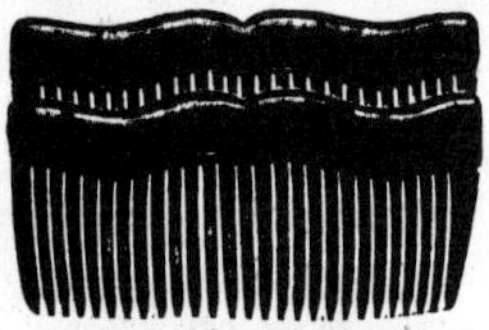

LARGE SIDE COMBS, 10c.
BX116—Large Side Combs. Size, 2x4¾ inches. Highly finished. Heavy waved top. Beveled teeth. Made from high grade celluloid. Weight, 1 ounce. Price, per pair **10c**

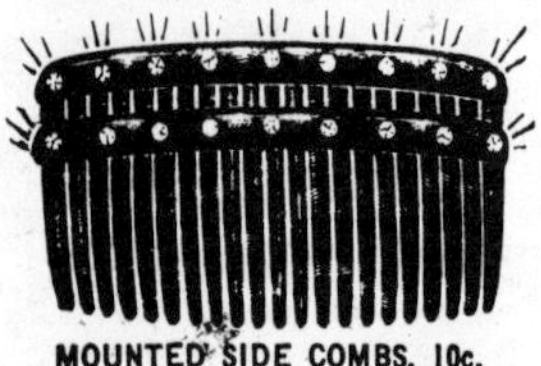

MOUNTED SIDE COMBS, 10c.
BX117—Mounted Side Combs. Size, 1⅞x4¼ inches. The narrow oval back of each comb is set with nine selected brilliants. Weight, ½ ounce. Price, per pair.......................... **10c**

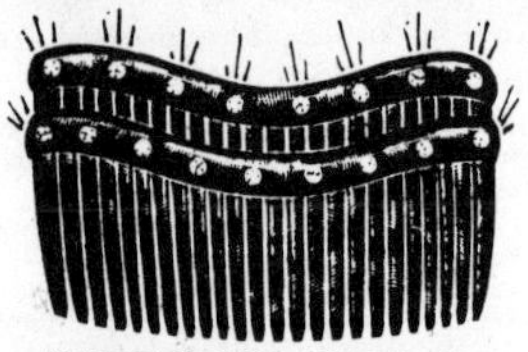

MOUNTED SIDE COMBS, 10c.
BX118—Mounted Side Combs. Size, 1⅞x4¼ inches. Extra quality celluloid. Saddle curved oval top, set with nine brilliants. Weight, ½ ounce. Price, per pair...................... **10c**

FANCY SIDE COMBS, 10c.
BX119—Fancy Side Combs. Size, 1¾x3¾ inches. Heavily embossed and cut out top. Highly polished. Beveled teeth. Made from heavy weight double celluloid. Weight, ½ ounce. Price, per pair...................... **10c**

SMALL SIZE SIDE COMBS, 10c.
BX120—Small Side Combs. Size, 1¾x3¾ inches. Made from fine highly polished celluloid. Reinforced heavy oval top. Fine teeth. Weight, ½ ounce. Price, per pair........ **10c**

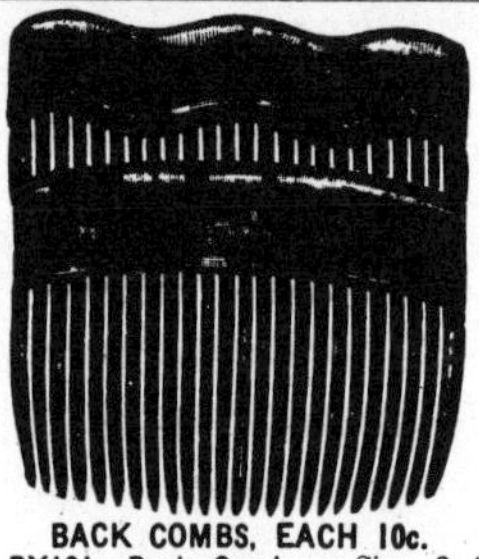

BACK COMBS, EACH 10c.
BX121—Back Comb. Size, 3x4½ inches. Very heavy oval top. Highly polished. Made from fine celluloid. Weight, 1 ounce. Price, each.. **10c**
BX122—Back Comb. Same as above except has waved top. Weight 1 ounce. Price, each **10c**

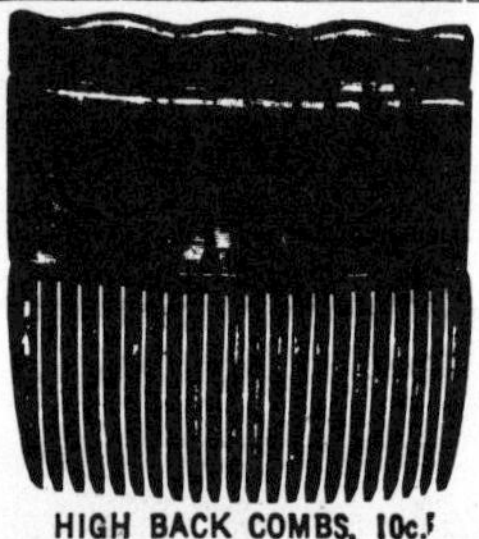

HIGH BACK COMBS, 10c.
BX123—High Back Comb. Size, 3¾x4½ inches. The teeth are widely separated and round finish. The broad plain finished top is beautifully polished. Weight, 1 ounce. Price, ea. **10c**
BX124—High Back Comb. Same as above, except has waved top. Weight, 1 ounce. Price, each.......... **10c**

SINGLE SIDE COMBS, 10c.
BX125—Single Side Comb. Size, 2½x5 inches. Finely constructed from heavy weight celluloid. Teeth separated, tapered and beveled. Strong oval top. Weight, 1 ounce. Price, each............................ **10c**
BX126—Single Side Comb. Same as above, except has waved top. Weight, 1 ounce. Price, each **10c**

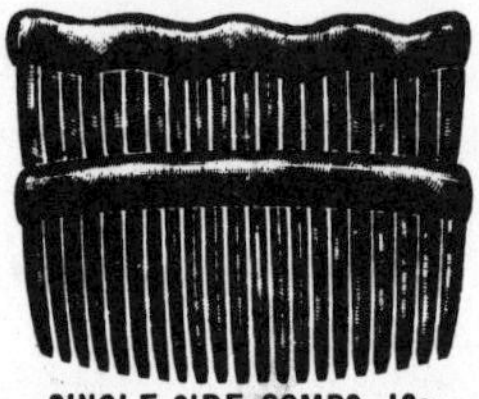

SINGLE SIDE COMBS, 10c.
BX127—Single Side Comb. Medium size, measures 2x4½ inches. Bright finish. Reinforced oval top. Made from extra quality celluloid. Weight, ½ ounce. Price, each.......... **10c**
BX128—Single Side Comb. Same as above, except waved top. Weight, ½ ounce. Price, each.......... **10c**

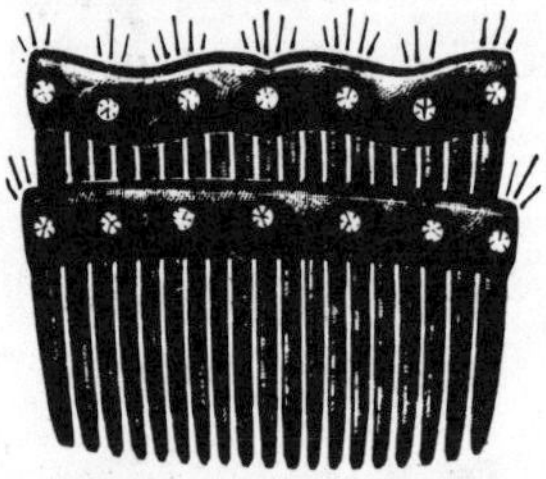

MOUNTED BACK COMBS, 10c.
BX129—Mounted Back Comb. Size, 2½x4½ inches. Oval top, each comb is set with seven first quality brilliants. Weight, ½ ounce. Price, each.. **10c**
BX130—Mounted Back Comb. Same as above, except waved top. Weight, ½ ounce. Price, each......... **10c**

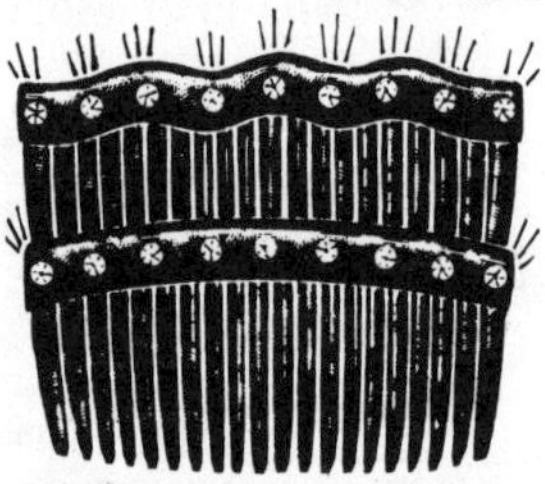

MOUNTED SINGLE SIDE COMBS, 10c.
BX131—Mounted Single Side Comb. Size, 2x4½ inches. The reinforced highly polished oval top is set with nine selected brilliants. Weight, ½ ounce. Price, each.................. **10c**
BX132—Mounted Single Side Comb. Same as above, except waved top. Weight, ½ ounce. Price, each.. **10c**

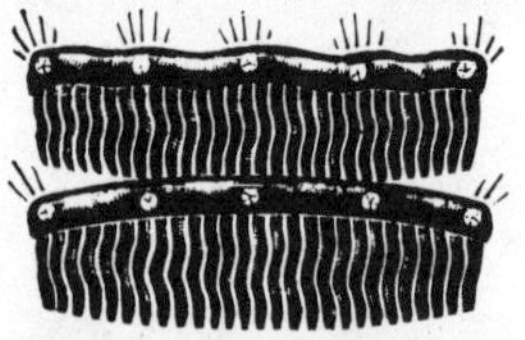

MOUNTED FORWARD COMB, 10c.
BX133—Mounted Forward Comb. Size, 1½x5 inches. Made from heavy highly polished celluloid. Has waved teeth to prevent comb from falling out. Mounted with five selected brilliants. Weight, ½ ounce. Price, each.. **10c**
BX134—Mounted Forward Comb. Same as above, except has waved top. Weight, ½ ounce. Price, each.. **10c**

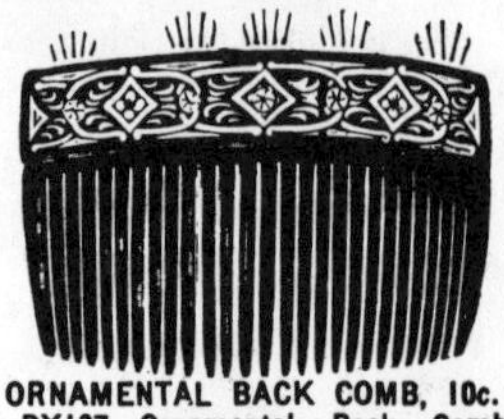

ORNAMENTAL BACK COMB, 10c.
BX137—Ornamental Back Comb. Size, 3x4¾ inches. Made of extra quality celluloid with beautiful inlaid design in gold, set with brilliants. Weight, ½ ounce. Price, each.. **10c**

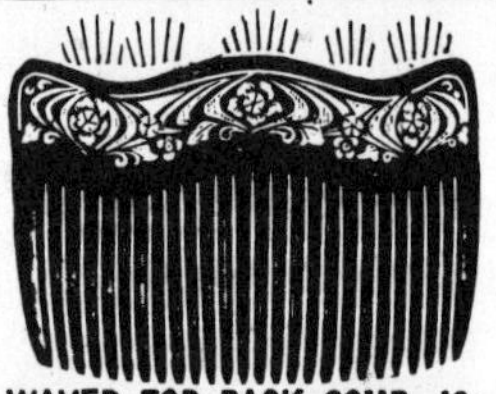

WAVED TOP BACK COMB, 10c.
BX138—Waved Top Back Comb. Size, 3x4½ inches. Beautiful gold inlaid design, mounted with five first quality brilliants. Weight, ½ ounce. Price, each **10c**

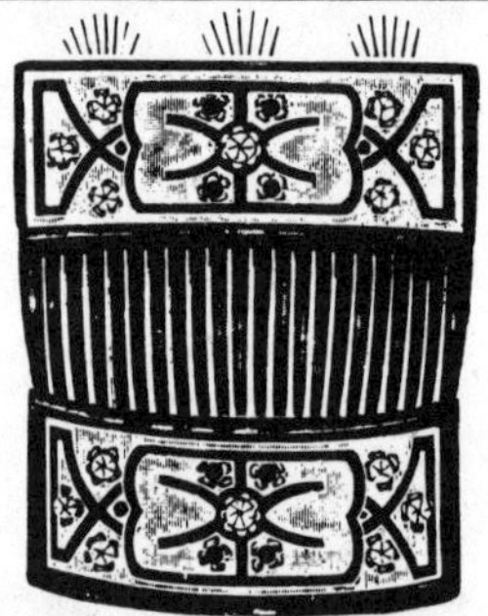

HIGH TOP BACK COMB, 10c.
BX139—High Top Back Comb. Size, 3½x5 inches. A large comb with rich Roman gold inlaid mounted with brilliants. Wt., 1 oz. Price, each.. **10c**
BX140—Barrette to Match Back Comb BX139. Size, 1¾x4¾ inches. Weight, ½ ounce. Price, each.. **10c**

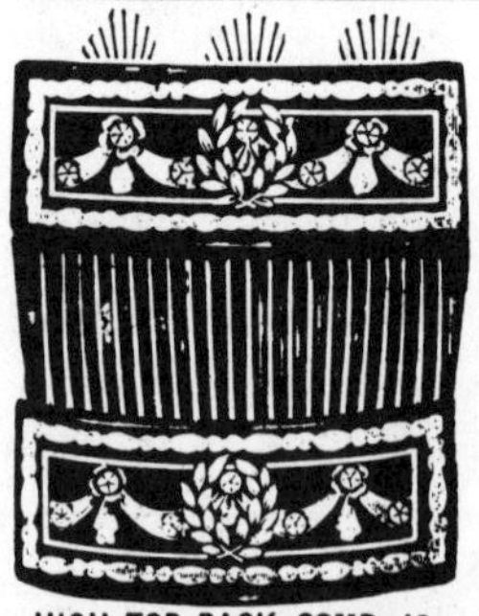

HIGH TOP BACK COMB, 10c.
BX141—High Top Back Comb. Grecian design in gold inlaid mounted with seven handsome brilliants. Weight 1 ounce. Price, each.......... **10c**
BX142—Barrette. To match back comb BX141. Size, 3½x4¾ inches. Weight, 1 ounce. Price, each.. **10c**

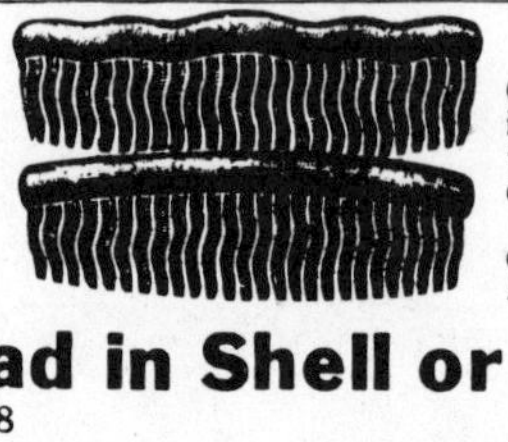

CELLULOID FRONT COMB, 10c.
BX135—Front Comb. Size, 1½x5 inches. Comb is made of heavy celluloid with reinforced top. Has waved teeth to prevent falling out. Weight ½ ounce. Price, each.............................. **10c**
BX136—Front Comb. Same as above, except waved top. Weight, ½ ounce. Price, each........................ **10c**

The Above Combs Can be Had in Shell or Amber Color

High Grade Combs and Barrettes at 10c

MEDIUM SIZE SIDE COMBS, 10c.

BX143—Side Combs. Medium size double side combs, measuring 1⅝x4 inches. Shown in pearl gray. Weight, ½ ounce. Price, per pair.......**10C**

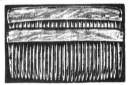

OVAL SIDE COMBS, 10c.

BX144—Side Combs. Medium size, measuring 1¾x4 inches. Oval top. Shown in pearl gray. Weight, ½ ounce. Price, per pair.......**10C**

SINGLE SIDE COMB, 10c.

BX145—Single Side Comb. Heavy quality, size 2x2¼ inches. Oval top. Shown in pearl gray only. Weight, ½ ounce. Price, each...........**10C**
BX146—Single Side Comb. Same as above, except waved top. Weight, ½ ounce. Price, each...........**10C**

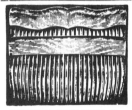

CELLULOID BACK COMB, 10c.

BX147—Back Comb. Size, 2½x4¾ inches. Made of fine quality pearl gray, celluloid, oval top design. Weight, ½ ounce.
Price, each..............**10C**
BX148—Back Comb. Same as above, except waved top. Weight, ½ ounce. Price, each **10C**

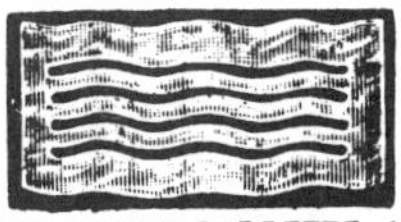

FANCY DESIGN BARRETTE, 10c.

BX149—Barrette. Size, 1⅜x3¾ inches. Five strand waved cut design, made from finest polished celluloid. Pearl gray only. Weight, ½ ounce. Price, each................**10C**

STRAND DESIGN BARRETTE, 10c.

BX150—Barrette. Size, 1⅜x3¾ inches. Five strand design. Made from high grade pearl gray celluloid. Weight, ½ ounce. Price, each..**10C**

FANCY DESIGN BARRETTE, 10c.

BX151—Barrette. Size, 1¾x4½ inches. Four strand heavy surf design in pearl gray. Weight, ½ ounce. Price, each....................**10C**

FANCY DESIGN BARRETTE, 10c.

BX152—Fancy Barrette. Size, 2x5¼ inches. Strand center, embossed and cut out lace border. Nicely finished. Weight, ½ ounce. Price, each..**10C**

FANCY EMBOSSED BARRETTE, 10c.

BX153—Fancy Barrette. Size, 2x4¾ inches. Artistically embossed and cut out design. Weight ½ ounce. Price, each....................**10C**

FANCY LARGE BARRETTE, 10c.

BX154—Large Barrette. Size, 2x4¾ inches. Six strand waved design. Highly finished. Weight, ½ ounce. Price, each...............**10C**

LARGE BARRETTE, EACH, 10c.

BX155—Large Barrette. Size, 1¾x5 inches. Plain design. Highly polished. Weight, 1 ounce. Price, each..**10C**

FANCY BARRETTE, EACH, 10c.

BX156—Fancy Barrette. Size, 2x4¼ inches. Graceful conventional design. Bright finish. Weight, ½ ounce. Price, each....................**10C**

FANCY LARGE BARRETTE, 10c.

BX157—Fancy Barrette. Large size. 2x4¾ inches. Embossed and cut out design. Made of finest celluloid. Very attractive shape. Weight, ½ ounce. Price, each.................**10C**

All of the above barrettes, unless otherwise stated, can be had in shell or amber. Amber is for blondes and shell for brunettes. Do not fail to see our bargains in fancy hair pins, combs, etc. on the following pages.

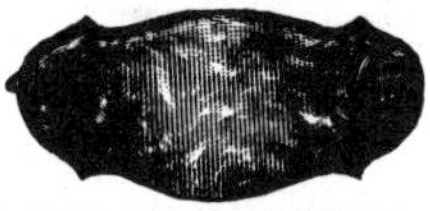

BEVELED SHAPE BARRETTE, 10c.

BX158—Barrette. Size, 1⅜x4½ inches. Conventional beveled shape. Made from fine extra heavy celluloid. Weight, ½ ounce. Price, each...**10C**

LARGE BARRETTE, EACH 10c.

BX159—Large Barrette. Size, 2x4⅞ inches. Fancy four strand effect with embossed center. Weight, ½ ounce. Price, each. **10C**

LARGE BARRETTE, EACH 10c.

BX160—Large Barrette. Size, 2x5 inches. Broad curved three strand effect in extra heavy celluloid, highly polished. Weight, 1 ounce. Price, each....................**10C**

MEDIUM SIZE BARRETTE, 10c.

BX161—Barrette. Medium size. Measures 1⅜x4½ inches. Curved cross strand effect. Weight, ½ ounce. Price, each....................**10C**

MEDIUM SIZE BARRETTE, 10c.

BX162—Fine Barrette. Medium size measures 1¾x4 inches. Five waved strand effect, set with six brilliants. Weight, ½ ounce. Price, each..**10C**

STRAND DESIGN BARRETTE, 10c.

BX163—Barrette. Medium size, measures 1¾x4 inches. Five strand design, wave effect. Very highly polished. Weight, ½ ounce. Price, each....................**10C**

OVAL BARRETTE, EACH, 10c.

BX164—Oval Barrette. Medium size, measures 1¾x4½ inches. Four strand design. Made of first quality celluloid. Weight, ½ ounce. Price, each.....................**10C**

SELECT JEWELED BARRETTE, 10c.

BX165—Mounted Barrette. Size: 1¾x4 inches. Five strand design, wave effect. Mounted with six selected brilliants. Weight, ½ ounce. Price, each.....................**10C**

MEDIUM SIZE BARRETTE, 10c.

BX166—Fancy Barrette. Medium size, measures 1¼x3¾ inches. Strand design, as shown. Open center. Highly polished. Weight, ½ ounce. Price, each. **10C**

FANCY DESIGN BARRETTE, 10c.

BX167—Fancy Barrette. Medium size, measures 1½x4 inches. Wave line cut out design. Made of best celluloid. Weight, ½ ounce. Price, eace....................**10C**

LIGHT WEIGHT BARRETTE, 10c.

BX168—Light Weight Barrette. Size, 1⅞x4¾ inches. Oval shape, strand effect. Open center. Very light and graceful. Weight, ½ ounce. Price, each....................**10C**

FANCY DESIGN BARRETTE, 10c.

BX169—Fancy Barrette. Size, 1⅜x4½ inches. Border strand design with three link center. Highly finished in extra quality celluloid. Weight, ½ ounce. Price, each...........**10C**

GOLD INLAID BARRETTE, 10c.

BX170—Fancy Barrette. Size, 1¼x4¾ inches. Strand design with gold inlaid, mounted with four selected brilliants. Very beautiful design. Weight, ½ ounce. Price, each..**10C**

SELECT JEWELED BARRETTE, 10c.

BX171—Mounted Barrette. Size, 1¾x2¼ inches. Broad beveled ring design, set with four first quality brilliants. Weight, ½ ounce. Price, each....................**10C**

Fine Quality Barrettes and Hair Pins, 10c

FANCY EMBOSSED BARRETTE, 10c.
BX172—Fancy Barrette. Size, 1½x4 inches. Elaborate conventional design, embossed and open work, highly polished. Extra quality celluloid. Weight, ½ ounce. Price, each.... **10c**

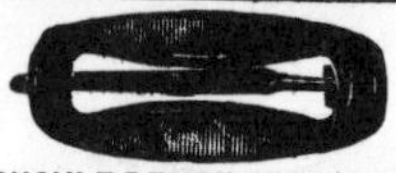

BUCKLE DESIGN RABRETTE, 10c.
BX173 — Barrette. Size, 1½x3¾ inches. Buckle design. Open center. Extra heavy celluloid. Highly polished. Weight, ½ ounce. Price, each.... **10c**

FANCY EMBOSSED BARRETTE, 10c.
BX174 — Barrette. Size 1½x4 inches. Beautiful strand and flower design, richly embossed and cut out. Weight, ½ ounce. Price, each **10c**

SMALL SIZE BARRETTE, 10c.
BX175—Barrette. Small size, measures 1⅛x3¼ inches. Five strand design. Made from highly polished celluloid. Weight, ½ ounce. Price, each..... **10c**

EXTRA FANCY BARRETTE, 10c.
BX176 — Fancy Barrette. Size, 1⅝x3¾ inches. Ornate strand design. Extra quality celluloid. Very fashionable. Weight, ½ ounce. Price, each.................. **10c**

OPEN WORK BARRETTE, 10c.
BX177 — Fancy Barrette. Size, 1½x3¾ inches. Open work and embossed four strand and fleur de lis design. Weight, ½ ounce. Price, each..... **10c**

FANCY OVAL BARRETTE, 10c
BX178 — Oval Barrette. Size, 1⅝x4 inches. Four waved strand design. Made from first quality celluloid. Popular style. Weight ½ ounce. Price, each... **10c**

SMALL SIZE BARRETTE, 10c.
BX179 — Small Barrette. Size 1⅝x2⅞ inches. Heavy broad strand design. Highly polished. Weight, ½ ounce. Price, each...................... **10c**

FANCY EMBOSSED BARRETTE, 10c.
BX180 — Fancy Barrette. Size, 1½x4 inches. Elaborate conventional design, cut out and embossed. Made from high quality celluloid. Weight, ½ ounce. Price, each..... **10c**

SMALL SIZE BARRETTE, 10c.
BX181 — Small Barrette. Size, 1⅛x3 inches. Five strand design with rounded ends. A well made article. Weight, ½ ounce. Price, each..... **10c**

SMALL OVAL BARRETTE, 10c.
BX182 — Small Barrette. Size, 1x3¼ inches. Oval open center design. Made from extra heavy celluloid. Weight, ½ ounce. Price, each..... **10c**

FANCY SMALL BARRETTE, 10c.
BX183 — Small Barrette. Size, 1x4 inches. Four strand design. Made from first quality high finished celluloid. Weight, ½ ounce. Price, each.... **10c**

SMALL OVAL BARRETTE, 10c.
BX184 — Fancy Barrette. Small size, measures 1⅜x2⅞ inches. Oval double link design. Highly polished. Weight, ½ ounce. Price, each..... **10c**

SMALL FANCY BARRETTE 10c.
BX185 — Small Fancy Barrette. Size, 1¼x2½ inches. Four linked ring design, embossed and cut out. Weight, ½ ounce. Price, each. **10c**

EMBOSSED OVAL BARRETTE, 10c.
BX186 — Oval Barrette. Small size, measures 1¼x3⅜ inches. Three link center. Embossed and cut out design. Weight, ½ ounce. Price, each..... **10c**

PLAIN OVAL BARRETTE, 10c.
BX187 — Plain Barrette. Size, 2¼x2⅞ inches. Broad band oval ring design in highly polished first quality celluloid. Weight, ½ ounce. Price, each..... **10c**

SMALL OVAL BARRETTE, 10c.
BX188 — Small Oval Barrette. Size, 1¾x2½ inches. Heavy strand ring design. Finely finished, high quality celluloid. Weight, ½ ounce. Price, each.................. **10c**

FANCY SMALL BARRETTE, 10c.
BX189 — Fancy Small Barrette. Size, ⅞x2¼ inches. Four oval linked ring design. Well made from highly polished celluloid. Weight, ½ ounce. Price, each.................. **10c**

EVERTIDY COMB, 10c.
BX190 — Evertidy Comb. Length, 4 inches. Well made from high grade polished celluloid. Weight, ½ ounce. Price, each.................. **10c**

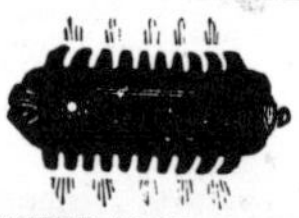

MOUNTED HAIR BINDERS, 10c.
BX191 — Mounted Hair Binders. (With elastic). Made of best celluloid, set with eight first quality brilliants. Weight, ½ ounce. Price, each... **10c**

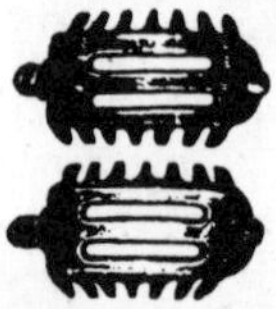

DANDY HAIR BINDERS, 2 FOR 5c.
BB192 — Dandy Hair Binder. (With elastic.) Made of best quality celluloid. Come in shell or amber. Small size. Very useful for fastening braid. State color wanted. Weight, ½ ounce. Price, 2 for **5c**

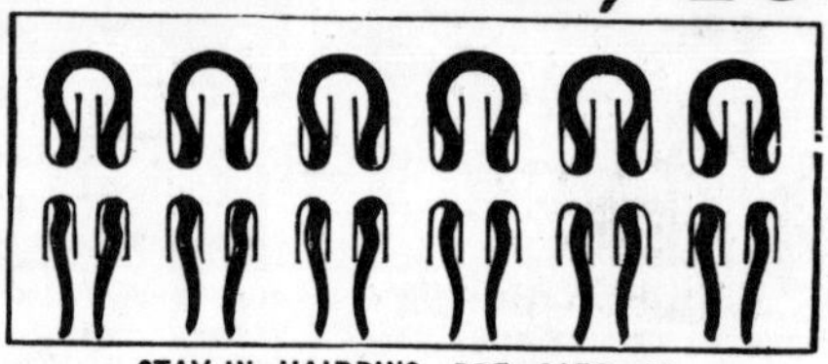

STAY-IN HAIRPINS, PER CARD, 10c.
BX193 — Stay-in Hairpins. Best celluloid. Thoroughly polished with tapered points. Six on a card. Weight, ½ ounce. Price, per card.............................. **10c**

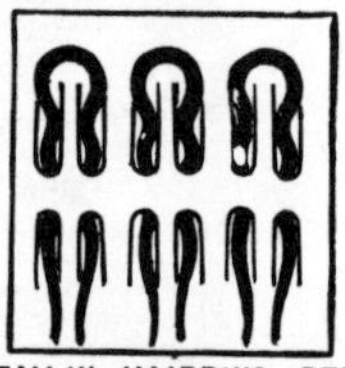

STAY-IN HAIRPINS, PER CARD, 10c.
BX194 — Stay-In Hairpins. Pearl gray color. Made from best quality celluloid. Very high grade hairpin at the price. Three on a card. Weight, ½ ounce. Price, per card.. **10c**

STAY-IN HAIRPINS, PER CARD, 10c.
BX195 — Stay-In Hairpins. Extra strong. Made from heavy celluloid. 3½ inches long. Three on a card. Weight, ½ ounce. Price, per card......... **10c**

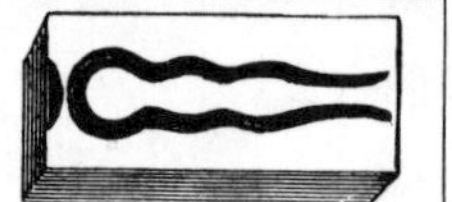

"OUR LEADER" HAIRPINS, 10c.
BX196 — "Our Leader" Hairpins. 3 inches long. Made of first quality celluloid. Stay-in design. Ten pins in box. Weight 1 ounce. Price, per box.. **10c**

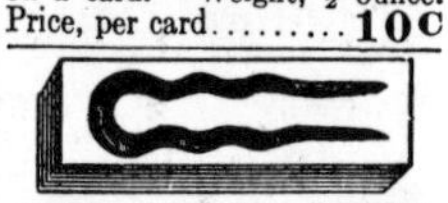

HORN HAIRPINS, PER BOX, 10c.
BX197 — Horn Hairipns. Waved design. 3 inches long. Extra quality horn. Eight pins in a box. Weight, ½ ounce. Price, per box.......... **10c**

HORN HAIRPINS, PER BOX, 10c.
BX198 — Horn Hairipns. Straight design. 3 inches long. Extra quality horn. Eight pins in a box. Weight, 1 ounce. Price per box. **10c**

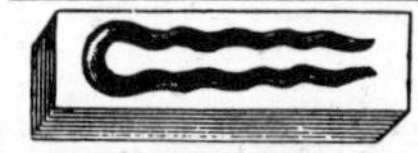

HORN HAIRPINS, PER BOX, 10c.
BX199 — Horn Hairpins. Waved design. 3 inches long. Nine pins in box. Weight, 1 ounce. Price, per box... **10c**

HORN HAIRPINS, PER BOX, 10c.
BX200 — Horn Hairpins. Waved design. 3¼ inches long. Five pins in box. Weight, 1 ounce. Price, per box... **10c**

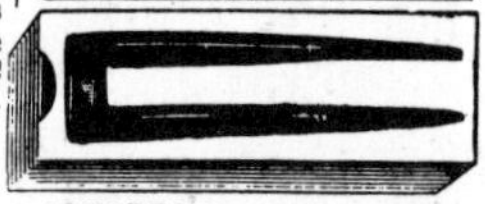

SQUARE TOP HAIRPINS, 10c.
BX201 — Square Top Hairpins. 3½ inches long. Made of selected horn. Five pins in box. Weight, 1 ounce. Price, per box **10c**

HORN HAIRPINS, PER BOX, 10c.
BX202 — Horn Hairpins. 3 inches long. Loop design. Nine pins in box. Weight, 1 ounce. Price, per box... **10c**

LARGE HORN HAIRPINS, PER BOX, 10c.
BX203. Large Horn Hairpins. 4½ inches long. Waved and loop design. Three pins in box. Weight, 1 ounce. Price, per box **10c**

FANCY BRAID PINS, 10c.
BX204 — Mounted Braid Pin. Loop and waved design. Each pin set with six selected brilliants. 4½ inches long. Weight, ½ ounce. Price, each..... **10c**

BX205 — Mounted Braid Pin. 4½ inches long. Square straight design. Each pin set with six selected brilliants. Weight, ½ ounce. Price, each **10c**

All of the articles shown on this page can be had in shell or amber except where otherwise stated. Amber is for blondes and shell for brunettes. Do not fail to state color and Katalog number when ordering. Combs and brushes are shown on the following pages. Nothing over 10c.

Extra Quality Hair Goods 5 & 10c

We list below some wonderful Bargains in hair goods, Hair Nets, Etc. In fact, similar goods are sold by Hair Goods Stores at from 10c to 50c. You can save money by ordering your Hair Goods from us. Nothing over 10c.

IMPORTANT! READ!

When ordering Hair Goods be sure to state shade desired, also send a sample of the hair you desire us to match and state Katalog number wanted.

EXTRA LARGE IMPORTED SILK HAIR NETS, 2 FOR 5c.

B B - 112 — Extra Large Imported Silk Hair Nets. Best quality silk. Each net is equipped with elastic band and guaranteed perfect in every respect. Each net in separate envelope. State shade wanted. Weight, 2 nets, 1 ounce. 2 for....... **5 C**

EXTRA LARGE SILK HAIR NETS, EACH, 5c.

B V - 110 — Extra Large Silk Hair Nets. Made of best quality silk, with fast knotted meshes.

Every net guaranteed perfect. Cannot be distinguished from real hair. Long wearing quality. State shade wanted. Weight, 1 ounce. Each...... **5 C**

EXTRA SPECIAL HUMAN HAIR SWITCHES, CHOICE OF ALL SHADES, 10c

FOR ONE SWITCH.

BX100 — Extra Special Human Hair Switches. These switches measure about 17 inches in length and are composed of best quality human hair. Shades are so natural that they will blend perfectly and cannot be told from the natural hair. These switches are extra full and can be had in the following shades: dark brown, medium brown, light brown, black, and blonde. State shade wanted. Weight, each, ½ ounce. Price of single switch only.. **10 C**

PSYCHE BUNS, MADE FROM HUMAN HAIR, 10c.

BX102 — Psyche Buns. Made from extra long selected human hair. These buns are made extra full and in a variety of shades that will match the natural hair perfectly. They are a necessity for the Psyche Coiffure. Strands are all carefully combed. State shade wanted when ordering. Weight, each, 2 ozs. Price, each. .... **10 C**

REGARDING EXTRA SHADES

We do not furnish hair goods in extra shades. In the description of each number, we state the shades we can furnish.

DOUBLE WIDTH HAIR NETS, 2 FOR 5c.

B B - 111 — Double Width Silk Hair Nets. Good quality silk with fast knotted meshes. Every net guaranteed perfect. Cannot be distinguished from real hair. Each net in separate envelope. State shade wanted. Weight, 2 nets, 1 ounce. 2 for. **5 C**

EXTRA QUALITY SILK HAIR NETS, EACH, 5c.

B V - 109 — Extra Quality Silk Hair Nets. Fast knotted meshes. Every net guaranteed perfect. Cannot be distinguished from real hair. Each net is equipped with elastic band. State shade wanted. Weight, each, 1 ounce. Price................. **5 C**

THREE ROSETTES ATTACHED, WIRE FOUNDATION, 10c.

BX101 — Rosettes. Wire foundation covered with fine quality waved wool crepe. Three attached to a set. Can be had in all shades to match the hair. State shade wanted when ordering. Weight, set, 2 ounces. Price .... **10 C**

MARCELLE FORM, 10c.

BX103 — Marcelle Form. Covered with extra fine waved wool crepe. These forms are made with wire foundation. Come in all shades. State shade wanted. Weight, each, 2 ounces. Price.... **10 C**

FINE QUALITY NET COVERED PSYCHE ROLL, 5c.

BV108 — Fine Quality Net Covered Psyche Roll. Full 8 inches long. Best quality waved wool crepe. All shades to match the natural hair. State shade wanted. Weight, each, 1 ounce. Price........ **5 C**

SANITARY WOOL CREPE HAIR ROLLS, EACH, 10c.

BX104 — Sanitary Wool Crepe Hair Rolls. Full 24 inches long and can be washed when desired. Light weight and very serviceable. State shade wanted. Weight, each, 3 ozs. Price................. **10 C**

LIGHT WEIGHT NET, COVERED HAIR ROLL, 10c.

BX105—Light Weight Net Covered Hair Roll. Made from fine quality waved wool crepe, all shades. Full 24 inches long and covered with strong netting. State shade wanted. Weight, 3 ounces. Price.... **10 C**

18-INCH NET COVERED HAIR ROLL, 10c.

BX106 — 18-inch Net Covered Hair Roll. Superior quality waved wool crepe. A light weight roll. Matches the natural hair nicely. A very serviceable roll. State shade wanted. Weight, 2 ounces. Price....................... **10 C**

SANITARY PSYCHE ROLLS, WAVED WOOL CREPE, 10c.

BX107 — Sanitary Psyche Rolls. Full 6 inches in length. Made of very fine waved wool crepe with ribbon wire. All shades to match natural hair. State shade wanted. Weight, each, 1 oz. Price... **10 C**

NOTE:—For sanitary reasons we do not exchange Hair Goods, Hair Nets, etc. We agree to match hair goods in the shades listed above, but cannot take them back, for exchange or refund.

NOTIONS ETC. AT 5 & 10¢

BE sure to look over this, and the following pages carefully. We have listed hundreds of useful articles, used in the home every day. Special attention is called to our line of scissors, curling irons, needle-cases, etc., shown on pages 73, 74, 75, 76 and 77. The values in this line of merchandise have contributed to the success of the Kresge Stores to a great extent. Millions of customers all over the country are daily purchasing these articles, with the knowledge that nowhere else can they obtain such bargains. Nothing over 10c. Your money returned if we fail to please you.

ATLAS STRAIGHT TRIMMER, 10c.

HX430—Atlas Straight Trimmer. 8 inches long. Finely nickel plated straight shears, made of high quality steel. Have keen edge and brass connecting bolt. Weight, 5 ounces. Price, each.................................**10C**

ATLAS BENT TRIMMER, 10c.

HX431—Atlas Bent Trimmer. 8 inches long. Finely nickel plated. Made with bent handles to cut materials on sewing table easily. Weight, 4 ounces. Price, each..**10C**

NICKEL PLATED TENSION SHEARS, 10c.

HX432—Tension Shears. 8 inches long. Fine nickel plated shears with special device for regulating tension in cutting different kinds of cloth. Weight, 2 ounces. Price, each.**10C**

BARBER SHEARS, SHARP EDGE, 10c.

HX433—Barber Shears. Length, 8 inches. Highly finished nickel plate, brass bolt. Have special finger hook and exceedingly sharp edge. Weight, 3 ounces. Price, each.................................**10C**

LADY'S FINE QUALITY SCISSORS, 10c.

HX434—Lady's Scissors. 6 inches long. Nickel plated, pointed blades. A good scissors for all around. Weight, 2 ounces. Price, each..................**10C**

POINTED POCKET SCISSORS, 10c.

HX435—Pointed Pocket Scissors. Length, 5 inches. Nickel plated, medium size, sharp pointed. Just right for the sewing basket. Weight, 1 ounce. Price, each....**10C**

EXTRA QUALITY BUTTON-HOLE SCISSORS, 10c.

HX436 — Buttonhole Scissors. 4½ inches long. Very strong with regulating screw set between handles. A necessity in the home. Weight, 2 ounces. Price, each.................................**10C**

SMALL LIGHT SCISSORS, 10c.

HX437 — Light Scissors. Length, 4½ inches. Fine nickel plate. The right size for light cutting, or for fine sheer materials. Weight, 1 ounce. Price, each..................**10C**

NICKEL PLATED EMBROIDERY SCISSORS, 10c.

HX438 — Embroidery Scissors. 4½ inches long. Nickel plated, sharp pointed. Well made and have very sharp edge. Special design for fancy work. Weight, 1 ounce. Price, each..........**10C**

BLUNT POINT POCKET SCISSORS, 10c.

HX439—Pocket Scissors. Length, 4 inches. Nickel plated. Have blunt points, so that they can be carried in pocket or handbag with safety. Weight 4 ounces. Price, each..**10C**

TRAVELER'S CURLING IRON, 10c.

HX440—Travelers' Curling Iron. Heavily nickel plated. Handles made to fold back. See illustration. 9 inches long when open. Hardwood polished handles, durable spring, and well made. Weight, 3 ounces. Price, each. **10C**

VASSAR CURLING IRON, 10c.

HX441—Vassar Curling Iron. 8½ inches long. Highly finished hardwood handles. Pointed iron. Strong spring. Light and serviceable. Weight, 3 ounces. Price, each **10C**

BRIGHT FINISH CURLING IRON, 5c.

HV442—Curling Iron. Highly polished shaped maple handles. Dull point. Bright finish. 6 inches long. Has strong spring of fine steel. Weight, 2 ounces. Price, each..........................**5C**

NIAGARA WAVING IRON, 10c.

HX443—Niagara Waving Iron. Produces a beautiful wave effect. Is strong, well made, heavily nickel plated. Metal handles. Weight, 5 ounces. Price, each........................**10C**

MANHATTAN MARCELLE WAVING IRON, 10c.

HX444—Manhattan Marcelle Waving Iron. Produces the popular Marcelle wave, which is so stylish at the present time. Both blades heavily nickel plated. Metal handles; also nickel plated. Weight, 5 ounces. Price, each.................................**10C**

ALVITA MARCELLE WAVING IRON, 10c.

HX445—Alvita Marcelle Waving Iron. Handsomely nickel plated. Has oak handles, and spring which keeps iron closed until released by pressure of the hand. Weight, 4 ounces. Price, each..............**10C**

OUR GUARANTEE: We guarantee every article in this Katalog to be exactly as represented. See our Money Back Guarantee on second page of cover. Be sure to read it.

THE ORIGINAL PARCEL POST   KRESGE'S KATALOG   FIVE AND TEN CENT STORE

Fine Quality Notions—Nothing Over 10c

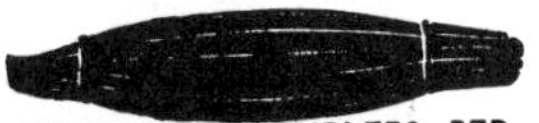

COLUMBIA KID CURLERS, PER BUNCH, 10c.

BX550—Columbia Kid Curlers. Flexible wire, padded, covered with black kid. Large size, 8½ inches long. 12 curlers in bunch. Weight, 1 ounce. Price, per bunch.............. **10c**

TAN KID COVERED CURLERS, PER BUNCH, 5c.

BV551 — Kid Curlers. Medium size. 5¼ inches long. Made of flexible wire, padded, covered with tan kid. 12 curlers in bunch. Weight, 1 ounce. Price, per bunch................ **5c**

MEDIUM SIZE KID CURLERS, 2 BUNCHES FOR 5c.

BB552-Kid Curlers. Medium size, 4½ inches long. Made of flexible wire, covered with tan leather. Weight, 1 ounce. 12 curlers in bunch. Price, 2 bunches for **5c**

WEST ELECTRIC HAIR CURLERS, 10c.

BX553—West Electric Hair Curlers. Patent hair curler, finely nickel plated. Made of rust proof steel, ever lasting. Unequaled for curling the hair. Come two curlers on card. Weight, 1 ounce. Price, per card.............. **10c**

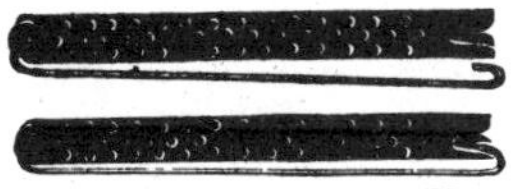

VENTILATED HAIR WAVERS, PER CARD, 10c.

BX554—Ventilated Hair Wavers. Each waver made of a black japanned, perforated metal tube. Wire attachment for holding together. A very excellent curler. Weight, 1 ounce. Come two on a card. Price, per card...................... **10c**

HAIR PIN CABINET, 5c.

BV555—Hair Pin Cabinet. A handsomely decorated box containing an assortment of 150 straight, crimped and invisible hairpins. A useful and decorative article for the dressing table. Weight, 3 ounces. Price, per box **5c**

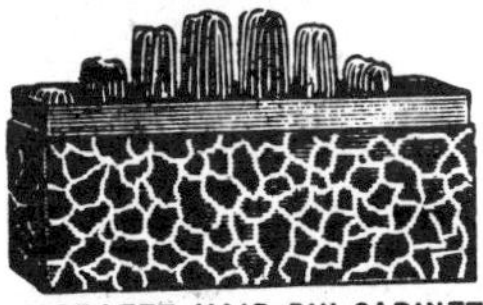

DECORATED HAIR PIN CABINET, 5c.

BV556 — Hair Pin Cabinet. Tastefully decorated box containing 200 assorted hairpins. Light weight pins, some straight and some crimped. Weight, 2 ounces. Price, per box. **5c**

FANCY HAIR PIN CABINET, 5c.

BV557 - Hair Pin Cabinet. Contains 200 assorted straight and crimped invisible hair pins. Highest quality, bright finished black Japan in fancy decorated box. Weight, 4 ounces. Extra value. Price, per box **5c**

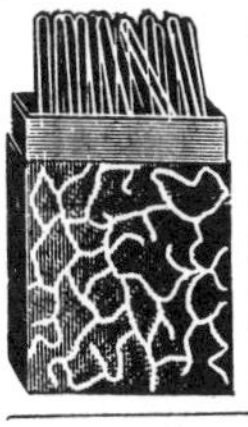

HAIR PIN CABINETS, 2 FOR 5c.

BB558 — Hair Pin Cabinet. Contains 60 assorted black japanned wire hair pins in fancy ornamented box. Weight, 2 ounces. Price, 2 boxes **5c**

FANCY HAIR PIN CABINETS, 2 FOR 5c.

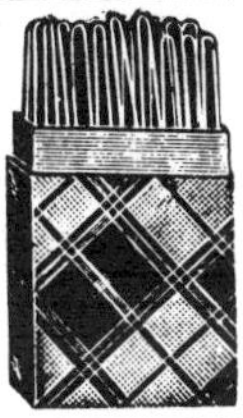

BB559 — Hair Pin Cabinet. Contains 60 assorted black japanned wire hair pins in fancy ornamented box. Weight, 2 ounces. Price, 2 boxes for............ **5c**

SQUARE HAIR PIN CABINET, 5c.

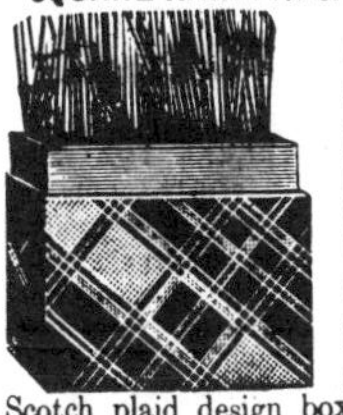

BV560 — Hair Pin Cabinet. Contains 150 assorted hair pins. Made of the best quality black japanned wire. Packed in a handsome square Scotch plaid design box. Weight, 3 ounces. Price, per box......... **5c**

BEST QUALITY IMPORTED HAIR PINS, 5c.

BV5605 — Hair Pins. Imported. Perfectly made, excellent finished black imported wire hair pins, wrapped in bunches of 10. Either straight or crimped, state which you want. Come 10 bunches to package. Weight, 3 ounces. Price, per package...................... **5c**

INVISIBLE WIRE HAIRPINS, 2 TUBES, 5c.

BB561. — Invisible Wire Hairpins. Very fine imported English made, black japanned wire hairpins. Packed in tubes, containing 50. Come in four lengths, straight or crimped, 1¾, 2, 2¼ and 2½-inch. State size and kind wanted. Weight, 1 ounce. Price, 2 tubes for........ **5c**

INVISIBLE HAIRPINS, 2 PKGS., 5c.

BB562 — Invisible Wire Hairpins. Best quality English manufacture. Straight or crimped, 50 in package. Four different sizes: 1¾, 2, 2¼ and 2½-inch. State size and kind wanted. Weight, 1 ounce. Price, 2 packages for.......................... **5c**

IMPORTED HAIRPINS, 2 PACKAGES, 5c.

BB564 — Imported Hairpins. Straight only. Genuine, imported black japanned wire hairpins of English manufacture. Come in seven sizes: 2¾, 3, 3¼, 3½, 4, 4½ and 5-inch. Paper packages, each containing 1 ounce. State size desired. Price, 2 packages for.................. **5c**

IMPORTED CRIMPED HAIRPINS, 2 PKGS., 5c.

BB565 — Imported Hairpins. Crimped only. Genuine, imported black japanned wire hairpins of English manufacture. Come in seven sizes: 2¾, 3, 3¼, 3½, 4, 4½ and 5-inch. Paper packages, each containing 1 ounce. State size desired. Price, 2 packages for................... **5c**

ENGLISH HAIRPINS, 2 PKGS., 5c.

BB566—English Hairpins. Superior quality, black japanned wire hairpins, imported. Come either straight or crimped in four sizes: 2¼, 2¾, 3 and 3½-inch. Wrapped in one ounce packages. State kind and size wanted. Price, 2 packages for.... **5c**

WHITE OR BLACK HEAD PINS, PER CARD, 5c.

BV567—Pin Card. Card like illustration containing 60 blue steel pins with your choice of jet, mourning or white glass head. State which you want, or whether you desire assorted colors. Weight, 1 ounce. Price, per card. **5c**

ROUND PIN CARD, 5c.

BV568 - Round Pin Card. Contains 60 blue steel pins in jet mourning, white or assorted colors. State color wanted. Weight, 1 ounce. Price, per card.................. **5c**

OVAL PIN CARD, 5c.

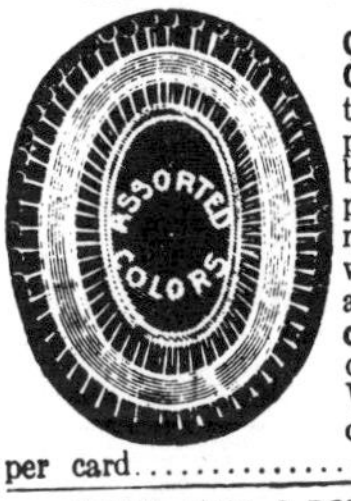

BV569 — Oval Pin Card. Containing 60 imported blue steel pins in jet, mourning, white or assorted colors. State color wanted. Weight, 1 ounce. Price, per card...................... **5c**

STEEL PINS, 3 BOXES, 5c.

B570 — Steel Pins. 60 in box. Come in black, white, and mourning. State which you want. Weight, 1 ounce. Price, 3 boxes for.......................... **5c**

LARGE IMPORTED PIN CUBE, 5c.

BV571 — Imported Pin Cube. Large Paper cubes containing 100 1½-inch glass headed pins. Come in three ways; black; mixed black and white and assorted colors. State which kind is wanted. Weight, 1 ounce. Price, per cube. **5c**

SMALL IMPORTED PIN CUBE, 5c.

BV572 —Imported Pin Cube. Small. Contains 100, 1½-inch glass headed pins. Come in three ways; black, mixed black and white and assorted colors. State which kind is wanted. Weight, 1 ounce. Price, per cube........ **5c**

IMPORTED HAT PINS, PER CARD, 5c.

BV573 - Imported Hat pins. Six pins on card. Fine blue steel hat pins. Come in three lengths, 8, 9 and 10-inch with black, or white heads. State length and color desired. Weight, 2 ounces. Price, per card **5c**

HORSESHOE NEEDLE BOOK, 5c.

BV574 — Horseshoe Needle Book. Contains five papers of assorted size needles, one paper of gold eye needles and ten assorted size darning needles, one steel bodkin or ribbon needle. This assortment is a very exceptional value. Weight, 1 ounce. Per book...... **5c**

FANCY NEEDLE CASE, 10c.

BX575 — Fancy Needle Case. Imitation padded leather case containing an assortment of needles as follows: 10 each of five different sizes gold eye needles, 10 assorted size darning needles, one bodkin or ribbon needle. This is not only a very useful but very attractive case. Weight, 1 ounce. Price, per case **10c**

LARGE EYE NEEDLE BOOK, 5c.

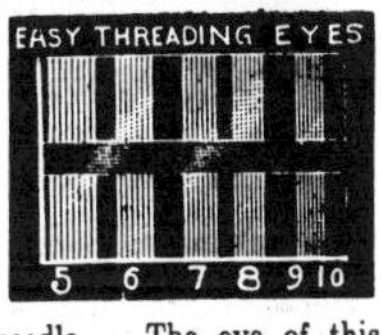

BV576—Needle Book. Containing five each of five sizes of the famous lightning needle. The eye of this needle is larger than in the average and the needle is tapered in such a manner as to make sewing easy. Weight, 1 ounce. Price, per book.......... **5c**

See page 71 for wonderful bargains in Hair Goods, Natural hair rolls, switches, etc., nothing over 10c.

Special Notion Bargains, 5c and 10c

EASY THREADING GOLD EYE NEEDLES, 2 PAPERS 5c

BB578 — Hanover Easy Threading Gold Eye Needles. Sizes, 4 to 8, 3 to 9, and 5 to 10, sharps. 25 needles in paper. A first class needle at a low price. Weight, ½ ounce. State size wanted. 2 papers for............5C

LARGE EYE EMBROIDERY NEEDLES PER PAPER, 5c.

BV579 — Crewel Needles with Large Eye, used for Embroidery work. Needles have gold eyes. 25 first quality needles in each paper. Sizes, 3 to 9 and 5 to 10. Sharp tapering points. State size wanted. Weight, ½ ounce. Per paper............5C

BEST QUALITY ENGLISH NEEDLES PER PAPER, 5c.

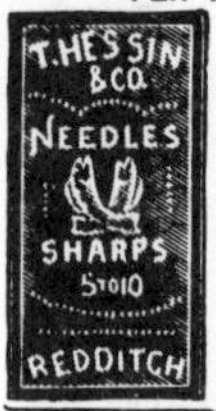

BV580 — Steel Eye English Needles. Made of best quality steel and have easy threading eye. Sharps only. Come in sizes, 4 to 8, 3 to 9 and 5 to 10. 25 needles to paper. A high quality needle. Weight, ½ ounce. State size wanted. Per paper............5C

ENGLISH GOLD EYE NEEDLES, PER PAPER, 5c.

BV581 — High grade English Gold Eye Needles. Made of best grade English steel. Come in sizes 4 to 8, 3 to 9, and 5 to 10, sharps. 25 needles in a paper. Many ladies prefer the gold eye needles to the ordinary steel. Weight, ½ ounce. State size wanted. Per paper............5C

20 HIGH GRADE DARNERS FOR 5c.

BB582 — Best quality English Darning Needles. Come in sizes 0 to 5. 10 needles in paper. Made of best English steel, highly polished. A good strong darning needle with fine sharp point. Good value. State size wanted. Wt., ½ ounce. 2 papers for............5C

EXTRA LARGE EYE DARNING NEEDLES, 2 PAPERS, 5c.

BB5822 — Extra Quality Darning Needles. Sizes, 14 to 18. Made with large eye for carrying heavy wool yarn. 10 needles to paper. State size wanted. Weight, ½ ounce. 2 papers for.5C

We guarantee the merchandise shown in this Katalog to be exactly as represented, and will exchange or refund your money on anything that does not give satisfaction.

NEEDLE POINT PINS, PER PAPER, 5c.

BV5788 — Crown Jewel Pins. Made of first quality brass wire. Each pin has needle point. Three sizes; MC large SC medium, F3½ small. A good quality pin that will give absolute satisfaction. 300 pins to paper. Weight, 2 ounces. State size wanted. Per paper.................5C

800 HIGH QUALITY PINS, 5c.

BB5799 — Gladiator Brand Pins. An excellent quality pin with perfect points. Pins are of large size. A good pin for everyday use. 400 to paper. Weight, 2 ounces. 2 papers for....5C

GOOD GRADE LARGE SIZE PINS, 4 PAPERS, 5c.

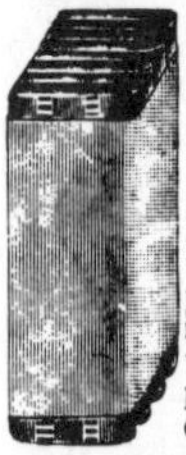

B5800 — A fine quality pin for everyday use. Made of good quality wire. Extra fine, sharp points. Large convenient size. An exceptional value at the price. 200 pins to paper. Weight, 2 ounces. 4 papers for.5C

24 NICKEL PLATED STEEL SAFETY PINS, 5c.

BB5811 — Good quality nickel plated steel safety pins. Good strong spring and sharp points. End has deep metal guard to hold point. Come in sizes, 2, 2½ and 3. 12 pins on card. State size wanted. Wt. ½ ounce. 2 cards for.5C

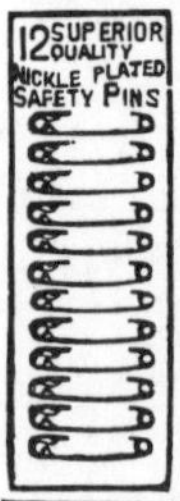

SHIELD COVERED SPRING SAFETY PINS, PER CARD, 5c.

BV5823 — High grade nickel plated safety pins. Made of best quality steel wire, firm sharp point. Deep metal guard on end. Each pin with shield covered spring. Come in sizes 0, 1, 2 and 3. 12 pins on card. Weight, ½ ounce. Per card 5C

BLACK JAPANNED SAFETY PINS, PER CARD, 5c.

BV583 — High quality japanned (black) safety pins. Preferred by many to the light colored safety pins, especially on dark cloth. Large size only. No. 3. Rust resisting. 12 pins on a card. Weight, 1 ounce. Per card............5C

ASSORTED NICKEL PLATED SAFETY PINS, PER CARD, 5c.

BV584 — Nickel plated Safety Pins with shield covered spring. 12 assorted pins on each card. Four each of three sizes. A size for every necessity around the house. It would be real economy to order several cards. Weight, ½ ounce. Per card 5C

RUST PROOF HOOK & EYES

48 HOOKS AND EYES, 5c.

BB585 — Good quality Hooks and Eyes. Four sizes, 0, 1, 2 and 3. Black or silver color. 24 hooks and eyes on a card. State size and color wanted. Weight, ½ ounce. 2 cards for....5C

RUSTPROOF HOOKS AND EYES, PER CARD, 5c.

BV586 — Extra quality Rustproof Hooks and Eyes. 24 hooks, 24 loops and 24 straight eyes on a card. Either black or silver. Sizes, 0, 1, 2 and 3. State size and color wanted. Weight, ½ ounce. Per card:.............5C

12 SNAP FASTENERS FOR 5c.

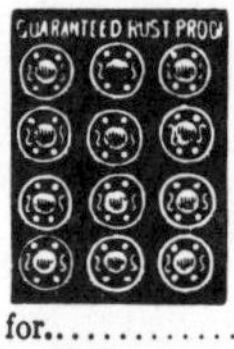

BV587 — Placket Fasteners. Used in place of hooks and eyes or buttons. An invisible fastener. Four sizes, 000, 00, 0 and 1. Black or silver. State size and color wanted. Weight, ½ ounce. 12 for............5C

HIGH GRADE PEARL BUTTONS PER CARD, 5c.

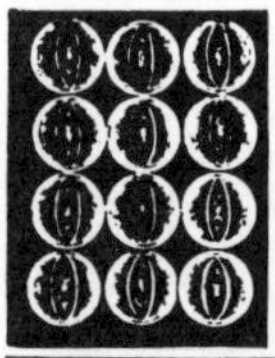

BV588 — High grade fresh water Pearl Buttons, fish eye pattern. 12 buttons on card. Five sizes: 14, 16, 18, 20 and 22 ligne. State size wanted. Wt., ½ ounce. Per card.......5C

BEVELED EDGE PEARL BUTTONS, PER CARD, 5c.

BV589 — Made of first quality fresh water pearl. Two holes. 12 buttons on card. Five sizes: 14, 16, 18, 20 and 22 ligne. State size wanted. Weight, ½ ounce. Per card....5C

PLAIN PEARL BUTTONS, PER CARD, 5c.

BV590 — High grade, fresh water Pearl Buttons, plain, 24 on a card. Two holes. Five sizes, 14, 16, 18, 20 and 22 ligne. State size wanted. Weight, ½ ounce. Per card....5C

---

24 GOOD QUALITY PEARL BUTTONS, 5c.

BB591 — Good quality fresh water Pearl Buttons. Come 12 two hole buttons on card. Diameter 7-16 in. Weight, 1 ounce. 2 cards for ..5C

24 FOUR HOLE PEARL BUTTONS, 5c.

BB592 — Fine quality fresh water Pearl Buttons. Come 12 four hole buttons on card. Diameter 7-16 in. Weight, ½ ounce. 2 cards for 5C

72 IMPORTED AGATE BUTTONS, 5c.

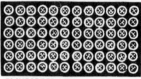

BV593 — Fine Imported Agate Buttons. Two sizes: 10 ligne (small), 30 ligne (large). 72 four hole buttons on card. State size wanted. Weight, 2 ounces. Per card..............5C

EXTRA QUALITY PEARL BUTTONS, PER CARD, 5c.

BV594 — Fish eye pattern Pearl Buttons. Three sizes: 24 ligne, ⅝ inch diameter. Six on card. 30 ligne, ¾ inch diameter. Four on card. 36 ligne, ⅞ inch diameter. Three on card. State size wanted. Weight, ½ ounce. Per card....................5C

24 HIGH GRADE BONE BUTTONS, 5c.

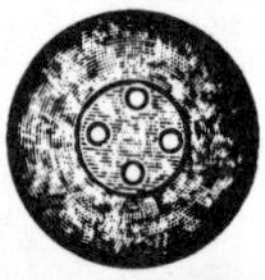

B595 — Good Grade Bone Button. 4 hole. Very useful for underwear. Children's garments, etc. Weight, 1 ounce. 24 buttons for.........5C

18 CORSET OR TAPE BUTTONS, 5c.

B596 — Fine Quality 2 Hole Bone Corset or Tape Button. Extra large eye for use with tape. Weight, 1 ounce. 18 buttons for........5C

36 METAL PANT BUTTONS, 5c.

B597 — Good Quality Metal Pant Buttons, 36 buttons in bunch. Weight, 1 ounce. Per bunch...5C

METAL BACHELOR BUTTONS, PER CARD, 5c.

BV598 — High Grade Metal Bachelor Buttons with patent Washburne Fastener. Two buttons on a card. Weight, ½ ounce. Per card.....................5C

Special Bargains in Notions at 5c and 10c

AUTOMATIC BACHELOR BUTTONS, PER BOX, 10c.

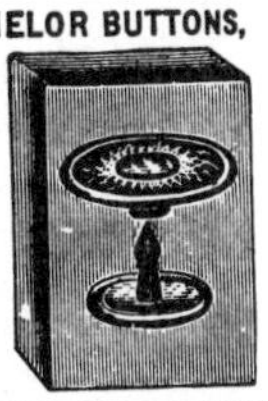

BX599 — Automatic Bachelor Buttons. Very easily attached or removed from garment. 12 buttons in a box. Weight, 1 ounce. Per box **10c**

WEDGE BACHELOR BUTTONS, PER BOX, 5c.

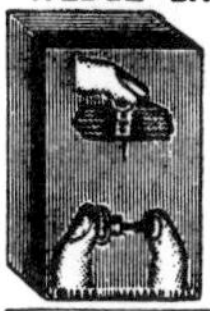

BV600 — Bachelor Buttons. Very easily attached to garment. Adjusted and detached with ease. 12 buttons and steel needle for attaching buttons. Wt., 1 ounce. Per box. **5c**

FINE BLACK VEST BUTTONS, 5c.

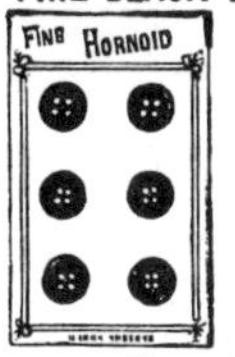

BV601 — Fine black hard rubber Vest Buttons. Made of best quality hard rubber, highly polished. 4 holes in each button. Six buttons on a card. Very convenient to have around the house. Weight, ½ ounce. Per card.. .... **5c**

BLACK COAT BUTTONS, CARD, 5c

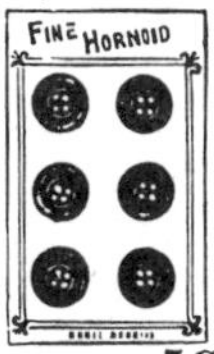

BV602 — Fine black hard rubber Coat Buttons. Made of best quality hard rubber and highly polished. Very smooth edges. 4 holes. Six buttons to a card. Good, serviceable buttons. Weight, ½ ounce. Per card.................. **5c**

HARD RUBBER OVERCOAT BUTTONS, 5c.

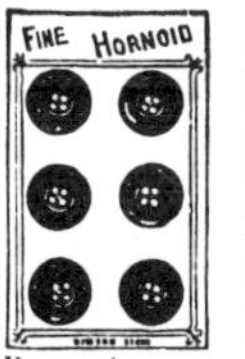

BV603 — Fine quality black hard rubber Overcoat Buttons. Nicely finished. Buttons very highly polished and edges finished very smooth. 4 holes. Six buttons to a card. Weight, ½ ounce. Per card...................... **5c**

200 YD. BEST MACHINE THREAD, 5c.

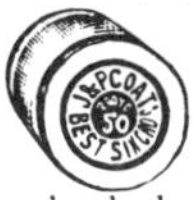

BV604 — Coat's, Clark's or O. N. T. Spool Machine Thread. Nos. 8, 16, 24, 36, 40, 50, 60, 70, 80 and 100. Black or white. State number, brand and color desired. Weight, ½ ounce. Per spool......................... **5c**

2 SPOOLS BEST MACHINE THREAD 5c.

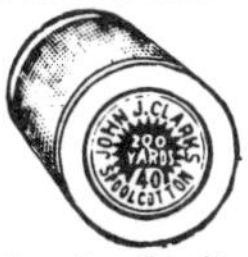

BB606 — John J. Clark's 200 Yd. Spool Machine Thread. Nos. 40, 50 and 60. Black or white. A fine quality spool thread. Specify number and color desired. Weight, 1½ ounces. 2 spools for............................ **5c**

3 SPOOLS BEST BASTING COTTON, 5c.

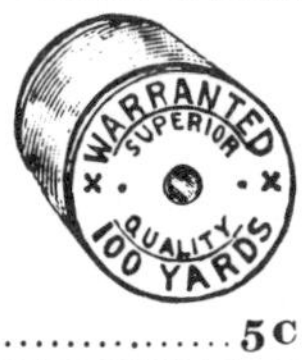

B608 — Excellent quality Basting Cotton, 100 yard spools. White only. Nos. 40, 50 and 60. State number wanted. Wt., 1 ounce. 3 spools for **5c**

500 YARD SPOOLS BASTING COTTON 5c.

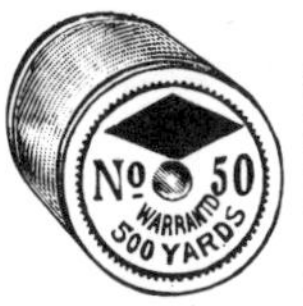

BV609 — Fine quality Basting Cotton, 500 yd. spools. White only. Can be had in following Nos., 40, 50 and 60. Specify number wanted. Weight, 1 ounce. Per spool..... **5c**

PURE LINEN THREAD, 100 YARD SPOOLS, 5c.

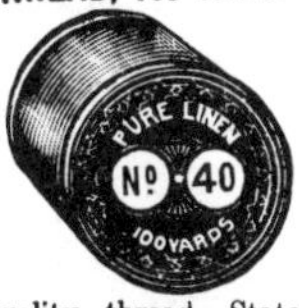

BV610 — Black or White, pure linen thread, 100 yds. to the spool. Comes in the following Nos.: 25, 30, 35 and 40. A good quality thread. State number and color desired. Weight, 1 ounce. Per spool............. **5c**

2 SPOOLS LINEN FINISH THREAD, 5c.

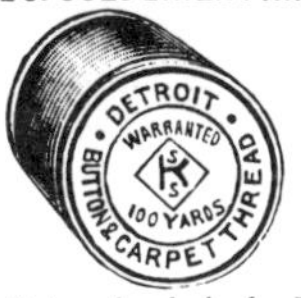

BB611 — Linen Finish Button and Carpet Thread, 100 yds. to the spool. Colors, black or white. A superior linen finish thread. State color desired. Weight, 3 ounces. 2 spools for.................. **5c**

EXTRA QUALITY LINEN FINISH THREAD, 5c.

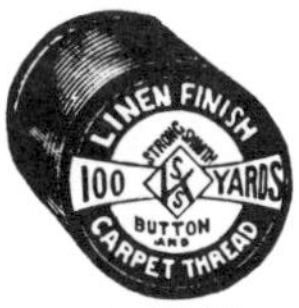

BV612 — Extra quality Linen Finish Button and Carpet Thread. 100 yd. spools. Black, white, brown or drab. A fine linen finish thread. State color wanted. Weight, 2 ounces. Per spool............ **5c**

DEXTER'S EMBROIDERY COTTON, 3 SPOOLS, 5c

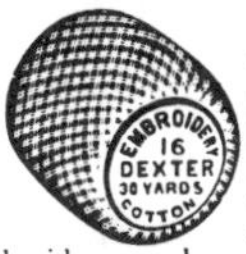

B613 — Dexter's Turkey Red Embroidery Cotton. 30 yards on spool. Fast color. Exceptional good quality for high class embroidery work. Weight, 1½ ounces. 3 spools for.................. **5c**

COAT'S DARNING COTTON, 2 SPOOLS, 5c.

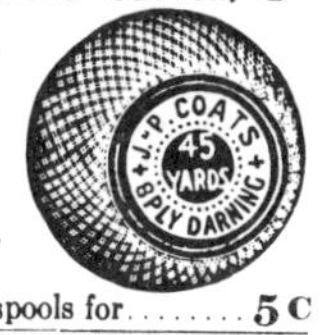

BB614 — J. & P. Coat's 8 Ply Darning Cotton. Comes in black, white or tan. Fine quality. State color wanted. Wt., 1½ ounces. 2 spools for....... **5c**

DEXTER'S DARNING COTTON, 2 SPOOLS, 5c.

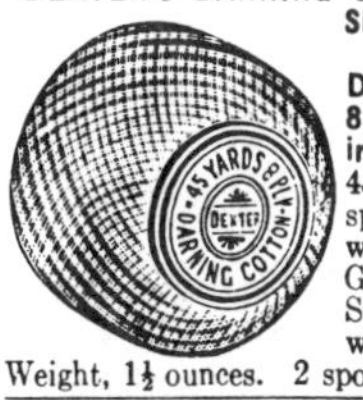

BB615 — Dexter's 8 ply Darning Cotton. 45 yards on spool. Black white or tan. Good value. State color wanted. Weight, 1½ ounces. 2 spools for. **5c**

DEXTER'S KNITTING COTTON, BALL, 5c.

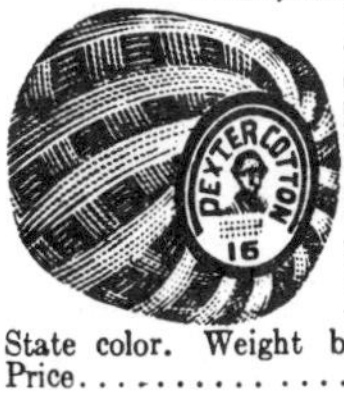

BV6001 — Dexter's Knitting Cotton. Best known and highest quality knitting cotton on the market. Black or white —fast colors. State color. Weight ball 1 ounce. Price............................ **5c**

CHILD'S FANCY EMBOSSED THIMBLE 2 FOR 5c.

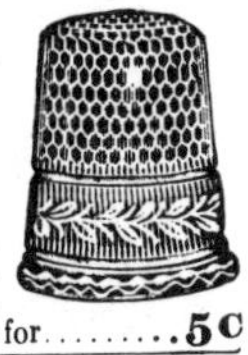

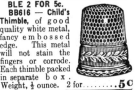

BB616 — Child's Thimble, of good quality white metal, fancy embossed edge. This metal will not stain the fingers or corrode. Each thimble packed in separate box. Weight, ½ ounce. 2 for......... **5c**

LADIES' EMBOSSED THIMBLES, 2 FOR 5c.

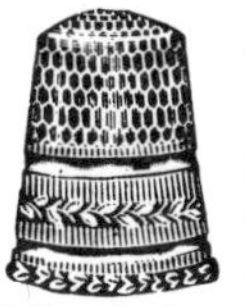

BB617 — Ladies' Thimble. Heavy quality, white metal, with fancy embossed rim. This metal will not stain the fingers or corrode. Very durable. Weight, ½ ounce. 2 Thimbles for................ **5c**

EXTRA HEAVY THIMBLES, 2 FOR 5c.

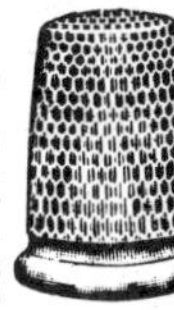

BB618 — Ladies' Extra Heavy White Metal Thimble. Plain rim. Very serviceable article. This metal will not stain the finger or corrode. Weight, ½ ounce. 2 Thimbles for............ **5c**

CELLULOID THIMBLE, GOLD BANDS, 2 FOR 5c

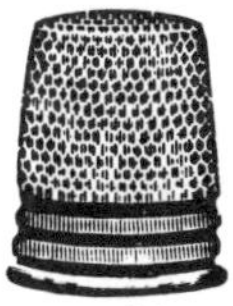

BB619 — Heavy celluloid Thimble, with plain rim and gold bands. Made of best quality white celluloid and tastefully decorated. Preferred by some to metal. Weight, ½ ounce. 2 for................. **5c**

STEEL CROCHET HOOK, 2 FOR 5c.

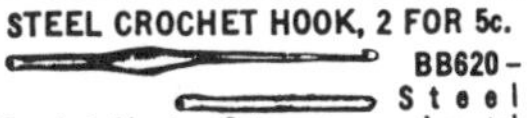

BB620 — Steel Crochet Hooks, flat center, and metal hook protector for covering hook. No danger of hook getting caught. Weight, ½ ounce. 2 hooks for........... **5c**

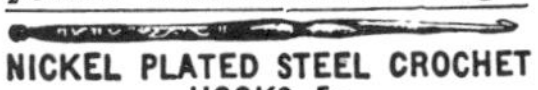

NICKEL PLATED STEEL CROCHET HOOKS, 5c.

BV621 — Steel Crochet Hook, heavily nickel plated, flat center, shaped handle. Best quality steel. Weight, ½ ounce. Each................ **5c**

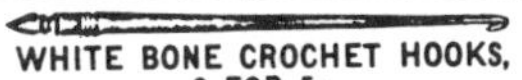

WHITE BONE CROCHET HOOKS, 2 FOR 5c.

BB622 — Fine White Bone Crochet Hook. 5 inches long. Will give excellent satisfaction. Weight, ½ ounce. 2 for **5c**

STEEL STILETTO, BONE HANDLE, EACH, 10c.

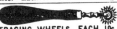

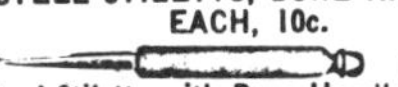

BX623 — Steel Stiletto with Bone Handle. Used largely for eyelet embroidery work. A necessary item. Weight, 1 ounce. Each.................... **10c**

3½-INCH BONE STILETTO, EACH, 5c.

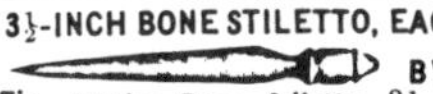

BV624 — Fine White Bone Stiletto, 3½ inches long. Fancy turned top. Weight, ½ ounce. Each **5c**

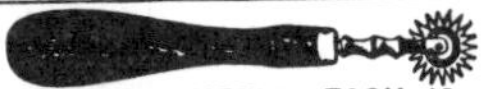

TRACING WHEELS, EACH 10c.

BX6244 — Tracing Wheels. About 6 inches over all. Steel wheel with good points. Polished hardwood handle with nickeled ferrule. Weight, 2 ounces. Price.......... **10c**

See our special bargains in Millinery Goods, Dry Goods, Etc. Nothing over 10c.

CELLULOID TATTING SHUTTLES, EACH, 10c.

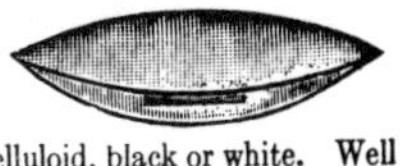

BX625 — Tatting Shuttles made of best quality celluloid, black or white. Well made. State color wanted. Weight, ½ ounce. Each................ **10c**

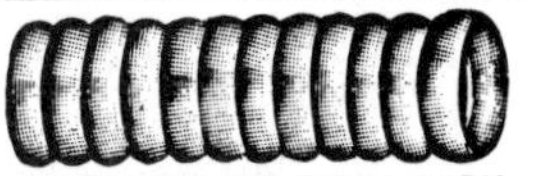

BONE RINGS FOR FANCY WORK, PER BUNCH, 5c.

B626 — Bone Rings. Made of good quality white bone. Four sizes; ½ in., ⅝ in., ¾ in. and ⅞ in. 12 rings in a bunch. Give size wanted. Weight, ½ ounce. Per bunch........... **5c**

BUTTON MOLDS, PER BUNCH, 5c

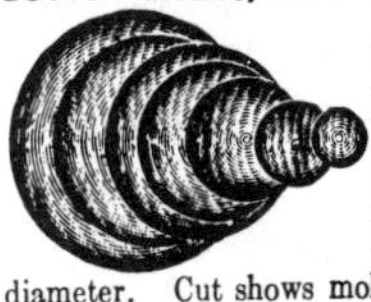

B627 — Wood Button Molds. Extra quality. Sizes, ⅜, 7/16, ⅝, ¾, ⅞, 1, and 1¼ inches diameter. Cut shows molds about ½ size. State diameter wanted when ordering. 36 molds in bunch. Average weight bunch 3 ozs. Bunch, **5c**

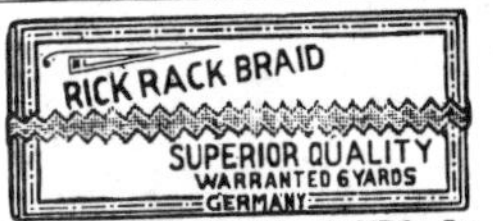

RICK RACK BRAID, 6 YDS, 5c.

BV628 — Fine Quality Imported Rick Rack Braid. 6 yards to piece. White only. Weight, ½ ounce. Per piece......................... **5c**

BIAS LAWN SEAM TAPE, PIECE, 5c.

BV629 — Fine lawn bias seam Tape. Best quality, white only. 6 yards to piece. Weight, ½ ounce. Per piece **5c**

HERRINGBONE COTTON TAPE, 5c.

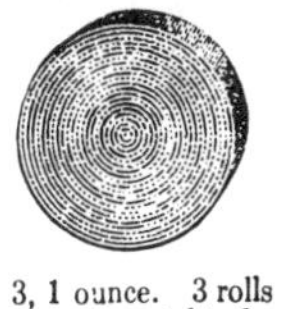

B630 — Colors, Black or White. Widths: 7-16 in., ½ in., 9-16 in., ⅝ in., ¾ in. and ⅞ in. 12 rolls in a bunch, two bunches to box. Give widths wanted. Weight, 3, 1 ounce. 3 rolls for **5c**, or box of 24 rolls, weight, 6 ounces, for..... **40c**

15 YARD ROLL COTTON TAPE, 5c.

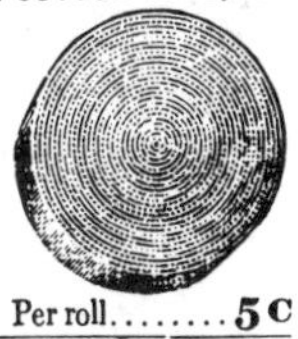

BV631. Cotton tape or stay Binding. 15 yards to roll. Widths, 7-16 in. and ½ in. Colors, black or white. Give color and width wanted. Weight, 1 ounce. Per roll........ **5c**

30 YARD ROLL COTTON TAPE, 10c.

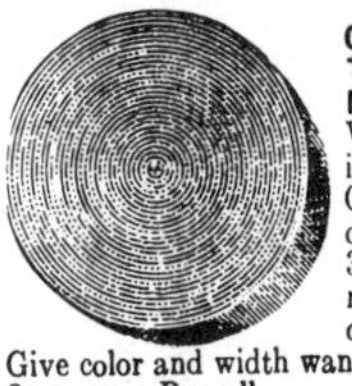

BX632 — Cotton Tape or Stay Binding. Widths, 7-16 in. and ½ in. Colors, black, or white. 30 yards to a roll. Good quality. Give color and width wanted. Weight, 3 ounces. Per roll........... **10c**

Bargains in Notions—Nothing Over 10c

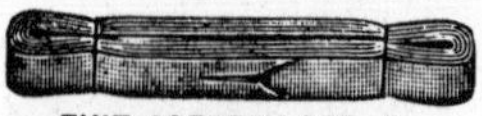

FINE CORSET LACE, 5c.

BV633 — Fine Corset Lace. Five yards long, ½-inch wide. Extra quality mercerized cotton. Comes in white only. Weight, 2 ounces. Price, each......5c

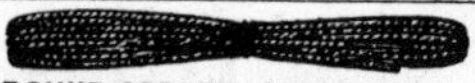

ROUND CORSET LACE, 6 FOR 5c.

B634 — Round Braided Corset Lace. 2½ yards long. High grade tubular weave. Metal tips. Comes in white only. Weight, 2 ounces. Price, 6 for......5c

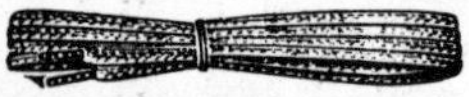

FLAT CORSET LACE, 6 FOR 5c.

B635 — Flat Corset Lace. Good quality. 2½ yards long. Web woven. Metal tips. Comes in white only. Weight, 2 ounces. Price, 6 for. 5c

ELASTIC CORSET LACE, 2 FOR 5c.

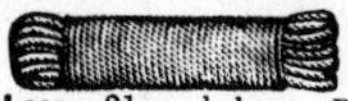

BB636 — Elastic Corset Lace. 2½ yards long. Round. Good quality. Metal tips. Comes in white only. Weight, 2 ounces. Price, 2 for......5c

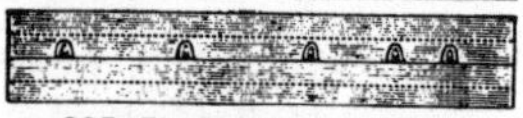

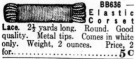

CORSET CLASP, EACH, 5c.

BV637 — Corset Clasp. 12 inches long, 5 hooks. Covered with extra quality white sateen. High grade steels. Comes in white only. Weight, 2 ounces. Price, each......5c

"EASYWAY" COLLAR SUPPORTERS 5c.

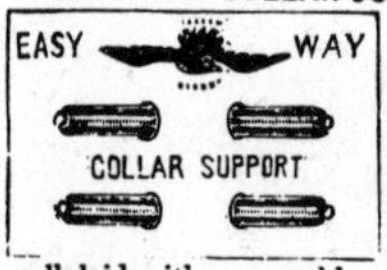

BV638 — "Easyway" Collar Supporters. Made from white celluloid with removable pins for adjusting to collar. Sizes, from 2 to 2¾ inches. Two on card. Weight 1 oz. Price per card......5c

"QUEEN" COLLAR SUPPORTERS, 5c.

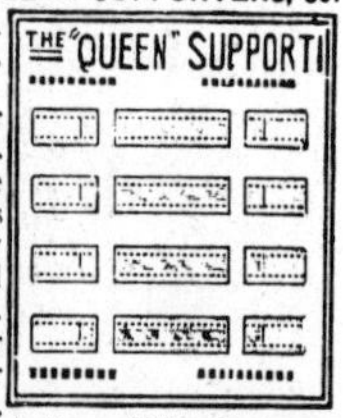

BV638 — "Queen" Collar Supporters. Removable celluloid stays. Easily stitched to collar. Black or white. Four on card. Sizes, 2 to 3½ inches. Wt., 2 ounces. Price, per card......5c

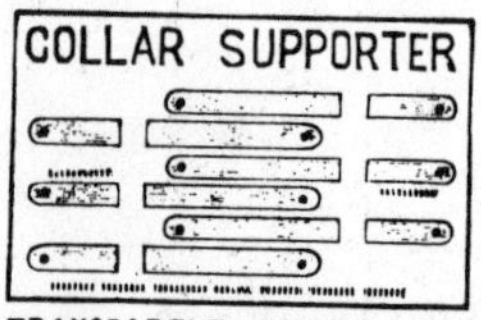

TRANSPARENT COLLAR SUPPORTERS, 2 CARDS, 5c.

BB640—Transparent Collar Supporters. Flexible, comfortable, easily attached. Six on card. Sizes, 2 to 3½ inches. Weight, 2 ounces. Price, 2 cards for......5c

"BLUE-BELLE" COLLAR SUPPORTERS, 5c.

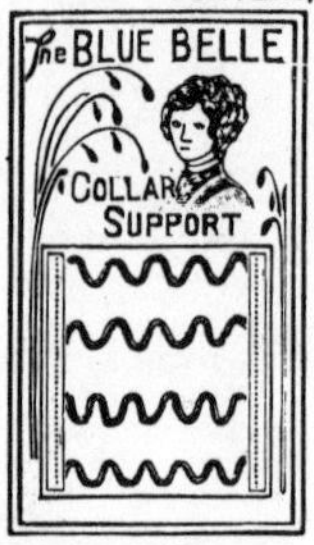

BV641 — "Blue-Belle" Collar Supporters. Serpentine shape, cotton covered. Adjustable. Can be lengthened or shortened as desired. Four on a card. White or black. Sizes, 2 to 3½ inches. Wt., 2 ounces. Price, per card......5c

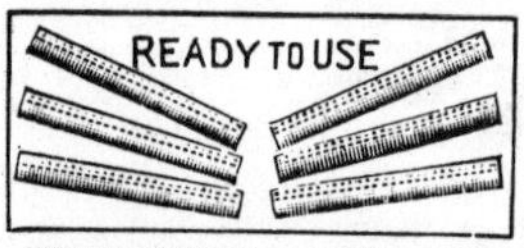

FEATHERBONE COLLAR SUPPORTERS, 5c.

BV642 — Featherbone Collar Supporters. Covered with gros-grain silk. Washable. Black or white. Six on card. Sizes, 2 to 3½ inches. Weight, 2 ounces. Price, per card......5c

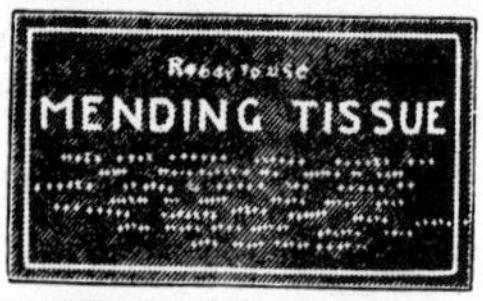

MENDING TISSUE PACKAGE, 5c.

BV643—Mending Tissue. Very useful article for mending torn garments or turning up hem at bottom of skirt or trousers. Black or brown. One piece 5x18 inches in envelope. Weight 1 ounce. Price, per envelope......5c

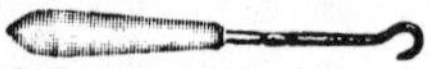

5-INCH BUTTON HOOK, 5c.

BV647 — Button Hook. 5 inches long. Highly finished nickel plated metal hook with 2½-inch genuine bone handle. A good, substantial button hook to have around every day. Weight, 2 ounces. Price, each......5c

STRAWBERRY SHAPE EMERY POLISHING CUSHION, 5c.

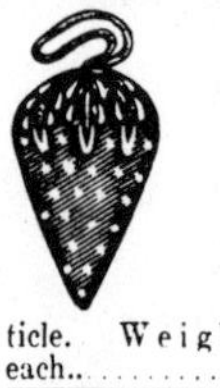

BV648½— Emery Cushion. Strawberry shape, silk covered and embroidered. Rusty needles brightened and sharpened by merely thrusting through cushion. Pays for itself in a short time. An indispensable article. Weight, 1 ounce. Price, each......5c

LARGE EMERY POLISHING CUSHION, 5c.

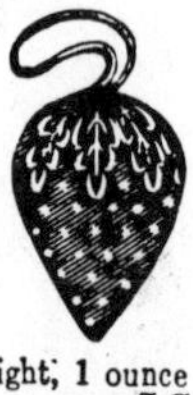

BV649 — Emery Cushion. Strawberry pattern. Cotton covered, large size. Rusty needles brightened and sharpened by merely thrusting through cushion. Filled with best qualty fine emery dust. Will not sift through covering with use. Weight, 1 ounce Price, each......5c

We guarantee every item in this Katalog to be strictly as represented, and should you be displeased with your purchases for any reason, we will ship you other goods, or refund money.

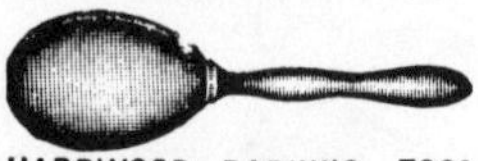

HARDWOOD DARNING EGGS, 2 FOR 5c.

BB651 — Darning Egg. With handle. Highly polished hardwood. Natural finished or japanned. Weight 3 ounces. Price, 2 for......5c

BV6511 — Same as above, except finished in hard white enamel. Price, each......5c

METAL SPOOL STAND, 10c.

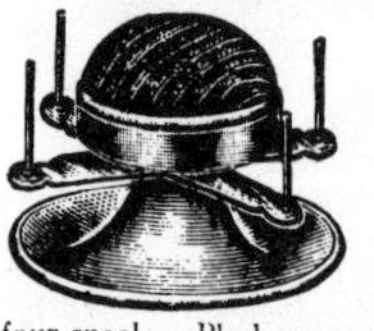

BX650 — Metal Spool Stand. Useful ornament for sewing table. Revolving. Holds four spools. Plush covered pin cushion in center. Nickel plated. Pin tray. Weight, 3 ounces. Price, each......10c

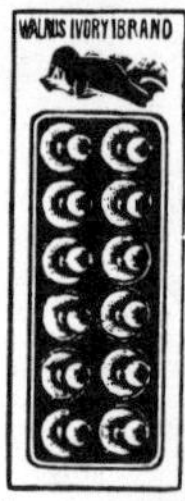

WHITE BONE COLLAR BUTTONS, PER CARD, 5c.

BV656 — Bone Collar Buttons. Warranted one piece. Made of best quality pure white bone. Will not discolor or break apart just when you need them most. Twelve buttons on card. Weight, 1 ounce. Price, per card......5c

SHOE LACES, 2 PAIRS, 5c.

BB657 — Shoe Laces. Banded in pairs. Double metal tips. Black or tan. Three lengths: 36, 45 and 54 inches. Extra fine quality. State length desired. Weight, 1 ounce. Price, 2 pairs for......5c

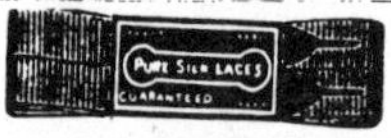

TUBULAR OXFORD SHOE LACES, 10c.

BX658 — Tubular Oxford Shoe Lace. All pure Silk. 30-inches long. Black only. Banded in pairs. Weight, 1 ounce. Price, per pair......10c

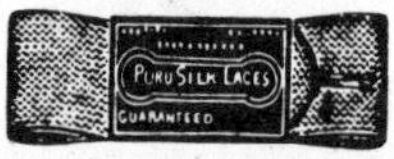

FLAT OXFORD LACES, 10c.

BX659 — Flat Oxford Lace. All pure Silk. 1¾ inches wide. 30 inches long. Black or tan. Banded in pairs. Weight, ½ ounce. Price, per pair......10c

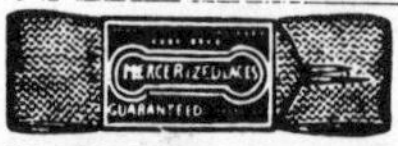

BLACK OR TAN OXFORD LACES, 5c

BV660—Oxford Lace. Very fine quality mercerized cotton. 30 inches long, 1½ inches wide. Selected metal tips. Black or tan. Weight, ½ ounce. Price, per pair......5c

OXFORD LACES, 2 PAIRS, 5c.

BB661 — Closely Woven Oxford Lace. Himalaya braided cotton. 1-inch wide, 30 inches long. Black or tan. Banded in pairs. Weight, ½ ounce. Price, 2 pairs for......5c

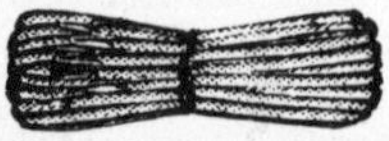

METAL TIP SHOE LACES, 12 FOR 5c

B662—Shoe Laces. Excellent quality cotton, with black metal tips. Two lengths: 45 and 54 inches. Black only. State length wanted. Weight, 1 ounce. Special price, 12 for......5c

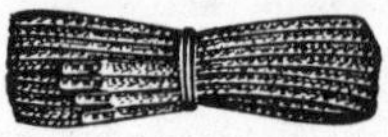

TUBULAR SHOE LACES, 8 FOR 5c.

B663 — Tubular Shoe Lace. Extra quality. Metal tips japanned in black. Comes in three lengths: 36, 45 and 54 inches. State length wanted. Weight, 1 ounce. Price, 8 laces for......5c

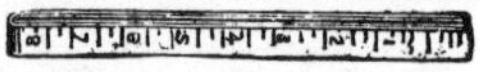

TAPE MEASURES, 2 FOR 5c.

BB644 — Tape Measure. 60-inch. Good quality, heavy glazed material. Large figures. Easy to read. Protecting metal end tips and bound edge. Weight, 1 ounce. Price, for 2......5c

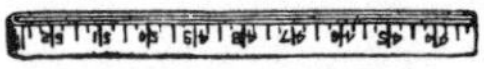

5-FOOT TAPE MEASURE, 5c.

BV645 — Tape Measure. 60-inch. Extra heavy glazed cotton. Large distinct figures, ⅛-inch divisions. Metal protected tip on each end, bound edges. Weight, 1 ounce. Price, each......5c

5-FOOT TAPE MEASURE, 10c.

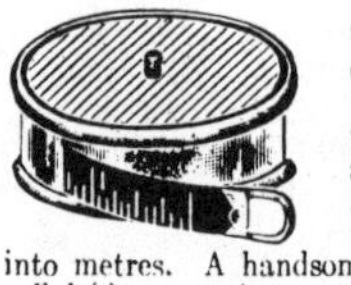

BX652 — Tape Measure 60 inches. Waterproof tape. One side divided into inches, the other into metres. A handsome metal and celluloid case. Automatic spring retractor. Weight, 1 ounce. Price, each......10c

60-INCH TAPE MEASURE, 10c.

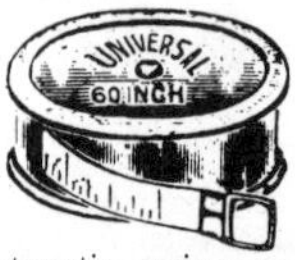

BX653 — Tape Measure 60 inches. Divided into ⅛-inch spaces. Highly nickel plated case. Strong automatic spring retractor. Weight, 1 ounce. Price, each......10c

NICKEL PLATED READY-CHANGE HOLDER, 10c.

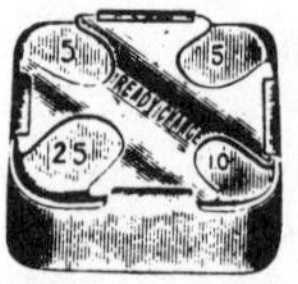

BX654 — Ready - Change Holder. Nickel plated. Compartments for nickels, dimes and quarters. 2 inches square. Each compartment has a spring to keep coin in place. Weight, 2 ounces. Price, each......10c

DIME BANK, CYLINDRICAL SHAPE, 10c.

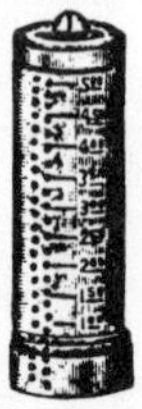

BX655 — Dime Bank. Nickel plated. Holds five dollars and cannot be opened until full. Figures on side and perforations indicate at all times amount of money in bank. A long screw pin in center keeps coins from rattling. Weight 1 ounce. Price, ea. 10c

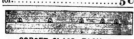

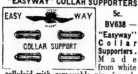

Dress Shields, Supporters, Elastic Webbing, Etc.

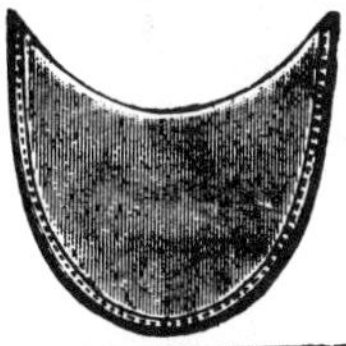

LIGHT WEIGHT DRESS SHIELDS, PER PAIR, 10c.

AX203 — Light Weight Dress Shields. Cambric covered, waterproof and odorless. Sizes, 3 and 4. A fine, durable shield. State size wanted. Weight, 2 ounces. Per pair... 10c

MERCERIZED DRESS SHIELDS, PER PAIR, 10c

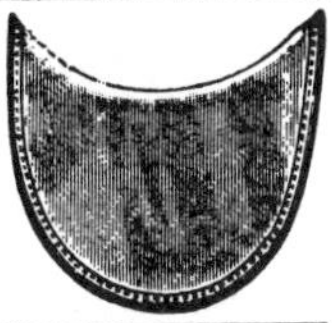

AX204 — Light Weight Dress Shield, covered with Mercerized Silk. A strictly high grade shield. Sizes, 3 and 4. State size wanted. Weight, 2 ounces. Per pair. 10c

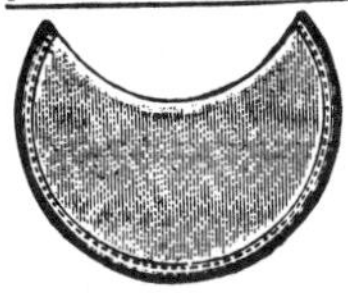

SHIRT WAIST SHIELDS, PER PAIR, 10c.

AX205 — Tape Bound Shields. Well made. Covered with fine cambric, bound with tape. Sizes, 3 and 4. Give size wanted when ordering. Weight, 2 ounces. Per pair... 10c

ALL ELASTIC SANITARY BELTS, 10c.

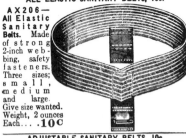

AX206 — All Elastic Sanitary Belts. Made of strong 2-inch webbing, safety fasteners. Three sizes; small, medium and large. Give size wanted. Weight, 2 ounces Each... 10c

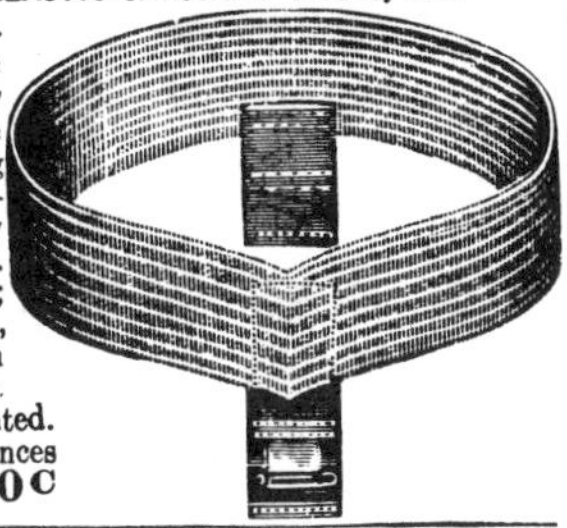

ADJUSTABLE SANITARY BELTS, 10c.

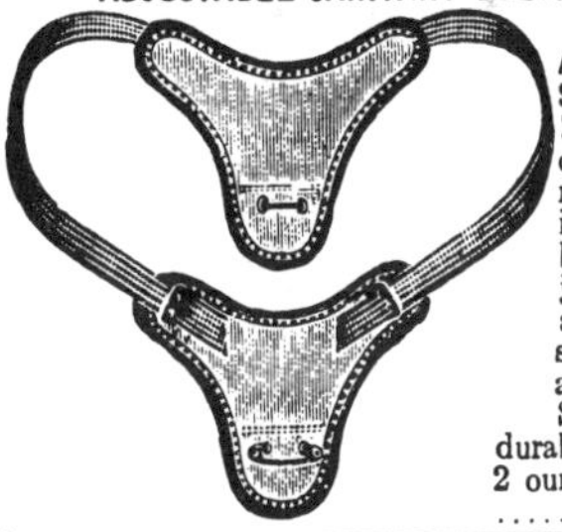

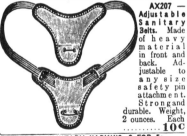

AX207 — Adjustable Sanitary Belts. Made of heavy material in front and back. Adjustable to any size safety pin attachment. Strong and durable. Weight, 2 ounces. Each 10c

SEAMLESS SANITARY NAPKINS, 2 FOR 5c.

AA208 — Seamless Sanitary Napkins. Full size.

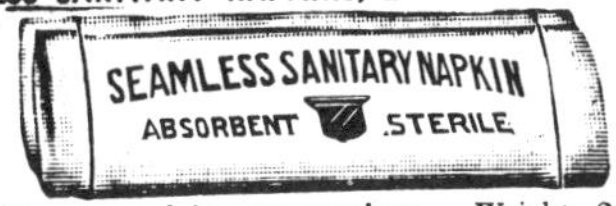

Each napkin wrapped in wax envelope. Weight, 2 ounces 2 for 5c

LADIES' SANITARY APRON, 10c.

AX209—Ladies' Sanitary Apron. Made of good quality rubber sheeting, bound with tape. Full size. Safety pin attachments and tape to tie around waist. This is one of the most practical articles ever made and a wonderful bargain at the price. Weight, 3 ounces Price, each....... 10c

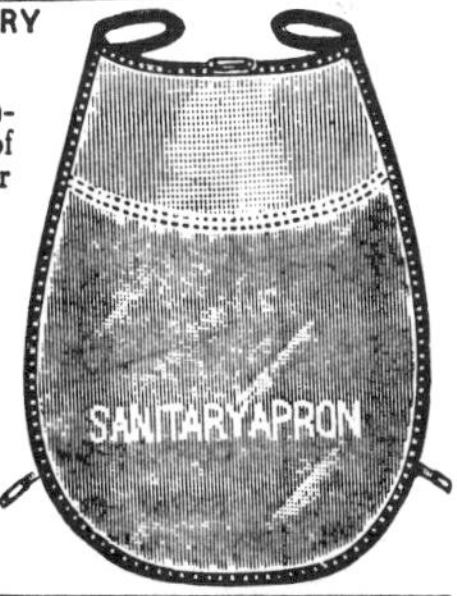

ADJUSTABLE SHIRTWAIST HOLDERS, EACH, 5c.

AV210 — Ladies' Elastic Shirt waist Holders. Made of ¾-inch elastic webbing, adjustable to any size. Dip pin attachment. Weight, 2 ounces. Each.................... 5c

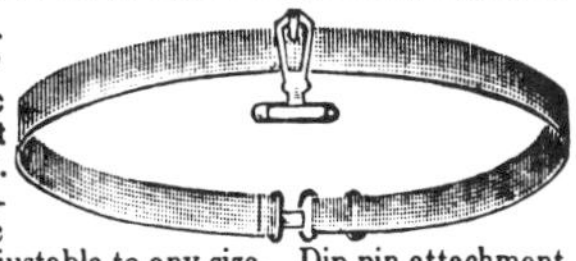

CHILDREN'S AND MISSES' HOSE SUPPORTERS PER PAIR, 10c.

AX216 — Children's and Misses' Hose Supporters. Best quality heavy elastic. Rubber cushion loop and rubber post buttons. All metal parts, such as buckles, loops, posts and fasteners are heavily nickel plated and rust-proof. Sizes, for infants, children, misses and young ladies. Colors, black and white. Give color and size wanted. Weight, 3 ounces. Per pair.................... 10c

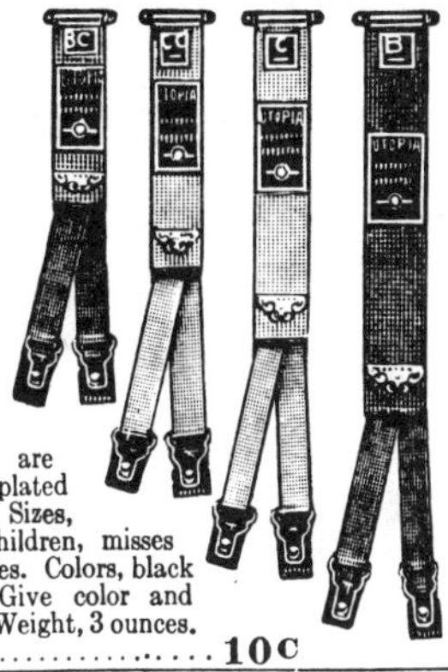

LADIES' ELASTIC HOSE SUPPORTERS, 10c.

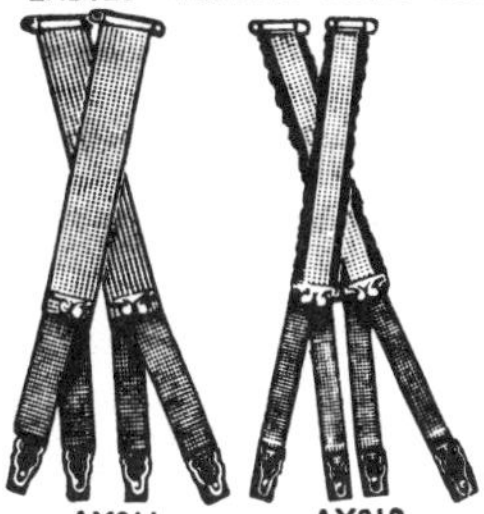

AX211 AX212

AX211 — Ladies' Elastic Hose Supporters. 1⅜-inch webbing, Adjustable nickel sliding buckle. Rubber post buttons, safety pin attachment. Colors: black, white, pink and blue. State color wanted. Weight, 2 ounces. Per pair...... 10c

AX212 — Fancy Side Hose Supporters. Made of good quality 1⅜-inch webbing, frilled, nickel fittings, post buttons. Colors, black, white, pink and blue. Give color wanted. Weight, 2 ounces. Per pr. 10c

MOIRE PAD HOSE SUPPORTERS, 10c.

AX213 — Moire Pad Hose Supporters. 1⅜-inch elastic supporters. White lined, double stitched. Nickel trimmings, adjustable belt. Rubber post buttons and velvet grip to prevent tearing hose. Supporters firmly attached to pad. Colors, black, white, pink and blue. Give color wanted. Weight, 4 ounces. Each............. 10c

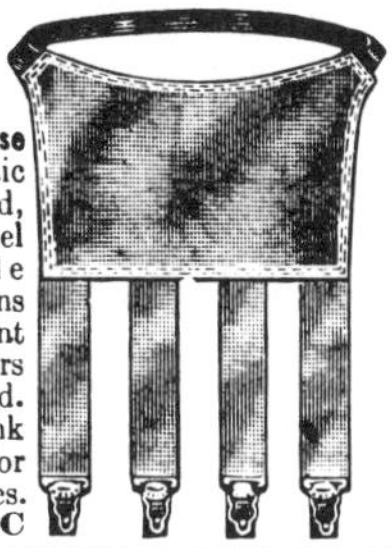

LADIES' SEW-ON SUPPORTERS, PER PAIR, 10c.

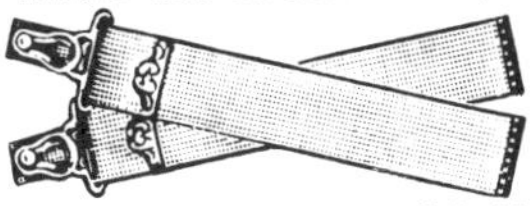

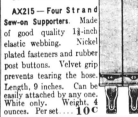

AX214 — Ladies' Sew-on Supporters. Just the thing for repair purposes. Easily attached by anyone and doubles the life of the corset. No danger of threads unravelling and supporter coming loose. Best quality 1⅜-inch heavy suspender web. Nickel slide buckle, flat loop, rubber button. Weight, 2 ounces. Per pair......... 10c

FOUR STRAND SEW-ON SUPPORTERS, 10c.

AX215 — Four Strand Sew-on Supporters. Made of good quality 1⅜-inch elastic webbing. Nickel plated fasteners and rubber post buttons. Velvet grip prevents tearing the hose. Length, 9 inches. Can be easily attached by any one. White only. Weight, 4 ounces. Per set.... 10c

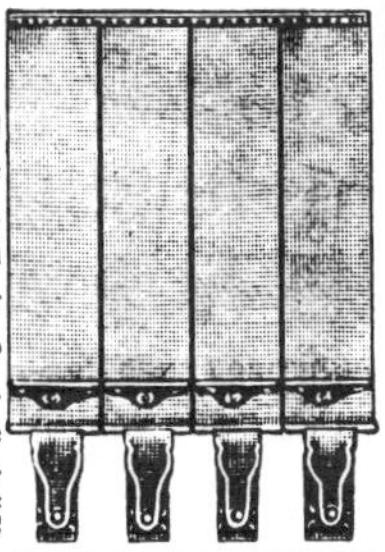

TRAVELER'S TOOTH BRUSH CASE, 10c.

AX217 — Traveler's Tooth Brush Case. Made of good quality rubber cloth, covered with fancy cretonne in floral design. Strongly bound at edges and closes with snap fastener. Weight, 1 ounce. Each.. 10c

TOURISTS' RUBBER COLTH SOAP CASE, 10c.

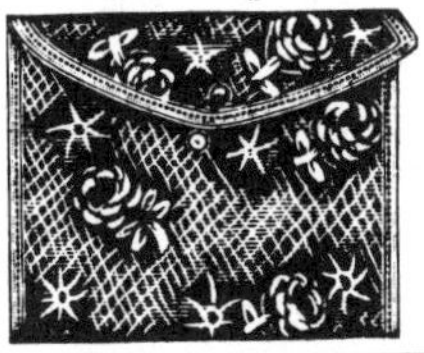

AX218 — Tourists' Soap Case. Made of good quality rubber cloth, covered with floral cretonne. Edges well bound with tape, closes with snap fastener. Weight, 1 oz. Each......... 10c

FANCY WASH CLOTH CASE, EACH, 10c.

AX219 — Wash Cloth Case. Made of good quality rubber cloth, covered with fancy cretonne, rich floral design. Strongly bound with tape, closes with snap fastener. An indispensable article. Weight, 1 ounce. Each............. 10c

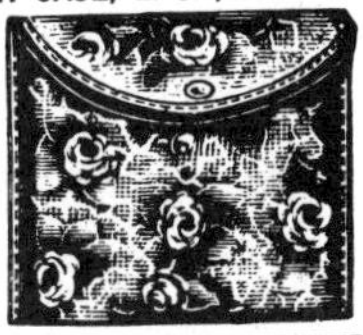

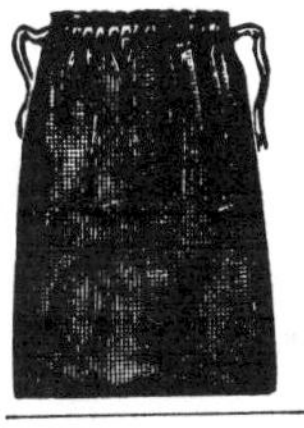

WELL MADE BATHING SUIT BAG, 10c.

AX220 — Bathing Suit Bag. Made of good quality black rubberized cloth. Size of bag, 10x14 inches. Has draw string at top. Strongly sewn. Just the thing to take along on vacations, outings, etc. Weight, 3 ounces. Each......... 10c

STRONG NET SHOPPING BAG, 10c.

AX221 — Shopping Bag. Made of heavy fancy jute cord, strongly reinforced. Size of bag, 14x18 inches. Indispensable for shopping, carrying parcels, etc. Color, black. Weight, 5 ounces. Each......... 10c

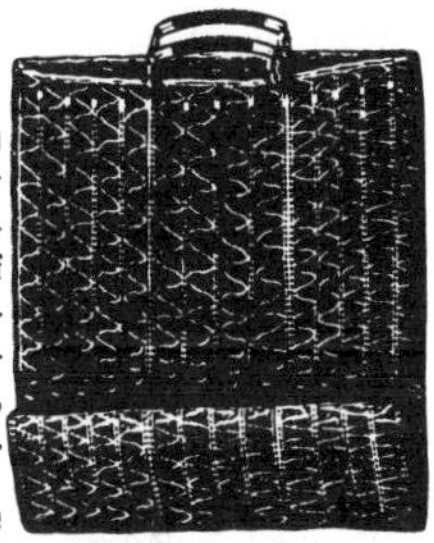

EXTRA HEAVY LISLE WEBBING, PER YD., 5c.

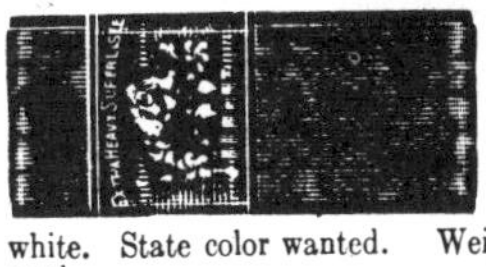

AV222 — Lisle Webbing. Made of extra heavy material, ¾- inch width. Guaranteed for one year. Colors, black and white. State color wanted. Weight, 1 ounce. Per yard.................................. 5c

LISLE ELASTIC WEBBING, PER YD., 5c.

AV 223 — Medium Quality Lisle Elastic. Guaranteed for one year. Colors, black and white. ⅞ inches wide. Give color wanted. Weight, 1 ounce. Per yard........ 5c

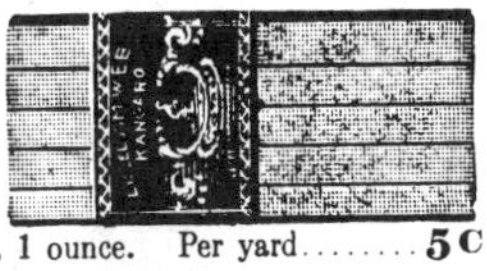

LISLE ELASTIC WEBBING, 2 YDS., 5c.

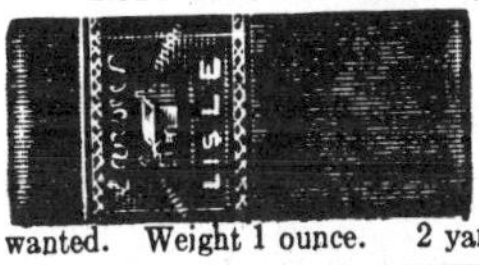

AA224 — This is a good quality lisle web. Colors, black and white. ½-inch wide. Give color wanted. Weight 1 ounce. 2 yards for......... 5c

When ordering notions, be sure to include enough other merchandise to make a profitable shipment. Order for the whole family at one time. Get your neighbors to order with you and get a valuable premium. See back page, also read page 3.

We fully guarantee every article shown in this catalog to be as represented, and will return your money if we fail to please you.

STATIONERY & SCHOOL SUPPLIES 5 & 10¢

IN listing our Stationery and School Supplies it was our aim to place before you a wide range of articles, and at the same time a line of the highest quality at the price. That we have succeeded in pleasing our customers is proven by the fact that this department is increasing tremendously.

The writing papers, envelopes, etc., are all exceptional values. School supplies such as note books, tablets, slates, pencils, pens, pen and pencil boxes, erasers, memorandum and account books, playing cards, score cards, etc., are listed in profusion. Nothing over 10c.

LINEN FINISH WRITING PAPER, 10c

BX750 — Linen Finish Writing Paper. Best quality linen finish ruled pages. Paper comes 24 sheets in a box with 24 linen finish envelopes to match. Size of sheet, 5¾x7½ inches. Weight, per box, 9 ounces. Price, per box **10C**

LINEN FINISH WRITING PAPER, 10c.

BX751 — Linen Finish Writing Paper. Best quality linen finish unruled pages. Comes 24 sheets in a box with 24 linen finish envelopes to match. Envelopes have the new long style flap. Size, 5½x7½ inches. Wt., per box, 9 ounces. Price......**10C**

NOVELTY WRITING PAPER, 10c.

BX752 — Novelty Finish Writing Paper. Made of best quality novelty finish paper, unruled pages. Paper comes 24 sheets in a box with 24 novelty finish envelopes to match. Envelopes have the long pointed flap. Weight per box, 8½ ounces. Price..................**10C**

CLOTH FINISH WRITING PAPER 10c.

BX753 — Cloth Finish Writing Paper. Made of best quality fabric finish paper. Ruled pages. Comes 24 sheets in a box with 24 fabric finish envelopes to match. Envelopes have the new long style flap. Weight, per box, 9 ounces. Price.........**10C**

SMOOTH FINISH WRITING PAPER, 10c.

BX754 — Smooth Finish Writing Paper. 24 sheets ruled paper in a box with 24 smooth finish envelopes to match. Cover of box is finished in fancy water color scene. Size page, 5½x7½ inches. Weight, per box, 11 ounces. Price.............**10C**

LINEN FINISH WRITING PAPER, 10c.

BX755 — Linen Finish Writing Paper. Made of best quality unruled paper with 24 linen finish envelopes to match. Envelopes have the new square flap. Box has unusually attractive cover. Size page, 5½x7½ inches. Weight, per box, 10 ounces. Price......................**10C**

LINEN FINISH MOURNING PAPER, 10c.

BX756 — Linen Finish Mourning Paper. 12 sheets of linen finish black bordered unruled writing paper in a box with 12 linen finish mourning border envelopes to match. Size of page 5½x7½ inches. Weight, per box, 7 ounces. Price **10C**

CORRESPONDENCE CARDS, 10c.

BX757—Correspondence Cards. 24 extra quality linen finish cards with 24 envelopes to match. Packed in a very attractive box. These cards are used for short personal notes that do not require the regular letter. Weight, per box, 7 ounces. Price.........**10C**

Always state Katalog Number when ordering.

High Grade Writing Tablets, at 5c and 10c

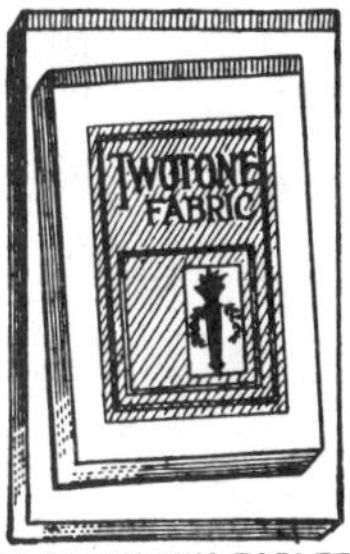

LINEN FINISH INK TABLETS, 5c.

BV759 — Linen Finish Ink Tablets. Fine smooth writing surface, unruled pages. Each tablet supplied with good blotter. Two sizes; note size, 5x8 inches, 55 leaves; two fold size, 6¾x10½ inches; 28 leaves. State size wanted. Weight, each, 4 ounces. Price **5c**

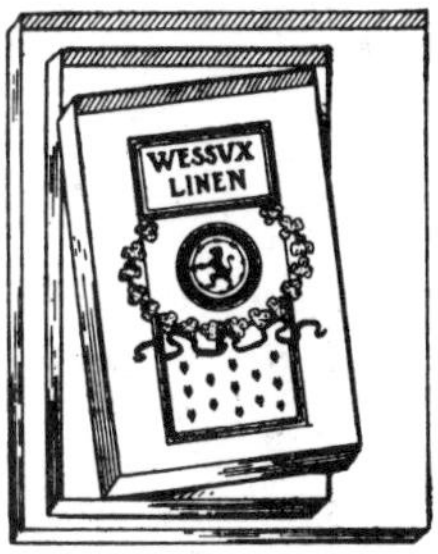

GOOD QUALITY INK TABLETS, 5c.

BV7577— Good Quality Ink Tablets. Fine smooth writing surface, conveniently ruled. Note size, 5x8 inches, 90 leaves; packet size, 5½x9 inches, 64 leaves; letter size, 8x10 inches, 36 leaves. State size wanted. Weight, note size, 6 ounces, letter and packet size, 5 ounces. Price, ea... **5c**

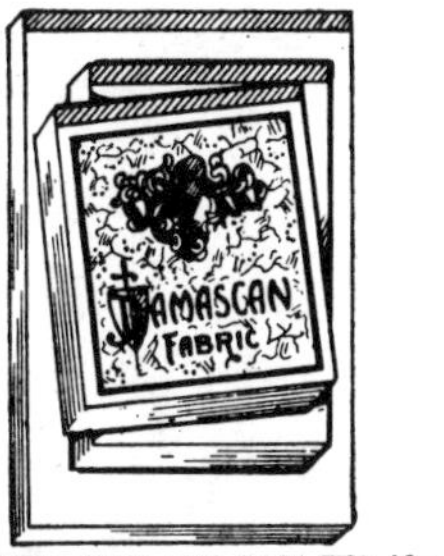

LINEN FINISH INK TABLETS, 10c.

BX760 — Linen Finish Ink Tablets. Made of extra quality unruled paper. Smooth writing surface. Note 5x8 inches, 80 leaves; one fold 5½x7 inches, 80 leaves; two fold, 6¾x10½ inches, 40 leaves. State size wanted. Weight, note and two fold size, 7½ ounces, one fold, 8 ounces. Price, each.......................... **10c**

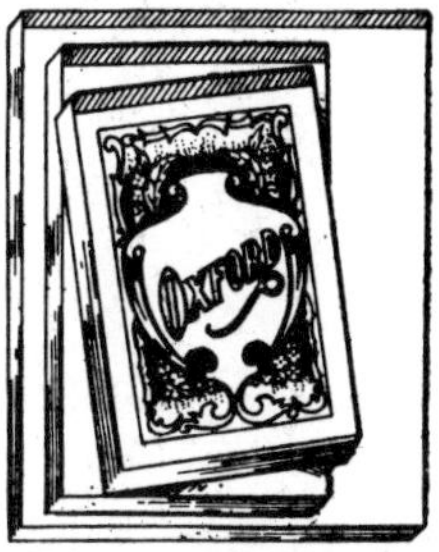

SMOOTH FINISH INK TABLETS, 5c.

BV758 — Smooth Finish Ink Tablets. Extra good writing surface, ruled pages. Note size, 5x8 inches, 100 leaves; packet size, 5½x9 inches, 70 leaves; letter size, 8x10 inches, 40 leaves. State size wanted. Weight, note size 8 ounces, packet and letter size, 7 ounces. Price, each............ **5c**

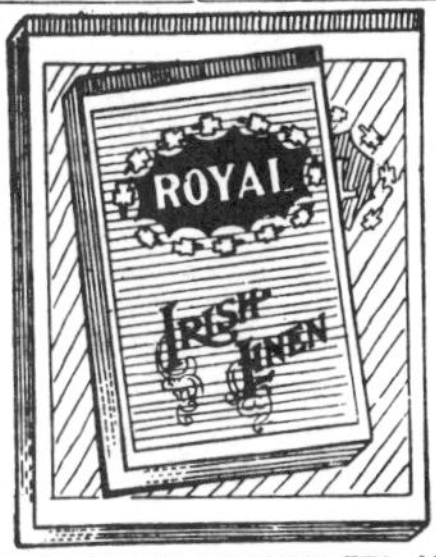

CLOTH FINISH INK TABLETS, 10c.

BX763 — Cloth Finish Ink Tablets. Made of extra quality smooth finish Irish linen paper, unruled pages. Good blotter and line guide. Two sizes; note 5x8 inches, 120 leaves; letter 8x10 inches, 48 leaves. State size wanted. Weight, each, 8 ounces. Price, each.................. **10c**

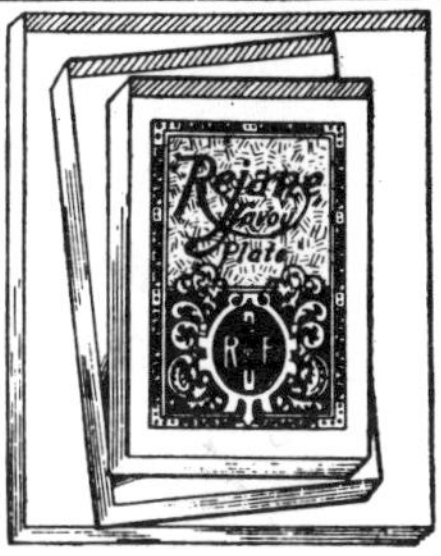

RULED PAGE INK TABLETS, 10c.

BX761 — Ruled Page Ink Tablets. Made of good quality extra smooth finish paper. Pages conveniently ruled. Three sizes; note size, 5x8 inches, 100 leaves; packet size, 5½x9 inches, 70 leaves; letter size, 8x10 inches, 40 leaves. State size wanted. Weight, 11 ounces each. Price, each.......................... **10c**

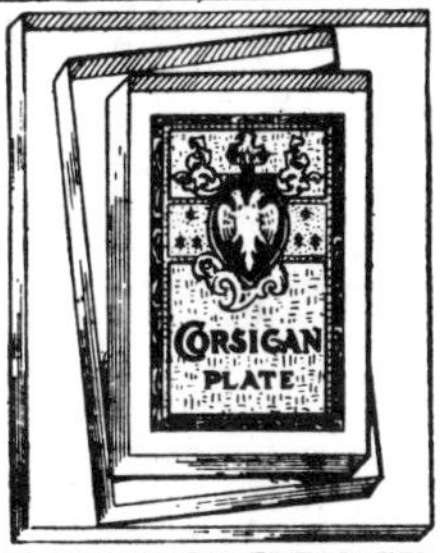

BEST QUALITY RULED TABLETS, 5c.

BV764— Best quality Ruled Tablets. Made of extra smooth finish, ruled paper. Each tablet has good blotter. Note size, 5x8 inches, 90 leaves; packet size, 5½x9 inches, 64 leaves; letter size, 8x10 inches, 35 leaves. State size wanted. Weight, each, 7 ounces. Price, each.................... **5c**

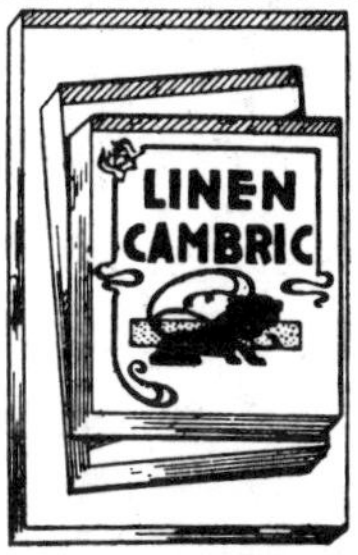

UNRULED PAGE INK TABLETS, 10c.

BX762 — Unruled Page Ink Tablets. Extra heavy quality linen finish unruled paper. Note, 5x8 inches, 60 leaves; two fold, 6¾x10½ inches, 30 leaves; one fold, 5¼x6¾ inches, 60 leaves. State size wanted. Weight. note and one fold size, 6½ ounces; two fold, 7½ ounces. Price, each.. **10c**

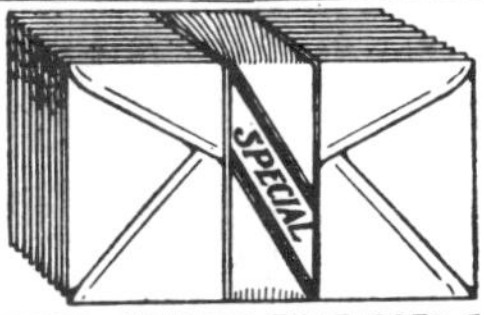

SPECIAL QUALITY ENVELOPES, 5c.

BV767 — Special Quality Envelopes. Made from high grade pure white paper. Three sizes; 3x5½, 3½x6 and 3⅜x6½ inches. 25 in package. State size wanted. Weight, 3 ounces. 2 packages for.................... **5c**

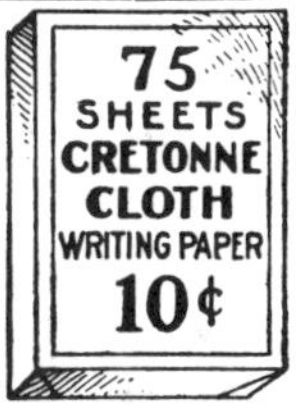

CRETONNE CLOTH WRITING PAPER, 10c.

BX765 — Cretonne Cloth Writing Paper. This paper is wrapped in separate packages containing 75 sheets each, 5¼x6¾ inches. Paper is unruled and has fine smooth writing surface. A convenient size note paper. Weight, 12 ounces. Price, per package.. **10c**

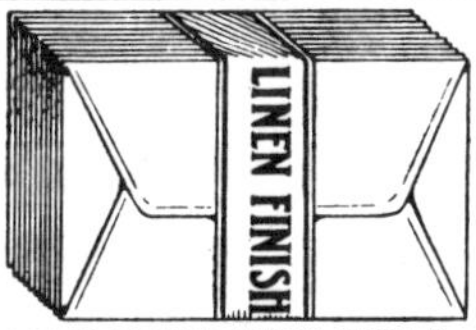

LINEN FINISH ENVELOPES, 5c.

BV768 — Linen Finish Envelopes. Made of best quality paper. New style straight edge flap. One size only. 3½x5½ inches. 25 in a package. Wt., 2½ ounces. Per package........ **5c**

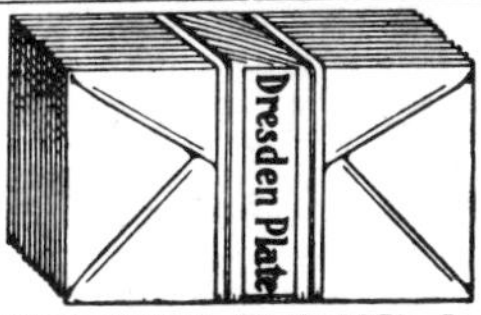

HIGH GRADE ENVELOPES, 5c.

BV766 — High Grade Envelopes. Dresden Plate smooth finish. Three sizes, 3x5½, 3½x6 and 3⅜x6½ inches. 25 in package. Weight, 3½ ounces per package. Give size wanted. Price, per package.......................... **5c**

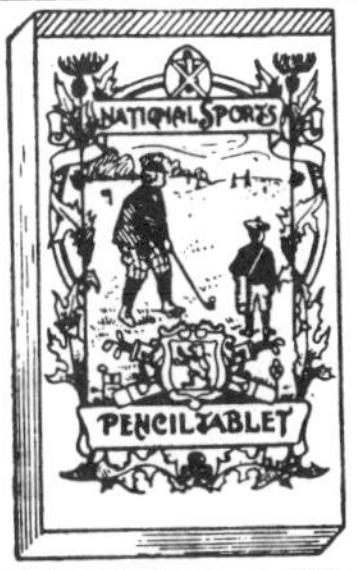

PENCIL TABLETS, 2 FOR 5c.

BB771 — Pencil Tablets. Made of best quality rough finish ruled paper. Good surface for pencil writing. Size of page, 5½x9 inches, 80 leaves. Comes in one size only. Weight, 2 tablets, 11 ounces. Special value, 2 for.......................... **5c**

Note: Always send an extra amount to pay transportation charges.

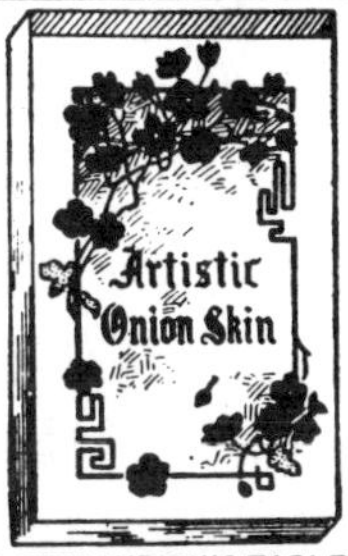

ONION SKIN WRITING TABLETS, 5c.

BV769 — Onion Skin Writing Tablet. Paper is light weight and very thin, almost transparent. Each tablet is furnished with good blotter. and ruled guide. Size, of page 5x8 inches, 60 leaves. Weight, 3 ounces. Price, **5c**

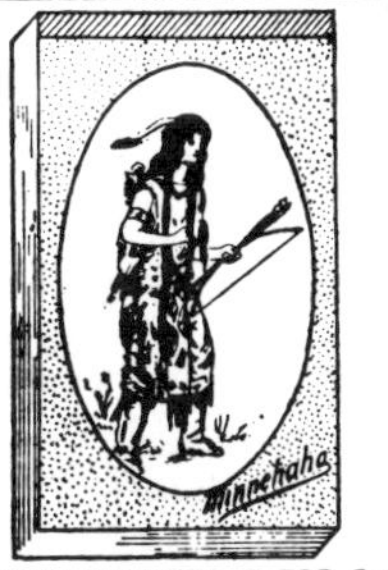

PENCIL TABLETS, 2 FOR 5c.

BB772 — Pencil Tablets. Made of best quality smooth finish ruled paper. Size of page, 5½x9 inches. 80 sheets in tablet. Stiff back and well bound. Weight, of two tablets 11 ounces. Special value, 2 for............ **5c**

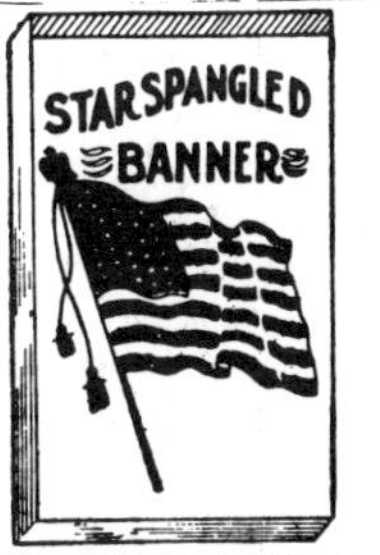

INK TABLETS, 2 FOR 5c.

BB770 — Ink Tablets. Extra quality smooth finish ruled paper, size, 5x8 inches. Comes in this size only. Tablet is supplied with a good blotter. Weight, 7 ounces for two tablets. 50 leaves. Special value, 2 for... **5c**

Be sure to order your hosiery from us. We show a complete line for Men, Women and Children at 10c per pair, on pages 47 to 49.

Writing Tablets and Memo Books 5c and 10c

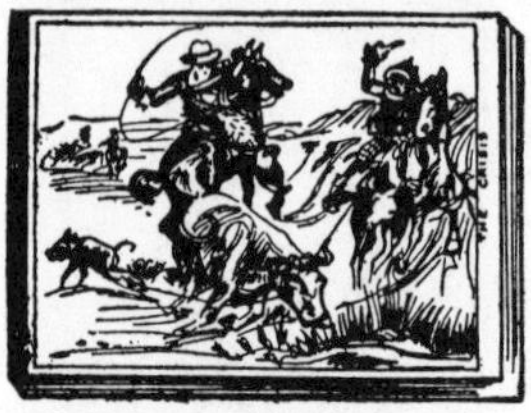

RULED PENCIL TABLET, 5c.

BV773 — Ruled Pencil Tablet. Size of tablet, 8x11 inches. Good quality smooth ruled paper. 100 leaves in each tablet. Weight, 12 ounces. Price........................**5c**

RULED PENCIL TABLET, 5c.

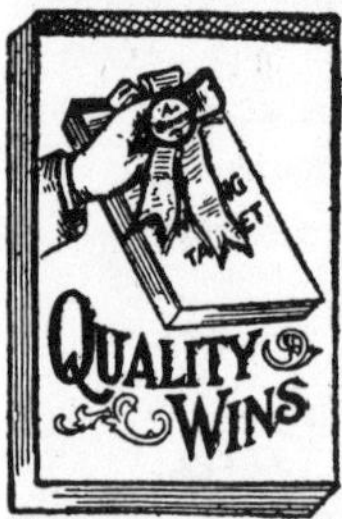

BV775 — Ruled Pencil Tablet, Size of tablet 6 x 9 inches. Contains 150 leaves of smooth pencil paper, nicely ruled. Leaves are perforated at top and tear out clean. Weight, 11 ounces. Price......**5c**

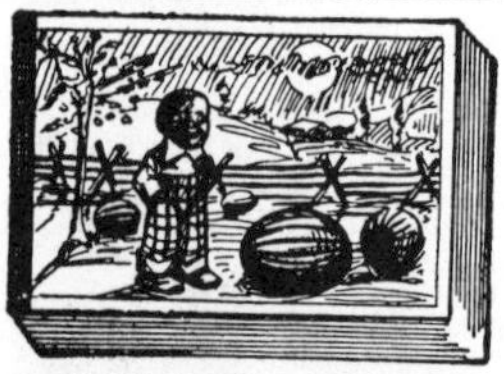

THICK PENCIL TABLET, 5c.

BV776 — Thick Pencil Tablet. 200 pages smooth finished leaves, nicely ruled. Size of tablet, 6 x 9 inches. Heavy board back, cloth bound edge. Fancy illustrated cover. A good quality pencil writing paper. Weight, of tablet, 13 ounces. Price, each....**5c**

LARGE PENCIL TABLET, 5c.

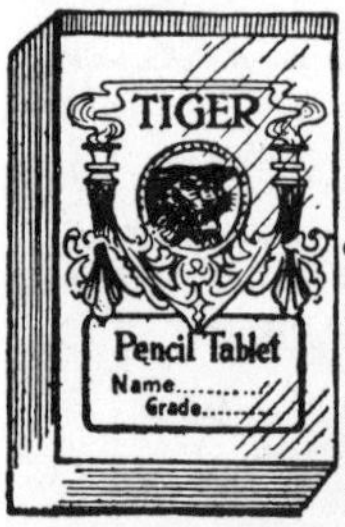

BV777 — Large Pencil Tablet. Contains 200 leaves of rough finished writing paper, evenly ruled. Size, 5½x9 inches. Strong board back. A good quality pencil tablet. Wt., 13 ounces. Price....**5c**

EXTRA THICK PENCIL TABLET, 5c.

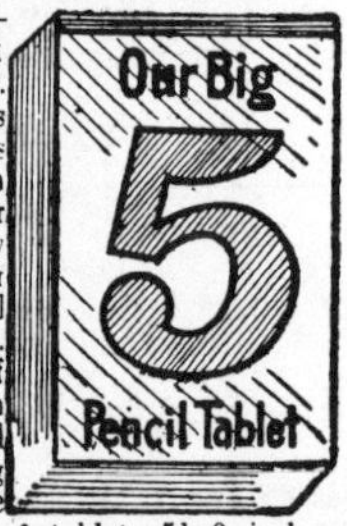

BV778 — Extra Thick Pencil Tablet. Contains 220 leaves of rough finished paper conveniently ruled for pencil writing. Heavy stiff back with cloth bound edge. Strong flexible cover. Size of tablet, 5½x9 inches. Weight, 14 ounces. Price......**5c**

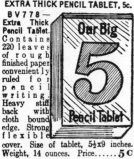

STUDENT'S NOTEBOOK, 5c.

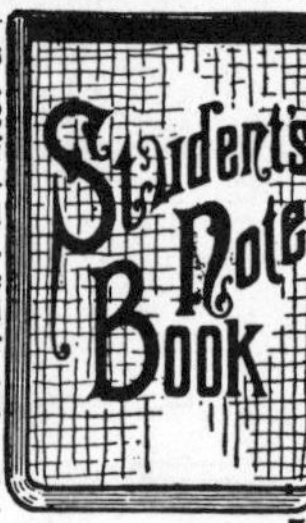

BV779 — Student's Note Book. Contains 72 leaves of smooth finished ruled ink paper. Has flexible front and back cover with cloth bound edge. Size, 6x8½ inches. Wt., 7 ounces. Price........................**5c**

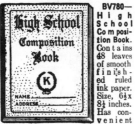

HIGH SCHOOL COMPOSITION BOOK, 5c.

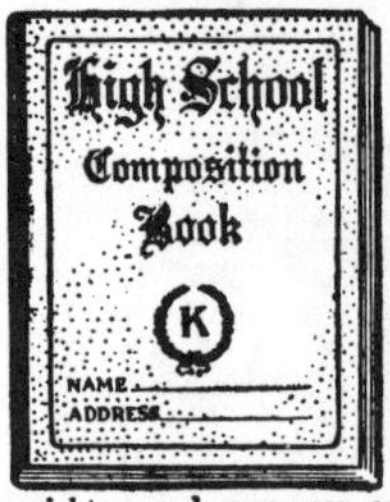

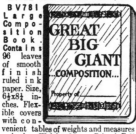

BV780 — High School Composition Book. Contains 48 leaves of smooth finished ruled ink paper. Size, 6½x 8½ inches. Has convenient weights and measures on back. Weight, 6 ounces. Price........**5c**

LARGE COMPOSITION BOOK, 5c.

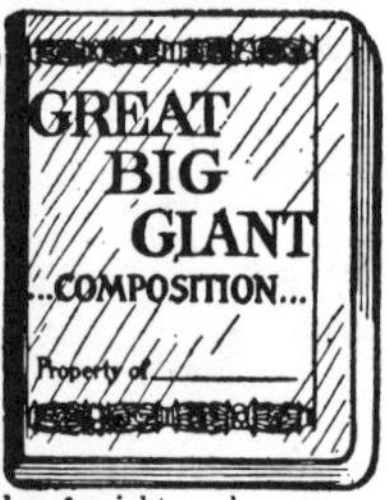

BV781 Large Composition Book. Contains 96 leaves of smooth finish ruled ink paper. Size, 6½x8½ inches. Flexible covers with convenient tables of weights and measures on back. Weight, 9 oz. Price...**5c**

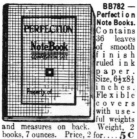

PERFECTION NOTE BOOKS, 2 FOR 5c.

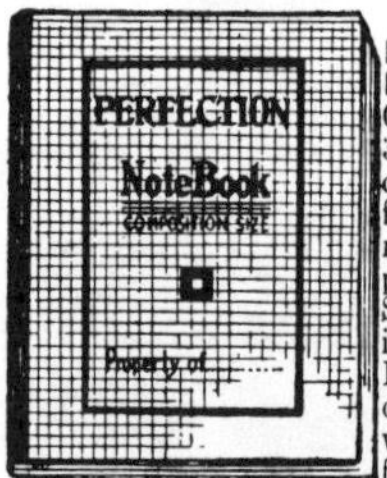

BB782 — Perfection Note Books. Contains 36 leaves of smooth finish ruled ink paper. Size, 6½x8½ inches. Flexible covers with useful weights and measures on back. Weight, 2 books, 7 ounces. Price, 2 for....**5c**

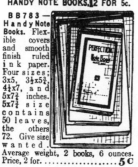

HANDY NOTE BOOKS, 2 FOR 5c.

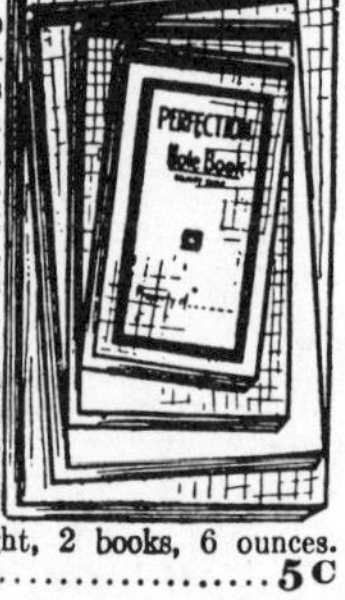

BB783 — Handy Note Books. Flexible covers and smooth finish ruled ink paper. Four sizes; 3x5, 3½x5¾, 4½x7, and 5x7¾ inches. 5x7¾ size contains 50 leaves, the others 72. Give size wanted. Average weight, 2 books, 6 ounces. Price, 2 for....................**5c**

STENOGRAPHER'S NOTE BOOK, 2 FOR 5c.

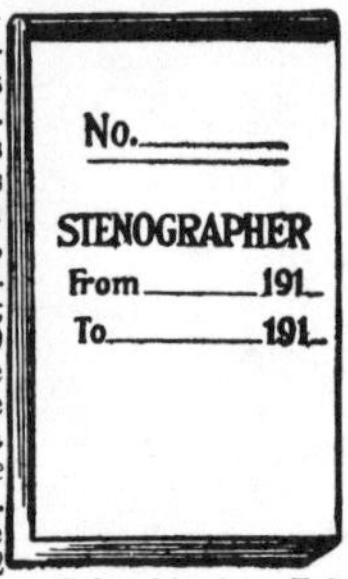

BB784 — Stenographer's Note Book. Contains 80 leaves smooth finish pencil paper, ruled in red. Two sizes; 4¾x9 and 6x9 inches. Have flexible Manila covers. State size wanted. Average weight, 2 books, 9 ounces. Price, 2 books..**5c**

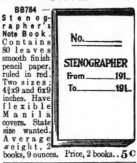

LOOSE LEAF MEMORANDUM BOOKS, 10c.

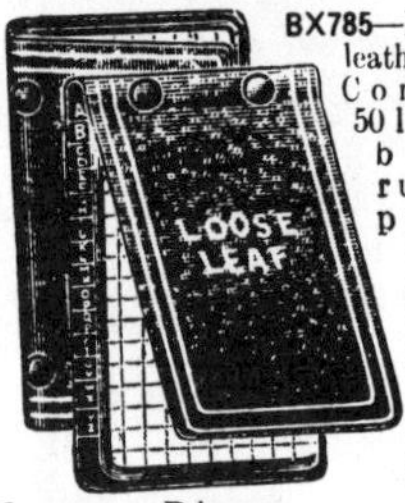

BX785—Imitation leather cover. Contains 50 leaves block ruled ink paper. Red or black. Alphabetical index. Open end. Weight, 2 ounces. Price............**10c**

BX7855 — Same as above, except open side. State color. Weight, 2 ounces. Price..............**10c**

Extra Fillers. 50 to a package. **BB785** O. E. — Fits open end book. **BB7855** O. S.—Fits open side book. State number of filler wanted. 2 Packages, 1 ounce. Price, 2 for..**5c**

INDEX MEMORANDUM BOOK, 10c.

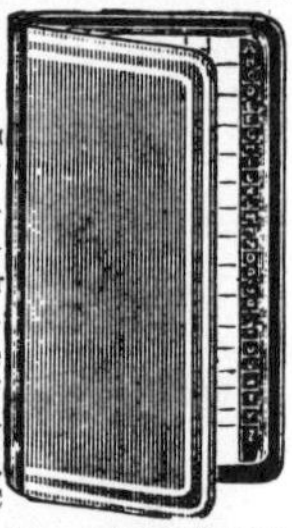

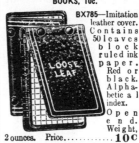

BX786 — Index Memorandum Book. Contains 100 pages of ledger ruled ink paper alphabetically indexed. Opens on side. Size, 3¾x6 inches. Red cover. Weight, 4 ounces. Price......**10c**

POCKET MEMORANDUM BOOK, 10c.

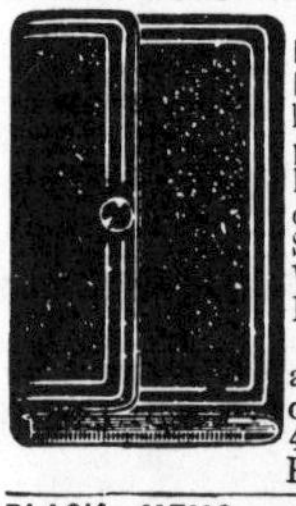

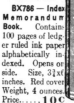

BX787 — Pocket Memorandum Book. 100 pages ledger ruled ink paper. Pencil loop, pocket and clasp. Open side. Size, 4x6 inches. Weight, 4 ounces. Price........**10c**

BX7877 — Same as above, but opens on end. Wt., 4 ounces. Price.....**10c**

BLACK MEMORANDUM BOOK, 10c.

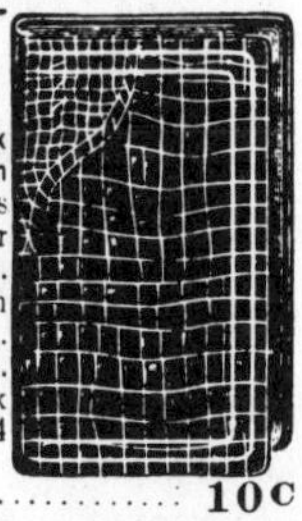

BX788 — Black Memorandum Book. Contains 100 pages of ledger ruled ink paper. Has imitation alligator cover. Size, 4x6¼ inches. Comes in black only. Weight, 4 ounces. Price..........................**10c**

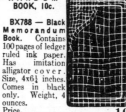

EXTRA THICK MEMORANDUM BOOK, 10c.

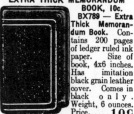

BX789 — Extra Thick Memorandum Book. Contains 200 pages of ledger ruled ink paper. Size of book, 4x6 inches. Has imitation black grain leather cover. Comes in black only. Weight, 6 ounces. Price......**10c**

POCKET MEMORANDUM BOOK, 5c.

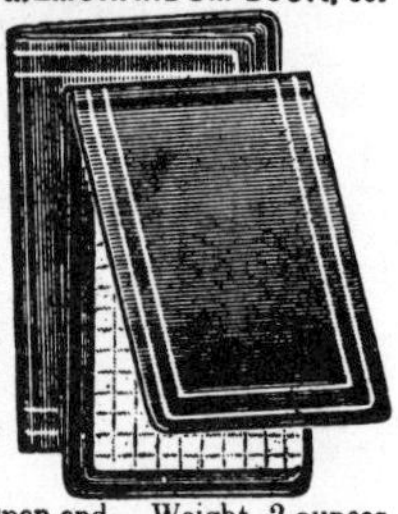

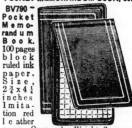

BV790 — Pocket Memorandum Book. 100 pages block ruled ink paper. Size, 2¾x4¼ inches Imitation red leather cover. Open end. Weight, 2 ounces. Price..........................**5c**

BV7900 —Same as above, open side. Weight, 2 ounces. Price........**5c**

VEST POCKET MEMORANDUM BOOK, 5c.

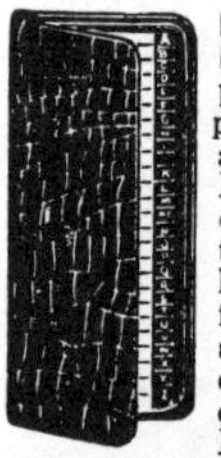

BV791 — Vest Pocket Memorandum Book. Contains 96 pages ledger ruled ink paper. Has convenient alphabetical index. Has black flexible cover stamped in imitation alligator leather. Convenient for farmers, builders, storekeepers and others. Comes in black only. Weight, 2 ounces Price...........**5c**

POCKET MEMORANDUM BOOK, 5c.

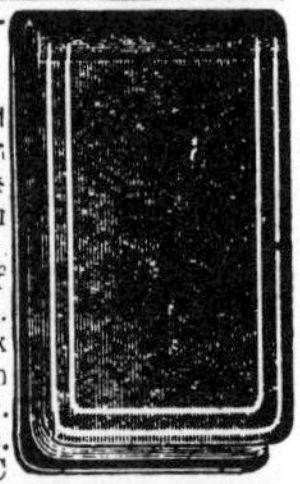

BV792—Pocket Memorandum Book. Contains 116 pages of ledger ruled ink paper Size of book, 3¾x6 inches. Open end. Has flexible black cover, stamped in imitation leather. Weight, 3 ounces. Price.......**5c**

VEST POCKET MEMORANDUM BOOKS, 4 FOR 5c.

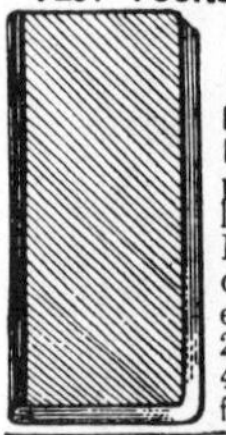

B793 — Vest Pocket Memorandum Books. Contains 96 pages of good quality ledger ruled ink paper. Have flexible paper covers and cloth bound edges. Size of book, 2½x5¼ inches. Weight, 4 books, 7 ounces. 4 for............**5c**

POCKET MEMORANDUM BOOKS, 2 FOR 5c.

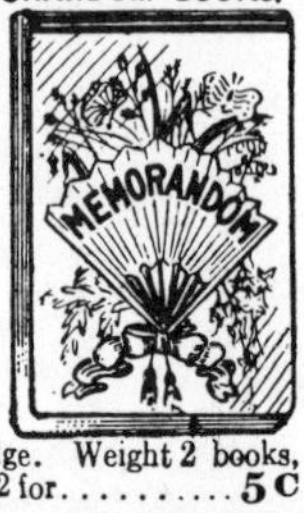

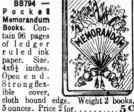

BB794 — Pocket Memorandum Books. Contain 96 pages of ledger ruled ink paper. Size, 4x6¼ inches. Open end. Strong flexible cover, cloth bound edge. Weight 2 books, 5 ounces. Price 2 for.........**5c**

Stationery and Supplies, 5 and 10c

OPEN SIDE MEMORANDUM BOOKS, 2 FOR 5c

BB795 — Open Side Memorandum Books. Contains 120 pages of good quality ledger ruled ink paper. Have strong, flexible covers. Size, 3½x6½ inches. Ruled in red and blue lines. Weight 2 books 6 ounces. Price, 2 for..**5C**

FLEXIBLE MEMORANDUM BOOK, 2 FOR 5c.

BB796 — Flexible Memorandum Book. This book has flexible linen cover, contains 48 leaves, ledger ruled ink paper. Size of book 3½x6 in. Weight, each 2 ounces. 2 books for..........**5C**

52 PAGE MONTHLY TIME BOOKS, 10c.

BX797 — 52 Page Monthly Time Book; Well bound. Size of book 4½x7 in. Ruled for each day of month or week. State whether weekly or monthly is wanted. Weight 5 ounces. Each....**10C**

CLOTH BOUND ORDER BOOKS, 10c.

BX798 — Cloth Bound Order Books. These books are cloth bound with stiff covers. Loop for pencil. 150 pages, ledger ruled ink paper. Size 4½x7 in. Weight 10 ounces. Each....**10C**

150 PAGE ORDER BOOKS, 10c.

BX799 — 150 Page Order Books. Cloth binding and stiff covers. Size of book 4½x7 in. 150 leaves, ledger ruled ink paper. Weight 10 ounces. Each....**10C**

FLEXIBLE COVER COUNTER BOOKS 5c.

BV800 — Flexible Cover Counter Books. Contain 90 leaves of Journal ruled pencil paper. Good tough cover. Size of book 5½x12 in. Can be used for entering orders, listing jobs, keeping accounts, etc. Weight 9 ounces. Each........**5C**

100 PAGE DAY BOOKS, EACH 10c.

BX801 — 1 0 0 Page Day Book. Size of book 6x14¾ in. Cloth bound, stiff cover. 100 pages of ruled ink paper. Very strong and substantially bound book. Weight 12 ounces. Each......**10C**

HIGH GRADE ACCOUNTING BOOKS, 10c.

BX802—High Grade Accounting Books. Choice of cash, Journal, Double Entry ledger; S. E. ledger, record book or day book. Cloth bound stiff covers. 100 pages ruled ink paper. State kind wanted. Weight 13 ozs. Each...**10C**

HANDY PERFORATED RECEIPT BOOKS, 2 FOR 5c.

BB803— Black stiff cover, perforated pages with convenient record stubs 2½x6½ inches. 50 receipts. Weight 3 ounces. 2 for..**5C**

BV8033— Same as above. 3x9 inches. Weight 3 ounces. Each.......**5C**

BX8034— Same as above. 3½x10½ inches. 100 receipts. Weight 4 ounces. Each......**10C**

ADJUSTABLE RUBBER DATE STAMP, 10c.

BX804—Adjustable Rubber Date Stamp. Dating stamp shows year, month and day, good until 1920. Good quality rubber. Well made. Date, month, years, and special lettering are on separate strips. Weight 1 ounce. Each......................**10C**

RUBBER TYPE PRINTING OUTFIT, 5c.

BV805—Rubber Type Printing Outfit. Handy for printing cards, stamping linen, marking books, etc. Clear rubber type, two row wood holder, tweezers and pad. An acceptable present to give a boy. Weight 2 ounces. Each....................**5C**

RUBBER TYPE PRINTING OUTFIT, 10c.

BX806—Rubber Type Printing Outfit. Contains 180 letters and figures, self-inking stamp pad, tweezers, three row wood holder. One of the best outfits for the boy. Weight 4 ounces. Each.....**10C**

AUTOMATIC RUBBER STAMP PRINTER, 10c.

BX807 — Automatic Rubber Stamp Printer. Contains good assortment of rubber letters, tweezers, and automatic printing outfit with self-inking pad. Just the thing for quick printing in quantities. Weight 6 ounces. Price.....................**10C**

EXTRA LARGE LETTERING OUTFIT, 10c.

BX808—Extra Large Lettering Outfit. Each letter mounted separately on polished wood base. Complete alphabet and figures, self-inking pad. Handy for printing show cards, price lists, etc. Weight 6 ounces. Price......**10C**

SELF-INKING STAMP PAD, 10c.

BX809—Self-inking Stamp Pad Size 2½x 4 inches. Wood base, with metal cover. Three colors: black, red or purple. State color wanted. Weight 4 ounces. Each........**10C**

CARTER'S WRITING INK, PER BOTTLE, 5c.

BV810 — Carter's Celebrated Writing ink. Square shaped 2 oz. bottle. Colors: red, koal black and blue black. State color wanted. Weight 6 ounces. Per bottle...................**5C**

DOOLEY'S WATERPROOF CEMENT, 10c.

BX8100—Dooley's Waterproof Cement. For mending china, cut glass, wood, leather, etc. Self sealing tubes. Best quality cement. Weight 1 ounce. Per package..................**10C**

CARTER'S LIBRARY PASTE PER BOTTLE, 5c.

BV811—Carter's Library Paste. White photo or library paste. Metal capped glass bottle. Keeps without drying. Weight 5 ounces. Per bottle.....**5C**

CARTER'S MUCILAGE PER BOTTLE, 5c.

BV812—Carter's High Quality Mucilage. Convenient round bottle. Full 2 ounces. A very high grade adhesive mucilage. Weight 6 ounces. Per bottle...**5C**

McCORMICK'S IRON GLUE 5c AND 10c.

BV813 — McCormick's Iron Glue. A liquid glue which will repair practically anything. Give size wanted. Weight 4 ounces. Each.....**5C**

BX8133—Weight 7 ounces. Each........**10C**

LePAGE'S LIQUID GLUE PER BOTTLE, 10c.

BX814—LePage's Liquid Glue. Put up in 1 oz. glass bottle with metal screw cap. Always ready for use. Will repair china, leather, glass, bric-a-brac, wood, etc. Weight 4 ounces. Per bottle...................**10C**

DENNISON'S LIQUID GLUE, PER TUBE, 10c.

BX815—Dennison's Liquid Glue in convenient lead tube. Useful on desk, at home or in workshop. No waste. Weight 2 ounces. Per tube.....**10C**

DENNISON'S ART PASTE, 5c & 10c.

BV816—Dennison's Art or Library Paste in lead tubes, with patent stopper. Never dries up. 1 oz. size. Weight 2 ounces....................**5C**

BX8166—2 oz. size, weight 3 oz. **10C**

DENNISON'S MUCILAGE PER TUBE, 10c.

BX817—Dennison's Mucilage. Full 2 oz. tube with needle stopper. A pure transparent mucilage. Self sealing tube. Weight 3 ounces. Each..**10C**

We Guarantee to Please You.

We guarantee the goods shown in this Katalog to be exactly as represented, and if for any reason you are not satisfied with your purchase you can return same and we will cheerfully ship you other goods or return your money.

Bargains in Pencils, Pens, Etc., 5 and 10c

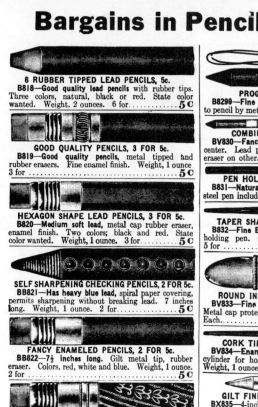

6 RUBBER TIPPED LEAD PENCILS, 5c.
B818—Good quality lead pencils with rubber tips. Three colors, natural, black or red. State color wanted. Weight, 2 ounces. 6 for............**5C**

GOOD QUALITY PENCILS, 3 FOR 5c.
B819—Good quality pencils, metal tipped and rubber erasers. Fine enamel finish. Weight, 1 ounce. 3 for **5C**

HEXAGON SHAPE LEAD PENCILS, 3 FOR 5c.
B820—Medium soft lead, metal cap rubber eraser, enamel finish. Two colors; black and red. State color wanted. Weight, 1 ounce. 3 for.......**5C**

SELF SHARPENING CHECKING PENCILS, 2 FOR 5c.
BB821—Has heavy blue lead, spiral paper covering, permits sharpening without breaking lead. 7 inches long. Weight, 1 ounce. 2 for...............**5C**

FANCY ENAMELED PENCILS, 2 FOR 5c.
BB822—7½ inches long. Gilt metal tip, rubber eraser. Colors, red, white and blue. Weight, 1 ounce. 2 for.........................**5C**

FANCY EMBOSSED LEAD PENCILS 2 FOR 5c.
BB823—Metal cap and rubber eraser. Good quality. No. 2 lead. Embossed design. Weight, 1 ounce. 2 for...............................**5C**

HEXAGON SHAPE PENCILS, 2 FOR 5c.
BB824—High enamel finish, metal cap and rubber eraser. Good quality No. 2 lead. Weight, 1 ounce. 2 for **5C**

HIGH GRADE LEAD PENCILS, EACH, 5c.
BV825—7½ inches long. Gilt metal cap, good quality red rubber eraser. A high grade pencil. Weight, 1 ounce. Each **5C**

HIGH GRADE PENCILS, EACH, 5c.
BV826—No. 2 medium soft lead. Gilt metal cap, white rubber eraser. Extra enamel finish. Weight, 1 ounce. Each **5C**

INDELIBLE LEAD PENCILS, EACH, 5c.
BV827—High grade imported indelible lead. Hard enamel tip. Perfect finish. Round shape. Weight, 1 ounce. Each **5C**

VERI-BLACK CARBON PENCILS, EACH, 5c.
BV828—Large soft black lead. 7 inches long. High enamel finish. Round shape. Weight, 1 ounce. Each...............................**5C**

EXTRA QUALITY CARPENTER'S PENCIL, 5c.
BV829—2x7½ inches. Extra heavy wide flat lead, high enamel finish. Weight, 1 ounce. Each....**5C**

PROGRAM PENCILS, 5 FOR 5c.
B8299—Fine enamel finish. 12-inch cord, attached to pencil by metal tip. Weight, 2 ounces. 5 for...**5C**

COMBINATION PEN AND PENCIL, 5c.
BV830—Fancy color enamel finish. Metal tube center. Lead pencil one end, pen and white rubber eraser on other. Weight, 1 ounce. Each......**5C**

PEN HOLDERS AND PENS, 5 FOR 5c.
B831—Natural Finish Wood with brass metal tip, steel pen included. Weight, 1 ounce. 5 for....**5C**

TAPER SHAPED PENHOLDERS, 5 FOR 5c.
B832—Fine Enamel Finish. Spring metal tube for holding pen. 6½ inches long. Weight, 1 ounce. 5 for..............................**5C**

ROUND INDELIBLE COPYING PENCIL, 5c.
BV833—Fine quality indelible or copying pencil. Metal cap protector, enamel finish. Weight, 1 ounce. Each...............................**5C**

CORK TIP PENHOLDER, EACH, 5c.
BV834—Enamel finish cork tip penholder. Metal cylinder for holding pen. Fine steel pen included. Weight, 1 ounce. Each **5C**

GILT PROPELLER PENCIL, 10c.
BX835—4-inch propeller pencil. Gilt finish. Has tube with three extra leads. Weight, 1 ounce. Price..............................**10C**

ALUMINUM FINISH PROPELLER PENCIL, 10c.
BX836—Fine aluminum, chased finish. Very convenient. Three extra leads. Weight, 1 ounce. Price..............................**10C**

BROWN ENAMEL PROPELLER PENCIL, 10c.
BX837—4 inches long. Very convenient for the vest pocket. Three extra leads. Weight, 1 ounce. Price..............................**10C**

GOOD QUALITY FOUNTAIN PEN, 10c.
BX838—Hard rubber case, chased finish. Perfect gold plated pen point. Two styles, plain, and gold band. State kind wanted. Weight, 1 ounce. Each..............................**10C**

ARTISTS' BRUSHES, 3 FOR 5c.
B839—7 inches long. Fine black handle, good quality camel's hair. Weight, 1 ounce. 3 for....**5C**

HEAVY BLACK MARKING CRAYONS, 3 FOR 5c.
B840—5 inches long. ⅜-inch diameter. Black only. Weight, 2 ounces. 3 for......................**5C**

METAL PENCIL SHARPENER, EACH, 5c.
BV841—Metal Pencil Sharpener, has steel blade to sharpen pencils to needle point. Weight, 1 ounce. Each..........**5C**

PEN OR PENCIL CLIP, EACH, 5c.
BV842—Pen or Pencil Clip. Has ball tip. Will fit any pen or pencil. Prevents pencil falling from pocket. Weight, 1 ounce. Each..........**5C**

SPENCERIAN STEEL PENS, 6 FOR 5c.
B843—Spencerian Steel Pens. Best quality, perfect writing pens. Come in four styles; Falcon, (B1), School (B2), Bank (B3), and Stub (B4). State style wanted when ordering. Indicate style by number. Weight, 6 pens, 1 ounce. Price, 6 for.........**5C**

HIGH GRADE STEEL PENS, 12 FOR 5c.
B844—High Grade Steel Pens. Made of fine quality steel with perfect writing points. Pens come in four styles; Falcon (B5), School (B6), Bank (B7), and Stub (B8). State style wanted when ordering. Indicate style by number. Weight, 12 pens, 1 ounce. 12 for.**5C**

WHITE RUBBER PENCIL ERASERS, 2 FOR 5c.
BB845—Made of high grade rubber. 1½ inches long, beveled end. Weight 1 ounce. 2 for...**5C**

RED RUBBER PENCIL ERASERS, 5 FOR 5c.
B846—Made of good quality red rubber. 2½ inches long. Weight, 1 ounce. 5 for.................**5C**

FINEST GRADE RED RUBBER ERASER, 5c.
BV847—Made of best grade ruby red rubber. Has beveled ends. 2½ inches long. Weight, 1 ounce. Each..............................**5C**

COMBINATION INK AND PENCIL ERASER, 5c.
BV848—⅞x2½ inches. One-half ink and one-half pencil eraser. Beveled ends. Weight, 1 ounce. Each..............................**5C**

SOFT RUBBER ERASERS, 2 FOR 5c.
BB849—Extra fine soft red rubber. 1-inch wide, 1½ inches long. Weight, 1 ounce. 2 for....................**5C**

CIRCULAR TYPEWRITER ERASERS, 5c.
BV850—Good quality rubber, beveled edge. Metal center shield. Weight, 1 ounce. Each **5C**

The pens, pencils, erasers and supplies listed on this page are extra values. When ordering, do not fail to include writing tablets, envelopes, memorandum books, etc., shown on Pages 78 to 81. Double the buying power of your nickels and dimes. Exceptional values—nothing over 10c.

A Variety of Bargains, Nothing Over 10c

BULLDOG PAPER CLIPS, 3 FOR 5c.

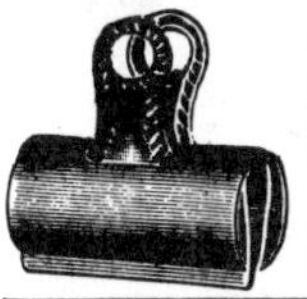

B851 — Bulldog Paper Clips. Made of heavy blued steel spring. Convenient for holding papers, Two sizes. State size wanted. Small size, 1¼ inches long. Weight, 1 ounce. 3 for **5c**

BB8511—Large size, 1¾ inches long. Weight, 1 ounce. Price, 2 for........................**5c**

PEN AND PENCIL RACKS, EACH, 10c.

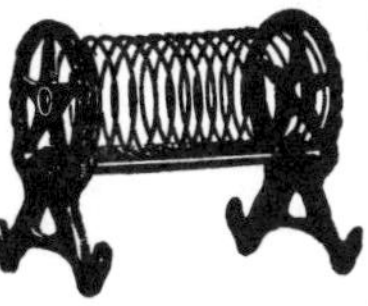

BX852—Pen and Pencil Racks. Made with copper spiral spring wire. Cast ends. 3½ inches long by 3 inches high. Convenient for the desk. Keeps pens and pencils handy. Weight, 5 ounces. Each..**10c**

WALL HANGER PAPER FILE, EACH, 5c.

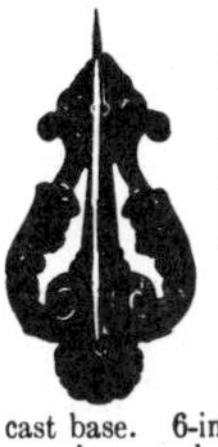

BV853 — Wall Hanger Paper File. Harp shape cast back, nicely japanned. Steel wire paper holder attached. A durable file. Weight, 6 ounces. Each...**5c**

SPINDLE PAPER FILES, EACH, 5c.

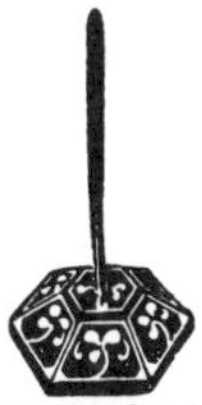

BV854 — Spindle Paper Files. Heavy cast base. 6-inch sharp, steel needle. Can be placed anywhere on desk. Weight, 4 ounces. Each....**5c**

BRASS HEAD THUMB TACKS, PER DOZEN, 5c.

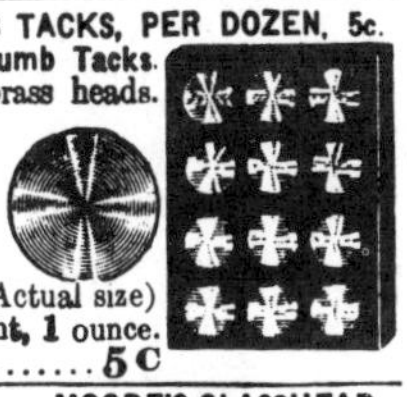

B855—Brass Head Thumb Tacks. Sharp points, ⅜-inch brass heads. 12 tacks on a block. Just right for the drafting board, for hanging pennants, etc., on walls without marring the plaster, and (Actual size) many other uses. Weight, 1 ounce. Per dozen....................**5c**

MOORE'S GLASSHEAD PUSH PINS, 10c.

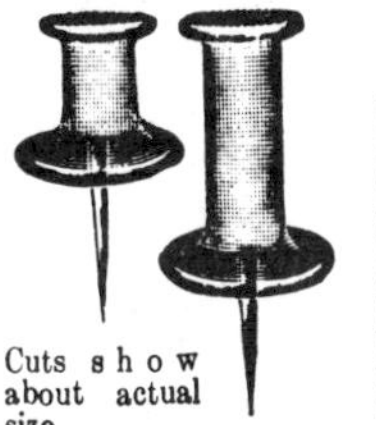

Cuts show about actual size

BX856 — Moore's Glass-head Push Pins. Needle points of tempered steel. Convenient for hanging pictures, etc., on wall without marring. Can be inserted and taken from walls many times without injury. Two sizes; ⅜-inch and ¾ inch long. State size wanted. Weight, 1 ounce. 6 for.....**10c**

GEM PAPER CLIPS, PER BOX, 5c.

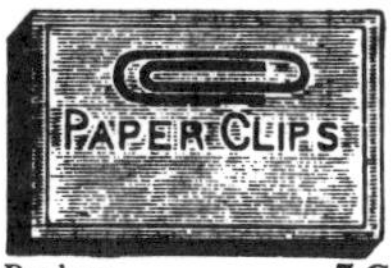
PAPER CLIPS

BV857 — Gem Paper Clips. Made of polished spring wire, 1¼ inches long. Very convenient for holding papers, bills, correspondence, etc. together. 100 clips in box. Weight, 3 ounces. Per box..............**5c**

PASSEPARTOUT BINDING, PER ROLL, 10c.

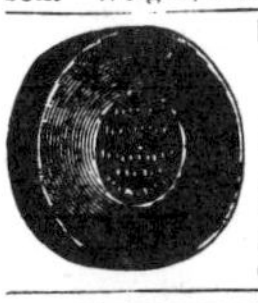

BX859 — Passepartout Binding. ⅞-inch wide. 12 yards in roll. Has pebbled finish. Two colors: red or black. State color wanted. Has a great variety of uses. Weight, 1 ounce. Per roll..........**10c**

WHITE BRISTOL VISITING CARDS, 10c.

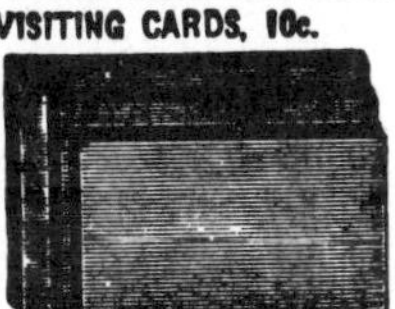

BV860—White Bristol Visiting Cards. Made of high grade white bristol. 25 in a package. Three sizes; gentlemen's, business, and Mrs. State size wanted. Weight, 1 ounce. Per package.......**5c**

LEATHER SUIT CASE TAGS, EACH, 10c.

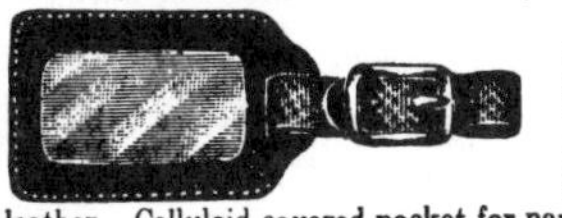

BX861 — Leather Suit Case Tags. Good quality black pebbled leather. Celluloid covered pocket for name card, strap and buckle for attaching to grip. Weight, 1 ounce. Each....................................**10c**

DENNISON'S BAGGAGE TAGS, PACKAGE, 10c.

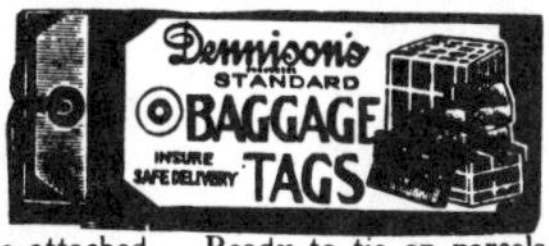
Dennison's
STANDARD
BAGGAGE
INSURE SAFE DELIVERY
TAGS

BX862 — Dennison's Baggage Tags. Made of tough Manila tag board with long flax twine attached. Ready to tie on parcels. 18 tags in package. Weight, 3 ounces. Per package.........................**10c**

HIGH GRADE SEA ISLAND TWINE, 5c.

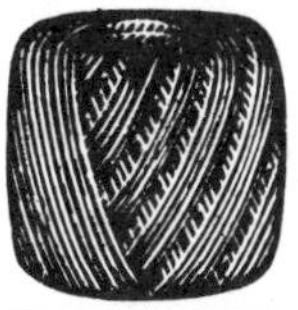

BV863 — High Grade Sea Island Twine. Made of good quality Sea Island Cotton. Three colors; red, white and green. A strong twine for every day use. State color wanted. Weight, 2 ounces. Per ball. **5c**

WHITE BONE DICE, 3 FOR 5c.

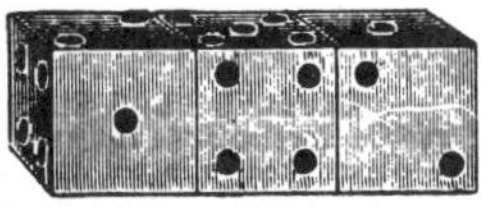

B864 — White Bone Dice. Made of good quality bone. 1½-inch cubes, black enameled spots. Perfectly cut and will roll evenly. Weight, 1 ounce. 3 for **5c**

35 BEST QUALITY COMPOSITION POKER CHIPS FOR 10c.

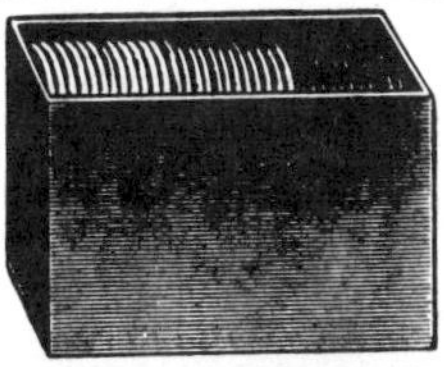

BX865—Composition Poker Chips. 1½-inch diameter. 20 white, 10 red, and 5 blue chips in a box. Weight, 10 ounces. Per box......**10c**

TOY PLAYING CARDS, PER PACKAGE, 10c.

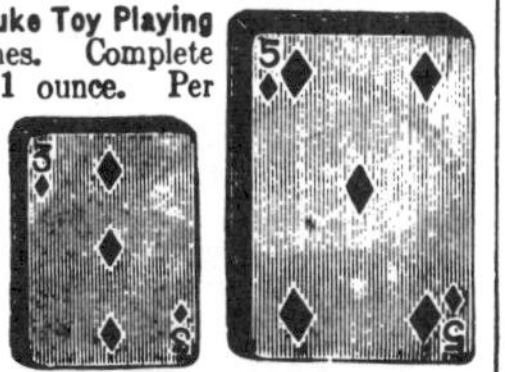

BX866—Little Duke Toy Playing Cards. 1¼x1¾ inches. Complete deck. Weight, 1 ounce. Per package...**10c**

BX867 — Cadet Size Playing Cards. 1¾x2½ inches. Complete deck of 52 cards. Weight, 2 ounces. Per package...**10c**

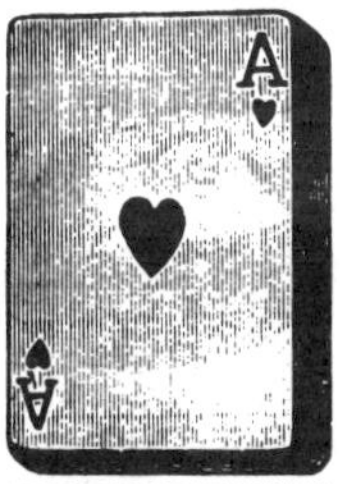

STEAMBOAT PLAYING CARDS, REGULAR SIZE, 10c

BX868 — High Grade Steamboat Playing Cards. Regular size deck of 52 cards. Weight, 3 ounces. Per package.....**10c**

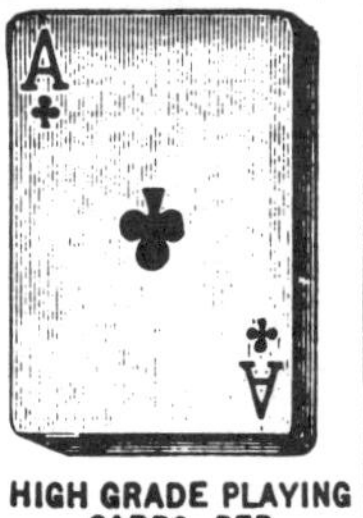

HIGH GRADE PLAYING CARDS, PER PACKAGE, 10c

BX869 — High Grade Playing Cards. Made of glazed finish stock. Pinochle and regular cards. State kind wanted. Wt., 3 ounces. Per package..............**10c**

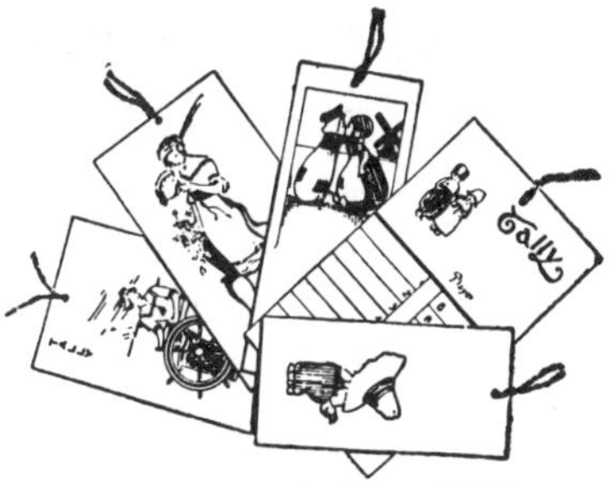

ARTISTIC TALLY CARDS, 6 FOR 5c.

B870—Artistic Tally Cards. Black and white figures, Dutch Kids, Fadeaway, Sunbonnet Series, and Progressive Euchre. An artistic tally card of a very high quality. State kind wanted. Weight 1 ounce. 6 for **5c**

HIGH GRADE PLACE CARDS, 6 FOR 5c.

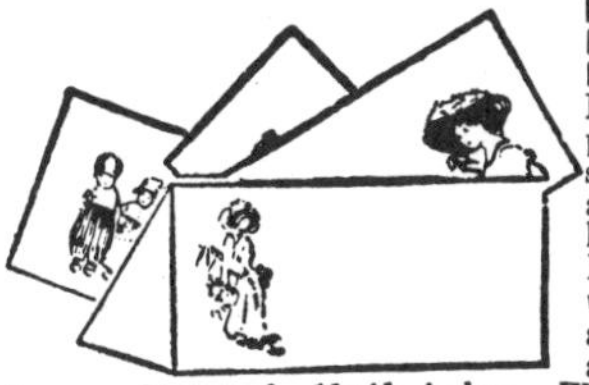

B871 — High Grade Place Cards. Have easel points. Four styles; black and white heads, Dutch figures, scenes and black and white figures. Size card, 1½x4½ inches. Weight of 6, 1 ounce. 6 for.............................**5c**

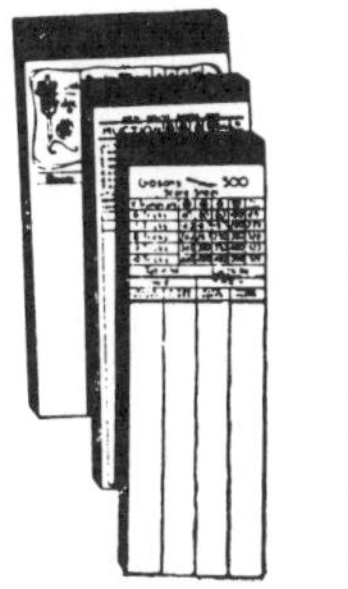

BOUND SCORE PADS, EACH, 10c.

BX872 — Bound Score Pads. Pads contain 38 sheets, properly ruled, with printed regulations for games. Three kinds; Bridge Whist, Auction Bridge, Five Hundred. State kind wanted. Wt., 3 ounces. Per pad **10c**

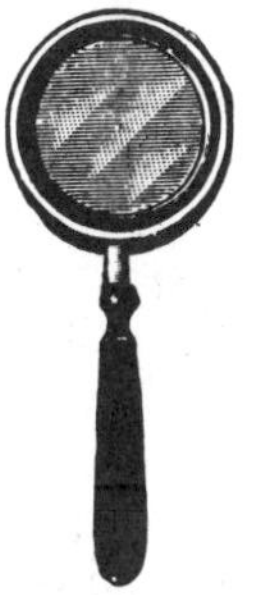

EXTRA QUALITY READING GLASS SPECIAL AT 10c.

BX873 — Extra quality Reading Glass. Made of extra heavy concave glass, 2¼ inches in diameter. Nicely finished wood handle. A convenient article. Weight, 2 ounces. Each..**10c**

BEST QUALITY SCHOOL SLATES, 10c.

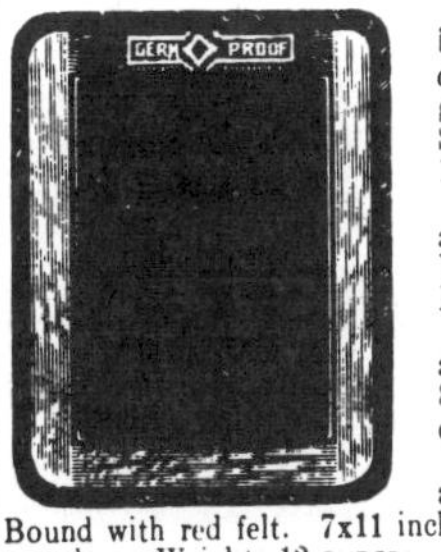
GERM PROOF

BX875 — Best Quality School Slates. Made of select smooth Bangor slate, felt bound. Size, 7x11 inches. Wt., 12 ounces. Each **10c**

BV8755 — Same as above, but 5x7 inches. Weight, 8 ounces. Each............**5c**

BV8756 — Same as above, but plain edge. 8x11 inches. Weight, 13 ounces. Each..**5c**

BZ8757 — Same as above, but double. Bound with red felt. 7x11 inches. Must be ordered together. Weight, 12 ounces. Price for 2....**20c**

BX8758—Double Slate. 5x7 inches. Weight, 8 ounces. Price **10c**

Read our Special Prepay Offer on page 3. We pay the freight on all orders amounting to $10 or more to the states named in the prepay list. Get your friends and neighbors to order with you and save transportation charges.

School Supplies, Etc., Nothing Over 10c

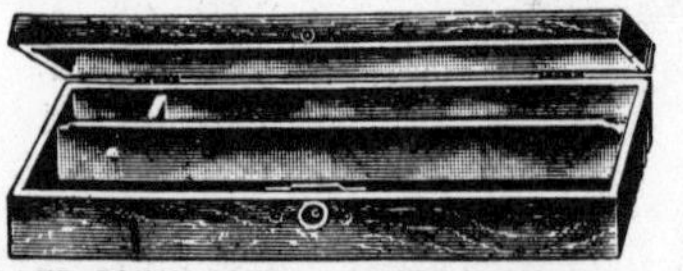

FILLED FANCY SCHOOL BOXES EACH, 10c.
BX876—Filled Fancy School Boxes. Size, $2\frac{1}{2}$x$8\frac{3}{4}$ inches. Nicely finished. Partitioned box contains pencil, penholder and ruler. Each box has lock and key. Weight, 6 ounces. Price.............. **10c**

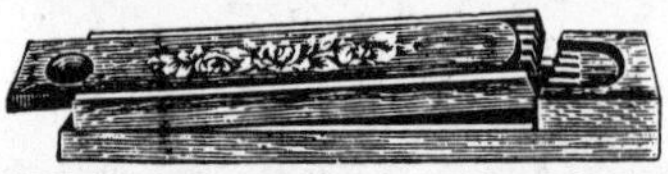

GOOD QUALITY IMPORTED PENCIL BOXES, 10c
BX877—Good Quality Imported Pencil Boxes. Made of strong walnut wood. Box has seven compartments and slide cover. Size, 2x$9\frac{1}{2}$ inches. Highly finished. Weight, 6 ounces. Price......... **10c**

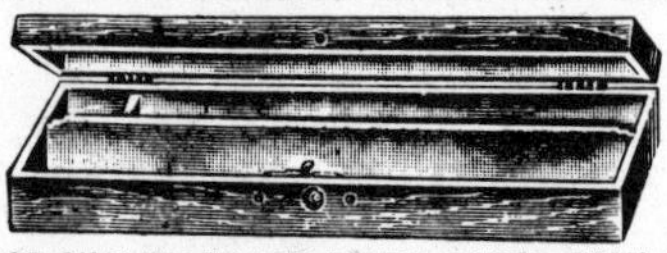

GOOD QUALITY FILLED PENCIL BOXES, EACH, 5c.
BV878 — Good Quality Filled Pencil Boxes. Made of good strong wood, nicely finished in cherry color. Size, $2\frac{1}{2}$x8 inches. Contains pencil, penholder and ruler. Locks with key. Weight, 5 ounces. Price. **5c**

WOOD COVERED SLATE PENCILS, 6 FOR 5c.
B879—Wood Covered Slate Pencils. Best quality smooth slate, 7 inches long. Finished in bright colored enamel. Good quality pencil. Weight, six, 3 ounces 6 for.. **5c**

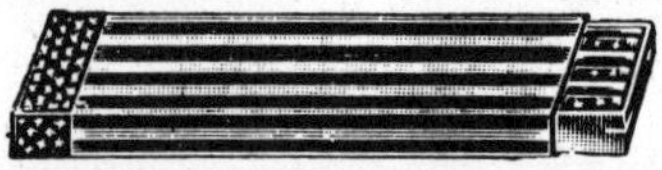

PAPER COVERED SLATE PENCILS, 24 FOR 5c.
BB880—Paper Covered Slate Pencils. Good quality smooth slate, $5\frac{1}{2}$ inches long. Paper covered. 12 in a box. Weight, two boxes, 6 ounces. Price, 2 bxs.. **5c**

ASSORTED COLORED WAX SCHOOL CRAYONS, 5c.

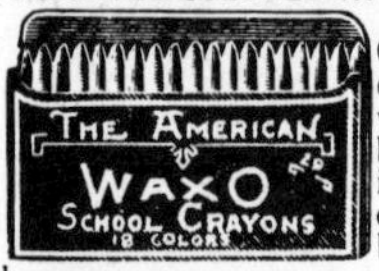

BB881 — Assorted Colored Wax School Crayons. 18 assorted colors, wax finish, crayons in a box. Each crayon is 2 inches long, and has tapered point. Weight, two boxes, 2 ounces. Price, 2 boxes....................... **5c**

CRAYONART ASSORTED WAX FINISHED SCHOOL CRAYONS, PER BOX, 5c.

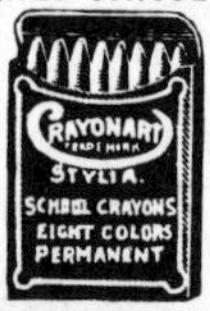

BV882 — Crayonart Assorted Wax Finished School Crayons. Eight assorted wax finished crayons in a box. $3\frac{1}{2}$ inches long. Good clear colors. Crayon bound with paper to prevent soiling the hands. Weight, per box, 2 ounces. Price.............................. **5c**

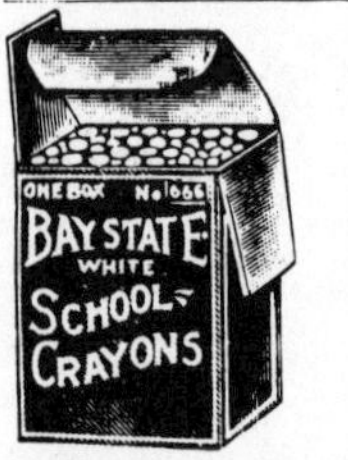

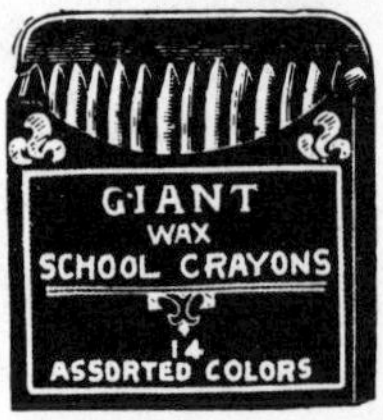

PLAIN WHITE SCHOOL CRAYONS, PER BOX, 5c.
BV886 — Plain White School Crayons. Each crayon is $3\frac{1}{4}$ inches long. 36 crayons to a box. Made of good white chalk and contains no grit. Smooth writing surface. Weight, per box, 7 ounces. Price.............. **5c**

GIANT ASSORTED SCHOOL CRAYONS, BOX. 5c.
BV884 — Giant Assorted School Crayons. Each crayon is $3\frac{3}{4}$ inches long. 14 assorted colors in a box. Fine waxed finish. Tapered end. All good permanent colors. Weight per box, 3 ounces. Price.............. **5c**

FINE QUALITY COLORED CHALK, PER BOX, 5c.

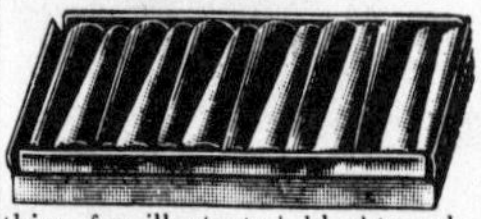

BV883 — Fine Quality Colored Chalk. 12 assorted colors in box. Each piece 3 inches long, tapered end. Just the thing for illustrated blackboard work in the school. Weight, per box, 3 ounces. Price.............. **5c**

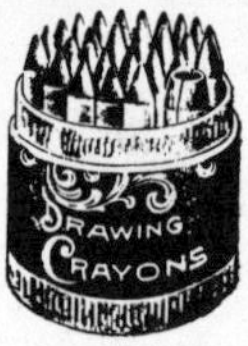

ASSORTED WAX CRAYONS AND HOLDER NEATLY PACKED, PER BOX, 5c.
BV885 — Assorted Wax Crayons. Each crayon over 2 inches long. 28 assorted colors in a box. Convenient wood holder. Fine for coloring maps, drawings, etc. Permanent colors. Weight, per box, 3 ounces. Price.............. **5c**

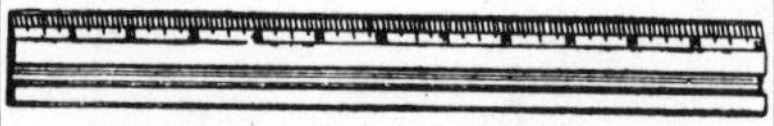

HARDWOOD RULER, BRASS EDGE, 5c.
BV887—Hardwood Ruler, Brass Edge. 12 inches long. Made of good quality wood, highly finished. Strong brass edge. Has groove in center for pencils. Weight, 2 ounces. Price...................... **5c**

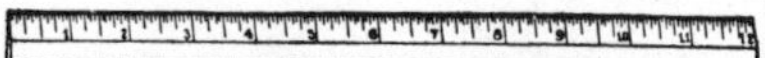

BEVELED EDGE RULERS, EACH, 5c.
BV888—Beveled Edge Rulers. Both edges beveled, one side marked in inches, the other side in metres. The side marked in inches has brass edge. Weight, 1 ounce. Price.. **5c**

CHILD'S GOOD QUALITY RUBBER FINISH SCHOOL BAG, 10c.

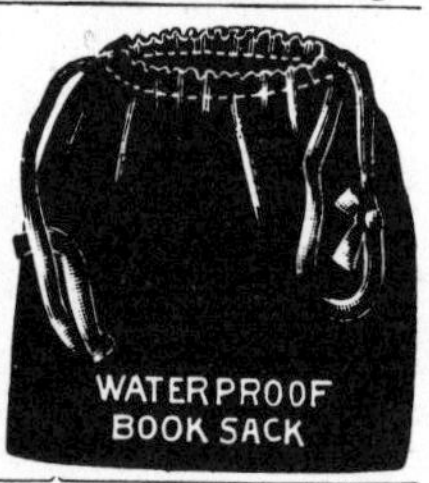

BX889 — Child's School Bag. Made of good quality rubber finished cloth. Size, 11x12 inches. Has draw string at the top for closing. Protects the books in rainy or snowy weather. Wt., 2 ounces. Price, each.......... **10c**

BROWN LINEN EYE SHADES, 10c.

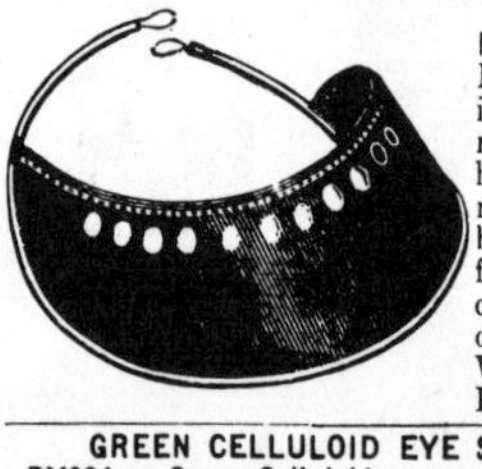

BX903 — Brown Linen Eye Shades. Made of good quality material. Have metal side clips for holding on head, and reinforced metal band. Invaluable for students and others who work under artificial light. Weight, 2 ounces. Price....... **10c**

GREEN CELLULOID EYE SHADE, 10c.

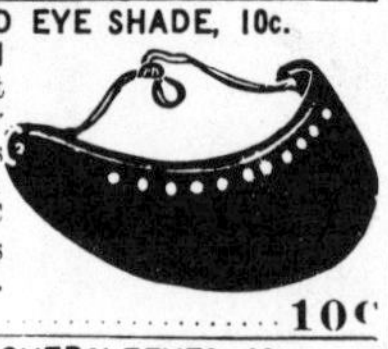

BX904 — Green Celluloid Eye Shade. Made of best quality celluloid. Very soothing to the eyes. Has elastic band. Weight, 1 ounce. Price...... **10c**
BX9044 — Same as above, with metal band. weight. 2 ounces. Price.............................. **10c**

BLACK OIL CLOTH OVERSLEEVES, 10c.

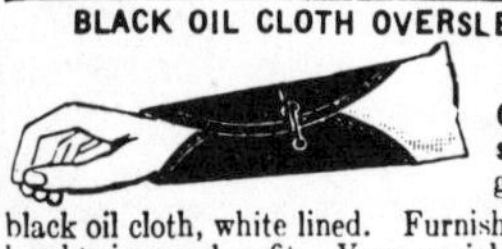

BX907 — Black Oil Cloth Oversleeves, Made of good quality black oil cloth, white lined. Furnished with an elastic band to insure close fit. Very special value. Weight, 4 ounces. Per pair.............................. **10c**

LADIES' BLACK SATEEN OVERSLEEVES, 10c.

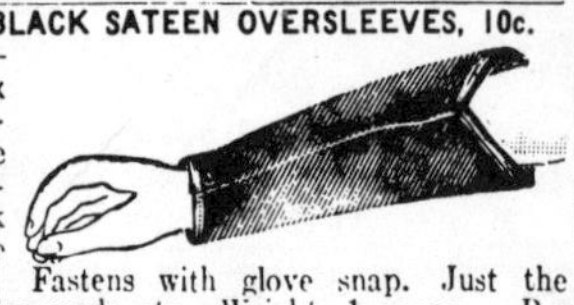

BX905 — Ladies' Black Sateen Oversleeves. Made of good quality black sateen. Close fitting wrist. Fastens with glove snap. Just the thing for office work, etc. Weight, 1 ounce. Per pair.. **10c**

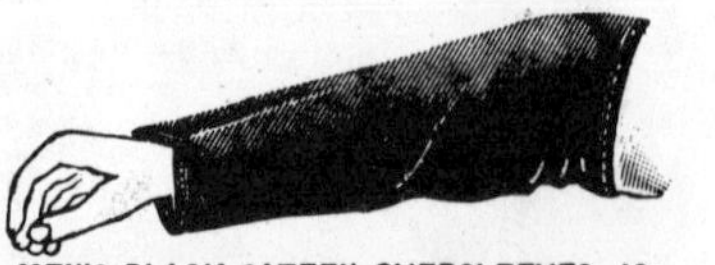

MEN'S BLACK SATEEN OVERSLEEVES, 10c.
BX906 — Men's Black Sateen Oversleeves. Made of good quality black sateen. Close fitting wrist. Reinforced edges. Weight, 2 ounces. Per pair..... **10c**

SPRING COVER SPECTACLE CASE, 10c.

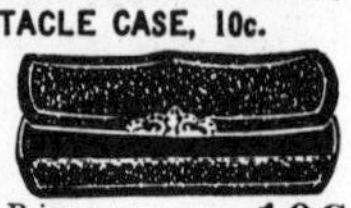

BX710 — Spring Cover Spectacle Case. Made of metal and covered with seal grain leather, plush lined. Inside measurements, $1\frac{1}{2}$x4 inches. Weight, 2 ounces. Price.......... **10c**

OPEN END SPECTACLE CASE, 5c.

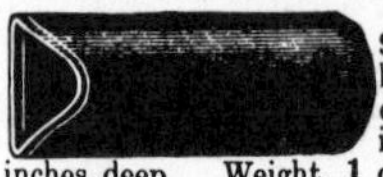

BV711 — Open End Spectacle Case. Made of heavy fibre, leatherette covered. Suitable for riding bow spectacles. $4\frac{3}{4}$ inches deep. Weight, 1 ounce. Price....... **5c**
BV712 — Same as above, but $6\frac{3}{4}$ inches deep. Proper size for straight temple spectacles. Weight, 1 ounce. Price.. **5c**

EYE GLASS CASE, 5c.

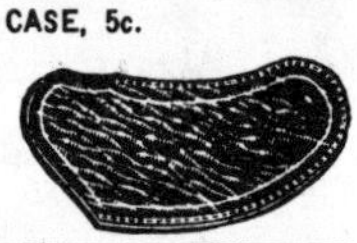

BV713 — Eye Glass Case. Has open end, felt lined, covered with black moire. Size, 2x$4\frac{1}{4}$ inches. Weight, 1 ounce. Price................ **5c**

SPRING COVER SPECTACLE CASE, 10c.

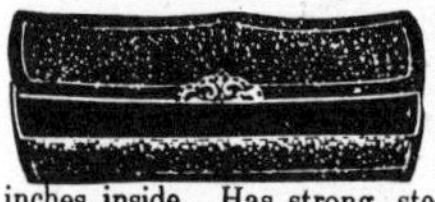

BX714 — Spring Cover Spectacle Case. Made of metal and covered with seal grain leather. Plush lined inside. Size, $1\frac{5}{8}$x$4\frac{3}{4}$ inches inside. Has strong, steel spring. Weight, 2 ounces. Price.............................. **10c**

CLEAR GLASS GOGGLES, EACH, 10c.

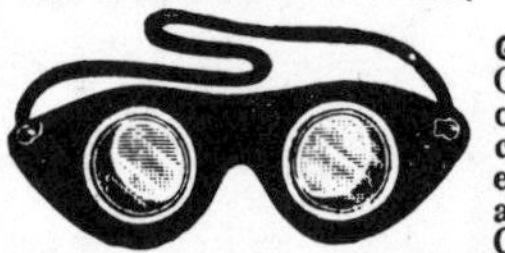

BX707 — Clear Glass Goggles. Goggles are made of best quality clear glass, mounted in ventilated aluminum cup. Cups are set in best quality tanned flexible leather. Fitted with elastic band. Weight, 2 ounces. Price.......... **10c**

BLACK LEATHER GOGGLES, EACH, 10c.

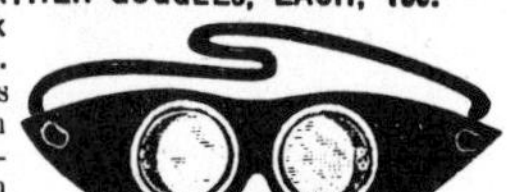

BX708 — Black Leather Goggles. $1\frac{3}{4}$-inch clear glass lens mounted in ventilated aluminum cups. Set in good quality flexible tanned leather. Just the thing for motoring, riding. Elastic band. Weight, 1 ounce. Price. **10c**

VELVET EDGE GOGGLES, EACH, 10c.

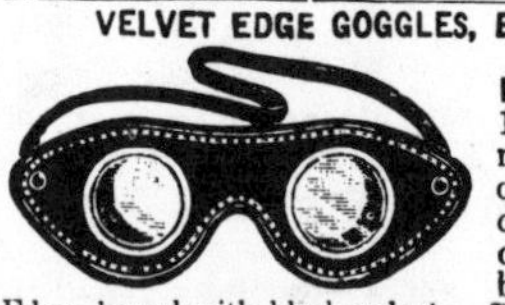

BX709 — Velvet Edge Goggles. $1\frac{7}{8}$-inch lens, mounted in extra deep aluminum cups. Set in best quality flexible black leather. Edges bound with black velvet. Fitted with elastic band. Weight, 2 ounces. Price............ **10c**

CREPE PAPER NAPKINS, DOZEN, 5c.

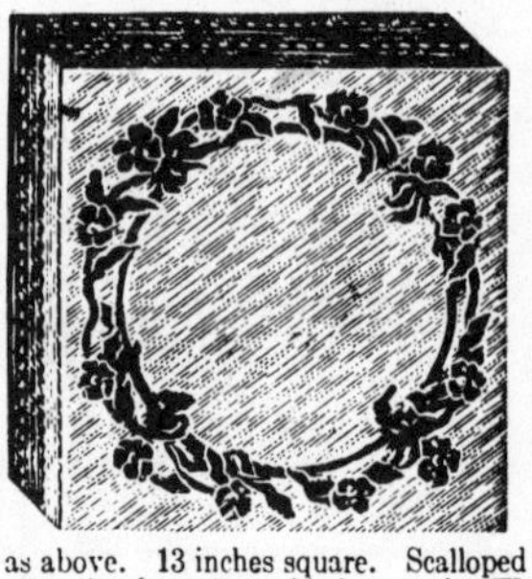

B895 — 14 inches square. Designs: Pansy, Sweet Pea, Japanese, Violet Cherry, Dutch Patriotic, Strawberry and Forget me-not. State design wanted. Weight, 1 oz. Per dozen, ... **5c**
B8955 — Same quality as above. 13 inches square. Scalloped edges, pink or green border. State kind wanted. Weight, 1 ounce. Per dozen.............................. **5c**

Crepe Paper, Jap Lanterns, Etc., 5c and 10c

ORNAMENTAL CREPE PAPER PER ROLL, 10c.
BX896 — Ornamental Crepe Paper. Design red, white and blue stripes. 10 feet in a roll. Best quality crepe paper, bright rich colors. Weight, per roll, 4 ounces. Price, per roll..................**10c**

DENNISON'S IMPERIAL CREPE PAPER, PER ROLL, 10c.
BX897 — Dennison's Imperial Crepe Paper. 10 feet long. Solid colors: white, ruby, orange, leaf green, Irish green, pink, blue, purple, lavender, black. State color wanted. Weight, 3 ounces. Price......**10c**

ORNAMENTAL CREPE PAPER, PER ROLL, 10c.
BX898 — Ornamental Crepe Paper. 20 inches wide, 10 feet in a roll. Designs; pink, carnation and gold, small rose, cherry, violet, blueflower, and dragon. State design wanted. Weight, 4 ounces. Price..**10c**

PAPER DOILIES, PER PACKAGE, 5c
BV890 — Paper Doilies. Embossed linen finished paper. Fancy scalloped edges. Lily-of-the-Valley design. 5½-inch diameter, 40 in a package. Weight, 2 ounces. Price.......**5c**
BV8900 — Same as above, except 6½ inches. 30 in a package. Weight, 2 ounces. Price.....**5c**

ASSORTED PAPER DOILIES, 10c.
BX891 — Assorted Paper Doilies. Made of good quality linen finish paper. Have scalloped edges and Lily of the Valley design embossed. Five assorted sizes in round and oval shapes in each package. Sizes 5½ to 8½ inches. Weight per package of 50, 5 ozs. Price.........**10c**

COMPLETE LUNCH SETS, EACH, 10c.
BX892 — Complete Lunch Stes. Consists of one large 56-inch paper table cover and one dozen paper napkins. Paper is sterilized. Neat design. Weight, per package, 4 ounces. Price....**10c**

STERILIZED PAPER LUNCH SETS, 10c.
BX893 — Sterilized Paper Lunch Sets. Consists of one large 56-inch paper table cover and one dozen paper napkins. Thoroughly sterilized. Sweet pea design. Weight per set, 4 ounces. Price.........**10c**

CREPE PAPER NAPKINS, 25 FOR 5c.
B894 — Crepe Paper Napkins. 14 inches square. Grecian border or Petunia design. Made of best quality crepe paper. Just the thing for parties, picnics and the like. Weight 25, 2 ounces. 25 for.....**5c**

WHITE CREPE PAPER NAPKINS 50 FOR 5c.
BB8944—White Crepe Paper Napkins. Best quality plain white crepe paper. Napkin is 13 inches square. Can be used for picnics, in the home, hotels, restaurants, and the like. Straight or scalloped edge. State kind wanted. Weight, 2 ounces. 50 napkins for........**5c**

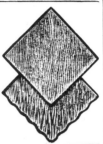

PURE WHITE WAX PAPER, PER ROLL, 5c.
BV899 — Pure White Wax Paper. 30 sheets in a roll. Size of sheet, 12x18 inches. Paper is odorless, tasteless and airproof. Weight, 4 ounces. Per roll......**5c**

LACE BORDER SHELF PAPER, PER FOLD, 5c.
BV900 — Lace Border Shelf Paper. Scalloped border, lace effect. Fold contains 5 yards 10½ inches wide. Colors: white, pink, or green. State color wanted. Weight, 3 ounces. Per fold.................**5c**

PAPER PICNIC PLATES, 24 FOR 5c.
B9001 — Paper Picnic Plates. Made of best quality sanitary pulp paper. Fine for picnics, outings, etc. Take up little space. Two sizes; 5 and 9-inch diameter. State size wanted when ordering. Weight, of 24 four ounces. Price, 24 for **5c**

WASTE PAPER BASKETS, EACH, 10c.
BX901 — Made of heavy double faced box board. Collapsible. Imitation wood finish. Have cut out for drawing ribbon through. Require about two yards of 2½-inch ribbon. Brown or green. State color wanted. Weight, 9 ounces. Price..**10c**

BX902 — Made of heavy double faced box board. Fancy wall paper design. Cut out for running ribbon through. Require about two yards of 2½-inch ribbon. State whether light or dark color is wanted. Weight, 9 ounces. Price..**10c**

JAPANESE LANTERNS, 2 FOR 5c.
EE240—Japanese Lanterns. Made of good quality paper, bamboo ribs. Wire handle and solid holder for candle. Weight, two, 2 ounces 2 for **5c**
EE241 — Same as above, except plain colors; red, green, pink and yellow. State color wanted. Weight, two, 2 ounces. 2 for........**5c**

ASSORTED JAP LANTERNS 5c.
EV242 — Assorted Jap Lanterns. These lanterns are made in fancy shapes and come in assorted Oriental decorations of Japanese design. Wire handle, candle holder, etc., are well made. Wt., per lantern, 5 ounces. Price, each. **5c**

JAPANESE LANTERNS, EACH, 10c.
EX243 — Japanese Lanterns, Extra large size and artistic shapes. Made of best quality paper, bamboo ribs, wire handle, and strong candle holder. Assorted Oriental decorations of Japanese design. Weight per lantern, 6 ounces. Price.........**10c**

JAP PAPER PARASOLS, 10c.
EX244—Jap Paper Parasols. These parasols are strongly made of best quality Japanese paper. When open they measure 30 inches across. Come in assorted Oriental decorations of Japanese design. Wt., 6 ounces. Price, ea.**10c**

CHINESE JOSS STICKS, 5c.
EV247—Chinese Joss Sticks. Sometimes called Chinese Incense. Have a delicate Oriental odor. A sure cure for the mosquito pest. Weight, 5 ounces. Per bundle **5c**

PRINTED MUSLIN U. S. FLAGS.
E256 — Size, 2½x4 inches. Mounted. Weight, 2 ounces. 24 for **5c**
E257 — Size, 6x9½ inches. Mounted. Weight, 2 ounces. 6 for....**5c**
EE258 — Size, 11x18 inches. Mounted. Weight, 3 ounces. 2 for....**5c**
EV259 — Size, 11x17 inches. Cadet. Cotton bunting. Mounted. Weight, 2 ounces. Each.............**5c**
EX260—Size, 16x24 inches. Infantry. Cotton bunting. Mounted. Weight, 3 ounces. Each.**10c**
EX261—Size, 24x36 inches. Cavalry. Cotton bunting. Mounted. Weight, 5 ounces. Each.**10c**
EX262—Size, 24x36 inches. Cavalry. Cotton bunting. Unmounted. Weight, 2 ounces. Each.**10c**

SILK HEMMED AMERICAN FLAGS.
E249—1½x2 inches. On brass pin. Weight, 1 ounce. 6 for.........**5c**
E250—2x3 inches. On wood spear. Weight, 1 ounce. 3 for.......**5c**
E251—2x3 inches. On brass pin. Weight, 1 ounce. 3 for......**5c**
EV252—4½x7 inches. On wood spear. Weight, 2 ounces. Each**5c**
EV253—6x9 inches. On wood spear. Weight, 3 ounces. Each.**5c**
EX254—8x10 inches. On wood spear Wt., 5 oz. Each.**10c**
EX255—9x13¼ inches. On wood spear. Weight, 8 ounces. Each..................**10c**

WHY WE CAN GIVE YOU SUCH REMARKABLE BARGAINS AT 5c AND 10c

We have made a specialty of buying and selling 5c and 10c merchandise for the past 16 years. In many instances we contract for the entire output of a factory, or we buy direct from the manufacturers, saving you the middlemen's profits in either case. Many of our lines are imported direct by us, enabling us to offer them at these remarkably low prices. Our aim is always—the best 5c and 10c bargains.

Popular Books, Printed on Good Quality Paper, Clear Type, Special at, Each Only, 10c

WEBSTER'S VEST POCKET DICTIONARY, 10c

BX930 — Webster's Vest Pocket Dictionary. Size, $2\frac{7}{8}$x$5\frac{3}{4}$ inches. Good, stiff cloth cover, convenient vest pocket size. Also contains valuable tables and other information. The dictionary for busy men. Weight, 3 ounces. Price.. **10c**

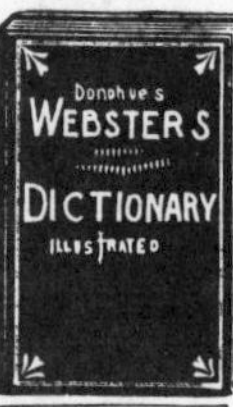

WEBSTER'S HANDY DICTIONARY, 10c.

BX931—Webster's Handy Dictionary. Size, 4x$5\frac{3}{4}$ inches. Contains 344 pages with instructive illustrations. The right size for the boy or girl who is attending school. Contains all words in common use. Weight 6 ounces. Price........................... **10c**

POPULAR UNIVERSAL HAND BOOKS, 10c.

BX932—Popular Universal Hand Books. Good cloth binding, heavy clear black type, good quality paper. These books are accepted as the best in their respective fields and are used and consulted every day in the year. Come in the following titles: Fortune Teller, Courtship and Matrimony, Guide to Beauty, Health, Manners and Rules of Good Society, Dream Book, and Economical Cook Book. State title wanted when ordering. Weight, each book, 7 ounces. Price................. **10c**

BOY SCOUT BOOKS, EACH, 10c.

BX933 — Boy Scout Books. These books are written by Major Robert Maitland, the well known writer of boy scout literature. Size of book is $4\frac{3}{4}$x7 inches. Good cloth binding, clear legible type on good quality paper. Every live red-blooded boy will want to read these books. They are full of the snap and dash that is inherent in every American boy. This list comprises the following well known titles: Boy Scouts in Camp, Boy Scouts to the Rescue, Boy Scouts on the Trail, Boy Scout Fire Fighters, Boy Scouts Afloat, Boy Scout Pathfinders, Boy Scout Automobilists, Boy Scout Aviators, Boy Scouts Champion Recruit, Boy Scouts Defiance, Boy Scouts Challenge, Boy Scouts Victory. Each book weighs 7 ounces. Per set of 12 books, $1.20, or each **10c**

BOOKS FOR RED-BLOODED BOYS, 10c.

BX934 — Books for Red-Blooded Boys. These books are all written by Horatio Alger, Jr., the well known writer of boys' books. They are written in plain every-day English and in such a manner that the boy cannot help but understand every word of them. Besides being full of snap and life they all teach a beautiful lesson. Handsomely bound in cloth and printed in plain clear type on good quality paper. Can be had in the following well known titles: Strong and Steady, A Street Boy, Try and Trust, Bound to Rise, Facing the World, Herbert Carter's Legacy, Sam's Chance, Jack's Ward, Joe's Luck, Wait and Hope, Paul the Peddler, Only an Irish Boy, Slow and Sure. A Cousin's Conspiracy, Tom the Bootblack, Struggling Upward, Risen from the Ranks, The Cash Boy, Making His Way, Tony the Tramp, Shifting for Himself, Do and Dare, Phil the Fiddler, The Young Salesman, Strive and Succeed, Andy Gordon, Bob Burton, Harry Vane, Hector's Inheritance, Mark Mason's Triumph, Brave and Bold, The Telegraph Boy, The Young Adventurer, The Young Outlaw, Sink or Swim, Luke Walton. Give title wanted. Weight, per book, 7 ounces. Price, each.. **10c**

WHEN ORDERING BOOKS, STATE KATALOG NUMBER and TITLE DESIRED. Books are mailed at the rate of 3 ounces for 1c to all points in the United States.

LONG LIST OF POPULAR FICTION, PER VOLUME, 10c.

BX938 — Long List of Popular Fiction. Paper binding. Includes masterpieces of some of the most popular writers. No better stories published at any price. We list these books below:

Kidnapped at the Altar, Laura Jean Libby.
The Woman Who Came Between, Caroline Hart.
Nameless Bess, Caroline Hart.
Married at Sight, Caroline Hart.
The Girl He Forsook, Laura Jean Libby.
Lil, The Dancing Girl, Caroline Hart.
For Love or Honor, Caroline Hart.
Love's Rugged Path, Caroline Hart.
Her Right to Love, Caroline Hart.
Della's Handsome Lover, Laura Jean Libbey.
A Handsome Engineer's Flirtation, Laura Jean Libbey.
Was She Sweetheart or Wife, Laura Jean Libbey.
Vendetta, Marie Corelli.
Redeemed by Love, Caroline Hart.
A Dangerous Flirtation, Laura Jean Libbey.
A Romance of Two Worlds, Maria Corelli
Her Ransom, Charles Garvice.
Vengeance of Love, Caroline Hart.
Pretty Rose Hall, Laura Jean Libbey.
Kathleen's Diamonds, Mrs. Alex. McVeigh Miller.
Little Sweetheart, Mrs. Alex. McVeigh Miller.
Littly Nobody, Mrs. Alex. McVeigh Miller.
Molly's Treachery, Mrs. Alex. McVeigh Miller
A Bitter Reckoning, Mrs. E. Burke Collins.
A Working Girl's Honor, Caroline Hart.
Her Husband's Ghost, Mary E. Bryan.
Sold for Gold, E. Burke Collins.
Irene's Vow, Charlotte Braeme.
Was It Wrong? Barbara Howard.
Was She His Lawful Wife, Barbara Howard.
The Ghost of Hurricane Hills, Mary E. Bryan.
Val, The Tomboy, Wenona Gilman.
Hearts of Fire, Caroline Hart.
Self Raised, E. D. E. N. Southworth.
Pretty Little Rosebud, Barbara Howard.
The Girl Wife, Mrs. Sumner Hayden.
Dora Thorne, Charlotte M. Breame.
India, or The Pearl of Pearl River, Mrs. Southworth.
Lost and Found, Charlotte M. Stanley.
The Curse of Clifton, E. D. E. N. Southworth.
The Lovers of Storm Castle, M. A. Collins.
Her Fairy Queen, Elizabeth Stiles.
Three Girls, Mary E. Bryan.
A Strange Marriage, Caroline Hart.
Wormwood, Maria Corelli.
Wicked Sir Dare, Charles Garvice.

State title wanted. Weight, 8 ounces. Price, each...................................... **10c**

GOOD BOOKS FOR GIRLS, 10c.

BX935 — Good Books for Girls. Handsomely bound in cloth and printed in clear type on good quality paper. These books are written by some of the best known writers of girls' stories. They will be appreciated by the young as well as the old. The following are some of the well known titles: Polly, A New Fashion Girl, A Girl in Ten Thousand, Good Luck, The Honorable Miss, Out of Fashion, Frances Kane's Fortune, A Sweet Girl Graduate, A Girl of the People, The Heart of Gold. State title wanted. Weight, 8 ounces. Price, each.................................. **10c**

POPULAR WORKS OF FICTION, EACH, 10c.

BX936 — These books are printed on good paper from clear type, and bound in genuine cloth. Beautiful covers stamped in colors from original and attractive designs. Titles stamped on the front and back. The books average nearly 300 pages and are 5x$7\frac{1}{2}$ inches in size. Embracing only the best selling titles of the most popular authors. Each title complete, unabridged and published in one volume, as for example, "Ishmael" is issued complete in one volume and so is "Self-Raised" and this is the only Cloth-Bound Edition on the market that contains these books to be retailed at the price quoted.

Aikenside..................... Mary J. Holmes
Beautiful Fiend .... E. D. E. N. Southworth
Black Beauty...................... Anna Sewall
Black Rock...................... Ralph Connor
Bride's Dowry........ ...E. D. E. N. Southworth
Camille................. Alexander Dumas, Jr.
Cousin Maud................ Mary J. Holmes
Dora Deane.................. Mary J. Holmes
Faithful Unto Death....... E. D. E. N. Southworth
Golden Heart, A................ Bertha M. Clay
Her Only Sin................... Bertha M. Clay
Inez........................... Augusta Evans
Ishmael.................. E. D. E. N. Southworth
King Solomon's Mines......... H. Rider Haggard
Mad Love, A.................... Bertha M. Clay
Maggie Miller.................. Mary J. Holmes
Mildred........................ Mary J. Holmes
Miss McDonald .... Mary J. Holmes
Self-Raised............ ...E. D. E. N. Southworth
Strange Case of Dr. Jekyll and Mr. Hyde......... Robert Louis Stevenson
Story of a Wedding Ring......... Bertha M. Clay
Ten Nights in a Bar Room.. .... T. S. Arthur
Treasure Island.......... Robert Louis Stevenson
Victor's Triumph .... E. D. E. N. Southworth
Woman Against Woman....... Mrs. M. E. Holmes

State title wanted. Weight, 9 ounces. Price, each.. **10c**

ST. ELMO, BY AUGUSTA J. EVANS, 10c.

BX937—St. Elmo, By Augusta J. Evans. This powerful and well known story can now be had at a popular price which will give every one a chance to read it. The book is printed in clean black type on good quality paper. Good stiff paper binding. The weight of the book is 9 ounces. Special value **10c**

ILLUSTRATED JUVENILE BOOKS, ASSORTED TITLES, COVERS IN ATTRACTIVE COLORS, 10c.

BX947—Illustrated Juvenile Books. These books are made with heavy stiff board covers, bound with cloth, and well illustrated. Printed in plain black type on good quality paper. Come in the following titles: Black Beauty, The Home Primer, Young Folks, Uncle Tom's Cabin, Young American Speaker, Father Goosey Gander, Mother Goose Melodies, Nursery Rhymes, Rhymes and Chimes, Mother Goose ABC, Jolly Jingles, and Mother Goose Tales. State title wanted. Weight each 10 ounces. Price.. **10c**

Children's Toy Books will be found in our Toy Department, Pages 90 to 93.

Large Collection of Post Cards at 5c and 10c

"I SHOULD WORRY" SERIES POST CARDS, 6 FOR 5c.

E551 — "I Should Worry" Series Post Cards. This assortment consists of 12 assorted phrases printed in colors. Very popular at the present time. Weight, 6 cards, 1 ounce. 6 for.................................5C

MOTTO POST CARDS, 6 FOR 5c.

E550 — Motto Post Cards. This assortment consists of 145 different well known phrases. Series has assorted borders in fancy designs and colors. Large clear type. Wt., six 1 ounce. 6 for.....5C

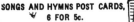

I would like to have your Photograph— For the center piece in my new crazy quilt.

"I'M THE GUY" COMIC POST CARDS, 6 FOR 5c.

E552 — "I'm The Guy" Comic Post Cards. 12 assorted designs. These cards are handsomely printed in colors. Appreciated by children as well as grown-ups. Just the cards for you to send to your friends. Weight, 6 cards, 1 ounce. Price, 6 for.....5C

SONGS AND HYMNS POST CARDS, 6 FOR 5c.

E554 — Songs and Hymns Post Cards. Splendid assortment of 75 designs in this series. These cards are printed in colors, and handsomely glazed. The songs are all popular and sung by everybody. Weight, 6 cards, 2 ounces. 6 for.......5C

SEPIA YAD KIDS POST CARDS, 6 FOR 5c.

E555 — Sepia Yad Kids Post Cards. This assortment contains a large variety of Yad Kids with appropriate phrases. Pictures and phrases all done in rich brown sepia color. A very good assortment. Weight, 6 cards, 1 ounce. 6 for.........5C

WOODEN SHOE DUTCH KIDS POST CARDS, 6 FOR 5c.

E556 — Wooden Shoe Dutch Kids Post Cards. A large assortment of comical Dutch Kids with witty and humorous phrases. The cards are of the best quality and printed in sepia color. Appreciated at all times. Weight, six cards, 1 ounce. 6 for.....................5C

Liff, luff, und lall mutch!

COMIC LOVERS' POST CARDS, 6 FOR 5c.

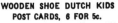

E557 — Comic Lovers' Post Cards. Handsomely printed in rich natural colors and have a highly glazed finish. Appropriate verse printed on each card. These cards are very much appreciated by young people. Weight, 6 cards, 2 ounces. 6 for.....................5C

We carry in stock at all times a large collection of Post Cards in the most popular styles and subjects.

Be happy Real happiness is found By passing A little happiness 'round.

WOODENETTE MOTTOES, EACH, 10c.

EX535 — Woodenette Mottoes. 12½ inches long, natural stained wood finish. Natural wood ends and silk cord for hanging. Lettered in attractive type, colored initials. Ten subjects. Wt., 4 ozs. 10C

ASSORTED GIRLS POST CARDS, 5 FOR 5c.

E564 — Assorted Girls Post Cards. This assortment contains photogravure cards for hand coloring, good poses, printed in soft tints. Weight, 5 cards, 1 ounce. 5 for 5C

NIPPLE NOVELTY POST CARDS, EACH, 5c.

EV566 — Nipple Novelty Post Cards. Choice of 12 subjects. Each card has a little humorous phrase, rubber nipple and safety pin attached with baby ribbon. Weight, each, 1 ounce. Price.....................5C

EMBOSSED BIRTHDAY CARDS, 6 FOR 5c.

E563 — Embossed Birthday Greeting Cards. Handsomely printed in colors. 100 assorted designs and greetings. A card that will be appreciated by your friends. Weight, 6 cards 1 ounce. 6 for.....................5C

EXTRA FINE BIRTHDAY CARDS, 2 FOR 5c.

EE565 — Extra Fine Birthday Cards. Handsomely finished in beautiful colors. Choice of 20 fine designs. Half of these cards have verses in addition to design. Weight, two cards, 1 ounce. Price, 2 for.......5C

JEWELED BIRTHDAY CARDS, EACH, 5c.

EV568 — Jeweled Birthday Cards. This assortment consists of 24 special designs highly embossed and finished in natural colors. Contain appropriate greetings. Roses, violets, pansies, and other subjects. Cards are nicely tinseled and studded with jewels. A very high class card, each in a separate envelope. Weight, 1 ounce. Each card...........5C

BIRTHDAY GREETING CARDS, 5 FOR 5c.

E560 — Birthday Greeting Cards. This assortment consists of 28 beautiful designs, such as Ivy, Primrose, Peach buds, Violets, Pansies, Bluebells, etc. Each card has a pretty verse in clear type. These cards come in natural colors and gilt. Cards have linen finish, and design is embossed. Weight, 5 cards 1 ounce. 5 for.............5C

COLORED BIRTHDAY POST CARDS, 5 FOR 5c.

E581 — Colored Birthday Post Cards. Consist of a series of landscapes and flowers, finished in beautiful natural colors. Each card has a short, sincere greeting. Wt., 5 cards, 1 ounce. 5 for....5C

STATE CAPITOL DESIGN POST CARDS, 6 FOR 5c.

E558 — State Capitol Design Post Cards. Capitol of every State in the Union. Bright colors with draped American flag and the seal of the state. Wt., 6 cards, 1 ounce. 6 for.............5C

INDIAN HEAD POST CARDS, 5 FOR 5c.

E5641 — Indian Head Post Cards. This assortment consists of Indian heads in black and white, suitable for hand coloring. Exceptional quality and figures readily lend themselves to hand painting. A choice assortment of heads. Weight, 5 cards, 1 ounce. 5 for 5C

ATHLETIC GIRL SERIES POST CARDS, 5 FOR 5c.

E5642 — Athletic Girl Series Post Cards. Consists of a splendid assortment of athletic girls in black and white, suitable for hand coloring. Rowing girls, swimming girls, basketball, etc. A very high quality card, suitable for framing. Weight, 5 cards, 1 ounce. 5 for........5C

GLAZED AND COLORED BIRTHDAY CARDS, 5 FOR 5c.

E562 — Glazed and Colored Birthday Cards. This assortment consists of plain colored gelatin post cards in colors. A very beautiful and popular card. 100 assorted designs. Appropriate greetings on each card. Weight, 5 cards, 1 ounce. Special value 5 for....5C

EMBOSSED BIRTHDAY POST CARDS, 6 FOR 5c.

E559 — Embossed Airbrush Post Cards. An assortment of 100 different designs, highly embossed. Birds, flowers, horseshoes, landscapes and other designs, finished in bright natural colors, richly gilted. Appropriate greetings in gilt on each card. Weight, 6 cards, 1 ounce. Price, 6 for 5C

METAL HORSESHOE BIRTHDAY CARDS, EACH 5c.

EV567 — Metal Horseshoe Birthday Cards. Variety of designs, such as flowers, landscapes, marines, and other patterns, highly embossed and finished in rich, natural colors. Large gilt metal horseshoe securely attached. Each card in separate envelope. Weight, 1 ounce. Price, each.....................5C

When ordering Post Cards, be sure to order other merchandise, such as Dry Goods, Notions, etc.

Wonder Water Color Outfit, 10c

EX625 — Wonder Water Color Outfit. This outfit consists of ten self-blending, transparent colors for tinting post cards, photographs, half tones, maps, pictures, burnt wood, etc. Full instructions for using are enclosed in every package. Each box contains one yellow, orange, flesh, bright red, leaf green, No. 2 green, sky blue, brown, purple and pearl gray color, together with one brush for painting. Weight, complete, 3 ounces. Price..........................10C

THE ORIGINAL PARCEL POST KRESGE'S KATALOG FIVE AND TEN CENT STORE

Photo Frames and Mirrors, Special at 10c

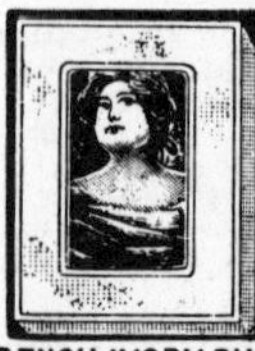

FRENCH IVORY PHOTO FRAMES, EACH, 10c.
EX517—Beautiful French Ivory Photo Frame. Size, 3x4 inches. Has easel attachment on back. Size of frame 3x4 inches. Frame only. Weight, 2 ounces. Price.......... **10c**

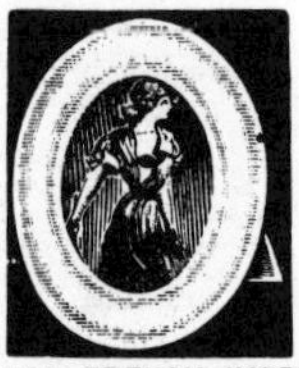

OVAL FRENCH IVORY FRAMES, EACH, 10c.
EX518—Beautiful French Ivory Photo Frame. Oval design. Size, 3½x4½ inches. Has easel stand. Can be placed on table, desk, etc. Frame only. Wt., 2 ounces. Price.. **10c**

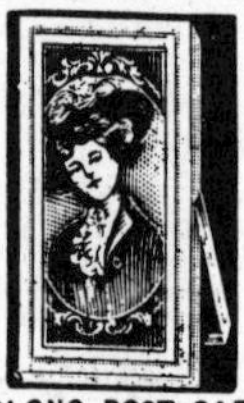

OBLONG POST CARD FRAMES, EACH, 10c.
EX519—Made of white French Ivory. Size, 2¾x5½ inches. Opening for picture, 1¾x4½ inches. Has folding easel for standing on desk, table, etc. Frame only. Wt., 1 ounce. Price... **10c**

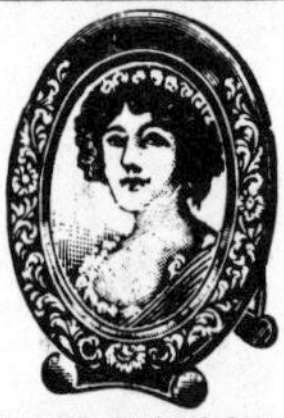

SILVER FINISH OVAL PHOTO FRAME, 10c.
EX520—Beautiful Silver Finish Embossed Photo Frame. Size, 4x5¼ inches. Opening for photo, 2¾x4 inches. Has folding easel back. Guaranteed not to tarnish. Weight, 3 ounces. Price........... **10c**

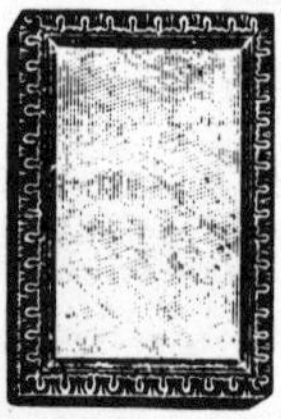

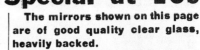

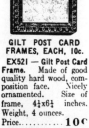

GILT POST CARD FRAMES, EACH, 10c.
EX521 — Gilt Post Card Frame. Made of good quality hard wood, composition face. Nicely ornamented. Size of frame, 4¼x6¼ inches. Weight, 4 ounces. Price........... **10c**

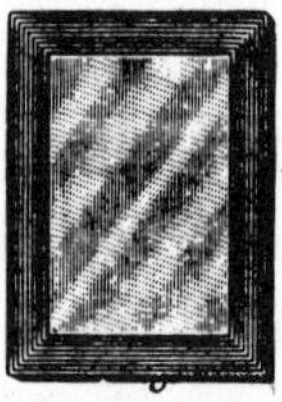

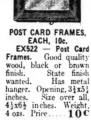

POST CARD FRAMES, EACH, 10c.
EX522 — Post Card Frames. Good quality wood, black or brown finish. State finish wanted. Has metal hanger. Opening, 3¼x5¼ inches. Size over all, 4½x6½ inches. Weight, 4 ozs. Price..... **10c**

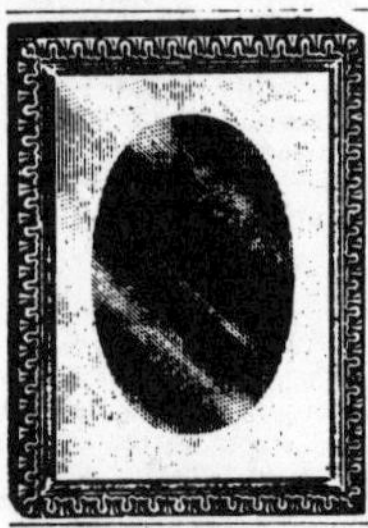

OVAL OR SQUARE EMBOSSED MOULDING PHOTO FRAMES, 10c.
EX523 — Heavy gilt frames, nicely embossed moulding. One opening, choice oval or square mats. Well made and neatly finished throughout. Size, 5¾x7¾. State kind of opening wanted. Weight, 8 ounces. Price.... **10c**

RAISED ORNAMENTAL GOLD FESTOON PHOTO FRAMES, EACH, 10c.
EX524—Gold Festoon Photo Frames. Size of frame, 7½x9½ inches. Ornamented with raised gilt festooning. Has high grade square cut mat. Size opening for picture, 3¼x5¼ inches. Weight, 9 ounces. Price ... **10c**

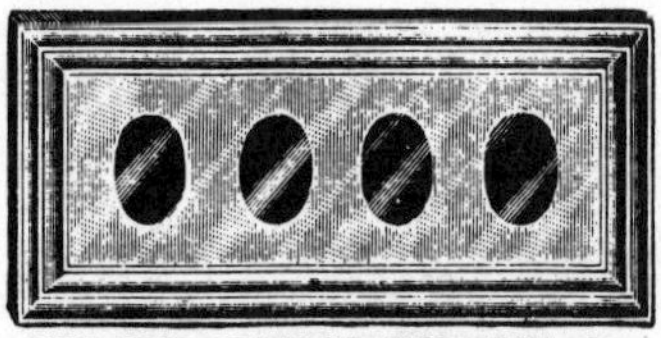

PING PONG PHOTO FRAMES, EACH, 10c.
EX525 — Ping Pong Photo Frames. Size of frame, 5x11 inches. Pure white mat with four oval openings. Nicely carved gilt frame. Very attractive. Weight, 7 ounces. Price.......................... **10c**

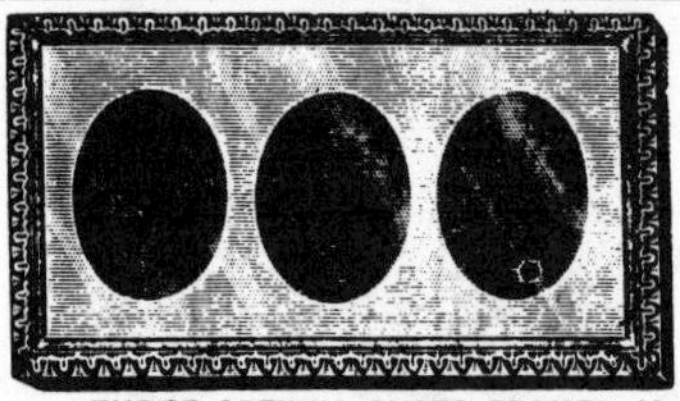

THREE OPENING PHOTO FRAMES, 10c.
EX526—Three Opening Photo Frames. Suitable for photos or post cards. Size of frame, 5⅞x10⅞ inches. Mat has three oval openings. Frame finished in fancy gilt. Weight, 9 ounces. Price............. **10c**

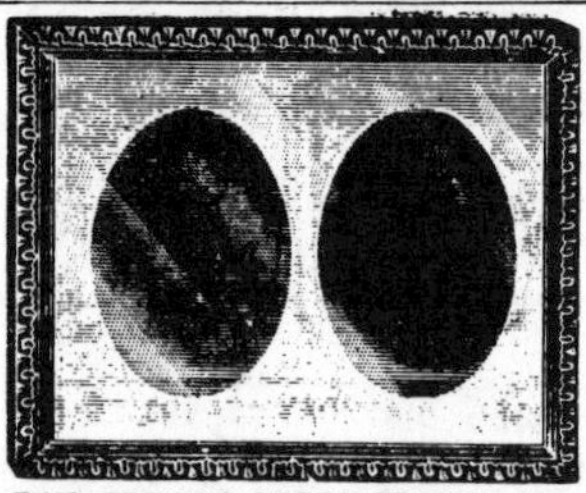

TWO OPENING PHOTO FRAMES, 10c.
EX527—Two Opening Photo Frames. Size of frame, 7¼x9¼ inches. Finished in fancy gilt design. Has two openings in mat. An ornament to any wall or room. Weight, 8 ounces. Price........... **10c**

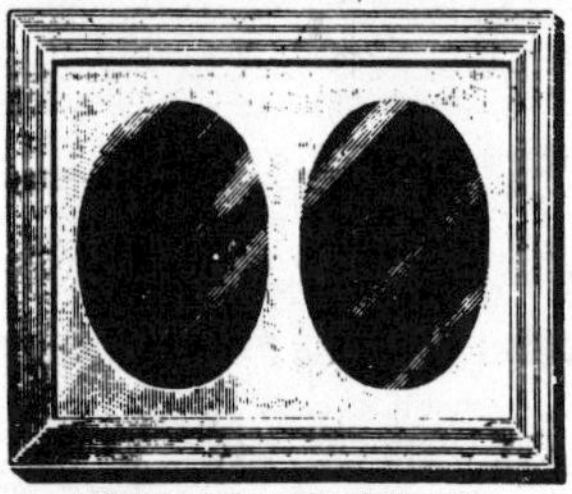

HEAVY GILT FRAMES, 10c.
EX528—Heavy Gilt Frames. Made of good, strong wood, composition finish, heavily covered with gilt. Size, 7½x9½ inches. Mat contains two openings, 3½x5 inches. Weight, 9 ounces. Price..... **10c**

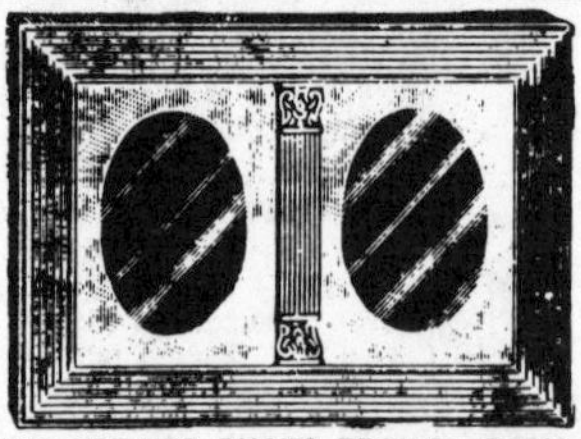

DOUBLE OPENING PHOTO FRAMES, EACH, 10c.
EX529—Double Opening Photo Frames. Size of frame, 8½x11½ inches. Made of ⅞-inch gilt moulding. Center bar and brass columns. Two oval openings, 3½x5¼ inches. Weight, 13 ounces. Price.... **10c**

Frames are made of good quality strong wood, stained or enameled. When ordering mirrors and frames be sure to include enough other merchandise to make a freight shipment. See our special prepay offer on Page 3.

The mirrors shown on this page are of good quality clear glass, heavily backed.

When ordering mirrors do not fail to include a few of the beautiful pictures shown on opposite page. A long list of subjects to select from.

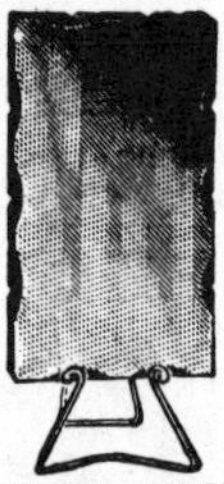

OBLONG CHIPPED GLASS MIRRORS, 10c.
EX531 — Oblong Chipped Glass Mirrors. Made of heavy, chipped, clear plate glass, backed with leatherette to prevent scratching. Strong wire easel standard frame. Special value. Size of glass, 4x6 inches. Weight, 11 ounces. Price........... **10c**

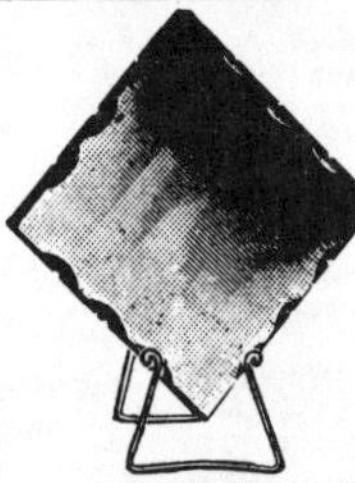

SQUARE GLASS CHIPPED MIRROR, 10c.
EX530 — Square Glass Chipped Mirror. Made of clear, heavy, plate glass, backed with leatherette binding. Strong wire easel standard frame. Convenient for shaving, etc. Size of mirror, 5x5 inches. Weight, 10 ozs. Price........... **10c**

FINE HEAVY GILT FRAME LARGE CLEAR GLASS MIRRORS, 10c.
EX532 — Made of good clear glass. 1-inch composition moulding frame, heavily gilted. Size of mirror, 7½x9½ inches. A dependable house mirror. Weight, 11 ounces. Price.. **10c**

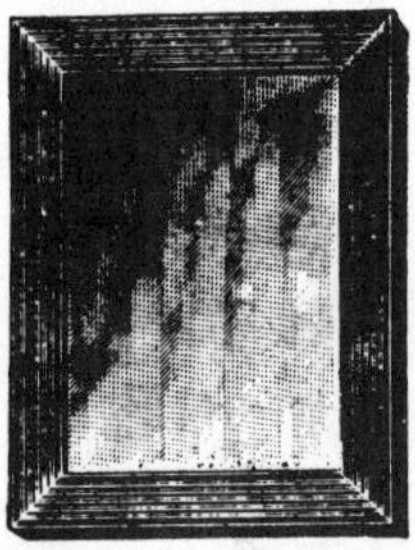

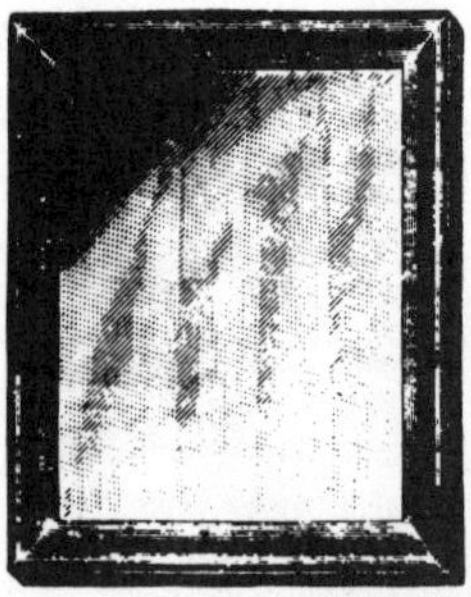

LARGE CLEAR GLASS MIRROR, 10c.
EX533—8½x10½ inches over all. Frame made of 1-inch heavy oak moulding. Best quality clear glass mirror. Frame is well made and neatly finished. Weight, 13 ounces. Price...... **10c**

IVORY WHITE ENAMEL FRAME BEST CLEAR GLASS MIRRORS, 10c.
EX534—Frame made of strong wood, nicely grained and enameled in ivory white. Mirror of good, clear glass. Size 9½x11½. Weight, 17 ounces. Price...... **10c**

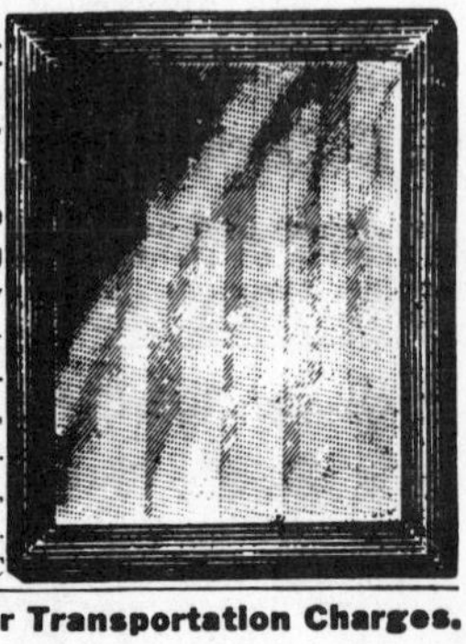

Be sure to state Katalog Number when ordering; also send an extra amount of money for Transportation Charges.

Beautiful Framed Pictures, Only 10c Each

CUPID AWAKE AND ASLEEP, 10c.

EX500 — This Beautiful Picture is 6 inches wide and 8 inches long. the frame is made of ⅝-in. moulding, corrugated finish and highly gilted. The picture is shown with two openings in gilt mat. A special value. Weight, 6 ounces. Price.........**10C**

CUPID AWAKE AND ASLEEP, 10c.

EX501 — This picture is mounted in two oval metal frames, joined in center. 5x8 inches. The frames are nicely finished and can be had in either gilt, brown or black. The pictures are in sepia. Brass chain for hanging. Weight, 5 ounces. Price......................**10C**

CUPID AWAKE AND ASLEEP, 10c.

EX502 — Picture is mounted in a single oval metal frame 5½x7 inches. Heavy mat with two oval openings. Frame may be had in gilt, brown or black. Brass ring on back. Weight, 5 ounces. Price, ...**10C**

CUPID OR MADONNA, 10c.

EX503 — These pictures are finished in a rich, dark, brown shade, 5x6½ inches. The frame is made of seasoned wood, richly tinted in brown, with a small gilt stripe. Best quality clear glass. A very artistic picture. State whether Cupid or Madonna is wanted. Weight, 5 ounces. Price.........**10C**

CUPID AWAKE AND ASLEEP, 10c.

EX504 — This picture is finished in an artistic brown color. Frame is of heavy metal in oval shape, 5½x7½ inches. Best quality clear glass. Frame can be had in either gilt, brown or black. State which is wanted. Brass ring on back. Weight, 5 ounces. Price.........**10C**

ASSORTED GAINSBORO HEADS, 10c.

EX505 — These pictures are copies of Gainsboro's masterpieces, in rich life-like colors. Assorted heads. Frame is of best quality heavy metal in gilt, brown, or black. Clear glass. Size of picture 5½x7½ inches, oval shape. Weight, 5 ounces. Price.................**10C**

OLD MASTERS IN COLORS, 10c.

EX506 — These pictures are copies of famous masterpieces. Eight subjects. Strong, oval shape metal frame, can be had in gilt, brown, or black finish. Size, 6½x8½ inches. Best quality clear glass. Brass ring for hanging on wall. Weight, 6 ounces. Price.**10C**

Every Picture shown on this page is a wonderful bargain at 10c,

---

When ordering pictures be sure to include enough other merchandise to make a freight shipment. See our special bargains in woodenware, hardware, mirrors, etc., shown elsewhere in this Katalog. Nothing over 10c.

Many of these pictures are copies of well-known subjects, and finished in rich, natural colors. The framing and workmanship is of a dependable kind, even though there is nothing on this page over 10c.

YOUNG MOTHER SERIES, EACH 10c.

Assorted Subjects.

EX507 — These pictures are finished in a rich dark sepia color. Frame is of plain, heavy metal and can be had in gilt, brown, or black finish. Oval shape. Clear glass. Size of picture, 6½x8½ inches. Weight, 6 ounces. Price.**10C**

YOUNG MOTHER SERIES, 10c.

EX508 — Two subjects, both finished in rich sepia color. Frame is made of good heavy metal, nicely stamped and finished in gilt, brown, or black. The size is 6x10½ inches, oval shape, clear glass. Brass ring in back for hanging on wall. Weight, 10 ounces. Price **10C**

DE LUXE GRAVURES, 10c.

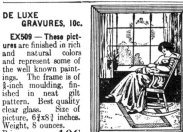

EX509 — These pictures are finished in rich and natural colors and represent some of the well known paintings. The frame is of ⅝-inch moulding, finished in neat gilt pattern. Best quality clear glass. Size of picture, 6¾x8½ inches. Weight, 8 ounces. Price.........**10C**

FAMOUS PICTURES IN COLORS, 10c.

EX510 — These pictures are copies of well known paintings finished in their original colors. The frame is made of 1-inch oak, stained a rich dark color, and finished with gilded composition ornaments. Size of frame, 7¼x9½ inches. Best quality clear glass. Weight, 9 ounces. Price.........**10C**

WOMEN, FAIR AND FAMOUS, 10c.

EX511 — This series represents well known pictures of famous women. They are finished in a rich sepia color with an oval mat. The frame is strongly made and nicely finished in a brown tint, 7x9 inches. Best quality clear glass. Weight, 10 ounces. Price.........**10C**

FAMOUS SCENES, 10c.

EX512 — This series represents a number of landscapes and marine scenes. Frame is made of 1¼-inch moulding, finished in gilt. Size, 8x10 inches. Best quality clear glass. Weight, 12 ounces. Price.................**10C**

DUTCH FLOWER GIRL, 10c.

EX513 — This picture represents a typical Dutch scene. The frame is made of solid oak, composition ornaments. Size, 7½x9½ inches. Best quality clear glass is used. Weight, 9 ounces. Price.................**10C**

YOUNG MOTHER, 10c.

EX514 — This beautiful picture is reproduced in the original colors. Frame is of 1-inch moulding, finished in heavy gilt. Clear glass. Size, 6½x16 inches. Weight, 13 ozs. Price.............**10C**

WESTERN LIFE, 10c.

EX515 — Indian and Cowboy Subjects. Frame is made of ¾-inch moulding, finished in dark tint. Best quality clear glass. Size, 6½x15½ inches. Wt., 12 ounces. Price.**10C**

THE GLEANERS, 10c.

EX516 — This beautiful series, represents an assortment of well known famous paintings such as "The Gleaners", etc. Frame is heavy oak moulding, neatly finished in a brown tint. Best quality clear glass. Size, 8½x10½ inches. Weight, 11 ounces. Price.................**10C**

THE DOCTOR, 10c.

EX5166 — This famous picture is finished in a warm sepia. Frame is heavy oak moulding, ⅞ inch wide, brown tint. Best quality clear glass is used. Size, 8½ x 10½ inches. Weight, 11 ounces. Price.........................**10C**

Toys for All The Children at 5c and 10c

On this and the following pages we show remarkable values in toys at 5c and 10c each. We sell enormous quantities of toys the year round in our many stores, because Kresge toys, like other Kresge merchandise, are wonderful bargains. Nothing over 10c.

DRESSED DOLL WITH TRIMMED HAT TO MATCH DRESS, 10c.

FX111—Dressed Doll. Pretty pink, red or blue dress and hat to match, all trimmed with lace. Painted shoes and stockings. White belt with little bow. China head, natural hair, and large eyes. Stands about 9 inches high. State color dress and hat wanted when ordering. Weight 3 ounces. Price......**10¢**

DRESSED DOLL WITH TRIMMED HAT TO MATCH DRESS, 10c.

FX112—Dressed Doll. Pretty pink, or blue dress and hat to match. Dress is lace trimmed. Rickrack braid on hat. Shoes and stockings can be taken off. China head, natural hair, and large eyes. Stands about 9 inches high. Weight 3 ounces. Price......**10¢**

DRESSED BOY DOLL, SHEPHERD PLAID DRESS SPECIAL, 10c.

FX113— Dressed Boy Doll. Pretty shepherd plaid dress with large white lace trimmed collar. Pretty straw hat. Shoes and stockings can be taken off. Good china head with large eyes. This doll stands about 9 inches high. Weight 3 ounces. Price......**10¢**

STUFFED DOLL UNBREAKABLE SPECIAL PRICE, 10c.

EX642— Unbreakable Stuffed Doll. Has celluloid face. Cloth covering is made of assorted red and blue colors. This doll can be thrown around without danger of breaking and is just the thing for the little folks. Stands about 11 inches high. Weight 4 ounces. Price.....**10¢**

BISQUE DOLL WITH NATURAL HAIR, 10c.

FX116 — Bisque Doll. Has movable arms and legs. Long natural hair in blonde, brunette and Tuscan shades. Painted shoes and stockings. Stands about 5 inches high. Weight, 2 ounces. Price...**10¢**

7-INCH DRESSED CHARACTER DOLL, 10c.

FX115—Dressed Character Doll. Very comical expression. Blue or pink striped dress with lace on sleeves. Painted shoes and stockings. Movable head, legs and arms. Head is of china. Stands about 7 inches high. Weight, 4 ounces. Price.....**10¢**

UNBREAKABLE CHARACTER FACE DOLL, SPECIAL PRICE, 10c.

FX110 — Unbreakable Character Face Doll. Has movable arms and legs with patent composition head. Dressed in long white shirt with lace trimming at neck. Stands about 12 inches high. Weight, 7 ounces. Price.....**10¢**

CHARACTER DOLL WITH MOVABLE HEAD, 10c.

FX114 — Character Doll. Composition body with movable arms and legs, and movable bisque head. Short hair. Dressed with white shirt. Stands about 6 inches high. Weight, 3 ounces. Price......**10¢**

BISQUE DOLL, MOVABLE ARMS AND LEGS, 10c.

FX117 — Bisque Doll. Has movable arms and legs. Painted shoes and stockings. Hair and ribbon also painted. Can be handled without danger of breaking. Stands about 7 inches high. Weight 5 ounces. Price......**10¢**

14-INCH UNBREAKABLE PAPER MACHE DOLL SPECIAL PRICE, 10c.

FX109—Unbreakable Paper Mache Doll. Head, legs and arms are made of paper mache. Legs and arms are movable. Painted shoes and stockings. Blonde, brunette or Tuscan hair. Chiffon dress with lace trimmed neck. Stands about 14 inches high. State shade hair wanted. Weight, 8 ozs. Price..**10¢**

BOY OR GIRL CLOTH DOLLS SPECIAL PRICE 10c.

EX673—Boy or Girl Cloth Dolls. Made of good strong cloth with printed face, dress, shoes and stockings in assorted colors. Well stuffed and strongly sewed. Stands about 12 inches high. When ordering state whether girl or boy is wanted. Weight, 5 ounces. Price.....**10¢**

ROLY POLYS, EACH 10c.

FX102 — Roly Polys. Celluloid cat or dog, with weighted bottom. Will always stand up. Come in brown or white. About 3½ inches high. State animal wanted and color desired when ordering. Weight 2 ounces. Price......**10¢**

WHITE RUBBER DOLL, 10c.

EX670— White Rubber Doll. Stands 5 inches high. Has whistle in back. Made of good quality white rubber neatly painted in parts. Weight 2 ounces. Price......**10¢**

RUBBER DOG OR CAT, 10c.

EX671 Rubber Dog or Cat. Made of good quality white rubber with painted features. Equipped with metal whistle. Length, 5 inches. State whether cat or dog is wanted. Weight, each 3 ounces. Price......**10¢**

STUFFED ANGORA DOG, 10c.

EX680 Stuffed Angora Dog. Has long white Angora ears, glass eyes and is mounted on four wood rollers. Small bell on neck. About 7 inches high. Weight, 13 ounces. Price............**10¢**

CELLULOID RATTLE, 10c.

EX607—Celluloid Rattle. Twisted handle with oval celluloid box on one end. Comes in pink and blue colors. State color wanted. Ribbon bow on handle. About 7 inches long. Weight 1 ounce. Price.............**10¢**

CAMPBELL RATTLE, 10c.

FX100—Campbell Rattle. Made of celluloid, with character face. Fancy handle with ring on end. About 7 inches long. Weight, 1 ounce. Price.....................**10¢**

HORSE RATTLE, 10c.

FX101—Horse Rattle. Made of celluloid with twisted handle. About 8 inches long. Weight 1 ounce. Price.....................**10¢**

EGG SHAPED RATTLE, 10c.

EX675—Egg Shaped Rattle. Made of celluloid. Twisted handle. Combination colors pink and white, or blue and white. State combination wanted. About 5 inches long. Weight, 1 ounce. Price.....................**10¢**

BABY RATTLE, 10c.

EV654—Baby Rattle. Four large nickel plated bells mounted on enameled wood handle. About 6 inches long. Weight, 2 ounces. Price....**5¢**

SPECIAL NOTE: It will pay you to make your order large enough to have same shipped by freight. Read our special prepay offer on page 3.

THE ORIGINAL PARCEL POST **KRESGE'S KATALOG** FIVE AND TEN CENT STORE

Special Bargains in Toys at 5c and 10c

EX655—Baby Rattle. Eight large nickel plated bells mounted on white enameled wood handle. About 6 inches long. Weight, 4 ounces.
Price......................**10c**

ROLLING CHIME, 10c.

EX658 Rolling Chime. Seven nickel plated bells mounted on two iron wheels. Indestructible. Weight, 7 ounces. Price..............**10c**

CHILD'S TEA SET, 10c.

FX118—Child's Tea Set. Made of good china, decorated with gold stripe and roses. Set consists of four cups and saucers, sugar, creamer, and tea pot, neatly packed in box. Weight complete 8 ounces. Price......**10c**

TOY KNIFE AND FORK SET, 10c.

FX135—Toy Knife and Fork Set. Set consists of three knives and forks, with three napkins in holders. Handles of knives and forks are of porcelain with neat blue decoration. Weight complete 5 ounces. Price......**10c**

TOY TEA SET, 10c.

EX678—Toy Tea Set. Set consists of two cups and saucers and one tea pot. Made of tin. Weight complete 7 ounces. Price..............**10c**

TIN TEA SET, 10c.

FX119—Tin Tea Set. Set consists of two cups and saucers, tea pot, creamer and cake tray, packed in a box. Weight 7 ounces. Price..............**10c**

Toys should be ordered with other merchandise in order to make a profitable shipment. See our special bargains in dry goods, notions, enamelware, tinware, etc. Be sure to read about our prepay offer on page 3.

TOY SEWING BOX, 10c.

FX136—Toy Sewing Box. Fancy box with picture on cover. Mirror on inside. Contains buttons, embroidery cotton, sewing silk, needles, and thimble. Size 4½x6½x1½ inches. Fastens with snap. Weight 4 ounces.
Price......................**10c**

TOY CLOTH PARASOL 10c.

EX618—Toy Cloth Parasol. Made of American Flag design cloth, bamboo handle, 8 strong wire ribs. About 20 inches long. Weight 3 ounces.
Price......................**10c**

JUMPING ROPE, 5c.

EV652—Jumping Rope. Good strong rope in variegated colors. Full 6 feet long. Has nicely varnished natural wood handle on each end. Weight 3 ounces Price........**5c**

JUMPING ROPE, 10c.

EX653—Jumping Rope. Variegated red, white and blue colors. Full 6 feet long. Nicely varnished red wood handles with brass bell on each handle. Weight 4 ounces Price....**10c**

TOY REINS, 10c.

EX657—Toy Reins. Made of white oil-cloth with double row stitching all over. Has horse's head on adjustable neck piece. Four large nickel plated bells. Weight, 4 ounces. Price..............**10c**

TOY SAD IRON, 10c.

EX695—Toy Sad Iron. Has detachable wooden handle. Iron heavily nickel plated. Can be used for ironing laces, etc. Weight, 11 ounces. Price..............**10c**

TOY SAD IRON, 10c.

EX630—Toy Sad Iron. Black enameled detachable handle. Heavily nickel plated. Equipped with metal stand. Weight, complete 14 ounces. Price..............**10c**

TOY COFFEE MILL, 10c.

EX605—Toy Coffee Mill. Made of strong cast iron painted red. Stands 4 inches high. Will actually grind coffee. Weight, 14 ounces. Price......**10c**

TUB AND BOARD, 10c.

EX608—Tub and Board. Made of heavy tin with heavy wire handles. Red, blue or green. State color wanted. Weight complete, 10 ounces. Price............**10c**

GIRL'S WATCH AND CHAIN, 10c.

FX121—Girl's Watch and Chain. Chain is set with four colored stones and has strong snap. Hands of watch can be turned. Weight complete, 1 ounce.
Price......................**10c**

BOY'S WATCH AND CHAIN, 10c.

FX122—Boy's Watch and Chain. Regular size watch and chain in rich gilt finish, hands turn automatically while winding. Weight, 2 ounces. Price....:....**10c**

NOVELTY CAMERAS, EACH 10c.

EX697—Novelty Cameras. Made like small camera, but has spring snake inside, which jumps out when box is opened. Very startling. Weight, 2 ounces. Price..............**10c**

TOY NURSING BOTTLE, 10c.

FX137—Toy Nursing Bottle. Has securely fitted cork, aluminum cap and bone nipple. Each packed in box and labeled "For my Doll." Weight, 1 ounce. Price..............**10c**

AUTOMATIC TOP, 5c

EV635—Automatic Top. Sides painted red, white and blue. Equipped with strong spring winder and will spin a long time with one winding. Weight, 2 ounces. Price............**5c**

HUMMING TOP, 10c.

EX636—Humming Top. Made of metal and finished in bright colors. Has strong spring winder, packed in separate box. Weight, 3 ounces.
Price......................**10c**

TIRELESS SPINNER TOP, 10c.

EX692—Tireless Spinner Top. Finished in red; white and blue spiral. Spins on little wood pedestal. Weight complete, 5 ounces.
Price......................**10c**

RUBBER BALLOONS, 5c.

EV643—Rubber Balloons. Self-closing valve prevents air or gas from escaping. Colors are red, blue or green. State color wanted. Weight, ½ ounce.
Each.....................**5c**

100 MARBLES, 5c.

EV681—Assorted Marbles. 100 assorted and colored marbles in net bag. Weight, 11 ounces. Per bag. ...**5c**

12 JACK STONES FOR 5c.

E606—Jack Stones. Medium size, made of good cast iron in one piece. Have copper colored finish and rounded points. Weight 12, 4 ozs.
Price 12.................**5c**
E669— Jack Stone Balls. Solid rubber, 1 inch in diameter. Weight 3, 2 ounces. 3 for..............**5c**

INFLATED COLORED BALLS, 10c.

EX666—Inflated Colored Balls. About 2½ inches in diameter. Come in assorted bright colors and pictures. Weight each, 2 ozs.
Price.....**10c**

GRAY RUBBER BALL, 10c.

EX664—Gray Rubber Ball. 2½ inches in diameter. Good quality gray rubber, inflated. For boys and girls. Weight each 2 ozs.
Price........**10c**

SOLID RUBBER BALL, 10c.

EX665—Solid Rubber Ball. Made of good quality gray rubber 2⅜ inches in diameter. Weight each, 7 ounces.
Price.......**10c**

RED RUBBER BALL, 10c.

EX667—Red Rubber Ball. 2½ inches in diameter. Good quality red rubber. Can be used for playing catch, and other games. Weight, 2 ounces.
Price.......**10c**

See Our Bargains in Harmonicas, Games, Etc.

RUBBER BASEBALL, 10c.
EX668—Rubber Baseball. Molded to represent regular baseball. Made of good quality gray rubber, inflated. About 2½ inches in diameter. Weight 2 ounces. Price....................**10c**

ROCKET BASEBALL, 5c.
EV637—Rocket Baseball. Good quality covered ball. Strong hand sewed. Just the thing for catch, knockout, or regular games. Weight each 4 ounces. Price....................**5c**

NATIONAL BASEBALL, 10c.
EX638—National Baseball. Regulation size. Good quality leather covering, hand sewn. Stands up well in regular game. Weight each, 5 ounces. Price....**10c**

CANARY WHISTLE, 5c.
EV672—Canary Whistle. Pewter canary bird whistle, with voice. A very loud and clear whistle. Weight each, 2 ounces. Price...............**5c**

NICKELOID FLUTE, 10c.
EX658—Nickeloid Flute. Key of C. 12½ inches long. Very clear musical tone. Heavily nickel plated. Weight, 2 ounces. Price............**10c**

NICKEL PLATED FIFE, 10c.
EX659—Nickel Plated Fife. Key of B. 15 inches long. Made of strong metal heavily nickel plated. Good mouth piece. Very clear notes. Weight 3 ounces. Price...........**10c**

WOOD CLARINET, 10c.
FX131—Wood Clarinet. Neatly turned, stained black and varnished. Wood mouth piece. Six nickel plated keys. Weight, 3 ounces. Price..**10c**

ACCORDIONS, EACH 10c.
FX127—Accordions. 6½x3½ inches. Made of wood with red paper cover. Four nickel plated keys. Weight, 4 ounces. Price...............**10c**

CONCERTINAS, EACH 10c.
FX128—Concertinas. Hexagon shape. Made of wood, covered with colored paper. Have nickel plated ends. Six reeds. About 4 inches across. Weight, 4 ounces. Price...........**10c**

CELLULOID HARMONICAS, 10c.
FX123—Celluloid Harmonicas. Has 28 reeds. About 5 inches long. Good tone. Imported instrument. Weight, 3 ounces. Price.................**10c**

NICKEL PLATED HARMONICAS, 10c.
FX124—Nickel Plated Harmonicas. 32 reeds. About 5 inches long. Imported instrument. Good clear tones. Weight, 3 ounces. Price.......**10c**

ORGAN HARMONICA, 10c.
FX125—Organ Harmonica. 28 reeds. Nickel plated casing. About 4½x2 inches. Loud tone. Imported instrument. Weight, 3 ounces. Price.................**10c**

OCEANIC HARMONICA, 10c.
FX126—Oceanic Harmonica. 32 reeds. Perforated nickel plated casing. Imported instrument. About 5 inches long. Good, clear tone. Weight, 2 ounces. Price.................**10c**

TIN TRUMPET, 10c.
FX129—Tin Trumpet. Made of bright heavy tin, wrapped with colored cord and tinsel. 11 inches long. Weight 3 ounces. Price.................**10c**

FLOATING DUCKS, 10c.
EX694—Floating Ducks. Set consists of one large, two medium and two small wax ducks. Packed in paste board box. Weight, 3 ounces. Price.................**10c**

LOTTO GAME, 10c.
EX815—Lotto Game. Set consists of numbered cards, wooden discs, and glass counters. All neatly packed in paste board box. Weight complete, 8 ounces. Price.................**10c**

OLD MAID, 10c.
EX621—Old Maid. Card game, which can be played by three to six players. Set consists of 41 cards. Very interesting. Wt. per box 6 ozs. Price.................**10c**

GAME OF AUTHORS, 10c.
EX622—Game of Authors. Set consists of ten books of three cards each. Three to six players can play this game. Educating and amusing. Weight per box, 5 ounces. Price....**10c**

TABLE CROQUET, 10c.
EX623—Table Croquet. Set consists of tape, mallets, balls, etc. Can be played by all the family. Weight complete in box, 10 ounces. Price....**10c**

PAINT BOX, 10c.
EX624—Paint Box. Buster Brown set. Consists of eight water colors, six crayons, brush and five cards for coloring. Weight in box, 5 ounces. Price.....................**10c**

TIDDLEDY WINKS, 10c.
EX616—Tiddledy Winks. Set consists of four colored bone snappers and 16 winks. Weight complete, 5 ounces. Price.....................**10c**

TRANSPARENT SLATE, 10c.
EX133—Transparent Slate. Strong wooden frame with ground glass. Any picture underneath may be traced with pencil. Size 9x11 inches. Weight, 15 ounces. Price.....................**10c**

NESTED BLOCKS, 10c.
FX134—Nested Blocks. Set consists of seven cubes with pictures, alphabet and numbers on blocks. 3½ inch cube. Weight, 7 ounces. Price **10c**

EMBOSSED ALPHABET BLOCKS, 10c.
EX631—Embossed Alphabet Blocks. 12 wooden blocks with letters, numbers, and pictures on each block. Weight per box, 18 ounces. Price.....**10c**

FLAT ALPHABET BLOCKS, 10c.
EX632—Flat Alphabet Blocks. 24 blocks with embossed pictures and letters, painted red and blue. Weight per box, 15 ounces. Price.........**10c**

NOTE.—Postage rates on toys, books, etc., 3 ounces for 1 cent, regardless of distance. Printed books cannot be sent by Parcel Post.

CHILDREN'S TOY BOOKS, EACH, 10c.
BX940—Children's Toy Books. Size, 7x9 inches, 12 pages. Cover and pages of linen, printed in plain type, with alphabet, numbers and pictures. Illustrated in colors. Weight, each, 2 ounces. Price **10c**

CHILDREN'S TOY BOOKS, EACH, 5c.
BV941—Children's Toy Books. Size, 4½x6½ inches, 12 pages. Cover and pages of linen, printed in plain type, with alphabet, numbers and pictures. Illustrated in colors. Weight, each, 1 ounce. Price...........**5c**

ILLUSTRATED TOY BOOKS, EACH, 10c.
BX943—Illustrated Toy Books. Size, 7½x14 inches. Fancy cut out shapes of boys and girls as illustrated. Illustrations in colors. 12 pages including cover. Weight, each, 4 ounces. Price......................**10c**

LARGE SIZE TOY BOOKS, EACH, 10c.
BX944—Large Size Toy Books. 9½x12 inches. 16 pages including cover, which is heavy flexible paper. Large clear print. Two subjects, fire department, and trains. State subject wanted. Weight, each, 6 ounces. Price......................**10c**

THE ORIGINAL PARCEL POST **KRESGE'S KATALOG** FIVE AND TEN CENT STORE

Practical Toys For Children at 10c Each

CHILDREN'S PAINTING BOOK, 10c.

BX945— Children's Painting Book. Size, 9¼x10¼ inches. Contains 24 pages of plain and colored illustrations. Paints for coloring plain pictures included with book. Weight each, 6 ounces. Price......................**10C**

MOTHER GOOSE BOOKS, EACH, 10c.

BX946— Mother Goose Books. Size, 10½ x 13 inches. Flexible cover with illustrations in beautiful colors. Three subjects: Mother Goose Melodies, Little Red Riding Hood, and Animals. State kind wanted. Weight, each, 5 ounces. Price.....................**10C**

WOOD TENPINS, 10c.

EX617— Wood Tenpins. Pins are 4¼ inches high, red and black stripes. Two wooden balls. Weight complete, 15 ounces. Price....**10C**

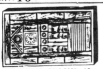

BUILDING BLOCKS, 10c.

EX601—Building Blocks. Set consists of 33 pieces in four colors. All packed in neat wooden box. Weight complete, 22 ounces. Price....**10C**

BUILDING BLOCKS, 5c.

EV600— Building Blocks. Set consists of 18 pieces in four colors. All packed in neat wooden box. Weight complete, 7 ounces. Price......**5C**

DOMINOES, PER BOX, 5c.

EV633—Dominoes. Made of black wood with painted white spots. All packed in neat box. Weight box, 6 ounces. Price, per box.........**5C**

DOMINOES PER BOX, 10c.

EX634—Dominoes. Made of composition ebonized wood with white enameled spots. American Flag on back. Neatly packed in cardboard box. Weight, 9 ounces. Price.**10C**

WATER PISTOL, 10c.

EX660—Water Pistol. An amusing toy. Has rubber bulb and shoots a fine stream of water. Metal parts nickel plated. Weight, 2 ounces. Price......**10C**

POP PISTOL, 10c.

EX609 Pop Pistol. Made of strong metal. Shoots a small cork which is attached to string. Loud report but absolutely harmless. Neatly packed in box. Weight, 5 ounces. Price, **10C**

TARGET SET, 10c.

FX108 Target Set. 6x10 inch pasteboard target, rubber tip arrow and Colt shape pistol, with japanned handle. Weight complete, 3½ ounces. Price.........................**10C**

BOY SCOUT GUN, 10c.

FX138—Boy Scout Gun. Strong metal parts with stained wood handle. Shoots wood arrow with vacuum bulb. Target and arrow included with gun. About 18 inches long. Weight complete, 7 ounces. Price........**10C**

PISTOL, HOLSTER AND BELT, 10c.

EX677—Pistol, Holster and Belt. Belt and holster of patent leather with harmless toy pistol. Nickeled buckle and loop. Something every boy wants. Weight complete, 6 ounces. Price....................**10C**

TOOL CHEST, 10c.

EX6022—Tool Chest. Size of chest 8x2½x1¼ inches. Contains saw, hammer, pinchers, square, and screw driver. Weight complete, 7 ounces. Price.....................**10C**

GARDEN SET, 10c.

EX645—Garden Set. Set consists of rake, hoe, and trowel. Handles 12 inches long. Strong and well made. Weight of set 10 ounces. Price..**10C**

HORSE SAVINGS BANK, 10c.

EX603 Horse Savings Bank. Made of heavy cast iron, nicely covered with gold paint. A very strong and serviceable bank. Weight, 11 ounces. Price......**10C**

Be sure to state Katalog Number when ordering.

PIG SAVINGS BANK, 10c.

EX604—Pig Savings Bank. Made of strong cast iron. Pig is in sitting position. All heavily gilted. Wt., 12 ounces. Price.....................**10C**

MECHANICAL MOUSE, 10c.

FX103—Mechanical Mouse. Very entertaining. Has wagging tail. Works mechanically and will travel by itself when started. Packed in neat pasteboard box. Weight, 2 ounces. Price.........................**10C**

MECHANICAL AUTO, 10c.

FX104 Mechanical Auto. Green body with red wheels. Man driver. Propelled by clock work and winds with key. About 4½ inches long. Weight complete, 3 ounces. Price.........**10C**

MECHANICAL TRICYCLE, 10c.

FX105 Mechanical Tricycle. Yellow body with red wheels. Lady driver About 5 inches long. Runs by clock work. Weight complete, 3 ounces. Price......**10C**

HOOK AND LADDER, 10c.

EX648—Hook and Ladder. Wagon painted red and ladder painted yellow. Detachable ladder, driver, and horse. About 11 inches long. Weight complete, 16 ounces. Price........**10C**

PASSENGER TRAIN, 10c.

EX649—Toy Passenger Train. Locomotive, tender, and two passenger cars. Locomotive painted black, cars red. Length of train 14 inches. Weight complete, 19 ounces. Price.....**10C**

TOY LOCOMOTIVE, 10c.

EX646—Toy Locomotive. Tender attached. Red wheels. Made of cast iron nicely enameled. 7 inches long. Weight, 14 ounces. Price......**10C**

PASSENGER COACH, 10c.

EX647—Toy Passenger Coach. Made of cast iron, painted red, with gold trimmings. Moving wheels. Matches EX646. About 7 inches long. Weight, 16 ounces. Price.......**10C**

EX685—Locomotive and Tender. Made of tin, black enameled, with red wheels. Length over all, 17 inches. Matches cars below. Weight, complete, 10 ounces. Price............**10C**

EX686 — Toy Passenger Car. Made of tin and painted red. Matches locomotive and tender above. Can be attached to make a train. 9 inches long, 4 inches high. Weight, each 7 ounces. Price.....................**10C**

EX687 — Toy Coal Cars. 11 inches long, 3 inches wide, and 2 inches deep. Marked Penn. R. R. Matches locomotive and passenger car above. Weight, each, 7 ounces. Price.**10C**

EX688 — Toy Oil Tank Car. Made of tin and neatly enameled. Looks like regular oil car. Lettered Standard Oil Line. Matches the cars above. 8¼ inches long, 4 inches high. Weight, 7 ounces. Price.................**10C**

EX689 — Toy Gondola Coal Car. Duplicate of large cars. Has automatic dump. 9 inches long. Neatly painted. Matches the numbers described above. Weight, 7 ounces. Price......**10C**

EX690 — Merchants' Despatch Freight Ca Exact duplicate of the large cars. 9 inches over all. Has sliding doors. Matches cars described above. Weight, 7 ounces. Price.**10C**

EX683 — Toy Automatic Dump Cart. Has single horse and driver. Made of tin and neatly painted. Body is released by automatic spring. 14 inches long over all. Wt., complete, 7 ozs. Price.................**10C**

EX679 — Panama Canal Derrick. Can be turned around on its base. Small shovel which raises and lowers automatically. 6 inches high, 6 inch crane. Weight, 5 ounces. Price **10C**

Aluminum Ware Bargains, 5 and 10c

CHILD'S ALUMINUM MUG, 10c.
HX366—Child's Mug. Large size. Highly polished, seamless aluminum. Handle securely riveted to cup. Will stand the hardest kind of treatment. Weight, 1 ounce. Price, each.............**10C**

GRADUATED MEASURING CUP, 10c.

HX367—Graduated Measuring Cup. One pint cup with divisions for $\frac{1}{4}$, $\frac{1}{3}$, $\frac{1}{2}$, $\frac{2}{3}$ and $\frac{3}{4}$ pints, plainly stamped on each side. Made of aluminum; riveted handle. Weight, 1 ounce. Price, each.......**10C**

CHILD'S ORNAMENTED MUG, 10c.

HX365 — Child's Ornamented Mug. Well made from one piece of pure aluminum. Decorated with bright band top and bottom, satin finished center. Weight, 1 ounce. Price, each............**10C**

ALUMINUM TEA PERCOLATOR, 10c.

HX361 — Tea Percolator of Aluminum. Medium size, perforated egg shape with chain. Easy and economical to prepare tea without getting leaves in cup. Weight, 1 ounce. Price, each............**10C**

ALUMINUM COFFEE PERCOLATOR, 10c.
HX362—Coffee Percolator. Large size. Top, bottom and middle sections closely perforated, screw top. Handle attached. No need of strainer to keep grounds from getting in cup. Weight, 2 ounces. Price, each.....................**10C**

ALUMINUM TEA BALL, 5c

HV364—Magic Tea Ball. Pure aluminum. Detachable wire handle, Holds top in place. You use less tea and get better results with these tea balls. Weight 1 ounce. Price, each **5C**

ALUMINUM SPOUT STRAINER, 5c.

HV363—Spout Strainer. Pure aluminum. To be attached to either tea or coffee pot. Has wire prong for inserting in spout. Strainer is bell shaped. Weight, 1 ounce. Price, each............**5C**

LEMON JUICE EXTRACTOR, 5c.

HV372—Lemon Juice Extractor. Very practical article. Pure aluminum. Will fit any size glass. Perforated bottom to permit juice to flow out, but keep back seeds. Weight, 1 ounce. Price, each.**5C**

COMBINATION DOUGHNUT CUTTER, 10c.
HX3722 — Combination Doughnut and Cookie Cutter. Inner ring for cutting hole in doughnuts is instantly removable. Made of solid aluminum with strong wooden handle. Weight, 2 ounces. Price, each...........**10C**

ALUMINUM JELLY MOLD, 5c.
HV381 — Jelly Mold. Dome shape design, stamped from solid aluminum. Opening $2\frac{1}{4}$ inches wide, $1\frac{3}{4}$ inches high. Has fluted sides and flat bottom. Weight, 1 ounce. Price, each..**5C**

SEAMLESS JELLY MOLD, 5c.
HV382 — Jelly Mold. Shell design, seamless, of pure aluminum. Opening, $2\frac{3}{4}$ inches wide, $1\frac{3}{4}$ inches high. Something that is always needed. Weight, 1 ounce. Price, each.............**5C**

1 PINT JELLY MOLD, 10c.
HX380 — One Pint Jelly Mold. Stamped from solid aluminum. Beautiful fluted design. Opening about 5 inches wide, $2\frac{3}{4}$ inches high. Has smooth flat bottom. Weight, 2 ounces. Price, each.......**10C**

ALUMINUM CLOTHES SPRINKLER, 5c.

HX383 — Aluminum Clothes Sprinkler. Strongly made of stamped pure aluminum with cork ring which fits ordinary size bottle. Sprinkles by simply shaking bottle. Wt. 1 ounce. Price, each..**5C**

ALUMINUM FUNNELS, 10c.
HX370 — Bell Shape Funnel. Highly polished, made from pure aluminum. Has ring for hanging up. Half pint size. Weight 1 ounce. Price, each **10C**
HX371 — Aluminum Funnel. Stamped from single piece of aluminum; riveted handle. Half pint size. Regular shape. Weight, 1 ounce. Price, each.**10C**

COLLAPSIBLE DRINKING CUP, 10c.
HX368 — Collapsible Drinking Cup. Three sections, with base and cover. Beautiful mottled finish. Etched border around top section and cover. Just the thing to carry with you on picnics, outings, and on trains. Weight, 1 ounce. Price, each...........**10C**

COLLAPSIBLE SMALL CUP, 10c.
HX369 — Collapsible Cup. In case. Four sections. Made of pure aluminum, milled edge top and bottom, decorated top. Easy to slip in the pocket or suitcase. Takes very little space. Weight, 1 ounce. Price, each. **10C**

ALUMINUM SOAP BOX, 10c.
HX375 — Aluminum Soap Box. Holds large size cake. Hinged top, satin finish, embossed. An indispensable article for travelers who prefer to take along their own soap. Weight, 1 ounce. Price, each....................**10C**

ALUMINUM PUFF BOX, FANCY EMBOSSED FINISH, SPECIAL AT 10c.

HX377 — Aluminum Puff Box. Bright finish. Large size. Handsomely decorated with ornamental bands. A very convenient article for any dresser. Will not scratch or mar the dresser top. Weight, 1 ounce. Price, each.........**10C**

ALUMINUM BON BON TRAY, 10c.

HX378 — Bon Bon Tray. Satin finish. Made of one piece aluminum, deeply embossed with rich floral design. $5\frac{1}{2}$ inches wide. Just the thing for parties, house gatherings, and the like. Weight, 1 ounce. Price, each **10C**

ORNAMENTAL MATCH SAFE, 10c.
HX379 — Ornamental Match Safe. Oak leaf and acorn design. Combination embossed and bright finish. Very artistic, an ornament for any wall. 6 inches high. Weight, 1 ounce. Price, ea.**10C**

ALUMINUM CIGAR CASE, 10c.
HX376 — New Style Aluminum Cigar Holder. Hinged top, well made. Prevents cigars being crushed in pocket. Holds three cigars. A useful article any man will appreciate. Weight, 1 ounce. Price, each **10C**

ALUMINUM WALL SOAP DISH, 10c.

HX384—Wall Soap Dish. Made of pure aluminum. A necessity in the kitchen or bathroom. 5 inches long, $3\frac{1}{2}$ inches wide. Bright finish. Can be attached and removed in a minute. Weight, 1 ounce. Price, each **10C**

ELECTRO-SILICON POLISH, 10c.

HX405 — Electro Silicon. An unrivaled polish for gold, silver. aluminum and other fine metals. One box will last a long time. Not wasteful and will not spoil by keeping. Weight, 4 ounces. Price, per box **10C**

ALUMINUM HOUSE NUMBERS, 2 FOR 5c.
HH386—House Numbers. Stamped and embossed from pure seamless, bright finish aluminum. Perforated for nailing on. Will not tarnish. When ordering, state the numbers you want. Numbers run from 1 to 0, also $\frac{1}{2}$. Weight, 2, 1 oz. Price, 2 for...**5C**

When ordering aluminum ware, tinware, etc., be sure to include enough dry goods, notions, woodenware, hardware, etc., to make a profitable shipment. We pay the freight on all orders amounting to $10 or more to all points in the states mentioned in our prepay list on Page 3 of this Katalog.

THE ORIGINAL PARCEL POST **KRESGE'S KATALOG** FIVE AND TEN CENT STORE

Silver Plated and Aluminum Ware, 5c and 10c

SILVER PLATED SALT AND PEPPERS, 10c.
HX339—Silver plated Salt and Pepper Shakers. Squat base. Heavy scroll base. A dependable article. State whether salt or pepper is wanted. Weight, 3 ounces. Price, each.................**10c**

TALL SILVER PLATED SHAKERS, 10c.
HX340—Tall Silver Plated Shakers. 3 inches high. Good, heavy plate. Rose engraved. Fancy scroll design top, and good, clean perforations. Salt shakers only. Weight, 3 ounces. Price,..**10c**

See page 96 for bargains in silver plated ware.

SILVER PLATED HOLY WATER FOUNT, 10c.
HX338 — Silver Plated Holy Water Fount. 5½ inches tall. Good heavy plate. Deep well. Perforated for hanging on wall. Weight, 5 ounces. Each..........**10c**

WHITE METAL CRUCIFIXES, EACH, 10c.
HX358 — White Metal Crucifixes. Good heavy base, good white metal. Stands 4¾ inches high. Metal is especially durable and will give good service. Weight, 5 ounces. Price, each.........................**10c**

SILVER PLATED CANDLE STICKS, 10c.
HX357—Silver Plated Candle Sticks. Good, heavy plate. Broad base prevents tipping. Will hold even the largest common candles without falling over. 4½ inches high. Weight, 6 ounces. Price, each..**10c**

HV397   HX398   HX399

TEA BELLS, 5 AND 10c. EACH.
HV397—5-inch Tea Bells. Nickel plated base. Polished black wood handle. Clear ring. Weight, 4 ounces. Price, each **5c**
HX398—Nickel Plated Tea Bells. Fancy base and handle. 3¾ inches high. A very artistic little bell. Weight, 3 ounces. Price, each.............**10c**
HX399—5½-inch Tea Bells. Heavy nickel plated. Plain base. Fancy handle. Highly finished. Weight, 4 ounces. Price, each **10c**

DOUBLE ACTION BICYCLE BELLS, 10c.
HX400 — Double Action Bicycle Bell. Easy to attach. Strong mechanism. Best quality metal, nickel plated. Wt., 4 ounces. Price, each..............**10c**

NICKEL PLATED CALL BELLS, 10c.
HX401 — Nickel Plated Call Bells. Highly finished nickel plated. Easy tap. Clear ring. 3-inch base. Weight, 4 ounces. Price, each...........**10c**

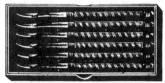

NICKEL PLATED NUT PICK SET, 10c.
HX404—Nickel Plated Nut Pick Set. Set comprises six picks. Best steel. Turned handles. Bent needle point picks. Weight, 4 ounces. Per set of 6..**10c**

NICKEL PLATED NUT CRACKERS, 10c.
HX403—Nickel Plated Nut Crackers. Fancy embossed, never-slip grip handles. Securely riveted to hinge. Good steel springs. Generous cracking space. Weight, 5 ounces. Price.....................**10c**

SILVER PLATED BABY SPOONS, 10c.

HX336— Silver Plated Baby Spoons. Troy pattern. Fully polished, heavy silver plate, handle is finished in a very artistic pattern. A good value. Weight, 1 ounce. Price.......................**10c**

CHILD'S SILVER PLATED MUG, 10c.
HX341 — Child's Silver Plated Mug. Fancy scroll bottom and handle. Nicely plated. Will give good, long service. A special value. Weight, 3 ounces. Price, each. **10c**

SILVER PLATED NAPKIN RINGS, 10c.
HX356 — Silver Plated Napkin Rings. Made of good quality metal base, heavily plated. Fancy scroll work border. A good, dependable ring. Wt., 3 ounces. Price, ea..**10c**

SILVER PLATED TOOTH PICK HOLDER, 10c.
HX355 — Silver Plated Tooth Pick Holder. Fancy engraving and scroll edge. Good, heavy plate and fine quality white metal base. A very useful article. Wt., 2 ounces. Price....**10c**

FANCY TOOTH PICK HOLDERS, 10c.
HX354 — Fancy Tooth Pick Holders. Basket shape, good, strong handle. Nicely engraved. Heavy plate and good quality white metal base. Weight, 3 ounces. Price.........**10c**

PURE ALUMINUM PEPPER SHAKER, 10c.
HX350 — Pure Aluminum Pepper Shaker. Made of best quality aluminum. Loaded bottom. Can't tip over. If salt shaker is wanted ask for HX351. Weight, 2 ounces. Price.....................**10c**

ALUMINUM SALT SHAKERS, 10c.
HX359 — Aluminum Salt Shakers. Best quality aluminum. Satin finish top. Polished base. If pepper shaker is wanted ask for HX360. Weight, 1 ounce. Price....**10c**

OCTAGON SHAPE ALUMINUM SHAKERS, 10c.
HX352 — Octagon Shape Aluminum Shakers. Made of pure aluminum. Weighted bottoms. Cannot tip over. If pepper shaker is wanted ask for No. HX353. Weight, 2 ounces. Price.............**10c**

3-INCH ALUMINUM SALT OR PEPPER SHAKERS, 10c.
HX348—3-inch Aluminum Salt Shakers. Large size. Pure aluminum. Loaded bottom. Cannot tip over. State whether salt or pepper is wanted. Weight 3 ounces. Price, each.......**10c**

SLOTTED ALUMINUM BASTING SPOON, 10c.

HX342—Slotted Aluminum Basting Spoon. 10 inches long. Made of pure aluminum. Three slots. Has hole in end of handle for hanging up. Weight, 2 ounces. Price, each......................**10c**

10-INCH ALUMINUM BASTING SPOONS, 10c.

HX343—10-inch Aluminum Basting Spoons. Made of pure aluminum, highly polished. Light but very strong. Weight, 2 ounces. Price............**10c**

PURE ALUMINUM TABLE SPOONS, 5c.
HV345—Pure Aluminum Table Spoons. Full size. Made of pure aluminum, highly polished. Something always used. Weight, 1 ounce. Price, each....**5c**

PURE ALUMINUM CREAM LADLE, 10c.

HX344—Pure Aluminum Cream Ladle. 7½ inches long. Made of pure aluminum, highly polished. Cream or gravy ladle. Deep bowl. Weight, 2 ounces. Price, each. **10c**

4-INCH ALUMINUM SUGAR SHAKER, SPECIAL AT 10c.
HX374 — Aluminum Sugar Shaker. Satin finish top, polished base. 4 inches high. Convenient for sugaring pies, cakes, etc., where only a sprinkle of sugar is wanted at one time. Weight, 1 ounce. Price. **10c**

All of our silver plated ware is made with good quality metal base. All of the aluminum ware shown on these pages is of the best quality, and we guarantee every article to be as represented.

THE ORIGINAL PARCEL POST KRESGE'S KATALOG FIVE AND TEN CENT STORE

Silver Plated Tableware—Special Values 10c

All of the items shown on this page have durable quality metal base, heavily silver plated. Come in Beautiful Colonial or Detroit patterns. We also show several pieces in the Antwerp pattern which is similar to the Colonial pattern.

SILVER PLATED DINNER KNIFE, 10c.
HX300—Medium size **Dinner Knife**, Sheffield pattern, triple silver plated, highly polished. Length, 9½ inches, Weight, 3 ounces. Special price........ **10C**
HX301—Sheffied **Dessert Knife**, same as above, but slightly smaller. Weight, 2 ounces. Price... **10C**

SILVER PLATED DINNER FORK, 10c.
HX302—Medium size **Dinner Fork**, Sheffield pattern; triple silver plated. Highly polished. Four tines. Length, 7½ inches. Weight, 2 ounces. Price, each **10C**
HX303—Silver plated **Dessert Fork**, same as above but slightly smaller. Length, 7½ inches. Weight 2 ounces. Price **10C**

SILVER PLATED TABLE FORK, 10c.
HX304—**Table Fork**, heavily silver plated. Four tines. Comes in Detroit pattern. Length, 7½ inches. Weight, 2 ounces. Price, each **10C**
HX305—Same as above in dessert size, length, 7 inches. Weight, 1 ounce. Price, each **10C**

SILVER PLATED TABLE FORK, 10c.
HX306—**Table Fork**, heavily silver plated. Highly polished. Four tines. Comes in Colonial pattern. Length, 7½ inches. Weight, 2 ounces. Price **10C**
HX307—Same as above in dessert size. Length, 7 inches. Weight, 1 ounce. Price, each **10C**

SILVER PLATED COLD MEAT FORK, 10c.
HX315—**Cold Meat Fork**, heavily silver plated. Made in beautiful Antwerp or Detroit pattern. Length, 8½ inches. Weight, 2 ounces. Price, each **10C**

SILVER PLATED OYSTER FORK, 10c.
HX316—**Oyster Fork**, heavily silver plated. Three tines. Long handle. Made especially for serving oysters. Comes in Detroit pattern. Length, 6½ inches. Weight, 1 ounce. Price, each **10C**
HX317—Same as above in Colonial pattern. Weight, 1 ounce. Price, each **10C**

SILVER PLATED PICKLE FORK, 10c.
HX318—**Pickle Fork**, heavily silver plated. Long handle. Three tines. Side tines barbed. Length, 7 inches. Comes in Detroit pattern only. Weight, 1 ounce. Price, each **10C**

SILVER PLATED BUTTER KNIFE, 10c.
HX319—**Butter Knife**, heavily silver plated. Transverse handle, vertical blade. Colonial pattern. Length, 6½ inches. Weight, 1 ounce. Price, each **10C**
HX320—Same as above in Detroit pattern. Weight, 1 ounce. Price, each **10C**

SILVER PLATED BUTTER SPREADER, 10c.
HX321—**Butter Spreader**, heavily silver plated. Highly polished. Broad thin blade. Detroit pattern. Length, 5½ inches. Weight, 1 ounce. Price, each **10C**
HX322—Same as above, in Colonial pattern. Weight, 1 ounce. Price, each **10C**

SILVER PLATED SUGAR TONGS, 10c.
HX325—**Sugar Tongs**, heavily silver plated. Buffed and polished. Deeply embossed rich Antwerp pattern. Length, 5 inches. Weight, 1 ounce. Price, each **10C**

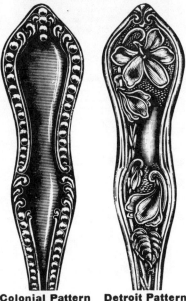

Colonial Pattern

The above design shows our Colonial pattern. The edges are of an artistically beaded design with highly polished centers. A very popular style.

Detroit Pattern

The above illustration shows our beautiful Detroit pattern, one of the most exquisite designs ever made. French gray finish handles with beautiful Lily design on front and back.

The pictures shown above illustrate tablespoon handles in actual size.
When ordering silverware which comes in Colonial or Detroit patterns, please state the patterns desired.

SILVER PLATED TEASPOON, 10c.
HX308—**Teaspoon**, heavily silver plated. Highly polished bowl. Comes in beautiful Detroit pattern. Length, 5¾ inches. Weight, 1 ounce. Price, each **10C**

SILVER PLATED DESSERT SPOON, 10c.
HX309—**Dessert Spoon**, same as above, except a little larger. Length, 7 inches. Weight, 1 ounce. Price, each **10C**

SILVER PLATED COFFEE SPOON, 10c.
HX310—Same as above in **Coffee Size**, which is a little smaller than a teaspoon. Weight, 2 ounces. Price, each **10C**

SILVER PLATED TABLESPOON, 10c
HX311—**Tablespoon**, same as HX308. Length, 7¾ inches. Weight, 2 ounces. Price, each.... **10C**

SILVER PLATED TEASPOON, 10c.
HX312—**Teaspoon**, heavily silver plated. Highly polished bowl. Comes in Colonial pattern. Length, 8 inches. Weight, 1 ounce. Price, each **10C**

SILVER PLATED DESSERT SPOON, 10c.
HX313—**Dessert Spoon**, heavily silver plated. Highly polished bowl. Comes in Colonial pattern. Length, 7 inches. Weight, 1 ounce. Price, each **10C**

SILVER PLATED TABLESPOON, 10c.
HX314—**Tablespoon**, heavily silver plated. Highly polished bowl. Comes in Colonial pattern. Length, 8 inches. Weight, 2 ounces. Price, each **10C**

OUR GUARANTEE

We guarantee the silver plated ware shown on this page to give splendid satisfaction in every particular. Be sure to state pattern desired when ordering.

SILVER PLATED SUGAR SHELL, 10c.
HX326—**Sugar Shell**, heavily silver plated. Oval shape bowl. Highly polished. Detroit pattern. Length, about 6 inches. Weight, 1 ounce. Price, each... **10C**
HX327—Same as above in Colonial pattern. Weight, 1 ounce. Price, each **10C**

SILVER PLATED BERRY SPOON, 10c.
HX328—**Large Berry Spoon**, heavily silver plated. Deeply embossed in rich Antwerp or Detroit pattern. Polished bowl. Length, 8 inches. Weight, 2 ounces. Price, each................. **10C**

SILVER PLATED PIE KNIFE, 10c.
HX329 — **Pie Knife**, heavily silver plated and highly polished. Size of blade, 3x4 inches long. Made in Antwerp pattern only. Length of knife, 9½ inches. Weight, 2 ounces. Price, each **10C**

SILVER PLATED GRAVY LADLE, 10c.

HX330—**Gravy Ladle**, heavily silver plated. Highly polished bowl. Made in Antwerp or Detroit pattern. Length, 6½ inches. Weight, 2 ounces. Price, each... **10C**

SILVER PLATED CREAM LADLE, 10c.
HX331—**Cream Ladle**, heavily silver plated. Highly polished bowl. Comes in Antwerp pattern only. Length, 5½ inches. Weight, 1 ounce. Price, each **10C**

SILVER PLATED ORANGE SPOON, 10c.
HX332—**Orange Spoon**, heavily silver plated. Oblong bowl, highly polished. For serving oranges or grape fruit. Detroit pattern. Length, 6 inches. Weight, 1 ounce. Price, each **10C**
HX333—Same as above, in Colonial pattern. Weight, 1 ounce. Price, each **10C**

SILVER PLATED FRUIT KNIFE, 10c.
HX334—**Fruit Knife**, heavily silver plated. Plain design. Sharp pointed blade. To be used when serving fruit. Length, 6½ inches. Weight, 1 ounce. Price, each **10C**

SILVER PLATED BOUILLON SPOON, 10c.
HX323—**Bouillon Spoon**, heavily silver plated. Round bowl, highly polished. Detroit pattern. Length, 6½ inches. Weight, 1 ounce. Price, each.. **10C**
HX324—Same as above, in Colonial pattern. Weight, 1 ounce. Price, each **10C**

CHILD'S KNIFE OR FORK, EACH 10c.
HX321—Detroit pattern. Child's fork. Heavily silver plated. Fancy handles. A very good, serviceable knife or fork. State which is wanted. Weight, each, 1 ounce. Price, each............... **10C**

CUTLERY, WIRE GOODS AT 5 & 10¢

IN listing our Cutlery and Wire Goods, we have endeavored to select only such items as have proven to be exceptional values for the money. We have been specializing in buying and selling 5c and 10c merchandise for the past 16 years, and the millions of customers patronizing our many 5c and 10c stores show their appreciation of our efforts by continuing to buy from us year after year. The Cutlery and Wire Goods departments in Kresge's 5c and 10c stores are visited daily by many thousands of customers.

Hundreds of dependable bargains in every-day necessities are shown on this and the following pages in Cutlery and Wire Goods, etc., nothing over 10c.

STEEL BLADE KNIFE, 5c.
HV500—Steel Blade Knife. Medium size. 5½-inch blade. Highly polished. Cocobola handle. Square end. Weight, 2 ounces. Price, each............**5C**
HV5000—Fork. To match knife above. Bright rustproof metal, three tines. Weight, 2 ounces. Price, each.................................**5C**

CHILD'S KNIFE AND FORK, 10c.
HX501—Child's Knife and Fork. Knife has bright steel blade, 4½ inches long, securely attached Cocobola handle. Three tined, bright steel fork to match. Weight, 2 ounces. Price, per pair............**10C**

CHILD'S KNIFE AND FORK, EACH, 10c.
HX502—Child's Knife and Fork. Selected white bone handle. 4½ inch blade. Heavy ornamental bolster where blade enters handle. Fork to match. Must be ordered in pairs. Weight, per pair, 3 ounces. Price, knife, **10C**. Fork.................**10C**

CHILD'S KNIFE AND FORK, EACH, 10c.
HX503—Child's Knife and Fork. Knife has bright steel blade, 4½ inches long, curved shape. Fancy bolster, selected Cocobola handle, shaped end. Three tined fork to match. Must be ordered in pairs. Wt., per pair, 3 ounces. Price, knife, **10C**. Fork.**10C**

TABLE KNIFE AND FORK, EACH, 10c.
HX504—Table Knife and Fork. Medium size. Knife has 5½-inch curved blade with beveled back. Heavy double bolster. Plain ebony handle. Four tined fork to match. Must be ordered in pairs. Weight, per pair, 5 ounces. Price, knife, **10C**
Fork **10C**

TABLE KNIFE AND FORK, EACH, 10c.
HX505—Table Knife and Fork. Medium size. 5½-inch scimeter steel blade, beveled back, ebony handle with heavy notch design bolster at each end. Four tined fork to match. Must be ordered in pairs. Weight, per pair, 5 ounces. Price, knife **10C**
Fork **10C**

KNIFE AND FORK, EACH, 10c.
HX506—Knife and Fork. Very fine. 5½-inch curved bright steel blade, beveled back, double crossed design bolster at each end. Carefully selected Cocobola handle. Fork to match. Must be ordered in pairs. Weight, per pair 6 ounces. Price, knife, **10C**
Fork **10C**

KNIFE AND FORK, EACH, 10c.
HX507—Knife and Fork. Fine thin curved steel blade, beveled back, fancy ring design bolster at each end. Selected Cocobola handle. Four tined fork to match. Must be ordered in pairs. Weight, per pair, 5 ounces. Price, knife, **10C**. Fork.......**10C**

TABLE KNIFE AND FORK, EACH, 10c.
HX508—Table Knife and Fork. Knife has fine polished steel convex blade, beveled back. Picked Cocobola handle, heavy bolstered handle end. Fork to match. Must be ordered in pairs. Weight, per pair, 5 ounces. Price, knife, **10C**. Fork....**10C**

Our Guarantee
We absolutely guarantee the cutlery represented on this page to be exactly as described, and we will cheerfully refund your money if you are not satisfied with your purchase. The blades and tines are highly polished; handles smooth and well made, riveted and bolstered. It would pay you to order at least six pairs—they are exceptional values at the price. Nothing over 10c.

WHITE HANDLED TABLE KNIFE AND FORK, EACH, 10c.
HX509—White Handled Table Knife and Fork. Polished steel blade, curved shape. Solid white bone handle, single bolster. Four tined fork to match. Must be ordered in pairs. Weight, per pair, 5 ounces. Price, knife, **10C**. Fork....................**10C**

FANCY TABLE KNIFE AND FORK, EACH, 10c.
HX510—Fancy Table Knife and Fork. Heavy, bright steel curved blade, beveled back. 5½-inch selected white bone handle, double ring design bolster. Four tined fork to match. Must be ordered in pairs. Weight, per pair, 6 ounces. Price, knife, **10C**
Fork **10C**

STAG HANDLE KNIFE AND FORK, EACH, 10c.
HX511—Stag Handle Knife and Fork. 5½-inch bright steel curved blade with beveled back. Plain stag handle, single bolster. Four tined fork to match. Must be ordered in pairs. Weight, per pair, 5 ounces. Price, knife, **10C**. Fork..................**10C**

6-INCH BUTCHER KNIFE, 10c.
HX512—Butcher Knife. Fine heavy steel 6-inch blade. Polished Cocobola handle. Blade goes all the way through handle. Weight, 5 ounces. Price, each..................................**10C**

7-INCH BUTCHER KNIFE, 10c.
HX513—Butcher Knife. 7-inch finely tempered bright steel blade. Cocobola handle. Blade goes all the way through handle. Weight, 5 ounces. Price, each..................................**10C**

8½-INCH BUTCHER KNIFE, 10c.
HX514—Butcher Knife. 8½-inch blade, 1¼ inches wide of finely tempered and highly polished steel. Selected Cocobola handle. Weight, 6 ounces. Price, each..................................**10C**

Carvers, Kitchen Knives, etc., Nothing Over 10c

TEMPERED STEEL HAM SLICER, 10c.

HX515 — Tempered Steel Ham Slicer. Has 9-inch tempered steel blade. Fine cutting edge. Round ebony handle. Average width of blade, ⅞-inch. Weight, 2 ounces. Price.. **10c**

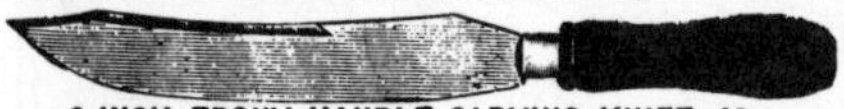

8-INCH EBONY HANDLE CARVING KNIFE, 10c.

HX516 — 8-inch Ebony Handle Carving Knife. Made of best tempered steel. French blade. Fine ebony handle. A strictly high grade carver. Good cutting edge. Weight, 3 ounces. Price.................................. **10c**

FLAT SIDE EBONY HANDLE CARVING KNIFE, 10c.

HX517 — Flat Side Ebony Handle Carving Knife. Tempered steel blade. Flat ebony handle. Scimeter edge. Good carver. Length of blade, 8½ inches. Weight, 3 ounces. Price.. **10c**

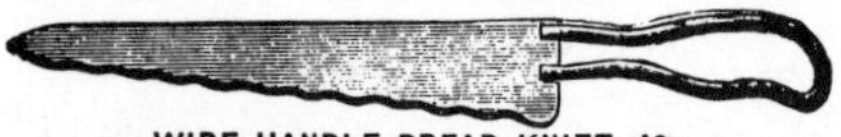

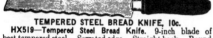

WIRE HANDLE BREAD KNIFE, 10c.

HX518 — Wire Handle Bread Knife. 10-inch tempered steel blade. Serrated edge. Nickel plated blade. Wire handle securely attached to the blade. Weight, 4½ ounces. Price.. **10c**

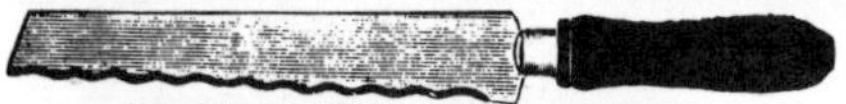

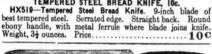

TEMPERED STEEL BREAD KNIFE, 10c.

HX519—Tempered Steel Bread Knife. 9-inch blade of best tempered steel. Serrated edge. Straight back. Round ebony handle, with metal ferrule where blade joins knife. Weight, 3½ ounces. Price........................ **10c**

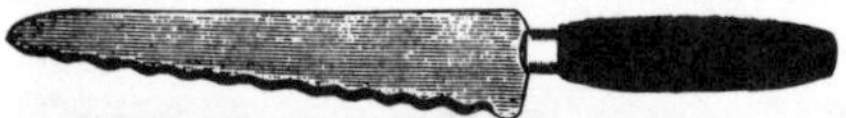

10-INCH TEMPERED STEEL BREAD KNIFE, 10c.

HX520—10-inch Tempered Steel Bread Knife. Blade made of best tempered steel, serrated edge. Sabatier shape. Round black enameled handle, with metal ferrule on handle. Weight, 3 ounces. Price................................ **10c**

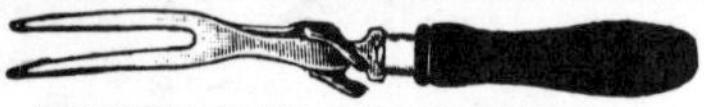

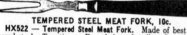

TEMPERED STEEL CARVING FORK, 10c.

HX521 — Tempered Steel Carving Fork. Made of best tempered steel. Two tines. Fitted with guard. Black enameled handle, with metal ferrule where tines join handle. Weight, 3 ounces. Price........................ **10c**

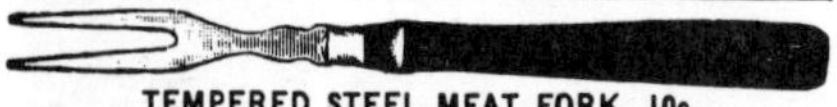

TEMPERED STEEL MEAT FORK, 10c.

HX522 — Tempered Steel Meat Fork. Made of best tempered steel. Two tines. Round ebony handle. Length, 14½ inches over all. Long handle is convenient for getting in oven, etc. Weight, 3 ounces. Price................ **10c**

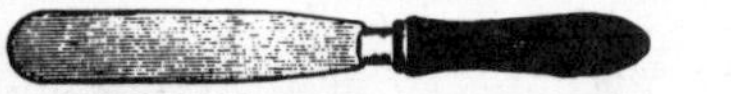

TEMPERED STEEL SPATULA, 10c.

HX523 — Tempered Steel Spatula. 6-inch pliable steel blade. Round black rubberoid handle. Length, 10½ inches over all. Very convenient article for a great variety of purposes. Weight, 1½ ounce. Price.............. **10c**

16-INCH NICKEL PLATED CAKE TURNERS, 10c.

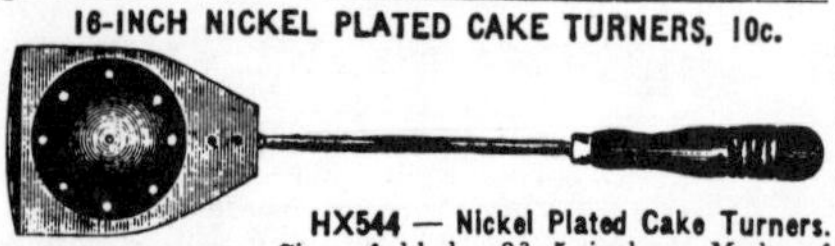

HX544 — Nickel Plated Cake Turners. Size of blade, 3⅜x5 inches. Made of perforated nickel plated steel. Circular depression. Black enameled handle. 16 inches over all. Weight, 3½ ounces. Price.. **10c**

Chopping knives, can openers, cleaners, ice picks, meat saws, etc., will be found with bargains in kitchen necessities on page 99.

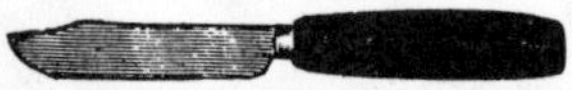

TEMPERED STEEL KITCHEN KNIFE, 5c.

HV524 — Tempered Steel Kitchen Knife. 3½-inch tempered steel blade. Round rosewood handle. A necessity in the kitchen. Weight, 1 ounce. Price.. **5c**

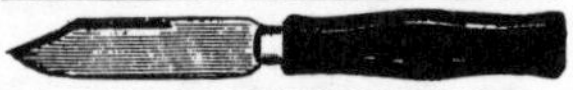

TEMPERED STEEL KITCHEN KNIFE, 5c.

HV5244 — 3-inch Tempered Steel Knife Blade. Made of tempered steel, swedged blade. Flat sided ebony handle. Weight, 1 ounce. Price.......... **5c**

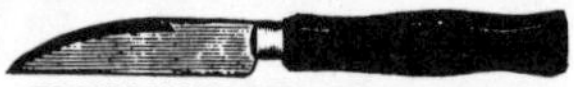

EBONY HANDLE KITCHEN KNIFE, 5c.

HV525—Ebony Handle Kitchen Knife. 3-inch tempered steel swedged blade. Flat sided ebony handle. Good cutting edge. Weight, 1 ounce. Price.... **5c**

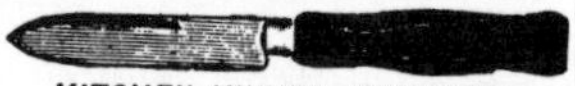

KITCHEN KNIVES, SWEDGED BLADES, 5c.

HV5255—Kitchen Knives. 3-inch tempered steel, swedged blades. Flat sided ebony handles. Sharp points. Weight, 1 ounce. Price.................... **5c**

CURVED EDGE KITCHEN KNIFE, 10c.

HX526 — Curved Edge Kitchen Knife. 4-inch tempered steel, swedged blade, riveted in Cocobola handle. Flat back. Weight, 1 ounce. Price......... **10c**

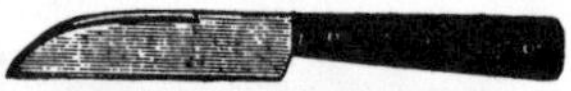

STEEL KITCHEN KNIVES, 10c.

HX527 — Steel Kitchen Knives. 3½-inch tempered steel blade. Back curved to edge. Riveted Cocobola handle. Weight, 1½ ounces. Price...... **10c**

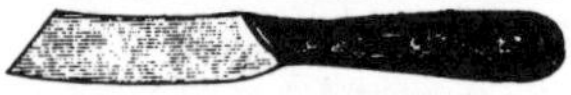

KITCHEN KNIFE, COCOBOLA HANDLE, 10c.

HX528 — Kitchen Knife. 3½-inch tempered steel blade, riveted on Cocobola handle. Curved back, sharp point. Weight, 1½ ounces. Price...... **10c**

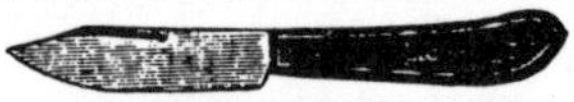

KITCHEN KNIFE, BOXWOOD HANDLE 10c.

HX529 — Kitchen Knife. 3-inch tempered steel blade. Sabatier shape. Good boxwood handle. Curved edge. Weight, 1 ounce. Price............... **10c**

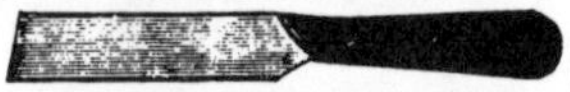

TEMPERED STEEL SHOE KNIFE, 10c.

HX530 — Shoe Knife. 4-inch tempered steel blade, straight edge and back, riveted in Cocobola handle. Weight, 1½ ounces. Price............... **10c**

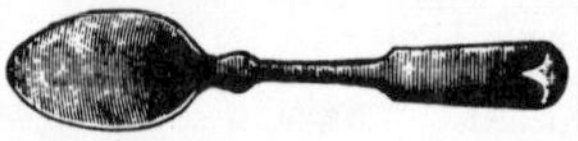

TEASPOONS, PLAIN PATTERN, 4 FOR 5c.

H531 — Teaspoons. Heavy, retinned on steel. Raised handle tip. Plain pattern. A good serviceable spoon. Weight, 1 ounce. 4 for.......... **5c**

HH532 — Dessert Spoon. Same as above. Weight, 2 ounces. 2 for.. **5c**

HH533 — Tablespoon. Same as above. Weight, 2 ounces. 2 for.......... **5c**

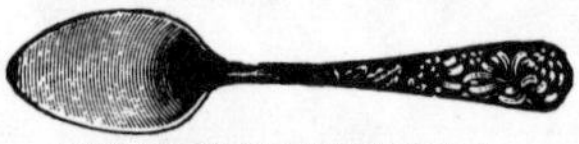

FANCY TEASPOONS, 3 FOR 5c.

H534 — Teaspoons. Heavy, retinned on steel. Fancy scroll leaf pattern. Weight, 1 ounce. 3 for.......... **5c**

HH5344 — Tablespoons. Heavy retinned on steel. Fancy scroll leaf pattern. Weight, 2 ounces. 2 for.......... **5c**

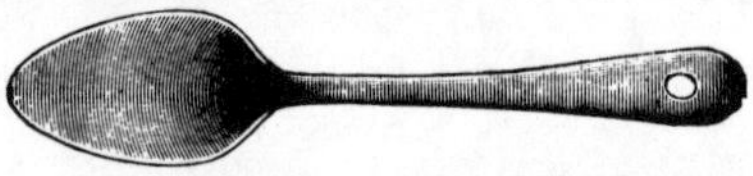

FORGED STEEL BASTING SPOON, 5c.

HV535—Basting Spoon. Made of extra heavy forged steel, retinned. Plain pattern. 10 inches long. Weight, 3 ounces. Price.. **5c**

HV5355 — Same as above. 12 inches long. Weight, 4 ounces. Each.. **5c**

HX536—Same as above. 18 inches long. Weight, 6 ounces. Price.. **10c**

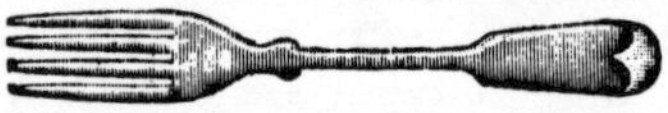

PLAIN PATTERN TABLE FORKS, 2 FOR 5c.

HH537—Four Tined Table Fork. Plain pattern, raised tip handle. Heavy, retinned on steel. Dependable fork for every day use. Weight, 2 ounces. 2 for.............. **5c**

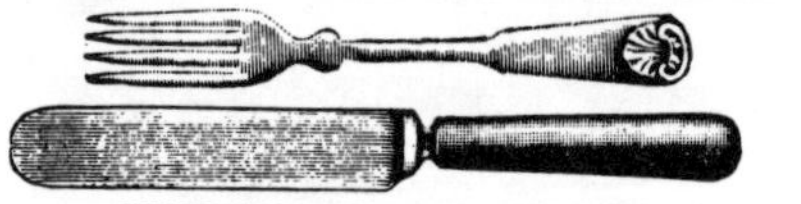

KNIFE AND FORK, PER PAIR 10c

HX538 — Medium Knife and Fork. Heavy, retinned on steel. Floral design tip on fork. Good cutting edge on knife. Weight, 5 ounces. Per pair........................ **10c**

STEEL BLADE CAKE TURNERS, 2 FOR 5c.

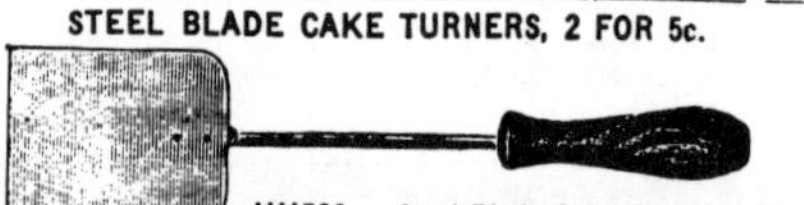

HH539 — Steel Blade Cake Turner. Size of blade, 2¾x3¼ inches. Highly finished oak handle. Weight, 2 ounces. 2 for.............. **5c**

PERFORATED BLADE CAKE TURNERS, 5c.

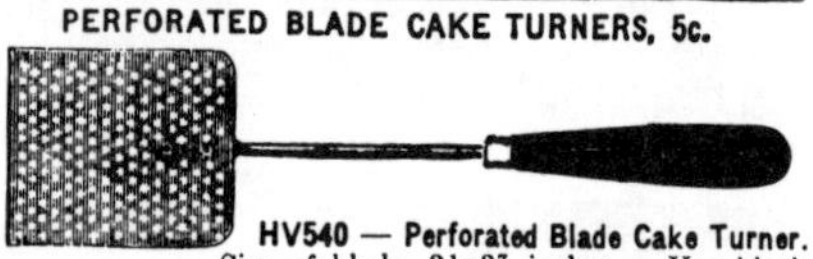

HV540 — Perforated Blade Cake Turner. Size of blade, 3¼x3⅞ inches. Has black enameled handle. Length, 13½ inches over all. Weight, 3 ounces. Price.. **5c**

14½-INCH CAKE TURNER, 5c.

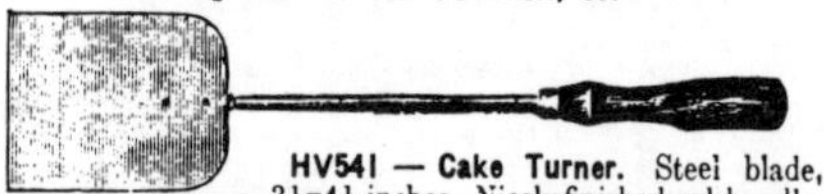

HV541 — Cake Turner. Steel blade, 3¼x4½ inches. Nicely finished oak handle. 14½ inches over all. Blade riveted to handle. Weight, 3 ounces. Price.. **5c**

PEAR SHAPED CAKE TURNERS, EACH, 5c.

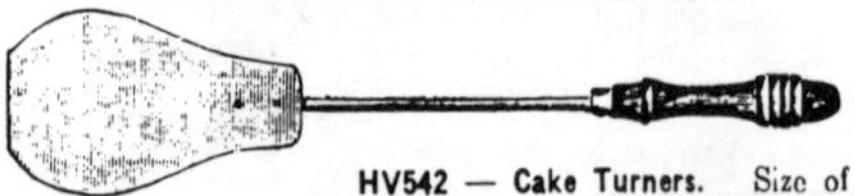

HV542 — Cake Turners. Size of blade, 3¾x6 inches, pear shaped. Blade riveted to handle of nicely turned oak. 17 inches over all. Weight, 4½ ounces. Price........................ **5c**

NICKEL PLATED CAKE TURNERS, EACH, 10c.

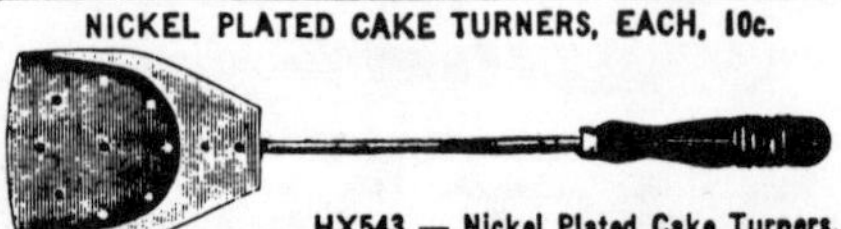

HX543 — Nickel Plated Cake Turners. 3⅜x5-inch blade, perforated nickel plated steel. Blade riveted to black enameled handle. 16 inches over all. Weight, 3½ ounces. Price........................ **10c**

Everything Needed in the Kitchen, 5 and 10c

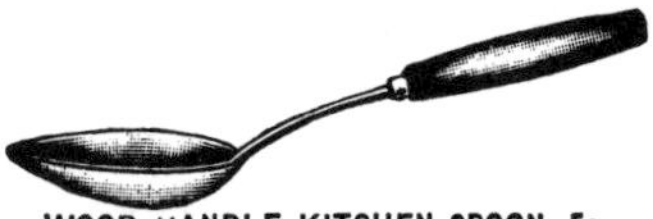

WOOD HANDLE KITCHEN SPOON, 5c.
HV545—Kitchen Spoon. Made of heavy retinned metal, solid bowl. Japanned wood handle. Length over all, 10½ inches. Weight, 3 ounces. Price each.. **5c**

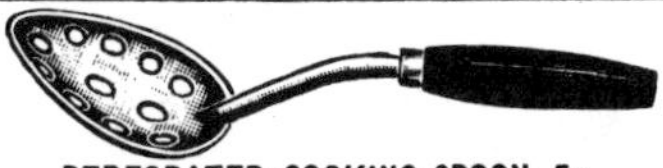

PERFORATED COOKING SPOON, 5c.
HV5455—Perforated Cooking Spoon. Made of heavy retinned metal, large bowl, wood handle. Bowl has large perforations. 10½ inches long. Weight, 3 ounces. Price, each........................ **5c**

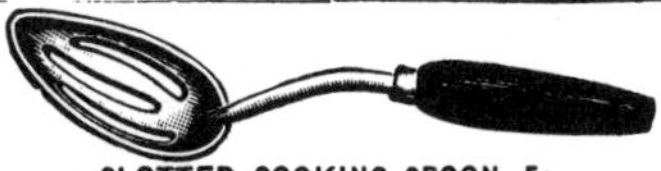

SLOTTED COOKING SPOON, 5c.
HV5450 — Slotted Spoon. Bowl 4 inches long by 2½ inches wide. Heavily retinned, wood handle. Has long oval perforations. Weight, 3 ounces. Price, each.. **5c**

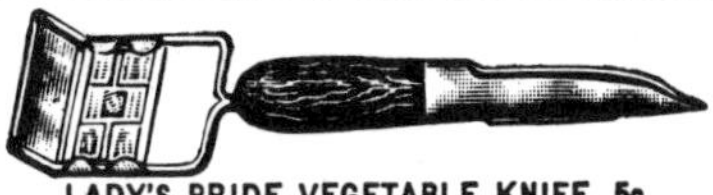

LADY'S PRIDE VEGETABLE KNIFE, 5c.
HV546 — Lady's Pride Vegetable Knife. A combination of slicer, peeler, slaw cutter, fruit corer, fish scaler and any number of other uses. Has rosewood handle. Weight, 2 ounces. Price, each................ **5c**

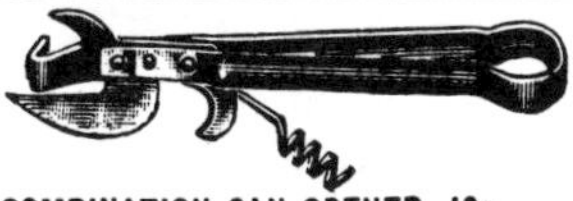

COMBINATION CAN OPENER, 10c.
HX5466 — Combination Can Opener. Can and bottle opener, cap remover, corkscrew, etc., combined in one tool. 5½ inches long. Weight, 2 ounces. Price, each **10c**

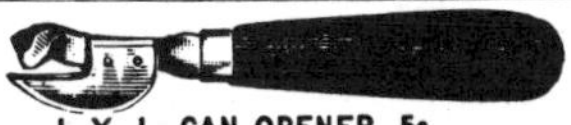

I. X. L. CAN OPENER, 5c.
HV547—I. X. L. Can Opener. Made of strong retinned steel, rosewood handle, 6 inches long. Straight blade. Weight, 2 ounces. Price, each........ **5c**
HX5477—Same as above, except highly finished, handle of black rubberoid and flaring blade. Weight, 2 ounces. Price, each...................... **10c**

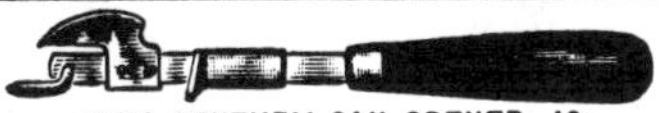

20TH CENTURY CAN OPENER, 10c.
HX548—20th Century Can Opener. Strong, highly finished combination can opener, with rubberized handle. Length over all, 8½ inches. Weight, 3 ounces. Price, each **10c**

DOUBLE CHOPPING KNIFE, 10c.
HX549 — Double Chopping Knife. Two finely tempered blades of steel, firmly attached to nickel plated supports and strong wooden handle. Weight, 7 ounces. Price, each. **10c**

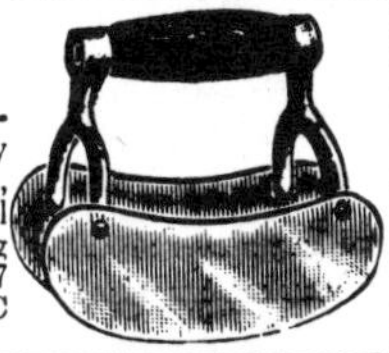

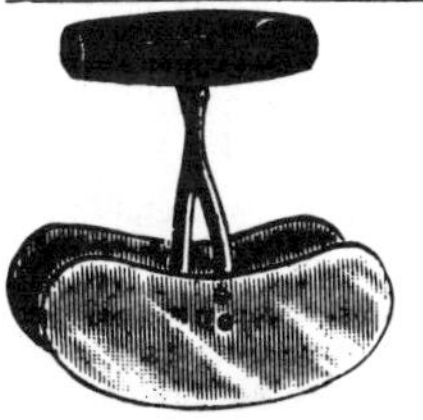

DOUBLE CHOPPING KNIFE, 5c.
HV550 — Double Chopping Knife. Two steel blades mounted on forked frame with single wood handle. 5¼ inches high, length the same. Weight, 5 ozs. Price, each. **5c**

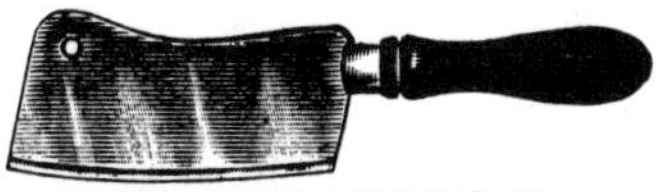

STEEL KITCHEN CLEAVER, 10c.
HX551—Kitchen Cleaver. Stiff tempered steel blade with firmly attached large black enameled handle. Blade is 6¼ inches long by 2¾ inches wide. Weight, 7 ounces. Price, each........................ **10c**

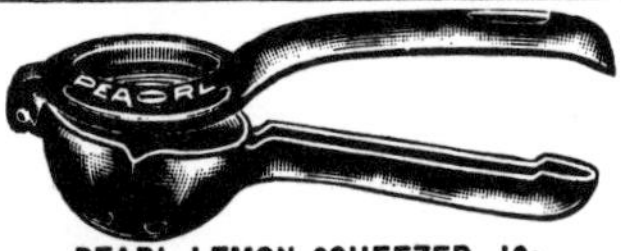

PEARL LEMON SQUEEZER, 10c.
HX552—Pearl Lemon Squeezer. Made of heavy cast retinned metal with wooden ball center and perforated bottom. Weight, 16 ounces. Price, each..... **10c**

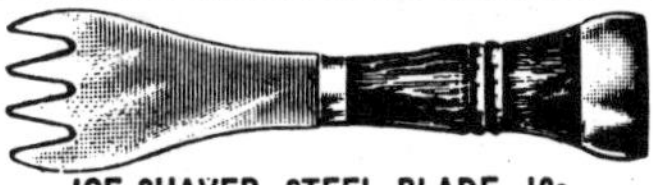

ICE SHAVER, STEEL BLADE, 10c.
HX553—Ice Shaver. Strong handle, reinforced by heavy metal cap. Four teeth, large tempered steel blade. 10 inches long. Weight, 10 ounces. Price, each...................................... **10c**

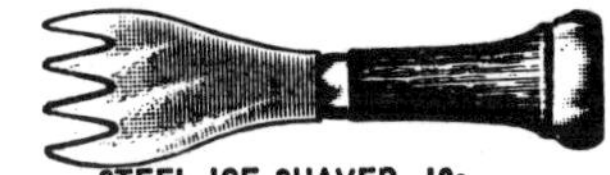

STEEL ICE SHAVER, 10c.
HX554—Ice Shaver. Same as above, except length over all, 7½ inches. Weight, 6 ounces. Price, each...................................... **10c**

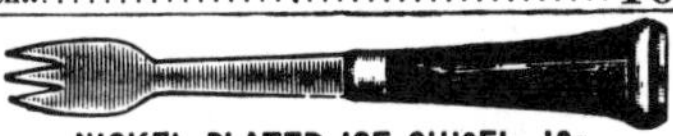

NICKEL PLATED ICE CHISEL, 10c.
HX555—Ice Chisel. Heavily nickel plated three pronged ice chisel. Rosewood handle with nickeled guard at end. Length, 8 inches. Weight, 4 ounces. Price, each. **10c**

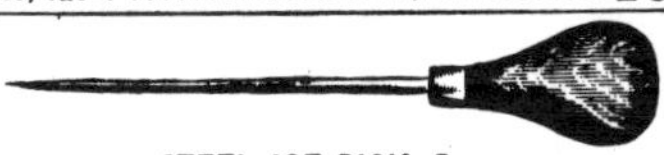

STEEL ICE PICK, 5c.
•**HV556 — Ice Pick.** Pear shaped, highly polished mahogany stained maple handle with extremely sharp steel point. Length, 9 inches. Weight, 2 ounces. Price, each. **5c**

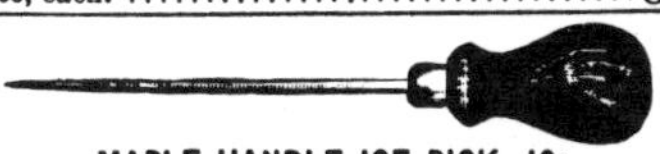

MAPLE HANDLE ICE PICK, 10c.
HX557—Ice Pick. Pear shaped, highly polished mahogany stained maple handle with extremely sharp steel point. Length, 9¼ inches. Weight, 3 ounces. Price, each. **10c**

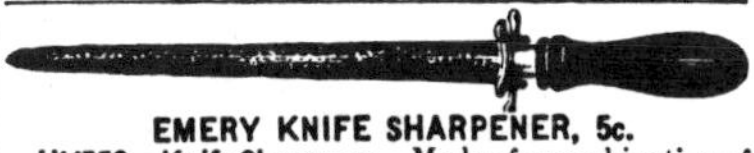

EMERY KNIFE SHARPENER, 5c.
HV558—Knife Sharpener. Made of a combination of emery and other grinding substances. Wooden handle stained red. 12 inches long. Weight, 3 ounces. Price, each. **5c**

EXTRA QUALITY KNIFE SHARPENER, 10c.
HX559 — Knife Sharpener. Extra quality. Special emery composition with five point guard, rubberoid handle. Length, 15 inches. Weight, 6 ounces. Price, each...................................... **10c**

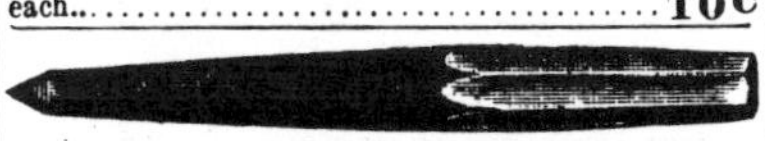

NATURAL STONE KNIFE SHARPENER, 10c.
HX560—Willow Creek Knife Sharpener. Gives a keen lasting edge to all carving, butcher or other steel knives. 12 inches long. Weight, 12 ounces. Price, each. **10c**

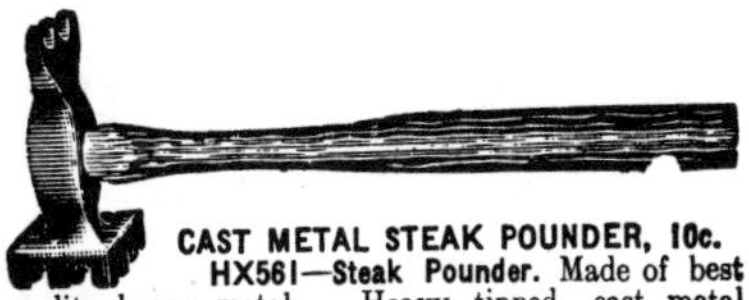

CAST METAL STEAK POUNDER, 10c.
HX561—Steak Pounder. Made of best quality heavy metal. Heavy tinned, cast metal steak hammer with securely seated natural wood handle. 11 inches long. Weight. 9 ounces. Price, each................................ **10c**

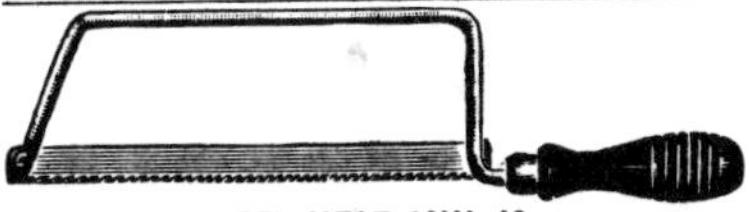

STEEL MEAT SAW, 10c.
HX562 — Armour Meat Saw. Strong, round, steel spring wire frame with highly tempered, detachable blade. Size, of blade, 8x½ inches. Weight, 5 ounces. Price, each................................ **10c**

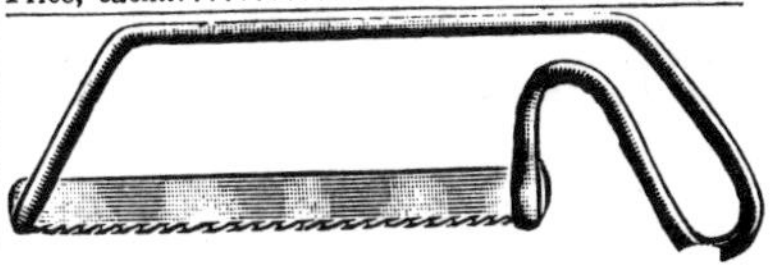

12-INCH STEEL MEAT SAW, 10c.
HX563—Morris Meat Saw. A highly tempered fine tooth steel blade attached to a round nickel plated steel frame. Length, 12 inches. Weight, 6 ounces. Price each................................ **10c**

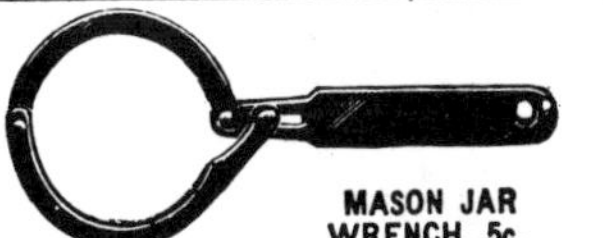

MASON JAR WRENCH, 5c.
HV5577—Grip Jar Wrench. Made of flat steel, heavily japanned. Length, 8 inches. Automatically adjusts itself to almost any size jar. Weight, 3 ounces. Price each........................ **5c**

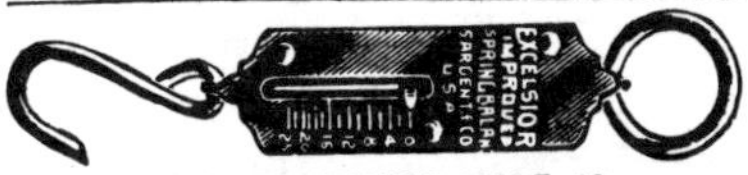

ACCURATE KITCHEN SCALE, 10c.
HX564—Spring Balance, or Kitchen Scale. Very accurate, heavy ring and hook, brass face, exposed parts finished in black Japan. 1¾x6 inches. Weight, 4 ounces. Price, each..................... **10c**
HX565—Same as above, except smaller. 1¼x4½ inches. Weight, 3 ounces. Price, each........ **10c**

DETACHABLE KETTLE KNOBS, 6 FOR 5c.

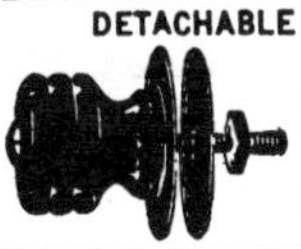

H572 — Kettle Knob. Black enameled kettle knob with two tin washers. 1½ inch bolt and nut. Fits any size cover. An inexpensive useful article. Wt. 1 ounce. Price, 6 for..... **5c**

ANTI-SPLASHER ATTACHMENTS.

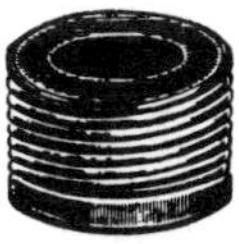

HH566—Eureka Anti-Splasher. Nickel plated. Two sizes; fitted with ¾ or ⅝ inch rubber washer. Weight 1 ounce. Price, 2 for... **5c**

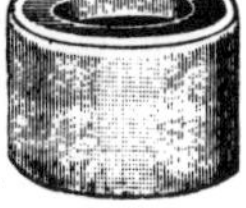

HV567—Made of white porcelain. Comes in two sizes, ¾ and ⅝ inch. Weight 1 ounce. Price, .. **5c**

FAUCET FILTER, 10c.

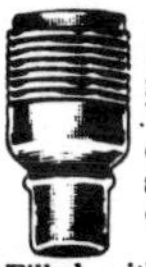

HX568—Charcoal Faucet Filter. Made of heavy nickel plate, rubber washer. Water is filtered through charcoal. Made to fit any size faucet. Weight 1 ounce. Price, each.. **10c**
HX569—Glass Filter. Filled with small pebbles through which water is perfectly filtered. Cleaned in one minute. 4 inches deep by 2½ inches wide. Weight 6 ounces. Price, each.................. **10c**

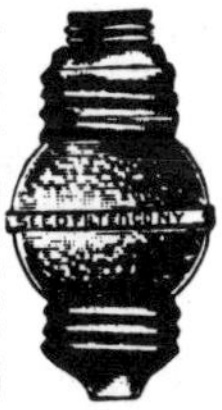

Practical Wire Goods at 5c and 10c

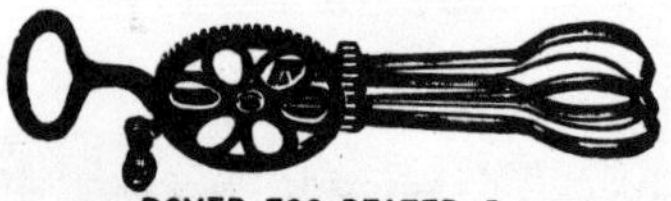

DOVER EGG BEATER, 5c.

HV570—Dover Egg Beater. $8\frac{1}{2}$ inches in length. Weight 6 ounces. Price, each. **5c**
HX571—Same as above, $10\frac{1}{2}$ inches in length. Weight 7 ounces. Price, each. **10c**

WIRE POTATO MASHER

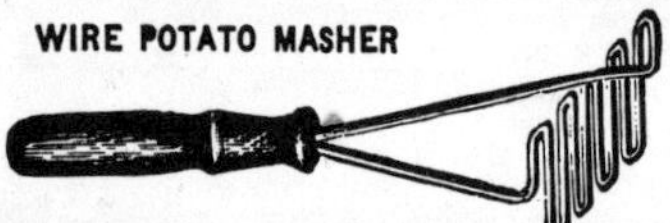

HX573—Potato Masher. Handle is of black rubberized wood. masher of strong steel wire, nickel plated. Length $10\frac{3}{4}$ inches. Weight 7 ounces. Price, ea. **10c**
HV5733—Same as above. Heavily retinned wire with large, highly polished wood handle. Weight 7 ounces. Price, each. **5c**

NICKEL PLATED TEA STRAINER, 10c.

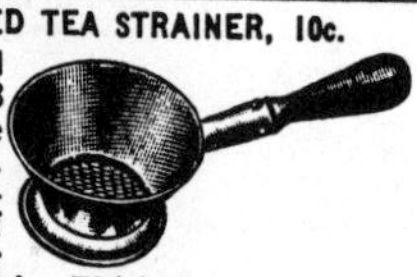

HX760—Nickel Plated Tea Strainer. 3 inch bowl with wire bottom. Flaring foot. Nicely finished hardwood handle. Size of strainer $6\frac{1}{2}$ inches over all. A dependable article. Weight 1 ounce. Price, each. **10c**

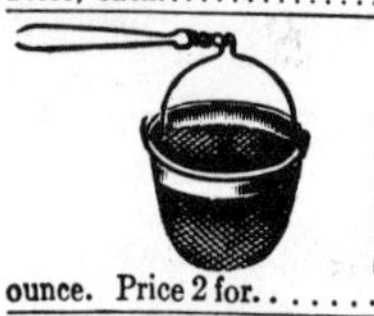

NICKELED TEA STRAINERS, 2 FOR 5c.

HH574—Tea Strainer. Tinned wired gauze bell strainer with wire prong to insert in spout of tea pot. $1\frac{3}{4}$ inches diameter. Very substantial. Weight 1 ounce. Price 2 for. **5c**

BOWL STRAINERS, 2 FOR 5c.

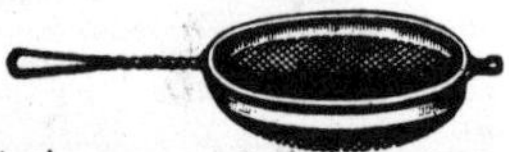

HH575 — Bowl Strainer. 4 inches diameter. Has heavy retinned band, bright wire coarse mesh strainer and wire handle. A very dependable strainer. Weight 2 ounces. Price, 2 for. **5c**

PLUNK TEA STRAINER, 5c.

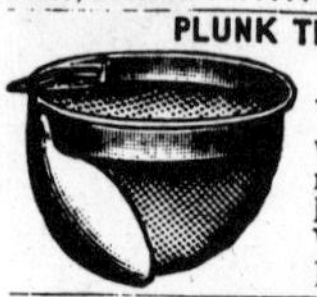

HV576—Plunk Tea Strainer. Very fine mesh strainer with wire attachment for spout and nickel plated drip shield. Strongly made and will last a long time. Weight 1 ounce. Price, each. **5c**

WIRE HANDLE TEA STRAINER, 5c.

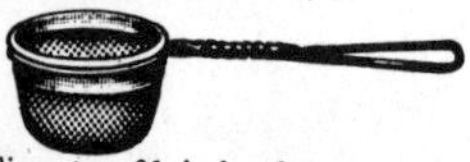

HV578—Tea Strainer with Wire Handle. Round bottom with fine mesh, retinned band. $2\frac{1}{4}$ inches diameter, $6\frac{1}{2}$ inches long. A very special value. Weight 1 ounce. Price, each. **5c**

LARGE BOWL KITCHEN STRAINER, 5c.

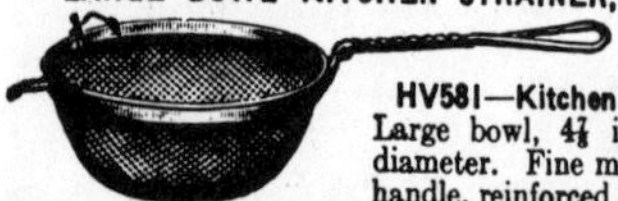

HV581—Kitchen Strainer. Large bowl, $4\frac{3}{4}$ inches in diameter. Fine mesh, wire handle, reinforced edge. 10 inches over all. Weight 2 ounces. Price, each. **5c**

LARGE KITCHEN STRAINER, 5c.

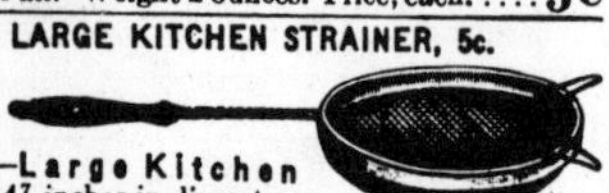

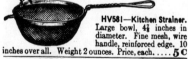

HV582—Large Kitchen Strainer. $4\frac{7}{8}$ inches in diameter. Black enameled wood handle. Two wire supports to rest on bowl. Fine mesh. Weight 3 ounces. Price, each, **5c**

FLAT BOTTOM TEA STRAINER, 10c

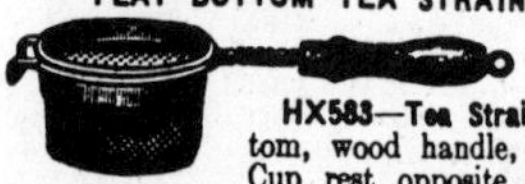

HX583—Tea Strainer. Flat bottom, wood handle, $2\frac{1}{2}$ inch bowl. Cup rest opposite handle. Reinforced edge. Fine mesh. $7\frac{1}{2}$ inches long. Weight 2 ounces. Price, each. **10c**
HV5833—Same as above, but smaller. Weight 2 ounces. Price, each. **5c**

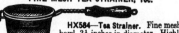

FINE MESH TEA STRAINER, 10c.

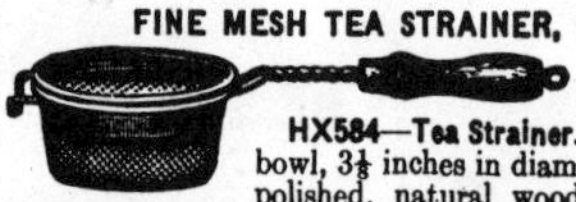

HX584—Tea Strainer. Fine mesh, bowl, $3\frac{1}{2}$ inches in diameter. Highly polished, natural wood handle. 9 inches long. Very high quality. Weight 2 ounces. Price, each. **10c**

LARGE KITCHEN STRAINER, 10c.

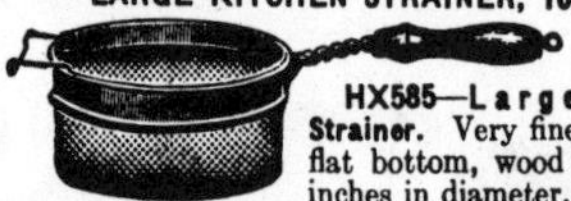

HX585—Large Kitchen Strainer. Very fine mesh. Has flat bottom, wood handle. $3\frac{7}{8}$ inches in diameter, cup rest opposite handle. Weight 3 ounces. Price, each. .. **10c**

FINE MESH BOWL STRAINER, 10c.

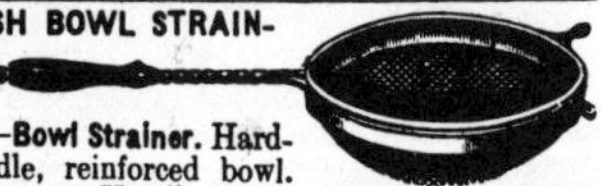

HX586—Bowl Strainer. Hardwood handle, reinforced bowl. Wire cup rests. Handle 6 inches long. $5\frac{1}{4}$ inches in diameter. Weight 3 ounces. Price, each. **10c**
HX587—Same as HX586, except has two wire guards running under and protecting bowl. Weight 4 ounces. Price, each. **10c**

COARSE MESH BOWL STRAINER, 10c

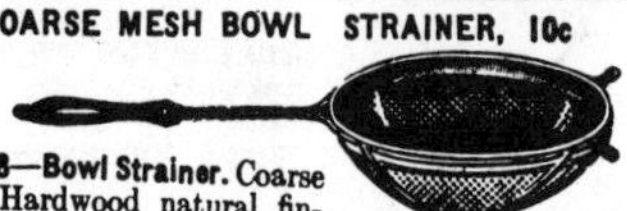

HX588—Bowl Strainer. Coarse mesh. Hardwood natural finished handle. Two wire cup rests. $5\frac{1}{4}$ inches in diameter. Weight 4 ounces. Price, each. **10c**
HX589—Same as HX588, except has two wire guards running under and protecting bowl. Weight 5 ounces. Price, each. **10c**

FRUIT PRESS, 10c.

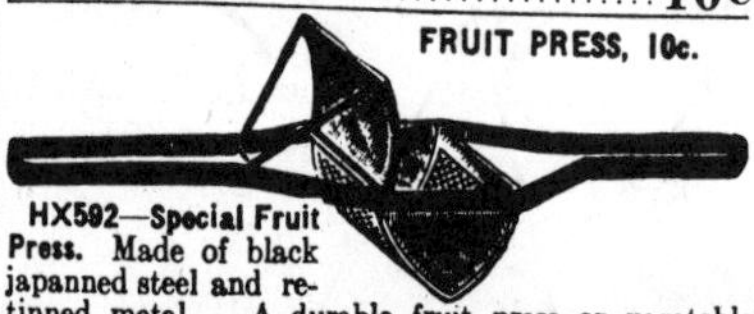

HX592—Special Fruit Press. Made of black japanned steel and retinned metal. A durable fruit press or vegetable masher. Holds about 1 pint. Weight 12 ounces. Price, each. **10c**

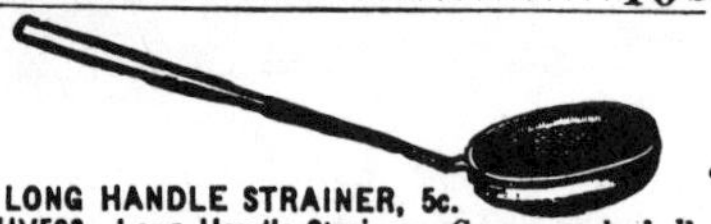

LONG HANDLE STRAINER, 5c.

HV593—Long Handle Strainer. Coarse mesh, ladle shaped strainer with 4 inch bowl and 10 inch wire handle. Weight 3 ounces. Price, each. **5c**

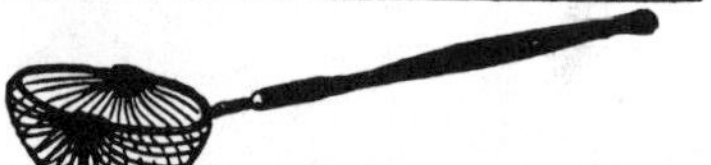

COARSE MESH VEGETABLE STRAINER, 5c.

HV594—Vegetable Strainer. Very coarse, all wire, ladle shaped. Long wood handle. $4\frac{1}{2}$ inch bowl, 12 inches over all. Weight 3 ounces. Price, each. ... **5c**

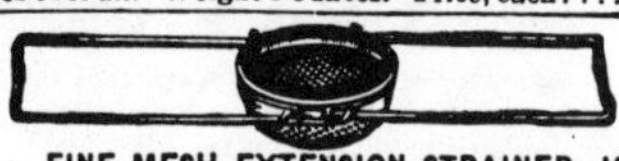

FINE MESH EXTENSION STRAINER, 10c.

HX590—Extension Strainer. Fine mesh. $5\frac{1}{4}$ inch bowl. Wire frame extends from 12 inches in width to 20 inches. Weight 6 ounces. Price, each. **10c**

FINE MESH WIRE PAN RIM STRAINER, 10c.

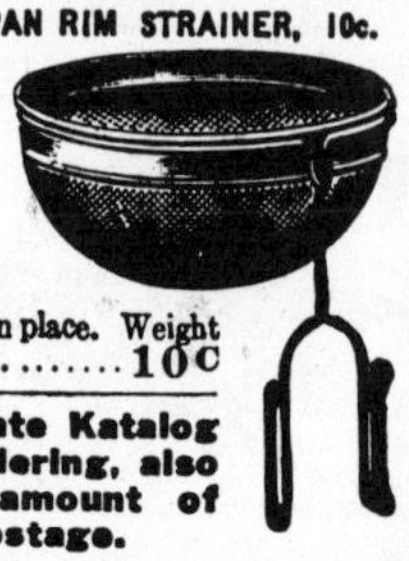

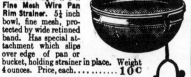

HX591—$5\frac{1}{4}$-Inch Fine Mesh Wire Pan Rim Strainer. $5\frac{1}{4}$ inch bowl, fine mesh, protected by wide retinned band. Has special attachment which slips over edge of pan or bucket, holding strainer in place. Weight 4 ounces. Price, each. **10c**

Be sure to state Katalog number when ordering, also send an extra amount of money to pay postage.

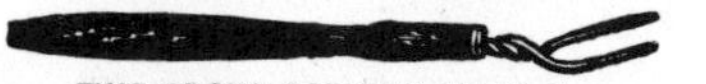

TWO PRONG COOKING FORK, 5c.

HV595—Cooking Fork. Heavy retinned two prong cooking fork with 9 inch mahogany finished wood handle. Strong and durable. Weight 2 ounces. Price, each. **5c**

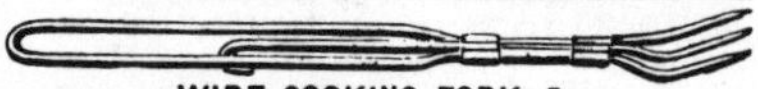

WIRE COOKING FORK, 5c.

HV596—Wire Cooking Fork. Strong wire fork, heavily retinned, 3 prongs, 16 inches long. Has kettle hook attached to handle. Weight 6 ounces. Price, each. **5c**

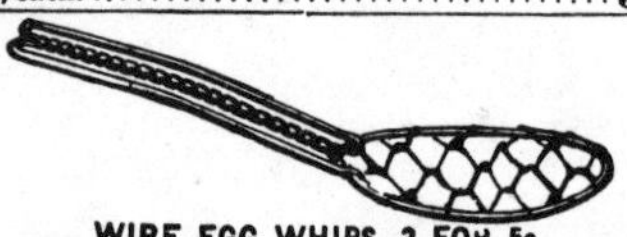

WIRE EGG WHIPS, 2 FOR 5c.

HH600—Egg Whip. Made of retinned, light twisted wire with cross lacing. $10\frac{1}{4}$ inches long. Very strong and stiff. Weight 2 ounces. Price 2 for. **5c**

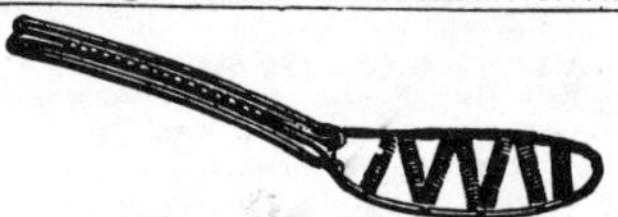

SPECIAL WIRE EGG WHIP, 5c.

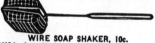

HV601—Special Egg Whip. Made of heavy retinned wire with recrossed coiled springs. Length $10\frac{1}{4}$ inches, blade $2\frac{7}{8}$ inches wide. Weight 3 ounces. Price, each. **5c**

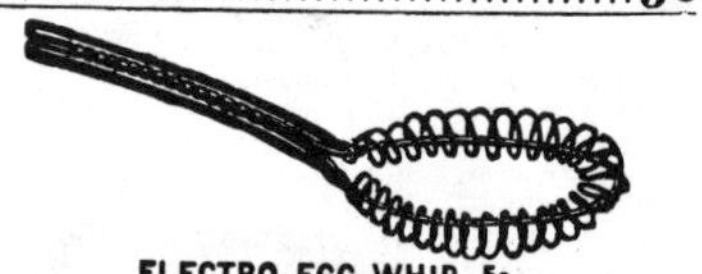

ELECTRO EGG WHIP, 5c.

HV602—Electro Egg Whip. Made of specially retinned wire with oval shaped coiled springs. 13 inches in length. Weight 2 ounces. Price, each. **5c**

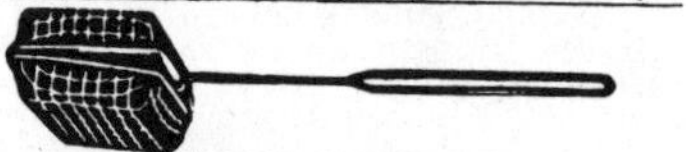

WIRE SOAP SHAKER, 10c.

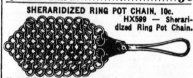

HX604—Soap Shaker. A wire screened box in which small pieces of soap can be retained and used to the last particle. Weight 5 ounces. Price, each. **10c**

4X6-INCH RING POT CHAIN, 5c.

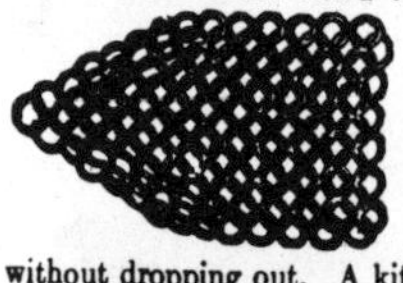

HV597 — 4x6-inch Ring Pot Chain. Heavily Sheraridized to prevent rusting. Size of chain, about 4x6 inches. Links are securely locked and will give the longest wear without dropping out. A kitchen necessity. Weight, $3\frac{1}{2}$ ounces. Price **5c**

SHERARIDIZED RING POT CHAIN, 10c.

HX599 — Sheraridized Ring Pot Chain.

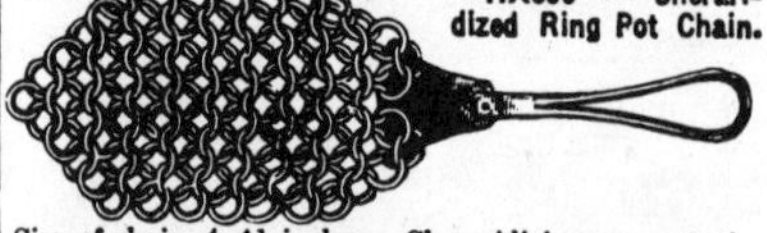

Size of chain, $4x4\frac{1}{2}$ inches. Sheraridizing prevents the chain from rusting. Has steel plate scraper attached. Total length over all, 10 inches. Weight, $4\frac{1}{2}$ ounces. Price. **10c**

HEAVILY TINNED VEGETABLE BOILER, 10c.

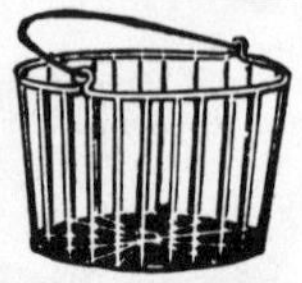

HX605 — Heavily Tinned Vegetable Boiler. Boiler is 7 inches in diameter and $4\frac{1}{2}$ inches high. Heavily retinned. Strong wire mesh. Will last a long time. Weight, 5 ounces. Price. **10c**

Read our Special Free Delivery Offer on Page 3. We pay all transportation charges on orders amounting to $10 or more to the various states named in the prepay list.

Wire Goods and Tinware, 5 and 10c

6-INCH TEA POT STAND, 10c.

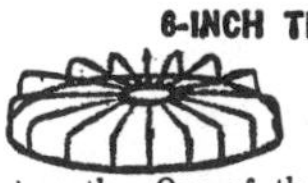

HX606 — 6-Inch Tea Pot Stand. Round tea pot stand heavily retinned. Made of twisted wire strands for extra strength. One of the most popular stands on the market. Weight, 3 ounces. Price........... **10c**

12X16-INCH DISH DRAINER, 10c.

HX607 — 12x16-inch **Dish Drainer.** Good, strong wire; heavily tinned. Has raised center. A very durable drainer. Prevents the dishes chipping or breaking and keeps them from sliding. Weight, 7½ ounces. Price.................. **10c**

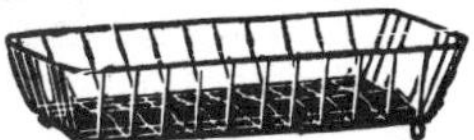

9X6-INCH HEAVY TINNED BROILER, 10c.

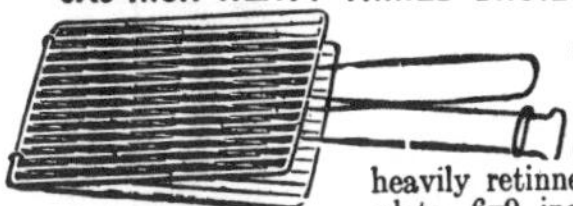

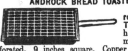

HX608— 9x6 - Inch Heavy Tinned Broiler. Made of strong wire heavily retinned. Size of plate, 6x9 inches. Bars ⅜-inch apart. Four strong center bars. Weight, 10½ ounces. Price............................ **10c**

9X10½-INCH HEAVY BROILERS, 10c.

HX610— 9x10½ - Inch Heavy Broilers. Made of heavily tinned strong wire. Four extra center bars. Bars ⅞-inch apart. Has long, convenient handle and clip for holding together. Weight, 10½ ounces. Price............................ **10c**

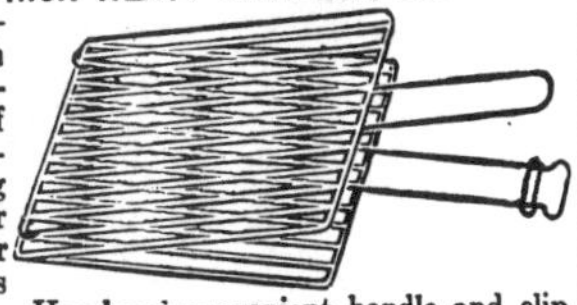

ANDROCK BREAD TOASTER, 10c.

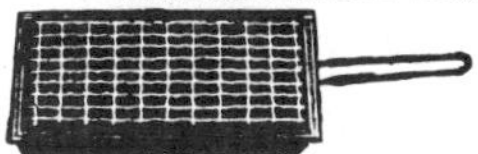

HX611—Androck Bread Toaster. Made of heavy sheet metal base, perforated. 9 inches square. Copper wire top. Has wire handle. Can be placed on any sort of stove or burner. Weight, 7½ ounces. Price.......... **10c**

PYRAMID BREAD TOASTER, PRICE, 10c.

HX612 — Pyramid Bread Toaster. One of the best toasters for gas stoves. Toasts four slices at one time. Heavy sheet steel base, sides and top. Toasts very evenly. Weight, 6 ounces. Price..... **10c**

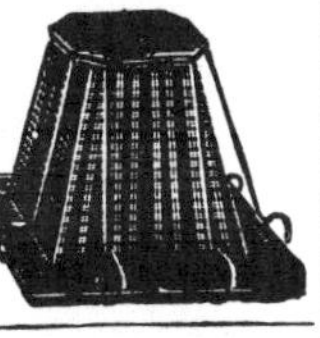

COCOANUT SHAPED DIPPERS, 5c.

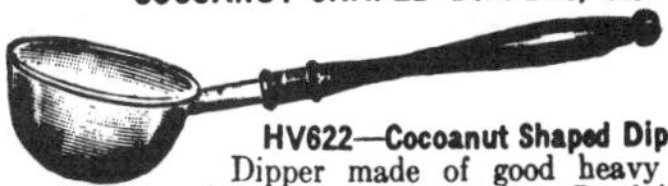

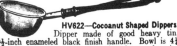

HV622—Cocoanut Shaped Dippers. Dipper made of good heavy tin, 10½-inch enameled black finish handle. Bowl is 4¼ inches deep and is neatly turned and strongly reinforced. Weight, 3 ounces. Price.............. **5c**

DOUGHNUT CUTTERS, 2 FOR 5c.

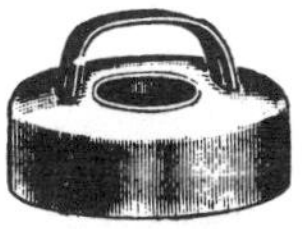

HH625—Doughnut Cutters. Made of good strong tin, with small circle inside. Good sharp cutting edges. 2½ inches diameter. Weight, 1 ounce. 2 for.................... **5c**

If 3-inch cutter is wanted, ask for No. HH626.

STAMPED BISCUIT CUTTERS, 2 FOR 5c.

HH627 — Stamped Biscuit Cutters. Stamped in good quality heavy tin. Good sharp cutting edges. Convenient handle for holding. 2½-inches diameter. Weight, 1 ounce. 2 for.................. **5c**

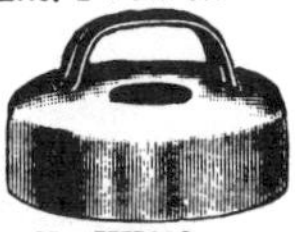

If 3-inch cutter is wanted, ask for No. HH628.

ANIMAL COOKIE CUTTERS, 2 FOR 5c.

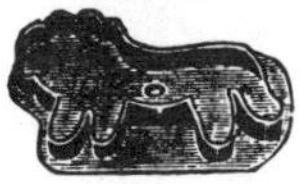

HH629 — Assorted Animal Cookie Cutters. Average size, 2½x4 inches. Heavily retinned. Children secure greater enjoyment from cakes cut with these animal cutters. Weight, 1 oz. 2 for.................. **5c**

COOKIE CUTTERS, 2 FOR 5c.

HH630 — Cookie Cutters. Size, about 2½x2½ inches. Made of best quality bright tin. Sharp, scalloped cutting edges. Come in heart, diamond, oval, round, and other shapes. Weight, 1 ounce. 2 for............ **5c**

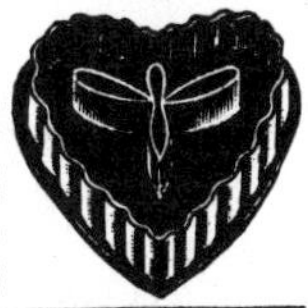

STAR SHAPED COOKIE CUTTERS, 2 FOR 5c.

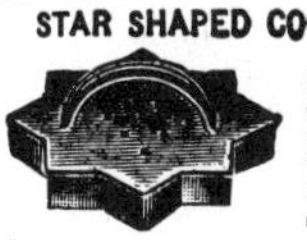

HH631 — Star Shaped Cookie Cutters. Made of good quality heavy tin. Diameter of cutter, about 3 inches. Just the thing for fancy cookies for parties, etc. Weight, each 1 ounce. 2 for.. **5c**

FRENCH BISCUIT CUTTERS, 2 FOR 5c.

HH632 — Stamped French Biscuit Cutters. Made of good quality metal, heavily tinned. Good sharp scalloped edges. 3 inches diameter. Large handle. Weight, each 2 ounces. 2 for................... **5c**

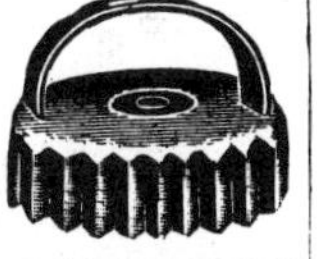

SCALLOPED COOKIE CUTTERS, 2 FOR 5c.

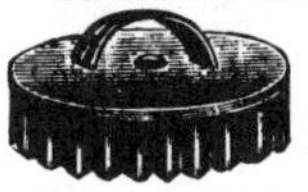

HH633 — Scalloped Cookie Cutters. Stamped from good quality tin, sharp scalloped edges. Convenient handle, strongly soldered to top of cutter. 3½ inches diameter. Weight, each 2 ounces. 2 for............... **5c**

SMALL RING SCOOP, 2 FOR 5c.

HH634—Small Ring scoop. Made of good quality tin. Nice convenient handle, size, 2¼x2¾ inches. Convenient for scooping flour, sugar, salt, teas, or other kitchen necessities. Weight, each 1 ounce. 2 for.. **5c**

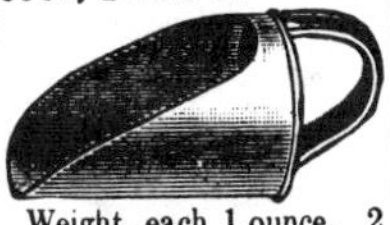

HEAVY RETINNED HANDLED SCOOPS, 5c.

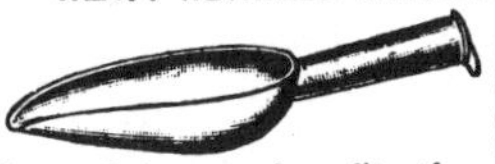

HH6355—Heavy Retinned Handle Scoops. Length of scoop, 5 inches; 8 inches over all. Stamped from good quality tin. Handle has hook on end for hanging up. Weight, 1 ounce. 2 for.. **5c**

LARGE GROCER SCOOPS, EACH, 10c.

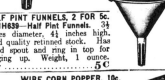

HX636—Large Grocer Scoops, 9½ inches over all. Made from best quality heavy tin. Large round scoop. Strong soldered handle. Bowl of scoop 6½ inches long. Weight, 4 ounces. Price.................. **10c**

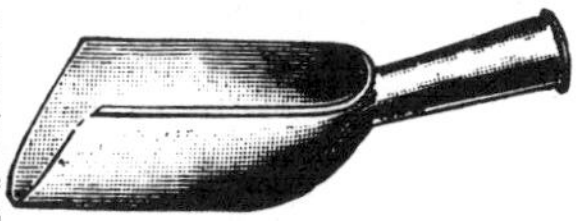

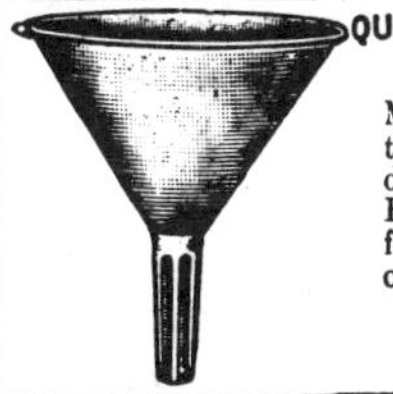

QUART FUNNELS, EACH 5c.

HV637—Quart Funnels. Made of good quality retinned stock. 5½ inches diameter. 6 inches high Have fluted spout and loop for hanging up. Weight, 3 ounces. Price, each... **5c**

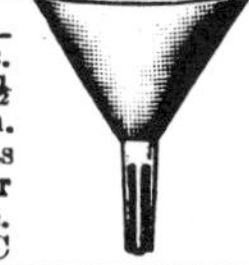

HALF PINT FUNNELS, 2 FOR 5c.

HH639—Half Pint Funnels. 3½ inches diameter, 4¼ inches high. Good quality retinned stock. Has fluted spout and ring in top for hanging up. Weight, 1 ounce. 2 for...................... **5c**

WIRE CORN POPPER, 10c.

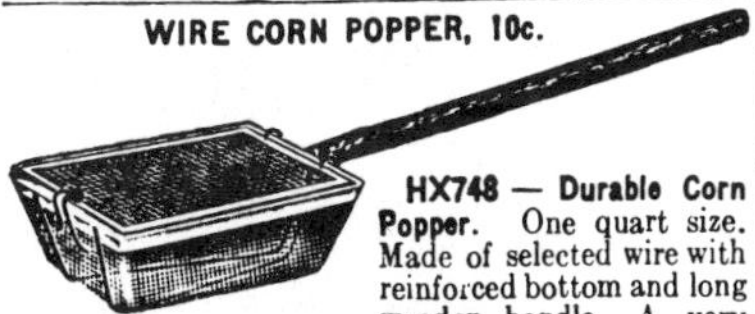

HX748 — Durable Corn Popper. One quart size. Made of selected wire with reinforced bottom and long wooden handle. A very practical article for home use. Well made throughout. Weight, 10 ounces. Price each....... **10c**

NUTMEG GRATERS, 2 FOR 5c.

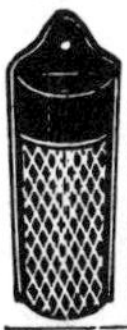

HH641—Nutmeg Graters. Made of good quality tin. Sharp cutting edges. Has nutmeg holder on top which is nicely japanned. Length over all, 5 inches. Weight, 2 ounces. 2 for.................. **5c**

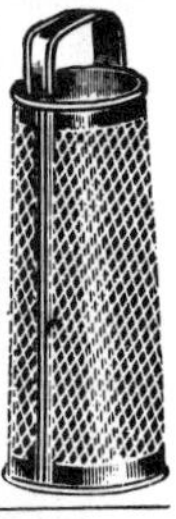

CONE SHAPED GRATERS, EACH, 5c

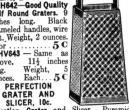

HV644 — Cone Shaped Graters. Heavily retinned. 7½ inches high, 3½ inches diameter. Has fine and coarse holes. Wt.. 2½ ounces. Price **5c**

9-INCH CONE SHAPED GRATER, SPECIAL AT 10c.

HX645—Same as above. 9 inches high. Weight, 4 ounces. Price... **10c**

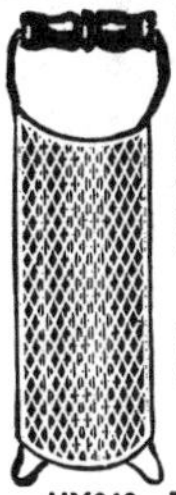

HALF ROUND GRATERS, 2 FOR 5c.

HH642—Good Quality Half Round Graters. 9 inches long. Black enameled handles, wire feet. Weight, 2 ounces. 2 for.......... **5c**

HV643 — Same as above. 11½ inches long. Weight, 5 ounces. Each... **5c**

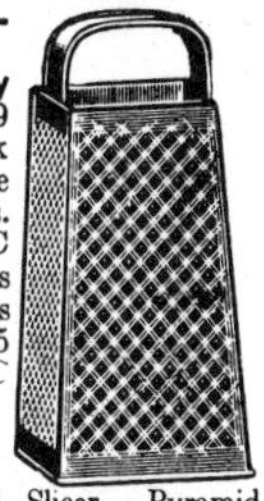

PERFECTION GRATER AND SLICER, 10c.

HX646—Perfection Grater and Slicer. Pyramid shape. Has four cutting sides. 9 inches over all. Best quality metal. Sharp perforations. Extra strong tin handle on top. Weight, 7 ounces Price................................ **10c**

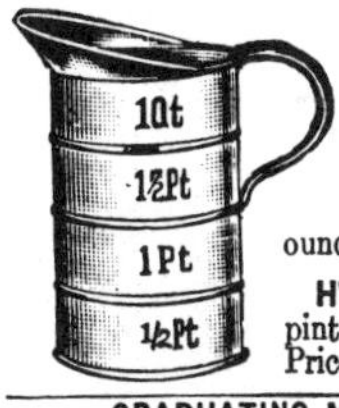

GRADUATED QUART MEASURE, 5c.

HV647 —Graduated Measure. Quart size. Specially made, retinned, rolled edge, handle and lip. Weight, 5 ounces. Price, each...... **5c**

HV648—Same as above, except pint size. Weight, 3 ounces. Price, each.............. **5c**

GRADUATING MEASURING CUP, 5c.

HV649 — Measuring Cup. specially retinned, rolled edge, securely attached handle. Quarter cup divisions stamped in metal. 2¾ inches high by 3 inches wide. Weight, 2 ounces. Price, each.......... **5c**

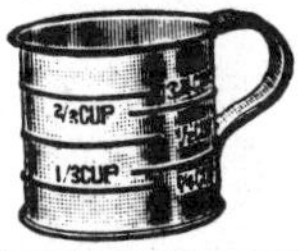

UTILITY MEASURES, EACH, 10c.

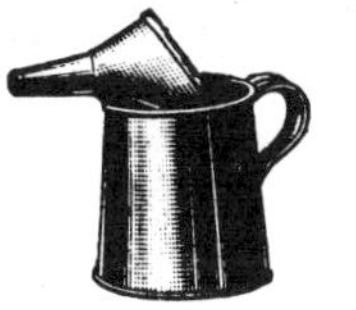

HX650 — Utility Measure. One pint size. Retinned. Has special funnel spout for pouring liquids into bottles. Weight 3 ounces. Price, each **10c**

HX651 — Same description as above, except half-pint size. Weight, 2 ounces. Price, each........ **10c**

SIMPLEX FLOUR SIFTER, 10c.

HX652 — Simplex Flour Sifter. Full size. Shaker action. Extra strong and well made of best quality bright tin. Has strong tin handle and large heavy wire shaker. Very simple to operate. Weight, 7 ounces. Price, each........ **10c**

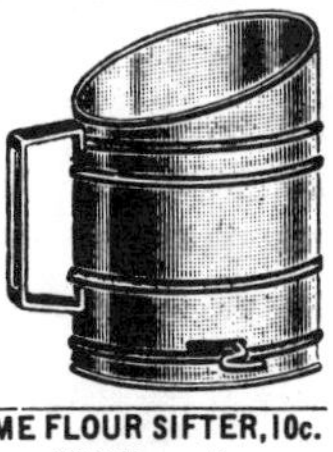

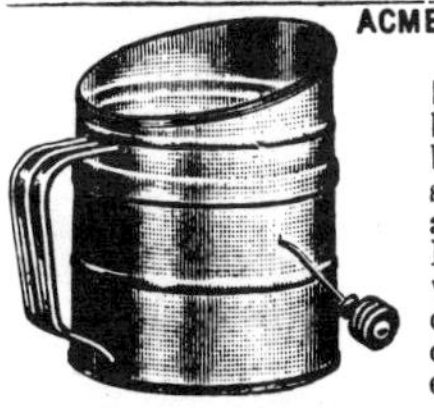

ACME FLOUR SIFTER, 10c.

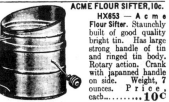

HX653 — Acme Flour Sifter. Staunchly built of good quality bright tin. Has large strong handle of tin and ringed tin body. Rotary action. Crank with japanned handle on side. Weight, 7 ounces. Price, each......... **10c**

Special Bargains in Tinware, 5 and 10c

DREDGE BOXES, EACH, 5c.

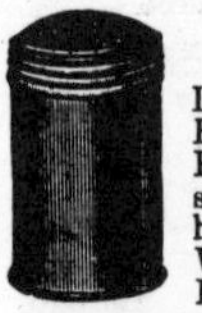

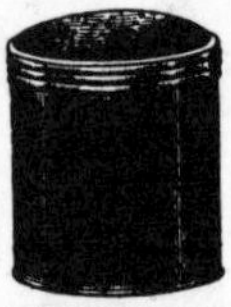

HV654 — Dredge Box. Durable, well made. Heavily japanned. Properly perforated screw top. $3\frac{1}{4}$ inches high by $2\frac{7}{8}$ inches wide. Weight, 3 ounces. Price, each..... **5c**

JAPANNED PEPPER BOXES, 2 FOR 5c.

HH655—Japanned Pepper Box. Large size. Screw top. Finely perforated. 3 inches high by $1\frac{7}{8}$ inches wide. Weight, 2 ounces. Price, 2 for.......... **5c**

HH656—Same as above, but smaller size. Weight, 1 ounce. Price, 2 for.......................... **5c**

TIN GRAVY STRAINER, 5c.

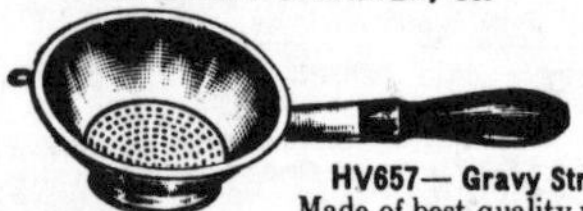

HV657— Gravy Strainer. Made of best quality metal, heavily retinned. $4\frac{1}{2}$-inch bowl. Specially punched strainer. $5\frac{1}{2}$-inch black enameled handle. A very useful article. Weight, 2 ounces. Price, each.... **5c**

CUP STRAINERS, 2 FOR 5c.

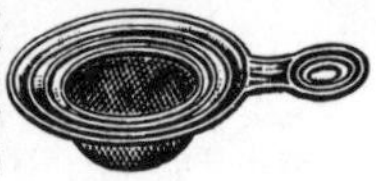

HH658 — Cup Strainer. To fit on top of cup when pouring. Wide fluted rim. Deep bowl. Gauze strainer. Handle at side. Weight, 1 ounce. Price, 2 for.. **5c**

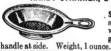

HANDY STRAINER, 2 FOR 5c.

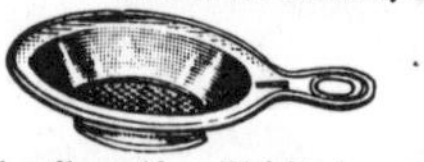

HH659 — Handy Strainer. Saucer shaped strainer with wide rim and wire gauze bottom. Has handle at side. Weight, 1 ounce. Price, 2 for.... **5c**

TIN CUPS, 2 FOR 5c.

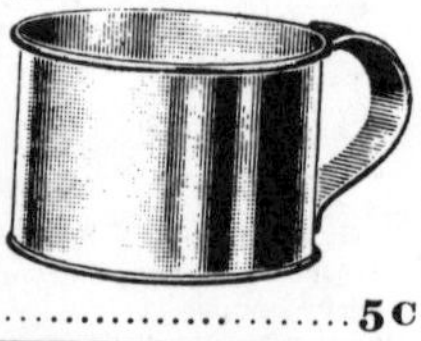

HH660. — Tin Cup. Half pint size. Specially retinned. Straight sides and flat bottom. Wt., 2 ounces. Price, 2 for.............. **5c**

HH661 — Pint Size. Otherwise same as above. Weight, 3 ounces. Price, 2 for.............................. **5c**

JELLY STRAINERS, EACH, 10c.

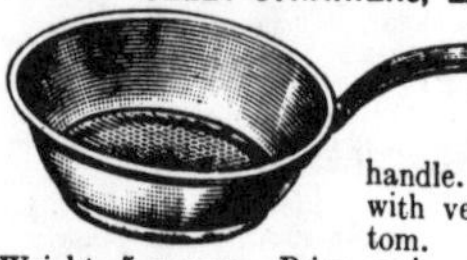

HX662– Jelly Strainer. Sauce pan shape. Long handle. Specially tinned with very fine screen bottom. 7-inch diameter. Weight, 5 ounces. Price, each.............. **10c**

CHAMPION SIEVES, EACH, 5c.

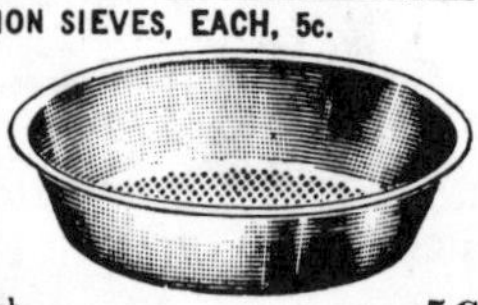

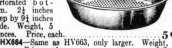

HV663 —Champion Sieve. Small size. Plain and easily cleaned, perforated bottom. $2\frac{1}{4}$ inches deep by $9\frac{1}{4}$ inches wide. Weight, 5 ounces. Price, each............................ **5c**

HX664—Same as HV663, only larger. Weight, 6 ounces. Price, each................................ **10c**

UTILITY SIEVE, 10c.

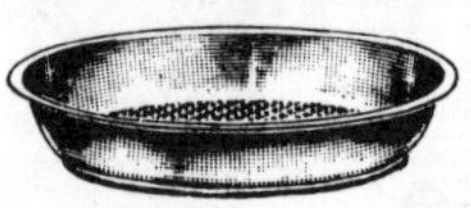

HX665 — Utility Sieve. Well made of best quality metal, heavily tinned. Fine wire sieve. $2\frac{1}{2}$ inches deep. An indispensable article in the kitchen. Weight, 9 ounces. Price, each.................................. **10c**

10-INCH COLANDER, 10c.

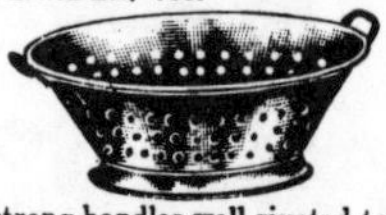

HX666 — Colander. 10 inches wide, made of best quality metal, heavily retinned. Strong reinforced footing. Perforated sides and bottom. Two strong handles well riveted to colander. Weight, 9 ounces. Price, each..... **10c**

MILK STRAINERS, EACH, 10c.

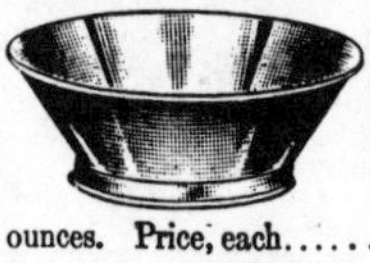

HX667 — Milk Strainer. 10-inch size. Made from good quality metal, specially retinned. Footed. Strongly made with 2-inch circular copper gauze screen in bottom. Weight, 8 ounces. Price, each..................... **10c**

SHALLOW PIE PLATES, 2 FOR 5c.

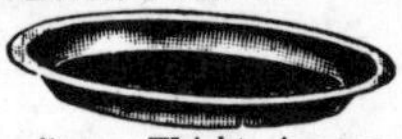

HH668 — Shallow Pie Plates. Specially tinned, wide rim plates. Come in 6, 7, 8 and 9-inch diameter. Extra quality. Weight, 4 ounces. Price, 2 for.................................. **5c**

HV6688—10 and 11-inch sizes. State size wanted. Weight, 4 ounces. Price, each................ **5c**

MOUNTAIN CAKE PANS, 5c.

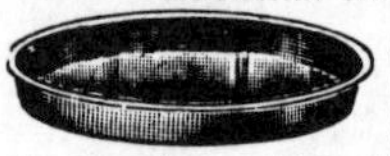

HV669—Mountain Cake Pans. Made of best quality metal, heavily tinned. Come in 9, 10 and 11-inch sizes. Always mention size desired. Weight, 5 ounces. Price, each **5c**

DEEP PIE PLATES, 5c.

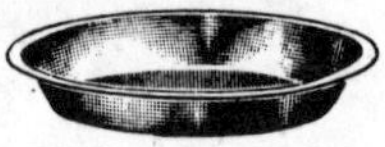

HV670—Deep Pie Plates. Stamped metal, heavily tinned extra deep pie plates. Come in 8, 9, 10 and 11-inch sizes. Always state what size you want. Weight, 4 ounces. Price, each.................................. **5c**

DEEP JELLY CAKE PANS, 5c.

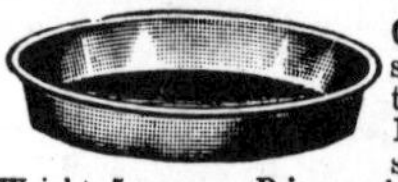

HV671 — Deep Jelly Cake Pans. Stamped from strong metal. Heavily tinned. Come in 8, 9 and 10-inch sizes. Always state size wanted. Weight, 5 ounces. Price, each.................. **5c**

"EZEOUT" PIE PLATES, 5c.

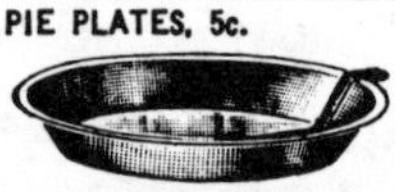

HV672 — "Ezeout" Pie Plates. Made of best quality tinned metal. 9 and 10 inch. Have bottom cutting blade. Simple, efficient. State size wanted. Weight, 4 ounces. Price, each........................ **5c**

"EZEOUT" JELLY CAKE PANS, 5c.

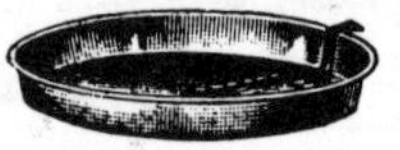

HV673 — "Ezeout" Jelly Cake Pans. 9 and 10-inch sizes. Made of best quality metal, heavily tinned. Have bottom cutting blade. State size desired. Weight, 5 ounces. Price, each.............................. **5c**

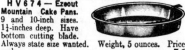

"EZEOUT" MOUNTAIN CAKE PANS, 5c.

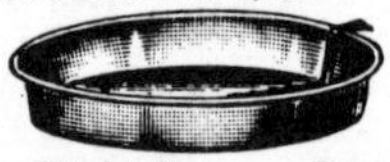

HV674 — Ezeout Mountain Cake Pans. 9 and 10-inch sizes. $1\frac{1}{4}$-inches deep. Have bottom cutting blade. Always state size wanted. Weight, 5 ounces. Price, each................................ **5c**

SEAMLESS SQUARE PAN, 5c.

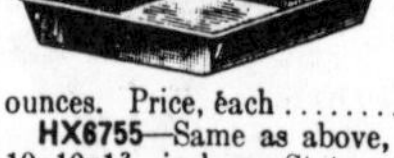

HV675—Seamless Square Pan. For bread or cake. Bright tin. $1\frac{5}{8}$ inches deep. $7\frac{1}{2}$ inches square. Weight, 6 ounces. Price, each.......................... **5c**

HX6755—Same as above, except $9x9x1\frac{1}{2}$ inches or $10x10x1\frac{3}{4}$ inches. State size wanted. Weight, 8 ounces. Price, each........................ **10c**

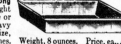

OBLONG CAKE PAN, 5c.

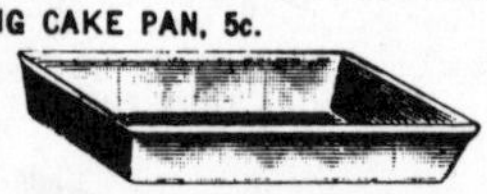

HV676 —Oblong Cake Pan. Bright tin oblong cake or biscuit pan. Heavy wired edge. Size, $7\frac{1}{2}x11\frac{1}{4}x1\frac{7}{8}$ inches. Weight, 8 ounces. Price, ea.. **5c**

HX6766—Same as above, except sizes are $8\frac{7}{8}x12\frac{1}{2}x1\frac{7}{8}$ inches and $10x14x2\frac{1}{4}$ inches. State size wanted. Weight, 11 ounces. Price, each **10c**

SEAMLESS BREAD PAN, 5c.

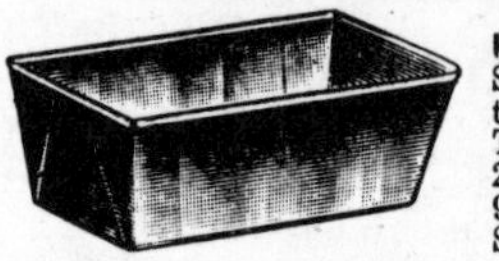

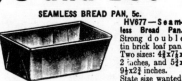

HV677—Seamless Bread Pan. Strong double tin brick loaf pan. Two sizes: $4\frac{5}{8}x7\frac{7}{8}x2$ inches, and $5\frac{3}{4}x9\frac{1}{2}x2\frac{7}{8}$ inches. State size wanted. Weight, 7 ounces. Price, each................ **5c**

HX6777 — Same as above, except two larger sizes, $5\frac{3}{4}x9\frac{3}{4}x3\frac{1}{2}$ inches and $6\frac{5}{8}x10\frac{1}{2}x2\frac{1}{2}$ inches. Weight, 9 ounces. State size wanted. Price, each...... **10c**

PUDDING PANS, 2 FOR 5c.

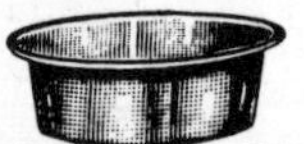

HH678 — Pudding Pans. Made of strong, plain tin. Come in three sizes, ½ quart, 1 quart, and 3 pint. Average weight, 4 ounces. Give size wanted. Price, 2 for.................................. **5c**

DAIRY PANS, 2 FOR 5c.

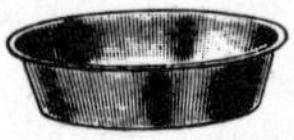

HH679 — Dairy Pan. Made of plain tin (like illustration). In four sizes, ½ pint, 1 pint, 1 quart and $1\frac{1}{2}$ quart. Average weight, 4 ounces. Give sizes wanted. Price, 2 for.. **5c**

PLAIN TIN PUDDING PAN, 5c.

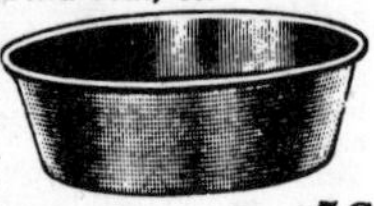

HV680 — Pudding Pan, Stamped from hard metal, heavily tinned. Comes in three sizes, 3, 4 and 5 quart. Average weight, 5 ounces. Give size wanted when ordering. Price, each.............. **5c**

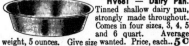

SHALLOW DAIRY PAN, 5c.

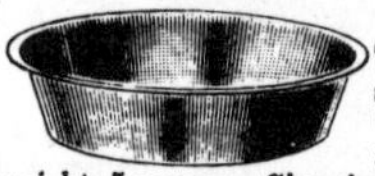

HV681 — Dairy Pan. Tinned shallow dairy pan, strongly made throughout. Comes in four sizes, 3, 4, 5 and 6 quart. Average weight, 5 ounces. Give size wanted. Price, each.. **5c**

HEAVY TINNED MUFFIN PAN, 10c.

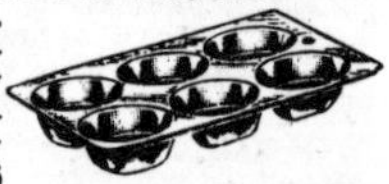

HX682 — Muffin Pan. Six cup muffin pan, substantially made and heavily tinned. Has hole for hanging up. $6\frac{3}{4}$ inches wide by $10\frac{1}{4}$ inches long. Weight, 6 ounces. Price, each...................... **10c**

CORN CAKE PANS, 10c.

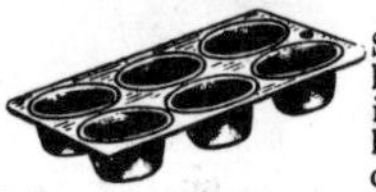

HX683 — Corn Cake Pan. Six cup, strongly made, heavily tinned pan. $6\frac{3}{4}$ inches wide by $10\frac{1}{4}$ inches long. Cups are $1\frac{1}{2}$ inches deep. Weight, 7 ounces. Price, each.............................. **10c**

HX6833.—Same as above, only eight cups instead of six. Weight, 9 ounces. Price, each.......... **10c**

TURK'S HEAD MUFFIN PAN, 10c.

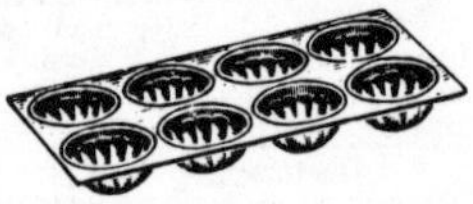

HX684 — Turk's Head Muffin Pan. Heavily tinned. Cups fluted in Turk's head pattern. Two sizes—six cups, $6\frac{3}{4}x10\frac{1}{4}$ inches; eight cups, $7x13\frac{1}{2}$ inches. Give size wanted. Weight, 7 ounces. Price, each.............. **10c**

OVAL SHAPED JELLY MOLD, 10c.

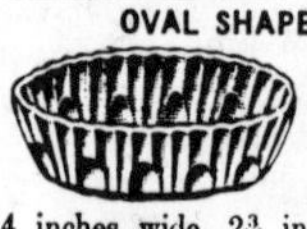

HX685 — Jelly Mold. Heavy retinned, oval shaped, large size jelly mold. Deeply stamped and embossed in fancy ornamental pattern. 6 inches long, 4 inches wide, $2\frac{3}{4}$ inches deep. Weight, 4 ounces. Price, each.............................. **10c**

ROUND CAKE PAN, 10c.

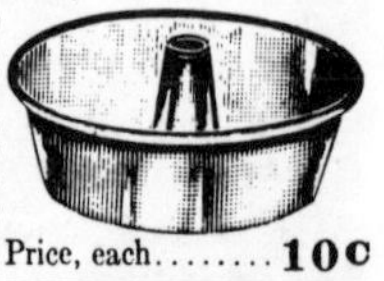

HX686 — Round Cake Pan. With center tube. Made from extra heavy retinned metal. Heavy, staunchly built pan designed to give long service. 9-inches diameter, 3 inches deep. Weight, 7 ounces. Price, each........ **10c**

Remember that you save money by having your goods shipped by freight. It costs as much to ship 20 pounds as it does to ship 100 pounds—so order for the whole family at one time.

Extra Values in Roasters and Tinware at 10c

OCTAGON CAKE PAN, 10c.

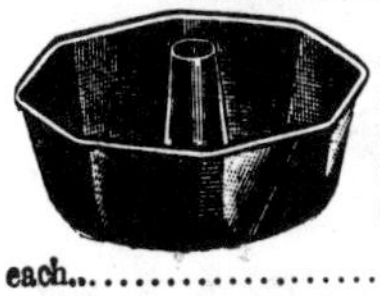

HX687 — Octagon Cake Pan. With center tube. Made from best quality retinned metal. Heavy, retinned octagonal pan with fancy bottom. 8-inch diameter, $2\frac{3}{4}$ inches deep. Weight, 6 ounces Price, each.................................... 10c

TURBAN CAKE PAN, 10c.

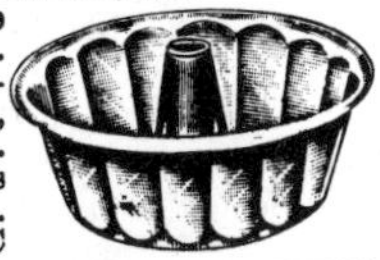

HX688 — Turban Cake Pan. With center tube. Stamped from heavy retinned metal. Round, with fancy fluted pattern. $3\frac{1}{4}$-inch deep by $8\frac{1}{2}$ inches wide. Weight, 6 ounces. Price, each........ 10c

HEAVY DOUBLE ROASTER, 10c.

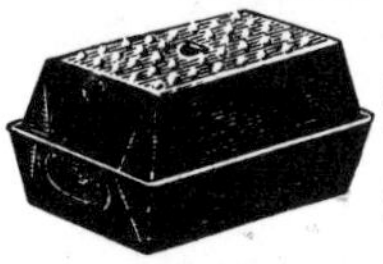

HX689 — Double Roaster. Made from best quality heavy black seamless sheet iron. $6\frac{1}{2}$x$9\frac{1}{2}$x$4\frac{3}{4}$ inches with drip top and strong wired edges and handles. Weight, 20 ounces. Price, complete..... 10c

LARGE DOUBLE ROASTER, EACH PAN, 10c.

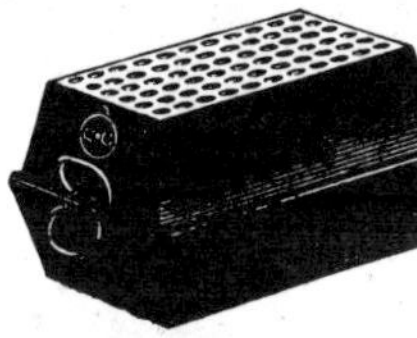

HZ690 — Double Roaster. Made of two heavy sheet iron pans with drip top and heavy wired edges. Size, 9x14x7 inches. Weight, complete, 3 pounds. Price, for two pans.............................. 20c

Note.—Both pans must be ordered, we cannot separate.

HZ691—Same as above, only larger. Size, 10x15x7 inches. Weight, complete, $3\frac{1}{2}$ pounds. Price, for two pans.............................. 20c

Note.—Both pans must be ordered, we cannot separate.

SHEET IRON DRIP PAN, 5c.

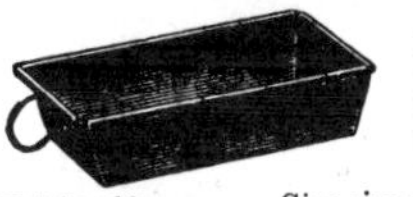

HV692 — Drip Pan. Heavy black sheet iron pan with strong wired edge. Two sizes, 6x9x$2\frac{1}{4}$ inches and 7x10x$2\frac{1}{4}$ inches. Weight, 10 ounces. Give size wanted. Price, ea. 5c

HX6922—Same as above, only larger—8x15x$2\frac{1}{2}$ inches. Weight, 13 ounces. Price, each...... 10c

HEAVY BLACK DRIP PAN, 5c.

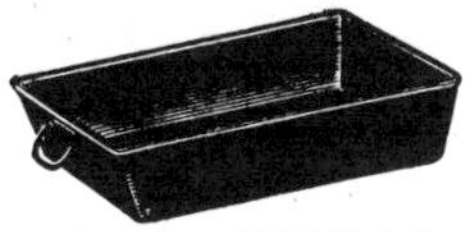

HV693 — Drip Pan. Heavy black sheet iron with strong wired edge. Size, 8x12x$2\frac{1}{2}$ in. Weight, 12 ozs. Price, each.. 5c

HX6933 —Same as above, but larger. Three sizes, 10x14x$2\frac{1}{2}$ inches, 10x17x$2\frac{1}{2}$ inches, and 10x19x$2\frac{1}{2}$ inches. Weight, 20 ounces. Give size wanted. Price, each...... 10c

PRESSED STEEL FRY PAN, 5c.

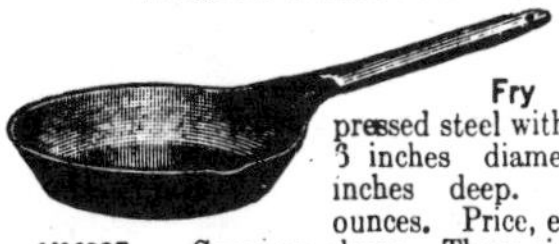

HV694 - Acme Fry Pan. Black pressed steel with cold handle. 3 inches diameter by $1\frac{1}{2}$ inches deep. Weight, 11 ounces. Price, each.... 5c

HX695 — Same as above. Three sizes, 8 inches, $9\frac{3}{4}$ inches and $10\frac{1}{4}$ inches. Average weight, 13 ounces. State size wanted. Price, each.............. 10c

BRIGHT TIN DISH PAN, 10c.

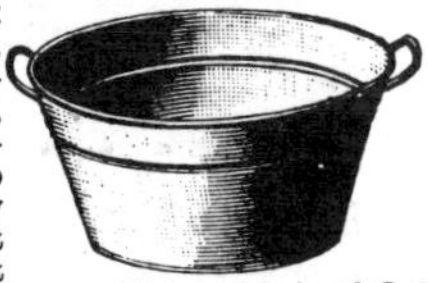

HX700 — Ten Quart Dish Pan. Bright tin, flat bottom. $12\frac{3}{4}$ inches in diameter at top, 9 inches bottom: 6 inches deep with two side handles. Heavily wired edges to prevent pan from sagging out of shape. Weight, 17 ounces. Price, each.... 10c

SEAMLESS RINSING PAN, 10c.

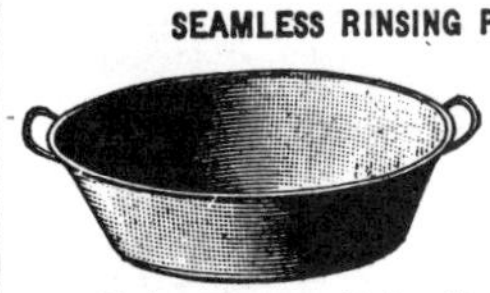

HX701 — Rinsing Pan. Holds eight quarts. Stamped seamless from heavily tinned metal. 14 in. diameter at top, 10 inches at bottom, 4 inches deep, two side handles. Weight 12 ounces. Price, each.............. 10c

HX7011. — Same as above, but size $14\frac{1}{2}$x$9\frac{1}{2}$x$4\frac{3}{4}$ in. Holds ten quarts. Average weight 15 ounces. Price, each......................... 10c

HEAVY TIN FLARING PAIL, 10c.

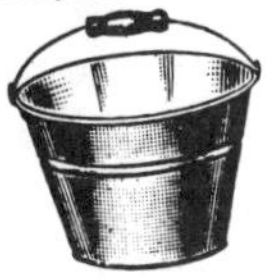

HX702 — Flaring Pail. Well made, bright tin pail with strong bail and wood handle. Two sizes, 8 quart and 10 quart. Give size wanted. Weight, 14 ounces. Price, each.... 10c

STRONG SUD DIPPER, SPECIAL AT ONLY 10c

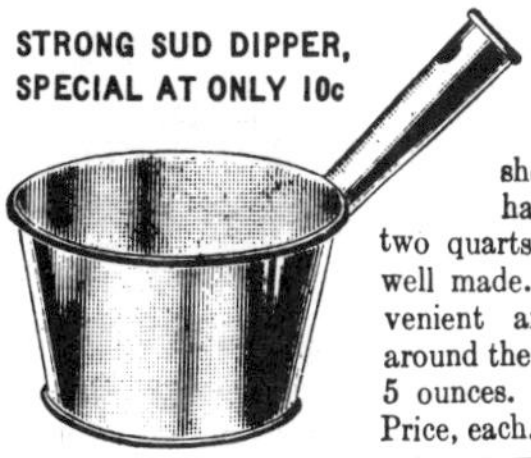

HX703 — Sud Dipper. Bright heavy tin with short round handle. Holds two quarts. Strong and well made. A very convenient article to have around the house. Weight, 5 ounces. Price, each. 10c

GALVANIZED IRON DIPPER, 10c.

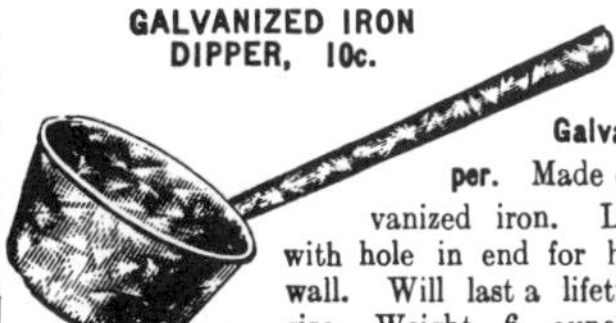

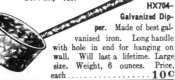

HX704— Galvanized Dipper. Made of best galvanized iron. Long handle with hole in end for hanging on wall. Will last a lifetime. Large size. Weight, 6 ounces. Price, each.................. 10c

TWO QUART EXTRA QUALITY TIN DIPPER, 10c.

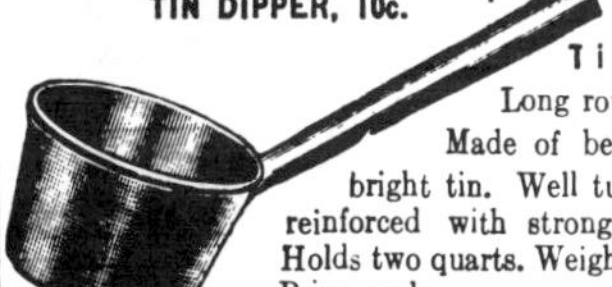

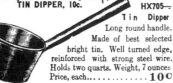

HX705— Tin Dipper Long round handle. Made of best selected bright tin. Well turned edge, reinforced with strong steel wire. Holds two quarts. Weight, 7 ounces Price, each............. 10c

EXTRA HEAVY WASH BASIN, 10c.

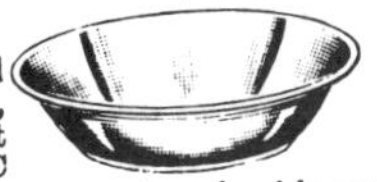

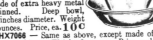

HX706 — Wash Basin Made of extra heavy metal retinned. Deep bowl, 12 inches diameter. Weight 8 ounces. Price, ea. 10c

HX7066 — Same as above, except made of heavy galvanized iron. Weight, 9 ounces. Price, each 10c

TIN POT COVERS, 2 FOR 5c.

HH725 — Pot Covers. Stamped from heavy bright tin, smooth turned edge, ring handle. Four sizes, 7, $7\frac{1}{2}$, 8 and $8\frac{1}{2}$ inches. Specify size desired. Average weight, 3 ounces. Price, 2 for.......................... 5c

HV7255 — Same as above, except larger. Eight sizes, 9, $9\frac{1}{2}$, 10, $10\frac{1}{2}$, 11, $11\frac{1}{2}$, 12 and $12\frac{1}{2}$ inches. Specify size desired. Average weight, 5 ounces. Price, each.......................... 5c

See our Special Bargains in kitchen knives, forks, basters, cake turners, etc., on page 98.

Tinware, Enamelware, Glassware, etc., should be shipped by freight as it is very bulky and will not make a profitable shipment by parcel post.

NICKELED TEA STEEPER, 10c.

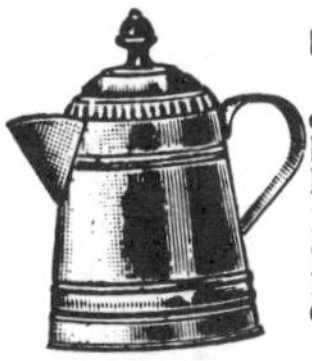

HX726 — Tea Steeper. Made of high grade nickeled tin, embossed around top, spout and handle firmly attached. Capacity, $1\frac{1}{2}$ pints. Good wearing quality. A special value at the price Weight, 5 ounces. Price, each.................. 10c

HEAVY TIN COFFEE POT, 10c.

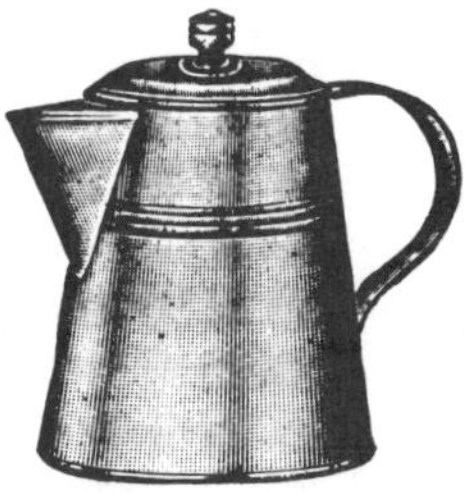

HX727—Coffee Pot. Made of high grade bright tin. Hinged top. Generous handle, wide open spout. Comes in three sizes, $1\frac{1}{2}$, 2 and 3 quart. Be sure to give size wanted when ordering. Average weight, 7 ounces. Price, each...... 10c

HEAVY TIN TEA POT, 10c.

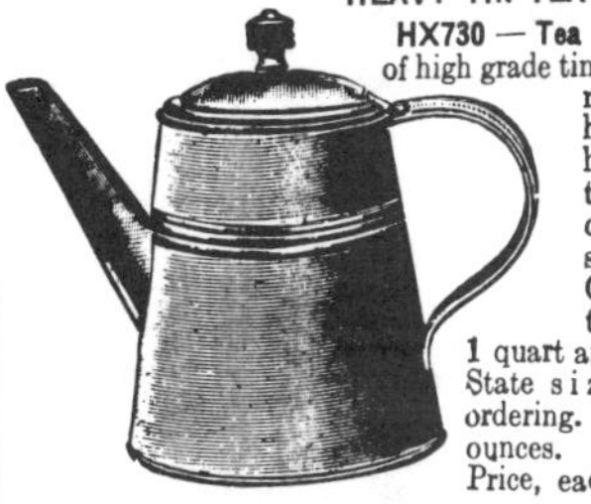

HX730 — Tea Pot. Made of high grade tin plate, with rolled handle, hinged top, long closed spout. Comes in two sizes, 1 quart and 2 quart State size when ordering. Weight, 7 ounces. Price, each.. 10c

OIL STOVE TEA KETTLE, 10c.

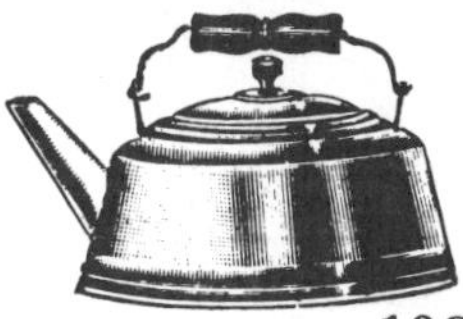

HX732 — Oil Stove Tea Kettle. Made of heavy, plain, durable tin. Low squat shape. Wire bail, wood handle. Separate cover, round spout. Capacity, 3 pints. Weight, 7 ounces. Price, each.......................... 10c

COVERED TIN BUCKET, 10c.

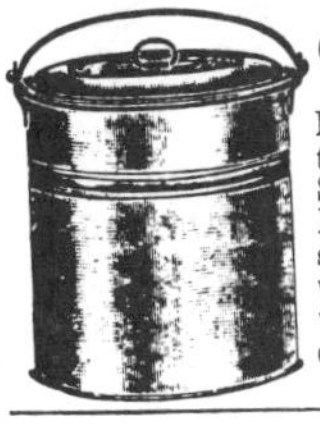

HX733 — Covered Bucket. Made of special grade, bright tin. Securely attached bail. Separate cover with ring handle. High pattern. Comes in two sizes, 2 and 3 quart. Give size wanted when ordering. Average weight, 9 ounces. Price, each.................. 10c

BRIGHT FINISH TIN MILK CAN, 10c.

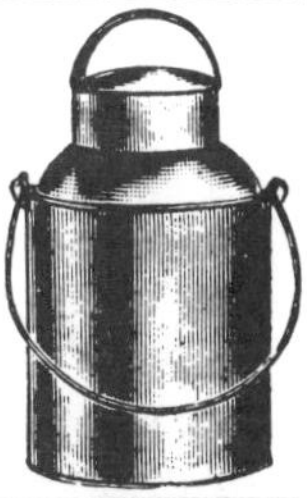

HX735 — Milk Can. Made of best grade bright tin, with wire bail handle, shaped top. Cup cover with handle. A strong and very durable can. One and two quart sizes. State size wanted. Average weight, 8 ounces. Price, each. 10c

TIN SPRINKLING CAN, 10c.

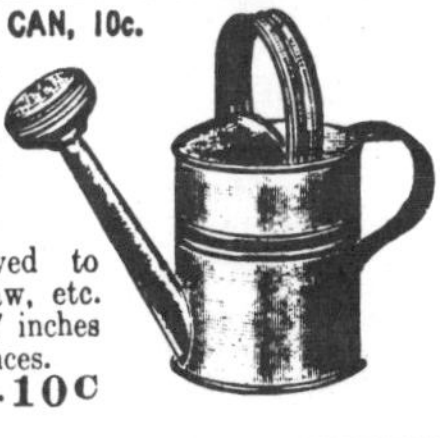

HX741—Tin Sprinkling Can. Made of good quality bright tin with fine spray top, bail and side handle. the spray top can be removed to take out leaves, straw, etc. $3\frac{3}{4}$ inches wide and 7 inches high. Weight, 8 ounces. Price, each......... 10c

Bargains in Tinware—Nothing Over 10c

TEA OR SUGAR CANISTER 10c.

HX737 — Tea or Sugar Canister. Cylindrical shape. Made of best quality bright metal, heavily japanned. Has hinged cover with neat device for locking if desired. Comes in two sizes, 3½ lbs. and 7 lbs. Mention size wanted. Weight, 7 ounces. Price... ....**10C**

COFFEE OR TEA CANISTER, 10c.

HX739 — Coffee or Tea Canister. Comes in one size of 2 pound capacity. Made of highest grade tin plate, enameled in assorted colors. One size only for either tea or coffee. Airtight lid, keeps the flavor in the coffee and tea. Weight, 9 ounces. Price, each. **10C**

FANCY PATTERN NICKEL PLATED TRAY, 5c.

HV761 — Fancy Pattern Nickel Plated Tray. 10 inches in diameter and center has very fancy engraved pattern. Scroll edge. Heavily nickel plated. Weight, 5 ounces. Price...................**5C**

LARGE FANCY NICKEL PLATED TRAY, 10c.

HX762 — Large Fancy Nickel Plated Tray. Round shape. Diameter of tray, 13 inches. Fancy etched pattern in center. Scroll edge. All heavily nickel plated. Weight, 8 ounces. Price............**10C**

NICKEL PLATED FANCY OBLONG TRAY, 10c.

HX763 — Nickel Plated Fancy Oblong Tray. Size, 10¼x14 inches. Center has fancy floral etching. Embossed edge. All heavily nickel plated. A very durable tray. Weight, 10 ounces. Price....................**10C**

ROUND JAPANNED FANCY TRAY, 10c.

HX764 — Round Japanned Fancy Tray. 13 inches in diameter. Made of best quality heavy metal, durable black japanning. Has rose painted in center. Very durable. Weight, 7 ounces. Price....................**10C**

OVAL BLACK JAPANNED TRAY, 10c.

HX765 — Oval Black Japanned Tray. Made of best quality heavy metal black Japan with two gold hair line stripes. Size, 13½x16 inches. Weight, 10 ounces. Price....................**10C**

ICE CREAM SCOOP, 10c.

HX747 — Ice Cream Scoop. Made of high quality, double tinned steel. Has side scraper. Comes in large or small size. State which you want. Weight, 4 ounces. Price, each. **10C**

EASY EGG POACHER, 10c.

HX746 — Egg Poacher. Maryland pattern. Poaches three eggs at one time. Rings lift up to allow easy removal of eggs. Weight, 4 ounces. Price, each. **10C**

HEAVY TIN CANDLE HOLDER, 5c.

HV754 — Candle Holder. Well constructed from heavy tin. Has large handle and flaring bottom. Dark enamel finish. Wt., 2 ounces. Price, ea...**5C**

CORNER SINK STRAINER, 10c.

HX744—Corner Sink Strainer. Made of good heavy quality tin, covered with fine blue enamel. Fits in corner of sink. Comes in two sizes; large and small. Give size wanted. Average weight, 6 ounces. Price, each. **10C**

PERFORATED SINK STRAINER, 10c.

HX743 — Sink Strainer. Made of high-grade tin plate, perforated, finished in blue enamel. Wire hook to fit over edge of sink. Wt., 8 ounces. Price, each. **10C**

WALL MATCH SAFE, 5c.

HV750 — Wall Match Safe. Made of tin plate. Stamped and embossed, decorated with colored enamel. Has hinged cover. Indispensable. Weight, 2 ounces. Price, each...................**5C**

TWIN MATCH SAFE, 5c.

HV751 — Twin Match Safe. Carefully constructed of ornamental embossed and enameled tin. Has two pockets with scratcher in between. Finished in blue enamel. Weight, 3 ozs. Price, each....**5C**

SELF-FEEDING MATCH SAFE, 10c.

HX753 — Self-Feeding Match Safe. Made of good quality heavy metal, nicely enameled. Large size, holds full box of matches, discharging few at a time. No danger of scattering matches all over the floor. Receptacle on the side for burnt matches. Weight, 4 ounces. Price, each. **10C**

SELECTED SANITARY GLASS, ONE PINT NON-BREAKABLE FLASK, 10c.

HX749 — Selected, non-breakable Sanitary Glass Flask in bolstered tin casing to prevent breakage. Capacity, 1 pint. Just right for the dinner basket, camping, picnics, outings, etc. Will carry coffee, tea, cocoa, milk or other liquids without danger of breakage. Weight, 12 ounces. Price, each..**10C**

FANCY DESIGN BRASS FINISH DECORATED FLUE STOP, 5c.

HV755 — Flue Stop. Decorative fancy design. Made of tin, brass finished, with wire attached for 6-inch flue. Needed in every home where stoves are used during the year. Weight, 3 ounces. Price, each **5C**

BRASS STOVE PIPE COLLAR, 5c.

HV775 — Stove Pipe Collar. Made of heavy brass finished tin, deeply embossed with a fancy ornamental design. Made to fit a 6-inch pipe. It keeps soot and ashes from falling out around stove pipe. Weight, 2 ounces. Price, each. **5C**

See our special bargains in dinnerware on page 109. When ordering be sure to include an extra amount to cover transportation charges.

DUST PAN, WITH GUARD, 10c.

HX776 — Dust Pan, with Guard. Made from extra heavy sheet iron, embossed and enameled in colors. Has 2-inch dust guard or half cover at back of pan, a special precaution to prevent dust from flying. Weight, 12 ounces. Price each. **10C**

SPECIAL DUST PAN, 5c.

HV777 — Special Dust Pan. Made of heavy sheet metal. Finished in black Japan and embossed. Has round handle with hole for hanging. Weight, 7 ounces. Price, each. **5C**

STAMPED TIN CUSPIDOR, 10c.

HX778 — Stamped Tin Cuspidor. Decorated with colored enamel and striped. 7 inches in diameter, 3⅜ inches high. Weight, 7 ounces. Price, each...**10C**

HX779 — Same as above, only larger. Weight, 9 ounces. Price, each...**10C**

SHEET METAL FIRE SHOVEL, 5c.

HV780—Sheet Metal Fire Shovel. Stamped from heavy sheet steel, finished in black Japan. Has round handle. 4½-inch blade, length, 14½ inches. Weight, 5 ounces. Price, each......**5C**

GALVANIZED IRON FIRE SHOVEL, 10c.

HX781 — Galvanized Iron Fire Shovel. Extra heavy. Long round handle. Made from selected material and will last a lifetime. Weight, 11 ounces. Price, each. **10C**

HX782 — Same as above, except finished in black Japan. Good quality. Wt., 10 ozs. Price, each **10C**

ASBESTOS STOVE MATS, 2 FOR 5c.

HH784 —Asbestos Stove Mats. Cut round, well bound with tin. Have ring handle on one side. Wt., 2 ounces. Price, 2 for.........**5C**

HV785 — Asbestos Toaster. Same as above, except has wire screen protecting one side. Weight, 4 ounces. Price, each...........**5C**

ROUND ASBESTOS TABLE MATS, 5c.

HV786 — Round Asbestos Table Mats. Extra heavy, well bound with tape. Come in three sizes, 7½, 8 and 8½-inch diameters. Weight, 6 ounces. Price, each..........**5C**

HH788 — Same as above, except 5½ inches in diameter. Weight, 4 ounces. Price, 2 for.........**5C**

OVAL ASBESTOS TABLE MATS, 5c.

HV790 — Oval Asbestos Table Mats. Extra heavy, well bound with tape. Size, 5½x9½ inches. Weight, 4 ounces. Price, each ..**5C**

HH789 — Same as above, except two sizes, 5x7 inches and 5x8½ inches. Weight, 3 ounces. Price, 2 for **5C**

HIGH GRADE GRAY ENAMELWARE AT 5 & 10¢

Look over these great bargains in our high-grade "Defiance" brand enamelware, shown on this and the following page. The body of "Defiance" ware is made of high-grade iron of extra heavy gauge. The enamel is of light gray color with beautiful mottling. This enamel ware is one of the most durable, sanitary and attractive lines made. Every piece guaranteed to be strictly as represented. Nothing over 10c.

When ordering enamelware do not fail to include hardware, woodenware, dry goods, notions, etc. Make a freight shipment and save on transportation charges. See our Free Delivery Offer on page 3.

GRAY ENAMEL TEA STRAINER, 5c.

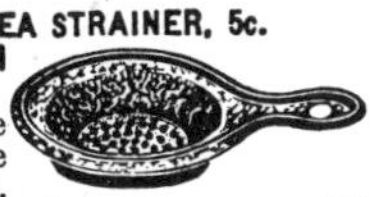

HV800 — Gray Enamel Tea Strainer. Made of heavy gray enamelware with rolled edge and side handle. Size, 3¼x5¾ inches. Weight, 2 ounces. Price, each..............5C

GRAY ENAMEL SOAP DISH, 10c.

HX801 — Gray Enamel Soap Dish. Large size. Heavy stamped steel, gray enamel covered wall soap dish with drainer. Very convenient dish for the kitchen or bathroom. Wt., 5 ounces. Price, each......10C

GRAY ENAMEL FUNNEL, 10c.

HX802 — Gray Enamel Funnel. Made of heavy stamped steel and covered with thick glazed gray enamel. Size of funnel, 4½x4½ inches, with ½-inch spout. A good funnel for everyday use. Weight, 3 ounces. Price, each..............10C

GRAY ENAMEL BEAN BOWL, 5c.

HV803 — Gray Enamel Bean Bowl. Small heavy gray enamel bowl for which the housewife will find many uses. 4½ inches wide by 2 inches deep. Weight 3 ounces. Price, each......5C

GRAY ENAMEL DRINKING CUP, 10c.

HX804 — Gray Enamel Drinking Cup. One pint size. Made of heavy gray enamelware, extra quality. Convenient large handle. Weight, 6 ounces. Price, each..............10C

ENAMELED CUP AND SAUCER, 10c.

HX805 — Enameled Cup and Saucer. Regular size. Made of heavy gray enamelware. Cup has handle and rolled edge. Saucer is generous in size. Weight, 6 ounces. Price, complete..............10C

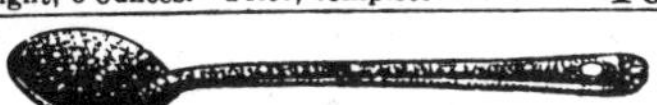

GRAY ENAMEL BASTING SPOON, 10c.

HX806 — Gray Enamel Basting Spoon. 16 inches in length. Made of heavy gray enamel. Concave handle to give strength. Hole in end. Weight, 4 ounces. Price, each..............10C

HV8066—Same as above, except 12 inches long. Weight, 4 ounces. Price, each..............5C

GRAY ENAMEL CAKE TURNER, 5c.

HV807 — Gray Enamel Cake Turner. Made of heavy gray enamelware. 15 inches long. Has round handle with hole in end. Weight, 5 ounces. Price, each..............5C

GRAY ENAMEL SKIMMER, 5c.

HV808 — Gray Enamel Skimmer. Made of good heavy, serviceable gray enamelware with broad perforated blade, 8 inches in diameter. Length over all, 14 inches. A useful kitchen utensil. Weight, 5 ounces. Price, each..............5C

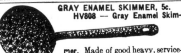

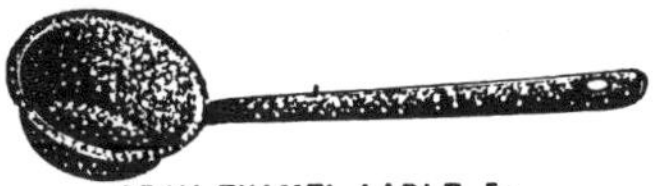

GRAY ENAMEL LADLE, 5c.

HV809 — Gray Enamel Ladle. Made of first quality gray enamelware with large bowl and half-round handle, with hole in end. Length over all, 13 inches. Weight, 5 ounces. Price, each.........5C

EXTRA DEEP LADLE, 10c.

HX810 — Extra Deep Ladle. A strong, heavy gray enamel kitchen utensil. Has long half-round handle. Bowl, 2 inches deep by 4½ inches wide. Length, 13½ inches. Weight, 5 ounces. Price, each..............10C

ENAMELED WINDSOR DIPPER, 10c.

HX811 — Enameled Windsor

Dipper. Made of extra heavy gray enamelware. Has seamless bottom. Capacity of dipper, 1½ pints. Length, 15 inches over all. Handle is firmly attached to dipper. Weight, 8 ounces. Price, each..............10C

ENAMEL PRESERVING KETTLE, 5c.

HV812 — Preserve Kettle. One quart size. Extra heavy gray enamel, rolled edge, tipping handle and lip. Strong wire bail securely attached. Weight, 10 ounces. Price, each..............5C

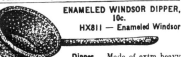

HX813 — Same as above, except larger. Four sizes, 2 quart, 2¾ quart, 3¼ quart, and 4 quart. Always mention size wanted. Average weight, 14 ounces. Price, each..............10C

SHALLOW STEW PANS, 5c.

HV832— Shallow Stew Pan. Made of extra heavy gray enamelware. 1 and 1½ qt. size, rolled edge, long handle, hole in handle. Weight, 7 ounces. Price each..............5C

HX8322—Same as above, except larger. Comes in two sizes, 2 and 3 quart. Always mention size wanted. Average weight, 13 ounces. Price, ea.10C

DEEP STEW PANS, EACH, 5c.

HV837— Deep Stew Pans. One quart size. Made of selected gray enamelware. Has long handle, rolled edge, pouring lip, and hole in handle. Weight, 10 ounces. Price, each...5C

HX838 — Same as above, only larger. Comes in four sizes, 2, 3, 4 and 5 quart. Always mention size wanted. Average weight, 18 ounces. Price, ea.10C

ENAMEL PUDDING PANS, 5c.

HV842 — Enamel Pudding Pans. Deep extra heavy gray enamelware pan, with wide flaring rim. One and 1½ quart sizes. Mention size wanted when ordering. Average weight, 10 ounces. Price, each..............5C

HX844 — Same as above, except larger. Four sizes, 3, 4, 5 and 6 quart. Always mention size wanted. Average weight, 15 ounces. Price, each......10C

ENAMEL SAUCE PANS, 5c.

HV817— Sauce Pan. One quart size. Made of extra heavy gray enamelware, with long handle and pouring lip. Weight, 10 ounces. Price, each. 5C

HX817 — Same as above, except larger. Come in four sizes, 2, 2¾, 3¼ and 4 quart capacity. Always mention size wanted. Average weight, 18 ounces. Price, each..............10C

GRAY ENAMEL DAIRY PANS, EACH, 5c.

HV848 — Gray Enamel Dairy Pans. Made of fine gray enamelware, extra heavy with rolled rim. Three sizes: 1, 1½ and 2 quart. Always mention size wanted when ordering. Average weight, 10 ounces. Price, each..............5C

HX851 — Same as above, except larger. Three sizes: 3, 4 and 6 quart. Always mention size wanted. Average weight, 18 ounces. Price, each......10C

THE ORIGINAL PARCEL POST **KRESGE'S KATALOG** FIVE AND TEN CENT STORE

High Grade Enamelware at 5c and 10c Each

GRAY ENAMEL DEEP BAKING PAN, 5c.

HV854 — Gray Enamel Deep Baking Pan. One quart size. Made of fine extra heavy gray enamel with wide rim and two side handles. Weight, 10 ounces. Price, each **5C**
HX855 — Same as above, except larger. Comes in four sizes: 2, 3, 4 and 5 quart. Always mention size wanted. Average weight, 15 ounces. Price...**10C**

GRAY ENAMEL SHALLOW BAKING PAN, 5c.

HV859 — Gray Enamel Shallow Baking Pan. One quart size. Made of extra heavy gray enamel with wide rim and two side handles. Weight, 10 ounces. Price, each..................**5C**
HX860 — Same as above, except larger. Comes in two sizes: 3 and 4 quart. Always mention size wanted. Average weight, 12 ounces. Price, each......**10C**

GRAY ENAMEL ENGLISH PUDDING POT, 10c.

HX862 — Gray Enamel English Pudding Pot. Deep, extra heavy gray enamel pan with rolled edge and two side handles. Comes in two sizes; 2½ and 4 quart. Always mention size wanted. Average weight, 13 ounces. Price, each...........

GRAY ENAMEL MIXING PANS, EACH, 5c.

HV864 — Gray Enamel Mixing Pans. One quart size. Extra heavy selected gray enamel, deep flat bottom pan. Weight, 7 ounces. Price, each............**5C**
HX865 — Same as above, except larger. Comes in three sizes: 2, 2½ and 4 quart. Always mention size wanted. Average weight, 12 ounces. Price, each.............**10C**

GRAY ENAMEL DUTCH BOWLS, EACH, 10c.

HX868 — Gray Enamel Dutch Bowls. Very deep, extra heavy gray enamel bowl with wide roll rim. Comes in three sizes; 1½, 2 and 3 quart. Always mention size wanted when ordering. Average weight 11 ounces. Price, each...................**10C**

GRAY ENAMEL COLANDERS, EACH, 10c.

HX871 — Gray Enamel Colanders. Made of extra heavy gray selected enamel properly perforated. Colander has heavy raised base. Made in one size only, 3½ quart. A good, serviceable colander. Weight, 13 ounces. Price......................**10C**

GRAY ENAMEL CAKE PANS, EACH, 10c.

HX872 — Gray Enamel Cake Pans. Round shape. Made of extra heavy gray enamel with wide rim. Has center tube. Size, 9⅞x3 inches. Good results can be obtained with this cake pan, as it distributes the heat evenly. Weight, 13 ounces. Price, each.................**10C**

GRAY ENAMEL BREAD PANS, EACH, 10c.

HX873 — Gray Enamel Bread Pans. Made of extra heavy gray enamel. Oblong cake or bread pan. 9 inches long, 6 inches wide, and 2½ inches deep. Weight, 11 ounces. Price, each. **10C**

We guarantee our enamelware to be of the highest quality and well made. All of these numbers will give the best of service and satisfaction, and we guarantee them to be just as represented, or we will cheerfully refund your money if you are not pleased with your purchase in every respect.

GRAY ENAMEL BREAD PANS, EACH, 10c.

HX874 — Gray Enamel Bread Pans. Brick loaf size. Made of heavy sheet steel, first quality gray coated enamel. 9½ inches long, 5¼ inches wide, and 2¾ inches deep. Weight, 11 ounces. Price..**10C**

PERFORATED KITCHEN STRAINER, 10c.

HX875 — Perforated Kitchen Strainer made of extra quality, heavy gray enamel, properly perforated. Has strong raised base and good heavy handle. Handle has hole in end to permit hanging up. Weight, 9 ounces. Price...........**10C**

GRAY ENAMEL SINK STRAINER, 10c.

HX876 — Gray Enamel Sink Strainer. Made of extra heavy gray enamel. Has perforated bottom with strong securely attached feet. Strainer is 8 inches in diameter. Weight, 9 ounces. Price, each **10C**

GRAY ENAMEL FRYING PAN, 10c.

HX877 — Gray Enamel Frying Pan. Stamped from heavy metal, gray enameled. Has long handle and pouring lip. 10½ inches in diameter. Weight, 12 ounces. Price, each.........**10C**

GRAY ENAMEL MOUNTAIN CAKE PAN, 10c.

HX878 — Gray Enamel Mountain Cake Pan. Made of extra heavy gray enamel, highly finished. 10½ inches wide by 1¾ inches deep. Weight, 10 ounces. Price..........**10C**

GRAY ENAMEL BOSTON PIE PAN, 10c.

HX879 — Gray Enamel Boston Pie Pan. Made of extra heavy quality gray enamel. Very deep pan. 10¼ inches wide. Very convenient size. Weight, 10 ounces. Price...........**10C**

GRAY ENAMEL JELLY CAKE PAN, 5c.

HV880 — Gray Enamel Jelly Cake Pan. Made of strong extra heavy gray enamel. Two sizes 9 and 10-inch. State size wanted when ordering. Weight, 7 ounces. Price, each.................**5C**

GRAY ENAMEL DEEP PIE PLATE, 5c.

HV881 — Gray Enamel Deep Pie Plate. Has wide flaring rim. Two sizes: 9 and 10-inch. State size wanted when ordering. Average weight, 7 ounces. Price......................**5C**
HX883 — Same as above, only larger. 11 inches in diameter. Weight, 9 ounces. Price, each....**10C**

GRAY ENAMEL SAUCE PANS, EACH, 10c.

HX884 — Gray Enamel Sauce Pans. Made of extra heavy gray enamel, seamless stamped steel. Has deep handle. 1½ quart size. Equipped with tin cover. A very serviceable enamel sauce pan. Weight, 11 ounces. Price, each..**10C**

GRAY ENAMEL GERMAN STEW CUP, 10c.

HX885 — Gray Enamel German Stew Cup. Made of extra heavy gray enamel, seamless stamped steel. Each cup is equipped with bright tin cover. Capacity, 3 pints. Average weight, 9 ounces. Price, each..................**10C**

GRAY ENAMEL COVERED BUCKET, 10c.

HX886 — Gray Enamel Covered Bucket. Heavy seamless gray enamel, with strong bail, and extra quality tin cover. Comes in two sizes, 1½ and 2 quart. Mention size wanted when ordering. Average weight, 12 ounces. Price, each.................**10C**

GRAY ENAMEL STOCK POTS, EACH, 10c.

HX888 — Gray Enamel Stock Pots. Made of carefully selected seamless heavy gray enamel. Supplied with first quality tin cover. Has two strong side handles. Two sizes; 1½ and 2 quart. State size wanted when ordering. Average weight, 13 ounces. Price, each.................**10C**

GRAY ENAMEL WASH BASINS, EACH, 10c.

HX890 — Gray Enamel Wash Basins. Made of fine quality extra heavy gray enamel. Has wide, deeply rolled edge. Three sizes, 2, 3 and 5 quart. Give size wanted when ordering. Average weight, 14 ounces. Price, each.........**10C**

GRAY ENAMEL KETTLE COVERS, EACH, 10c.

Made of extra heavy gray enamel, stamped knobs. Come in the following numbers and designed to fit kettles and pans as mentioned.
HX821 — Fits HX817 and HX813. Price.**10C**
HX822 — Fits HX818 and HX814. Price, each...............**10C**
HX823 — Fits HX819 and HX815. Price, ea.**10C**
HX824 — Fits HX820 and HX816. Price, each **10C**
HX825 — Fits Kettle 10 inches across top. Ea..**10C**
HX826 — Fits kettle 10½ inches across top. Each..................**10C**
HX827 — Fits kettle 11 inches across top. Each..................**10C**
HX828 — Fits kettle 11½ inches across top. Each..................**10C**
Average weight of the above lids is 9 ounces. The merchandise mentioned for which these lids are intended will be found on this page and page 105.

Such articles as enamelware, crockery, woodenware, tinware, etc., are very bulky and should be shipped by freight. When ordering, be sure to include enough merchandise to make at least 100 lbs., as the freight rate is no more on 100 lbs. than on 20 lbs. Get your friends to order with you. Read page 3 and back cover of Katalog for special offers.

GENUINE SWEDISH WHITE ENAMELWARE AT 10¢

This ware is made of fine quality sheet steel, triple coated with pure white porcelain enamel, with fine light blue hair line edge. It is very durable, sanitary and light. It is easily cleaned, and in every respect gives complete satisfaction. Every piece is seamless.

WHITE ENAMEL SAUCE PAN, 10c.

HX900 — Sauce Pan. Pure white Swedish enamel, decorated with brilliant blue edge $4\frac{1}{2}$ inches wide, $2\frac{3}{4}$ inches deep. Capacity, 1 quart. Strong, straight handle. Wt., 6 ounces. Price, each........................ 10c

OVAL ENAMEL BAKING DISH, 10c.

HX901 — Deep oval Baking Dish. Made of imported Swedish enamel, all white with fine blue edge, withstands heat perfectly. Size, $8\frac{3}{4}$x7 inches. Weight, 7 ounces. Price, each........................ 10c

WHITE ENAMEL PUDDING PAN, 10c.

HX902 — Pudding Pan. Genuine Swedish imported enamel, all white with blue edge decoration. 6-inch diameter, about $2\frac{1}{2}$ inches deep. Weight, 5 ounces. Price, each. 10c

WHITE ENAMEL FRYING PAN, 10c.

HX903 — Frying Pan. Seamless imported Swedish enamel, long handle $6\frac{1}{2}$ inches wide, $1\frac{1}{4}$ inches deep. Decorated with fine blue edge. Weight, 7 ounces. Price, each.............. 10c

HX904—Same as HX903, only smaller. Weight, 7 ounces. Price, each.............. 10c

WHITE ENAMEL SAUCE PAN, 10c.

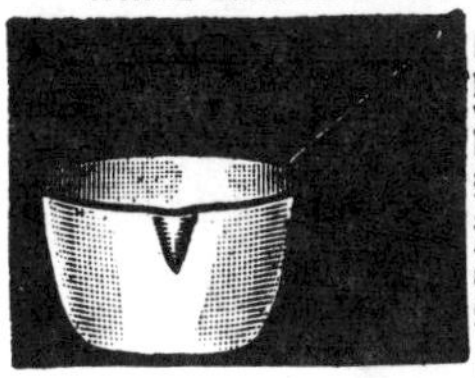

HX905—Sauce Pan. Made of imported Swedish white enamel with blue edge, wider at top than bottom. Lipped. Has long handle. Comes in sizes, 1 and $1\frac{1}{2}$ pints. State size wanted. Weight, 7 ounces. Price, each.. 10c

WHITE ENAMEL MIXING BOWL, 10c.

HX907 — Mixing Bowl. Made of all white imported Swedish enamel with blue edge. Comes in two sizes, 1 and $1\frac{1}{2}$ pint capacity. When ordering, state capacity wanted. Weight, 7 ounces. Price, each.................. 10c

WHITE ENAMEL BASIN, 10c.

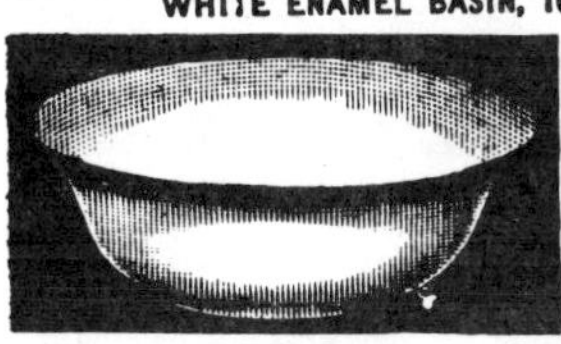

HX909 — White Enamel Basin Made of genuine Swedish enamel, pure white, blue edge decoration, flared bowl. 8-inch diameter. A strong durable basin for every day use. Weight, 7 ounces. Price, each.............................. 10c

WHITE ENAMEL FLARED BOWL, 10c.

HX910 — Flared Bowl. Made of pure white imported Swedish enamel with blue decoration on edge. $7\frac{1}{2}$ inch diameter. Capacity, 3 pints. Wt., 5 ounces. Price. each.............. 10c

ALL WHITE IMPORTED SWEDISH NESTING TUMBLERS, 10c.

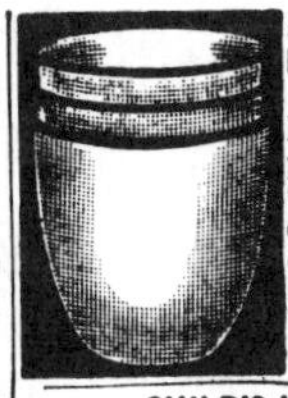

HX911 — Nesting Tumblers. Made of best quality all white imported Swedish enamel. Size of tumbler, 3x3 inches. Has fine blue edge. Just the thing for picnics, outings, etc, where a number of tumblers can be put in a small space. Weight, 3 ounces. Price, each tumbler.................... 10c

CHILD'S WHITE ENAMEL CUP, 10c.

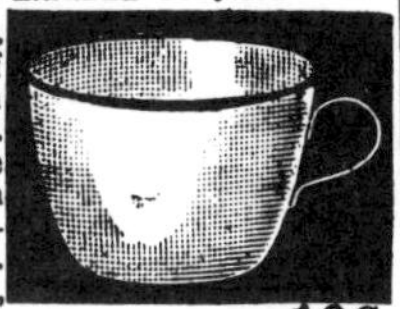

HX912 — Child's Cup. Flared, sanitary. Made of imported all white Swedish enamel, $3\frac{1}{2}$ inch diameter. Capacity, $\frac{1}{2}$ pint. Can be taken to school, picnics, on trains and wherever an individual cup is wanted. Weight, 4 ounces. Price, each.................................... 10c

GENUINE IMPORTED SWEDISH WHITE ENAMEL CUSTARD CUP, 10c.

HX913 — Genuine Imported Swedish White Enamel Custard Cup. Made of genuine imported pure white Swedish enamel with fine blue edge. $3\frac{3}{4}$-inch diameter, $2\frac{1}{2}$ inches high. Capacity, $\frac{1}{2}$ pint. Weight, 3 ounces. Price, ea.. 10c

WHITE ENAMEL STRAIGHT CUP, 10c.

HX914 — Straight Cup. Genuine Swedish enamel, straight cup, $3\frac{3}{4}$ inches in diameter, $3\frac{1}{2}$ inches high. Capacity, 1 pint. Has fine blue edge. Weight, 6 ounces. Price, each.......... 10c

HX915 — Same as above, except smaller. Weight, 4 ounces. Price, each.......... 10c

HX916 — Same as above, except still smaller. Weight, 3 ounces. Price, each.............. 10c

WHITE ENAMEL CUP AND SAUCER, EACH, 10c.

HX917 — Cup, Saucer to match. All white imported Swedish enamel. Cup has handle. Both ornamented with fine blue edge. Weight, complete, 6 ounces. Must be ordered in pairs. Price, cup, 10c; saucer.. 10c

IMPORTED SWEDISH ENAMEL SOUP PLATES, 10c.

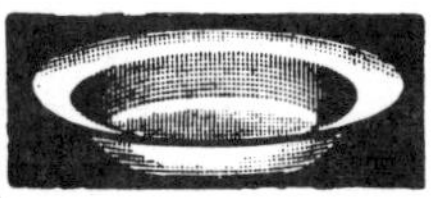

HX918 — Imported Enamel Soup Plates. Made of best quality imported Swedish enamel. Plates are 8 inches in diameter and $1\frac{1}{4}$ inches deep. Has fine blue edge all around plate. Weight, 5 ounces. Price.............................. 10c

FINE IMPORTED SWEDISH WHITE ENAMEL DINNER PLATE, 10c.

HX920 — Dinner Plate. All white imported Swedish enamel with dark blue edge Comes in two sizes: $7\frac{3}{4}$ and $8\frac{5}{8}$-inch diameters. State whether large or small size is wanted. Weight, 4 ounces. Price, each.......... 10c

WHITE ENAMEL PIE PLATE, 10c.

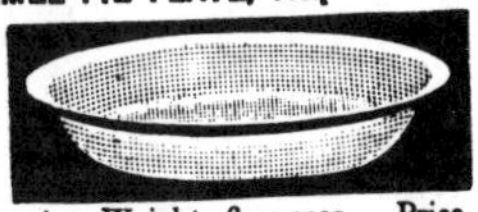

HX922—White Enamel Pie Plate. 9-inch size. Wide rim; deep body. Made of pure white imported Swedish enamel. Weight, 6 ounces. Price, each.................................... 10c

WHITE ENAMEL RICE DISH, 10c.

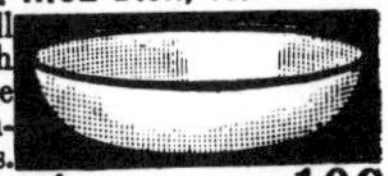

HX923 — Rice Dish. All white imported Swedish enamel with blue edge decoration. $6\frac{1}{2}$-inch diameter. Capacity, 3 pints. Weight, 5 ounces. Price, each.............. 10c

WHITE ENAMEL PHOTOGRAPHER'S TRAY, 10c.

HX924—Photographer's Tray. Made of all white genuine Swedish enamel. A necessity in the office of photographer or physician. Size, $5\frac{1}{2}$x$7\frac{1}{2}$ inches. Weight, 7 ounces. Price, each.................................... 10c

WHITE ENAMEL POT COVER, 10c.

HX925 — Pot Cover. Flanged edge, made of all white genuine imported Swedish enamel. Comes in two sizes, $8\frac{1}{2}$ and $9\frac{1}{4}$ inches. When ordering, state whether large or small size is wanted. Weight, 8 ounces. Price, each.................................... 10c

WHITE ENAMEL SKIMMER, 10c.

HX927—Skimmer. Made of pure white imported Swedish enamel. Perforated. Bowl is $4\frac{1}{2}$ inches in diameter. Handle, $10\frac{1}{2}$ inches long with hook at end. Weight, 5 ounces. Price, each........ 10c

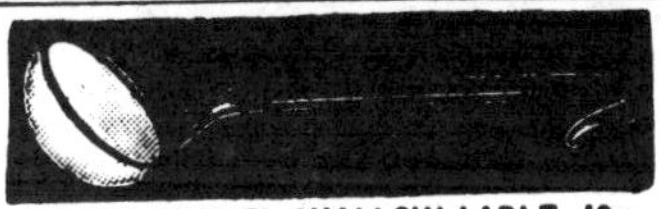

WHITE ENAMEL SHALLOW LADLE, 10c.

HX928 — Shallow Ladle. Made of imported Swedish white enamel. Seamless. 10-inch hooked handle, 3-inch bowl. Weight, 5 ounces. Price, each.................................... 10c

WHITE ENAMEL DEEP LADLE, 10c.

HX929—Deep Ladle. All white imported Swedish enamel. Bowl, 4 inches wide; has long, strong hooked handle. Length, over all, 14 inches. Weight, 6 ounces. Price, each.............................. 10c

FINE IMPORTED SWEDISH WHITE ENAMEL BOWL SHAPED FUNNEL, 10c.

HX930 — Bowl shaped Funnel. Seamless. Made of all white imported Swedish enamel. Comes in two sizes, 4-inch diameter and $3\frac{1}{2}$-inch diameter. When ordering, state whether large or small size is wanted. Weight, 4 ounces. Price, each.............. 10c

Extra Quality Semi-Porcelain Dinnerware

Gold Loop Pattern, Per Piece, Only

5c and 10c

Every piece is of pure white semi-porcelain, with fast underglazed colors. This means that it will give excellent service. The body of this dinnerware is made of the best potter's clay, imported from England, and made up in America's largest potteries. Every piece is decorated with a continuous gold loop pattern and gold edge. The illustrations in natural colors will be found on page 13. This dinnerware is an open stock pattern which means that you can buy any piece or pieces listed below, at any time. It has stood the test with millions of customers who have purchased it from our many stores. The following pieces come in gold loop pattern only.

EV209 — Fruit Saucer. 4½ inches in diameter. Weight, 7 ounces. Price.....5 C

EV210 — Oatmeal Dish. 5 inches in diameter. Weight, 7 ounces. Price.....5 C

EV211 — Bread and Butter Plate 4 inches in diameter. Weight, 6 ozs. Price.....5 C

EV212 — Pie Plate. 5 inches in diameter. Weight, 6 ounces. Price.....5 C

EX213 — Tea Plate. 7 inches in diameter. Weight, 6 ounces. Price.....10C

EX214 — Soup Plate. 7 inches in diameter. Weight, 17 ounces. Price.....10C

EX215 — Dinner Plate. 8 inches in diameter. Weight, 15 ounces. Price.....10C

EX216 — Salad Bowl. 6 inches in diameter. Weight, 12 ounces. Price.....10C

EX217 — Salad Bowl. 7 inches in diameter. Weight, 15 ounces. Price.....10C

EX219 — Baker. Oval shape, 6 inches long. Weight, 9 ounces. Price.....10C

EX220 — Baker. Oval shape, 7 inches long. Weight, 10 ounces. Price.....10C

EX221 — Platter. 7x10 inches. Weight, 17 ounces. Price, each.10C

EX222 — Platter. 8x10¾ inches. Weight, 20 ounces. Price.....10C

EX223 — Platter. 9x11¾ inches. Weight, 22 ounces. Price.....10C

EX224 — Creamer. Capacity 1½ pints. Weight, 12 ounces. Price 10C

EX225 — Fancy Bowl. Size, 3½x5½ inches. Weight, 12 ounces. Price.....10C

EX226 — Cup and Saucer. Ovoid shape. Weight, 12 ounces. Price for cup and saucer.....10C

Morning Glory Pattern, Per Piece, Only

5c and 10c

This set is decorated with beautiful Morning Glory vine and flowers, with gold edge, fast underglazed colors. Illustrations of this pattern in rich, natural colors will be found on page 13. The body of this dinnerware is made of the best imported English potter's clay, and manufactured in America. This dinnerware is also an open stock pattern, and you can order one or a hundred of the pieces listed below, with the assurance that every piece will match perfectly. Select a complete set for your dinner table. You will be surprised at the low cost, and the excellent values you can get from us at 5c and 10c each. The following pieces come in Morning Glory pattern only.

EV191 — Fruit Saucer. 4½ inches in diameter. Weight, 7 ounces. Price.....5 C

EV192 — Oatmeal Dish. 5 inches diameter. Weight, 7 ounces. Price.....5 C

EV193 — Bread and Butter Plate. Diameter, 4 inches. Weight, 5 ounces. Price.....5 C

EV194 — Pie Plate. 5 inches in diameter. Weight, 6 ounces. Price.....5 C

EX195 — Tea Plate. 7 inches in diameter. Weight, 6 ounces. Price.....10C

EX196 — Soup Plate. 7 inches in diameter. Weight, 16 ounces. Price.....10C

EX197 — Dinner Plate. 8 inches in diameter. Weight, 15 ounces. Price.....10C

EX198 — Salad Bowl. Size, 2½x6 inches. Weight, 12 ounces. Price.....10C

EX199 — Salad Bowl. Size, 3x7 inches. Weight, 15 ounces. Price.....10C

EX201 — Baker 6-inch oval shape. Weight, 9 ounces. Price.....10C

EX202 — Baker 7-inch oval shape. Weight, 10 ounces. Price.....10C

EX203 — Platter. 7 inches wide by 10½ inches long. Weight 17 ounces. Price.....10C

EX204 — Platter. 8 inches wide by 10¾ inches long. Weight, 20 ounces. Price.....10C

EX205 — Platter. 9 inches wide by 11¾ inches long. Weight, 22 ounces. Price.....10C

EX206 — Creamer. Capacity 1½ pints. Weight, 12 ounces. Price 10C

EX207 — Fancy Bowl. Size, 3½x5½ inches. Weight, 12 ounces. Price.....10C

EX208 — Cup and Saucer. Fancy Shape. Weight, 12 ounces. Price for cup and saucer.....10C

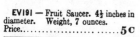

Read our Special Free Delivery Offer on Page 3.   **All Dinnerware should be shipped by Freight.**

Flow Blue Pattern, Dinnerware at 5c and 10c

The dinnerware illustrated above is known as our Flow Blue pattern. See page 13 for actual colors. The body is made of high-grade imported potter's clay. The pattern consists of a dark blue edge, graduating into a lighter shade; gold edge and neat gold decorations over the blue. The colorings are fast and all underglazed, and will give splendid wear and satisfaction. This is an open stock pattern and supplied in the various pieces listed below, in Flow Blue Pattern only.

EV800 — Fruit Dish. 4 inches in diameter. Weight, 4 ounces. Price, each..................5 C

EV801 — Fruit Dish. 5 inches in diameter. Weight, 7 ounces. Price, each..................5 C

EX802 — Tea Plate. 7 inches in diameter. Weight, 6 ounces. Price, each..................10 C

EX803 — Dinner Plate. 8 inches in diameter. Weight, 17 ounces. Price, each..................10 C

EX804 — Savoy Nappy. 7 inches wide. Weight, 16 ounces. Price, each..................10 C

EX805 — Soup Plate. 7 inches in diameter. Weight, 15 ounces. Price each..................10 C

EX806 — Baker. Size, 6½x8½ inches. Weight, 13 ounces. Price, each..................10 C

EX807 — Platter. Size, 7x11 inches. Weight, 15 ounces. Price, each..................10 C

EX808 — Bowl. Size, 5 inches in diameter, 2½ inches deep. Weight, 14 ounces. Price, each..................10 C

EX809 — Jug. 8 inches high. Wt., 13 ounces. Price, each..................10 C

EX810 — Cup and Saucer. Regular size. Not sold separately. Weight, 11 ounces. Price, for Cup and Saucer..................10 C

State Katalog number when ordering, also how you want your order shipped

Plain White Crockery—Nothing Over 10c

FRUIT SAUCERS, 2 FOR 5c.

EE170 — Fruit Saucers. 5 inches in diameter, smooth high-grade finish. Weight, two 8 ounces. Price, 2 for..................5 C

BAKING DISH, 5c.

EV174 — Baking Dish. 3-inch baking or side dish. White crockery. Weight 5 ounces. Price, each..................5 C

OAT MEAL DISH, 5c.

EV181 — Oat Meal Dish. Best white crockery. Fancy shape. Smooth finish. Weight, 5 ounces. Price, each..................5 C

FANCY SHAPED BOWL, 10c.

EX185 — Fancy Shaped Bowl. Best white crockery. 8 inches in diameter. Very useful article. Weight, 2 pounds. Price, each..................10 C

BUTTER CHIPS, 3 FOR 5c.

EE182 — Butter Dishes. Best white crockery. 3½ inches in diameter. Regular size. Weight, for three, 3 ounces. Special value, 3 for..................5 C

SPECIAL BARGAINS IN USEFUL PLAIN WHITE CROCKERY PLATES.

EV177 — Pie Plate. 6 inches in diameter. Weight, 10 ounces. Price, each..................5 C

EV178 — Plain White Tea Plate. 7 inches in diameter. Weight, 13 ounces. Each..................5 C

EE176 — Bread and Butter Plate. 5 inches in diameter. Best white crockery. Wt., 6 ounces. Price, 2 for..................5 C

EV179 — Soup or deep Plates. 7 inches in diameter. Weight, 10 ounces. Price, each..................5 C

EV180 — Large Dinner Plate. 8 inches in diameter. Weight, 16 ounces. Price, each..................5 C

OYSTER BOWL, 5c.

EV173 — Oyster Bowl. Best white crockery, deep pattern. Footed. Weight, 12 ounces. Price, each..................5 C

ST. DENNIS BOWL, 5c.

EV172 — St. Dennis Bowl. White crockery, plain shape. 5 inches in diameter, 3½ inches high. Weight, 12 ounces. Price, each..................5 C

IMPORTED CHINA EGG-CUPS, 2¼ INCHES HIGH, 2 FOR 5c.

FF160 — Plain white. Fancy design. Weight, 4 ozs. 2 for..................5 C

FF161 — Gold Band and gold hairline. Weight, 4 ounces. 2 for..................5 C

FRUIT BOWLS, EACH, 5c.

EV171 — Fruit Bowls. Best white crockery. 6 inches in diameter. Weight, 15 ounces. Price, each..................5 C

HANDLED MUG, 5c.

EV175 — Handled Mug. Best quality plain white crockery. No saucer. Can be used for many purposes. Very special value. Weight, 9 ounces. Price, each..................5 C

CUP AND SAUCER, 5c.

EV183 — Holland Tea-Cup and Saucer. Best white crockery. High-grade finish. Cup has round smooth handle. Weight, complete, 12 ounces. Cup and saucer..................5 C

CUP AND SAUCER, 5c.

EV184 — Cup and Saucer. Handled cup, deep saucer. Best white crockery, high-grade finish. Not sold separately. Weight, complete, 12 ounces. Cup and Saucer..................5 C

HANDLED PITCHER, 10c.

EX186 — Handled Pitcher. Fancy shape with strong handle and pouring lip. About 8 inches high. Made of white crockery, high-grade finish. Fancy turned top and bottom. Weight, 3 pounds. Price..................10 C

MIXING BOWLS, 5c.

EV227 — Mixing Bowls. 7 inches in diameter. Fancy green decoration. A splendid value. Weight, 3 pounds. Price, each..................5 C

MIXING BOWLS, 10c.

EX228 — Mixing Bowls. Same as above, except 9 inches in diameter. Deep pattern. Fancy green decoration. An excellent value. Weight, 3½ lbs. Price, each..................10 C

Crockery and Glassware — Nothing Over 10c

BLUE BRISTOL GLAZE MIXING BOWL, 10c.

EX229—Blue Bristol Glaze Mixing Bowl. 9 inches in diameter. Neat blue decoration with blue band around center. Weight 2 pounds. Each.. **10c**

MIXING OR STIRRING BOWLS, EACH 10c.

EX230—Mixing or Stirring Bowls. Neat blue decoration, Bristol glaze. 9 inches in diameter. A handy kitchen utensil. Weight 2 pounds. Each.................. **10c**

SHALLOW MILK BOWLS, EACH 10c.

EX231—Shallow Milk Bowls. 9 inches in diameter, fluted pattern. Blue decoration with high Bristol glaze. Good quality bowl, very serviceable. Weight 3 pounds. Each.................. **10c**

BEAN POT WITH COVER, 10c.

EX236—Bean Pot with Cover. Two quart capacity. Decoration half red on white body. The regulation New England Bean Pot. Weight each 3½ pounds. Price.. **10c** Strong and well made.

GOOD QUALITY SALT BOX, 10c.

EX235—Good Quality Salt Box. Best quality stoneware with cover. Has blue tinted decoration. A very convenient article. Weight 3 pounds. Each...... **10c**

HALL BOY JUGS EACH, 10c.

EX233—Hall Boy Jugs. Capacity 2 quarts. Good quality stoneware, blue mottled decoration. Large handle and lip. Weight 3 pounds. Price............... **10c**

FANCY DECORATED TANKARDS, 10c.

EX232—Fancy Decorated Tankards. Two quart capacity. Handsome willow pattern, blue tinted on Bristol glaze. Inside is white finish. Has large convenient handle and pouring lip. Strong and well made. Weight 3½ pounds. Price............... **10c**

The weights on crockery make it advisable to ship by freight and save transportation charges. Read our Prepay Offer on Page 3.

GOOD STONEWARE ROLLING PIN, 10c.

EX234—Good Stoneware Rolling Pin. Roller is of stoneware with blue decoration on Bristol glaze. Large polished wood handles. Weight 2½ pounds. Price................**10c**

SOLID COLOR JARDINIERES, 10c.

EX238—Solid Color Jardinieres. Made of good quality stoneware with decoration in solid color glazes. Glazed inside and out. 7 inch size. Weight 2½ pounds. Price....................**10c**

STONEWARE CUSPIDORS, EACH 10c.

EX237—Stoneware Cuspidors. Neatly decorated with green and brown blended colors. Highly glazed. 7 inch size. Strong and well made. Heavy flaring edge. Weight 2½ pounds. Each......**10c**

DECORATED MUSTARD POTS, EACH 10c.

EX1900—Decorated Mustard Pots. Good quality Delph ware with neat blue decorations. Convenient handle, mustard spoon and lid. Weight 7 ounces. Price......**10c**

DECORATED GINGER POTS, EACH 10c.

EX1902—Decorated Ginger Pots. Good quality Delph ware with neat blue pattern. Highly glazed inside and out. Comes in the following: Ginger, Spices, Allspice, Pepper, Nutmeg, Cinnamon, Cloves — state kind desired. Weight 8 ounces. Price...........**10c**

GLAZED STONEWARE FUNNEL 10c.

EX1904—Glazed Stoneware Funnel. Made of good quality heavy Delph-ware with neat blue decoration. Heavily glazed inside and out. Convenient handle. 4 inches over all. Weight 4 ounces. Price....................**10c**

GLAZED STONEWARE STRAINER, 10c.

EX1906—Glazed Stoneware Strainer. Very sanitary. Made of good quality Delph ware, neat blue decoration, heavily glazed. Has polished wood handle. 9 inches long. Weight 3 ounces. Price....................**10c**

PLAIN WHISKEY GLASSES 2 FOR 5c.

EE122—Plain Whiskey Glasses. Good quality thin blown. Two ounce capacity. Crystal clear glass with nice smooth edge. Convenient size. Weight each 2 ounces. Price 2 for.....**5c**

GOOD QUALITY TABLE TUMBLERS, 2 FOR 5c.

EE116—Good Quality Table Tumblers. Fine finish. Neat and attractive. Made of best quality clear glass. Very smooth edge. Weight each 3 ounces. 2 for.**5c**

TABLE TUMBLERS 2 FOR 5c.

EE121—Thin Blown Table Tumblers. Made of good quality crystal clear glass. Capacity of tumblers 9 ounces. Smooth finish edge. An extra good value. Weight each 3 ounces. Price 2 for.......**5c**

FLUTED TABLE TUMBLERS, 3 for 5c.

EE150—Fluted Table Tumblers. Good quality clear glass with optic flute. Capacity of tumbler 8 ounces. A good quality serviceable tumbler for every day use. Weight each 9 ounces. Price 3 for.................**5c**

HAND POLISHED TABLE TUMBLERS EACH 5c.

EV1500—Hand Polished Table Tumblers. Best quality crystal clear glass. Capacity of tumblers about 9 ounces. Fancy ground bottom with star design. Good value. Weight 11 ounces. Each....................**5c**

TEA TUMBLERS EACH 5c.

EV117—Iced Tea Tumblers. Made in attractive Colonial fluted design with round bottom. Capacity of tumbler about 12 ounces. Handy for iced tea or lemonade. Weight 13 ounces. Each.......**5c**

TAPER SHAPED SODA GLASS, 5c

EV118—Taper Shaped Soda Glass. Made of best quality clear crystal glass, tapered shape. Capacity of glass about 12 ounces. Regular soda fountain size and will fit any standard holder. Weight 14 ounces. Price, each...**5c**

TABLE TUMBLERS, EACH 5c.

EV125—Thin Blown Table Tumblers. Made of clear crystal glass, thin blown. Has five hair lines ground on each glass. A very neat design. Capacity about 9 ounces. Weight each 3 ozs. Price, each....**5c**

DECORATED TABLE TUMBLERS, EACH 5c.

EV126—Decorated Table Tumblers. Best quality thin blown glass with four bands and two hair lines ground in glass. Neat, attractive pattern. Capacity about 9 ounces. Weight each glass 3 ounces. Price..........**5c**

DECORATED TABLE TUMBLERS, EACH 5c.

EV127—Decorated Table Tumblers. Made of good quality thin blown glass with four hair lines and two bands ground in glass. A very desirable pattern. Capacity about 9 ounces. Weight each 3 ounces. Price, each....................**5c**

GLASS TUMBLERS EACH 5c.

EV812—Blown Glass Tumblers. Very neat scroll and band design, needle etched. Neat pattern and a popular size. Capacity 9 ounces. A very good value for the price. Weight each 4 ounces. Price.........**5c**

NEEDLE ETCHED TUMBLERS EACH 5c.

EV814—Needle Etched Tumblers. Made of clear blown glass, with neat scroll design around top, needle etched. Good smooth edge. Capacity 9 ounces. A good tumbler for every day use. Weight 4 ounces. Price.........**5c**

GLASS TUMBLERS EACH 5c.

EV813—Blown Glass Tumblers. Made of good quality clear crystal glass with fancy scroll design around top, needle etched. Medium heavy weight. Capacity 9 ounces. Weight each 4 ounces. Price.........**5c**

GLASS TUMBLERS, EACH 5c.

EV815—Blown Glass Tumblers. Made of good quality clear crystal glass with smooth edge. Decorated with fancy scroll and band design on upper half of tumbler. Capacity 9 ounces. Weight 4 ounces. Each.........**5c**

Extra Special Bargains—Nothing Over 10c

NEEDLE ETCHED TUMBLERS, 5c.

EV816—Fine Cut Glass Tumblers. Good quality blown glass tumblers with grape design, nicely cut. Capacity of tumbler about 8 ounces. Bell shape. Attractive pattern. Weight each 4 ounces. Price........5C

CUT GLASS TUMBLERS, EACH, 5c.

EV817—Cut Glass Tumblers. Best quality clear blown glass with three cut star designs. Medium weight bottom. Smooth edge. A very attractive pattern for the dinner table. Wt., each glass, 4 ozs. Price........5C

TABLE TUMBLERS, 3 FOR 5c.

E148—Plain Glass Table Tumblers. Made of good quality clear plain glass. with horseshoe design in bottom. A good glass for every day use. Capacity, 8½ ozs. Weight, each, 4 ounces. 3 for 5C

FLUTED TABLE TUMBLERS, 3 FOR 5c.

E149—Fluted Table Tumblers. Made of good quality clear glass, half fluted design. Capacity, about 9 ozs. Good smooth finished top. A good serviceable glass for every day use. Weight, 4 ozs. 3 for..5C

PLAIN FOOTED GOBLETS, EACH, 5c.

EV115—Plain Footed Goblets. Made of good serviceable clear glass Capacity, about 10 ounces. A good serviceable Goblet. Weight, 12 ounces. Each........5C

See page 112 for descriptions and prices of imitation cut glass goblets.

PLAIN JELLY GLASSES, 3 FOR 5c.

E128—Plain Jelly Glasses. Tin top. Six oz. capacity. Weight, of 3, 17 ounces. 3 for........5C

E1288—Same as above, but 8 ounce capacity. Weight, of 3, 17 ounces. 3 for 5C

JELLY MOULDS, 3 FOR 5c.

E129—Jelly Moulds. Flat shape with tin cap. Makes a smooth mould. Weight of 3, 20 ounces. 3 for..5C

FOOTED SHERBET GLASS, 5c.

EV114—Footed Sherbet Glass. Made of good quality glass in neat Colonial design. Medium heavy weight. 4½ ounce capacity. Weight, 8 ounces. Each...............5C

CUSTARD CUPS, EACH, 5c.

EVI13—Custard Cups. Made of good quality clear glass in plain design. Capacity of cup, 4 ounces. Convenient article. Weight, 5 ounces. Price...5C

HEAVY CUT CREAMER, 10c.

EX131—Heavy Cut Creamer. Good quality heavy glass. Cut wreath design. Good heavy handle. and neatly turned lip. Matches EX-130. Weight, 9 ounces. Price...10C

HEAVY CUT SUGAR, 10c.

EX130—Heavy Cut Sugar. Good quality heavy glass. Cut wreath design. Neat attractive pattern. Matches EX131. Weight, 10 ounces. Price...............10C

HORSERADISH JARS, EACH, 5c.

EV155—Horseradish Jars. Made of good quality glass, fluted design. Round hollow top. Each jar is nicely finished throughout and a special value at the price. Weight, 11 ounces. Price....5C

INDIVIDUAL SALT DIPS, 3 FOR 5c.

E1111—Individual Salt Dips. Made of good quality heavy glass in Colonial design. Has fluted round top. A table necessity. Weight, of 3, 8 ounces. 3 for...............5C

CASTOR SET COMPLETE, 10c.

EX140—Castor Set. Made of good quality glass. Salt and pepper shaker with silver plated tops. Both set in individual castor. Castor is in neat Colonial design. Weight, 8 ounces. Complete 10C

CRYSTAL GLASS SUGAR SHAKER, 5c.

EV132—Crystal Glass Sugar Shaker. Good quality glass, fluted design. Celluloid top. Weight, each, 8 ounces. Price........5C

EV133—Same as above, but equipped with metal top, highly nickeled. Weight, 8 ozs. Price..5C

SALT AND PEPPER SHAKERS, 2 FOR 5c.

EE134—Salt and Pepper Shakers. Made of good quality glass, Colonial design. Sides have concave shape. Good metal top, highly nickel plated. Weight, each, 5 ozs. 2 for 5C

SALT AND PEPPER SHAKERS, 2 FOR 5c.

EE135—Salt and Pepper Shakers. Made of good quality glass. Barrel shape, octagon pattern. Nickeled top with celluloid inlay. Weight, each, 4 ozs. 2 for 5C

SALT AND PEPPER SHAKERS, 2 FOR 5c.

EE136—Salt and Pepper Shakers. Made of good quality medium heavy glass, graduated shape. Has nickeled top with celluloid inlay. A very special value. Weight, each 4 ounces. Price, 2 for...........5C

SALT AND PEPPER SHAKERS, 2 FOR 5c.

EE154—Salt and Pepper Shakers. Made of good quality opal glass. Round shape. Good metal top, heavily nickeled. Weight, each, 3 ounces. 2 for.5C

OPAL GLASS SUGAR SIFTER, 5c.

EV137—Opal Glass Sugar Sifter. Made of best quality opal glass. Barrel shape. Stands about 4 inches high. Has good nickeled top with celluloid inlay. A very attractive grape design. Weight, 8 ounces. Price......5C

GOOD QUALITY FISH GLOBES, 2 FOR 5c.

EE144—Fish Globes of clear glass. ½-pint. Heavy flared top. Weight, each, 4 ounces. 2 for......5C

EV145—Capacity, 1 pint. Weight, 8 ounces. Price..5C

EX146—Capacity, 1 quart. Weight 13 ounces. Price 10C

EX147—½ gallon. Weight, 21 ounces. Price...........10C

CEMETERY VASES, 10c.

EX119—10-inch Spike Shape, to hold flowers on graves. Weight, 16 ounces. Each 10C

GLASS VASE 10c.

EX120—Made of good quality glass with neat flared top, scalloped edge. 16 inches tall. Wt., 28 ounces. Price......10C

ATTRACTIVE GLASS CANDLE-STICK, 10c.

EX112—Attractive Glass Candlestick. Made of good quality glass in the popular Chippendale style. Two handles. Square base. Medium heavy bottom to prevent tipping. Height, over all, 7 inches. Weight, 12 ounces. Price...............10C

NEST EGGS, 3 FOR 5c.

EE153—Nest Eggs. Made of opal glass. Size of regular egg. Weight 3, 2 ounces. 3 for 5C

GLASS POULTRY FOUNTAIN, 10c.

EX139—Glass Poultry Fountain. Made of clear glass. Bowl stands 7 inches high. Holds about 3 pints. Automatic water level. Absolutely sanitary. Weight 30 ozs., complete Price......................10C

PLAIN GLASS PITCHER, 10c.

EX143—Plain Glass Pitcher. Plain design with fluted handle. Good quality clear glass. 3 pint capacity. Weight, 2 pounds. Price.....10C

Read our free delivery offer on page 3. All glassware, etc. should be shipped by freight.

Page 111

Serviceable Glassware—Nothing Over 10c

EE100 — Fruit Saucer. 4 inches across top. About 2½ inches deep. Rich cut glass design. Weight for 2, 5 ounces. Price, 2 for.......**5C**

EX106—Celery Tray. 11½ inches long. Artistic buzz-saw design. A very beautiful and highly finished tray. An exceptional value. Weight, 25 ounces. Price, each........**10C**

EX104 — 6½ inch olive dish with handle. Heart shape design. A very useful and attractive dish. Weight, 11 ounces. Price, each....................**10C**

■**EIII** — Individual salts. Round shape. Beautiful buzz-saw pattern. An extra special value. Weight, of three, 6 ounces. Price, 3 for ...**5C**

EX163—Olive or pickle dish. 8 inches long. Rich Nu-cut glass design. An ornament to any dinner table. Looks like fine cut glass. Weight, 14 ounces. Price, each. **10C**

EX166 — Relish or pickle dish. 6½ inches in diameter. Deep oval shape. Rich Nu-cut glass pattern. Weight, 14 ounces. Price, ea.**10C**

EX160 — Beautiful glass dish. 6 inches in diameter. Rich Nu-cut glass pattern. Can be used for many purposes. Wt., 23 ozs. Price,**10C**

EX167 — Round shape olive dish with handle. 5½ inches in diameter. Beautiful Nu-cut glass pattern. A splendid value. Weight, 16 ounces. Price,**10C**

EX161 — Glass plate. 7½ inches in diameter. Nu-cut glass pattern. Buzz-saw design. An excellent value for the price. Weight, 25 ounces. Price, each................**10C**

EX159 — Deep glass bowl. 6½ inches in diameter. Nu-cut glass pattern. Useful for bon bons, etc. Weight, 20 ounces. Price, each........................**10C**

EX164 — Spoon tray. 7½ inches long. Oval shape. Comes in Nu-cut glass design. A very useful tray. Weight, 20 ounces. Price, each.................**10C**

EX162 — Heart-shape bon-bon dish. 6 inches long. Very attractive. Beautiful Nu-cut glass pattern. Weight, 18 ounces. Price, each........................**10C**

CUT GLASS PATTERN MOLASSES CAN, 10c.

EX103—Molasses can with extra quality highly polished metal top. Holds 13 ounces. About 8 inches high. Comes in beautiful buzz-saw design. Looks like cut glass. Weight, 15 ounces. Price, each......**10C**

EX109 — Creamer in buzz-saw design. Matches sugar. EX108. 4⅞ inches high; 3½ inches deep. Special value. Weight, 20 ounces. Price, each.**10C**

EX108 — Sugar with cover. Oval shape buzz saw pattern. Matches creamer EX109. 6 inches deep, 4½ inches across top. Weight 25, ounces..**10C**

EV101—Regular size table tumbler. Rich buzz-saw pattern around center. Flaring shape. An extra special value. Weight, 10 ounces. Price, each..............**5C**

BUZZ SAW PATTERN OIL CRUET.

EX105 — Oil and Stopper in buzz-saw pattern. Very attractive shape. Capacity 8 ounces. A very useful article. Can be used for vinegar or olive oil. Weight, 15 ounces. Price, each..**10C**

EX107 — Butter dish and cover. Buzz-saw pattern. Butter retainer, 7½ inches in diameter. Weight, complete, 2½ pounds. Price, each.................**10C**

EX169 — Creamer. Flaring shape. 3 inches high, 4 inches in diameter. Matches EX168. Weight, 16 ounces. Price, each..................**10C**

EX168—Sugar. Nu-cut glass design. Matches creamer EX169. 3 inches high, 3¾ inches in diameter. Weight 15 ounces. Price, each.......**10C**

EX110 — Salad bowl. Round shape 8½ inches in diameter. Comes in beautiful buzz-saw design. Looks like real cut glass. Special value. Weight, 2 lbs. Price, each....................**10C**

EE141 — Wine glass. Nu-cut glass design, popular size. Weight, for two, 8 ounces. Price, 2 for..**5C**

EX165 — Footed Jelly Glass. Rich Nu-cut glass design. 6 inches high, 4 inches in diameter. Weight, 19 ounces. Price..**10C**

EX1044 — Handled basket. Beautiful buzz-saw design. 6½ inches high, 4 inches in diameter. Oblong shape. Looks like real cut glass. An extra special value. Weight, 20 ounces. Price, each..**10C**

EX102 — Water pitcher. 8 inches high. Capacity, 1 quart. Beautiful buzz-saw design. Weight, 2½ lbs. Price, each. **10C**

EE142 — Wine glass. Nu-cut glass design. This glass is larger than EE141. Wt., for two, 8 ounces. Price, 2 for **5C**

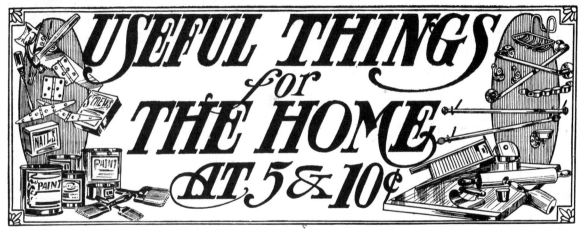

USEFUL THINGS *for* THE HOME AT 5 & 10¢

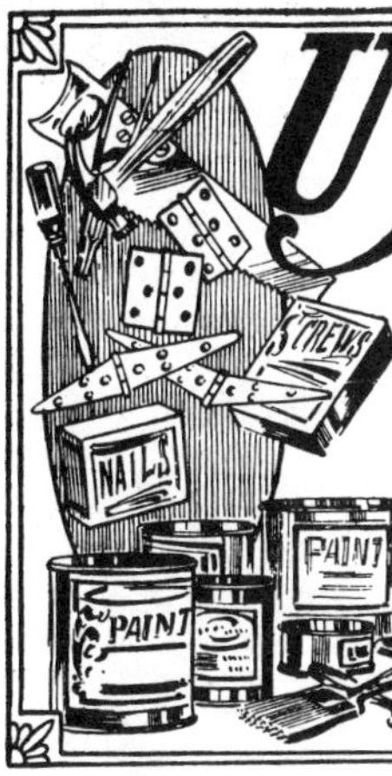

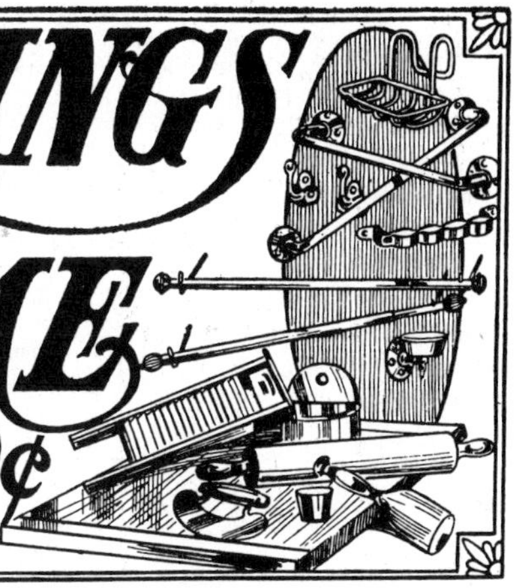

THIS and the following pages are filled with wonderful bargains in curtain rods, garment hangers, bathroom fixtures, gas fixtures and globes, hardware, woodenware, paints, brushes, etc., nothing over 10c

From this Katalog you can order many useful things for the home, at prices that enable you to effect a great saving. Everything that is shown on these pages is guaranteed to be just as represented, and if for any reason you are not perfectly satisfied with your purchase we will gladly exchange the article, or refund your money if you desire.

For years these lines of merchandise have been sold in Kresge's many 5c and 10c Stores throughout the country, and have been bought by millions of customers who appreciate the quality of the merchandise we sell.

As these articles are rather bulky, it will pay you to include enough drygoods, notions, enamelware, etc., to make a freight shipment and save on the cost of transportation charges. Get your friends and neighbors to order with you.

BRASS PLATED SASH RODS, 2 FOR 5c.
HH1075 — Brass Plated Sash Rods. Unpolished, extension sash rods. Has solid rod inside. Extends from 24 to 44 inches. Weight, each, 3 ounces. Price, 2 for **5c**

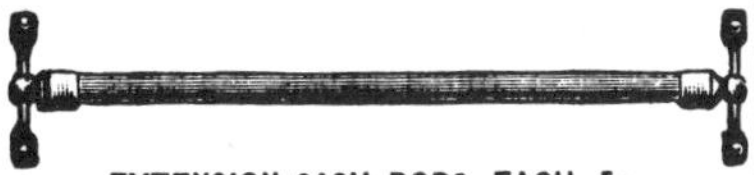

EXTENSION SASH RODS, EACH, 5c.
HV1076—Extension Sash Rods. Has solid rod inside with strong swivel ends. Extends from 24 to 44 inches. Strong and substantially made. Weight, 3 ounces. Price, each. **5c**

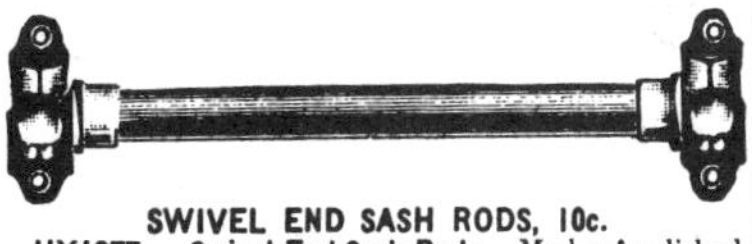

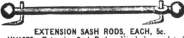

SWIVEL END SASH RODS, 10c.
HX1077 — Swivel End Sash Rods. Made of polished brass plated metal tube 5-16 inch in diameter. Has strong swivel end. Extends from 24 to 44 inches. Weight, 4 ounces. Price, each **10c**

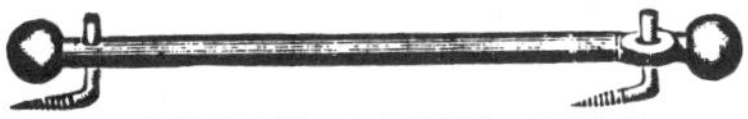

EXTENSION SASH RODS, EACH, 5c.
HV1078—Extension Sash Rods. Nicely brass plated with solid ball ends. Has solid rod inside. Extends from 24 to 44 inches. Very strongly made. Weight, 3 ounces. Price, each **5c**

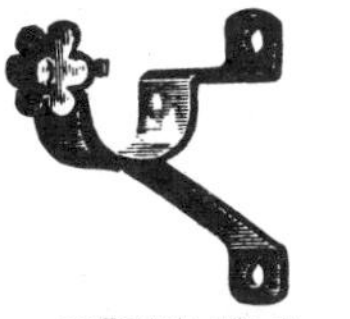

CURTAIN POLE BRACKETS, PAIR, 5c.
HV1087 — Curtain Pole Brackets. Made of extra heavy metal, brass plated. Has thumb set screws to prevent pole from slipping. Fits 1½-inch pole. Weight, pair, 3 ounces. Price, pr. **5c**

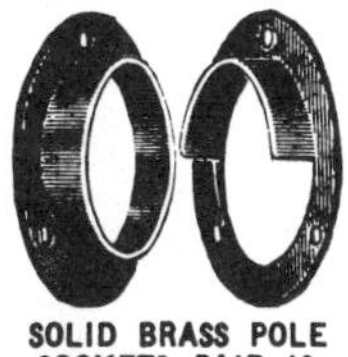

SOLID BRASS POLE SOCKETS, PAIR, 10c.
HX1092 — Solid Brass Pole Sockets. Made of heavy cast solid brass, highly polished and lacquered. Sockets fit 1½-inch pole. Has three holes for screws or nails. Weight, pair, 2 ounces. Price, per pair.. **10c**

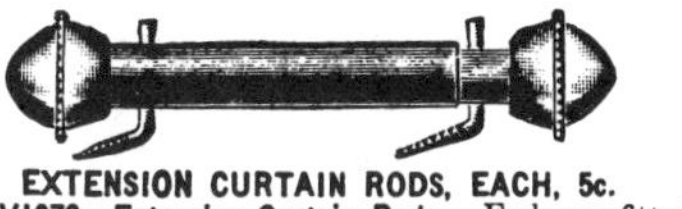

EXTENSION CURTAIN RODS, EACH, 5c.
HV1079—Extension Curtain Rods. Ends are fitted with 1-inch polished knob. Rod is well made and nicely plated. Extends from 30 to 54 inches. Weight, 4 ounces. Price, each **5c**

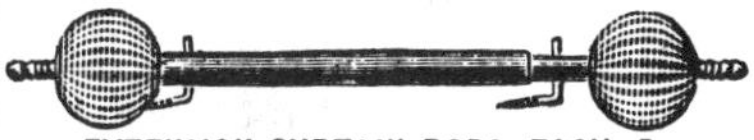

EXTENSION CURTAIN RODS, EACH, 5c.
HV1080—Extension Curtain Rods. Brass plated tube, ⅜-inch diameter. Extends from 30 to 54 inches. Has silver corrugated ball ends. Weight, each 4 ounces. Price. **5c**

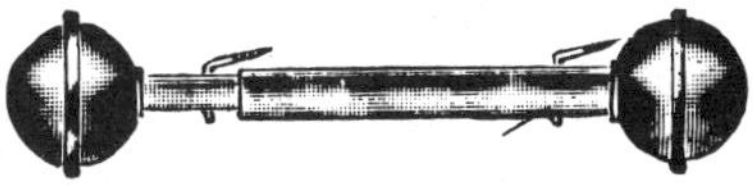

EXTENSION CURTAIN RODS, EACH, 10c.
HX1081—Extension Curtain Rods. 1⅜-inch polished brass ball ends. Made of strong 7-16 inch tube. Extends from 30 to 54 inches. Weight, each, 4 ounces. Price. **10c**

HX1082—Same as above. But finished in oxidized. Weight, each, 4 ounces. Price, each **10c**

GOOSENECK EXTENSION RODS, EACH, 10c.

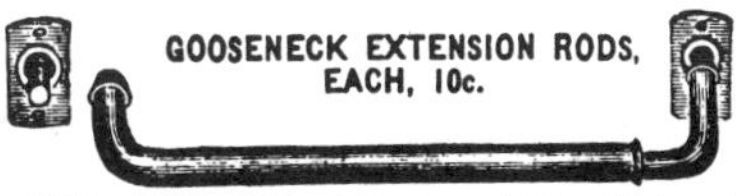

HX1086—Gooseneck Extension Rods. Made of extra heavy metal, brass plated. Fitted with curved gooseneck brackets, plunger ends. Extends 30 to 54 inches. Weight, each, 5 ounces. Price..... **10c**

SOLID BRASS POLE SOCKETS, PAIR, 10c.
HX1094 — Solid Brass Pole Sockets. Stamped from solid brass, nicely polished and lacquered. Cylindrical shape. Fit 1½ inch pole. Perforations are on the inside and either screws or nails can be used for attaching socket. Weight, pair, 1 ounce. Price, per pair **10c**

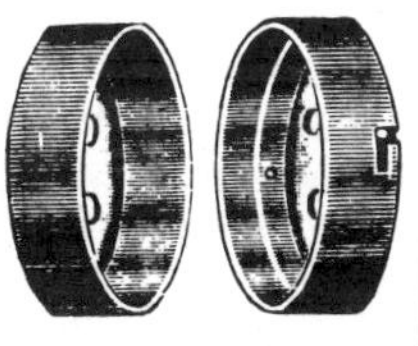

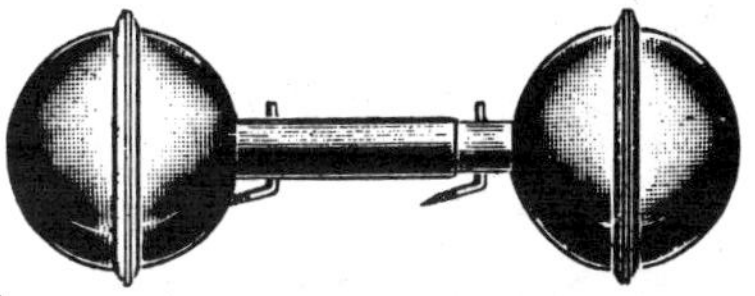

CURTAIN ROD BALL END, EACH, 10c.
HX1083—Curtain Rod Ball End. ½-inch tube, 1¾-inch pure brass ball end, highly polished. Extends 30 to 54 inches. Weight, each, 4 ounces. Price, each **10c**

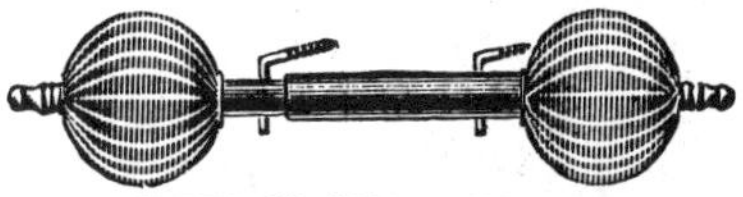

EXTENSION CURTAIN ROD, 10c.
HX1084—Extension Curtain Rod. Has 1⅝-inch silver corrugated ends. 7-16 inch tube. Extends 30 to 54 inches. Very attractive. Weight, each, 5 ounces. Price, each. **10c**

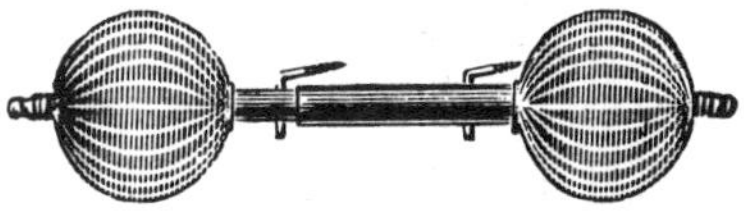

ATTRACTIVE CURTAIN RODS, EACH, 10c.
HX1085—Attractive Curtain Rods. Fitted with 2-inch silver corrugated ends. Will not tarnish. Extends 30 to 54 inches. Weight, each, 4 ounces. Price.. **10c**

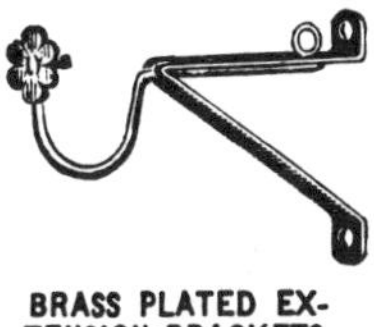

BRASS PLATED EXTENSION BRACKETS, PAIR, 10c.
HX1090 — Brass Plated Extension Brackets. Made of extra heavy metal, brass plated. Fits 1½-inch pole. Bracket can be extended from 4 to 7 inches. Weight, pair, 5 ounces. Price, pair. **10c**

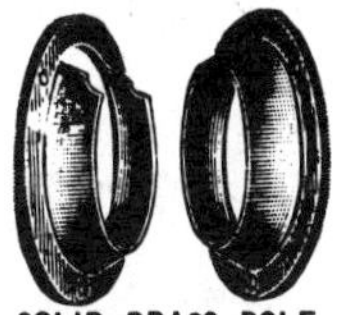

SOLID BRASS POLE SOCKETS, PAIR, 5c.
HV1093 — Solid Brass Pole Sockets. Stamped from good quality metal, highly polished and lacquered. These sockets fit 1½-inch pole. Can be attached in a few moments. Weight, pair, 1 ounce. Price, pair **5c**

Curtain Fixtures, Garment Hangers, 5 & 10c

SOLID BRASS POLE ENDS, PAIR, 10c.

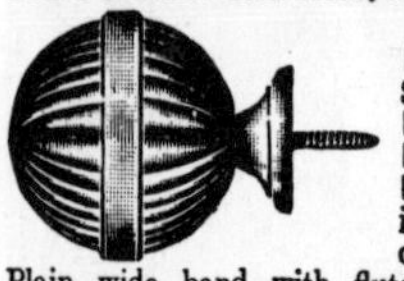

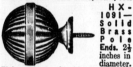

HX-1091—Solid Brass Pole Ends. 2½ inches in diameter. Plain wide band with fluted sides. Fits 1½ inch pole. Weight, pair, 2 ounces. Price pair.......... **10c**

CURTAIN POLE RINGS, 8 FOR 5c.

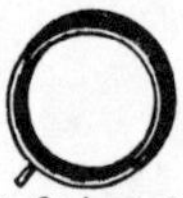

H1095—Curtain Pole Rings. Stamped from solid brass with fine satin finish. Will fit 1½-inch curtain pole. Has loop for attaching drapery hook. Weight, 8 rings, 2 ounces. 8 for................ **5c**

CURTAIN POLE RINGS, 2 FOR 5c.

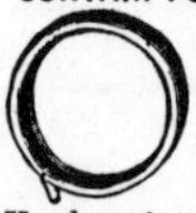

HH1096 — Curtain Pole Rings. Stamped from extra heavy solid brass, highly polished and lacquered. Fits 1½-inch curtain poles. Has loop for attaching drapery hook. Weight two, 1 ounce. 2 for...... **5c**

DRAPERY HOOKS, 36 FOR 5c.

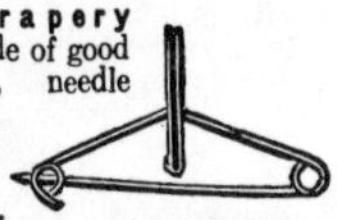

H1097—Drapery Hooks. Made of good spring steel, needle point, brass plated. A very good quality pin. Weight, 36, two ozs. 36 for.. **5c**

BRASS CURTAIN RINGS, 36 FOR 5c.

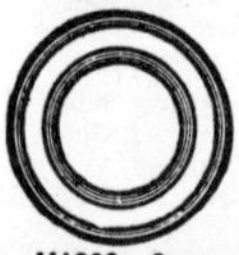

H1098—Brass Curtain Rings. Solid brass. ½-inch diameter. Curtain or fancy work ring. Wt., 36, one ounce. 36 for.......... **5c**

H1099—Same as above, but 1-inch diameter. Weight, 12, one ounce. 12 for.............................. **5c**

CLOSED BRASS BELLS, 12 FOR 5c.

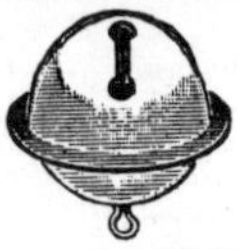

H1100— Closed Brass Bells. Made of solid brass ½-inch in diameter. Used for fancy work or masquerade suits. Weight 12, one ounce. 12 for.................. **5c**

OPEN BRASS BELLS, 6 FOR 5c.

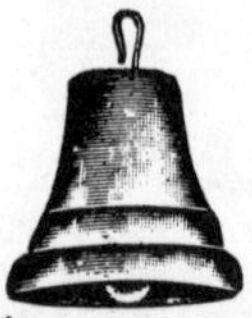

H11011—Open Brass Bells. Made of solid brass, ½-inch open bell. Used for fancy work or masquerade suits. Clear, pleasant ring. Weight 6, one ounce. 6 for.......................... **5c**

CURTAIN BRACKETS, 12 FOR 5c.

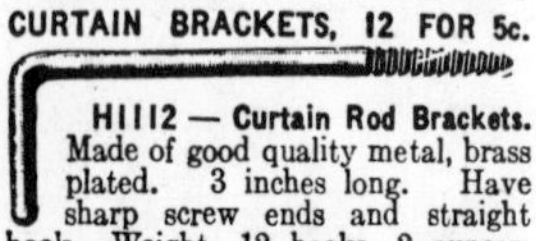

H1112 — Curtain Rod Brackets. Made of good quality metal, brass plated. 3 inches long. Have sharp screw ends and straight hook. Weight, 12 hooks, 2 ounces. 12 for........................ **5c**

PLAIN MOULDING HOOKS, 24 FOR 5c.

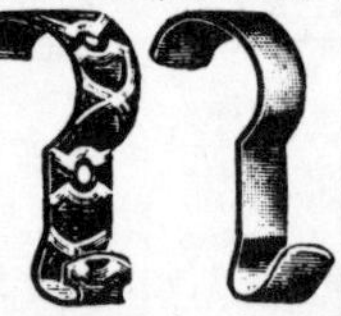

H1103 — Plain Moulding Hooks. Brass plated ½-inch. Wt., 24, four ozs. 24 for. **5c**

H1104—Same as above, except ¾-inch and embossed. Weight, 12, two ounces. 12 for.............................. **5c**

EMBOSSED MOULDING HOOKS, 6 FOR 5c.

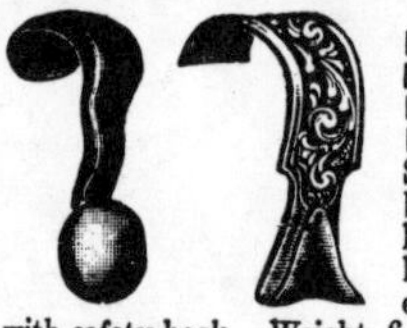

H1105—Embossed Moulding Hooks. Solid brass, heavily lacquered. Made with safety hook. Weight, 6 hooks, 2 ounces. 6 for................ **5c**

H1106 — Same as above, except extra heavy cast. Ball knob end. Weight, each, 1 ounce. 3 for.... **5c**

PORCELAIN HEAD PICTURE NAILS, 6 FOR 5c.

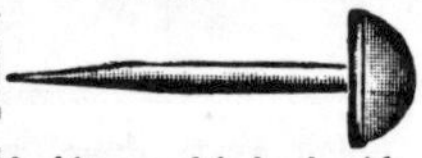

H1107—Porcelain Head Picture Nails. Have solid white porcelain heads with brass screw cap. Nail can be driven into wall and head fitted on after. Weight, six, 3 ounces. 6 for.... **5c**

SOLID BRASS CUP HOOKS, 12 FOR 5c.

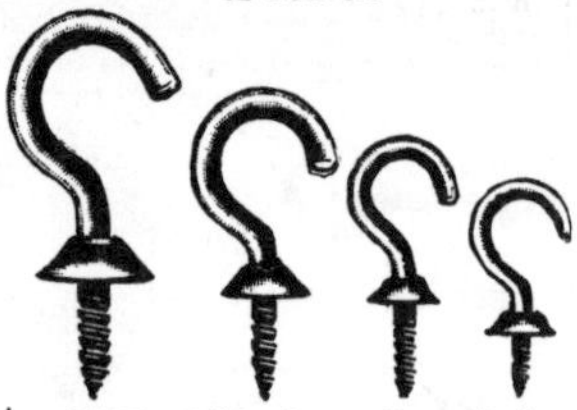

H1108—Solid Brass Cup Hooks. Made of solid brass with sharp screw ends. Fitted with ornamental brass guards. Weight, 12 one ounce. ¾-inch long. 12 for.............. **5c**

H1109—Same as above except ⅞-inch long. Weight 12, one ounce. 12 for.............................. **5c**

H1110 — Solid Brass Cup Hooks. 1⅛ inches long. Made of solid brass with sharp screw ends. Used in china closets and the like. Weight six, 1 ounce. 6 for.............. **5c**

H1111 — Same as above, but 1¼ in. long. Weight six, 1 ounce. 6 for.. **5c**

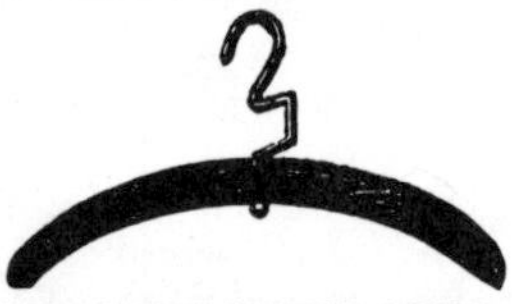

WOODEN COAT HANGERS, 2 FOR 5c.

HH1000 — Wooden Coat Hangers. Stained wood, wax finish. Has off-set coppered wire hook to prevent clothes from touching the wall. Weight, each, 5 ounces. 2 for................ **5c**

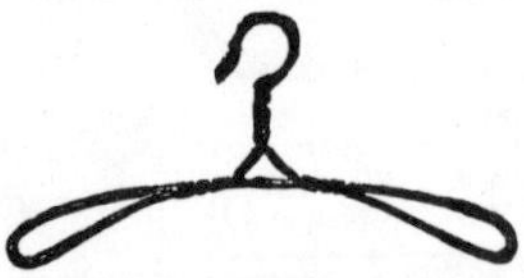

WIRE COAT HANGERS, 2 FOR 5c.

HH1101 — Wire Coat Hangers. Made of good heavy tinned wire with off-set hook. Broad at ends to keep shoulders in shape. Weight, each, 3 ounces. 2 for................ **5c**

Additional bargains in bathroom fixtures will be found on page 115. **If possible always order enough hardware, etc., to make a freight shipment.**

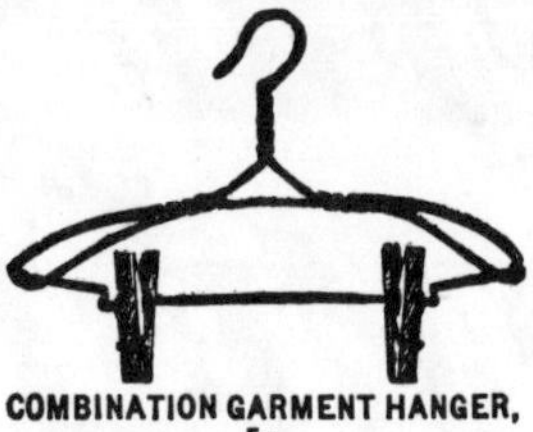

COMBINATION GARMENT HANGER, 5c.

HV1002 — Combination Garment Hanger. Made of heavy tinned wire, off-set hook. Has two spring wire clothes pins to hold trousers. Weight, each, 6 ounces. Price.......... **5c**

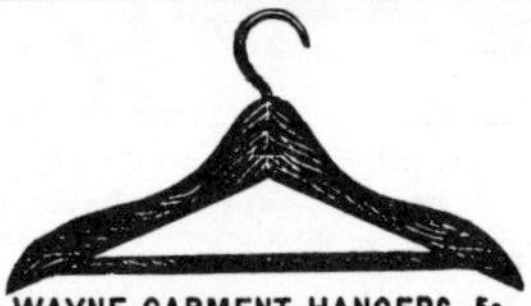

WAYNE GARMENT HANGERS, 5c.

HV1003—Wayne Garment Hanger. Combination coat and trouser hanger. Well shaped shoulders. Edges nicely smoothed. Wire hook. Weight, each, 8 ounces. Price.............. **5c**

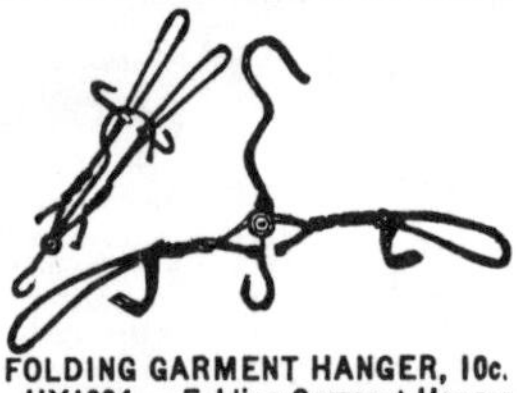

FOLDING GARMENT HANGER, 10c.

HX1004 — Folding Garment Hanger. Made of heavy wire, nickel plated and polished. For coat and trousers. Can be folded and placed in suitcase when traveling. Weight, each, 6 ounces. Price........................ **10c**

ACME TROUSER HANGER, 10c.

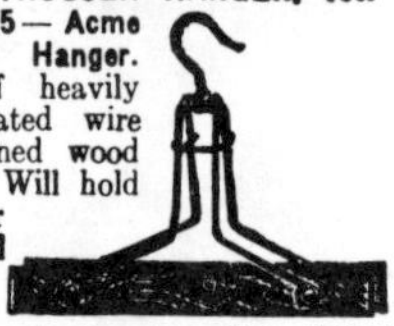

HX1005 — Acme Trouser Hanger. Made of heavily nickel plated wire with stained wood clamps. Will hold one or several pairs of trousers. Weight, each, 3 ounces. Price **10c**

SPRING STEEL TROUSER HANGER, 5c.

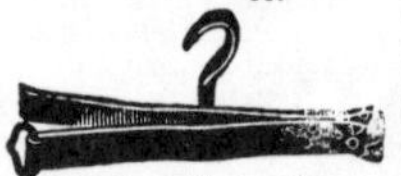

HV-1006—Spring Steel Trouser Hanger made of good quality spring steel, nicely japanned. Has flat hook which can be folded down. Weight, each, 5 ounces. Price.............. **5c**

WIRE TROUSER HANGERS, 2 FOR 5c.

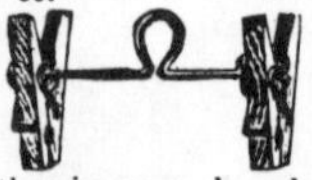

HH1007—Wire Trouser Hangers. Made of strong coppered wire with spring clothespin on each end. Has convenient loop for hanging up. Weight, each, 1½ ounces. 2 for.. **5c**

WIRE CEILING HOOKS, 3 FOR 5c.

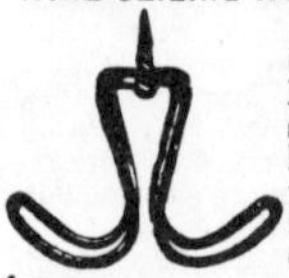

H1008—Wire Ceiling Hooks. Made of good strong wire, heavily nickel plated. See illustration. Wt., each, 1 ounce. 3 for.............................. **5c**

H1009 — Same as above, but heavy coppered wire. Weight, each, 1 ounce. 6 for.............................. **5c**

COAT AND HAT HOOKS, 6 FOR 5c.

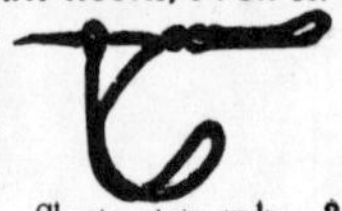

H1010—Coat and Hat Hooks. Made from good strong wire, heavily nickel plated. Sharp screw ends. 3 inches long. Weight, each, 1 ounce. 6 for.............................. **5c**

COAT AND HAT HOOKS, 8 FOR 5c.

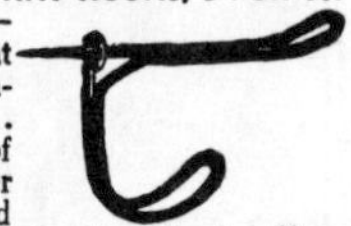

H1011—Coat and Hat Hooks. 3 inches long. Made of heavy copper wire, twisted top. Double wire, lower hook. Sharp screw point. Weight, each, 1 ounce. 8 for.............................. **5c**

COAT AND HAT HOOKS, 12 FOR 5c.

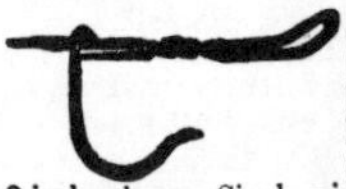

H1012—Coat and Hat Hooks. Made of heavy coppered wire. 3 inches long. Single wire lower hook. Sharp screw point. Weight, each, 1 ounce. 12 for................ **5c**

COAT AND HAT HOOKS, 10c.

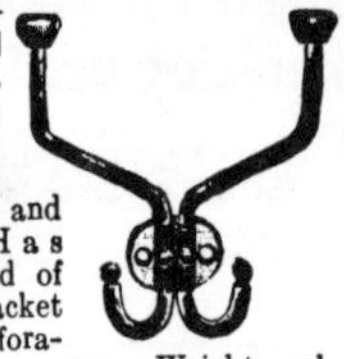

HX1013—Coat and Hat Hooks. Double bracket pattern. Heavily brass plated and lacquered. Has knobs on end of hooks. Bracket has two perforations for nails or screws. Weight, each, 6 ounces. Price.............. **10c**

TOOTH BRUSH HOLDERS, EACH, 10c.

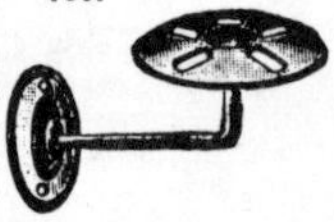

HX1025—Tooth Brush Holders. Strong metal, heavily nickel plated with stamped wall plate. Holds five brushes. Can be attached instantly with screws or nails. Weight, each, 2 ounces. Price........................ **10c**

NICKEL PLATED TUMBLER HOLDER, 10c.

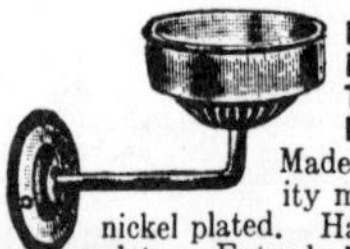

HX1026—Nickel Plated Tumbler Holder. Made of good quality metal, heavily nickel plated. Has round wall plate. Extends 5 inches from wall. Weight, each, 3 ounces. Price........................ **10c**

WALL SOAP DISH, 10c.

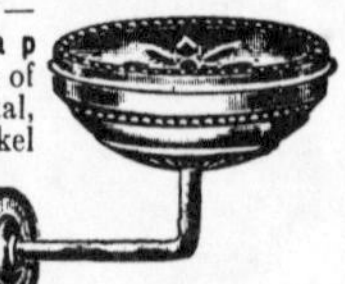

HX1027—Wall Soap Dish. Made of strong metal, heavily nickel plated. Has removable top. 4¾ inches in diameter. Round wall plate. Can be cleaned by removing top. Weight, each, 5 ounces. Price...... **10c**

WIRE TUMBLER HOLDER, 5c.

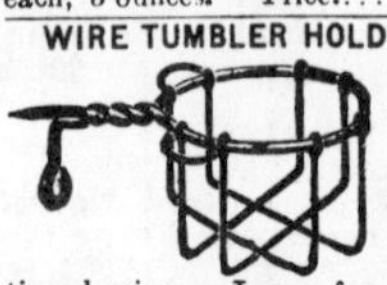

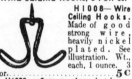

HV-1028—Wire Tumbler Holder. Made of heavy tinned wire. Loops for two tooth brushes in addition. Sharp screw point for attaching to wall. Weight, 2 ounces. Each.................. **5c**

Bathroom Fixtures, Gas Globes, Etc., 5 and 10c

WIRE SOAP DISHES, 2 FOR 5c.

HH1030— Wire Soap Dishes. Made of light retinned wire with strong wire frame. Has loop for hanging on wall. Weight, each, 2 ounces. 2 for...................**5 C**

WIRE WALL SOAP DISH, 5c.

HV-1031— Wire Wall Soap Dish. Made of heavy retinned wire with strong wire frame. Can be used for hanging on wall or standing up. Weight, each, 3 ounces. Price....**5 C**

HEAVY WALL SOAP DISH, 10c.

HX-1032— Heavy Wall Soap Dish. Made of extra heavy retinned wire, finely finished. All joints electro-welded. Two loops for hanging on wall. Weight, each, 5 ounces. Price........................**10 C**

STANDING SOAP DISH, 10c.

HX-1033— Standing Soap Dish. Made of extra heavy retinned wire, finely finished. Four strong wire feet. All joints electro-welded. Weight, 4 ounces. Price.................**10 C**

WALL SOAP BRACKET, 5c.

HV1034— Wall Soap Bracket. Made of light retinned wire with high back and loop for hanging on wall. Convenient for the kitchen. Weight, each, 10 ounces. Price.........**5 C**

WIRE SOAP BRACKET, 10c.

HX-1035— Wire Soap Bracket. Made of heavy retinned wire with strong wire frame. For bath tub use. Has curved wire loops to fit tub. Weight, each, 4 ounces. Price........................**10 C**

HEAVY WIRE SPONGE BASKET, 10c.

HX1036—Heavy Wire Sponge Basket. Made of extra heavy retinned wire with curved brackets to fit tub. All joints strongly electro-welded. Weight, each, 7 ozs. Price.......**10 C**

HEAVY WIRE TOWEL RING, 10c.

HX-1029— Heavy Wire Towel Ring. Made of extra heavy wire, nicely nickel plated. Two movable rings. Wire loops for attaching to wall. Weight, 7 ounces. Price......**10 C**

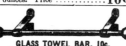

WALL TOWEL RACK, 10c.

HX1037 — Wall Towel Rack. Three arms 12 inches long, with oblong wall plate, all heavily nickel plated. Arms can be swung in any position. Weight, 7 ounces. Price.............**10 C**

GLASS TOWEL BAR, 10c.

HX1038 — Glass Towel Bar. Made of fine opal glass. ½-inch in diameter. with heavy nickel plated brass ends, and brackets. 15 inches long. Splendid value. Weight, 5 ounces. Price........................**10 C**

NICKEL PLATED TOWEL BAR, 10c.

HX1039 — Nickel Plated Towel Bar. Made of good strong metal, heavily nickel plated. Bar is 5-16-inch in diameter. 18 inches long. Round wall supports. Weight, 11 ounces. Price........................**10 C**

NICKEL PLATED TOWEL BAR, 10c.

HX1040 — Nickel Plated Towel Bar. 24 inches long. Solid metal bar and brackets, heavily nickel plated. Bar is 5-16-inch in diameter. Weight, 12 ounces. Price..............**10 C**

SAFETY MATCH HOLDER, 10c.

HX1041 — Safety Match Holder. Made of good quality metal with wide weighted bottom, all heavily nickel plated. Bottom used for ash tray and has wide flare. Weight 6 ounces. Price ....**10 C**

FANCY EMBOSSED COMB CASE, 10c

HX-1042— Fancy Embossed Comb Case. Made of good retinned metal. Has match holder on each side, and mirror in center. Weight, 8 ounces. Price..........................**10 C**

TOILET PAPER HOLDER, 5c.

HV1045— Toilet Paper Holder. Solid cast back, nicely nickel plated. Fitted with oak roller. Strong wire flange. Holes for nails or screws. Weight, 4 ounces. Price........................**5 C**

GEM TOILET PAPER HOLDER, 10c.

HX1046—Gem Toilet Paper Holder. Back is made of good quality bent steel, heavily nickel plated. Flange is of strong heavy wire. Has black wood roller. Weight, 5 ounces. Price..........................**10 C**

EXTRA HEAVY TOILET PAPER HOLDER, 10c.

HX1047— Extra Heavy Toilet Paper Holder. Heavy steel back and cast arms, all heavily nickel plated. Back has fashioned cigar rest. Black enameled wood roller. Weight, 6 ounces. Price........................**10 C**

JAPANESE CREPE TOILET PAPER. 2 ROLLS, 5c.

HH1048— Japanese Crepe Toilet Paper. Made of good quality Japanese crepe paper. Each roll weighs 3½ ozs. Special value.
2 rolls for.................**5 C**

WALDORF TOILET PAPER, ROLL, 5c.

HV1049— Waldorf Toilet Paper. A very soft and thoroughly antiseptic paper. 9 oz. roll. Per roll....**5 C**
HX1050— Same as above, but 17 ounce roll. Price per roll ....**10 C**

DAISY BATH STOPPERS, 5c.

HV1051 — Daisy Bath Stoppers. Made of good quality white rubber, nickel plated ring. 2¾ inches in diameter. Weight, 2 ounces. Price........................**5 C**

DAISY SINK STOPPER, 10c.

HX1052 — Daisy Sink Stopper. Made of best quality gray rubber, with nickel plated ring. 4¾ inches in diameter. A very convenient article for kitchen use. Weight, 3 ounces. Price.....**10 C**

COMPOSITION RUBBER BATH STOPPERS, 2 FOR 5c.

HH1053 — Composition Rubber Bath Stoppers. Nickel plated ring. Come in the following sizes: 1, 1⅛, 1½ and 1¾ inches in diameter. State size wanted when ordering. Weight, each, 1 ounce. 2 for.............**5 C**

NICKEL PLATED BATH SPRAY, 10c

HX1043 — Nickel Plated Bath Spray. 2½ inches in diameter. Has small perforations for fine spray. Weight, 2 ounces. Price.............**10 C**
HV1044 — White Rubber Hose for the above. Weight, per foot, 1 ounce. Price, per foot.................**5 C**

RUBBER FORCE CUP, 10c.

HX1056 — Rubber Force Cup. These cups are intended to clean the waste pipes of washstands, bath tubs, wash tubs, etc. Very efficient. Weight, each, 5 ounces. Price.......**10 C**

INVERTED GAS GLOBE, 10c.

HX100— Inverted Gas Globe. Round shape, open bottom half frosted, half clear. Made of good quality glass. These globes are exceptional values for the price. Weight, each, 6 ounces. Price.........................**10 C**

INVERTED GAS GLOBE, 10c.

HX101 — Inverted Gas Globe. Round shape, half frosted, open bottom. This globe has a fancy border where the clear glass joins the frosted. These globes reflect an excellent light. Wt., each, 6 ounces. Price....**10 C**

MISSION PATTERN INVERTED GAS GLOBE, 10c.

HX102 — Mission Pattern Inverted Gas Globe. The entire globe is frosted with the exception of the lines which divide the panel. Globes have air holes. Weight, each, 10 ounces. Price.............**10 C**

INVERTED GAS GLOBES, 10c.

HX103 — Balloon Shape Inverted Gas Globes. The entire globe is frosted with the exception of the fancy lines shown in illustration which are clear. Globes have air holes. Weight, each, 10 ounces. Price.**10 C**

PEAR SHAPED INVERTED GAS GLOBES, 10c.

HX104— Pear Shaped Inverted Gas Globes. Upper half frosted, lower half clear glass with air holes. This is a popular shape globe. Weight, each, 9 ounces. Price. each...................**10 C**

GRAPE CLUSTER INVERTED GAS GLOBES, 10c.

HX105—Grape Cluster Inverted Glass Globe. This globe is made in a very attractive grape cluster pattern, entirely frosted. Has air holes in bottom. A very pretty style. Weight, each, 10 ounces. Price......**10 C**

UPRIGHT GAS GLOBE, 10c.

HX107— Upright Gas Globe. Round pattern with frosted top. Reflects a soft clear light. Has small flaring top and extended bottom which sets in support. Weight, each, 7 ounces. Price.**10 C**

Gas Globes, Mantles and Fixtures, 5c and 10c

UPRIGHT GAS GLOBE, 10c.

HX108—Upright Gas Globe. Made of good quality opal glass. Has air holes in bottom. Helps the mantle to give a strong, steady light. Has small flaring top and extended bottom. Weight, 8 ounces.
Price.....................**10¢**

MISSION PATTERN UPRIGHT GAS GLOBE, 10c.
HX109—Mission Pattern Upright Gas Globe. Has all frosted panels with clear lines where panels join, as illustrated. A very attractive pattern. Weight, each, 8 ounces. Price..............**10¢**

BELL SHAPE GAS SHADE, 10c.

HX110 — Bell Shape Gas Shade. Made of good quality glass in a prismatic pattern. Has flaring bottom to fit 4½-inch ring. Weight, 16 ounces.
Price.....................**10¢**

PRISM PATTERN GAS SHADE, 10c.

HX111 — Prism Pattern Gas Shade. Bell shape. Made of good quality glass with flaring bottom to fit 4½-inch ring. Pattern as illustrated. Weight, 16 ounces. Price..............**10¢**

STAR PATTERN GAS SHADE, 10c.

HX112 — Star Pattern Gas Shade. Made of good quality glass, bell shape, with beautiful star pattern as illustrated. Weight, each, 16 ounces. Price..............**10¢**

PRISMATIC GAS SHADE, 10c.

HX106 — Prismatic Gas Shade. Made of good quality clear glass, prismatic pattern. Has flaring bottom to fit 4½-inch ring. Weight, each, 17 ounces. Price..............**10¢**

PRISMATIC PATTERN ELECTRIC SHADE, 10c.

HX113 — Prismatic Pattern Electric Shade. Made of good quality glass and fits 2½ inch ring. Matches No. HX110. Can be used on combination fixtures. Weight, each, 9 ounces.................**10¢**

PRISM PATTERN ELECTRIC SHADE, 10c.

HX114 — Prism Pattern Electric Shade. Made of good quality glass, pattern as illustrated. Fits 2½-inch ring Matches No. HX111. Can be used on combination fixtures. Weight, 9 ounces.
Price, each...............**10¢**

STAR PATTERN ELECTRIC SHADE, 10c.

HX115 — Star Pattern Electric Shade. Fits 2½-inch ring. Good quality glass. Matches No. HX-112 and can be used on combination fixtures. Wt., 9 ounces. Price, each.......**10¢**

MICA GAS CHIMNEY, 10c.

HX157 — Mica Gas Chimney. Made of good quality clear mica, reinforced top and bottom. 7 inches high. Weight, ½ oz. Price.....**10¢**

UPRIGHT GAS CHIMNEY, 10c.

HX119 — Upright Gas Chimney. Good clear glass. Air holes in bottom. 7 inches high. Withstands the heat. Weight, 3 ounces. Price.....**10¢**

JUNIOR MANTLE AND CHIMNEY, 10c.

HX133 — Junior Mantle and Chimney. Gives a very powerful light. to be used in connection with HX134. Weight, ½ ounce. Price, complete.......**10¢**

JUNIOR GAS BURNER, 10c.

HX134 — Junior Gas Burner. A very economical gas user. To be used in connection with HX133. Weight, 1 ounce. Price..............**10¢**

GAS TUBING, PER FOOT, 5c.

HV166—Gas Tubing. Cotton lined. single dipped gas tubing. Can be ordered only in 4, 6, 8 or 10 foot lengths. State length wanted Weight, per foot, 2 ounces. Price, per foot....................**5¢**

INVERTED GAS MANTLES, 10c.

HX129 — Inverted Gas Mantles. Made for either natural or artificial gas. Single weave. A good quality mantle. Weight, each, 1 ounce. Price......**10¢**

TRIPLE WEAVE INVERTED MANTLES, 10c.

HX132 — Triple Weave Inverted Mantles. Made for natural or artificial gas. Gives a clear, bright and steady light. Weight, 1 ounce. Price.......**10**

UPRIGHT GAS MANTLES, 10c.

HX131 — Upright Gas Mantles. Triple weave. For natural or artificial gas. Gives a clear, bright light. Weight, 1 ounce. Price.....**10¢**

UPRIGHT GAS MANTLES, 10c.

HX130 — Upright Gas Mantles. Single weave. State whether for natural or artificial gas. Weight, 1 ounce. Price.....**10¢**

GAS BURNER, 5c.
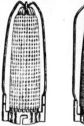
HV150 — Gas Burner. Double Jumbo burner with fine lava tip. Gives a clear bright flame. Weight, ½ ounce. Price.........**5¢**

BRASS PILLARS, 6 FOR 5c.
H151 — Brass Pillars. Made of good quality brass. Can be attached to any bracket. Weight, six, 2 ounces. 6 for..............**5¢**

GAS TIPS, 6 FOR 5c.

H152—Gas Tips. Best grade lava tips. Gives a clear, broad flame. Weight, six, 1 ounce. 6 for.........**5¢**

ALUMINUM TIPS, 3 FOR 5c.
H153 — Aluminum Tips. Made of good quality aluminum. Give a soft, steady light. Wt., 3, 1 oz., 3 for.**5¢**

INNER CUP FOR INVERTED BURNER, 5c.

HV121 — Inner Cup for Inverted Burner. Made of thin glass. Can be used on any inverted burner and doubles the life of the mantle. Weight, 3 ozs. Price.........**5¢**

BRASS BY PASS, 10c.

HX180 — Brass By Pass. Made of good quality brass with lever and chain. Can be regulated for high or low flame. Weight, each, 2 ounces. Price.......**10¢**

UPRIGHT GAS BURNER, 10c.
HX136 — Upright Gas Burner. Needle point. Made of good quality brass. Cuts down the gas bill. Mantle support is made in open design. Weight, 2 ounces..............**10¢**

BRASS PLATED BRACKET, 10c.

HX145 — Brass Plated Bracket. 6 inches long. Straight, stiff arm. Equipped with easy turning lever. Can be attached to pipe by anyone. Weight, 4 ounces. Price.........**10¢**

FEMALE HOSE COCK, 10c.

HX146 — Female Hose Cock. Brass plated. Convenient for attaching hose of gas iron or reading lamps. Easily attached. Holds the hose firmly without stretching. Weight, 3 ounces. Price...........**10¢**

L BURNER COCK, 10c.

HX147—L Burner Cock. ¾-inch brass plated. Can be attached in a few moments. Wt., 3 ounces. Price **10¢**
HX148 — Same as above, but ½-inch brass plated. Weight, 3 ounces. Price.10¢**

GAS SHADE RING, 5c.
HV143 — Gas Shade Ring. Made of good, heavy metal, brass plated. 4 inches in diameter. Has three set screws for holding shade in ring. Wt., each, 1 ounce. Price..........**5¢**

INVERTED GAS BURNER, 10c.

HX135 — Inverted Gas Burner. Has lava tip for holding mantle in place. Equipped with regulator to mix air with gas. Very economical. Weight, 3 ounces. Price...........**10¢**

GAS TUBING, 2 FEET, 5c.
HH170 — Gas Tubing. Cotton lined, single dipped gas tubing. Can be ordered only in 4, 6, 8 or 10 foot lengths. State length wanted. Weight, per foot, 2 ounces.
Price, 2 feet....................**5¢**

Gas Cord, Lamp Chimneys, Etc., 5c and 10c

FLEXIBLE METALLIC TUBING, FOOT, 5c.

HX174 — Flexible Metallic Tubing. "Can't wear Out" kind. Can be ordered only in 4, 6, 8 or 10 foot lengths. State length wanted. Weight, per foot, 6 ounces. Price, per foot........**10c**

JUNIOR PORTABLE TUBING, PER FOOT, 5c.

HV181 — Junior Portable Tubing. Cotton lined, green silkaline covered, 6 foot length. Weight, 9 ounces. Per piece, 30c.; per foot............**5c**
HV182 — Same as above, but 8 foot length. Weight, 12 ounces. Per piece, 40c.; per foot............**5c**

GOOSE NECK COMBINATION, 10c.

HX149 — Goose Neck Combination. Brass plated stork or goose neck combination, fits inside of pillar. Weight, 1 ounce. Price **10c**

ONE BURNER GAS STOVE, 10c.

HX160 — One Burner Gas Stove. Made of best quality white metal in two pieces. Plenty of heat and uses little gas. Weight, 20 ounces. Price........................**10c**

SAFETY GAS LIGHTER, 10c.

HX154 — Safety Gas Lighter. Always ready. A metal lighter which does away with flying match heads and fire risk. Weight, 1 ounce. Price......**10c**

ELECTRIC SHADE HOLDER, 5c.

HV144— Electric Shade Holder. Good quality, heavily brass plated. 2½ inches in diameter. Has thumb screw for holding shade tight, with clamp for attaching to socket. Weight, 1 ounce. Price...........................**5c**

REFILLED ELECTRIC BULB, 10c.

HX183 — Refilled Electric Bulb. 8 candle power. Gives a good steady light. Fits any screw socket. Weight, 1 ounce. Price **10c**
HX184 — Same as above, but 16 candle power. Weight, 2 ounces. Price.......**10c**

MICA CANOPY, 10c.

HX155— Mica Canopy. Made of best quality pure mica with three brass supports. 5 inches in diameter. Prevents scorched ceilings. Weight, 1 ounce. Price...........................**10c**

WAX TAPERS, PER PACKAGE, 5c.

HV179 — Wax Tapers. 30 full length wax tapers in a package. Well pressed to prevent wax from dropping while taper is lighted. Weight, 3 ounces. Per package...........**5c**

WAX TAPER HOLDER, 10c.

HX178 — Wax Taper Holder. Made of good quality metal, highly polished, with stained wood handle. Has catch on end for turning on gas. Weight, 7 ounces. Price. **10c**

BRACKET FOUNT WITH HANDLE, 10c.

HX124 — Bracket Lamp Fount with Handle. No. 2 bracket lamp fount of good quality heavy glass. Has convenient handle for carrying, if desired. Weight, 20 ounces. Price....**10c**

PLAIN FOOTED LAMP FOUNT, 10c.

HX125—Plain Footed Lamp Fount. Heavy pattern. Made of good quality glass. Stands 7½ inches high. Fits No. 1 burner. A good, strong lamp fount. Weight, 23 ounces. Price **10c**

It is advisable to have all glassware shipped by freight.

PLAIN FOOTED LAMP FOUNT, 10c.

HX126— Plain Footed Lamp Fount. Made of good quality heavy glass and stands 9 inches high. Fits No. 00 burner. Has large broad foot. Extra size and will light a large room. Weight, 3¼ pounds. Price, **10c**

NUTMEG LAMP CHIMNEYS, 3 FOR 5c.

H120—Nutmeg Lamp Chimneys. Fits nutmeg burner. Height, 3½ inches, bottom diameter 1¼ inches. Weight, for 3, 3 ounces. 3 for....**5c**

FANCY NIGHT LAMP, 10c.

HX122 — Fancy Night Lamp. Stands 9½ inches over all. Made of good quality crystal glass. Complete with nutmeg burner and chimney. Weight, 12 ounces. Price...........................**10c**
HX123 — Same as above but 9½ in. over all. Green glass. Weight, 12 ounces. Price...........**10c**

FANCY LAMP CHIMNEY, 10c.

HX116— Fancy Lamp Chimney. Good quality glass with fancy etched designs. Crimped top. Fits No. 2 burner. Chimney has extra wide spreading center. Wt., 7 ounces. Price..**10c**

SUN PLAIN LAMP CHIMNEY, 5c.

HV117 — Sun Plain Lamp Chimney. Made of good quality clear glass, crimped top. Fits No. 2 burner. Wt., 5 ozs. Price **5c**

PLAIN LAMP CHIMNEY, 5c.

HV118 — Plain Lamp Chimney. Made of good quality clear glass, crimped top. Fits No. 1 burner. Wt., 4 ounces. Price........**5c**

BRASS PLATED LAMP BURNER, 10c.

HX139 — Brass Plated Lamp Burner. Eagle lamp burner. Strong and well made. Fits No. 3 lamp wick and No. 2 lamp. Weight, each, 3 ounces. Price. **10c**

STRONG LAMP BURNER, 10c.

HX140 — Strong Lamp Burner. Brass plated. Gives a clear, steady light. Fits No. 3 wick and No. 2 lamp. Weight, 3 ozs. Price...........................**10c**

EAGLE LAMP BURNER, 5c.

HV138 — Eagle Lamp Burner. Made of good quality metal, heavily brass plated. Fits No. 2 lamp. Has four plated wire flanges. Weight, 2 ounces. Price.......**5c**

BANNER LAMP BURNER, 5c.

HV137 — Banner Lamp Burner. Made of good heavy metal, brass plated. Four wire flanges for holding chimney. Fits No. 1 lamp. Weight, 1 ounce. Price...........................**5c**

NUTMEG LAMP BURNER, 5c.

HV141—Nutmeg Lamp Burner. Made of good quality metal, heavily brass plated. Fits nutmeg lamp. Wt., 1 ounce. Price.............**5c**

HORNET LAMP BURNER, 5c.

HV142—Hornet Lamp Burner. Made of good quality metal, brass plated. Fits the Gem lamp chimney. Weight, 1 ounce. Price.............**5c**

LAMP WICKS, 12 FOR 5c.

H164 — Lamp Wicks. Good quality lamp wicks. Nos. 1 and 2. State size wanted when ordering. Weight of 12, 2 ounces. 12 for............**5c**
H1655 — Same as above, but for nutmeg lamps. Weight, 12, 2 ounces. 12 for **5c**

LAMP WICKS, 6 FOR 5c.

H163 — Lamp Wicks. Best quality No. 3 wick. Clear and steady burning. No unnecessary waste. Easy to trim. Will fit burner without crowding. Weight, 6, 1 ounce. 6 for **5c**

ROCHESTER LAMP WICKS, 2 FOR 5c.

HH162 — Rochester Lamp Wicks. For No. 2 Rochester lamps. Good quality woven wick. Insures a clear and steady light. Weight, two, 2 ounces. 2 for **5c**

OIL STOVE WICKS, 2 FOR 5c.

HH161 — Oil Stove Wicks. Size of wick, 4x8 inches. Gives clear, steady flame and is very economical in the use of oil. Weight, two, 2 ounces. 2 for **5c**

Birthday Candles, Drawer Pulls, Etc., 5 and 10c

CANDLE HOLDER, 10c.

HX159— Candle Holder. Low style, brass plated. Has convenient handle for carrying and flaring bottom to catch drippings. Weight, 2 ozs. Price.............**10¢**

CANDLE SHADE HOLDERS, 5c.

HV156—Candle Shade Holders. Good quality metal, brass plated. Length, 4½ inches and can be extended to 7 inches. Weight, 1 ounce. Price.......**5¢**

PLATED CANDLE STICK, 10c.

HX158 — Plated Candlestick. 5½ inches high. Made of good quality metal, heavily brass plated. Broad base to prevent tipping over. Weight, 7 ounces. Price.....**10¢**

PAPER LAMP SHADE, 5c.

HV207 — Paper Lamp Shade. 10 inches in diameter. Come in assorted colors. Edges nicely bound. Wt. 2 ounces. Price .... **5¢**

ROSE ENGRAVED CUIRASS, 10c.

HX208 — Rose Engraved Cuirass. Silver plated, plain top and bottom edge. Weight, 1 ounce. Price...............**10¢**

BRASS PUNCTURED CUIRASS, 10c.

HX209— Brass Punctured Cuirass. Iris flower design. A very neat pattern. Exceptional value for the money. Weight, 2 ounces. Price............**10¢**

CANDLE SHADE LININGS, 10c.

HX210 — Candle Shade Linings. Good quality linen with silk fringe. Colors: Yellow, Pink, Red, or White. State color wanted when ordering. Weight, 1 ounce. Price......**10¢**

MIDGET BIRTHDAY CANDLES, PER BOX, 5c.

HV188— Midget Birthday Candles. 2 inches long. 24 to a box. Fits HX196. Red, White, Pink or Yellow. State color wanted. Weight, 1 ounce. Price............

MIDGET CANDLE HOLDERS, 5 FOR 5c.

H200 — Midget Candle Holders. Made of good quality white metal. Have drip pan and convenient ring for carrying. Weight, of 5, 6 ounces. 5 for............**5¢**

BIRTHDAY CANDLES, PER BOX, 10c.

HX192— Birthday Candles. 3¼ inches long. 20 to a box. Fit rosebud candle holder HX201. Weight, per box, 6 ozs. Price..**10¢**

FANCY TWISTED PARAFINE CANDLES, 3 FOR 5c.

H187 — Fancy Twisted Parafine Candles. Pink, Red, White or Green. State color wanted. Weight, three, 5 ounces. 3 for............**5¢**

WHITE PARAFINE CANDLES, 2 FOR 5c.

HH185 — White Parafine Candles. 1x10 inches. Good quality parafine, slow burning. Weight, two, 5 ounces. 2 for ....**5¢**

H186 — Same as above, but ¾x5 inches. Weight, six, 6 ounces. 6 for............**5¢**

ROSEBUD CANDLE HOLDERS, BOX, 10c.

HX201 — Rosebud Candle Holders. Colors: Pink, Red, White, or Yellow. State color wanted when ordering. Fit candles No. HX-192. 6 to a box. Weight, 2 ozs. Per box...**10¢**

BIRTHDAY CANDLE HOLDERS, BOX, 10c.

HX196—Birthday Candle Holders. Red, White, Pink or Yellow. State color wanted. Fits No. HV-188, midget candles. 10 to a box. Weight, per box, 2 ounces. Price............**10¢**

JEWEL TOY LANTERN, 10c.

HX127 — Jewel Toy Lantern. Stands 7 inches high. Complete with crystal globe, burner, and wire handle for carrying. Lamp gives a good, clear light and uses very little oil. Weight, 7 ounces. Price............**10¢**

HX128 — Same as above, but green globe. Weight, 7 ounces. Price.................**10¢**

BRASS SCREW RINGS, 12 FOR 5c.

H1113— Brass Screw Rings. Have good sharp threads. Rings ¾-inch in diameter. Weight, 12, one ounce. 12 for............**5¢**

H1114 — Same as above, but with ¾-inch brass rings. Weight, six, 1 ounce. 6 for............**5¢**

BRASS HEAD TACKS, PACKAGE, 5c.

HV1115 — Brass Head Tacks. Polished brass headed upholstery tacks. Packed 50 in a box. Weight, per box, 1 ounce. Price............**5¢**

UPHOLSTERY TACKS, 50 FOR 5c.

H1155 — Upholstery Tacks. ½-inch top, metalline enameled to represent leather. Colors: Black, Olive Green or Tan. State color wanted. Weight, 1 ounce. 50 for............**5¢**

PLUMBER'S CHAIN, PER YARD, 5c.

HV1116 — Plumber's Chain. Good strong chain, seamless links. Heavily brass plated. Weight, per yard, 2 ounces. Price, per yard............**5¢**

SINGLE JACK CHAIN, PER YARD, 5c.

HV1117 — Single Jack Chain. Large double links, heavily brass plated. Good, strong, durable chain. Weight, per yard, 1 ounce. Price, per yard............**5¢**

RETINNED PICTURE WIRE, 2 PACKAGES, 5c.

HH1118—Retinned Picture Wire. 25 feet in a package. Four strands. Weight, two packages, 3 ozs. Price, 2 for .....**5¢**

HH1188 — Same as above, but 8 strand. Weight, per package, 2 ozs. Price, 2 for............**5¢**

HV1189 — Same as above, but 16 strand. Weight, per package, 2 ounces. Price............**5¢**

HV1180 — Same as above, eight strand, gilt picture wire. Weight, package, 2 ounces. Price............**5¢**

BRASS PLATED SASH LIFT, 5c.

HV1119 — Brass Plated Sash Lift. Heavy cast metal, brass plated. Size, 4x1½ inches. Four screw holes. Weight, 2 ounces. Price............**5¢**

HV1199 — Same as above, but oxidized finish. Weight, 2 ounces. Price............**5¢**

LACQUERED DOOR PULL, 5c.

HV1120 — Lacquered Door Pull. Good quality stamped metal, brass plated. Nicely lacquered. 5 inches over all. Rounded corners. Weight, 1 ounce. Each............**5¢**

FANCY BRASS DRAW PULLS, 2 FOR 5c.

HH1121— Fancy Brass Draw Pulls. Satin finish. Good quality metal with a raised polished center. Weight, two, 3 ozs. 2 for............**5¢**

BRASS PLATED DRAW PULLS, 2 FOR 5c.

HH1122— Brass Plated Draw Pulls. Fancy pattern. Nicely polished brass with fancy embossed drop handle. Weight, each, 2 ounces. 2 for............**5¢**

OXIDIZED DRAW PULLS, 2 FOR 5c.

HH1123— Oxidized Draw Pulls. Fancy pattern oxidized copper, fancy beaded solid drop handle. Matches mission furniture. Weight, each, 2 ounces. 2 for............**5¢**

SOLID BRASS DRAW PULLS, EACH, 5c.

HV1124— Solid Brass Draw Pulls. Made of good quality brass, fancy pattern. Solid handle with beaded design. Weight, each, 2 ounces. Price............**5¢**

EXTRA LARGE DRAW PULLS, EACH, 5c.

HV1125— Extra Large Draw Pulls. Made of good quality polished brass, very artistic pattern. Solid drop handle neatly embossed. Weight, each, 2 ounces. Price, each. ....**5¢**

SOLID BRASS DRAW PULLS, EACH, 10c.

HX1126— Solid Brass Draw Pulls. Heavy cast metal, fancy pattern, fine Etruscan finish. Heavy cast drop handle, fancy design. Weight, each, 3 ounces. Price, each. ....**10¢**

LION HEAD PATTERN DRAW PULL, 10c.

HX1127— Lion Head Pattern Draw Pull. Made of solid brass, fine polished finish. Heavy cast drop handle of fancy pattern. Weight, each, 3 ounces. Price..**10¢**

Bargains in Dependable Hardware, 5c and 10c

GLASS DRAW KNOBS, EACH, 10c.

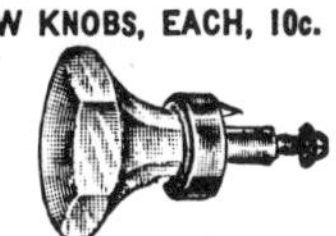

HX1128—Glass Draw Knobs. 1-in. plain hexagonal. Set in brass mounting. Smooth finished corners. Weight, each, 1 ounce. Price. . **10c**

HX1129 — Same as above, but $1\frac{3}{8}$ inches. Weight, 1 ounce. Price. **10c**

HX1130 — Same as above, but $1\frac{3}{4}$ inches. Weight, 1 ounce. Price **10c**

DROP RING DRAW PULLS, 2 FOR 5c.

HH1131—Drop Ring Draw Pulls. Made of good quality stamped brass, Etruscan finish. Diameter of plate, $1\frac{3}{8}$ inches ring $1\frac{1}{8}$ inches. Weight, each 1 ounce. 2 for **5c**

DRAW KNOBS WITH BOLT, 2 FOR 5c

HH1132—Draw Knobs with Bolt. Made of plain polished brass with bolt and nut attached. $1\frac{1}{4}$-inch top. Weight, each, $\frac{1}{2}$ ounce. 2 for **5c**

HH1133 — Same as above. but $1\frac{3}{8}$ inch top. Weight each, 1 ounce. 2 for **5c**

EBONY DROP HANDLES, EACH, 5c.

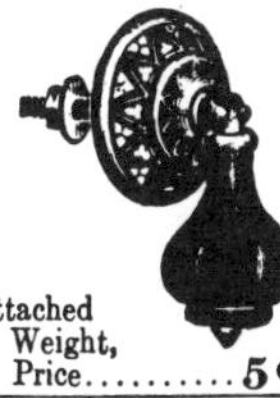

HV1134—Ebony Drop Handles. Base made of highly polished brass. Has nicely finished ebony drop handle attached to strong bolt. Weight, each, 2 ounces. Price **5c**

PORCELAIN DOOR KNOBS, 6 FOR 5c.

H1147 — Porcelain Door Knobs. Diameter of knob, 1-inch, fitted with $1\frac{3}{8}$-inch galvanized screws. Useful for cupboards, drawers, screen doors, etc. Wt., six, 3 ounces. 6 for. **5c**

HOOK SASH LIFTS, 2 FOR 5c.

HH1135—Hook Sash Lifts. Made of best quality stamped steel, oxidized copper finish. $1x1\frac{3}{8}$-inch base. Beveled edges, two screw holes. Wt., two, 1 ounce. Price, 2 for **5c**

HH11355 — Same as above, except old brass plated. Weight, two, 1 ounce. 2 for **5c**

HALF ROUND DRAW PULLS, 2 FOR 5c.

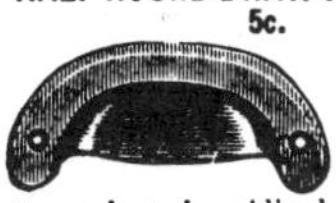

HH1136—Half Round Draw Pulls. Made of best quality stamped steel, oxidized copper finish. 3 inches across. Weight, each, 1 ounce 2 for **5c**

HH11366 — Same as above, except brass finished. Weight, each, 1 ounce. 2 for **5c**

NARROW BRASS HINGES, 2 PAIR, 5c

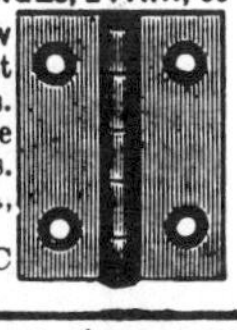

H1137 — Narrow Brass Hinges. Best quality solid brass. Highly polished. Size opened, $1x\frac{3}{4}$ inches. Four screw holes. Wt., two, 1 ounce. 2 pairs **5c**

SOLID BRASS HINGES, PER PAIR, 5c.

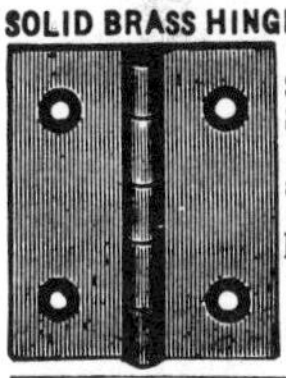

HV1138—Solid Brass Hinges. Size opened, $1\frac{1}{2}x$ $1\frac{1}{2}$ inches. Four screw holes. A well made brass hinge. Highly polished. Weight, pair, 3 ounces. Pair. **5c**

MEDIUM BRASS HINGES, PER PAIR, 5c.

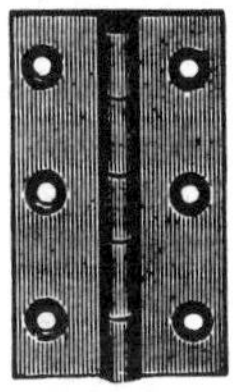

HV1139—Medium Brass Hinges. Made of good quality solid brass with six screw holes. Size opened, $1\frac{1}{2}x2$ inches. A very substantial hinge. Weight, pair, 2 ounces. Per pair. **5c**

FANCY SHAPE BRASS HINGES, PAIR, 5c.

HV-1140—Fancy Shape Brass Hinges, Made of solid brass, highly polished. Fancy shape, as illustrated. Six screw holes. Size, opened, $1\frac{1}{2}x2\frac{1}{2}$ inches. Weight, pair, 1 ounce. Price, pair. **5c**

LONG BRASS HINGES, PAIR, 10c.

HX1141 — Long Brass Hinges. Made of solid brass, heavily polished. Eight screw holes. Size, opened $\frac{3}{4}x3\frac{1}{2}$ inches. Weight, pair, 2 ounces. Price, pair. **10c**

SOLID BRASS HASP AND STAPLE, 5c.

HV1142 — Solid Brass Hasp and Staple. Highly polished. Three screw holes in end. Size, $\frac{3}{4}x2\frac{3}{4}$ inches. Weight, each, 1 ounce. Price **5c**

BRASS HASP, STAPLE AND HOOK, 10c.

HX1143 — Brass Hasp, Staple and Hook. Hinged hasp with heavy hook attached. Three screw holes in end. Highly polished. Size, $3x\frac{3}{4}$ inches. Weight, each, 1 ounce. Price. . **10c**

POLISHED BRASS CORNERS, 2 FOR 5c.

HH1144 — Polished Brass Corners. Solid brass fancy design For shirtwaist boxes, etc. $1\frac{1}{4}x1\frac{1}{4}x\frac{3}{8}$ inches. Weight, two, 1 ounce. 2 for **5c**

HV1145 — Same as above, but $1\frac{3}{8}x1\frac{3}{8}x\frac{3}{8}$ inches. Weight, each, 1 ounce. Price. **5c**

HV1146 — Same as above, but $1\frac{1}{4}x1\frac{1}{4}x1\frac{1}{4}$ inches. Weight, each, 1 ounce. Price. **5c**

JAPANNED CUPBOARD CATCH, 5c.

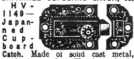

HV-1149—Japanned Cupboard Catch. Made of solid cast metal, nicely japanned. Has brass knob. Size, $3x1\frac{1}{4}$ inches. Weight, each, 3 ounces. Price. **5c**

OXIDIZED CUPBOARD CATCH, 10c.

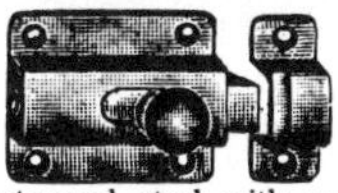

HX1150 — Oxidized Cupboard Catch. Made of good quality stamped steel with oxidized copper finish. Has strong spring. Size, $2x1\frac{3}{8}$ inches. Weight, each, 2 ounces. Price. **10c**

COPPER FINISH CUPBOARD CATCH, 10c.

HX1151 — Copper Finish Cupboard Catch. Made of good quality stamped steel, oxidized copper finish. Has large turn knob and strong spring. Size, 2x2 inches. Weight, each, 3 ounces. Price, ... **10c**

HX11511 — Same as above, except old brass finish. Weight, 3 ounces. Price. **10c**

JAPANNED BARREL BOLT, 5c.

HV-1152—Japanned Barrel Bolt. Made of best quality stamped steel, nicely japanned. Brass plated knob. 3 inches long. Weight, each, 2 ounces. Price **5c**

HV11522 — Same as above, but 4 inches long. Weight, each, 3 ounces. Price. **5c**

NICKEL PLATED BARREL BOLT, 10c

HX1155 — Nickel Plated Barrel Bolt. Heavy cast metal, fancy pattern, nickel plated. 5 inches long. Weight, each, 6 ounces. Price **10c**

HEAVY DOOR FASTENERS, 10c.

HX1156 — Heavy Door Fasteners. Heavy cast base, nicely japanned. Has 7-inch heavy steel chain. Keeps out intruders. Weight, each, 7 ounces. Price. **10c**

JAPANNED DOOR BUTTONS, 4 FOR 5c.

H1148 — Japanned Door Buttons. Made of good heavy cast metal, nicely japanned. Size, $2\frac{1}{2}$ inches. Weight, four, 6 ounces. 4 for. **5c**

BRONZE SASH FASTENERS, 5c.

HV1157 — Bronze Sash Fasteners. Made of heavy cast metal, Tuscan bronze finish. Strong spring. Keeps windows closed tight. Wt., each, 4 ounces. Price **5c**

NICKELED LETTER PLATE, 10c.

HX-1158—Nickeled Letter Plate. Made of heavy cast metal, nicely nickel plated. Has four screw holes. Beveled edges. Size, $2\frac{1}{4}x6$ inches. Weight, 7 ounces. Price. **10c**

OAK DOOR STOPS, 2 FOR 5c.

HH-1160—Oak Door Stops. Made of selected oak, nicely finished. Rubber tips. Good sharp screw points for attaching to wall. Weight, two, 3 ounces. 2 for **5c**

WROUGHT STEEL BARREL BOLT, 10c.

HX1153 — Wrought Steel Barrel Bolt. Heavy bronze plated. Four screw holes. Size, $1\frac{1}{4}x4$ inches. Wt., each, 6 ounces. Price. **10c**

HX1154 — Same as above, but $1\frac{1}{4}x5$ inches. Weight, 7 ounces. Price **10c**

BALL BEARING CASTERS, 2 FOR 5c.

HH1161 — Ball Bearing Casters. Heavy steel plate. Good ball bearings. Size of plate, $1\frac{1}{4}x1\frac{1}{2}$ inches. Four holes for attaching. Weight, each, 2 ounces. 2 for **5c**

HEAVY STEEL CASTERS, 2 FOR 5c.

HH1162 — Heavy Steel Casters. Good ball bearings. Size plate, $1\frac{1}{4}x2$ inches. Four holes for attaching. Weight, each, 3 ounces. 2 for. **5c**

HV11622 — Same as above, except brass plated finish. Weight, 3 ounces. Each. **5c**

HARD MAPLE WHEEL CASTERS, 2 FOR 5c.

HH1163—Hard Maple Wheel Casters. Tooth neck grip. Size of wheel, $1\frac{1}{4}$ inches. Weight, each, 2 ounces. 2 for. **5c**

BALL BEARING BED CASTERS, 2 FOR 5c.

HH1164 — Ball Bearing Bed Casters. Hard maple wheel, $1\frac{1}{4}$ inches diameter. For iron beds. Wt. each, 2 ozs., 2 for. . **5c**

ECLIPSE STEEL CASTERS, 2 FOR 5c.

HH1165 —Eclipse Steel Casters. Made of good heavy steel, $1\frac{1}{4}$-inch wheel. Tooth neck grip. Can be attached by anyone. Weight, each, 3 ounces. 2 for. **5c**

HV11655 — Same as above. Except brass plated. Wt., each, 3 ounces. Price, each. **5c**

WROUGHT STEEL SHELF BRACKETS, PAIR, 5c.

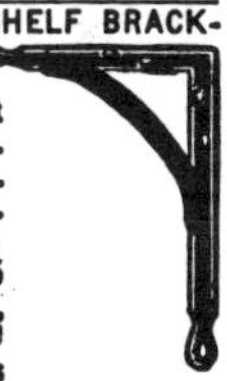

HH1167 — Wrought Steel Shelf Brackets. Strong center brace. Nicely japanned. State size wanted. Sizes, 3x4 and 4x5 inches. Weight, each, 2 ounces. Per pair **5c**

HX11677—Same as above, except 6x8 and 8x10 inches. Average weight, each, 4 ounces. Price, pair. **10c**

Kitchen Hardware, Etc.—Nothing Over 10c

NICKEL PLATED SLEEVE IRON, 10c.

HX11688 — Nickel Plated Sleeve Iron. Solid cast metal, Heavily nickel plated highly polished bottom. For sleeves and shirt waists. Weight, each, 25 ounces. Price...............**10C**

SAD IRON HANDLES, EACH, 5c.

HV-1168 — Sad Iron Handles. Solid cast bottoms, neatly japanned. Nicely finished wooden handle and knob. Weight, each, 6 ounces. Price....................**5C**

SAD IRON HANDLES, EACH, 10c.

HX-1169 — Sad Iron Handles. Heavy cast base highly nickel plated. Nicely finished wood handle and knob. Weight, each, 10 ounces. Price............**10C**

SAD IRON HANDLES, EACH, 10c.

HX-1170 — Sad Iron Handles. Heavy cast base, nicely nickel plated. Natural finished wood handle and knob, as illustrated. Weight, each, 8 ounces. Price..**10C**

UNIVERSAL IRON HOLDER, 10c.

HX-1171 — Universal Iron Holder. Made of wrought steel, highly nickel plated. Has enameled wood handle. Fits any style iron. Weight, each, 6 ounces. Price.......**10C**

JAPANNED IRON STAND, 5c.

HV-1173 — Japanned Iron Stand. Made of heavy cast iron with high rimmed edge. Nicely japanned. Weight, each, 9 ounces. Price...........**5C**

ASBESTOS IRON HOLDER, 5c.

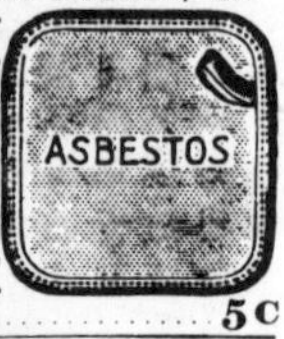

HV1172 — Asbestos Iron Holder. Double thickness, asbestos lined, Jersey covered iron holder. Just the thing for solid irons. Wt., each, 1 ounce. Price....................**5C**

STOVE PIPE DAMPER, 10c.

HX1175 — Stove Pipe Damper. Made of heavy cast metal. 6 inches in diameter. Has heavy nickeled turn. Weight, 11 ounces. Price......**10C**

COLD HANDLE STOVE LIFTER, 5c.

HV1176 — Cold Handle Stove Lifter. Heavily nickel plated, bent coiled wire handle. Will not get hot. 8 inches long. Weight, 5 ounces. Price..........................**5C**

NICKEL PLATED STOVE LIFTER, 5c.

HV1177 — Nickel Plated Stove Lifter. 9 inches long. Cast metal, nickel plated. Handle of coiled wire, bent in loop. Will not get hot. Weight, each, 7 ounces. Price................**5C**

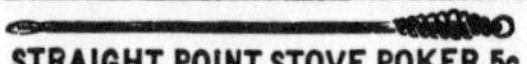

STRAIGHT POINT STOVE POKER, 5c.

HV1178 — Straight Point Stove Poker. 20 inches long. Nickel plated, spring coiled cold handle. Weight, each, 7 ounces. Price..........**5C**

HV1179 — Same as above, but bent point. 18 inches long. Weight, 7 ounces. Price.............**5C**

HX11799 — Same as above, bent point, 21 inches long. Weight, 14 ounces. Price **10C**

UPHOLSTERY TACKS, 6 PACKAGES, 5c. **MATTING TACKS, 3 PACKAGES, 5c.**

H1180 — Upholstery Tacks. 2 and 6 ounce size. Flat head, blued 75 to a box. Wt., 1½ ounces. 6 boxes............**5C**

H1181 — Matting Tacks. Blued steel, double pointed. Take strong, firm hold. Easy to remove. Weight, per box, 1½ ounces. 3 for.........**5C**

CARPET TACKS, 2 BOXES, 5c.

HH1182 — Carpet Tacks. 8 ounce size. 250 in a box. Bright flat heads. ½ in. long. Weight, per box, 7 ounces. 2 for...........**5C**

HH11822 — Same as above, but 10 ounce. ⅝-inch long. Weight, per box, 7 ounces. 2 for...........**5C**

CARPET TACKS, PER BOX, 5c.

HV-1183 — Carpet Tacks. 8 ounce. Bright, flat headed. Sharp ½-inch points. 500 to a box. Weight, per box, 7 ounces. Price, per box.**5C**

HV11833 — Same as above, but 10 ounce. Points ⅝-inch long. Weight, per box, 8 ounces. Price........**5C**

WIRE NAILS, POUND BOX, 5c.

HV1185 — Wire Nails. Made of bright wire, flat heads. 2 inches long. A very good quality nail, one that will drive into the wood easily. Special value at the price. Weight, per box, 16 ounces........**5C**

WIRE NAILS, POUND BOX, 5c.

HV1184 — Wire Nails. Made of good quality wire with flat heads, good sharp points and strong body which keeps them from bending while being driven into the wood. Nails are 1½ inches long. Weight, per box, 16 ounce. Price.**5C**

BRASS WOOD SCREWS, 12 FOR 5c.

H1186 — Brass Wood Screws. Flat heads. Good quality brass. Sharp points. ⅝-inch long. Weight, 12, two ounces. 12 for..........**5C**

H11866 — Same as above, but 1-inch long. Weight, 12, 3 ounces. 12 for...................**5C**

BRIGHT WOOD SCREWS, 36 FOR 5c.

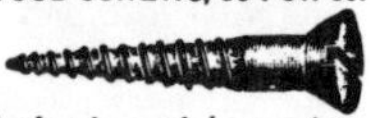

H1187 — Bright Wood Screws. Flat heads, good sharp points, nicely finished. ½-inch long. Weight, 36, 2 ounces. 36 for..........**5C**

H11877 — Same as above, but ⅞-inch long. Weight, 36, 2 ounces. 36 for.................**5C**

BRIGHT WOOD SCREWS, 36 FOR 5c.

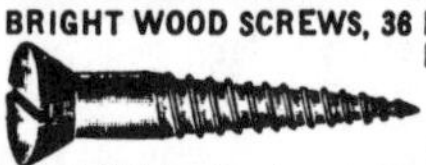

H1188 — Bright Wood Screws. No. 8, flat heads, sharp points, nicely finished. ¾ inches long. Weight, 36, 3 ounces. 36 for.................**5C**

H11888 — Same as above, 1-inch long. Weight, 36, 3 ounces. 36 for.................**5C**

HEAVY WOOD SCREWS, 24 FOR 5c.

H1189 — Heavy Wood Screws. No. 10, flat heads, sharp points, and threads. 1½-inch long. Weight, 24, 4 ounces. Price, 24 for...**5C**

ROUND HEAD WOOD SCREWS, 12 FOR 5c.

H1190 — Round Head Wood Screws. Nickel plated. No. 4. ½-inch long. Sharp points. Weight, 12, 1 ounce. 12 for...........**5C**

H11900 — Same as above, but 1-inch long. Weight, 12, 1 ounce. 12 for...................**5C**

ROUND HEAD STOVE BOLTS, 12 FOR 5c.

H1191 — Round Head Stove Bolts. Good sharp threads. Nuts attached. 3-16x½ inches. Weight, 12, two ounces. 12 for...................**5C**

H11911 — Same as above, but 3-16x1 inches. Weight, 12, three ounces. 12 for...................**5C**

H11912 — Same as above, but ¼x1½ inches. Weight, 12, four ounces. 12 for...................**5C**

WIRE SCREW EYES, 24 FOR 5c.

H1192 — Wire Screw Eyes. Sharp points and threads. Strong eye. 1⅜ inches long, ⅝-inch eye. Weight, 24, three ounces. 24 for.......................**5C**

H11922 — Same as above, but 1½-inch long, ½-inch eye. Weight, 24, three ounces. 24 for..........**5C**

H11923 — Same as above, but ⅞-inch long, ⅜-inch eye. Weight, 24, two ounces. 24 for................**5C**

BRIGHT WIRE SCREW HOOKS, 24 FOR 5c.

H1193 — Bright Wire Screw Hooks. Made of good quality bright wire, sharp threads. 2 inches long. Weight, 24, 5 ounces. 24 for....**5C**

H11933 — Same as above, but 2¾ inches long. Weight, 12, 4 ounces. 12 for...................**5C**

BRIGHT WIRE SCREW HOOKS, 6 FOR 5c.

H1194 — Bright Wire Screw Hooks. Made of good bright wire, sharp threads 4¼ inches long. Weight, six, 3 ounces. 6 for.......................**5C**

H11944 — Same as above, but 5 inches long. Weight, three, 2 ounces. 3 for...................**5C**

GATE HOOKS AND EYES, 6 FOR 5c.

H1195 — Gate Hooks and Eyes. Made of strong, bright wire, sharp threads. 1½ inches long. Weight, 6, three ounces. 6 for..........**5C**

H11955 — Same as above, but 3 inches long. Weight, six, 4 ounces. 6 for...................**5C**

BLACK SPOOL WIRE, 4 SPOOLS, 5c.

H1196 — Black Spool Wire. Fine black hair wire. 28 feet on spool. Weight, spool, ¾ ounce. 4 for..**5C**

H11966 — Same as above, but tinned wire. Weight, spool, ¾ ounce. 4 for...................**5C**

BRASS SPOOL WIRE, SPOOL, 5c.

HV1197 — Brass Spool Wire. Fine quality brass wire, 12 feet on a spool. Weight, per spool, 1 ounce. Price........**5C**

CLOTHES LINE HOOKS, 2 FOR 5c.

HH1198 — Clothes Line Hooks. Heavy cast metal, nicely japanned. Plate 2x2 inches. Four screw holes. Good strong hook. Weight, each, 4 ounces. 2 for.....................**5C**

HEAVY HAMMOCK HOOKS, 5c.

HV-1199 — Heavy Hammock Hooks. Stamped plate. Four screw holes. Hook made of 5-16 inch heavy rod, all heavily retinned. Weight, each, 5 ounces. Price....................**5C**

See page 123 for bargains in gas pliers, hatchets and dependable carpenter tools. Nothing over 10c. Don't fail to read our special offer of Free Silverware for getting three or more of your friends to send their order with yours.

Bargains in Hardware—Nothing Over 10c

CLOTHES LINE PULLEYS, 2 FOR 5c.

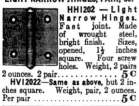

HH1200—Clothes Line Pulleys. Made of heavy cast metal, black japanned. 3/4-inch opening, 2½ inches over all. Weight, each, 4 ounces. 2 for.....**5C**

HV12001—Same as above, but 1½ inch opening. Weight, each, 1 ounce. Price.....**5C**

WOOD CLOTHES LINE PULLEY, 5c.

HV1201—Wood Clothes Line Pulley. Heavy cast frame, retinned. Solid wood roller. 3⅜ inches over all. 1-inch diameter. Weight, 4 ounces. Each **5C**

LIGHT NARROW HINGES, PAIR, 5c.

HH1202—Light Narrow Hinges. Fast joint. Made of wrought steel, bright finish. Sizes, opened, 1½ inches square. Four screw holes. Weight, 2 pairs 2 ounces. 2 pair.....**5C**

HV12022—Same as above, but 2 inches square. Weight, pair, 2 ounces. Per pair.....**5C**

MEDIUM STEEL HINGES, PAIR, 5c.

HV1203 — Medium Steel Hinges. Made of good quality wrought steel. Fast joint, bright finish, six screw holes. Size, opened, 2x3 inches. Weight, pair, 5 ounces. Pair.....**5C**

HEAVY STEEL HINGES, PAIR, 5c.

HV1204—Heavy Steel Hinges. Loose pin, reversible. Made of good wrought steel, bright finish. Size, opened, 3x3 inches. Weight, pair, 10 ounces. Price, pair.....**5C**

LIGHT STRAP HINGES, PAIR, 5c.

HV1205—Light Strap Hinges. Made of good quality wrought steel, bright finish. Six screw holes. Length, opened, 6 inches. Weight, pair, 4 ounces. Pair.....**5C**

HV12055 — Same as above, but 8 inches open. Weight, pair, 6 ounces. Pair.....**5C**

HEAVY STRAP HINGES, PAIR, 5c.

HV1206—Heavy Strap Hinges. Made of good quality wrought steel, eight screw holes. Bright finish. Length, opened, 10 inches. Weight, pair, 9 ounces. Price, pair.....**5C**

HX1206 — Same as above, but extra heavy. 12 inches open. Weight, pair, 25 ounces. Pair.....**10C**

STEEL T HINGES, PAIR, 5c.

HV1207—Steel T Hinges. Good quality wrought steel, bright finish. Six screw holes, 3 inches long. Weight, pair, 4 ounces. Pair.....**5C**

See our bargains in bath room fixtures and supplies on pages 114 and 115. Nothing over 10c.

LARGE T HINGES, PAIR 5c.

HV1208—Large T Hinges. Good quality wrought steel, bright finish. 5 inches long. Weight, pair, 7 ounces. Pair.....**5C**

HX12088 — Same as above, but 6 inches long. Weight, pair, 9 ounces. Pair.....**10C**

HINGE AND HASP COMPLETE, 5c.

HV1209 — Hinge and Hasp. Good quality wrought steel, bright finish. Four screw holes. Length, 8 inches over all. Weight, complete, 5 ounces. Price.....**5C**

HV12099 — Same as above. but 6 inches over all. Weight, complete, 4 ounces. Price.....**5C**

HASP AND STAPLE, 2 FOR 5c.

HH1210—Hasp and Staple. Made of good quality wrought steel with flat catch attached. Good sharp staple. Weight, complete, 4 ounces. 2 for.....**5C**

SCREEN DOOR SPRINGS, EACH, 5c.

HV1211—Screen Door Springs. Made of flexible coiled wire, black japanned. ⅞-inch diameter. 17 inches long. Weight, 6 ounces. Price.....**5C**

DOOR SPRING

HH12111—Same as above. but 5-16 inch diameter. Weight, each, 4 ounces. 2 for.....**5C**

SCREEN DOOR HINGES, PAIR, 10c.

HX1212—Screen Door Hinges. Made of heavy cast metal with strong spring, all black japanned. Size opened, 2½x3½ inches. Weight, pair, 14 ounces. Price, pair.....**10C**

JAPANNED RIM LATCH, 10c.

HX1213—Japanned Rim Latch. Made of heavy cast metal, black japanned. Three screw holes. Size, 2x4 inches. Weight, 9 ounces. Price **10C**

PORCELAIN DOOR KNOBS, 10c.

HX1214 — Porcelain Door Knobs. Full size. Black cast trimmings and steel connecting rod. White porcelain knobs. Fits HX1213. Weight, each, 14 ounces. Price.....**10C**

CAST BRONZE PADLOCKS, EACH 10c.

HX1215 — Cast Bronze Padlocks. Small size. Highly polished. Two keys. Suitable for dog collars, mail boxes, etc. Weight, complete, 1 ounce. Price.....**10C**

BLACK JAPANNED PADLOCK, 10c.

HX1216—Black Japanned Padlock. 1½-inch wrought steel case. Heart shape. Round spring shackle. Two keys furnished with each lock. Strong and well made. Weight, each, 2 ounces. Price.....**10C**

BRASS PLATED PADLOCKS, EACH, 10c.

HX1217—Brass Plated Padlocks. Made of wrought steel, brass plated. Spring shackle. Large size. Two keys furnished with each lock. Weight, complete, 5 ounces. Price.....**10C**

WROUGHT STEEL PADLOCKS, EACH, 10c.

HX1218—Wrought Steel Padlocks. 2-inch wrought steel case, black japanned. Malleable iron spring shackle. Each lock furnished with two keys. Weight, complete, 5 ounces. Price.....**10C**

BRASS PLATED PADLOCKS, EACH, 10c.

HX1219—Brass Plated Padlock. Wrought steel case, brass plated. 2 inches in length. Oval shape, strong malleable shackle. Weight, complete 2 ounces. Price.....**10C**

HX12199 — Same as above, except black japanned. Weight, complete, 2 ounces. Price.....**10C**

LARGE SIZE PADLOCKS, EACH, 10c.

HX1220—Large Size Padlocks. Best quality wrought steel case, brass plated, square shape. Round malleable iron shackle. 2 inches square. Two keys. Weight, complete, 5 ounces. Price.....**10C**

HX12200—Same as above, except black japanned. Weight, complete, ounces. Price.....**10C**

NICKEL PLATED PADLOCK, 10c.

HX1221—Nickel Plated Padlock. Heavy cast case and shackle. Square shape. Key enters at bottom. 1½ inches square. Two keys furnished with each lock. Weight, complete, 3 ounces. Price.....**10C**

HEAVY CAST PADLOCKS, EACH, 10c.

HX1222—Heavy Cast Padlocks. Case is heavily brass plated, square shape. Key enters at bottom. Engraved design. Size, 1½x2 inches. Complete with two keys. Weight, 6 ounces. Price.....**10C**

BRASS PLATED PADLOCKS, EACH, 10c.

HX1223 — Brass Plated Padlocks. Heavy cast case and shackle. 2½ inches, round shape. Key enters at bottom. Patent shackle. Very strong. Weight, complete with two keys, 6 ounces. Price.....**10C**

SMALL OIL CAN, 5c.

HV1225—Small Oil Can. Made of good quality polished zinc. 2-inch base, 3¾ inch bent spout. Convenient for oiling phonographs or sewing machines. Weight, each, 1 ounce. Price.....**5C**

ZINC OIL CANS, 5c.

HV1226 — Zinc Oil Can. Made of good quality polished zinc. 2¼ inch base, 2-inch straight spout. For oiling sewing machines or other small machinery. Weight, 1 ounce. Price.....**5C**

LARGE ZINC OIL CAN, 10c.

HX12277—Large Zinc Oil Can. Made of good quality polished zinc. 4-inch base. 5-inch spout. 8½ inches over all. For oiling large heavy machinery. Weight, 4 ounces. Price.....**10C**

When ordering hardware, do not fail to include woodenware, etc., and make a freight shipment. Get your friends to order with you and reduce transportation charges. It is not profitable to you or us to ship hardware, etc., by parcel post.

Bargains in Useful Hardware, 5 and 10c Each

COPPER PLATED OILERS, 10c

HX1228 — Copper Plated Oilers. Good quality metal, heavily copper plated. 3¼-inch base, 4-inch straight spout. 7½ inches over all. For oiling heavy machinery, etc. Weight, 3 ounces. Price..... **10c**

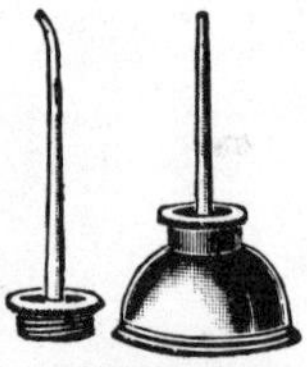

DOME SHAPE OIL CAN, 10c.

HX1227—Dome Shape Oil Can. Made of good quality metal, heavily coppered. 3-inch base, 3¼-inch straight spout, 7¼ inches over all. Large oil reservoir. For mowing machines, traction engines, etc. Wt. 4 ounces. Price...... **10c**

COPPER PLATED OIL CAN, 10c.

HX1229 —Copper Plated Oil Can. 3½-inch base, 2½-inch spout, 4½ inches over all. Weight, 4 ounces. Price..... **10c**

HX12299—Same as above, except 8-inch bent spout. Weight, 5 ounces. Price..... **10c**

FOLDING POCKET RULES, 10c.

HX-1255—Folding Pocket Rules. Round brass center joints, heavy brass ends. 24 inches long. Divided into 1-16 inches. 1-inch wide when folded. Weight, 2 ounces. Price.............. **10c**

FOLDING POCKET RULE, 10c.

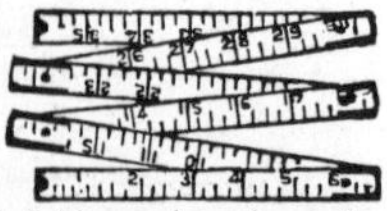

HX-1256—Folding Pocket Rule. Made of natural finish wood, spring locks, metal tips. 3 feet long. Divided into ⅛ and 1-16 inches. 1-inch thick when folded. Weight, 2 ounces. Price....................... **10c**

WOOD POCKET LEVEL, 10c.

HX-1250—Wood Pocket Level. 5 inches long. Made of imported wood. Spirit level, mitred ends. Heavy brass top. Spirit glass can be read from top or side. Weight, 2 ounces. Price.............. **10c**

HARDWOOD SPIRIT LEVEL, 10c.

HX1251 — Hardwood Spirit Level. Made of good quality maple, oil finish. 12 inches long. Spirit glass is protected by nickel plated top plate. Weight, each, 7 ounces. Price........ **10c**

POLISHED STEEL BALL BRACE, 10c.

HX1268 — Polished Steel Ball Brace. Has stained wood handle and ball end. 8-inch sweep. Will hold any size bit. Weight, 11 ounces. Price.... **10c**

TEMPERED STEEL AUGER BITS, 10c.

HX1267 — Tempered Steel Auger Bits. Double cut, sharp point, bright finish, tempered steel. Fine boring tool. Sizes, 4-16, 6-16, 8-16, 10-16 and 12-16. State size wanted when ordering. Average weight, 4 ounces. Price, each....................... **10c**

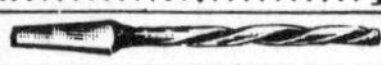

TEMPERED BIT STOCK DRILLS, 10c.

HX1266 — Tempered Bit Stock Drills. Made of best quality tooled steel. Can be used for either wood or metal. Fits any brace chuck. Sizes, 2-32, 4-32, 6-32 and 8-32. State size wanted when ordering. Average weight, 1 ounce. Price...... **10c**

TEMPERED STEEL PRICK PUNCHES 5c.

HV1270 — Tempered Steel Prick Punches. Extra fine quality tempered tool steel. Highly polished point and head. Knurled center. 3¾ inches long. Weight, each, 1 ounce. Price....................... **5c**

TEMPERED STEEL NAIL SET, 5c.

HV1271 — Tempered Steel Nail Set. Made of best quality tempered tool steel. Highly polished point and head with knurled center. 3½ inches long. Weight, each, 1 ounce. Price... **5c**

TEMPERED STEEL CENTER PUNCH, 5c.

HV1272 — Tempered Steel Center Punch. 3¾ inches long. Made of fine quality tempered tool steel. Highly polished point and head with knurled center. Weight, 1 ounce. Price.. **5c**

TEMPERED STEEL COLD CHISELS, 5c

HV1273 — Tempered Steel Cold Chisels. Extra quality tool steel. 5-16x6 inches and ⅜x6 inches. State size wanted. Average weight, 9 ounces. Price........................ **5c**

HX12733—Same as above, but ¾x6 inches. Average weight, 12 ounces. Price....................... **10c**

SLIM TAPER FILES, 5c.

HV1240—Slim Taper File. First quality steel, properly tempered and cut. 5 inches long. A very good cutting file. Weight, each, 1 ounce. Price....................... **5c**

REGULAR TAPER SAW FILE, 5c.

HV1241 — Regular Taper Saw File. Made of best quality steel, properly tempered and cut. 6 inches long. Weight, each, 3 ounces. Price.. **5c**

DOUBLE END SAW FILE, 10c.

HX1242 — Double End Saw File. Made of best quality steel, highly tempered. 10 inches long. Double end, one end fine, the other coarse. Weight, each, 3 ounces. Price. **10c**

HALF ROUND BASTARD FILES, 5c.

HV1243—Half Round Bastard Files. Made of best quality steel, properly tempered and cut. 6 inches long. Weight, 2 ounces. Price....... **5c**

HX12433 — Same as above, but 10 inches long. Weight, 3 ounces. Price....................... **10c**

FLAT MILL FILES, EACH, 5c.

HV1244 — Flat Mill Files. Made of best quality tool steel, properly tempered and cut. 6 inches long. Weight, 2 ounces. Price............ **5c**

HX1245 — Same as above, but 10 inches long. Weight, 8 ounces. Price........................ **10c**

HX12446 — Same as above, but 12-inch bastard. Weight, 10 ounces. Price....................... **10c**

NICKEL PLATED PLUMB BOB, 10c.

HX1269 — Nickel Plated Plumb Bob. Lined hole through side and top of center. ½-lb. bob. Heavily nickel plated. Well made and balances nicely. Wt., 4½ ounces. Price.. **10c**

IRON HANDLE GLASS CUTTER, 5c.

HV-1257—Iron Handle Glass Cutter. Red painted. Highly tempered cutting wheel. Three sizes glass breaking teeth. Weight, each, 1 ounce. Price......................... **5c**

RED ENAMELED GLASS CUTTER, 10c.

HX-1258—Red Enameled Glass Cutter. Made of extra quality cast steel, heavy ball end. Fine quality cutting blade. Three sizes glass breaking teeth. Wt., 2 ounces. Price............. **10c**

ROSEWOOD HANDLE GLASS CUTTER, 10c.

HX-1259-Rosewood Handle Glass Cutter. Extra quality cutting blade. Three sizes glass breaking teeth, nickel ferrule. Polished rosewood handle. Weight, 1 ounce. Price.............. **10c**

STEEL PUTTY KNIFE, 5c.

HV-1260—Steel Putty Knife. Made of polished steel, tapered blade. Red varnished handle, nickeled ferrule. Blade 1¼x3½ inches. Weight, 2 ounces. Price.. **5c**

EXTRA QUALITY PUTTY KNIFE, 10c.

HX-1261—Extra Quality Putty Knife. Flexible tapered, polished steel blade. Cocobola handle with three rivets and bolster. Blade 1¼x3¾ inches. Weight, each, 3 ounces. Price....................... **10c**

FINE QUALITY WALL SCRAPER, 10c.

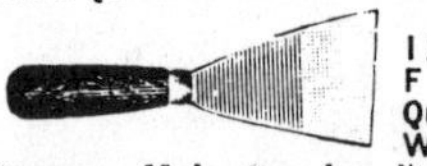

HX-1262—Fine Quality Wall Scraper. Made of good quality steel. 2⅞x3¾ inches. Nickel ferrule and round varnished rosewood handle. Weight, 3 ounces. Price.............. **10c**

HANDY SCREW DRIVERS, 5c.

HV1263 — Handy Screw Drivers. Good quality blades, varnished wood handles, nickel ferrules. ¼-inch diameter. 3, 4 and 5-inch blades. Average weight, 4 ounces. State length wanted. Price....................... **5c**

BABY CHALLENGE SCREWDRIVER, 10c.

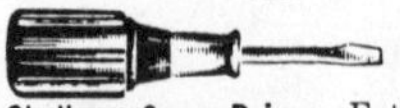

HX-1264-Baby Challenge Screw Driver. Extra quality tempered steel. 1½-inch blade. Steel ferrule. For sewing machines, typewriters. Black wood handle. Weight, 1 ounce. Price.............. **10c**

BEST QUALITY SCREWDRIVERS, 10c.

HX1265 — Best Quality Screwdrivers. Crucible steel blade, tempered in oil. Long steel ferrule. Fluted hardwood cherry finish handle. Lengths of blades 2, 3, 4, 5 and 6 inches. State length wanted. Average weight, 5 ounces. Price....................... **10c**

TEMPERED STEEL GIMLET, 10c.

HX1249 — Tempered Steel Gimlet. Large size. Double cut. Fine point. Natural wood handle. 7½ inches over all. Weight, 2 ounces. Price...... **10c**

TEMPERED STEEL GIMLET, 5c.

HV1248—Tempered Steel Gimlet. Double cut. Varnished wood handle. 4½ inches over all. A very convenient tool for every day use. Weight, 1 ounce. Price. **5c**

BARBER'S RAZOR HONE, 10c.

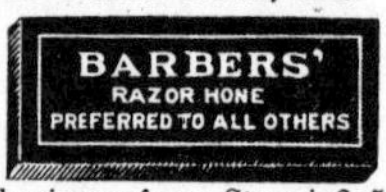
BARBERS'
RAZOR HONE
PREFERRED TO ALL OTHERS

HX-1253—Barber's Razor Hone. Extra fine honing surface. Stone is 2x5 inches. May be used with lather, water, or oil. Weight, 6 ounces. Price....................... **10c**

EXTRA QUALITY RAZOR HONE, 10c.

O-SO-EZE
RAZOR HONE
BARBERS'AND PRIVATEUSE

HX-1254—Extra Quality Razor Hone. O-So-Eze brand. Fine quality stone with perfect surface. Size, 2x6 inches. Guaranteed to give satisfaction. Weight, 7 ounces. Price....................... **10c**

NICKEL PLATED BICYCLE WRENCH 10c.

HX1281 — Nickel Plated Bicycle Wrench. One piece steel. Jaws open to 1⅜ inches. 5 inches over all. Weight, 5 ounces. Price...... **10c**

BLUED STEEL BICYCLE WRENCH, 10c.

HX1282 — Blued Steel Bicycle Wrench. Extra heavy one-piece steel. Jaws open to 1¾ inches. 5½ inches over all. Weight, 6 ounces. Price....................... **10c**

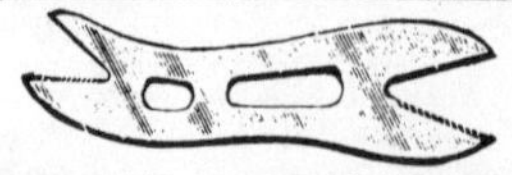

CAST STEEL ALLIGATOR WRENCH, 10c.

HX1283 — Cast Steel Alligator Wrench. Made of best quality steel, highly polished. Two size jaws. A very serviceable tool. Weight, 5 ozs. Price....................... **10c**

NOTE—All orders for hardware, crockery, glassware, tinware, enamelware, etc., should be shipped by freight. Read our special free delivery offer on page 3. We guarantee to please you or promptly return your money.

Bargains in Household Tools, 5c and 10c

CAST STEEL S WRENCHES, 5c.
HV1284 — Cast Steel S Wrenches. Polished double ends. Fits 3-16 and $\frac{1}{4}$-inch, $\frac{1}{4}$ and 5-16-inch nuts. State size wanted. Average weight, 4 ounces. Price.......................... 5c
HX12844—Same as above, but fits $\frac{3}{8}$ and 7-16-inch and 7-16 and $\frac{1}{2}$-inch nuts. State size wanted. Average weight, 6 ounces. Price...... 10c

SPRING TICKET PUNCH, 10c.
HX1276 — Spring Ticket Punch. Made of cold rolled steel with tool steel cutter. Cuts round hole, 3-32 inch diameter. $4\frac{1}{2}$ inches over all. Weight, 3 ounces. Price............ 10c

STEEL COMBINATION PLIER, 10c.
HX1275 — Steel Combination Plier. Made of cold rolled steel, highly polished. Flat nose and wire cutting sides. 5 inches over all. Weight, 3 ounces. Price...... 10c

POLISHED STEEL PLIER, 5c.
HV1274—Polished Steel Plier. Flat nose, knurled jaw. 4 inches over all. Weight, 3 ounces. Price 5c
HX12744—Same as above, but 5 and 6 inches over all. State size wanted. Weight, 3 ounces. Price...... 10c

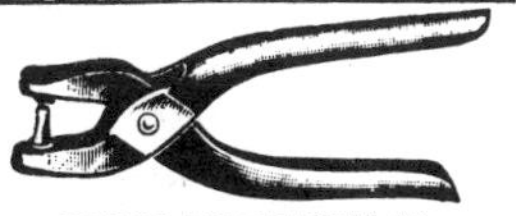

SPRING BELT PUNCH, 10c.
HX1277 — Spring Belt Punch. Made of cold rolled steel with tool steel cutter. Brass stop plate. 6 inches over all. Weight, 4 ounces. Price...... 10c

ADJUSTABLE GAS PLIER, 10c.
HX1278 — Adjustable Gas Plier. Made of best quality cast steel, highly nickel plated. Can be adjusted to various sizes. Gas or auto plier. $6\frac{1}{2}$ inches over all. Weight, 9 ounces. Price.......................... 10c

NICKEL PLATED GAS PLIERS, 10c.
HX1279 — Nickel Plated Gas Plier. Made of heavy cast steel with two sizes of jaws. 8 inches over all. A handy tool. Weight, 9 ounces. Price 10c

INSULATING TAPE, PACKAGE, 10c.

1-4 LB. 3-4 IN.
TIRE
TAPE

HX1280 — Insulating Tape. $\frac{3}{4}$-inch wide. For tires or electric wire. About 75 feet in roll. Wt., per package, 4 ozs. Price 10c

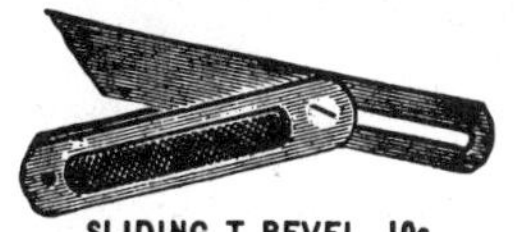

SLIDING T BEVEL, 10c.
HX1285 — Sliding T Bevel. 6-inch steel blade. Cast handle, heavily nickel plated. A first quality bevel. Weight, 6 ounces. Price...... 10c

STEEL TRY SQUARES, 10c.

HX1286 — Steel Try Squares. 6-inch blade, cast arm, heavily nickel plated. Marked in $\frac{1}{8}$-inch. Weight, 7 ounces. Price.................. 10c

HEAVY STEEL SQUARES, 10c.
HX1287 — Heavy Steel Squares. Made of good quality steel, nickel plated. 7x12 inches. Marked in 1-16-inch. Figures on both sides. Weight, 6 ounces. Price........ 10c

STEEL BLOCK PLANE, 10c.
HX1290—Steel Block Plane. Japanned finish; sharp adjustable blade. Size, 5x1$\frac{3}{4}$ inches. A good, practical tool. Weight, 10 ounces. Price. 10c

SUPERIOR KEYHOLE SAW, 10c.
HX1302—Superior Keyhole Saw. 10-inch polished steel blade. Teeth set and filed. One piece shaped varnished beechwood handle. Weight, 4 ounces. Price.......................... 10c
HX13022 — Compass Saw. 14-inch blade. Weight, 5 ounces. Price. 10c

STEEL HAND SAWS. EACH, 10c.
HX1304 — Steel Hand Saws. Polished steel blade. Has set and filed teeth. One piece varnished beechwood handle. Length of blade, 12, 14 or 16 inches. State length wanted. Average weight, 9 ounces. Price.............. 10c

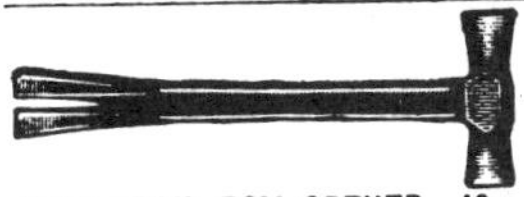

CAST IRON BOX OPENER, 10c.
HX1293 — Cast Iron Box Opener. Good quality gray iron, heavily nickel plated. Claw end. 9 inches over all. A useful tool. Weight, 11 ounces. Price.......................... 10c

CLAW TACK HAMMER, 5c.
HV1294 — Claw Tack Hammer. Nickel plated with varnished hardwood handle. Handy size for ladies' use. For everyday use about the house. Weight, 7 ounces. Price.......................... 5c

UPHOLSTERER'S HAMMER, 5c.
HV1295 — Upholsterer's Hammer. Good quality cast iron, heavily nickel plated. Varnished hardwood handle. Quality and finish equal to much higher priced hammers. Weight, 6 ounces. Price.......................... 5c

BELL-FACED HAMMER, 10c.
HX1296 — Bell-Faced Hammer. Good quality cast iron, heavily nickel plated. Bell-faced claw hammer. Has varnished hardwood handle. Weight, 11 ounces. Price.................. 10c
HX12966 — Same as above, except 16 ounce weight. Price........ 10c

NICKEL PLATED CLAW HAMMER, 10c.
HX1297—Nickel Plated Claw Hammer. Adze shape. Made of good quality cast steel. Varnished hardwood handle. Weight, 20 ounces. Price.................. 10c
HX12977 — Same as above, except 16 ounce weight. Price...... 10c

TOY HATCHETS, EACH, 5c.

HV1298 — Toy Hatchets. Nicely polished blade, $\frac{3}{4}$ gold painted. 2x3 inch blade. Polished hardwood handle. 8$\frac{3}{4}$ inches long. Weight, 5 ounces. Price.................. 5c

SHINGLING HATCHETS, EACH, 10c.
HX1299—Shingling Hatchets. Good quality cast iron heads. Half blade polished, balance painted red. Oval hardwood handle. Useful for repair purposes around the house or barn. Wt., 16 ounces. Price.. 10c

CAST IRON HATCHET, 10c.
HX1300—Cast Iron Hatchet. Full size. Half polished blade, balance painted red. Oval hardwood handle. Can be used for nail driving or chopping purposes equally well. Weight, 21 ounces. Price.................. 10c

BOY SCOUT'S AXE, 10c.
HX1301—Boy Scout's Axe. Made of good quality heavy cast iron. Half blade polished, balance painted red. Hardwood oval handle. Useful for camping parties, hunters, etc. Weight, 17 ozs. Price.......................... 10c

MAPLE HATCHET HANDLE, 5c.
HV1291 — Maple Hatchet Handle. Made from selected wood. Nicely shaped and finished. 14 inches long. Weight, 7 ounces. Price........ 5c

MAPLE HAMMER HANDLE, 5c.
HV1292 — Maple Hammer Handle. Made from selected maple. Nicely shaped and finished. 14 inches long. Weight, 6 ounces. Price........ 5c

When ordering tools do not fail to include household paints and brushes. See pages 126 and 127.

QUILT FRAME CLAMP, 5c.

HV-1288—Quilt Frame Clamp. Heavy cast metal, two pieces, black japanned. 3-inch opening. Weight, 8 ounces. Price.......................... 5c
HH12888—Same as above. $2\frac{1}{2}$-inch opening. Weight, each, 6 ounces. Price, 2 for.................... 5c

ANVIL BENCH VISE, 10c.

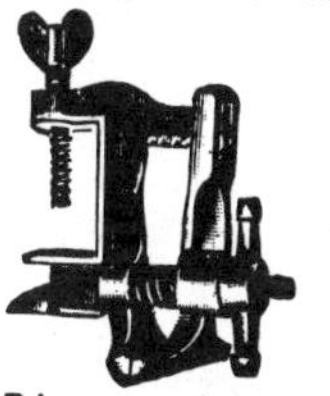

HX1289 — Anvil Bench Vise. Made of cast iron, japanned finish. Jaws open to 1 inch. Bench opening, $1\frac{3}{4}$ inches. Weight, 10 ounces. Price.......................... 10c

POINTED STEEL TROWEL, 5.
HV1230 — Pointed Steel Trowel. Blade $2\frac{1}{2}$x$5\frac{1}{2}$ inches. Polished maple handle with steel ferrule. Weight, 4 ounces. Price.................. 5c

STEEL BRICK TROWEL, 10c.
HX1231 — Steel Brick Trowel. Good quality steel blade, $4\frac{1}{2}$x$9\frac{1}{2}$ inches. Maple handle and steel ferrule. Weight, 9 ounces. Price 10c

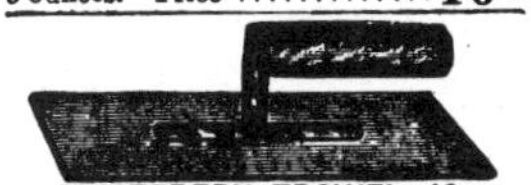

PLASTERER'S TROWEL, 10c.
HX1232 — Plasterer's Trowel. Blade of good quality steel, $4\frac{1}{2}$x10 inches. Heavy maple handle, with rivet through center. Weight, 15 ounces. Price.......................... 10c

LADIES' FLOWER TROWEL, 10c.
HX1233 — Ladies' Flower Trowel. Made of good quality rolled steel, rounded blade. Hardwood handle and nickel ferrule. $1\frac{1}{2}$x6 inch blade. Weight, 4 ounces. Price...... 10c

STEEL GARDEN TROWEL, 5c.
HV1234 — Steel Garden Trowel. 3x6 inch rounded steel blade. Natural wood handle and nickel ferrule. Wt., 5 ounces. Price 5c

HEAVY STEEL GARDEN TROWEL, 10c.
HX1235 — Heavy Steel Garden Trowel. $3\frac{1}{2}$x$6\frac{1}{2}$-inch. Extra heavy rolled steel blade. Varnished handle and brass ferrule. Weight, 8 ounces. Price.......................... 10c

MALLEABLE IRON WEEDING HOOK, 5c.
HV1236 — Malleable Iron Weeding Hook. Made of good quality malleable iron, heavily tinned. Five prongs. Black enameled handle. $9\frac{1}{2}$ inches over all. Weight, 4 ounces. Price.... 5c

Practical Articles—Special at 5c and 10c

CAST STEEL SPADING FORK, 5c.
HV1237 — Cast Steel Spading Fork. Three tines, 2½x3½ inches. Varnished wood handle, with nickeled ferrule. 9 inches over all. Weight, 4 ounces. Price..................5C

FOUR TINED SPADING FORK, 10c.
HX1238 — Four Tined Spading Fork. Good quality cast steel, 2½x4 inches. Extra heavy maple handle with brass ferrule. 10 inches over all. Weight, 7 ounces. Price..................10C

STEEL PRUNING SHEARS, 10c.
HX12455 — Steel Pruning Shears. Detachable steel cutting blade. Heavy cast handles, black japanned. Strong spring. Weight, 12 ounces. Price..................10C

CAST STEEL TINNER'S SHEARS, 10c.
HX12466 — Cast Steel Tinner's Shears. Made of heavy cast steel in two pieces, fastened with good stout bolt. Black japanned handles. 11 inches over all. Weight, 16 ounces. Price..................10C

SELF-SHARPENING GRASS SHEARS, 10c.
HX1247 — Self-Sharpening Grass Shears. Made of cold rolled crucible steel. Spring handle. Effective grass cutter. 13 inches over all. Weight, 11 ounces. Price..................10C

HOUSEHOLD SOLDERING SET, 10c.
HX1252 — Household Soldering Set. Consists of coppered soldering iron, prepared rosin and piece of solder. Iron is 10½ inches long. A household necessity. Weight, 5 ounces. Price..................10C

STEEL CURRY COMBS, EACH, 10c.
HX1411 — Steel Curry Combs. Solid steel back, eight bars strongly riveted to back. All nicely japanned. Large round wood handle, stained red. Nickeled ferrule. Handle riveted to comb. Weight, 11 ounces. Price..................10C

OPEN BACK CURRY COMBS, 10c.
HX1412 — Open Back Curry Comb. Made of best quality pressed steel, finished with lacquer. Has eight bars securely riveted. Heavy wire support with black enameled wood handle, securely attached. Brass ferrule. Wt., 8 ounces. Price..................10C

BLACK JAPANNED MAIL BOX, 10c.
HX1413 — Black Japanned Mail Box. Made of best quality heavy sheet iron. Weatherproof, top. Can be secured with a small lock. Wire holder for newspapers. 11 inches long, 5 inches wide, 1½ inches in thickness. Weight, 11 ounces. Price.....10C

COMBINATION STORM GLASS AND THERMOMETER, 10c.
HX1406 — Combination Storm Glass and Thermometer. Good quality barometer and tested thermometer mounted on nicely finished wood frame with nickeled guards. Easy reading. Weight, each, 4 ounces. Price......10C

EASY READING THERMOMETER, 10c.
HX1407 — Easy Reading Thermometer. Large plain figures on white enameled metal back. Entire thermometer of heavy metal, black japanned. 10 inches high. Weight, 3 ounces. Price......10C

WHITE MAPLE TOOTH PICKS, PER BOX, 5c.
HV1575 — White Maple Tooth Picks. Round picks with one point sharpened. Made of best white maple. 500 picks in a box. Wt. per box 3 ounces. Price......5C

DETROIT TOOTH PICKS, 2 BOXES 5c
HH1576 — Detroit Tooth Picks. Good hardwood picks, pointed one end, the other end flat. 1,500 picks in a box. Weight, per box, 4 ounces. 2 for......5C

EUREKA TOOTH PICKS, 2 BOXES, 5c.
HH1577 — Eureka Tooth Picks. Made of good hard wood, one end sharp, the other end flat. 2,500 in a box. A good quality pick. Weight, per box, 5 ounces. 2 for......5C

BOXWOOD MUSTARD SPOONS, 4 FOR 5c.
H1578 — Boxwood Mustard Spoons. Made of polished boxwood with deep bowl and round, turned handle. Good value. Weight 4, one ounce. 4 for......5C

HARDWOOD SALAD SET, 10c.
HX1579 — Hardwood Salad Set. Set consists of salad spoon and fork. Made of good hardwood stained yellow finish. 9 inches long over all. Weight, pair, 1 ounce. Price..........10C

MASON JAR CAPS, 3 FOR 5c.
H1580 — Mason Jar Caps. Genuine Boyd cap for Mason jars. Made of polished zinc with porcelain lining. Weight, each, 2 ounces. 3 for..................5C

RUBBER JAR RINGS, 24 FOR 5c.
H1581 — Rubber Jar Rings. Good quality black rubber, light weight. Weight 24, 12 ozs. 24 for......5C
H15811 — Heavyweight, Weight, 12, 5 ounces, 12 for..................5C
H15812 — Same as above, but white rubber. Weight, 12, 5 ounces. 12 for..................5C
H15813 — Same as above, but red rubber. Weight 12, 5 ounces. 12 for..................5C
H15814 — Extra heavy, white rubber. Weight, 12, 5 ounces. 12 for......10C

COTTON DISH MOP, 5c.
HV1582 — Cotton Dish Mop. Small size, round polished hardwood handle. 12 inches over all. Weight, 3 ounces. Price..................5C
HX15822 — Same as above, but large size. 16 inches over all. Weight, 4 ounces. Price..................10C

WHITE COTTON DISH CLOTH, 5c.

HV1583 — White Cotton Dish Cloth. Red striped border. Bound edges. Size 15x15 inches. Weight 2 ounces. Price..................5C
HX15833 — Same as above but 21x21 inches. Weight, 3 ozs. Price 10C

DOUBLE KNIT COTTON MOP, 10c.

HX1584 — Double Knit Cotton Mop. Made from heavy white cotton, double knit. Absorbent. Tubular shape. Wt. 4 ounces. Price..10C

HARDWOOD KNIFE TRAY, 10c.
HX1585 — Hardwood Knife Tray. Nicely varnished. Center bar lift. Size, 8x12 inches. Beveled sides. Weight, 13 ounces. Price..................10C

HARDWOOD POTATO MASHER, 5c.
HV1586 — Hardwood Potato Masher. Round handle with knob on end. 2½ inches diameter. 9½ inches over all. Weight, 6 ounces. Price..................5C
HX15866 — Same as above, but better quality. 10 inches over all. Weight, 9 ounces. Price..................10C

REVOLVING ROLLING PIN, 10c.
HX1587 — Revolving Rolling Pin. Made of selected hardwood. Revolving handles. All smoothly sand papered. 2½x19 inches. Weight, 25 ounces. Price..................10C

HARDWOOD MEAT BOARD, 10c.
HX1588 — Hardwood Meat Board. Made of selected hardwood with nicely finished handle. Handle is perforated for hanging. Size, 8½x16 inches. ¾ inch thick. Weight, 34 ounces. Price..................10C

IMPORTED SALT BOX, 10c.

HX1589 — Imported Salt Box. Made of alternate pieces of light and dark wood. Back 9¾x5½ inches. Perforated for hanging. Has nickeled plate attached with word "SALT" stamped on it. Weight, 13 ounces. Price.....10C

HARDWOOD TOWEL RACK, 10c.
HX1590 — Hardwood Towel Rack. Nicely finished. Three arms. Block back with nail holes. Arms 12 inches long. Weight, 7 ounces. Price..10C

SINGLE TOWEL RINGS, EACH, 5c.
HV1591 — Single Towel Rings. Made of good quality hardwood walnut finish. 6-inch diameter. Weight, each, 4 ounces. Price..................5C

DOUBLE TOWEL RINGS, EACH, 10c.
HX1592 — Double Towel Rings. Made of good quality hardwood, walnut finish. Rings 5 inches in diameter, fitted in wall bracket. Bracket has two nail holes. Weight, complete, 6 ounces. Price..................10C

PAIL SIZE WASHBOARDS, EACH, 10c
HX1593 — Pail Size Washboards. Zinc lined and well made. Size, 7x16 inches. Handy for baby clothes, handkerchiefs, laces, ribbons, etc. Weight, 16 ounces. Price..10C

SPRING CLOTHES PINS, 12 FOR 5c.
H1594 — Spring Clothes Pins. Galvanized spring. Good strong pin. 3 inches long. Will last a long time. Weight, 12, 8 ounces. 12 for..................5C

Chair Seats, Scrub Brushes, Etc., at 5 and 10c

EXCELSIOR CLOTHES PINS, BOX, 5c.

HV1595 Excelsior Clothes Pins. A good hardwood clothes pin, nicely finished. 4 inches long. 36 pins packed in a box. Weight, per box, 10 ounces.
Price.........................**5c**

FIBRE CLOTHES LINE, 10c.

HX1597 — Fibre Clothes Line. Made of good quality sisal fibre, extra strong. 50 feet in a hank. Weight, per hank, 7 ounces. Price **10c**

BRAIDED HEMP CLOTHES LINE, 10c.

HX1598 — Braided Hemp Clothes Line. Hard braided, smooth finish. Will not stain the clothes. 40 feet in a hank. Weight, per hank, 10 ounces. Price.................**10c**

MONARCH CLOTHES RACK, 10c.

HX1639 — Monarch Clothes Rack. Consists of six adjustable wooden bars, 18 inches long. Has nickel plated wall bracket. Bars securely attached to bracket. Can be dropped down when not in use. Weight, 15 ounces. Price.**10c**

PURE REFINED PARAFINE, BOX 10c.

HX1599 —Pure Refined Parafine. Used for washing and ironing, sealing fruit jars, jelly glasses, etc. Full directions for using on each box. Weight, per box, 18 ounces.
Price, ...**10c**

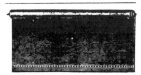

HEAVY PAPER WINDOW SHADE 10c.

HX1602 — Heavy Paper Window Shade. Made of heavy paper, dark green color. 37½ inches wide, 5 feet, 6 inches long. Weight, 5 ounces. Price.........................**10c**

WINDOW SHADE BRACKETS, 4 PAIRS, 5c.

H1102 – Window Shade Brackets. Stamped from good quality metal, heavily coppered. 1-inch over all. Easy to set in and take out shade. Weight, pair, 2 ounces. 4 pairs for....................**5c**

HARDWOOD FOLDING HAT RACK, 10c.

HX1600 — Hardwood Folding Hat Rack. Made of good quality hardwood, nicely finished and varnished. Rack is fitted with ten hooks. Very strongly built. Weight, 18 ounces.
Price **10c**

SIX HOOK HAT RACK, 10c.

HX1601 — Six Hook Hat Rack. Size, 4x33 inches with six cast iron copper hooks. Rack is walnut stained. Weight, 15 ounces. Price....**10c**

UPHOLSTERED CHAIR SEAT, 10c.

HX1624 — Upholstered Chair Seat. Made of black imitation leather. 12 inches square. Regular price, 25c. Weight, 12 ounces. Price..**10c**

HX16244 — Same as above, but 13 inches square. Weight, 14 ounces. Price.......................**10c**

IMITATION LEATHER CHAIR SEAT.

HX1625 — Imitation Leather Chair Seat. Diner shape, tufted pattern. Made of extra heavy fibre board. Oak or black finish. Sizes, 12, 13, 14, 15 and 16 inches, at front. State size and color wanted. Average weight, 9 ounces. Price **10c**

BALL TOP CHAIR SEAT, 10c.

HX1626 — Ball Top Chair Seat. Made of extra heavy fibre board in imitation leather. Oak or black finish. Sizes, 12, 13, 14, 15 and 16 inches at front. State size and color wanted. Average weight, 9 ounces. Price...........................**10c**

IMITATION LEATHER CHAIR SEATS, 10c.

HX1627— Imitation Leather Chair Seats. Round style. Made of heavy fibre board. Colors oak or black. Tufted pattern. Sizes, 12, 13 and 14 inches. State size and color wanted. Average weight, 8 ounces. Price.......**10c**

BIRCH VENEER CHAIR SEAT, 10c.

HX1629— Birch Veneer Chair Seat. Perforated and varnished. Oak or walnut stain. 12, 13, 14, 15 and 16 inch front measure. Square shape. State size and color. Average weight, 11 ounces. Price...........**10c**

BALL TOP CHAIR SEAT, 10c.

HX1628 — Ball Top Chair Seat. Made of best quality birch veneer, perforated and varnished. Oak and walnut finish. Sizes, 12, 13, 14 and 15-inch front measure. State size and finish wanted. Average weight, 9 ounces. Price.................**10c**

BIRCH VENEER ROCKER SEAT, 10c.

HX1630— Birch Veneer Rocker Seat. Made of best quality birch veneer, perforated and heavily varnished. Oak or walnut finish. Two sizes, 18 and 20 inches front. State size and color wanted. Average weight, 16 ounces. Price.................**10c**

ROUND CHAIR SEAT, 10c.

HX1631— Round Chair Seat. Made of best quality birch veneer, round shape. Oak or walnut finish. 13, 14 and 15-inch diameter. State size and color wanted. Average weight, 12 ounces. Price **10c**

SQUARE SHAPED CHAIR SEAT, 10c.

HX1632— Square shaped Chair Seat. Made of best quality birch wood veneer. Oak or walnut finish. 14 and 15-inch front measure. State size and color wanted. Average weight, 13 ounces. Price, each.**10c**

Brushes at 5c and 10c

We show a large line of brushes for various uses at 5c and 10c.

HANDY HOUSE BRUSH, 5c.

HV1525 Handy House Brush. 4 x 15 rows white tampico, securely fastened in hardwood, sanded block. Convenient shaped handle. Weight, 3 ozs. Price........................**5c**

S SHAPE SCRUB BRUSH, 10c.

HX1531 — S Shape Scrub Brush. Good quality white tampico securely set in heavy polished block. Has two winged ends. Weight, each, 7 ounces. Price.............................**10c**

EXTRA LARGE SCRUB BRUSH, 10c.

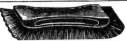

HX1532 — Extra Large Scrub Brush. Good quality white tampico securely set in polished, grooved grip block. Pointed ends. 10½ inches long. Weight, 9 ounces. Price.**10c**

MEDIUM SIZE SCRUB BRUSH, 10c.

HX1533 — Medium Size Scrub Brush. Made of rice root set in heavy concave back. Square ends. Length. 9 inches. Weight, 7 ounces. Price.........................**10c**

RICE ROOT SCRUB BRUSH, 5c.

HV1534 — Rice Root Scrub Brush. Selected rice root, securely set in hardwood block. Both ends pointed. 9 inches long. Weight, 5 ounces. Price.........................**5c**

PALMYRA STOCK SCRUB BRUSH, 5c

HV1535 — Palmyra Stock Scrub Brush. Heavy oval hardwood block. Pointed on both ends. 8¼ inches long. Weight, 5 ounces. Price......**5c**

SQUARE SHAPE SCRUB BRUSH, 5c.

HV1536 — Square Shape Scrub Brush. Good quality white tampico, securely set in hardwood block. Square ends, grooved sides. 2¾x6¼ inches. Weight, 5 ounces. Price.**5c**

GRAY FIBRE SCRUB BRUSH, 10c.

HX1537 — Gray Fibre Scrub Brush. Extra quality. Hardwood polished block. Pointed ends. For scrubbing stairs and corners. 7½ inches long. Weight, 5 ounces. Price......**10c**

GENUINE PALMETTO SCRUB BRUSH 10c.

HX1538 — Genuine Palmetto Scrub Brush. Hardwood block. Square ends. Size, 2x8 inches. Weight, 9 ounces. Price.........................**10c**

WHITE TAMPICO BATH BRUSH, 10c.

HX1539— White Tampico Bath Brush. Very soft. Rounded oval hardwood block with heavy strap for hand. 3x5¼ in. long. Weight, 5 ounces. Price.**10c**

NOTE—Woodenware is quite bulky, therefore it should be shipped by freight. You will save money on transportation charges by having tinware, glassware, woodenware, etc., shipped by freight.

Bargains in Brushes, Paints, Etc., 5 and 10c

LONG HANDLED BATH BRUSH, 10c.

HX15399 — Long Handled Bath Brush. Good quality soft white tampico set in polished hardwood oval block. Long loose handle. 17 inches long. Weight, 7 ounces. Price **10¢**

BATH TUB BRUSHES, EACH, 10c.

HX1540 — Bath Tub Brushes. Long white tampico stock, securely set in heavy hardwood block. Bath tub or milk can brush. Winged ends. Weight, 8 ounces
Price ....**10¢**

BLACK FIBRE SOAP BRUSH, 10c.

HX1541 — Black Fibre Soap Brush. 11 inches long, 2¼ inches wide. Polished hardwood block. Has dauber on turn-up end. Shaped wood handle. Weight, 8 ounces. Price .....**10¢**

GRAY FIBRE STOVE BRUSH, 10c.

HX1542 — Gray Fibre Stove Brush. Gray mixed fibre set in heavy block. Yellow stained edges, red top. Rocker shape. Finished handle. 2½x9 inches. Weight, 6 ounces. Price .....**10¢**

GENUINE PALMETTO HORSE BRUSH, 10c.

HX1543 — Genuine Palmetto Horse Brush. 4x8½ inches oval hardwood block with patent leather hand strap. A good quality brush. Weight, 9 ounces. Price ....**10¢**

GENUINE PALMYRA HORSE BRUSH, 10c.

HX1544 — Genuine Palmyra Horse Brush. Heavy coarse stock. 2½x10-inch hardwood block with grooved sides, pointed on both ends. Weight, 9 ounces. Price.................**10¢**

ANCHOR SINK BRUSH, 10c.

HX1545 — Anchor Sink Brush. Good quality red fibre with heavy tinned ferrule. Black enameled handle. 10 inches over all. 5 inches wide at bottom. Weight, 3 ounces. Price.....**10¢**

COMBINATION BRUSH AND SHOVEL 10c.

HX1546 — Combination Brush and Shovel. Red fibre on one end and tin shovel on other. Heavy nickeled ferrule on brush. 11 inches long over all. Weight, 4 ounces. Price..**10¢**

GENUINE PALMETTO SINK BRUSH, 10c.

HX1547 — Genuine Palmetto Sink Brush. Heavy bristles. Size brush, 2¼ inches square. 12-inch hardwood handle. For sinks or cuspidors. Wt., 5 ounces. Price ....**10¢**

TOILET BOWL BRUSH, 10c.

HX1549 — Toilet Bowl Brush. Heavy gray mixed fibre, wire drawn, horseshoe shape end. Mahogany finished handle with nickeled ferrule. 20 inches long over all. Weight, 6 ounces. Price.....................**10¢**

MILK BOTTLE BRUSH, 10c.

HX1548 — Milk Bottle Brush. All bristle, wire drawn, round end. Has stiff fibre on end. 13 inches over all. Weight, 3 ounces. Price......**10¢**

FIBRE COUNTER DUSTER, 10c.

HX1553 — Fibre Counter Duster. Long gray mixed fibre, wire drawn, round shape with bent end. Walnut stained varnished handle. 16 inches over all. Weight, 5 ounces. Price....................**10¢**

NURSING BOTTLE BRUSH, 5c.

HV1554 — Nursing Bottle Brush. All white bristles with twisted wire handle. Diameter of brush, 2 inches, 11 inches over all. Will fit neck of any nursing bottle. Weight, 1 ounce. Price........................**5¢**

REFRIGERATOR BRUSH, 5c.

HV1555 — Refrigerator Brush. All white bristles, wire drawn. For cleaning out refrigerator waste pipe. Diameter of brush, 1 inch, 33 inches long. Weight, 3 ounces. Price.......**5¢**

STAIR OR COUNTER DUSTER, 10c.

HX1552 — Stair or Counter Duster. Extra full black tampico. 1½x12½-inch polished hardwood back. A very good quality brush. Weight, 7 ounces. Price.............**10¢**

PIANO OR FURNITURE DUSTER, 10c.

HX1550 — Piano or Furniture Duster. Long wool end. Black enameled wood handle. 13 inches over all. Will not scratch or mar furniture. Weight, 3 ounces. Price...................**10¢**

STANDARD FEATHER DUSTER, 10c.

HX-1551 — Standard Feather Duster. Full feather duster with black enameled handle. 18 inches over all. Good quality Turkey feathers. Weight, 4 ounces. Price **10¢**

JOKER MOUSE TRAPS, 3 FOR 5c.

H1633 — Joker Mouse Traps. Extra strong copper plated spring, trip lever. Catches them every time. Weight, each, 1 ounce. Price, 3 for......**5¢**

JOKER RAT TRAP, 10c.

HX1634 — Joker Rat Trap. Extra strong spring of copper plated wire, copper plated trip lever. Easy to set. The surest rat trap made. Weight, each, 8 ounces. Price.........**10¢**

PENNSYLVANIA RAT TRAP, 10c.

HX1635 — Pennsylvania Rat Trap. Upright back. Very powerful spring, heavily galvanized. A very strong and efficient trap. Easy to bait and set. Weight, each, 15 ounces. Price....**10¢**

FIVE HOLE TIN OR WOOD MOUSE TRAP, 10c.

HX1636 — Five Hole Mouse Trap. Made of good quality tin with coppered spring wire. Catches five mice at one time. Weight, each, 3 ounces. Price.........**10¢**

HV1637—Same as above. Made of wood, Weight, 5 ounces. Price......................**5¢**

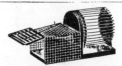

TOY WHEEL MOUSE TRAP, 10c.

HX1638 — Toy Wheel Mouse Trap. Trap made of heavy galvanized wire on wood base. Has revolving wheel on one end. Weight, 8 ounces. Price...................**10¢**

HOUSEHOLD PAINT, PER CAN, 10

HX1675 — Household Paint. Composed of extra quality dry colors and pure raw linseed oil, varnish and dryer, containing pure lead and zinc. Produces brilliant color with a hard, lasting, durable finish. Colors, inside white, outside white, black, medium Vermont, medium blue, vermillion, imperial red, clear gray, brown drab, straw, and light slate. State color wanted. Put up in half pint cans. Average weight, per can, 13 ounces. Price, per can.......**10¢**

VARNISH STAIN, PER CAN, 10c.

HX1676— Varnish Stain, Fine quality varnish stain composed of earth color, ground in fine quality grinding varnish. Produces a high grade varnish finish in various wood effects. Quick drying and hard lasting. Colors, light oak, dark oak, walnut, mahogany, light cherry, and dark cherry. State color wanted. Put up in half pint cans. Weight, per can, 12 ounces. Price, per can..**10¢**

ENAMELED PAINT, PER CAN, 10c.

HX1677 — Enameled Paint. Extra quality enamel, can be used for both iron and wood work. Contains pure zinc, raw linseed oil and dryer. Produces a high grade enameled finish. Colors especially brilliant, white, black, pale blue, ivory, vermillion, yellow, dark olive, emerald green, and Princeton. State color wanted. Put up in ¼-pint cans. Average weight, per can, 7 ounces. Price.................**10¢**

BLACK SCREEN PAINT, 10c.

HX1678— Black Screen Paint. Put up in ½ pint cans. Can be used on woodwork, as well as wire screen cloth. Contains asphaltum and carbon black. Will not clog the meshes. Average weight, per can, 10 ounces. Price....................**10¢**

GOLD PAINT OUTFIT, 10c.

HX1681 — Gold Paint Outfit. Contains one bottle gold bronze, one bottle of lacquer, one brush, and mixing saucer, all neatly packed in a box with full instructions for using. Weight, complete, 6 ounces. Price.........**10¢**

READY MIXED ALUMINUM PAINT, 10c.

HX1682—Ready Mixed Aluminum Paint. Especially suitable for radiators, pipes, iron railing, iron beds, etc. Easy to apply. Weight, per can, 4 ounces. Price ....**10¢**

Paint and Varnish Brushes, Etc., at 5c and 10c

We list on this page some extra special values in Gold Paints, Stove Polish, Etc., at 10c.

READY MIXED GOLD PAINT, 10c.

HX1683 — Ready Mixed Gold Paint. Composed of fine quality bronze powder, mixed with lacquer. Will work equally well on any surface. 2 ounces in a bottle. Weight, per bottle, 6 ounces. Price....10c

BARREL GOLD PAINT, 10c.

HX1684 — Barrel Gold Paint. Extra fine quality ready mixed gold paint, and brush. All in fancy polished wood barrel. This is a good quality gold paint and very durable. Weight, complete, 5 ounces. Price............10c

LA BELLE METAL POLISH, 10c.

HX1685 —LaBelle Metal Polish. Contains no poison or acid to injure the hands or metal surface. Polishes brass, copper, tin, zinc plated ware or any other metal. Put up in screw top can. Wt., per can, 10 ounces. Price..........10c

WALL PAPER CLEANER, 10c.

HX1686 —Wall Paper Cleaner. This cleaner makes no streaks on the paper. Is a thorough disinfectant. Easily applied and gives excellent results. Put up in round tin cans. Weight, per can, 16 ounces. Price....10c

VELVET FURNITURE POLISH, 10c.

HX1687 —Velvet Furniture Polish. For use on furniture, pianos, automobiles, etc. Put up in attractive package with full instructions for using. Weight, package, 10 ounces. Price 10c

FLOOR OIL PER CAN, 10c.

HX1689 — Floor Oil. For renewing floors, mops, and all dustless dusters. Contains no injurious acids. Polishes furniture, etc. Screw top can. Weight, 11 ounces. Price.....10c

SPERM OIL, PER BOTTLE, 10c.

BX874—Sperm Oil. A high grade oil for lubricating sewing machines, bicycles, typewriters, guns, machinery, etc. Weight per bottle, 6 ounces. Price......10c

3-IN-1 OIL BOTTLE, 10c.

HX1414— 3-in-1 Oil. Small size bottle. Lubricates sewing machines, guns, typewriters, etc. Can also be used for polishing furniture, pianos, etc. Weight, 4 ounces. Price......10c

DUSTLESS DUST CLOTH, 10c.

HX1688 — Dustless Dust Cloth. Size, 27x36 inches. Black color. Chemically treated. Bound edges. Absorbs the dust, does not scratch and leaves no lint. Weight, 2 ounces. Price 10c

BLACK WOOL DUSTLESS MOP, 10c.

HX1690 — Black wool Dustless Mop. Chemically treated; for polishing hardwood floors, furniture, pianos, etc. Absorbs the dust. 15 inches long over all. Weight, 4 ounces. Price........................10c

STOVE PIPE ENAMEL, CAN, 10c.

HX1679—Stove Pipe Enamel. Composed of black asphaltum base, ground in specially prepared liquid. Produces a high grade, glossy finish on stove pipes, gas ranges, etc. ½ pint cans. Weight, 10 ounces. Price..............10c

STOVE POLISH, PER CAN, 10c.

HX-1680—Stove Polish. A good quality liquid stove polish. Produces a brilliant, durable finish. Put up in ½ pint cans. Easy to apply. Weight, per can, 9 ounces. Price........................10c

Brushes at 5c and 10c — **We show a large line of popular styles in Paint and Varnish Brushes at 5c and 10c.**

SOFT BRISTLE BRUSH, 10c.

HX1651 — Soft Bristle Brush. Made of good quality soft black bristle, round shape, with nickeled ferrule. Has pointed red varnished handle. 7¾ inches over all. Weight, 1 ounce. Price......................10c

CAMEL'S HAIR BRUSH, 5c.

HV1652 — Camel's Hair Brush. Made of soft camel's hair. Half round. For lacquering, etc. Round, pointed, green painted handle. 7½ inches long. Weight, 1 ounce. Price................................5c

BRISTLE VARNISH BRUSH, 10c.

HX1653—Bristle Varnish Brush. Good quality black bristle, 1 inch wide, set in rubber. 7½ inches long. Nickeled ferrule. Fancy shaped handle, yellow stained. Weight, 1 ounce. Price..........10c

WHITE BRISTLE VARNISH BRUSH, 10c.

HX1654 — White Bristle Varnish Brush. Double thick. 1-inch wide. Long soft bristles. 7½ inches long. Yellow varnished handle and nickeled ferrule. Weight, 2 ounces. Price....................10c

FLAT VARNISH BRUSH, 5c.

HV1655—Flat Varnish Brush. Long black bristles, 1-inch wide. Finished cedar handle and nickeled ferrule. 7½ inches over all. Weight, 2 ounces. Price..5c

FLAT VARNISH BRUSH, 5c.

HV1656 — Flat Varnish Brush. Good quality white bristles, 1½ inches wide. Yellow stained wood handle and nickeled ferrule. 7½ inches long. Weight, 2 ounces. Price..............................5c

FLAT VARNISH BRUSH, 10c.

HX1657—Flat Varnish Brush. Good quality white bristles, 2½ inches wide. Fancy yellow stained wood handle. 9½ in. over all. Wt., 2 ozs. Price....10c

HX16577—Same as above, but 3 inches wide. Weight, 2 ounces. Price..............................10c

THICK VARNISH BRUSH, 10c.

HX1658 — Thick Varnish Brush. Long black bristles, double thickness, 2 inches wide. Round black enameled handle. 8¾ in. over all. Wt., 3 ozs. Price 10c

FLAT VARNISH BRUSH, 5c.

HV1659 — Flat Varnish Brush. Long black bristles, black enameled wood handle. 1-inch and 1½ inches wide. State width wanted. Weight, 2 ounces. Length, 8 inches. Price....5c

HX16599—Same as above. Except 2½ or 3 inches wide. State width wanted. Wt., 3 ozs. Price..10c

DOUBLE BRISTLE VARNISH BRUSH, 10c.

HX1660—Double Bristle Varnish Brush. Long black bristles, 2 inches and 2½ inches wide. Orange stained wood handle, nickeled ferrule. 8½ inches long. Weight, 3 ounces. Price.......................10c

BLACK BRISTLE SASH BRUSH, 5c.

HV1661—Black Bristle Sash Brush. Long black bristle, nearly round, 1-inch wide. Red stained wood handle with nickeled ferrule. 9¼ inches over all. Weight, 1 ounce. Price.......................5c

WHITE BRISTLE SASH BRUSH, 5c.

HV1662—White Bristle Sash Brush. Good quality white bristles, round shape. Heavy steel ferrule. 9 inches over all. Weight, 2 ounces. Price......5c

HX1663 — White Bristle Sash Brush. Good quality white bristles, nearly round, 1-inch wide. Polished orange stained wood handle. Heavy ferrule. 9½ inches over all. Weight, 2 ounces. Price....10c

HX1664—Heavy Sash Brush. Long black bristle. Oval shape, 1¾ in. wide. Red stained wood handle with heavy ferrule. 11 in. over all. Wt., 3 ozs. Price 10c

OVAL PAINT BRUSH, 10c.

HX1665—Oval Paint Brush. Long black bristles, oval shape, 1½ inches wide. Extra heavy ferrule. pointed natural wood handle. 8½ inches over all. Weight, 2 ounces. Price....................10c

ELECTRIC WALL BRUSH, 10c.

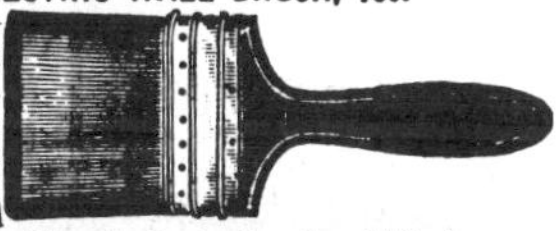

HX1666—Electric Wall Brush. Long white tampico, 3½ inches wide Varnished red stained wood handle, heavy ferrule. 9½ inches over all. Weight, 5 ounces. Price..............10c

WALL PAPER BRUSH, 10c.

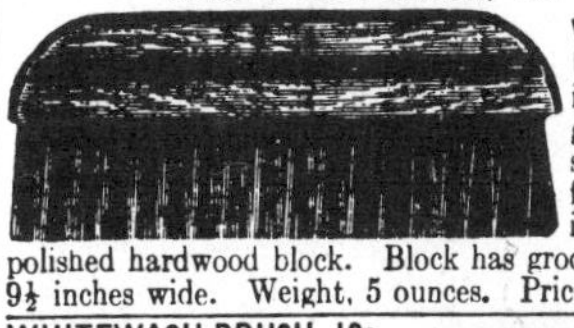

HX1668—Wall Paper Brush. 2-inch mixed gray fibre, securely fastened in heavy polished hardwood block. Block has grooved handle. 9½ inches wide. Weight, 5 ounces. Price....10c

WHITEWASH BRUSH, 10c.

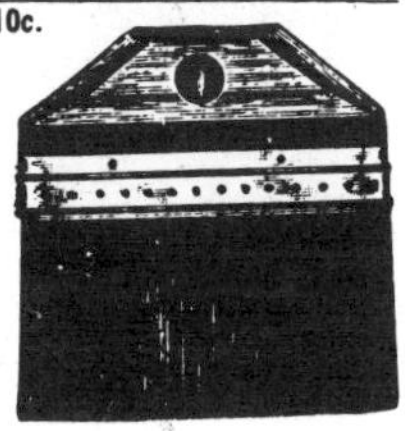

HX1667 — Whitewash Brush. Made of 2½-inch white tampico securely set in stained wood block. Heavy brass plated ferrule. Brush is 6 inches wide. Weight, 7 ounces. Price.........10c

HX16677 — Same as above except 7 in. wide. Wt., 9 ozs. Price 10c

Cobbler Outfits and Supplies, 5c and 10c

SHOE DAUBERS, EACH, 5c

HV1350▼—Shoe Daubers. Good quality black tampico, natural wood finished handle. $2\frac{1}{4}$x6 inches over all. Weight, 2 ounces. Price...**5c**

HX13500—Black Bristle, long oval handle. Polished back. $2\frac{1}{2}$x$7\frac{1}{4}$ inches over all. Weight, 3 ounces. Price....................................**10c**

FELT POLISHING BRUSH, 10c.

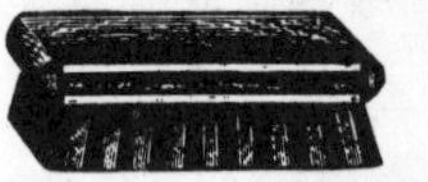

HX1351 — Felt Polishing Brush. Composed of alternate pieces of red and black felt, securely glued to polished wood back. Gives a very high polish. Size, $1\frac{1}{2}$x2x6 inches. Weight, 4 ounces. Price....................**10c**

HEAVY SHOE BRUSH, 10c.

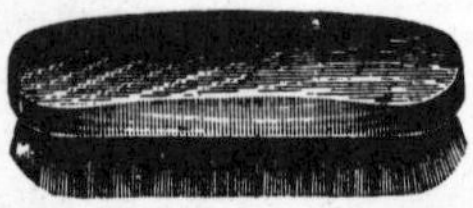

HX1353 — Heavy Shoe Brush. Good quality black tampico securely set in oval wood back. 8 inches over all. Fine natural finish. Weight, 6 ounces. Price....................................**10c**

SHOE BRUSH WITH DAUBER, 10c.

HX1354—Shoe Brush with Dauber. Good quality black tampico set in natural finish wood back. Polished wood handle. Size, 11 inches over all. Weight, 8 ounces. Price............**10c**

DANDY POLISHING SET, 10c.

HX1352 — Dandy Polishing Set. Fleeced brush and dauber mounted on nicely finished wood. Fleece has leather side turned in, giving a very long, serviceable life to the brush. Size of brush, $1\frac{1}{2}$x2x6 inches. Dauber 6 inches over all. Weight, complete, 4 ounces. Price..........**10c**

TWO IN ONE SHOE PASTE 10c.

HX1368 — Two In One Shoe Paste. One of the best known shoe pastes on the market. For black, tan or white shoes. Easily applied and gives a high polish. State kind wanted when ordering. Weight, box, 3 ounces. Price.........**10c**

JET OIL POLISH PER BOTTLE, 10c.

HX1357— Jet Oil Polish. A superior liquid polish which softens, water - proofs, and preserves black leather. Weight, per bottle, 10 ozs. price...**10c**

COMBINATION SHOE POLISH, 10c.

HX1356—Combination Shoe Polish. Consisting of liquid cleaner and separate paste. For all black shoes, softens and preserves the leather. Wt., complete, 12 ozs. Price**10c**

SATINOLA COMBINATION POLISH, 10c.

HX1355—Satinola Combination Polish. Each box contains liquid cleaner and box of paste. For tan shoes and fancy colored leather. Weight complete, 12 ounces. Price....**10c**

THREE BEE SHOE POLISH, 5c.

HV-1380—Three Bee Shoe Polish. Small size can with patent handle. Opens easily. A good quality shoe blacking. Weight per can, 5 ounces. Price....**5c**

SHUWITE CREAM, PER BOTTLE, 10c.

HX1381—Shuwite Cream. A liquid cream for white canvas shoes or any article made of canvas. Easily applied. Weight, per bottle, 11 ounces. Price........**10c**

CAST IRON STAND FOR LASTS, 10c.

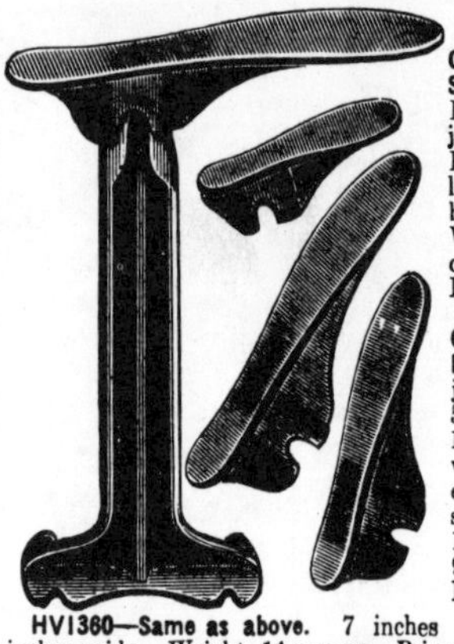

HX1358—Cast Iron Stand for Lasts. Black japanned. Fits all lasts, listed below. Weight, 32 ounces, Price..**10c**

HV1359—Cast Iron Last. Black japanned. 5 inches long, $1\frac{5}{8}$ inches wide at ball of foot. Fits stand HX-1358. Wt., 9 ounces. Price....**5c**

HV1360—Same as above. 7 inches long by $2\frac{1}{8}$ inches wide. Weight, 14 ounces. Price........**5c**

HX1361 — Same as above. $8\frac{1}{2}$ inches long, $2\frac{3}{4}$ inches wide. Weight, 20 ounces. Price............**10c**

HX1362 — Same as above. $9\frac{1}{2}$ inches long, $2\frac{7}{8}$ inches wide. Weight, 25 ounces. Price......**10c**

HEAVY LEATHER SLABS, PAIR, 10c.

HX1373—Heavy Leather Slabs. Extra quality. Acorn brand, tanned oak leather. $3\frac{1}{2}$x$5\frac{1}{2}$ inches. Weight, pair, 3 ozs. Price**10c**

MEN'S TAPS, PAIR, 10c.

HX1371—Men's Taps. Extra quality "Wilco-Acorn" brand leather. Each pair has full instructions for use. Weight pair, 3 ounces. Price....**10c**

WOMEN'S TAPS, PAIR, 10c.

HX1372—Women's Taps. Extra quality "Wilco-Acorn" brand leather. Each pair has full instructions for using. Weight, pair, 3 ounces. Price....**10c**

RUBBER HEELS, PER PAIR, 10c.

LEATHER HEELS, PER PAIR, 5c.

HX-1376—Rubber Heels. Made of good quality black rubber with small nail holes. Good grip. Heels complete in package with nails for attaching. When ordering draw diagram of heel on piece of white paper and send to us. Average weight, 6 ounces. Per pair..........**10c**

HV1374 — Leather Heels. Fine quality leather. Women's size. Weight, pair, 1 ounce. Price..**5c**

HV1375—Same as above. Except men's size. Wt., pair, 2 ounces. Price............................**5c**

GOOD QUALITY SHOE KNIFE, 5c.

HV1364 — Good Quality Shoe Knife. $3\frac{1}{2}$-inch square pointed blade. Round handle, stained and varnished. Nickeled ferrule. Weight, each, 2 ounces. Price..**5c**

EXTRA QUALITY SHOE KNIFE, 10c.

HX1365—Extra Quality Shoe Knife. Made of extra quality steel. 4-inch square pointed blade. Cocobola handle. Blade extends through handle and is secured by three rivets. Weight, 2 ounces. Price **10c**

BENT POINT SEWING AWL, 5c.

HV1366 — Bent Point Sewing Awl. $2\frac{1}{2}$-inch bent steel point. Varnished hardwood handle with brass ferrule. Weight, 2 ounces. Price..............**5c**

PEG AWL, HAFT AND WRENCH, 5c.

HV13666—Peg Awl, Haft and Wrench. Good heavy hickory handle, nicely varnished. Weight, complete, 3 ozs. Price..**5c**

COBBLER CLINCHING NAILS, 2 PACKAGES, 5c.

HH1369 — Cobbler Clinching Nails. Made of best quality steel, good clinching points. Sizes, $\frac{3}{8}$, $\frac{5}{8}$ and $\frac{7}{8}$ inches. Average weight, per package, 4 ounces. 2 for. **5c** State size wanted.

BRASS CLINCHING NAILS, PACKAGE, 5c.

HV1370 — Brass Cobbler Clinching Nails. Made of good quality brass with fine clinching points. Size, $\frac{3}{8}$, $\frac{5}{8}$ and $\frac{7}{8}$ inches. State size wanted. Average weight, per box, 4 ounces. Package..............**5c**

CAST IRON SHOE HAMMER, 10c.

HX1363 — Cast Iron Shoe Hammer. Made of very good quality gray cast iron, nicely finished. Black japanned. Has stained oval hardwood handle. $1\frac{1}{4}$ inches face. Length over all, $8\frac{1}{2}$ inches. An excellent hammer at the price. Weight, 12 ounces. Price......**10c**

BOSTON HEEL PLATES 6 PAIRS, 5c.

H1367 — Boston Heel Plates. Gray cast iron. Sizes, $\frac{7}{8}$, 1, $1\frac{1}{8}$, $1\frac{1}{4}$ and $1\frac{1}{2}$ inches. State size wanted when ordering. Plates have sharp points for fastening. Can be attached by any one in a few minutes with a hammer. Average weight, 6 pairs 2 ounces. 6 pairs. **5c**

SHOE BUTTON KIT, 5c.

HV1378 — Shoe Button Kit. Outfit consists of 24 good quality black enameled medium size shoe buttons with steel needle and strong thread for attaching buttons to shoes. Can be attached by anyone in a few moments and will stay fastened. Weight, 1 ounce. Price............**5c**

For bargains in shoe laces see page 76. **It will pay you to order other merchandise with your shoe supplies.**

We list below the latest and most popular songs and instrumental sheet music. When ordering give name of each piece of music you desire; add 1c per copy for postage, 11c in all per copy. All orders filled promptly.

Popular Songs

As The Years Roll By
Always Take a Girl Named Daisy
A Little Bunch of Shamrocks
As Long as the Shamrock Grows Green
Bring Me Back My Honey Boy
Curse of An Aching Heart
'Cross the Great Divide
Down by the Old Mill Stream
Dear Old Girl
Daddy Has a Sweetheart
Dream Days
Don't Blame It all on Broadway
Don't You Wish You Were Back Home Again
Floating Down The River
Good-Bye Summer, So Long Fall, Hello Winter Time
Good-Bye Little Girl of My Dreams
Good-Bye Boys
Good-bye My Love Good-bye
He'd Have to Get Out and Get Under
He Wants Someone to Call Him Papa
Hour That Gave Me You
In My Harem
Isch Ga Bibble
I Don't Want To, Oh, Come On
It Takes a Little Rain with the Sunshine, etc.
Isle D'Amour
I Am Afraid I'm Beginning to Love You
I Love Her, Oh! Oh! Oh!
I'll Change the Shadows to Sunshine
If They Don't Stop Making Them So Beautiful
I'm Crying Just For You
I Miss You Most of All
In Dreams My Own

Popular Songs

In the Harbor of Home Sweet Home
Just for To-night
Killarney, My Home O'er the Sea
Kiss Me Good Night
Love Me While the Loving is Good
Last Night Was The End Of The World
My Melancholy Baby
No One Else Can Take Your Place
Not Till Then Will I Cease to Love You
On a Honeymoon Express
On the Old Front Porch
Paradise For Two
Peg O' My Heart
Sunshine and Roses
Swanee Rose
Sailing Down the Chesapeake Bay
Somebody Else is Crazy About Me
The Little Church Around the Corner
The Song That Reaches Irish Hearts
Those Songs My Mother Used to Sing
There's One in a Million Like You
'Til the Sands of the Desert Grow Cold
That International Rag
There's A Girl In The Heart Of Maryland
To Have, To Hold, To Love
That's How I Need You
That Old Girl of Mine
That Tango Tokio
The Big Red Motor and the Little Blue Limousine
Trail of the Lonesome Pine
There's a Girl in Arizona
Underneath the Cotton Moon
Way of the Cross (Sacred Song)

Popular Songs

When I Dream of Old Erin
We Have Much to be Thankful For
Where the Red, Red Roses Grow
Where the River Shannon Flows
When I Lost You
When It's Apple Blossom Time In Normandy
When the Maple Leaves are Falling
When the Twilight Comes to Kiss the Rose Good-Night
Where Did You Get That Girl
Why Did You Make Me Care
Will the Roses Bloom in Heaven
Won't You Take Me Back Again
You Can't Get Away From it
You Made Me Love You
You're a Great Big Blue-Eyed Baby
You're The Most Wonderful Girl
You've Got Your Mother's Big Blue Eyes

INSTRUMENTAL

Burning of Rome
Chapel Chimes (Reverie)
Day Dreams (Syncopated Waltz)
Dream Girl Waltzes
Evening Chime (Reverie)
Fairy Kisses Waltz
Garden of Allah Waltz
Hesitation Waltz
Jamaica Ginger Rag
Marriage Market Waltz
Napoleon's Last Charge
Peg O'My Heart Waltzes
Rose Dream Waltz
Some Smoke (Turkey Trot)
Too Much Mustard (Tres Moutarde)
Wedding of the Winds Waltzes

Give name of each selection desired and send all orders to

S. S. KRESGE COMPANY, Detroit, Mich.

The Original Parcel Post 5c and 10c Store with over 100 Branch Stores

This set of 6 beautiful
heavily silverplated
Teaspoons

FREE

(THIS CUT SHOWS ACTUAL SIZE OF SPOONS)

These Beautiful Sets Free!

*You can get these beautiful sets of silver plated tableware
Free by doing a few minutes' work among your friends*

We want a million customers for our New Parcel Post 5c and 10c Store. Yes, a million people to know about the wonderful 5c and 10c bargains they can get from us by mail. That is why we make the following Special Free Offers. No time limit whatever is put on these special offers. Anyone can have the sets Absolutely Free for helping us to get new customers.

Read our Special Free Offers below and see how easily and quickly you can get a set of beautiful silver plated ware Free. Each set is heavily silver plated and with care will last for several years. The pattern is a very artistic lily and leaf design, deeply embossed, made in French gray finish.

SPECIAL FREE OFFER No. 1

The set of six beautiful silver plated Teaspoons shown above will be given to you Absolutely Free if you will show this Katalog of wonderful 5c and 10c bargains to your friends and get three of them to give you an order amounting to $1.00 or more each and send their orders to us together with your own order amounting to $1.00 or more—four orders in all, each amounting to $1.00 or more. The four orders must be packed and shipped to one address. The names and addresses of the parties ordering with you must be written on a plain piece of paper and enclosed with your order. The set of Teaspoons will be sent to you securely packed with your order.

SPECIAL FREE OFFER No. 2

The illustration to the left shows a beautiful five piece set of useful silver plated ware which you can get Absolutely Free by showing this Katalog to your friends and getting five of them to give you an order amounting to $1.00 or more each and sending the orders to us, together with your own order amounting to $1.00 or more—six orders in all, each amounting to $1.00 or more. The six orders must be packed together and sent to one address. The full name and address of each of the parties ordering with you are to be plainly written on a sheet of paper and enclosed with your order. Each piece of this set is full regular size and consists of Butter Knife, Cold Meat Fork, Sugar Shell, Berry Spoon and Gravy Ladle.

Remember, we give you these sets of silverware free for a few minutes' easy work among your neighbors and friends. Our 5c and 10c bargains are so remarkably good and so many to select from that it will only take a few minutes of your time to show our Katalog to your friends and get their orders.

We guarantee everything to be just as represented, or will promptly refund the full amount sent us, including transportation charges.

Be sure to read our Free Delivery Offer on orders amounting to $10.00 or more on page 3.

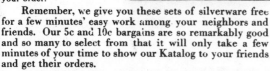

S. S. KRESGE COMPANY, Detroit, Mich., U. S. A.

The Original Parcel Post 5c and 10c Store with Over 100 Branch Stores